ADOLESCENTS, SEX, AND THE LAW

The LAW AND PUBLIC POLICY: PSYCHOLOGY AND THE SOCIAL SCIENCES series includes books in three domains:

Legal Studies—writings by legal scholars about issues of relevance to psychology and the other social sciences, or that employ social science information to advance the legal analysis;

Social Science Studies—writings by scientists from psychology and the other social sciences about issues of relevance to law and public policy; and

Forensic Studies—writings by psychologists and other mental health scientists and professionals about issues relevant to forensic mental health science and practice.

The series is guided by its editor, Bruce D. Sales, PhD, JD, University of Arizona; and coeditors, Stephen J. Ceci, PhD, Cornell University; Norman J. Finkel, PhD, Georgetown University; and Bruce J. Winick, JD, University of Miami.

***

ADOLESCENTS, SEX, AND THE LAW

PREPARING ADOLESCENTS FOR RESPONSIBLE CITIZENSHIP

ROGER J. R. LEVESQUE

AMERICAN PSYCHOLOGICAL ASSOCIATION
Washington, DC

Published by
American Psychological Association
750 First Street, NE
Washington, DC 20002

Copies may be ordered from
APA Order Department
P.O. Box 92984
Washington, DC 20090-2984

In the UK and Europe, copies may be ordered from
American Psychological Association
3 Henrietta Street
Covent Garden, London
WC2E 8LU England

Typeset in Times Roman by GGS Information Services, York, PA

Printer: United Book Press, Inc., Baltimore, MD
Cover Designer: DRI Consulting, Chevy Chase, MD
Editor/Project Manager: Debbie K. Hardin, Reston, VA

Library of Congress Cataloging-in-Publication Data
Levesque, Roger J. R.
    Adolescents, sex, and the law : preparing adolescents for
responsible citizenship / by Roger J. R. Levesque
      p. cm. — (Law and public policy)
    Includes bibliographic references and index.
    ISBN: 1-55798-609-6 (alk. paper)
    1. Teenagers—Legal status, laws, etc.—United States. 2. Sex and
law—United States. I. Title. II. Series.
KF479.L48   1999
346.7301'35—dc21   99-38670
                                  CIP

British Library Cataloguing-in-Publication Data
A CIP record is available from the British Library

Printed in the United States
First Edition

For my parents, Marc and Isabelle Levesque

CONTENTS

ACKNOWLEDGMENTS

I owe much to Bruce Sales. Submission of a manuscript to his journal, *Psychology, Public Policy, and Law,* quickly led to a book proposal. I was so fueled by his good humor, intellectual passion, and commitment to getting things done that I completed the first draft in a fraction of the time we had envisioned. I also owe much to the American Psychological Association's editorial staff. Susan Reynolds deserves considerable credit for encouraging me to cut my original draft in half and streamline arguments. Two anonymous reviewers provided incredibly thorough and insightful feedback. One reviewer—Gerald Koocher— even decided to no longer remain anonymous; he faxed me a copy of his encouraging review. His quick comments reinforced my belief in the worth of the manuscript. Adrian Harris Forman, the development editor in charge of the book, helped put the reviews in perspective and charted a way to actually rethink the presentation of the entire manuscript. She provided the nuturing feedback that made writing the sort of intellectual process it is supposed to be and, along the way, managed to help turn the project into a much more engaging text. Lastly, Debbie K. Hardin shepherded the manuscript through the production process. Her close reading of the text, attention to detail, remarkable efficiency, and ability to give new meaning to passages by simply changing a few words certainly did much to improve the final draft's content, presentation, and accessibility.

As with any worthwhile outcome, it is important to consider its source. Although the text was written with significant guidance from reviewers and editors, I owe much to Dan Freedman, Gilbert Herdt, Bert Cohler, and Daniel Offer for their unstinting support throughout my four years in the University of Chicago's unique doctoral program in cultural psychology. My early research on adolescents' romantic relationships continues to fuel my current interests that now center more on law, policy, and human rights. For the extension of my understanding of adolescent life to adolescents' unique place in the legal system, I feel much gratitude for having studied with several professors at Columbia Law School, especially Martha Fineman, Phil Genty, and Louis Henkin. They made me struggle with difficult human rights issues, learn to love the law, and realize the need to examine the rights of those excluded from dominant legal thought. Colleagues at the University of Nebraska's Law & Psychology Program, particularly Gary B. Melton, Alan J. Tomkins, and Mark Fondacaro, deserve credit not just for their continued personal support but also for solidifying my interest in adolescence.

For my focus on responsibility, citizenship, and need to rethink how society treats people, two college professors deserve credit. Lowell Eayrs Daigle and T. Franklin Grady both fostered the type of learning and commitment to treating others that form the experimental basis for the proposals championed in this book. My life would be far less eventful and less fulfilling if it were not for them. Both passed away last year, but their memories continue to encourage me.

My family deserves much credit for also providing the type of environment that allowed me to explore the possible roles for adolescents in society. Marc and Henry, my two sons, made me think of the challenges they will face when they reach adolescence. Helen, my wife, helped me trust that life's challenges always work themselves out and that much room exists for hope. Her gentle love for us ensures that we find the world a deeply meaningful place and that we feel very optimistic about life and our children's sexual development. As Catholic parents, we sincerely strive to provide an environment that encourages children to not engage in premarital sexual activity. As any parent knows, our children live in a sexualized world and their resistance to sexual activity requires much more than simple legal prohibitions mandating, for example, that they should not engage in sexual activity, not gain access to contraceptives, not be exposed to sexualized media, and so forth. Instead, they need supportive environments that promote self-respect, concern for others, hope for the future, and a sense that they have a secure place in a rapidly changing and constantly challenging world. This book aims to develop a legal system that would foster those supportive environments, rather than envisioning a legal system that simply (and ineffectively) lists prohibitions. As we will see, supportive environments actually have to do with treating adolescents as human beings, not just sexual beings. As human beings, adolescents, from my view, have corollary obligations, such as the fundamental civic obligation not to victimize others and not to place themselves in circumstances that could lead to harm. This is actually not a very radical position; it is what we as human beings and our human rights are all about. My parents, Marc and Isabelle, served as an example of the type of parents I envisioned, parents who foster responsibility and a sense of obligation for others. For my parents' ability to do so, for enabling me to end up where I am today, and, more important, simply because they are my parents, I dedicate this book to them.

INTRODUCTION: Sexuality and the Rights of Adolescents

Until a few decades ago, parents exclusively controlled adolescents' rights and were charged with the control of adolescent sexual development. The rationale for that control was simple. The law considered adolescents nonpersons. The legal system considered adolescents' rights only when parents absolutely failed in their caretaking or when adolescents were emancipated from their parents.[1] Theories of sexuality and societal views of sexual experiences reflected the view that parents controlled adolescents. Adolescent development was considered an autonomous biological process in which hormones and basic instincts drove changes in sexual behavior.[2] Parents, as guardians, had the obligation to restrain their children's premarital sexual behavior and experimentation. The guiding assumption was that adolescents only became active sexual beings once they had matured enough to be beyond adult control.

Although these traditional views still guide perceptions of adolescents and their rights, both laws and the understanding of adolescent sexuality have undergone important developments that challenge traditional views. Social scientists now view the natural process of sexual development as more flexible and influenced by forces beyond parental or caretaker control. For example, despite the belief that parents control their adolescents, partners play a powerful role in the initiation to sexual activity and its outcomes.[3] Likewise, parents deny or do not realize the extent of their children's sexual activity.[4] To a considerable degree, the law now recognizes that parents no longer do or must control adolescents' rights. For example, access to contraceptives, testing for sexually transmitted diseases, and abortions reveal how the control of access to modern technologies have such profound consequences for adolescents and society that the legal system *allows* states to limit the parental right to control adolescents' decisions and actions.[5] Although states do not necessarily move to reform their laws with what developments in adolescents' rights permit and social sciences support, legal systems do increasingly provide adolescents with control of their sexual rights to address the reality that sexual activity and development largely occurs prior to the age of majority.

Despite important changes in laws and the understanding of sexual behaviors and development, progress in defining adolescents' legal rights still fails to keep pace with the current realities of adolescent sexuality. Legal systems, for example, pervasively *fail* to facilitate adolescents' access to the previously mentioned medical technologies,[6] to protect adolescents from their partners' coercive behaviors,[7] to promote supportive family environments,[8] to limit harmful community influences on adolescent sexuality,[9] and to provide adolescents with resources to respond to the failure of legal and other social systems in addressing adolescents' needs.[10] The disjuncture between the apparent reality of adolescent sexual life and the development of adolescents' rights provides the rationale for this book.

The text fundamentally concerns itself with the extent to which adolescents' rights could better reflect the reality of adolescent sexual life. Of particular concern are the rights of adolescents deemed "minors" or "juveniles" by law—those who have not achieved legal majority and general legal emancipation from their parents and other adults. Admittedly and despite impressive social changes in sexual attitudes and recognition of individual rights, any investigation of adolescent sexuality and adolescents' rights remains loaded with ethical and political concerns. Yet the changing reality of adolescent life warrants a reconsideration of laws that control adolescents' lives. This introduction enumerates these changes, highlights the law's failure to respond, and emphasizes the need to address disjunctures between myths and realities.

Adolescent Sexuality and Social Reality

The past several decades witnessed the transformation of the naturalistic view of sexual development and sexuality. Since the 1950s basic experimental, sociological, and cross-cultural research drew attention to social and individual differences in sexual development.[11] The social sciences now view sexual maturation as a process of social learning, the main goal of which involves the acquisition of social and communicative skills that will enable youth to deal with their sexuality as well as a variety of questions that enlarge their horizons.[12] In that development, parents do not solely control sexual experiences; communities and adolescents themselves play an active role that influences adolescents' sexual maturation and interactions with their surroundings.

The view that adolescents affect their own environment and development, and the proposal that sociocultural forces affect adolescent life, finds support from reports of changes in the nature and extent of sexual activity. Rates of sexual activity among adolescents have increased dramatically.[13] National samples report that by the age of 15, more than half of both boys and girls will have engaged in sexual intercourse.[14] By the time they are high school seniors, about three fourths of adolescents will have experienced sexual intercourse at least once.[15] In addition to higher rates of sexual activity, the age of onset of sexual intercourse continues to decrease.[16] Although rates vary according to racial and minority status,[17] reports indicate that for all youth the decade prior to the mid-1990s witnessed a drop in age of onset of sexual activity to a low mean age of 16½.[18] Likewise, teenagers mature reproductively earlier and engage in higher frequencies of sexual intercourse, as reflected in higher rates of pregnancy.[19] Lastly, a sizable percentage of those who do become sexually active, more than 15%, report six or more different sexual partners during their adolescent years.[20] Much of these changes support recent evidence that adolescents feel sexual urges much earlier than researchers and the general public once thought,[21] and that they increasingly act on those urges.[22]

The results of sexual activity—pregnancies, abortions, childbearing, and sexually transmitted diseases—also have changed during the past several decades. The changes point toward one direction: increasing rates and heightened risks for negative outcomes. The number of pregnancies continues to increase as well as the number of teenagers who opt to become parents.[23] Likewise, since the legalization of abortions, teenagers abort pregnancies at high rates, which vary considerably among those in social groups who respond to different sociocultural forces.[24] Perhaps the most negative outcome involves the emergence of HIV/AIDS, as well as changes in the transmittance of sexually transmitted diseases that signal how adolescents continue to engage in risky sexual activity.[25] The Centers for Disease Control, for example, has reported early adolescents as recording the highest rate increases for some sexually transmitted diseases—nearly half of the sexually active 10- to 14-year-old boys and more than half of the girls from the same age group have been infected with gonorrhea.[26]

In addition to the outcomes of sexual activities, the nature of sexual relationships and gender relations have changed, or at least become better understood. Sexual harassment, dating violence, and rape are much more prevalent in adolescent populations than previously perceived; researchers now view these phenomena as ubiquitous to the adolescent period.[27] The realization that adolescents can be victims of sexual violence previously viewed as limited to adults has led to the recognition that adolescents also make up a large percentage of those who commit sexually violent acts and acts that were before seen as only part of adult relationships. Given that sexual awakenings and sexual maturity come earlier, it can no longer be assumed that perpetrators are unaware of their behaviors, a recognition that challenges the use of the traditional juvenile justice system as a way to deal with immature offenders.[28] In addition to these developments, society and the legal system continue to fail to address the plight of those who already have been recognized as needing assistance. Most notably, for example, the manner the mental health, foster care, and other therapeutic interventions disproportionately harm gay and lesbian youth illustrates well not only the challenge to recognize diversity but also the challenge of responding to harms by the very systems created to assist.[29]

Adolescent sexuality also emerges in a markedly changed social context. Family and cultural life dramatically have been altered within the past two decades. As detailed in chapter 1, adolescents now live in more diverse family structures. Adolescents also are more likely to grow up in poverty. They face more risk to their health, particularly in terms of health conditions resulting from earlier drug use. Difficulties find expression in the rapid transformation of popular media, as it capitalizes on dramatic changes in adolescents themselves. In addition, adolescents face the risk of not being adequately prepared for the next century. Educational institutions fail to meet the basic needs and fulfill the rights of American adolescents, especially those already facing difficult circumstances—the poor, certain minorities, and adolescents who adopt nontraditional sexual lifestyles face limited educational opportunities.[30] In sum, cultural values have changed. Adolescents have to deal with conflicting values in their peer relationships, families, and schools, as well as conflicting values found in social policies and broader society. And society fails to prepare adolescents to confront conflicting pressures and oppressive conditions.

Legal Developments

Legal developments in adolescents' rights have yet to reflect and adapt to transformations in family structures, shifts in cultural life, and changes in adolescent sexuality. Despite claims that adolescents increasingly have been bestowed rights and that adolescents are more autonomous than they were before the rights revolution of the 1960s, laws generally have remained static. Parents or the state, not adolescents themselves, control adolescents' rights. The point that adolescents generally do not control their rights, despite important developments in attempts to protect adolescents, is worth emphasizing.

It would be erroneous to suggest that the rights of adolescents, those generally referred to as "minors" or "juveniles" by the law, have not developed. Merely a few decades ago adolescents were considered "nonpersons" under the law; adolescents did not possess constitutional rights. The U.S. Supreme Court transformed that position through a series of landmark cases involving juvenile justice systems,[31] schools,[32] and families.[33] At a minimum, and even though adolescents' autonomous rights do not gain as much respect as those of adults, states must now aim to protect adolescents from state intrusion into rights recognized as protected for adults. The burgeoning recognition is quite significant. The new status of adolescents' rights provides the legal impetus to consider reconceptions of laws and policies related to adolescent sexuality and development.

Although recent developments are significant, it is critical to emphasize that parents still retain the plenary right to determine their children's daily routines, religion, education, health care, discipline, and even where and with whom they live.[34] By controlling the everyday domains of adolescent life, parents and guardians essentially control adolescents' sexual rights. In exchange for these plenary rights, parents also face many responsibilities for their children, including the provision of financial support, physical needs, and emotional care. These parental rights and obligations, however, are not absolute. Although parental rights are ''fundamental'' and receive the utmost protection from legal institutions, parental rights are far from unequivocal. States also retain a number of rights and responsibilities for children's welfare. Most notably, states can act in the best interests of the child and intrude into family life to act on behalf of children when parents fail to meet their basic responsibilities.[35] Before states may intervene, however, they typically aim to use the least intrusive means to respect, as much as possible, the rights of family members. The general rule, then, is that parental rights adequately protect adolescents' rights; and when parents fail, the state has the right and responsibility to control adolescents.[36] These rules are noteworthy. Developments in adolescents' rights do not necessarily aim to bestow on adolescents more rights to control their own lives. Instead, developments in adolescents' rights frequently mean that legal developments protect the rights of adolescents by having parents or the state responsible for controlling and protecting adolescents. Justice Antonin Scalia stressed well the limits of adolescents' rights in the most recent case involving minors' rights to freedom from adult control and laws that treat adolescents more like children than adults:

> Traditionally at common law, and still today, unemancipated minors lack some of the most fundamental rights of self-determination—including even the right of liberty in its narrow sense, *i.e.,* the right to come and go at will. They are subject, even as to their physical freedom, to the control of their parents or guardians.[37]

Developments in adolescents' rights often mean clarification of who among parents, adolescents, or other adults has the right to control adolescents. The fundamental issue confronting society revolves around the extent to which adolescents should control their own rights.

The Role of Social Scientists in the Law

This book challenges the fundamental assumption that adolescents should not control their rights, particularly in the context of sexual development and sexual activity. The task remains undoubtedly formidable. No other aspect of adolescent life reflects clashes in ''who controls?'' and fuels sociopolitical debates than issues that surround adolescent sexuality. Left to be determined is the extent to which adolescents can be free to engage in various forms of sexual behavior, to purchase or simply watch sexually charged materials, to obtain medical care and counseling for a variety of sex-related health needs, to obtain sexual information and education, to have access to contraception and abortion services, and to receive protection from harmful sexual relationships. It is important to note that not all domains of adolescents' rights and jurisdictions deny adolescents their own rights. Changes in the right to obtain abortions reflect fundamental developments in adolescents' rights to privacy in the context of family life and parental rights.[38] However, the differences across jurisdictions, particularly in terms of states' approaches to adolescent sexuality, raise concerns about whether states' policies and laws are accessible to reform that would be more consistent with the empirical reality of adolescent life.

The extent to which empirical findings may contribute to legal and policy movements remains to be determined. The state of law and its divergence from the understanding of adolescent sexuality suggest that laws only slowly adapt to changing realities, if laws do change at all. Numerous factors account for the reticence to adapt social policies and laws to empirical understandings of adolescent life. Five points are particularly illustrative. First, symbolism and intuitive beliefs guide the law. The general belief is that parents determine their children's upbringing, despite strong evidence to the contrary.[39] Second, our society exhibits profound cultural attachment to privacy and family life. Americans value individualism, self-sufficiency, and independence; those values are reflected in the venerable tradition of noninterference with the rights of the family, such that governments remain leery to involve themselves. Third, social sciences and legal systems use and offer conflicting paradigms.[40] For example, the Supreme Court must base legal decisions on legal principles, a process that frequently becomes hostile to social science analyses and even leads several Justices to view, for example, the most robust psychological findings from leading journals on adolescent development (as well as the Justices who use the evidence) as ''psychology practiced by amateurs.''[41] Fourth, when social science evidence has been used, such as to support greater intervention, results have not been uniformly positive. History is replete with innovations gone wrong and those who inform policy making are not free from their own political agendas.[42] Fifth, the innovations demand a reconception of rights. Adolescents are in the unique position of being both dependent and independent, and the law's insistence on narrow conceptions of rights has trouble accommodating such uncertainty.

Despite these clashes between law and the social sciences, social scientists have an interest in evaluating and determining alternative approaches to current legal mandates. First, the law frequently emphasizes psychological and social factors in deciding cases that deal with adolescents' sexual rights. The Supreme Court's approach to abortions for adolescents who have not attained the age of legal majority—although exceedingly controversial—illustrates the potential significance of empirical research.[43] Second, courts and legislatures need assistance in evaluating the validity of assumptions that determine whether any compelling basis exists for age-based regulation of sexual activity and its consequences. Similarly, only sound research can evaluate legal procedures to ensure that they remove rather than create unintended negative effects. Third, social scientists assist adolescent clients or health professionals in their interactions with one another. Those interactions are ubiquitous to adolescent life; psychologists, for example, interact with adolescents as clinicians, counselors in schools, as mental health center experts, in health care settings, and as experts who guide what parents do. Fourth, the numerous professional fields that interact with adolescents continue to commit themselves to the promotion of human welfare.[44] Social workers and psychologists, for example, seek to ensure adolescents and families access to services to assist them in understanding alternatives to dealing with crises. All are ethically bound to respect individual privacy, protect the civil rights of their clients, and even challenge social injustice.[45] Thus although the law may often clash with social science realities, important opportunities and professional mandates spur investigations of the design, implementation, evaluation, and reform of legal approaches to adolescent life.

Overview

Despite difficulties and because of social scientists' obligations, this book seeks an alternative vision and legal conception of adolescent life, with special emphasis on sexuality. This book explores alternatives in light of existing research and evaluates whether it is possible to overcome stumbling blocks. The book examines numerous areas of dispute as it illuminates the complexity of adolescent sexual activity. The discussion is descriptive, analytical, normative, and prescriptive. The descriptive component discusses the emergence

and contemporary doctrine of adolescents' rights along with the current empirical understanding of the place of adolescents in society and the law. The analytical component
examines the legal reasoning employed by courts, legislative and other policy efforts, and
the controversies regarding adolescent sexual life. The normative component considers the
legal status of adolescents, the proper parameters of their rights, and the role of institutions
and individuals in ensuring adolescents' rights. Finally, the prescriptive component involves
the delineation of a model that addresses the general place of adolescents in the law and
society as well as the particular regulation of adolescents' sexual rights.

Chapter 1 examines the historical and current social construction of adolescence. The
chapter draws from social science investigations of adolescence to highlight major sociocultural forces that lead to the invention of adolescence, changes in those forces, and emergence
of new conceptions of adolescence. Although current conceptions are marked by diversity
and reflect adolescents' different social conditions, the chapter briefly analyzes major
themes that guide responses to adolescence and how those themes relate to major social
transformations in the place of youth in society and family life. The analysis ends by
exploring how the major themes are challenged by empirical reconceptions of adolescents,
their abilities, and recent conceptions of social service delivery to foster adolescent
development.

Chapter 2 explores major historical developments in adolescents' rights and the
persistent need to balance adolescents' rights with state and parental interests. The review
reveals that there exists no systematic and comprehensive jurisprudence of adolescents'
rights. Although important recent attempts aim to protect youth from state interference and
extend some due process rights to juveniles, no parallel development systematically
addresses adolescents' private relationships. Adolescents' rights remain largely undeveloped, and where they are settled, they tend to be viewed as coterminous with parental rights.

Chapters 3 and 4 begin the rethinking of adolescents' rights with an investigation of
adolescents' sexual rights in the context of family and other social relationships. The
chapters examine the manner laws generally aim to give parents and society control over
adolescents' sexual development, including access to health services, information, parenthood, and certain forms of sexual relationships. Within each context of regulation, the
chapters present laws that guide the differential control of adolescents' rights and then
compare that control to the current empirical understanding of adolescent sexual development and sexual experiences. The empirical evidence suggests that current legal approaches
remain problematic and increasingly fail to address adolescents' needs. The findings suggest
that, although reform of current approaches could guide adolescents toward more positive
outcomes, the pressing need for more effective policies and less politically charged reforms
necessitates a focus on other efforts. The need for a refocus provides the springboard for and
centerpiece of the following chapters, which aim to increase adolescents' access to
information and protection, broaden societal obligations, and recognize youths' citizenship
in society.

Chapter 5 examines adolescents' right to sexuality education—a broad view of "sex
education" that would provide adolescents with opportunities to understand and respond to
various influences on their sexual, gender, and social development. To do so, this chapter
details the justifications for sexuality education, its successes and failures, and emerging
suggestions for reform. That analysis suggests the need for different approaches to the
manner adolescents receive, learn, and practice information relating to their sexual
development and intimate relationships. The chapter presents current laws and alternative
approaches to sexuality education. The chapter delineates specific, alternative approaches to
sexual education that would rebalance parental control of adolescents' rights to adolescents

themselves. The alternative suggests that schools must develop adolescents' decision-making skills, include adolescents in the design of programs, play down parental interests, and strive for broad community involvement in supporting adolescent development. These proposals rest on the democratic notion that society must prepare adolescents for their future and immediate social participation.

Chapter 6 investigates how laws regulate adolescents' exposure to sexually charged media. The chapter highlights how existing efforts pervasively fail and provides an empirical analysis of the powerful impact of diverse media on adolescents' sexual attitudes and behaviors. The chapter closes with an alternative approach to dealing with policy failures. The proposal begins with the recognition that the media plays a central role in adolescents' sexual socialization. From that starting point, the chapter suggests how alternative models still must balance that need with parental–state interests while building on participatory models of adolescents' rights and the various forms those rights may take to deal with potentially negative consequence of access to a sexually charged media.

Chapters 7 and 8 address issues concerning adolescent sexual victimization. Chapter 7 focuses on sexual exploitation by adults and chapter 8 details victimization by adolescents, particularly in the form of harassment, relationship violence, and sexual assault. Evaluations of social and legal responses to these forms of victimization reveal a persistent failure to recognize victims' needs and denial of adolescents' access to legal and social services. To address the sexual victimization of adolescents, chapter 8 presents alternatives to increase adolescents' access to services and addresses challenges that alternatives unduly extend the rights of adolescents at the expense of parental rights and social interests. Again, the chapter adopts a participatory model that focuses on the need to include adolescents in their own protection not only in formal legal systems but also in societal arrangements that otherwise foster exclusion and victimization.

Chapter 9 explores adolescent sexual offending. The chapter first examines available social science literature dealing with the development of sexual offenders, treatment models, and prevention efforts. That analysis serves to highlight that current laws regulating adolescent sexual offending, although marked by important developments, generally reflect a narrow approach to adolescents offending. Current analyses and discussions of adolescents' rights in the context of sexual offending essentially center on protections from governmental intrusion in the lives of alleged offenders. To explore a more expansive view of rights and offer alternative approaches to dealing with adolescent sex offenders, the analysis suggests a need to broaden conceptions of offending and redirect current trends in legal intervention. The chapter offers proposals that adopt an ecologically focused array of legal intervention that aims for broad societal reforms that recognize adolescents' individuation needs. The proposals complement the previous chapters' suggestions regarding reforms and supportive interventions that would foster adolescents' abilities to exercise responsible self-determination.

Chapter 10 provides the last substantive analysis as it highlights an outcome of sexual activity that particularly overshadows and fuels recent policy debates: adolescent parenthood. The chapter first discusses the determinants and correlates of pregnancy resolutions that lead to early parenting and their consequences. That analysis serves as a background for examining developments in adolescents' rights. Although commentators and the law tend to focus on the right to parent, the chapter broadens the focus to understand how laws may affect adolescents' actual parenting and redirect intervention strategies. As with previous chapters, the alternatives reveal the need to recognize adolescents' citizenship and their peculiar place in society to develop more comprehensive and effective approaches to adolescent sexuality.

Chapter 11 addresses the future of adolescents' rights and ways to support sociolegal reform. The chapter emphasizes that the law is at a critical juncture. For the first time, those who evaluate adolescents' rights for protection and autonomy may do so by reference to new legal principles and empirical evidence. At the same time, the nature of those rights are increasingly controversial in nature. No simple calculus determines the nature of those rights and how they may be balanced with the rights of others. Lack of a simple rule makes inevitable the need to rethink adolescents' place in society and the law. Regardless of the political stance taken by policy makers, those who carry out legal mandates, and those who unwittingly follow existing laws, all must address adolescents' changing place in society. The chapter highlights how alternatives presented throughout the text may create new opportunities to address adolescents' needs and ensure their basic human rights. As revealed throughout the book, the alternatives do much more than foster respect for adolescents' rights and acknowledge their particular needs. The alternatives chart a path to prepare adolescents for responsible citizenship in an increasingly changing and challenging world.

Notes

1. Roger J. R. Levesque, *Adolescents, Society and the Law* (Chicago: American Bar Association, 1997).
2. A. Chris Downs and Lisa Scarborough Hillje, "Historical and Theoretical Perspectives on Adolescent Sexuality: An Overview." In *Adolescent Sexuality,* ed. Thomas P. Gullotta, Gerald R. Adams, and Raymond Montemayor (Newbury Park, CA: Sage, 1993).
3. Arland Thornton, "The Courtship Process and Adolescent Sexuality," *Journal of Family Issues* 11 (1990):239–273; Raye Hudson Rosen, "Adolescent Pregnancy Decision-Making: Are Parents Important?" *Adolescence* 15 (1990):43–54.
4. *See, e.g.,* James Jaccard and Patricia Dittus, *Parent–Teen Communication: Towards the Prevention of Unintended Pregnancies* (New York: Springer-Verlag, 1991).
5. *See, e.g.,* Carey v. Population Servs. Int'l, 431 U.S. 678 (1977) (regarding contraceptives); Planned Parenthood v. Casey, 505 U.S. 833 (1992) (regarding abortions).
6. *See, e.g.,* Suellyn Scarnecchia and Julie Kunce Field, "Judging Girls: Decision Making in Parental Consent to Abortion Cases," *Michigan Journal of Gender and Law* 3 (1995):75–123.
7. *See, e.g.,* Michelle Oberman, "Turning Girls Into Women: Re-Evaluating Modern Statutory Rape Law," *Journal of Criminal Law and Criminology* 85 (1994):15–79.
8. Roger J. R. Levesque, "Emotional Maltreatment in Adolescents' Everyday Lives: Furthering Sociolegal Reforms and Social Service Provisions," *Behavioral Sciences & the Law* 16 (1998):237–263.
9. *See, e.g.,* Victor C. Strasburger, *Adolescents and the Media: Medical and Psychological Impact* (Thousand Oaks, CA: Sage, 1995).
10. Roger J. R. Levesque, "Educating American Youth: Lessons From Children's Human Rights Law," *Journal of Law & Education* 27 (1998):173–209.
11. Alfred C. Kinsey, Wardell B. Pomeroy, and Clyde E. Martin, *Sexual Behavior in the Human Male* (Philadelphia: Saunders, 1948); Alfred C. Kinsey, Wardell B. Pomeroy, Clyde E. Martin, and Paul H. Gebhard, *Sexual Behavior in the Human Female* (Philadelphia: Saunders, 1953); Clellan S. Ford and Frank A. Beach, *Patterns of Sexual Behavior* (London: Eyre and Spottiwoode, 1952).
12. Gullotta et al., *Historical and Theoretical Perspectives on Adolescent Sexuality.*
13. Sandra Hofferth, Joan R. Kahn, and Wendy Baldwon, "Premarital Sexual Activity Among U.S. Teenagers Over the Past Three Decades," *Family Planning Perspectives* 19 (1987):46–53.
14. The Centers for Disease Control reports in its 1990 Youth Risk Behavior Survey that about 49% of ninth-grade boys (whose model age is 14 at the beginning of the school year) have had sex. Centers for Disease Control, "Sexual Behavior Among High School Students—U.S., 1990," *Morbidity and Mortality Weekly Report* 40 (1992):885–888. For girls, 32% of 9th-grade girls and 43% of 10th-grade girls report having had sex. Other national samples report similar results. The National

Longitudinal Survey of Youth reports that about 31% of adolescents say they have had sex before age 15 and that by age 16, 55% say they have. See Frank L. Mott, Michell M. Fondell, Paul N. Hu, Lori Kowaleski-Jones, and Elizabeth G. Menaghan, ''The Determinants of First Sex by Age 14 in a High-Risk Adolescent Population,'' *Family Planning Perspectives* 28 (1986):13–18.

15. Centers for Disease Control, ''Sexual Behavior Among High School Students.''

16. Cheryl D. Hayes (Ed.), *Risking the Future: Adolescent Sexuality, Pregnancy, and Childrearing.* Vol. 1 (Washington, DC: National Academy Press, 1987); Elizabeth C. Cooksey, Ronald R. Rindfuss, and David K. Guilkey, ''The Initiation of Adolescent Sexual and Contraceptive Behavior During Changing Times,'' *Journal of Health and Social Behavior* 37 (1996):59–74.

17. Studies of urban minority youth indicate that the median age of onset of sexual activity may be as low as 12 to 14. Bonita Stanton, Xiaoming Li, Maureen Black, Izabel Ricardo, Jennifer Galbraith, Linda Kaljee, and Susan Feigelman, ''Sexual Practices and Intentions Among Preadolescent and Early Adolescent Low-Income Urban African-Americans,'' *Pediatrics* 93 (1994):966–973.

18. Susan Sprecher, Anita Barbee, and Pepper Schwartz, '' 'Was It Good for You Too?': Gender Differences in the First Sexual Intercourse Experiences,'' *Journal of Sex Research* 32 (1995): 3–15.

19. Lynda M. Sagrestano and Roberta L. Paikoff, ''Preventing High-Risk Sexual Behavior, Sexually Transmitted Diseases, and Pregnancy Among Adolescents.'' In *Enhancing Children's Wellness,* ed. Roger P. Weissberg, Thomas P. Gullotta, Robert L. Hampton, Bruce A. Ryan, and Gerald R. Adams (Thousand Oaks, CA: Sage, 1997).

20. *See, e.g.,* Robing G. Sawyer and Nancy Gray Smith, ''A Survey of Situational Factors at First Intercourse Among College Students,'' *American Journal of Health Behavior* 20 (1996): 208–217.

21. Martha K. McClintock and Gilbert Herdt, ''Rethinking Puberty: The Development of Sexual Attraction,'' *Current Directions in Psychological Science* 5 (1996):178–183.

22. Sharon K. Araji, *Sexually Aggressive Children: Coming to Understand Them* (Thousand Oaks, CA: Sage, 1997).

23. Kristine A. Moore, Brent C. Miller, Dana Glei, and Donna Ruane Morrison, *Adolescent Sex, Contraception, and Childbearing: A Review of Recent Research* (Washington, DC: Child Trends, 1995).

24. *Id.*

25. Roger J. R. Levesque, ''The Peculiar Place of Adolescents in the HIV-AIDS Epidemic: Unusual Progress & Usual Inadequacies in 'Adolescent Jurisprudence,' '' *Loyola University Chicago Law Journal* 27 (1996):701–739.

26. Centers for Disease Control, ''Special Focus: Surveillance for Sexually Transmitted Diseases,'' *Morbidity & Mortality Weekly Report* 42, no. SS-3 (Aug. 13, 1993).

27. Levesque, ''Emotional Maltreatment in Adolescents' Everyday Lives.''

28. Sander N. Rothchild, ''Beyond Incarceration: Juvenile Sex Offender Treatment Programs Offer Youths a Second Chance,'' *Journal of Law and Policy* 4 (1996):719–758.

29. Colleen A. Sullivan, ''Kids, Courts and Queers: Lesbian and Gay Youth in the Juvenile Justice and Foster Care Systems,'' *Law & Sexuality* 6 (1996):31–62.

30. Levesque, ''Educating American Youth: Lessons From Children's Human Rights Law.''

31. In re Gault, 387 U.S. 1 (1967).

32. Tinker v. Des Moines Indep. Community Sch. Dist., 393 U.S. 503 (1969).

33. Bellotti v. Baird, 443 U.S. 622 (1979).

34. Levesque, *Adolescents, Society and the Law.*

35. Prince v. Massachusetts, 321 U.S. 158 (1944).

36. Levesque, *Adolescents, Society and the Law.*

37. Vernonia Sch. Dist. v. Acton, 515 U.S. 646, 654 (1995).

38. *See, e.g.,* Carey v. Population Servs. Int'l, 431 U.S. 678 (1977); Planned Parenthood v. Casey, 505 U.S. 833 (1992).

39. Judith R. Harris, ''Where Is the Child's Environment? A Group Socialization Theory of Development,'' *Psychological Review,* 102 (1995):458–489.

40. Craig Haney, ''Psychology and Legal Change: On the Limits of a Factual Jurisprudence,'' *Law and Human Behavior* 4 (1980):147–200.

41. *See* Scalia's scathing dissent, joined by Chief Justice Rhenquist and Justices White and Thomas, in Lee v. Weisman, 505 U.S. 577, 636 (1992).

42. Roger J. R. Levesque, ''The Failures of Foster Care Reform: Revolutioning the Most Radical Blueprint,'' *Maryland Journal of Contemporary Legal Issues* 6 (1995):1–35.

43. Gary B. Melton and Anita J. Pliner, ''Adolescent Abortion: A Psycholegal Analysis.'' In *Adolescent Abortion: Psychological and Legal Issues,* ed. Gary B. Melton (Lincoln: University of Nebraska Press, 1986).

44. American Psychological Association, ''Ethical Principles of Psychologists,'' *American Psychologist* 36 (1981):633–638.

45. *Id.* For an analysis of social workers' obligations indicated in several codes of ethics, *see* David G. Gill, *Confronting Injustice and Oppression: Concepts and Strategies for Social Workers* (New York: Columbia University Press, 1998).

PART I

Conceptions of Adolescents and Their Place in the Law

Chapter 1
THE INVENTION AND REINVENTION OF ADOLESCENCE

Politicians, professionals, and the lay public widely debate the place of adolescents in families and society. Adolescents figure prominently in discussions of sexuality, crime, poverty, education, and economic development.[1] Although the debates about the proper place of adolescents certainly pervade numerous points of discussion, all discussions necessarily reveal contemporary changes in adolescent life and the place of adolescents in society. The discussions also pervasively exhibit a societal failure to match views of adolescents with the realities they face. The failure involves the manner changes in the realities of contemporary life require adolescents to adopt characteristics attributed more to adults, and how society fails to adapt and rethink the manner it imagines adolescents as vulnerable, child-like, and unable to cope with those adult demands. The reality of adolescent life and the traditional image that adolescents need protection and control requires policy makers to address the gap between images and reality.

This chapter explores how society portrays images of adolescents and addresses adolescents' concerns—how the realities of contemporary adolescent life increasingly challenge traditional societal views of adolescence. To do so, this chapter details how two ideological responses to the manner adolescents deal with adult issues—one response that fosters relative dependency on and control by adults and another that promotes relative autonomy from adults—have played critical roles in the development and current conceptions of adolescence. The analysis demonstrates how the invention of the notion of adolescence equated adolescents with children, and how that conception constitutes the "traditional" view of adolescents. The analysis further reveals how, in several societal domains, the contemporary realities of adolescent life challenge traditional conceptions. These contemporary challenges reveal society's increasing obligation to foster adolescents' competency, adolescents' need to acquire it, and the need to temper the traditional models' hold on images of adolescent life.

Although historical analyses always shed light on contemporary issues, it is important to emphasize the significance and narrowness of the discussion that follows. The chapter presents the historical roots of reigning ideologies of adolescents to reveal four points. First, the reigning image of how society should approach adolescent life seeks to impose adult authority over youth as it views adolescents as in need of control so that they may gain protection from society and themselves. Second, despite the reigning image, contemporary life challenges the traditional image of adolescents. Third, recent social science evidence and some legal developments respond to new challenges and recognize adolescent competency to control their own lives and the need to foster autonomous competency. Fourth, the new findings and developments clash with traditional ideologies and the failure to address the clash stifles the development of a more comprehensive and appropriate youth policy, of a more coherent and effective conception of adolescents' rights. Thus understanding the formal recognition of adolescent personhood helps highlight important and predictable disjunctions between the legal regulation and eventual reality of adolescent life, an elucidation that serves as the foundation on which to foster reform that would close the gap between adolescents' everyday experiences and sociolegal understandings of those experiences.

The Emergence of Adolescent Personhood

The emergence of the notion of adolescence reflects the complexity of adolescence as well as the creation of organizations designed to monitor youths' social and moral behavior. Each era's attitudes about gender, race, and class shaped social responses and images of adolescents. Although different social and spatial locations contributed to different experiences for adolescents, similar demographic and ideological shifts led to the sociolegal invention of adolescence that allegedly emerged in the 19th and early 20th centuries.[2] Those forces resulted in models of family life that were unlike the families and adolescents of the preceding century and contributed to the currently reigning paradigm of the traditional family and adolescent. This section uncovers the forces that led to the modern conception of adolescence, the different meanings and experiences attached to the term, and the new opportunities and constraints produced by the social construction of the adolescent period.

A growing body of literature suggests that colonial Americans did manifest a conception of adolescence and that sociocultural changes led to the development of an adolescent "subculture."[3] Research reveals that colonial adolescence had its gestation in English adolescence and that the notion of adolescence stretches back to even before the Medieval period. In terms of adolescent life, several have argued, the teenage years in numerous ways were similar to those of modern adolescents.[4] Like today, the adolescent transition could stretch from approximately age 10 to age 21 and often older.[5] The period involved movement away from complete social and economic dependence on the family of origin to an extended state of semidependence. No common age-graded experiences predetermined when a child would leave home, become apprenticed, obtain gainful employment, or get married.[6] Becoming an adult entailed an ongoing process rather than a discrete sequence of sharing common experiences of a distinctive legal status. In addition, patterns of work, play, and premarital sexual flirtation were similar enough to sustain the belief that a subculture existed with its own age-bounded rituals and rules that led to the potential for unruly behaviors. Indeed, the manner that period in life was observed as plagued by the many temptations and sins of the world partly led Puritans to leave for the New World.[7] It would not be an overstatement to propose that attempts to control youth contributed to the founding of the nation. Thus even though life in the American frontier was rapid and rigorous, even it allowed for a distinct "adolescent" period.[8]

Although the adolescent period during colonial times seemed distinct, commentators find this part of the life course too undifferentiated to actually constitute a formal and sociolegally recognized period. Historians do tend to agree, however, that colonial Americans had conceptual vocabularies that distinguished youth from adults, but the phrase for this stage of life connoted neither a uniform set of experiences nor a fixed age span. The category of youth lumped together apprentices, schoolchildren, farmhands, servants, slaves, and spanned the ages of 10 up to 30.[9] In addition to lack of differentiation, social institutions and peer groups encompassed a broad range of ages and did not distinguish particularly between adults, children, and youth. The heterogeneity reflected in the diversity and absence of age differentiation in social gatherings is precisely to what historians attribute the imprecision of the term *youth* and lack of formal conception of adolescence.[10] Thus colonists did not themselves recognize an adolescent period, but much of what would later mark the period of adolescence existed in colonial times.[11]

Although not yet conceived as consisting of a readily identifiable group that could be called adolescents, colonial "adolescents" posed enough concern that colonists molded three key institutions to control them: family, church, and work. As with today, the patriarchal family served as a primary means to govern youth. To the colonists, the family was hierarchical and patriarchal.[12] Unlike today, however, parents had considerably more control over their children. In 1646 Massachusetts passed an important "stubborn child" law, a statute that made a child's stubbornness a capital offense.[13] The law, which several of the other colonies quickly adopted, applied only to "stubborn or rebellious son[s], of sufficient years and understanding (*viz.*) sixteen years of age."[14] By applying to what we clearly would consider adolescents, the legislation sought to enforce traditional authoritarian relationships, to ensure rigid conformity of thought and action in future generations, and to sustain the community's allocation of responsibilities among appropriate spheres in the social order—all of which would limit broader social conflict and maintain established authority.[15] As with today, religion also significantly affected the lives of asolescents and their families. Unlike today, however, the church played a much more overt, forceful, pervasive, and significant role in efforts to control youth in family and community life.[16] Church leaders and other community members actively oversaw child rearing, so much so that the colonists viewed child rearing as a communal endeavor in which religious, community, and private responsibilities overlapped.[17] Work, the third domain, also is significant for modern youth, but it generally does not operate today as much of a powerful force as it did in colonial times. Colonists placed out orphaned, wayward, destitute, or dependent children to work with other families' production of their needed goods; or integrated them into their own families; or involved them in the family economy of their masters.[18] The significant role of servitude for colonial society cannot be underestimated—indentured servitude in the Chesapeake mirrored the commanding socializing force of the patriarchal household in New England.[19] Unlike for modern youth, work in the form of family-based labor, but particularly apprenticeships and servitude, were often used as a form of punishment for youths' unruly and immoral behavior.[20] Regardless of the reasons for and forms of labor, children became adults by working with, acquiring the skills of, and by functioning as adults. The extensive focus on labor reveals more than the primary manner individuals became adults; it indicates well the communal, rather than the exclusively nuclear, familial character of child rearing in colonial times. Even when young people left their own parental homes, they lived with their master's household or with other families, which provided stability and demanded accountability. The powers and functions of church, work, and family all interlocked to provide cohesion and maintain informal social controls over adolescents. The manner these institutions served as focal points of control over adolescent life, and the changes in these institutions, would contribute to the construction of a distinct adolescent period. Indeed, the perceived need to control youth, and the difficulty of accommodating that need, played the central part in the late 19th- to early 20th-century recognition that youth could constitute a group of individuals with similar experiences subsumable under the rubric of the "adolescent" experience.

Despite these three omnipresent institutions' control, much variation still existed in the colonial experience of adolescence. One of the most striking differences historians note between the experiences of adolescents of this period and of the eras that would follow is the remarkable control of adolescence despite lack of formal, state-sponsored institutions that sought to control them. Instead of governmental regulatory institutions, adolescents faced adults' erratic but harsh authority.[21] Although punishment for deviance could be harsh, the hierarchic and patriarchic control found in key institutions did not control youth as much as may have been hoped. Although adults expected deference and the prevailing ideology of child-rearing fostered the control of youth, youth still managed to escape control. Considerable evidence reveals how adolescents actively resisted whenever possible. For example, many report how the experience of youth involved more "patterns of disorderliness and violence" rather than the romanticized picture of stability, control, and order.[22] Indeed, it was in the 1690s that a hysteria spread among a group of adolescent girls in Salem, Massachusetts, and led to the most notorious of witch trials. These trials exemplified the tumultuousness of adolescence and how changing social life shaped the adolescent experience.[23] Commentators frequently propose that the afflicted projected on the accused unacknowledged sexual and material worldly impulses that lay within themselves.[24] Further signs of the institutions' lack of control emerge from reports of a surge in adolescent sexual activity by the early 1700s, as evidenced by premarital conceptions.[25] Several attribute the apparent surge in sexual activity to increases in geographic mobility and the declining ability of families and churches to reach and constrain youth.[26] Rather than to religious declension and social change, others credit the change to adolescence itself.[27] Regardless of the reasons for the apparent sexual activity and deviance, both real and imagined, characterizations of adolescents of the late 1700s and early 1800s continue to describe them as restless, and society began to view young people as a new social problem.

The shift in views of the young as constituting a period of social concern emerged from profound demographic, social, and economic changes of the late 1700s and early 1800s. Structural changes transformed America from a rural, agricultural society into an urban, industrial society.[28] Although the structural changes emerged from the predominantly household-based manufacturing of consumer goods to more mass production that differed among regions of the country, industrialization transformed the economy which in turn revolutionized family life. As explored later, changes in economic production greatly influenced family structure, family dynamics, images of families, and images of child development. All of these changes contributed not only to the formal recognition of an adolescent period, they also reaffirmed the image of adolescents as individuals who must be controlled and protected from the harsh realities of life, an image that reflects the essence of the traditional—and now reigning—model of adolescent life.

Changes in the very structure and composition of families contributed immensely to the traditional model of adolescent life that now serves as the dominant model of how society should approach the adolescent period. Before the late 1800s, families essentially produced what they needed to consume. That mode of production joined people within working households. The result was that families were rather extended; families consisted of parents, children, other relatives, as well as apprentices and perhaps journeymen.[29] In response to industrialization, families lost their productive capacity and became, instead, units of consumption.[30] As a result, family patterns changed; families declined in size and intergenerational influences waned. Changes in family structures and economic production also affected family dynamics that, in turn, contributed to a different need for children. That change weakened patriarchal authority and allowed for new images of nurturing mothers to compete with traditional images of parentage, and new images of childhood emerged to reflect and reinforce the gentler image of parenting. This transformation was made possible by the advent of smaller families that allowed them to disconnect family life from community life. In the community, the metaphor of the marketplace increasingly characterized interactions. That vision viewed adults as individuals who prized liberty and individuality, as individuals perceived as autonomous and unconnected.[31] As the community was envisioned as an arena of choice, the family was seen as the opposite. Families increasingly were differentiated from the community and viewed as social units that were enduring and connected; unlike the community, the family prized hierarchy and dependency over equality and autonomy. In separating community and family life, explicit roles emerged to guide adults and children within families. Caring husbands were supposed to provide economically for their families and caring women were expected to provide sanctuary for their beleaguered husbands and for the spiritual and physical nourishment of their children.[32] Caring parents were those who placed children at the center of family life. The value of families became inextricably intertwined with the production and socialization of emotionally and physically healthy children. Children served to justify both the husband's renumerative efforts in the marketplace and the wife's nonrenumerative efforts in the home. Children became so integral to families that families without children were not characterized as families.[33]

These changes signaled a different image of family life. Rather than being like the community, the family was imaged as a safe haven from the harsh realities of communities. However, the family was still one marked by parental control over children. Society structured family life so that children were under the charge of parents obligated to maintain and educate children and help society produce healthy adults. It is important to note that the image of parental and societal obligations was omnipresent, even though the actual socialization process was not experienced uniformly by all groups in American society. Class and ethnicity, which were interrelated, affected positively the ages of leaving home and duration of familial residence, length of schooling, and age of entry into the workforce.[34] Despite these diverse experiences, reform was spurred by the vision of middle-class childhood—an image of children who were not expected to participate in the formal productive process.[35] The result was that children became viewed as valuable property and a vulnerable class in need of protection, a class inclined toward neither good nor evil, but essentially malleable.[36] Thus even though several children did not easily fit into its projection, the image of family life's role in child development became settled with changes in economic production, family structure, and parental roles.

The role of mothers in child rearing warrants special emphasis. As the traditional networks of families, communities, and churches weakened, and social and economic changes separated work from the home, the new image of women's proper role in society emerged to complement the image of childhood as a period of dependency, vulnerability, and postponement of adult roles. The prolonging of children's dependency consigned women to greater domestic life and bestowed on them a central role in molding, shaping, and preparing children and realizing their potentials.[37] As the families insulated themselves from the surrounding world, women's roles in caring for children increased, so much so that a "cult of true womanhood" emerged and defined women solely in terms of their domestic functions.[38] The dramatic changes in the perception of women is found most keenly in legal reform: Anglo-American law traditionally granted fathers the unlimited right to the custody of their minor children, but by the early 19th century judges increasingly gave mothers custody.[39] Society defined mothers' primary functions in terms of the need to provide for the healthy and moral development of children. The corollary of this view was that fathers were inherently unfit to nurture their children.[40] The emphasis on women's natural abilities and need to care for children provided the impetus to make the world in which their children lived a better place. That emphasis eventually would allow women to enage in social and moral welfare reform, to particpate in public causes such as the temperance that led to child labor, education, and child protection laws[41]—all of which would affect greatly the formal recognition of the adolescent period.

Given the previously discussed images of ideal domesticity, adolescents and families who did not fit into mid-19th-century, middle-class conceptions were viewed as problematic. Middle-class adults sought to differentiate the middle-class adolescents from their more dangerous working-class counterparts. Most notably, new attention to gender differentiation is characterisitic of this era, with much concern focused on the need to protect middle-class daughters from precocious sexuality[42]—a concern that would eventually spread to other classes. Also subjected to much middle-class adult concern were the gangs of lower-class and working-class youths who became more visible in urban street life; these groups were seen as dangerous because of their focus on physical prowess, rowdy and potentially violent behavior. Concern also was placed on dramatic increases in immigrants from Europe who brought with them languages, religions, political heritages, and cultures different from the Anglo-Protestant Americans who had preceded them.[43] Societal changes, massive immigration, and growing industrialization and urbanization created undesirable conditions perceived as threats to the foundation of society.[44] Industrialization encouraged migration and fostered population changes that weakened the informal systems of social control based on families, churches, and family-based labor; those changes in systems of control produced cultural conflict and threatened traditional value systems of the middle-class. These features of early 19th-century America increased the potential for youth's autonomy and independence and rendered problematic their social control and integration. The changes in family, community, and work life meant that the traditional methods of informal social control no longer proved as effective.

The contrast between middle-class and the more dangerous lower- and working class fostered a new image of child development. As we have seen, even though several youth did not fit into prevailing images of what children were like or what children did, all were viewed as malleable and valuable. These two features were critical and needed to support the dramatic social reconstruction of childhood. The notion of malleability was used as a means to secure help for children, especially those of poor immigrant families, and for society itself.[45] Children were seen as humanity's redeemers, and this role was reflected in the prevailing notion that children would mature and determine society's future. The solution envisioned by adult reformers was to construct a more regulated, age-segregated environment during the perilous years of growing up. Reformers articulated an ideology of developmental perils without proper intervention at the same time that a parallel ideology emerged that pronounced children as priceless and vulnerable.

Historians view the child-saving movement, which ranged from the later 1800s to the early 1900s, as the solution to the perceived threat of lower classes and the somewhat contradictory perceptions of all children as priceless innocents. That movement involved an amalgam of middle-class reformers, professionals, and philanthropists, but particularly middle-class Protestant women of Anglo-Saxon descent. These activists championed the need to recognize the special, vulnerable position of children in families and society and sought greater control of both children and the lower classes, which were deemed in need of assistance to raise their children into productive citizens. The orientation that aimed to ensure and better provide for children's health and welfare resulted in child labor reform, compulsory education, and the juvenile justice system.[46] These reforms renewed community interest in children's lives and fostered the recognition that communities are inextricably connected to family life. Rather than simply reflecting family life, these reforms were seen as complementing and reinforcing the important roles of families or simply acting in their stead.

Schools were designed to advance the potential person status of children by developing competencies for the child as a future adult and a productive member of society. Schools were meant simply to assist parents in the upbringing of their children. In assisting parents, however, the transfer of children from work to educational settings clearly involved a projection of middle-class childhood and middle-class needs onto individuals and families from other social spheres.[47] This development signaled a severe limitation in parental power that did not fit the mold of middle-class family life. Reformers viewed schools as an ideal environment to inculcate individuals into middle-class values. Common schools served as a tool for a moral crusade to ''Protestantize'' immigrants, to instill democratic values, and to transform the masses into productive citizens imbued with virtues of industry, temperance, and frugality.[48] School reform allowed the state to abrogate parental prerogatives and grant its power of *loco parentis,* the state power to act in the place of parents, to its ideological apparatus, the schools. As societal changes removed children's economic value derived from child labor, schools became children's major work setting. The powerful role work had played in socializing individuals into adulthood and community life, as described earlier, was now replaced by schooling. Rather then encouraging incorporation into adult and community institutions, the state enforced the segregation of youth. The devlopment in compulsory schooling, coupled by the necessary child labor legislation, was rapid: By the early 1900s virtually every state passed laws that excluded youth from most employment and required them to attend secondary schools.[49] The result was that legislation effectively and systematically excluded youth from adult roles, deprived them of adult status, and prolonged their dependency well into their teenage years. With that exclusion came the ability to control and mold children, to protect them from exploitation, and to oversee their parents.[50]

These shifts were so prominent that it was within that period that a truly fundamental change in the sociolegal image of childhood occurred—the more formal invention of adolescence. By the early 1900s the term *adolescence* was popularized, most notably by G. Stanley Hall.[51] Hall and other experts viewed childhood as consisting of a series of developmental stages that differentiated children deemed immature and vulnerable from the more mature and malleable adult. Couched between childhood and adulthood was the period of adolescence, which was now conceived as a natural and universal developmental stage. This development in the formal invention of adolescence resulted from the same forces that had spurred the progressive, child-saving efforts. The child-saving metastructure enforced age segregation, prolonged dependency, and promulgated rules that governed the social lives of youth.[52] The focus on mutability, vulnerability, and inherent worth contributed to views of adolescence that constituted a period not close to adulthood but rather as a part of childhood. The developments reflected the centrality of and cultural emphasis on childhood that must be allowed to progress through developmental tasks to achieve full physical, psychological, and moral maturity.[53] Adolescence was conceived as a stage that routinely produced crises, which if left unattended to and unregulated could generate more crises and social turmoil. For example, vulnerable girls who engaged in precocious sexual activity jeopardized their futures as well as those of their children and the future of all generations.[54] The focus on potential crisis and need for direction produced a concept of adolescence that would serve to justify the prolonged social and economic dependency of youth and rationalize the differentiation, separation, and segregation of adolescents from adults, until the adolescents were mature enough to be deemed adults. This broad-gauged standardization of youthful experiences into age-segregated activities removed adolescents from the remainder of adult society and created what is now viewed as a distinct adolescent subculture.[55]

As part of the way adolescence was defined during the social reforms of the early 1900s, extending children's attributes to the postpubescent period, laws governing infants were applied to adolescents. In essence, adolescents became children under adult control and choice and subject to adults' parental attention.[56] Although the early 1900s witnessed a great deal of compulsory legislation for youth, the most influential impact of the child-saving efforts has been felt most explicitly in the institutionalization of the juvenile court and the impact it has had on adolescent life. The courts provided a means by which to define and control youthful deviance and support other child-saving endeavors, namely the ability to intervene in the event of parental deviance from the ideal way to prepare children for life.

The formal beginning of the current juvenile justice system, at least its basic ideology of reform, actually had emerged in the early 1800s. The 1820s witnessed the establishment of the first publicly funded and legally chartered custodial institutions for juvenile offenders— the Houses of Refuge and Houses of Reformation.[57] These houses were the first urban institutions to adopt age-segregate responses to adolescents who otherwise would have been treated as criminal adults if deemed adult-like or who would have avoided criminal liability and social control if deemed more child-like. These houses reflected many of the same elements of the common school movement that sought to bring adolescents under the formal control of public authority. By allowing for the removal of children considered directly or potentially delinquent, the houses provided a new means of control and containment that allowed the removal of children of urban immigrants and lower classes whose families did not provide adequate moral direction.[58] By saving children, activists literally intended the houses as sanctuaries and havens that sheltered youth, much as the ideal families were supposed to do. Indeed, the houses were molded after the family, which granted the houses of refuge and reform all the discretionary authority of the family, with the additional legitimation of formal law. The houses, though, quickly fell in disrepute as they became more like warehouses for deviant youth rather than ideal families that could foster healthy moral development. Much of that decline in reputations has been attributed to reformers' conflicts over the mode of family discipline, one harsh and another nurturing.[59] Regardless of that conflict, juvenile institutions would retain the houses' fundamental goals—to achieve a better imitation of ideal family life, and through that achievement the rehabilitation and prevention of problematic behavior.[60]

These efforts, which culminated in the modern juvenile court system—a separate system designed for the special needs of youth—replicated other efforts to impose middle-class views of child rearing. The system mirrored, reinforced, and extended previous efforts in three important ways. First, and as we have seen earlier, the basic ideology for reform allowed for intervention in immigrant and poor families derived from images of middle-class childhood. Second, the removal of youth from the criminal justice system reflected the previous effort to socially differentiate children from adults and emphasized benevolent assistance to children as a means to control their behavior and the child-rearing patterns of their parents and communities. Third, the new system *legally* allowed public officials to intervene in the family and determine what actions they should take. The development of the houses of refuge and reform, and the ensuing juvenile court system, reflected the creation of a strong, centralized state government that formally regulated social problems previously addressed informally and locally. Indeed, by 1928 all but two states had a juvenile court system.[61] Reformers had sought and achieved legislative sanctions to pursue their goals, and those sanctions would allow for the legal redefinition of juvenile deviance and solidify the creation of the period of adolescence.

Numerous examples of the concern for deviance reflect the juvenile justice system's focus on monitoring and responding to youthful behaviors indicative of further problems, such as a potential idle or immoral life. A key example involves attempts to control girls' behaviors.[62] Girls were clear losers in juvenile justice reform efforts. Many of the activities of the child savers and the juvenile justice system involved monitoring the behavior of young girls, especially of working-class and immigrant girls, to prevent their straying from normative, middle-class boundaries of social order.[63] Thus girls who failed to conform with ideals were labeled as "wayward" and deemed in need of juvenile court assistance. As several have revealed, almost all of the girls who appeared in juvenile court were found wayward and in need of reform, which involved placement in training schools and reformatories.[64] The cultural stereotypes of womanhood reinforced judicial efforts and allowed the isolation of sexually active girls. The stereotypes allowed the control to safeguard girls from exploitation, to preserve their "marriageability," to prevent them from reproducing, and to protect society. Again, it was the middle-class, Protestant view of sexuality that allowed for the control: A leading study of the first training school for girls in Massachusetts found that the institution housed primarily the daughters of Irish Catholic parents.[65] Other studies report that parents themselves frequently initiated court proceedings against their daughters, in attempts to restrain autonomous social and sexual behavior.[66] The control of girls' sexuality exemplifies how the state had institutions and the force of law available to control youth who exhibited adult behaviors—how state systems aimed to ensure that adolescents were in fact dependent children in need of control and supervision.

The impact of the juvenile justice system, as well as the educational system, reached beyond efforts to control adolescents when parents had failed or when youth did not fit into the middle-class social mold. The system provided important institutions that gained significance in the manner they served as the eventual source of adolescents' individual rights. These institutions, explicitly designed to control youth, ultimately and ironically served as primary sources of efforts to liberate adolescents from parental and social control. Although much of the juvenile justice and educational systems still reflect and retain traditional images of adolescence, the development of these systems spurred the adolescents' rights movement.

The development of what may be deemed an adolescents' rights movement (most often viewed as the juvenile rights revolution) began by the mid-1900s.[67] It was in that period that reformers had become increasingly concerned about the juvenile court's abuse of its powers to correct youthful behavior and concerned that schools' inculcation of youth thwarted the development of responsible democratic citizenship. That need to respond to abuses and concerns contributed directly to the legal recognition of adolescents' rights within public, state-controlled systems. Thus by the late 1960s adolescents had acquired independent rights in juvenile justice systems[68] and schools.[69] Concern for abuses and need to protect adolescents' individual rights even infiltrated the more private aspects of youths' lives—family relationships. In the late 1970s adolescents had acquired limited but nevertheless independent rights within their families, which allowed adolescents to exert control over their lives when parent–child relationships failed to protect adolescents.[70] This new status was reflected by the Supreme Court's eventual recognition that minors were "persons" protected by the Constitution,[71] a protection that inevitably led to an increase in adolescents' legal status.

These developments dramatically departed from traditional approaches in that the law sought to distinguish the rights of adolescents as separate from those of their families, parents, or other institutions controlled by adults. Although the developments did not forcefully and unequivocally recognize adolescents' own rights, the developments have *allowed* for greater adolescent autonomy and considered adolescents more complete human beings under the Constitution.[72] By the late 1970s the legal system reflected institutional changes as it became charged with alternative images of adolescence that began to compete openly with the more traditional ideology focused on adult control of adolescents. This legal development within social systems, explored more directly in the following chapter, resulted in an unprecedented position of adolescents in the law. The force of law that had helped move the control of adolescents away from church, work, and family life to schools, families, and other institutions now reflected and spurred another development in the place of adolescents in society. Although hesitantly and often barely perceptively, the force of law now moves the control of adolescents to adolescents themselves.

That new development, one that seeks to recognize the adult nature of adolescence rather than impose on adolescence the status of childhood, leads to polarized ideologies of who should primarily control adolescent life. The more recent and still emerging model, with roots in the 1960s and 1970s, views adolescents as more independent, capable of choice and benefiting greater autonomy. The traditional model, with roots in the early 1900s, views adolescents as dependent and under the control of authority. Unlike the traditional model, the emerging model presents adolescents as relatively complete human beings, capable of making their own decisions and thus as being responsible for their consequences.

The two contrasting visions loom prominently. In the context of family life, the traditional model views adolescents as living in private, hierarchical settings that leave youth essentially without choices and families with little outside influences.[73] The model reinforces strong parental authority and, with few exceptions, assumes that parents rightly may displace the choices of their adolescent children. The emerging vision perceives youth as existing in more egalitarian families that understand parent–adolescent relationships as grounded in autonomy, greater choice, and increased freedom to engage with more public, external influences.[74] In their everyday dealings with students, schools also vacillate between the traditional extreme that aims to control adolescents in a hierarchical environment and the emerging view that aims to include youth in school authority structures and foster adolescent participation and control over their own educational experiences.[75] Likewise, juvenile justice systems alternate between similar opposites. The traditional approach posits that adolescents are under the control of their parents, and that the juvenile court acts as good parents as it flexibly involves youth in dispositions and acts in children's best interests. Despite that view, juvenile justice system's pervasively switch toward the ultimately modern antipode as it attempts to assimilate adolescents into an egalitarian view of interactions that prizes autonomy and denies any fundamental distinction between adolescence and adulthood.[76] Allowing adolescents to be viewed as autonomous, competent, mature, and adult permits society to impose ''get-tough'' measures in response to perceptions of youth as violent and prone to uncontrollable behavior.[77] Although the law tends to fluctuate in institutions outside of the domestic sphere, the law is much less hesitant to redefine the proper place, roles, and rights of youth in public institutions.

These contrasting images of youth and the social institutions that they interact with infiltrate and guide social policies and affect the extent to which systems act in adolescents' own interests. The traditional image insists that adolescents benefit from being treated as innocent and vulnerable children separated from the harsh realities of adult life. Because adolescents are vulnerable both to the demands of the world outside domestic order and to their own immaturity, society assigns adolescents a preferred status and offers protection from the vagaries of adult life. However, the traditional images seem less compelling as the familial and societal contexts that were once thought to have actualized those images disappear and the law faces the plight of actual adolescents. The traditional images also lose much of their rhetorical power in light of current developmental psychological research that questions the premises about adolescents' incompetencies and the way they gain competencies. We now turn to those contemporary challenges and the extent to which adolescents' competencies constitute a malleable social construct rather than an immutable scientific fact.

The Reinvention of Adolescent Personhood

We thus far have sketched a link between the emergence of the adolescent period and the concomitant reflection of that recognition in the manner families and society treat their adolescents. These developments that occurred over the span of centuries, however, recently have been revisited by rapid changes. Two dominant developments in the reinvention of adolescence directly determine the challenges youth face and opportunities for positive outcomes. The first critical transformation involves the lengthening of the period of adolescence. The extension comes in several forms. Control of infection and better nutrition have lowered the average age at which physical maturity begins.[78] At the same time, social changes—primarily economic changes—have postponed the end of adolescence and stretched the period of dependency much longer. This elongated period of adolescence introduces much uncertainty. At least a decade of transition now exists between childhood and adulthood.[79]

The second transformation deals with the increasing disjuncture between biological and social development. Although adolescents actually reach reproductive maturity and pervasively acquire sexual interests in early adolescence,[80] cognitive capacities attain characteristics of fuller stages only in the middle-adolescent period.[81] It is only between the ages of 14 and 16, for example, that adolescents begin to be able to think abstractly enough to adopt a sophisticated view of other people's perspectives and move beyond egocentrism and personal fables characterized by biased and incomplete images of themselves.[82] The lag in cognitive capacity ensures a concomitant lag in social maturity. These developments also reveal sizeable sex, class, and cultural differences.[83] These social, psychological, cognitive, and biological changes result in the development of increasingly distinct adolescent periods, now frequently delimited as early, middle, and late adolescence. Exactly how to deal with these different stages of adolescence remains unclear. What does seem clear is that adolescents make many fateful decisions that affect their entire life course, that societal conditions challenge adolescents' abilities to embark on healthy courses of development, and that the social sciences increasingly agree about what contributes to youths' competency—the ability to engage in mature decision making—and supports trajectories toward healthy development and responsible societal membership.

Challenges to Adolescent Competency

Although the vast majority of adolescents successfully negotiate the path from childhood to adulthood,[84] the developmental path has been marked by several changes. While transformations in the period increase, adolescents experience an erosion of family and social support networks. Traditionally, families and communities provided durable networks, familiar human relationships, and cultural guidance for youth. In times of stress, such networks offered support and the skills necessary for successful coping and adaptation. In contemporary societies, such social support networks have eroded and their absence challenges adolescents' efforts to gain competence.

Numerous commentators canvass the dramatic change from nuclear families to different permutations of families that cannot be assumed to nourish, treasure, and safeguard adolescents.[85] The new families, premised on the equality and choices of adults presumed free to negotiate the terms of their relationships and the terms of their relationships' demise, result in widespread social disruption for children. Many of the qualities viewed as prerequisite for individual health and professional success strain the central qualities of modern parenting: spending time with family members, maintaining empathic and child-centered relationships, thinking about and dealing with children's problems, and providing consistency and stability for children.[86] A single look at current research on family life reveals the failure to meet these simple yet necessary needs. The structure of families has changed dramatically. These changes relate directly to the capacity and resources of caretakers who affect youths' emotional development. By the time they are 16, approximately half of all children in the United States will experience their parents' divorce.[87] This transformation relates to the major social shift in maternal employment. Mothers increasingly work outside the home, and those with the fewest social and personal resources— single mothers—are especially more likely to work outside the home.[88] Fewer than 7% of families now reflect the two-parent model of husband as breadwinner and wife as homemaker.[89] Commentators link these changes to threats to children's development as they produce latchkey children who more likely experience emotional problems and engage in risk behaviors.[90] Equally illustrative of the changes are youth outside of families. The major example is the number of adolescents who runaway or reside in alternative-care placements. Although the number of adolescents in foster care, group care, or institutional care is unknown, what is known is that they may be in need of extra care and that their lives are placed at extra risk, and those risks arise from the failed familial bonds that were either overtly abusive or nonresponsive to the adolescents' needs and from deficiencies in alternative care systems.[91]

Changes in family life and less stable environments compound adolescents' exposure to increasing risks. Approximately half of U.S. adolescents place within moderate or greater risk categories of those who engage in a host of disruptive practices: unsafe sexual behaviors, teenage pregnancy, and teenage childbearing; drug and alcohol use and abuse; school underachievement, failure, and dropout; and delinquency, crime, and violence. Fifty percent of today's 10- to 17-year-olds engage in two or more of these types of risk behaviors, and 10% of youth in this age range engage in all of these risks.[92] Although youth always had access to potentially life-threatening substances, weapons, and activities, societal changes exacerbate their risk; for example, the last five years of the 1980s saw the average age of gang members drop from 15 to 13.[93] These transformations gain considerable significance in light of our understanding of adolescent development. Early adolescents increasingly encounter more ambiguity and complexity about what constitutes preparation for effective adulthood; foreseeing years ahead increasingly becomes more difficult for everyone.

Numerous risks arise from increased rates and changing consequences of sexual activity. Health risks involved in sexual activity are high, as are the long-term risks associated with parenthood and certain sexually transmitted diseases. Statistics regarding pregnancy and parenting present a situation of difficulty and disadvantage. One million U.S. teenage women become pregnant each year.[94] Teenage mothers are more likely to rely on public assistance, obtain less education, receive inadequate prenatal care, and rear high-risk children than their non–early-child-rearing peers.[95] The costs of early pregnancy accrue not only to the adolescent herself but to her children, parents, partners, and society.[96] The statistics regarding sexually transmitted diseases (STDs) are equally grim. Each year three million teenagers acquire a sexually transmitted infection, with adolescents accounting for 25% of the new sexually transmitted infections in the United States.[97] An estimated 40% of students in grades 9 through 12 have a history of a STD.[98] The number of adolescents with acquired immunodeficiency syndrome (AIDS) has increased 77% since 1989, and the latency period suggests that many AIDS patients were probably infected as teenagers.[99] For girls, early intercourse, repeated sex-related infections, and multiple partners greatly increase the risk of cervical cancer and infertility.[100] Again, the costs are not only personal. It is estimated that $4 billion to $5 billion are spent each year treating the sequelae of STDs.[101]

Increasing risks reflect other transformations, particularly the increasing likelihood of being raised in poverty. Forty percent of those living in poverty are children,[102] and 16% of children between ages 12 and 17 live in households with incomes below the poverty line.[103] It is important to note that existing data sets do not even cover the most problematic poor adolescents: those who are homeless.[104] Yet evidence suggests that the number of homeless youth continues to increase, a result of a combination of factors, including changes in family structure, changes in the labor market economy, and decreases in governmental assistance to the poor.[105] These changes differentially affect children from different ethnic and minority groups. Most problematically, poverty represents a constellation of risk factors for children's physical and mental health development.[106] In addition, poverty also means growing up in dangerous environments: not only do poor people have the most health problems, they gain the least access to health care[107] and are at highest risk for educational failure, which further limits economic opportunities.[108] Economic forces also strain relationships within families: Financial problems undermine parental involvement and supportive parenting.[109] At extremes, adolescents face homelessness, an outcome of poverty that increases a wide range of other problems.[110]

Forces that place adolescents at risk do not only derive from social forces seemingly far from adolescents' immediate families. Substance abuse presents important threats to families and impinges on youth development in two ways. When parents abuse drugs and alcohol, a host of negative outcomes arise. Children of alcoholic parents, for example, are at risk for numerous possible problems, particularly relational, behavioral, emotional, and academic problems.[111] When children themselves start using drugs as adolescents, less predictable problems arise. Youth who use drugs experience increased pressure to sell drugs; higher rates of behavioral, cognitive, and emotional impairments; and more violence than their peers.[112] Substance abusing adolescents are more likely to die violent deaths through homicides, suicides, and motor vehicle accidents.[113] It is important to note that those who report on trends in drug use find increases; estimates now show that nearly 20% of 12- to 17-year-olds have used illicit drugs, and nearly 90% have used alcohol, with more than one fourth of eighth graders reporting that they have been drunk.[114]

In addition to substance abuse, domestic violence poses another pervasive threat to youth within families. Adolescents who simply witness domestic violence report more social, cognitive, emotional, and behavioral problems than children from nonviolent homes.[115] These findings are significant. Evidence mounts that these situations place youth at risk for continuing behaviors into their own relationships and that their communities reinforce negative outcomes.[116] Likewise, available data indicate that up to 70% of youth who are exposed to domestic violence also are themselves physically abused, sexually abused, or both.[117] Despite negative outcomes, the domestic violence movement has yet to address the needs of secondary victims.[118]

Adolescents face other hazards. When overall prevalence rates are taken into consideration, nearly one third of all youth in the United States suffers from a chronic illness.[119] Chronic and disabling physical conditions affect up to 15% of all youth, and another 10 to 25% exhibit serious mental health disorders.[120] These disabling conditions pose challenges for youth. Up to 80% of those with mental health disorders receive no mental health care.[121] The effects reverberate. Many experience school failure and drop out of school. Nationwide, more than 12% of adolescents are high school dropouts, a finding that ranges widely depending on race, ethnic backgrounds, and geographical locations.[122] Severe emotional problems and related abuses place youth at higher risk of suicide, which currently is the third leading cause of death for late adolescents (following accidents and homicide).[123]

Adolescents also suffer social exclusion from the benefits of major civil rights initiatives. For example, the recent policy efforts to address the HIV/AIDS crisis, guided by response to an adolescent who championed reform even to the extent to which the major act was named after him—The Ryan White Comprehensive AIDS Resources Emergency (CARE) Act of 1990[124]—fails to include adolescents in the programs that were funded and policies that were encouraged: The Act focused on young children and adults.[125] The failure reflects how major civil rights movements have largely ignored the adolescents who constitute the groups in need of protection. Efforts to better the place of gay and lesbian members of society also illustrate well how social movements largely ignore the plight of youth, as does the manner the women's movement's attempt to halt domestic violence largely ignores adolescent dating violence.[126] Yet the adolescent experiences of both of these groups reveal that the period of adolescence provides an opportune time for intervention that would foster development and healthier responses to social pressures and personal stresses.

A last major transformation in the lives of adolescents involves the need to adapt to an increasingly multiethnic and global society. This change in cultural life gains considerable significance and challenges current conceptions of youth. Adolescents may live in familial contexts culturally distinct from the ecology of the broader society. Roles appropriate for adolescents may differ within racial–ethnic and socioeconomic groups and lead to dissonance between the demand of bicultural contexts.[127] Likewise, within each specific ethnic–racial group or subgroup, cultural values and ideologies that mark passages into adulthood may diverge from the majority context.[128] Various cultural practices, family values, and role expectations affect different groups' perspectives on the relevance and timing of developmental tasks and needs.[129] These changes do not only create difficulties for adolescents, they also challenge responses to adolescents' needs and crises. For example, the child welfare and juvenile justice systems continue to be marked by subtle and overt discrimination that results in remarkable disproportions in outcomes for youths of minority status.[130] Responses to such acknowledged discrimination remain difficult to envision, let alone implement.

Given the rapid transformation of contemporary life and the challenges youth face, it becomes understandable that policies fluctuate between efforts to protect and efforts to liberate from special protections. The circumstances youth face also make understandable the reason the most forceful ideologies continue to champion protection at the expense of even moderate liberation. The irony of the desire to protect is that it seemingly results in the creation of the problems that fuel protective impulses. Of equal irony is the manner the desire to protect contributes to the failure of protective efforts and disables the development of competency to deal with troubling life circumstances.

Pathways to Adolescent Competency

Although several researchers and commentators report on the tasks youth face in their adolescent transition, all generally focus on youth's sense of self and relationships to others and the necessary balance between independence and dependence, or between protection and liberation.[131] As with previous time periods, adolescents must find a place in a valued group that provides a sense of belonging. Adolescents also must identify tasks generally recognized by the group as adaptive, and acquire skills to cope with the task if they are to earn respect and self-worth. In addition, adolescents still must establish reliable and predictable relationships with other people, especially some close relationships, and find ways to be useful to others. Adolescents must develop a basis for making informed, deliberate decisions, particularly decisions that have life-long consequences. Neither last nor least, adolescents must accept the enormous diversity of modern society and find constructive expression of curiosity and exploration that characterizes modern adolescence.

Despite the numerous tasks and challenges, healthy outcomes derive from predictable paths. Social scientists increasingly concur that several conditions more likely ensure the development of positive adolescent competence.[132] The most widely accepted research on prototypic parenting styles consistently demonstrates their relationship to psychosocial and behavioral adjustment in offspring.[133] These findings continue even after adjustments for such usual influences as gender, socioeconomic status, family structure, and ethnicity.[134] The wide range of behavioral and psychosocial characteristics associated with parenting style include social competence, academic achievement, self-reliance, psychosocial distress and delinquency, substance use, adolescent drinking, peer group selection, and mental health. In general, adolescents who rate their parents as *authoritative* experience the most favorable adjustment, those who view their parents as more neglectful have the least favorable outcomes, and those with parents who adopt the middle-ground (authoritarian and indulgent) exhibit mixed adjustments.[135] The findings are far from surprising. Successful parenting practices revolve around the management of relationships, encouragement of the child's sense of control within the parent–child relationship, provision of support for mutual coregulation, and teaching of sophisticated skills for expressing resistance and negotiation.[136]

The forms of interactions needed for successful relationships and community membership simply reflect effective parenting and interactions with youth that support self-determination and adjustment to society. Lessons learned from family life transfer to other institutions examined by researchers as critical to adolescent life. Various areas of society that directly intervene in adolescent life, ranging from schools, penal systems, health organizations, to leisure and recreation, all succeed when they follow a model that includes youth in developing and structuring programs that foster self-determination.[137] Positive and competent development derives from and is maintained under conditions of autonomy support, structure, and knowledge about and involvement in the adolescents' life.[138]

Although supported by the challenges of reality, the new image of adolescent life gains recognition and approval by society and the legal system only with ambivalence and much hesitancy. Despite hesitancy, the law is more ready than it was even a few decades ago to define adolescents, in various contexts and for various purposes, as autonomous individuals with their own legal personhood. The willingness, especially for adolescents in public contexts, contributes an element of modern law that opens unusual opportunities for reform efforts. Equally significant, the courts and legislatures dealing with actual adolescents increasingly are unable to rely on traditional assumptions about the character of domestic life and other institutions that once protected youth. These two changes reflect and encourage shifts in the legal personhood of adolescents.

Conclusion

The early 1900s marked the initial disappearance of the notion that, on reaching puberty, a child could assume a status independent of his or her parents or other dominant social institution. This new status for youth who became viewed as "children" meant that adolescents, like children, were assumed to be vulnerable, malleable, and in need of adult guidance, control, and training. This new potential-person status had evolved as the notion of child-oriented family life emerged and as forces external to the family, most notably child labor laws, compulsory schooling provisions, and juvenile justice systems began to influence the care of children. As the enforced prolongation of childhood was settled, the invention of adolescence emerged as it simply added a second childhood to childhood.

Contemporary changes challenge the traditional, child-like view of adolescents. The change from the traditional to an emerging model that focuses on recognizing and ensuring adolescent competence reveals several important points about the social recognition of adolescence. First, the current understanding of adolescence suggests that there exists multiple pathways through adolescence, a diversity that must be addressed if laws will foster adolescents. Second, society no longer assumes, nor allows, parents to control their children to the extent that history suggests. As the abilities of families to perform traditional roles decrease, society increasingly takes the obligation of families in educating, guiding, and preparing youth for their future. Third, despite continued attempts to preserve traditional images of adolescents, society and the law continue to redesign the lives of most adolescents, and the very notion of adolescence itself. Fourth, recognition that adolescents are affected by transformations in society and family life places pressure on the need to recognize and foster adolescent competence.

The end of the 1900s now mark a massive change in the reality of adolescent life. Like adults, adolescents have increased their independence through a number of individual choices available to them and have been faced by increasing challenges. Despite changes in the realities of adolescent life, traditional images that contributed to the invention of adolescence still pervade societal beliefs and perceptions of adolescents. Likewise, traditional images pervasively guide responses to adolescents' circumstances and policy responses to adolescent life. Policy responses follow the same ideological conflicts found in society; both remain conflicted between the need and desire to foster adolescents' dependence or independence. Fluctuations between traditional or emergent approaches also are prominent in the development of adolescents' rights, as the legal system recognizes some aspects of adolescents' changing place in society and family life but still hesitates to recognize many of adolescents' situations. The next chapter examines these developments in adolescents' rights to reveal the manner conflicting images of youth constrain how the law approaches the adolescent period and ensures, as we will see and attempt to counter in the remaining chapters, that society inadequately addresses adolescents' sexuality.

Endnotes

1. Roger J. R. Levesque, *Adolescents, Society, and the Law* (Chicago: American Bar Association, 1997).
2. Commentators generally suggest that the term *adolescence* as understood today, emerged as a creation of the 19th-century social and industrial order; *see, e.g.,* John Demos, *Past, Present and Personal: The Family and the Life Course in American History* (New York: Oxford University Press, 1986); Joseph Kett, *Rites of Passage: Adolescence in America, 1790 to the Present* (New York: Basic Books, 1977). Others, however, argue that the notion of adolescence merely transformed the parameters of an existing category of social identity; *see, e.g.,* Roger Thompson, "Adolescent Culture in Colonial Massachusetts," *Journal of Family History* 9 (1984):127–144.
3. *See* Harvey Graff, *Growing Up in America: Historical Experiences* (Detroit, MI: Wayne State University Press, 1987); Joseph M. Hawes and N. Ray Hiner (Eds.), *American Childhood: A Research Guide and Historical Handbook* (Westport, CT.: Greenwood Press, 1985).
4. Barabara A. Hanawalt, *The Ties that Bound: Peasant Families in Medieval England* (New York: Oxford University Press, 1986).
5. Kett, *Rites of Passage: Adolescence in America, 1790 to the Present.*
6. Burton J. Bledstein, *The Culture of Professionalism: The Middle Class and the Development of Higher Education in America* (New York: Norton, 1976).

7. Steven R. Smith, "Religion and Conception of Youth in Seventeenth-Century England," *History of Childhood Quarterly* 2 (1974):493–516.

8. Kett, *Rites of Passage: Adolescence in America, 1790 to the Present;* Oscar Handlin and Mary F. Handlin, *Facing Life: Youth and Family in American History* (Boston: Little, Brown, 1971).

9. Kett, *Rites of Passage: Adolescence in America, 1790 to the Present.*

10. *Id.*

11. Thompson, "Adolescent Culture in Colonial Massachusetts."

12. Michael Grossberg, *Governing the Hearth: Law and the Family in Nineteenth-Century America* (Chapel Hill: University of North Carolina Press, 1985).

13. Lee E. Teitelbaum and Leslie J. Harris, "Some Historical Perspectives on the Governmental Regulation of Children and Parents." In *Beyond Control: Status Offenders in the Juvenile Court,* ed. Lee E. Teitelbaum and Aidan R. Gough (Cambridge, MA: Ballinger, 1977), pp. 1–44.

14. *See* John R. Sutton, *Stubborn Children: Controlling Delinquency in the United States* (Berkeley: University of California Press, 1988), p. 10.

15. Teitelbaum and Harris, "Some Historical Perspectives on the Governmental Regulation of Children and Parents." *See also* Sutton, *Stubborn Children: Controlling Delinquency in the United States.*

16. Daniel Scott Smith and Michael S. Hindus, "Premarital Pregnancy in America 1640–1971: An Overview and Interpretation," *Journal of Interdisciplinary History* 4 (1975):537–570.

17. Sutton, *Stubborn Children: Controlling Delinquency in the United States.*

18. Joseph Hawes, *The Children's Rights Movement: A History of Advocacy and Protection* (Boston: Twayne, 1991).

19. David Galenson, *White Servitude in Colonial America: An Economic Analysis* (Cambridge, MA: Cambridge University Press, 1981).

20. Robert H. Bremner (Ed.), *Children and Youth in America* (Cambridge, MA: Harvard University Press, 1970).

21. Demos, *Past, Present and Personal: The Family and the Life Course in American History.*

22. Kett, *Rites of Passage: Adolescence in America, 1790 to the Present,* at 60–61.

23. Paul Boyer and Stephen Nissenbaum, *Salem Possessed: The Social Origins of Witchcraft* (Cambridge, MA: Harvard University Press, 1974).

24. John Demos, "Underlying Themes in the Witchcraft of Seventeenth-Century New England," *American Historical Review* 75 (1970):1311–1326.

25. Smith and Hindus, "Premarital Pregnancy in America 1640–1971: An Overview and Interpretation." *See also* Maris A. Vinovskis, *An "Epidemic" of Adolescent Pregnancy?: Some Historical and Policy Perspectives* (New York: Oxford University Press, 1988).

26. Robert V. Wells, "Illegitimacy and Bridal Pregnancy in Colonial America." In *Bastardy and Its Comparative History,* ed. Peter Laslett, Larla Oosterveen, and Richard M. Smith (Cambridge, MA: Harvard University Press, 1980).

27. Roger Thompson, *Sex in Middlesex: Popular Mores in a Massachusetts County, 1649–1699* (Amherst: University of Massachusetts Press, 1986).

28. Robert H. Wiebe, *The Search for Order, 1877–1920* (New York: Hill and Wang, 1967).

29. Demos, *Past, Present and Personal: The Family and the Life Course in American History.*

30. Grossberg, *Governing the Hearth: Law and the Family in Nineteenth-Century America.*

31. *Id.* at 31.

32. Steven Mintz and Susan Kellogg, *Domestic Revolutions: A Social History of American Family Life* (New York: Free Press, 1988).

33. David M. Schneider, *American Kinship: A Cultural Account* (Englewood Cliffs, NJ: Prentice Hall, 1968), p. 33.

34. Harvey J. Graff, "Early Adolescence in Antebellum America: The Remaking of Growing Up," *Journal of Early Adolescence* 5 (1985):411–427. For example, some groups of children were obligated to support their parents and families. As society was defining the ideal of childhood as separate from the interactions with the working world, poor children were being exploited by the industrial enterprise. *See also* Viviana A. Zelizer, *Pricing the Priceless Child: The Changing*

Social Value of Children (New York: Free Press, 1985). Throughout much of the early American history of childhood and the social construction of the adolescent period, not much remains known or written about how children's slaves experienced adolescence; for an important analysis comparing Black children's experiences with other groups, *see* Priscilla Ferguson Clement, *Growing Pains: Children in the Industrial Age, 1850–1890* (New York: Twayne, 1997).

35. The movement toward innocence and reduced economic worth of children was supported and channeled by professional organizations, especially health professionals who championed their fields of expertise and labor unions ready to assist and protect adult laborers' interests. Herbert M. Likebard, "Psychology . . . The Teacher's Blackstone: G. Stanley Hall and the Effort to Build a Developmental Curriculum for Youth," *Journal of Early Adolescence* 5 (1985):467–478; Barbara Bennett Woodhouse, " 'Who Owns the Child?': *Meyer* and *Pierce* and the Child as Property," *William and Mary Law Review* 33 (1992):995–1122.

36. Kett, *Rites of Passage: Adolescence in America, 1790 to the Present;* Anthony Platt, *The Child Savers: The Invention of Delinquency.* 2d ed. (Chicago: University of Chicago Press, 1977).

37. Carl Degler, *At Odds: Women and the Family in America From the Revolution to the Present* (New York: Oxford University Press, 1980).

38. Brigitte Berger and Peter L. Berger, *The War Over the Family: Capturing the Middle Ground* (New York: Anchor Books, 1984).

39. Clement, *Growing Pains: Children in the Industrial Age, 1850–1890.*

40. *Id.*

41. Degler, *At Odds: Women and the Family in America From the Revolution to the Present.*

42. Betty G. Farrell, *Family: The Making of an Idea, an Institution, and a Controversy in American Culture* (Boulder, CO: Westview Press, 1999).

43. Richard Hofstadter, *The Age of Reform: From Bryan to F.D.R.* (New York: Knopf, 1955).

44. Frank A. Fasick, "On the 'Invention' of Adolescence," *Journal of Early Adolescence* 14 (1994):6–23.

45. *Id.*

46. Woodhouse, " 'Who Owns the Child?': *Meyer* and *Pierce* and the Child as Property."

47. Several view schooling as the manner to deploy youth within the economic sphere and serve as an important way to instill the culture's authority structure and to ease adolescents' passage into the world of work. *See* Raymond E. Callahan, *Education and the Cult of Efficiency* (Chicago: University of Chicago Press, 1962); Daniel K. Lapsley, Robert D. Enright, and Ronald C. Serline, "Toward a Theoretical Perspective on the Legislation of Adolescence," *Journal of Early Adolescence* 5 (1985):441–466; Selwyn K. Troen, "Technological Development and Adolescence: The Early Twentieth Century," *Journal of Early Adolescence* 5 (1985):429–439.

48. Michael Katz, *The Irony of Early School Reform: Educational Innovation in Mid-Nineteenth Century Massachusetts* (Boston: Beacon, 1968).

49. David Tyack, "Ways of Seeing: An Essay on the History of Compulsory Schooling, *Harvard Educational Review* 46 (1976):355–389.

50. David J. Rothman, *Conscience and Convenience: The Asylum and Its Alternative in Progressive America* (Boston: Little, Brown, 1980).

51. G. Stanley Hall, *Adolescence: Its Psychology and Its Relations to Anthropology, Sociology, Sex, Crime, Religion, and Education* (New York: Appleton, 1904).

52. David I. Macleod, *The Age of the Child: Children in America, 1890–1920* (New York: Twayne, 1998).

53. Lamar T. Empey, "The Social Construction of Childhood and Juvenile Justice." In *The Future of Childhood and Juvenile Justice,* ed. LaMar T. Empey (Charlottesville: University of Virginia Press, 1979).

54. Farrell, *Family: The Making of an Idea, an Institution, and a Controversy in American Culture.*

55. Demos, *Past, Present and Personal: The Family and the Life Course in American History.*

56. Roger J. R. Levesque, "The Internationalization of Children's Human Rights: Too Radical for American Adolescents?" *Connecticut Journal of International Law* 9 (1994):237–293.

57. Sutton, *Stubborn Children: Controlling Delinquency in the United States.*

58. Rothman, *Conscience and Convenience: The Asylum and Its Alternative in Progressive America.*

59. Sutton, *Stubborn Children: Controlling Delinquency in the United States.*

60. *Id.*

61. Platt, *The Child Savers: The Invention of Delinquency.*

62. Mary E. Odem, *Delinquent Daughters: Protecting and Policing Adolescent Female Sexuality in the United States* (Chapel Hill: University of North Carolina Press, 1995).

63. *Id. See also* Linda Gordon, *Heroes in Their Own Lives: The Politics and History of Family Violence: Boston, 1880–1960* (New York: Viking, 1988).

64. Meda Chesney-Lind and Randall G. Shelden, *Girls, Delinquency, and Juvenile Justice* (Belmont, CA: Wadsworth, 1998).

65. Barbara Brenzel, "Domestication as Reform: A Study of the Socialization of Wayward Girls, 1856–1905," *Harvard Educational Review* 50 (1980):196–213.

66. Ruth M. Alexander, *The "Girl Problem": Female Sexual Delinquency in New York, 1900–1930* (Ithaca, NY: Cornell University Press, 1995).

67. Levesque, *Adolescents, Society and the Law.*

68. *In re* Gault, 387 U.S. 1 (1967).

69. Tinker v. Des Moines Ind. Community Sch. Dist., 393 U.S. 503 (1969).

70. Bellotti v. Baird, 443 U.S. 622 (1979).

71. *Tinker,* 393 U.S. at 511.

72. The recognition of autonomy can be considered to reinforce the traditional notions of family autonomy insofar as the adolescents in the major cases of *Tinker* and *Gault* were not opposed by their parents but were supported by them; *In re* Gault, 387 U.S. at 4–5 (1967) (demonstrating support for child by parent through attendance at hearing and subsequent suit for *habeas corpus*); *Tinker,* 393 U.S. at 504 (noting complaint filed on behalf of petitioners by their fathers). Likewise, in the abortion case that apparently recognizes autonomy, *Bellotti,* 443 U.S. at 622, the result upholds traditional notions in that it allows judicial bypasses for mature adolescents but preserves the family for those who are immature and creates a system in which even the mature adolescents are encouraged, if not arguably required, to obtain parental permission or consent. Existing systems allow for the belief that parents control their children. *Id.*

73. Levesque, *Adolescents, Society and the Law.*

74. *Id.*

75. Roger J. R. Levesque, "Educating American Youth: Lessons From Children's Human Rights Law," *Journal of Law & Education* 27 (1998):173–209.

76. Roger J. R. Levesque, "Is There Still a Place for Violent Youth in Juvenile Justice?" *Aggressive and Violent Behavior* 1 (1996):69–79.

77. *Id.*

78. Francoise D. Alsaker, "Annotation: The Impact of Puberty," *Journal of Child Psychology and Psychiatry* 37 (1996):249–258.

79. Jeffrey Jensen Arnett and Susan Taber, "Adolescence Terminable and Interminable: When Does Adolescence End?" *Journal of Youth and Adolescence* 23 (1994):517–537.

80. Martha K. McClintock and Gilbert Herdt, "Rethinking Puberty: The Development of Sexual Attraction," *Current Directions in Psychological Science* 5 (1996):178–183.

81. For leading social science analyses of these developments, *see* Elizabeth S. Scott, N. Dickon Reppucci, and Jennifer L. Willard, "Evaluating Adolescent Decision Making in Legal Contexts," *Law and Human Behavior* 19 (1995):221–244; Laurence Steinberg and Elizabeth Cauffman, "Maturity and Judgment in Adolescence: Psychosocial Factors in Adolescent Decision Making," *Law and Human Behavior* 20 (1996):249–272.

82. *See* William Damon, *Social and Personality Development: Infancy Through Adolescence* (New York: Norton, 1983).

83. *See, e.g.,* Jari-Erik Nurmi, "How Do Adolescents See Their Future? A Review of the Development of Future Orientation and Planning," *Developmental Review* 11 (1991):1–59.

84. For ground-breaking research noting the claim, *see* Daniel Offer, Eric Ostrov, Kenneth I.

Howard, and Robert Atkinson, *The Teenage World: Adolescents' Self-image in Ten Countries* (New York: Plenum Press, 1988).

85. James Garborino and John Eckenrode, *Understanding Abusive Families: An Ecological Approach to Theory and Practice* (San Francisco: Jossey-Bass, 1997).

86. Sylvia Ann Hewlett, *When the Bough Breaks: The Cost of Neglecting Our Children* (New York: Basic Books, 1991).

87. Paul R. Amato and Bruce Keith, "Parental Divorce and the Well-Being of Children: A Meta-Analysis," *Psychological Bulletin* 110 (1991):26–46.

88. Children's Defense Fund, *The State of America's Children: Yearbook 1994* (Washington, DC: Author, 1994).

89. Louise B. Silverstein, "Transforming the Debate About Child Care and Maternal Employment," *American Psychologist* 46 (1991):1025–1032.

90. Edward Zigler and Martha Finn-Stevenson, *Children: Development and Social Issues* (Lexington, MA: Heath, 1987).

91. Bonita Evans, *Youth in Foster Care: The Shortcomings of Child Protection Services* (New York: Garland, 1997).

92. Joy G. Dryfoos, *Adolescents at Risk: Current Prevalence and Intervention* (New York: Oxford University Press, 1990).

93. Gaylen M. Kelton and J. Christopher Shank, "Adolescent Injury and Death: The Plagues of Accident, Self-Infliction and Violence," *Adolescent Medicine* 25 (1998):163–177.

94. Centers for Disease Control and Prevention, "Pregnancy, Sexually Transmitted Diseases, and Related Risk Behaviors Among U.S. Adolescents," *Adolescent Health: State of the Nation Monograph Series, No. 2* (1994), CDC Publication No. 099-4630.

95. Barbara B. Tobias and Rick E. Ricer, "Counseling Adolescents About Sexuality," *Adolescent Medicine* 25 (1988):49–70.

96. Rebekah Levine Coley and P. Lindsay Chase-Lansdale, "Adolescent Pregnancy and Parenthood: Recent Evidence and Future Directions," *American Psychologist* 53 (1998):152–166.

97. Centers for Disease Control and Prevention, "Pregnancy, Sexually Transmitted Diseases, and Related Risk Behaviors Among U.S. Adolescents."

98. Centers for Disease Control, "Sexual Behavior Among High School Students—United States 1990," *Morbidity and Mortality Weekly Report* 40 (1990):885–888.

99. Donna Futterman, Karen Hein, Nancy Rueven, Ralph Dell, and Nathan Shafer, "Human Immunodeficiency Virus-Infected Adolescents: The First 50 Patients in a New York City Program," *Pediatrics* 91 (1993):730–735.

100. M. Schydlower and M-A Shafer (Eds.), "AIDS and Other Sexually Transmitted Diseases," *Adolescent Medicine: State of the Art Reviews* 1 (1990):409–647.

101. Scot Lappa, Mary T. Coleman, and Anna-Barbara Moscicki, "Managing Sexually Transmitted Diseases in Adolescents," *Adolescent Medicine* 25 (1998):71–110.

102. Children's Defense Fund, *The State of America's Children: Yearbook, 1994;* Vonnie C. McLoyd, "Socioeconomic Disadvantage and Child Development," *American Psychologist* 53 (1998):185–204.

103. Gretchen T. Cornell and Samuel M. Curtis, "The Demographic Context of U.S. Adolescence." In *Early Adolescence: Perspectives on Research, Policy, and Intervention,* ed. Richard M. Lerner (Hillsdale, NJ: Lawrence Erlbaum, 1993).

104. *Id.*

105. Greg J. Duncan, "The Economic Environment of Childhood." In *Children in Poverty,* ed. Aletha C. Huston (New York: Cambridge University Press, 1991).

106. Vonnie C. McLoyd, "Socioeconomic Disadvantage and Child Development," *American Psychologist* 53 (1998):185–204.

107. National Commission on Children, *Beyond Rhetoric: A New American Agenda for Children* (Washington, DC: Author, 1991).

108. *Id.*

109. Ronald L. Simons, Frederick O. Lorenz, Rand D. Conger, and Chi-In Wu, "Support From

Spouse as Mediator and Moderator of the Disruptive Influence of Economic Straining on Parenting," *Child Development* 63 (1992):1282–1302.

110. Yvonne Rafferty and Marybeth Shinn, "The Impact of Homelessness on Children," *American Psychologist* 46 (1991):1170–1179; Les B. Whitbeck, Danny R. Hoyt, and Kevin A. Auckley, "Abusive Family Backgrounds and Later Victimization Among Runaway and Homeless Adolescents," *Journal of Research on Adolescence* 7 (1997):375–392.

111. Martina Tomori, "Personality Characteristics of Adolescents of Alcoholic Parents," *Adolescence* 29 (1994):949–959.

112. Nathan L. Centers and Mark D. Weist, "Inner City Youth and Drug Dealing: A Review of the Problem," *Journal of Youth and Adolescence* 27 (1998):395–411.

113. Michael R. Liepman, David M. Keller, Richard J. Botelho, Alicia D. Monroe, and Mark A. Sloane, "Understanding and Preventing Substance Abuse by Adolescents," *Adolescent Medicine* 25 (1998):137–162.

114. U.S. Department of Health and Human Services, *National Survey Results on Drug Use From the Monitoring the Future Study, 1975–1993: Vol 1: Secondary Students* (Washington, DC: National Institute on Drug Abuse, 1994).

115. Jerome R. Kolbo, Elennor H. Blakely, and David Engleman, "Children Who Witness Domestic Violence: A Review of the Literature," *Journal of Interpersonal Violence* 11 (1996):281–293.

116. Beth S. Warner and Mark D. Weist, "Urban Youth as Witnesses to Violence: Beginning Assessment and Treatment Efforts," *Journal of Youth and Adolescence* 25 (1996):361–377.

117. Einat Peled, "The Experience of Living With Violence for Preadolescent Children of Battered Women," *Youth & Society* 29 (1998):395–430.

118. *Id.*

119. Robert W. Blum, "Transition to Adult Health Care: Setting the Stage," *Journal of Adolescent Health* 17 (1995):3–5.

120. National Commission, *Beyond Rhetoric: A New American Agenda for Children*; Doug Post, Chris Carr, and John Weigand, "Teenagers: Mental Health and Psychological Issues," *Adolescent Medicine* 25 (1998):181–192.

121. *Id.*

122. Rosalind R. Bruno and Andrea Adams, *School Enrollment—Social and Economic Characteristics of Students: October 1993* (Washington, DC: Bureau of the Census, 1994).

123. Barry M. Wagner, "Family Risk Factors for Child and Adolescent Suicidal Behavior," *Psychological Bulletin* 121 (1997):246–298; Kelton and Shank, *"Adolescent Injury and Death."*

124. Pub. L. No. 101-381, 104 Stat. 576 (1998) (codified at 42 U.S.C.A. § 300ff-90 (West Supp. 1998)).

125. For a thorough analysis and citations, *see* Roger J. R. Levesque, "The Peculiar Place of Adolescents in the HIV-AIDS Epidemic: Unusual Progress & Usual Inadequacies in 'Adolescent Jurisprudence,'" *Loyola University Chicago Law Journal* 27 (1996):701–739.

126. Roger J. R. Levesque, "Dating Violence, Adolescents, and the Law," *Virginia Journal of Social Policy and Law* 4 (1997):339–379.

127. Craig C. Brookins and Tracy L. Robinson, "Rites-of-Passage as Resistance to Oppression," *Western Journal of Black Studies* 19 (1995):172–179.

128. Patricia Bell-Scott and Ronald L. Taylor, "Introduction: The Multiple Ecologies of Black Adolescent Development," *Journal of Adolescent Research* 4 (1989):119–124.

129. Cynthia García Coll, Contran Lamberty, Renee Jenkins, Harriet Pipes McAdoo, Keith Crnic, Barbara Hanna Wasik, and Heidie Vazquez Garcia, "An Integrative Model for the Study of Developmental Competencies in Minority Children," *Child Development* 67 (1996):1891–1914.

130. For child welfare, *see* Evans, *Youth in Foster Care: The Shortcomings of Child Protection Services;* for juvenile justice, *see* R. Cohen, D. Parmelee, L. Irwin, and J. Weisz, "Characteristics of Children and Adolescents in a Psychiatric Hospital and Corrections Facility," *Journal of the American Academy of Child and Adolescent Psychiatry* 29(1990):909–913.

131. Ann S. Masten and J. Douglas Coatsworth, "The Development of Competence in Favorable and Unfavorable Environments: Lessons From Research on Successful Children," *American Psychologist* 52 (1998):205–220.

132. *Id.*

133. Larry Steinberg and Nancy Darling, "The Broader Context of Social Influence in Adolescence." In *Adolescence in Context: The Interplay of Family, School, Peers, and Work in Adjustment,* ed. Rainer K. Silbereisen and Eberhard Todt (New York: Springer-Verlag, 1994).

134. *Id.*

135. *Id.*

136. Joan E. Grusec and Leon Kuczynski, *Parenting and Children's Internalization of Values: A Handbook of Contemporary Theory* (New York: John Wiley, 1997).

137. This was, e.g., John Dewey's most important message about schools that continues to be shown true by research today; *see* Levesque, "Educating American Youth: Lessons From Children's Human Rights Law." For a recent empirical analysis of the need to consider adolescents' self-determination concerns in families, schools, and the workplace, *see* Timothy J. Owens, Jeylan T. Mortimer, and Michael D. Finch, "Self-Determination as a Source of Self-Esteem in Adolescence," *Social Forces* 74 (1996):1377–1404.

138. *See* Grusec and Kuczynski, *Parenting and Children's Internalization of Values: A Handbook of Contemporary Theory.*

Chapter 2
ADOLESCENCE AND THE LAW

Several commentators have reviewed the rise of children's rights in American jurisprudence and the place of children in the legal system.[1] Yet comprehensive reviews of the development of adolescents' legal rights and the place of adolescents in the legal system do not exist. Reviews limit themselves, for example, to distinguishing adolescents' abilities to make decisions in legal contexts[2] or to exploring specific areas of law that relate to juveniles, such as the juvenile justice system.[3] Discussions and the actual legal conception of adolescents' rights, just like social conceptions of adolescence, reviewed in chapter 1, remain tied to the period of childhood. Although no comprehensive effort exists that reviews and distinguishes the entire panoply of adolescents' rights from those of children, landmark cases in children's rights actually often deal with adolescents. Those "children's rights" cases, and the many cases that frequently lump adolescents with children under the rubric of "minors" or "juveniles," serve as the necessary starting point to delineate overriding themes in current conceptions of adolescents' rights.

As the general themes of the children's cases and numerous commentators on sociocultural images of children attest, adolescents have moved from property to person status.[4] Thus just as the previous chapter focused on tensions between traditional and modern conceptions of the place of adolescents in society, the place of adolescents in the legal system follows a similar pattern. The contours of the rights of adolescents actually reflect the images reviewed in chapter 1. The history of adolescents' rights documents the progression from the mid-19th-century paternalistic concern with protection and paternalistic control of youth to latter-20th-century recognition of adolescents' individual rights, particularly adolescents' rights to self-determination. Understanding adolescents' rights, then, fundamentally entails an appreciation of the tension between traditional social control and individual autonomy more characteristic of modern conceptions of adolescence.

Although the development of adolescents' rights clearly aims toward greater recognition of adolescents' own personhood and individual autonomy, the move remains limited in three general ways. First, the so-called "parental presumption" reigns. That is, when balanced against the family, particularly the rights of parents, the law pervasively remains reluctant both to interfere in the family domain and to recognize that adolescents even have their own rights. Second, when balanced directly against state's interests, adolescents' rights find limits in the states' *parens patriae* power to act as parents would. That is, adolescents' rights to autonomy and self-determination now give way to the general state interest of protecting youth from their autonomy and enhancing the broad social control of adolescents. Third, adolescents' rights also are balanced against states' broad police power that rules both adults and minors. That power authorizes the state to act as protector of the community—to make laws to protect the public health, safety, welfare, and morals. Although these three general powers may be theoretically distinct, they remain similar in reality. Thus courts may intervene to ensure that a child will develop into a healthy and civic-minded adult, which coincides with the state police power to protect community interests in upholding moral and legal standards and support parental authority to guide their children's development. The result is that, although adolescents' rights have been recognized, they have not been fashioned in ways that substantially alter the distribution of power between adolescents, parents, and state: Parents and the state largely control the content and expression of adolescents' rights. Although history does suggest that adolescents have become visible individuals who may hold and exercise rights independent of the family or the state, little effort has been made to amplify the scope, meaning, control, and nature of those rights.

The following review details the rise and limits of adolescents' rights. The analysis highlights important points to lay a foundation from which to expand recent trends in the development of adolescents' rights and offers suggestions for future developments that comport with contemporary understandings of adolescent life. Before exploring the leading cases, it is worth stating more precisely the specific reasons that make the review a significant exercise for understanding the nature of adolescents' rights. First, the early cases reveal what is meant by recognition. That is, even though adolescents may be recognized as people who possess rights, it is important to consider who controls the nature and exercise of those rights. Second, the cases reflect how adolescents' rights necessarily involve familial interests as well as greater societal–state interests. Third, the cases project an image of how far the state or parents may go to protect and develop adolescents so that they conform with a particular image of both the adolescent and the eventual adult. Fourth, the cases set the trend for current jurisprudence, which must recognize and address early precedents and still confront the necessary balance between external control of adolescents' rights and adolescents' need for self-determination in a rapidly changing society. Fifth, the review suggests why, although there may be general themes in the development and current status of adolescents' rights, the U.S. Supreme Court and commentators have yet to develop a jurisprudence that addresses adolescents' peculiar interests and social status.

The Evolution of Adolescents' Rights

The earliest constitutional cases that at least indirectly dealt with the rights of adolescents involved the extent to which parents may dictate the nature of adolescents' rights and the extent to which states play an active role in guiding the allocation of rights between adolescents and their parents. The analysis suggests that the early cases lay the foundation for the current jurisprudence of adolescents' rights that places the control of those rights under the authority of parents or those of the state that act *parens patriae,* as parent surrogates, to ensure the protection of adolescents from both themselves and their various social and institutional relationships.

The first recognition of adolescents' rights emerged in the context of educational cases. Rather than establishing adolescents as independent rights holders, these cases stand for the principle that parents hold adolescents' rights against the state and that those rights are rooted in the indirect right of parents to control and raise their children. For example, the earliest of the so-called children's rights opinions reflected how the rights of minors belong to their parents. In *Meyer v. Nebraska,*[5] the Supreme Court addressed the rights of parents vis-à-vis the state to control their children and obtain foreign language instruction in the private and public schools. At the center of the controversy was a young adolescent, all we know of whom is that he was a 10-year-old student at a school maintained by a Zion Evangelical Lutheran Congregation. Although the Court did refer to the "opportunities of pupils to acquire knowledge," the *Meyer* Court ruled that a statute that forbade schools from teaching children a foreign language prior to their completion of the 8th grade infringed on parents' due process rights under the Fourteenth Amendment.[6] The Court interpreted the Fourteenth Amendment to denote "not merely freedom from bodily restraint but also the right of the individual to contract, to engage in any of the common occupations of life, to acquire useful knowledge, to marry, establish a home and bring up children, [and] to worship God according to the dictates of his own conscience . . ."[7] The Court also recognized the legitimate power of the state to compel school attendance and to establish minimum curricular requirements; but it refused to extend this power to a standardized program required in instances in which the parents have other compelling concerns. The case, then, addressed the rights of minors through the interests, rights, and obligations of parents and the state. The case offers few reflections on the rights of adolescents who are the concern of the statutory restriction and presents no testimony from the adolescents who were affected by the challenged law. Even though the state retained considerable rights and the case forms the foundation of analyses that deal with children's rights, the case continues to be viewed as a "parental rights" case, one in which parents have the right to dictate the upbringing of their minor children.

Two years later, in *Pierce v. Society of Sisters*,[8] the parental rights approach was reaffirmed in a case that involved Oregon parents who wished to educate their children outside the public school system. The Court again recognized the legitimate power of states to regulate schools and to require school attendance. It found, however, that any state's power was limited by the "liberty of parents and guardians to direct the upbringing and education of children under their control."[9] The Court held that a state law that required all children between the ages of 8 and 16 to attend public schools violated parents' due process rights because the state deprived parents of the opportunity to regulate the educational upbringing of their children and of the decision to send their children to a religious school. The Court continued and declared in an often-cited phrase: "The child is not the mere creature of the State; those who nurture him and direct his destiny have the right, coupled with the high duty, to recognize and prepare him for additional obligations."[10] Although the Court had heard arguments that focused on the liberty interests of the minors involved, the Court paid no apparent heed to these assertions as it rendered an opinion that ignored the voices or independent interests of youth. It is important to note that before declaring that children belong to their parents as well as the state, the Court restated the limits of the state's power to intrude in parental functions: "The fundamental theory of liberty upon which all governments in this Union repose excludes any general power of the State to standardize its children by forcing them to accept instruction from public teachers only."[11] The Court grounded its opinion in the commanding metaphor of a communistic world in which parents could relinquish control of their children's upbringing to the state. The Court reaffirmed *Meyer's* forceful rejection of the state power to control child development. In *Meyer*, the Court had rejected as proper the communistic family presented by Plato in the *Republic*. The Court had found that such relationship between parent, child, and state, even though impressive to people of great genius, contrasted and clashed absolutely with the American ideal. To hold otherwise would offend "the letter and spirit of the Constitution."[12] The Constitution demanded parental autonomy and parental liberty to raise children as parents saw fit.

Like *Meyer, Pierce* established that adolescents were creatures belonging to parents and the state. In neither of these cases, which would have a profound and continuing impact on adolescents' rights, did the Court view minors as individuals who possessed their own rights. The Court made it clear that these cases were resolved without regard to the interests of the minors involved. Moreover, neither of these cases involved a contest between parental authority and their children's discretion; both dealt with parents asserting, and gaining, fundamental family rights against the state. Both found for a parent's authority to speak for and through the child. The Court envisioned a world in which parents were free to direct the socialization of their children and in which parents enjoyed the Constitution's protection to choose deviation from state assessments of how best to achieve that end. The decisions were premised on a deep-seated fear of state control and presumption of parental control over their children that allowed the law to condone adolescents' voicelessness and isolation from the community.

Other seminal, yet often ignored, cases illustrate the extent to which the Courts went to protect parental rights in educational settings. *Farrington v. Tokushinge*[13] well illustrates the power bestowed on parents, as it further established the broad principle that states could not preempt the role of parents in determining their children's educational and cultural experiences. The principle provided the Court with the rationale to invalidate a Hawaiian statute that regulated almost every aspect of private schooling. In particular, the statute effectively banned private after-school classes that were taught in Japanese and the subject matter, which included, among other matters, Japanese culture and language. Citing *Meyer* and *Pierce,* the Court held that the law unreasonably interfered with the parents' ability to direct and control the upbringing of their children by denying them the opportunity to teach their children Japanese. The case stood for the simple proposition that the state must allow parents some control over their children's educations at least to the extent that the parents must be able to augment and direct that education.

This trilogy of cases, all involving parental challenges to state attempts to monopolize education, established that the state must allow parents some control to broaden and direct their children's education. The cases did not, however, address what steps parents could take to protect their domain from a state's program that disrupts educational functions traditionally left to the family, such as religious and sexual education. When the Court finally did address the issue, it used the opportunity to step beyond previous cases and crystalize the power of parents to control the life course of their children.

The Court addressed the issue only 50 years after *Meyer, Pierce,* and *Farrington.* It was only in the 1970s that the Court began to grapple with whether parents may object to state educational programs that seemingly undermine traditional parent-initiated education. The now principal case in this area, *Wisconsin v. Yoder,*[14] involved Amish parents' challenge of a compulsory education law that required children to attend school until they reached the age of 16. The parents challenged the statute on the grounds that it violated their religious faith, which held that children should attend school only through the 8th grade. The parents argued that mandatory attendance until age 16 "takes [children] away from their community, physically and emotionally, during the crucial and formative adolescent period of life,"[15] and that such mandatory education "was contrary to the Amish religion and way of life" and thereby jeopardized both their children's salvation and their own.[16] The Court agreed and rested its conclusion on intertwined principles of religious freedom and parental prerogatives. The principles allowed the Court to reaffirm and establish "beyond debate as an enduring American tradition" the importance of parental liberty to guide their children's upbringing.[17] The distinctive failure to consider adolescents' rights, however, did not go unnoticed. Justice Douglas, in his dissenting opinion, properly complained about the lack of consideration given to the students' interests: "It is the student's judgement, not his parents', that is essential if we are to give full meaning to what is said about the Bill of Rights and of the rights of the students to be masters of their own destiny."[18] For Justice Douglas, the Constitution demanded respect for children's voices, which required the children to participate in decision making about their education. Yet despite Justice Douglas' spirited opinion, the Court found that the rights of parents take precedence over those of their children. The argument that it was not the best choice for the children involved was insufficient to override parental choice. The Court found that the statute violated Amish parents' constitutional rights to direct the religious and moral upbringing of their children. The unusual mention of adolescence as the period that increases the importance of parental control over their children's rights continues to be celebrated as a victory for parental rights.[19] The underlying theme that parents and adolescents have closely aligned, if not identical, interests continues to define the current understanding of minors' rights.

Yoder steps beyond previous cases' firm balance of parental rights against the state's broad societal interests and obligations to specific children. In apparent favor of parental rights, *Meyer* aborted attempts to prohibit the teaching of modern foreign languages below 8th grade, *Pierce* banned efforts to prohibit attendance at parochial schools, and *Farrington* thwarted a quest to proscribe all parental attempts to supplement their children's educations beyond state-sponsored instruction. The spirit of those cases, although recognizing the power of parents, also had projected the image that the state's interest in compulsory education must be compatible with open and diverse educational opportunities. *Meyer* opposed Plato's deep paternalistic theory of education in the interest of protecting a diverse curriculum, *Pierce* repudiated efforts to forbid parochial school attendance as an infringement on diverse educational experiences as the Court unequivocally condemned "any general power of the State to standardize its children,"[20] and *Farrington* upheld the teaching of "foreign" cultural values at a time of intense social conflict. *Yoder,* on the other hand, allows attempts to limit students' exposure to a wide range of subjects and viewpoints. The case questions the value of education as it allows parents to insulate their children from a diverse education that would foster their children's difference, independence, and knowledge. The Court was well aware that, if anything, the factual record of Amish objection to high school education suggested that Amish parents feared precisely the kind of diverse experience that might enable their children to develop personal independence. The Court even conceded the state's argument that the Amish were "fostering 'ignorance' from which the child must be protected by the State," and admitted that the state has a "duty to protect children from ignorance."[21] Despite such concessions and awareness, the Court found the case one of fundamental parental rights. The Court carefully and explicitly avoided any recognition of a minor's own rights: It was the parents' "right to free exercise, not that of children," that was critical to the ultimate decision.[22]

Although respect for parental rights may be fundamental to the fabric of society and the Constitution itself, it is far from absolute. Despite respect for parental rights, the parent–child relationship does not lie entirely beyond the reach of state control. In these cases, the Courts concluded that only legislative action that reasonably related to a legitimate state interest could interfere with the parental liberty interest to raise their children as they see fit. The ability of states and communities to control parental rights was first articulated in the now often-cited case of *Prince v. Massachusetts.*[23] *Prince* involved the constitutionality of a statute used to convict a custodian who allowed her 9-year-old ward to accompany and assist her in selling religious pamphlets. The custodian appealed the law with a claim that it interfered with her right to deal with her child as she saw fit. Her arguments rested on two points. The first challenge rested on the undue interference by the state with her parental right to control the activities of her children. The second challenge proposed that the state action unduly inhibited her exercise of religion. Although both of these arguments had proven controlling before, the case reveals that they were insufficient to override the state's interest in protecting its children.

In a direct limit to expansion of parental rights, the Court upheld the guardian's conviction for permitting the child to sell religious pamphlets in violation of state child labor laws. The Court found that the "interest of society to protect the welfare of children, and the state's authority to that end" stood against parents' "sacred private interests, basic in a democracy."[24] In strictly applying the state's child labor law, the Court reasoned that "[a] democratic society rests . . . upon the healthy, well-rounded growth of young people into full maturity as citizens" and that "the power of the State to control the conduct of children reaches beyond the scope of its authority over adults.''[25] The Court set the enduring standard that states must be allowed to interfere in family life to protect states' interests in their children. In dramatic fashion, the Court further stated that parents are ''free to become martyrs themselves but not to make martyrs of their children before they have reached the age of full and legal discretion.''[26] The state, not the child, had an interest in securing the ''healthy, well-rounded growth of young people into full maturity as citizens, with all that implies.''[27] Thus although the Supreme Court recognizes the profound role parents play in shaping their children's behaviors, it allows for state intervention not necessarily to protect youths' rights but to protect the rights of society. It is the state's interests acting *parens patriae* to guard the general interest in youth's well-being that matter and justify the limitation of certain parental prerogatives, whether religiously grounded or not.

The *Prince* Court's protectionist approach to children was not adopted without awareness of adolescents' interests and potential rights. The dissenting opinion, much like those in the cases before it, championed the rights of minors. For example, Justice Murphy did not find the potential harm sufficient to deny a child the right to practice his or her religion. He found that ''if the right of a child to practice its religion in that manner is to be forbidden by constitutional means, there must be convincing proof that such a practice constitutes a grave and immediate danger to the State or to the health, morals or welfare of the child.''[28] Thus under this line of reasoning the minor could exercise fundamental rights to the extent that they are not placing themselves or the state's interests in ''grave or immediate danger.''[29] Although the opinion may stand as an early effort to recognize the rights of youth to exercise fundamental rights viewed as sacred when practiced by adults, the view was ignored by the majority of the Court. Although the majority opinion noted the attitude and beliefs of the 9-year-old niece and referred to the rights of minors at several points, the ultimate judicial holding was defined in terms of a confrontation between the power of the state versus the rights and responsibilities of parents. All opinions of the *Prince* decision agreed on one fundamental point, for which the *Prince* decision now stands: Parental authority is not without its limits. The case crystallized the idea that a state can exercise authority over parents' control of their children's upbringing. In this way, the case asserted protection of *societal interests* as defined and commanded by the state.

The redefinition of who ultimately controls adolescents' rights constituted an important development, and also provided the foundation of the ultimate limitation on adolescents' rights. Although the move to limit parental authority may be seen as a recognition of adolescents' legal personhood, the previously discussed cases simply helped define the limits of parental authority rather than revoke it. Thus in these landmark cases, the state's ''parental authority'' over children only superseded parental authority when parents failed to protect their children. Equally important, it is the state that acts as the ultimate parent and sets the broad parameters that guide the standard for how parents must behave. Just as the Amish parents had requested only a limited exemption for their children past the 8th grade, Mrs. Prince had invited the Court to exempt children for religiously motivated street sales only under direct parental supervision. Likewise, the same psychological virtues in the parent–child relationship had been evident in *Prince* that the *Yoder* Court previously had praised in the Amish practices. Although the cases resulted in different outcomes, they do reflect one unbending aspect of judicial policy: Regardless of whether it overtly approves of suspect parental practices or disdains parental values, the Court still remained overtly inattentive to adolescents' expressed desires.

The years prior to the *Prince* decision also involved two other important cases that dealt with the power of parents to have their children conduct themselves contrary to state mandates and the extent to which the Court went out of its way to not carve a jurisprudence tailored to adolescents. These two cases involved challenges to compulsory flag-salute exercises in public schools. In the first case, *Minnersville School District v. Gobitis,*[30] two adolescents who were 15 and 16 years old by the time the Supreme Court decided the case steadfastly refused to attend school if it meant saluting the flag. Although the lower courts all framed the issues in terms of children's rights, the controlling majority of the Court fashioned the case as one of conflict between the parents and the state.[31] As with other seminal cases that dealt with adolescents' rights, only the dissent considered how the law sought to coerce the children to violate their deepest religious convictions.[32] The majority viewed nothing suspect with saluting the flag, which summarized the kind of ordered society that allows for "preciousness of the family relation, [and] the authority and independence which give dignity to parenthood."[33] Indeed, the Court viewed not only nothing improper with encouraging students to show respect for their country but also an opportune moment to do so because the children were at the receptive age to gain an appreciation of the country's aspirations to protect liberties. Thus it was because minors were at a formative period in the development of citizenship that the Court allowed states to infringe their rights. The failure to consider children's rights directly was even more obvious in the Court's quick reversal of *Gobitis.* In *West Virginia v. Barnette,*[34] the Court did not even mention adolescents' rights specifically. Instead of specific children, a series of organizations had challenged the mandatory flag salute. Thus even though the Court noted that the case was one of "compulsion of students to declare a belief,"[35] the Court necessarily framed the issue in terms of the broad individual liberty to not bestow on states the power to make anyone salute the flag irrespective of their reasons for not doing so. In its often-quoted phrase, the Court found that

> if there is any fixed star in our constitutional constellation, it is that no official, high or petty, can prescribe what shall be orthodox in politics, nationalism, religion, or other matters of opinion or force citizens to confess by word or act their faith therein. If there are any circumstances which permit an exception, they do not now occur to us.[36]

Although the Court itself footnoted pervasive exceptions to its expansive proclamation, such as times of national emergency, the broad holding was used to find nothing peculiar with adolescents' rights. Rather than finding that adolescents had individual rights, the Court found that no officials could impose matters of opinion and political attitudes.

To recapitulate, by the beginning of this century the Court reflected the prevailing beliefs of its time. It had not begun to recognize that adolescents have assertable rights outside of and perhaps contrary to those of parents and families. The recognition of adolescents' interests was indirect and, to a large extent, inconsequential to the Court's ultimate decisions. The Court either overlooked adolescents' rights or viewed them as trivial. Although the Court couched language in the context of the parent–child relationship, the opinions centered on the legitimacy of parental authority. When the Court did recognize adolescents' rights, the rights were viewed as significant only when parents failed. At the point of parental failure, the state would assert its own authority and act as parent. In acting as parents, the Court offered numerous reasons to interfere with parental and adolescents' rights. Parents have the right to control the upbringing of their children, a right that reaches constitutional status. Because parents have the right to raise their children as they see fit, they have the right and obligation to mold them as they wish. Those parental rights, however, remain limited to the extent that the state may regulate both parental and adolescent's rights in the interest of society. Thus although state interests may include parents and adolescents' own interests as factors in the general societal interest, those interests must be weighed against the societal interest in the development of healthy, moral, and well-rounded citizens, ''and all that implies.''[37] Even when the state intervenes on behalf of a minor exposed to neglect or abuse, the state does so as a substitute parent—in other words, under the state's *parens patriae* power. The state moves to provide more of the guidance traditionally supplied by parents, and the boundaries between the rights of parents and the powers of the state remains unclear. What does remain clear is the remarkable extent to which parents and the state still control the nature and content of adolescents' rights.

The Limitations of Adolescents' Rights

The notion that the state must serve as the ultimate guarantor and standard bearer of adolescents' rights led to what has been characterized as the rights revolution of the 1960s and 1970s and to the eventual retrenchment of those developments by the end of the 1980s. During the earlier years of these three decades, the Supreme Court decided numerous cases that involved adolescents' right to protection by the U.S. Constitution. Seminal cases dealing with juvenile justice, health, and educational systems led the Court to conclude that adolescents were now persons under the Constitution. The cases signaled the Court's move toward a new conception of adolescents' rights, one that emphasized the adolescent's, rather than the parent's, relationship with the state. These cases initially suggested a groundswell of support for recognizing adolescents' rights and led numerous commentators to conclude that adolescents had achieved legal personhood. Yet even the initial recognition remained limited, and those limitations grew as the Supreme Court revisited cases dealing with adolescents' rights.

Before considering the cases, it is important to situate them in terms of the extent to which they seemingly respect adolescents' rights. As we will see, the cases certainly increased recognition that adolescents do possess rights. However, the cases substantially failed to alter the superior authority of parents or the state in regard to adolescents. In relationship to parents, the rights of adolescents, as conceived by the courts, generally remain anchored to family authority. That limit pervades the otherwise dramatic developments in adolescents' rights, even though there are numerous instances in which it seems that the Court recognized the juridical personality of adolescents. That is, although numerous Supreme Court cases have examined adolescents' right to constitutional protection, even those cases that uphold such protection have avoided the issue of how the child's constitutional rights would be affected by competing constitutional claims of the child's parents or others having a similar relationship to them. In relationship to the state, the limit may be characterized as the general view that adolescents are always in some form of custody. That subordinate position is significant for two reasons. First, it justifies a lower threshold for addressing challenges to potential violations of adolescents' constitutional rights. Second, it allows for considering the extent to which the state may use its dual powers of acting as parents or as protectors of community interests. Both of these considerations are significant in that the recent cases reemphasize the relationship of adolescents to the state as one that protects communities and one that aims to inculcate youth so that they become productive citizens who adjust and contribute to democratic life. Thus although great strides have been made in recognizing adolescents' rights, much remains to be determined and limited.

The early recognition that adolescents have due process rights occurred a year before in *In re Gault,* the case most often heralded as establishing the independent legal personhood of youth.[38] The earlier case, *Kent v. United States,*[39] involved the procedural safeguards required when the state seeks to treat a 16-year-old minor as an adult for purposes of criminal prosecution. (See chapter 9 for a discussion of *Kent*.) In that case, a latent fingerprint left at the scene of a the robbery and rape led to Kent's apprehension. After a seven-hour interrogation, Kent confessed to numerous break-ins. Given the seriousness of the crime and the nature of the evidence, Kent's case was transferred to adult court. Although such transfers may now be routine, the way the transfer occurred led to the legal precedent. The court failed to hold a formal hearing and did not provide Kent with notice that his case was transferred to adult court. On discovering a trial in adult court, Kent's attorney attempted to remove the case from adult court. To support his request, he also sought a psychiatric evaluation and requested receipt of social reports in the juvenile court's possession. The motions were denied, and Kent was found guilty of six counts of housebreaking and robbery resulting in a sentence of 30 to 90 years in prison. On appeal to the Supreme Court, Kent alleged three issues relating to his waiver to adult court: failure to hold a waiver hearing, failure to provide reasons for the waiver, and denial of access to social reports that would have been used by the judge in his decision to waive Kent to adult court. The Court found Kent's waiver invalid as it held that the due process clause applied to judicial waivers. Specifically, the Court ruled that Kent was entitled to representation by an attorney; to a meaningful hearing, even if informal; to access to records that would be used by the court in deciding the waiver; and to be apprised of the reasons for the waiver decision. Despite the possibility of a life sentence, the Court actually provided only modest constitutional protection. There was no constitutional right to a full adversarial hearing. More important, whatever constitutional rights a youth may have in a judicial waiver proceeding, virtually none exist if waiver of juvenile jurisdiction to adult court is either legislatively determined or is the product of the discretion of the prosecutor. For example, and as we will see in chapter 9, most states permit the use of adult court jurisdiction for certain crimes and most states also give power to the prosecutor to charge the crimes as an adult crime. If these two methods are used, the juvenile has no right to question the transfer to adult court. The result is that several states have moved toward by-passing the demands of *Kent* and proceeding directly into adult court and adult punishment.[40]

Regardless of the immediate impact of *Kent,* it was quickly eclipsed by *In re Gault,* a case that would have a much broader impact and fundamentally strain existing conceptions of adolescents' rights. *Gault* involved a challenge to the structure of the juvenile justice system. Fifteen-year-old Gerald Gault was accused of making an obscene telephone call. Finding that Gault had disturbed the peace by making the call and that he was "habitually involved in immoral matters,"[41] the juvenile court confined him to a juvenile detention facility for the remaining six years of his minority—the same crime for which an adult would have been subject to a fine and only up to 60 days in prison. The Supreme Court heard his *habeas corpus* petition and used it to alter the inherently discretionary nature of the juvenile justice system. The Supreme Court found that the juvenile court had denied basic procedural rights and declared that "under our Constitution, the condition of being a boy does not justify a kangaroo court."[42] The case ultimately culminated in the Court's mandate that juvenile court proceedings must provide minors a constitutional right to counsel, a right against self-incrimination, a right to specific notice of charges brought against them, and a right to confront and cross-examine accusers.

Although arguably a dramatic recognition of adolescents' rights, the celebrated case itself evidences the general failure to recognize adolescents' rights as their own. Although *Gault* broke ground by awarding extensive due process protections to juvenile delinquents and recognizing minors as individuals in their own right, *Gault* did not significantly displace traditional structures of authority over adolescents. Two points bolster this proposition. *Gault's* progeny reveals the accepted view that minors have the responsibilities of adults under some conditions without any special safeguards relative to their constitutional status as minors. The eventual erosion of the safeguards established in *Kent* illustrate the point. As highlighted previously, even though the Court may provide rights at certain events that involve due process, there are numerous ways to circumvent the need for due process, such as the elimination of the event and substitution with procedures that do not entail juveniles' due process rights. Equally illustrative of *Gault's* limits is the Court's treatment of minors as adults when they waive their rights. *Fare v. Michael C.* [43] held that a 16-year-old has the capacity to waive the right to counsel and confess to alleged crimes, despite evidence that adolescents may be especially susceptive to the entreaties of law enforcement figures and that even civil law allows 16-year-olds to void otherwise binding contracts because of their legal incapacity.[44] In addition, the constitutionality of imposing the death penalty on adolescents reflects how juveniles may not reach full maturity yet be held accountable as adults and pay the ultimate penalty while the Court does not afford them Constitutional protections at the transfer and sentencing stages to ensure that only mature juveniles find themselves on death row. In *Stanford v. Kentucky,*[45] the Court held that execution of juveniles who committed crimes at 16 and 17 does not offend the Eighth Amendment's prohibition against cruel and unusual punishment. Simply put, then, *Gault* failed to protect youth from other parts of juvenile justice processes, let alone from abolishing the juvenile court and removing special protections traditionally held by adolescents and conferred on youth because of their peculiar place in society and their developmental status.

The second major illustration of the Court's failure to alter substantially traditional structures of authority involves the manner the Court assumes minors are subordinate to both parents and the state. The Court disapproved of the lower court's approach to juvenile proceedings that reflected utter disregard for the traditional parent–state partnership in raising children and failure to respect the assumptions that parents remain best suited to restrain and mold youth. The Court noted that

> under traditional notions, one would assume that in a case like that of Gerald Gault, where the juvenile appears to have a home, a working mother and father, and an older brother, the juvenile judge would have made a careful inquiry and judgment as to the possibility that the boy could be disciplined and dealt with at home.[46]

Thus given that Gerald Gault had parents, it could be assumed that they could deal with the matter in their home. The Court, however, went even further. When addressing the parent–child relationship as a matter of law beyond the current facts, the Court noted, "If his parents default in effectively performing their custodial functions—that is, if the child is 'delinquent'—the state may intervene. *In so doing, it does not deprive the child of any rights, because he has none.*"[47] Those words are striking—a parent who fails in his duties has children with no rights. Although it would be imprudent to exaggerate the importance of this language, such language reflects well the notion that a minor's rights are essentially derivative of parents or parent substitutes. In other words, in this case the Court saw the teenager only in relation to his family or state and not as an individual who possessed separate constitutional status and rights.

The proposition that adolescents' rights are coterminous with those of their parents remains rather striking and actually resurfaces in other important cases involving the rights of adolescents. In 1984, for example, in the case of *Shall v. Martin,*[48] the Court decided that a state can authorize detention for juveniles who pose a serious risk of committing a crime because "juveniles, unlike adults, are always in some form of custody."[49] Unlike adults, then, adolescents always are under the authority of outside control. That authority is significant enough to allow the preventive detention of minors in a manner much broader than for adults. In reaching the decision on preventive detention, the Court gave weight both to the impulsivity and the immaturity of adolescents to conclude that

> our society recognizes that juveniles in general are in the earlier stages of their emotional growth, that their intellectual development is incomplete, that they have only limited practical experience, and that their value systems have not yet been clearly identified or firmly established.[50]

The impulsivity and immaturity was enough to justify the conclusions that society may preventively detain youth because they may, if released, commit more of the same criminal acts than adults who would have been charged with the crime and released to the community.

The apparent conflict with the Court's view of minors becomes pronounced in its analysis of the state's police powers. In *Michael C.,* for example, the Court did not question the defendant's intellectual and experiential competence to waive the right to counsel. Nor did the Court question such immaturity in cases that involve the death penalty as if the minor were an adult. These cases reflect the important point that what the state wishes to accomplish in its invocation of police powers largely dictates whether youth are viewed as immature, impulsive adolescents or as competent, responsible adults. If the state wishes to protect community interests through preventive detention, young persons are seen as children. Or if the state wishes, in the name of protecting the community, to accept quick confessions or harsher sentences, youth are seen as adults.

The general rule that adolescents are under the control of others may seem appropriate in the context of dealing with juvenile delinquents. In those instances, concern centers on protecting the community, protecting youth from undue state interference, protecting families from undue interference in their private family affairs, and even arguably protecting adolescents from themselves. The intrusion could come in the form of parental rights to control their children or in the form of parental protection of juveniles from undue state intrusion. However, the rule has been applied in other contexts in which adolescents may claim a right to act independently of parents, adults, and others acting on behalf of the state.

The extent to which parents still retain considerable rights is exemplified by the Court's grant of substantial parental authority over adolescents' medical decisions, including decisions that involve the fundamental right to liberty and freedom from confinement. In a 1979 ruling, *Parham v. J. R.,*[51] the Court upheld a Georgia statute that allowed the admittance and commitment of minors to a mental institution by parents and the staff. Under the challenged procedures, the minor had no right to notice, hearing, or counsel; and no legal right to challenge his or her involuntary confinement. Once the minor was observed, the facility could admit the minor "for such period and under such conditions as may be authorized by law."[52] The Court let stand the minimal procedures; minors' rights would be protected through parents and third parties, not through formal hearings. Although the Court agreed that minors had a substantial and constitutionally protected liberty interest in not being confined unnecessarily, that interest was outweighed by the state's interest in avoiding "time-consuming procedural minuets" and the state's "*parens patriae* interest in helping parents care for the mental health of their children" in a manner that would not be "too onerous, too embarrassing, or too contentious."[53] The Court also noted that the natural affinity of interest between parent and child, long recognized by law, properly allowed the "presumption that parents possess what a child lacks in maturity, experience, and capacity for judgment required for making life's difficult decisions."[54] That natural affinity would lead parents to act in their children's best interests. The Court not only reviewed and applauded traditional understandings of the parent–child relationship but also wrote that "the statist notion that governmental power should supersede parental authority in *all* cases because *some* parents abuse and neglect their children is repugnant to the American tradition."[55] That presumption of parental interest, combined with the staff's review authority, adequately protected youth from the possibility of parental abuse of commitment powers. Thus in the Supreme Court's view, parents acted in their children's best interests, admitting staff acted in a selfless capacity, hospitals ignored economic consequences of admittance, and other state agents acting as guardians were attentive substitute parents. The questionable nature of these assumptions has been revealed in the skyrocketing admission rates of youth after the opinion, which suggests the need to consider the conflicting legal, economic, and psychological interests at stake in the involuntary commitment process.[56] In addition to a dubious foundation, the Court's approach to the liberty interests of minors disregards and expressly declares irrelevant the choices and voices of children who would act contrary to their parents:

> We cannot assume that the result in *Meyer v. Nebraska* and *Pierce v. Society of Sisters* would have been different if the children there had announced a preference to learn only English or a preference to go to a public, rather than a church, school. The fact that a child may balk at hospitalization or complain about a parental refusal to provide cosmetic surgery does not diminish the parents' authority to decide what is best for the child.[57]

Though clearly concerned with the desire to reinforce the traditional understandings of the parent–child relationship, the Court does not rest its decision conclusively on those understandings; the Court still includes the extra protection of state officials and staff in adolescents' voluntary admission to mental institutions. The justification for reliance on those authorities, though, rests with a limited image of adolescents. The Court deemed minors incapable "even in adolescence" of "mak[ing] sound judgements concerning many decisions, including their need for medical care or treatment."[58] Although the Court suggested that the incapacity results in having parents make those judgments, the Court also used the incapacity to justify the exercise of *adult* authority. Adults, state officials, and hospital staff actually serve two functions: They afford children the treatment similar to what their parents would and actually guard against parents who would not act in their children's interests. The mix of protection and autonomy reflected in these cases move toward protection justified by parental authority, professional expertise, and important state interests. The Court recognizes a substantial proxy role for adults in making critical decisions on behalf of adolescents; adults are not only permitted, but obligated, to make judgments for adolescents. It does not matter whether adolescent's choices are subsumed by those of parents or by those of other adults.

Another landmark case often interpreted as guaranteeing adolescents constitutional rights and authoritatively establishing the legal personhood of minors also illustrates well the failure to recognize adolescents as subjects of their own rights. That is the case of *Tinker v. Des Moines Independent Community School District.*[59] In *Tinker,* the Court declared unconstitutional a school rule that prevented three adolescents, aged 13, 15, and 16, from expressing their political views at school by wearing black armbands to protest the Vietnam War. School authorities argued that the armbands created a disruption in the school. The Court dismissed the schools' assertion that the students' acts created a risk of disruption: "The Constitution says we must take this risk . . . that is the basis of our national strength and of the independence and vigor of Americans who grow up and live in this relatively permissive, often disputatious, society.''[60] Given the suggestion that the classroom was the ''training ground for the marketplace of ideas,'' it was not surprising that the Court held that ''neither students nor teachers shed their constitutional rights to freedom of speech or expression at the schoolhouse gate.''[61] According to the Court, students were persons who had rights found in the Constitution. In language that has been widely repeated, Justice Fortas continued to find, in dictum, that ''students in school as well as out of school are 'persons' under our Constitution.''[62]

Although courts and commentators often cite the *Tinker* opinion as proof of adolescents' full constitutional status, history and the case itself tell a different story. The '''persons' under our Constitution''[63] dictum was not as precedent-setting as some had hoped. The *Tinker* decision was very narrow for three reasons. First, the actual basis of the opinion was unclear. The opinion could easily be viewed as a parental rights or family rights case because the views of the children mirrored those of their parents, a possibility evidenced by commentators who view *Tinker* as a symbolic battle between adults, each using children as sacrificial pawns.[64] The outcome could have been different if the school officials had argued that they were acting not to impose their political views on students but rather on behalf of the root values of the First Amendment—tolerance, diversity of thought, individual autonomy—against parental impositions on children. Second, a dictum does not bind the court for further decisions; Courts are bound by the rule of law applied to the individual facts of the instant case. Regardless of the simple rule of legal interpretation, the dictum certainly did not apply to the entire Constitution. Third, despite the assertion of constitutional imperatives in dramatically broad terms, the freedom of expression that was protected was seen as ''closely akin to 'pure speech' which . . . is entitled to comprehensive protection under the First Amendment,'' and the case allegedly did not involve ''aggressive, disruptive action or even group demonstrations.''[65] The Court revealed in its cautionary language that had any such disruption occurred or been imminent, the outcome of the case might well have been different. Indeed, the Court recently narrowed those rights by adopting a differential approach to school administrators' rights and obligations.

Current jurisprudence dealing with students' educational rights accords school officials increasing power in educational policy making. The first of three foundational decisions, *Board of Education v. Pico*,[66] involved a suit brought by the parents of five high school and junior high students who challenged the school board's removal of nine books from the school library. In a vigorous and heated exchange, the Court ruled that, although they could not remove books based on partisan politics, school boards did have discretion to remove books based on educationally relevant criteria.[67] The Court construed the school board's rights as ''vitally important 'in the preparation of individuals for participation as citizens' and . . . for 'inculcating fundamental values necessary to the maintenance of a democratic political system.'''[68] The Court recognized school boards' broad control over curricular matters, even to the extent that boards ''might well defend their claim of absolute discretion'' to transmit community values.[69] Two important cases that followed firmly established school official control of school governance when students assert their own First Amendment rights. In *Bethel School District v. Fraser*,[70] a 17-year-old senior delivered a sexually charged speech to nominate a fellow student for elective office.[71] The Court pronounced that the speech was lewd, vulgar, and possibly damaging, and therefore subject to limitation. Under this line of reasoning, school officials may curb forms of speech deemed threatening to others, disruptive, and contrary to ''shared values,''[72] and contrary to the mission of schools to inculcate 'fundamental values necessary to the maintenance of a democratic political system.''[73] It is important to note that there was no need to muster evidence of disruption or damage to other students. The only rationale needed for the censure was that the school could disassociate itself from the content of the speech in a way that would communicate to other students that such vulgarity was "wholly inconsistent with the 'fundamental values of public school education.'"[74] The power of school authorities, acting as the inculcators of proper community values, was supported and developed further in *Hazelwood School District v. Kuhlmeier*.[75] In this case students alleged that their free speech rights had been violated when the principal deleted two articles from a school paper. The principal and school countered that the actions properly censored objectionable materials that dealt with issues of teenage pregnancy and the impact of parental divorce on students.[76] The Court upheld the authority of school officials to control the content of school-sponsored speech based on "legitimate pedagogical concerns."[77] The majority emphasized the role of schools as the primary vehicles for transmitting cultural values and their discretion in refusing to sponsor student speech that might be perceived as advocating conduct otherwise inconsistent with "the shared values of a civilized social order."[78] Thus a school need not tolerate student speech that is not consistent with its educational mission, even though the government could not censor similar speech outside the school. These developments reveal how the Court now approaches values from two perspectives to reaffirm (a) the authority of school officials to uphold the values of the community and (b) the mission of the schools to promote the fundamental values of a democratic society. Thus although students may not "shed their constitutional rights . . . at the schoolhouse gate,"[79] in practice the Court accords the government considerable license to control public school classrooms in general and secular curriculum in particular. The state has the special responsibility to inculcate youth.

These developments reflect how public school officials play the key role of arbiters and protectors of community values or preferences, both in the sense of common values shared throughout society and in a particular community. The decisions emphasize the inculcative or indoctrinative nature of schooling for a given purpose; according to these decisions, public schools not only may but should influence their students to adopt particular beliefs and values. Although other cases recognized and fostered the socialization function of schooling, the current approach looks to socialization as a mechanism both to preserve community interests and preferences and to prepare students for citizenship in the larger society. These jurisprudential developments challenge the prevailing belief that parents (and sometimes students) control the nature of public education.

The control given to school officials is most obvious in the context in which they may cause *deliberate harm* to certain students. Three instances are on point. The first example of state-sponsored harm involves school suspensions and the extent to which the rights of minors will be respected. In *Goss v. Lopez*,[80] numerous students had been suspended for up to 10 days for disruptive behavior. The legal challenge involved the suspension without benefit of a hearing. After determining that the minors involved had constitutionally protected property and liberty interests in public education and that substantial risks could develop from erroneous fact finding, the Court held that in suspensions for up to 10 school days, the student must "be given oral or written notice of the charges against him and, if he denies them, an explanation of the evidence the authorities have and an opportunity to present his side of the story."[81] The Court, however, noted that compliance with the standard simply involved "requirements which are, if anything, less than a fair minded principal would impose upon himself in order to avoid unfair suspension."[82] Thus if minors have rights in cases of school suspension, the rights operate at a minimal level: The Court, in effect, only requires a momentary verbal interchange between principal and student prior to suspension, and suspension for shorter periods does not assume any constitutional dimensions.

The second instance that involves deliberate harm entails arguably greater harm than suspension, yet still concerns essentially no due process rights. These cases deal with corporal punishment in schools. The leading case, *Ingraham v. Wright,*[83] involved students who had been subjected to such severe physical abuse and injury as to be grounds for an official state report for child abuse: One student had received more than 20 hits with a wooden paddle, resulting in severe hematoma, and another had been struck in the arm so severely that he was unable to exercise full use of the arm for a week. Yet the Court refused to apply even the momentary verbal interchange required by *Goss.* The Court found that the students had enough protection without requiring any proceedings prior to punishment. Rather than being found in the basic principles of the Constitution, the protections were to be found in the openness of the school, the professionalism of those who impose punishment, and the civil and criminal remedies available to those who get severely beaten. Minors only have voice after their rights have been violated; they can be subject to unwarranted punishment without any voice whatsoever. Although commentators and the dissent note that the opinion leaves youth without rights and without realistic remedies, states are allowed and do continue to impose corporal punishment in the schools.

The third instance that clearly entails deliberate harm involves the rights of adolescents who may be subject to invasive searches in public schools. The leading case, *New Jersey v. T. L. O.,*[84] concerned a student who was suspected of smoking in the girls' bathroom. When she denied that she smoked, the principal told her to empty her purse, which allegedly revealed evidence of the more serious crime of drug trafficking. The Court found that the Fourth Amendment proscription on illegal search and seizure applied to searches of adolescents in public schools. Yet the Court used the opportunity to lower the standard for conducting legal searches by school personnel:

> Accommodation of privacy interests of schoolchildren with the substantial need of teachers and administrators to maintain order in schools does not require strict adherence to the requirement that searches be made on probable cause. . . . Under ordinary circumstances the search of a student will be justified at its inception when there are reasonable grounds for suspecting that the search will turn up evidence that the student violated the law or rules of the school.[85]

Under all of these holdings, adolescents are all vulnerable to unwanted searches. School authorities only have to reach for a reasonable suspicion to effect an intrusive but still legal search, a much lower threshold than probable cause or reasonable belief that would be needed for intrusive searches with adults. The lower threshold has led numerous district courts to uphold strikingly invasive strip searches of adolescents, so long as administrators can establish that the students' conduct created a reasonable suspicion of a specific violation and the search would produce evidence of that violation.[86] The lower threshold has been so low that, for some intrusive searches, school officials no longer need to even have reasonable suspicion. The drug testing of students illustrates the extent to which the Court permits intrusion under justifications that are no longer particularized to the individual adolescents who are not necessarily individually suspected of inappropriate or illegal activity.[87] In terms of respect for individual student's own privacy and protection of students from harm, the school has become a much less secure place.

The development and current status of adolescents' rights in school settings do not purport to shield adolescents from state officials at a level students would enjoy if they were viewed as full-fledged legal persons. The cases' significance emerges from the two-fold powers held by school officials. First, they have power to protect students from themselves and other students as well as the power to protect societal interests in safety. Thus they are able to quickly mete out punishment and intrusively infringe on adolescents' rights to privacy to protect themselves and others. Second, they are entrusted with molding students, with the ultimate end of respecting basic constitutional principles. Both of these rationales provide school officials with considerable discretion in the extent to which they will respect adolescents' individual rights. Simply put, adolescents are not the constitutional persons the Court has held them up to be.

Just as the *Gault* and *Tinker* cases eventually revealed that adolescents may be controlled in schools and institutions, even the celebrated cases that substantially and incontrovertibly recognized adults and adolescents' right to privacy allow for important limits on adolescents' rights. These cases, all of which involve adolescents' reproductive rights, reveal that the Court has not transformed the legal regulation of parent–child relationships as dramatically as commentators suggested and that the Court has failed to affect markedly the extent to which adolescents may act as autonomous individuals within families and in cases involving intrafamily disputes. The cases reflect the remarkable extent to which states may control, and allow parents to control, adolescents' rights and the Court's continued preference for protection over autonomy.

Early cases dealing with adolescents' reproductive rights illustrate the Court's concerns with parental control of adolescents and the control of both by the state. For example, in the mid-1960s and 1970s the Court signaled its recognition of adolescents' right to autonomy and seemingly granted considerable power to adolescents. The Court first stressed the constitutional principle of adolescents' individual autonomy in *Carey v. Population Services International.*[88] In that case the Court struck down a New York statute that prohibited the distribution of nonprescriptive contraceptives to minors under the age of 16 years. Equally signaling recognition of adolescents' autonomy was the early right-to-abortion case, *Bellotti v. Baird.*[89] In that case, the Court struck down a state statute that required parental consent for minors who sought an abortion. In terms of reproductive rights, it would be difficult to underestimate the significance of these two cases. States reserve the right to limit and review parental authority in decisions about a child's health and welfare; and states must ensure consideration of adolescents' autonomy.

Although undoubtedly worthy of landmark status in the development of adolescents' rights, the two decisions that apparently provided adolescents with considerable reproductive rights actually remain significantly narrow. Four points are worthy of emphasis at this juncture, because we will return and more fully analyze these cases in chapter 4. First, the Court has upheld parental consent and notification provisions when coupled by a judicial bypass alternative that allows an adolescent to obtain an abortion if she can convince a court that she is mature and capable of giving informed consent to the proposed abortion. Although seemingly expansive, the bestowal of rights remained considerably narrow. For example, the case in which the notification by-pass was approved only made the by-pass available if the minor alleged parental abuse and neglect, which is the same low standard that the Court uses to intervene and infringe on parental rights. Second, the decisions define girls as vulnerable and immature yet place demands that require considerable maturity if they wish to exercise their rights and terminate their pregnancies: At a time of turmoil, the girls must petition the courts and respond to judges' intimate questions about their lives and choices, a burden on girls that may be greater than actually obtaining parental consent. Thus pregnant girls seeking abortions have not been granted autonomy as the term usually connotes; rather, they have been granted a peculiar sort of burdened autonomy that substitutes state authority for parental authority and that asks girls to show far more initiative and competence than the Court asks of adult women who seek abortions. Third, the extension and characterization of the right to privacy as potentially possessed by minors remains limited. For example, instances in which the girl is not viewed as mature mandate that the judge substitute his or her own decision regarding what would be in her best interests. That substitution inevitably results in the application of a judge's individual values on a case-by-case basis. Fourth, in the name of protecting parental rights, the Court has let stand policies that prohibit the distribution of condoms in public schools, which reflects the tenuous grounds on which *Carey v. Population Services International* was decided: Only four of the justices would have found that the ''constitutionality of a blanket prohibition on the distribution of contraceptives to minors is *a fortiori* foreclosed.''[90] The Court assumes that a state may regulate the sexual behaviors of minors, that a minor's right to privacy may suffer intrusion if such intrusion rationally relates to a legitimate governmental interest. Thus although adolescents may have some autonomous sexual rights, their rights nevertheless remain subject to control by the state and parents. The Court has not declared that adolescents have the constitutional authority to protect themselves from harm by gaining access to contraceptives; and the Court provides the opportunity for limited autonomy relative to abortion decisions for those willing to obtain judicial permission.

Decisions that clearly separate the interests of parents from those of minors provide an interesting glimpse into the power of parents when states take it on themselves to enhance their authority to safeguard adolescents from harm. *Ginsberg v. New York*[91] was the first case after *Gault* to narrowly limit only the minor's interests. That case involved the constitutionality of a New York law that accorded minors under the age of 17 a more restricted right to purchase pornography than that assured to adults. However, the case actually did not involve an adolescent's petition. Instead, the Court heard the appeal of a stationery store owner convicted for selling ''girlie'' magazines to a 16-year-old-boy.[92] Although the statute was challenged by a private business, the Court recognized that minors' rights were at stake and expounded on the rights of the state to control adolescents. The Court found nothing improper with the state's attempt to shield adolescents from harm. Largely because the statute still left considerable discretion to parents to control the upbringing of their children, the Court found the state's attempt to shield and protect youth permissible. Thus the Court not only affirmed the adolescent-versus-state framework of analysis established in *Gault* but also noted that it did not intrude on parental rights: The law left considerable discretion to parents and ''[did] not bar parents who so desire from purchasing the magazines for their children.''[93] *Ginsberg* contributes to the line of decisions that affirm the existence of a constitutional parental right against undue, adverse interference by the state into family matters. The state must tread more lightly on parental than on adolescents' rights.

Conclusion

The conclusion that emerges from an analysis of adolescents' legal rights reveals the continuing need to deal with the tension characteristic of adolescents' place in society. The tension involves the need to ensure protection for vulnerable, innocent, and immature youth while, at the same time, ensuring enough protection of their need for autonomy so that they may engage society as competent citizens. The tension manifests itself throughout the legal regulation of adolescents' lives and helps explain why the jurisprudence of adolescents' rights is more a jurisprudence of the *limits* of those rights. Although the rights of adolescents may be limited, as can and are the rights of adults, the adopted rationale for the limitation is significant. The reason for the limit determines the nature and extent of the limit.

Because of the ''peculiar vulnerability of children,''[94] the state arrogates to itself the ability to adjust its legal system to account for children's vulnerability and their need for concern. Where the Court realizes that parents may fail, they still maintain the image of parents controlling their children but allow substitute authorities to act in adolescents' best interests. Chief among these authorities has been the state, in various guises that often take the form of a judge, hospital personnel, physician, and teacher. In most cases, the court holds the final power to decide what constitutes adolescents' best interests, the parent next, and the adolescent last.[95] Thus although we learn that adolescents do have some legal rights under the Constitution, where the constitutional rights of adolescents have been recognized, the Supreme Court still remains far from solicitous of adolescents, and subsequent decisions often make the Court's expansive rhetoric ring hollow.

Although largely unchampioned, other rationales emerge to counter dominant views that bestow adolescents with limited control over their own rights because of adolescents' particular vulnerabilities. An alternative rationale for regulating adolescents' rights derives from the state's active responsibility to monitor adolescent development and offer safeguards against forces that might prevent their growth into free and independent well-developed men and citizens.[96] From this perspective, the regulation of adolescents' rights rests on the societal interest for future citizens who are able to act democratically. Although not dominant, the approach is not devoid of precedent. To ensure that interest, for example, the Court currently allows for greater community control of adolescents' rights, so long as communities do so democratically and aim to ensure the democratic development of adolescents. Thus the Court allows intrusion in adolescents' privacy interests in schools, for example, because officials act *in loco parentis* and have the duty to "inculcate the habits and manners of civility."[97] Likewise, the Court restrains state interference in family life because parents possess the right to control their children so long as they prepare them for civil society: The state has an interest in securing "healthy, well-rounded growth of young people into full maturity as citizens, with all that implies."[98] At heart, the state's claim for all of its substitute-parenting authority rests on an assertion that important social values would be served if the state allowed youth to develop toward self-reliant and civil adulthood. From this perspective, the state has the special duty to inculcate youth and to do so in a democratic fashion.

Much remains to be charted in efforts to articulate and develop the alternative rationale and accompanying system into an actual approach to adolescents' rights. The pervasive failure to explore alternative approaches to adolescents' rights reflects the failure to consider the current position of adolescents in society. As we will see, recent jurisprudence, empirical research, and social demands actually challenge the notion that all minors are vulnerable and in need of protection; those challenges also support a move away from third-party control of adolescents' rights. The following analysis of the regulation of adolescent sexuality takes advantage of these developments to rethink the traditional reasons for the control of adolescents' rights and offer an alternative model of who or what should control adolescents' rights and how they should do so.

Unlike the existing trend that focuses on parental obligations and rights to their children, the proposed model champions adolescents' right to self-determination in a democratic society. The proposal suggests that the most effective way the law may assist in producing citizens who abide by basic democratic principles and foster development consistent with democratic ideals is to take adolescents' individual rights seriously and ensure adolescents' civic participation in society. That conception of rights includes the right to consideration of needs separate from familial needs, to inclusion in decisions that involve them, to development of decision-making skills, to adaptation to a democratic society, and to more active community support. The rest of the text is devoted to these issues.

Endnotes

1. *See, e.g.,* Samuel M. Davis, Elizabeth S. Scott, Walter Wadlington, and Charles H. Whitebread, *Children in the Legal System.* 2d ed. (Westbury, NY: Foundation Press, 1997).

2. *See, e.g.,* Elizabeth S. Scott, N. Dickon Reppucci, and Jennifer L. Willard, 'Evaluating Adolescent Decision Making in Legal Contexts,'' *Law and Human Behavior* 19 (1995):221–244; Thomas Grisso, ''The Competence of Adolescents as Trial Defendants,'' *Psychology, Public Policy, and Law* 3 (1997):3–32.

3. Gary B. Melton, ''Taking *Gault* Seriously: Toward a New Juvenile Court,'' *Nebraska Law Review* 68 (1989):147–181.

4. *See, e.g., id.*

5. 262 U.S. 390 (1923).

6. *Id.* at 401.

7. *Id.* at 399.

8. 268 U.S. 510 (1925).

9. *Id.* at 534–535.

10. *Id.* at 535.

11. *Id.*

12. Meyer v. Nebraska, 262 U.S. 390, 402 (1923).

13. 273 U.S. 284 (1927).

14. 406 U.S. 205 (1972).

15. *Id.* at 211.

16. *Id.* at 209.

17. *Id.* at 232.

18. *Id.* at 243–244 (Douglas, J., dissenting).

19. Stephen G. Gilles, ''Liberal Parentalism and Children's Educational Rights,'' *Capital University Law Review* 26 (1997):9–44.

20. 268 U.S. 510, 535 (1925).

21. 406 U.S. 205, 222 (1972).

22. *Id.* at 231.

23. 321 U.S. 158 (1944).

24. *Id.* at 165.

25. *Id.* at 168, 170.

26. *Id.* at 170.

27. *Id.* at 168.

28. *Id.* at 174.

29. *Id.*

30. 310 U.S. 586 (1940).

31. Gobitis v. Minnersville Sch. Dist., 24 F. Supp. 271, 274 (1938) (reference to court's observation that it found the children's testimony persuasive in its earnestness and sincerity); Minnersville Sch. Dist. v. Gobitis, 108 F.2d 686, 693 (1938) (appellate court finds the appellant school board's failure to treat the conscientious scruples of the children appropriately).

32. *Minnersville Sch. Dist.* 310 U.S. at 601 (1940) (Stone, J., dissenting).

33. *Id.* at 600.

34. 319 U.S. 624 (1943).

35. *Id.* at 637, 642.

36. *Id.* at 642.

37. 321 U.S. 158, 168 (1944).

38. 387 U.S. 1 (1966).

39. 383 U.S. 541 (1966).

40. Grisso, ''The Competence of Adolescents as Trial Defendants.''

41. 387 U.S. 1, 9 (1966).

42. *Id.* at 17.

43. 442 U.S. 707 (1979).
44. *See* Grisso, "The Competence of Adolescents as Trial Defendants."
45. 499 U.S. 973, 980 (1989).
46. 387 U.S. 1, 28 (1966).
47. *Id.* at 17 (emphasis added).
48. 467 U.S. 253 (1984).
49. *Id.*
50. *Id.* at 264–265.
51. 442 U.S. 584 (1979).
52. *Id.* at 591.
53. *Id.* at 605.
54. *Id.* at 602.
55. *Id.* at 603.
56. Lois A. Weithorn, "Mental Hospitalization of Troublesome Youth: An Analysis of Skyrocketing Admission Rates," *Stanford Law Review* 40 (1988):773–838.
57. 442 U.S. 584, 603–604 (1979) (citations omitted).
58. *Id.* at 603.
59. 393 U.S. 503 (1969).
60. *Id.* at 508–509.
61. *Id.* at 506.
62. *Id.* at 511.
63. *Id.*
64. Robert Burt, "Developing Constitutional Rights of, in, and for Children," *Law and Contemporary Problems* 39 (1975):118–143.
65. *Tinker,* 393 U.S. at 505–506, 508.
66. 457 U.S. 853 (1982).
67. *Id.* at 870–871. The school board would have acted unconstitutionally if it would have been a substantial factor in removal.
68. *Id.* at 864 (quoting Ambach v. Norwick, 442 U.S. 68, 76–77 (1979)).
69. *Id.* at 869.
70. 478 U.S. 675 (1986).
71. *Id.* at 687.
72. *Id.* at 683.
73. *Id.* at 681.
74. *Id.* at 685.
75. 484 U.S. 260 (1988).
76. *Id.*
77. *Id.* at 273.
78. *Id.* at 272 (quoting *Fraser,* 478 U.S. at 683).
79. Tinker v. Des Moines Indep. Community Sch. Dist., 393 U.S. 503, 506 (1969).
80. 419 U.S. 555 (1975).
81. *Id.* at 581.
82. *Id.* at 583.
83. 430 U.S. 651 (1977).
84. 469 U.S. 325 (1985).
85. *Id.* at 341–342.
86. For a thorough review of strip-search cases that appeared before and after *T. L. O., see* David C. Bickenstaff, "Strip Searches of Public School Students: Can *New Jersey v. T.L.O.* Solve the Problem?" *Dickinson Law Review* 99 (1994):1–55.
87. Vernonia Sch. Dist. 47J v. Acton, 515 U.S. 646 (1995).
88. 431 U.S. 678 (1977).
89. 443 U.S. 622 (1979).
90. 431 U.S. 678, 694 (1977). For the important cases involving condom-availability programs in

public schools, *see* Alfonso v. Fernandez, 606 N.Y.S.2d 259 (N.Y. App. Div. 1993); Curtis v. School Committee, 652 N.E.2d 580 (Mass. 1995).

91. 390 U.S. 629 (1968).
92. *Id.* at 631, 634.
93. *Id.* at 639.
94. Bellotti v. Baird, 443 U.S. 622, 634 (1979).
95. For a similar observation, *see* Jopen D. Goetz, ''Children's Rights Under the Burger Court: Concern for the Child but Deference to Authority,'' *Notre Dame Law Review* 60 (1985):1214–1232.
96. Prince v. Massachusetts, 321 U.S. 158, 165 (1944).
97. *Vernonia Sch. Dist.,* 515 U.S. at 646.
98. *Prince,* 321 U.S. at 168.

PART II

The Regulation of Adolescent Sexuality

Chapter 3
REGULATING THE TRANSITION TO ADOLESCENT SEXUALITY

The study of adolescent sexual behavior and development increasingly expands its conceptualization of sexuality to reflect the complex and multidetermined features of adolescent sexuality. Although research on adolescent sexuality still overwhelmingly responds to society's concern with sexual behaviors that place adolescents at risk for pregnancy or sexually transmitted diseases,[1] research broadly expands beyond the focus on outcomes of sexual relations and the impact of social forces on those outcomes. Research now focuses on a wide range of relationships and sexual behaviors. Most notably and as we will see in the discussion that follows, research on adolescent sexuality now includes how gender roles affect sexual relationships and beliefs, how different sexual orientations affect adolescent life, how adolescents follow different developmental paths to sexual activity and intercourse, and how understanding sex involves understanding the forces that affect individuals' development and position in society. Simply stated, research has moved from the study of "sex"—whether adolescents have had or are having "it"—to the study of sexuality, which encompasses a much broader view of adolescents' sexual attitudes, behaviors, perceptions, development, as well as societal responses to those facets of adolescent sexuality.

This broader view and understanding of adolescent sexuality challenges current approaches to the regulation of adolescent life. The legal system's view of adolescents' sexual rights, and legal analyses of adolescent sexual life, tend not to approach adolescents' sexual rights in a similarly expansive and comprehensive manner. Yet to a large extent laws that regulate adolescent life all affect adolescent sexuality, and addressing adolescent sexuality necessitates addressing the position of adolescents in the law. This chapter and the next examine the legal regulation of adolescent sexuality that bears most directly on what tends to be considered societal and legal efforts to deal with the transition to adolescent sexuality and its outcomes. Both chapters examine laws in light of the current understanding of adolescent sexual development and behavior. Although dividing the discussion into chapters that separately focus on the transition to adolescent sexuality and on sexual activity in adolescence imposes a break in the continuity and diversity of sexual development, this analysis does so for the simple reason that it helps highlight different legal, policy, and research themes. Although offering different themes, both chapters do support the need for legal reform more consistent with the current understanding of adolescent sexuality and the place of adolescents in law and society.

This chapter details current directions of laws in various domains that relate to the transition to adolescent sexual behavior. Although it is important to understand that adolescent sexual behavior undoubtedly has important roots in child development, the analysis focuses on the manner various influences affect precursors to adolescents' sexual debut—their early efforts to engage in sexual activity, adolescents' actual sexual activity, and the medical issues relating to sexual activity that may not involve actual intercourse. The regulation of adolescent sexual development and the transition to adult legal status presents three important themes. First, family law generally views adolescents and their sexual development as under the control of their parents, when reality reveals that adolescent sexuality is much more multidetermined. Second, although the law bestows on parents the plenary right to control their adolescents' social environments, adolescents still retain the "right" to engage in sexual activity; and research reveals that the vast majority of adolescents do engage in sexual behavior. Third, the extent to which society grants adolescents the right to deal with negative outcomes of sexual activity, in this instance through obtaining medical testing and treatment, reflects less a concern with adolescents' individual situations or parental rights and more of a concern with the need to protect society from diseases and deter other social costs. These themes, and those developed in the following chapter, serve as a foundation to begin rethinking adolescents' sexual rights.

Regulating Precursors to Sexual Debut

Commentaries on adolescents' sexual rights frequently ignore an appropriate starting point: the dynamics that influence early sexual development and sexual experiences. Legally, the general rule that emerges from analyses of early adolescent development organizes the legal approach to family law around the assumption that parents directly govern family experiences. The ubiquitous assumption of parental power operates even to the extent that parents are given considerable control over outside forces that may infiltrate family life and influence their children's development. This section examines this basic legal rule and the extent to which it reflects the reality of the influences on adolescents' sexual lives.

The Law and Adolescents' Sexual Debut

The law generally assumes that adolescents do not control their rights, and the legal conception of adolescents' familial rights provides no exception. Adolescents do not have direct legal control over the family and social environment that lays the foundation for their sexual development and future sexual behaviors. Rather than bestowing the rights on adolescents, the legal system grants parents the right to control family life and adolescents' everyday interactions. For example, chapter 2 already reviewed how parents have the legal right to control the upbringing of their children, a right that reaches constitutional status. The Court announced that status in one of the earliest parental rights case, *Meyer v. Nebraska,*[2] which interpreted the Fourteenth Amendment to include the right "to marry, establish a home and bring up children."[3] Because the right to control the upbringing of their children reached a highly protected constitutional status, the Court also concluded that only legislative action that reasonably related to a legitimate state interest could interfere with the parental liberty interest to raise children as parents see fit. That is, states need a compelling interest to intervene into families and must tailor intervention narrowly to serve that interest. Both of these principles are important to understand and form this section's center of discussion.

In terms of intervention, the law assumes two points that mesh into one constitutional threshold to favor parental rights. First, legal systems presume that parents behave in their children's best interests. Second, legal systems generally do not require that parents be "good" parents. Parents simply must not be abusive. That considerably low threshold emerged from important constitutional interpretations established in *Prince v. Massachusetts.*[4] The case provided the Court with the opportunity to uphold a state's power to enact otherwise sweeping child labor ordinances and to announce the lowest standard to which states can hold parents accountable. Through the Court's often-cited phrase, the symbolic standard to which parents could be held would be one of martyrdom: Parents may be martyrs themselves, but they cannot make martyrs of their children. The case symbolizes how the Supreme Court respects the profound manner parents may shape their children's behaviors, but still recognizes the need for state intervention to protect the societal interest in child protection from maltreatment.

Although the constitutional threshold for parental obligations may be low, societal concern about child protection from exploitation contributed to the most notable and systematic limits on family life: statutory responses to child maltreatment. States have proceeded beyond low constitutional thresholds and have enacted extensive laws to combat, react to, and prevent the abuse of children. For example, all jurisdictions provide for state intervention to protect physically and sexually abused children.[5] Although these laws have been subjected to considerable criticisms—some argue that they are too intrusive and punitive, others argue that they are too ineffective, and others argue both[6]—these legal developments do reflect the extent to which society has established systems of laws aimed at child protection and social service delivery. Indeed, these traditional child abuse and neglect laws have been complimented by even more comprehensive laws that allow for extensive intervention into family life. The move to recognize and respond to emotional maltreatment illustrates the potentially broad state power to intervene in families. New statutes allow for intervention even though parents may not have caused the harm. For example, some statutes specifically reference what could be construed as emotional abuse by making "mental injury" or "harm to mental health" impermissible and do not explicitly require those who intervene in families to consider the cause of the harm.[7] Other statutes refer to psychological maltreatment and offer a standard for ascertaining its occurrence that focuses only on child outcomes and plays down the causes of harm.[8] These important developments reflect the extent to which states continue efforts to protect children. Despite Supreme Court mandates establishing that families deserve special protection and that parents have significant rights to protection from intrusive governmental attempts to raise their children, these statutes provide state officials with considerably broad authority to interfere in families in the name of protecting their own children.

Although states have enacted potentially very intrusive laws that aim to protect children in families, equally rigorous laws aim to remove children from their families and terminate parental claims to their children. Again, instead of encouraging such efforts, important Supreme Court dicta aim to *limit* the state's power to act on a child's behalf. In a concurrence in *Smith v. Organization of Foster Families,* which dealt with the due process rights to be accorded foster parents and children before termination of foster care placement, Justice Stewart asserted that the state could not break up a family over both the parents and children's objection just to further the "children's best interests."[9] Similarly, the majority in *Stanley v. Illinois,* a case involving the rights of putative fathers, found that the state's interest in the care and custody of a child would be *"de minimis"* if the child were in the custody of "fit" parents.[10] In the line of cases that ensued from *Stanley,* the mere showing of an interest in raising the child was enough to show fitness so long as the child was not in a more traditional family. The dicta found in these cases reveal the obstacles states must overcome to remove children from parents who fail to discharge their obligations and to act in their children's interests. Given such constitutional mandates, states must offer parents considerable protection. The burden placed on the state in efforts to terminate parental rights illustrates two significant points: the limited assistance child abuse and neglect laws can offer adolescents and the extent to which parents legally control their families. States must tread prudently when intervening to assist.

The most notable protection of parental rights that mandate prudent state action comes in two forms. The first form of protection derives from the manner the Constitution and state statutes heavily burden state officials who seek to terminate parental rights. The strong presumption of parental adequacy translates into a need to respect a heightened standard of evidence to terminate parental rights. In *Santosky v. Kramer* the Court held that the "clear and convincing" evidence standard (rather than the preponderance of the evidence standard) must be used in hearings regarding the termination of parental rights due to abuse or neglect.[11] The majority explained that "the fundamental liberty interest of natural parents in the care, custody, and management of their child does not evaporate simply because they have not been model parents or have lost temporary custody of their child to the State."[12] The prominence of parental rights has been reaffirmed in the most recent Supreme Court case to deal with child welfare issues. That case, *M. L. B. v. S. L. J.,*[13] reveals the second way states must protect parental rights.

In that case, a natural father (S. L. J.) sought to terminate the parental rights of his exwife because she allegedly failed to maintain visitation of their children and had discontinued child support. Given her alleged failures, he also wanted their children's birth certificates amended to name his new wife as their mother. The natural mother (M. L. B.) counterclaimed that her exhusband simply had not allowed reasonable visitation, despite their divorce decree that he do so. Given his alleged failures, she sought primary custody of the children. At trial the chancellor (judge) declared the mother unfit as he ruled in favor of the father. His ruling, however, failed to provide any elaboration about why the mother had been found unfit and the father had won. The mother sought to appeal. Unable to pay the $2000 cost of preparing and transmitting the record for appeal, she further sought to proceed *in forma pauperis,* which would require the state to provide her with the requisite funds. Because it was a civil case, however, Mississippi law provided the right to proceed *in forma pauperis* only at the trial level, not at the appellate level. Having been deemed unable to proceed *in forma pauperis,* she appealed that narrow issue to the U.S. Supreme Court. The Court found in her favor. In doing so, the Court ruled that an indigent parent possesses a right to have his or her court fees waived in proceedings to terminate their parental rights. The Court's decision was based on an equal protection and due process doctrine developed in a series of cases that guaranteed indigent criminal defendants access to the courts. In making the arguments, the Court stated that "choices about marriage, family life and the upbringing of children are among associational rights this Court has ranked as 'of basic importance in society,' . . . rights sheltered by the Fourteenth Amendment against the State's unwarranted usurpation, disregard or disrespect."[14] Given the fundamental nature of parental rights, the Court mandated the institution of a series of protections that the Court historically granted in proceedings that deal with the outright deprivation of property and physical liberty through criminal sanctions. Thus not only must states prove allegations to a heightened degree, states also must provide parents legal assistance—two protections that highlight the profound interest parents have in raising their children.

Without doubt, legal systems currently focus on providing children with minimal protections and require parents to follow minimal standards. However, legal systems also encourage parents to foster healthy development in a more affirmative manner. Two attempts are illustrative. The most prominent attempt to foster family responsibility involves parental responsibility laws, enacted in numerous jurisdictions, that hold parents liable for their children's failures. Such laws have been used to deal with juvenile delinquency, including sexual acting out and pregnancy as well as such broad conduct as growing up to lead an "idle, dissolute, or immoral life."[15] Although not necessarily meant to visit criminal sanctions on parents who fail, several states have enacted parental responsibility laws that intend to do so,[16] and several statutes provide a high level of intent on the part of parents who contribute to their children's problem behavior that would allow courts to uphold criminal sanctions.[17] The second prominent attempt to foster supportive parenting involves families that legally dissolve or never materialized. These laws, for example, deal with ensuring child support for children and placing children in custody situations that would be determined by their own best interests.[18] Both of these attempts provide powerful incentives for parents to act properly. Yet they still remain difficult to evaluate. Parental responsibility laws, for example, may simply translate into greater parental control, exacerbation of problems that cause delinquency, and the suppression of problems until youth reach the age of majority. The custody and support laws, for example, do not necessarily deal effectively with parental disharmony or with the basic problem that parents sometimes lack material resources to support youth.[19] When applied, these laws tend to return to a focus on minimal protections and minimal supports rather than affirmatively moving youth toward wellness. Indeed, these laws tend to not even be considered child protection laws. Despite considerable limitations and the pervasive failure to recognize their implications for adolescents' welfare, attempts to foster obligations and positive relationships continue to be made and actually can challenge the narrow mandates that laws historically have imposed on parents.

In sum, one major trend guides the legal allocation of familial rights that would affect an adolescents' early family life: parental control. The courts and legislatures provide parents with considerable freedom in their attempts to raise children as they see fit. The overriding principles of family privacy and parental rights seek to prevent state intrusion in family life, and some movement to hold parents responsible for their children's failures prompts parents to act in their children's interests. How this legal reality reflects the social reality of the precursors of adolescents' sexual experiences becomes the next topic of inquiry.

Realities of Adolescent Life

At first glance, the legal assumption that parents control their adolescents' early lives finds support from empirical research. Parents do exert a powerful influence on their children's sexual debut and the extent to which adolescents will engage in certain forms of sexual activities. However, the manner in which parents affect adolescent sexuality does not necessarily comport with popular perceptions. This section explores the extent to which parental influences do and do not comport with popular perceptions that justify the legal rule in the first place. As the existing research suggests, trends in findings reveal a need to consider the impact of forces beyond family life and parental control.

Parental Influences Largely Beyond Parental Control

A most remarkable finding that emerges from research deals with the extent to which parents do affect their children's eventual sexual and intimate relationships and the large extent to which those influences are not directly under the control of parents. Important research establishes that parents affect their children's sexual development by their own sexual, marital, and other child-bearing behaviors. These powerful influences indirectly affect a wide range of sexual behavior and beliefs. The most significant factors that provide and support models for adolescents' sexual development include parents' experiences with divorce, remarriage, living arrangements, and apparent behaviors toward the opposite sex.

Numerous fields of research suggest that parents may provide and support role models for young people. Research suggests that adolescents who experience the breakdown of their parents' marriages during childhood have differing experiences from those who do not. For example, parental marital disruption links to earlier onset of sexual activity for their children.[20] Adolescents—daughters in particular—from single-parent families are more likely to begin sexual intercourse at younger ages than their peers from two-parent families.[21] Adolescents from "blended families"—families with step-parents or step-children—tend to have sexual activity rates that rank between adolescents who come from single-parent and two-parent families.[22] This research relates to demographic and socioeconomic studies that consistently find significant associations between early sexual activity and factors such as family economic disadvantage, large family size, minority group status, unstable family environment, and low maternal education.[23]

In addition to research on family structure, considerable research reveals the impact of parental discord on child sexual development and experiences. This area of research recognizes that viewing marital disruption as a sudden event ignores a complicated series of family processes that influence the shape of children's lives and the course of their development.[24] Regardless of the approach taken to understanding divorce, few doubt that the disruption has an impact. Research focused on discord finds support in research that reveals the critical role family closeness plays in influencing sexual activity. Studies that relate to the initiation of early sexual activity to lack of family closeness and lack of parental support suggest that adolescents who seek independence early because of unsatisfactory familial relationships regard sex as part of the expression of independence. An important longitudinal study revealed that parents who foster restraint are those with more supportive families, accepting fathers, and less indulgent parents.[25] Thus a negative association between relationship satisfaction and the initiation of sexual intercourse may occur because poor relationships with parents encourage adolescents to engage in risky behaviors.[26] In general, as adolescents' satisfaction with parent–child relationships increase, the probability that they have engaged in intercourse decrease. Rejecting fathers and unsupportive or indulgent parents have been associated with early sexual behavior in boys and girls.[27] Research consistently associates nonvirginity among young people with nonauthoritative and permissive parenting, lack of parental support and control, and family stress.[28] Families marked by noncommunicative parents who do not exchange affection and with very strict fathers tend to provide environments that foster less healthy sexual relations—those more likely to involve younger adolescents, direct consent to early sexual experiences, and make less use of contraceptives.[29]

Researchers report two other often ignored but important ways parents may model and affect adolescent sexuality through forces beyond direct parental control. The first deals with the extent to which siblings model sexual activity. Siblings share similar sexual attitudes and ages at first sexual intercourse.[30] Adolescents with older sexually active siblings are more likely to begin sexual activity at an earlier age.[31] Researchers report the "striking" influence of older brothers on the initiation of sexual activity of both boys and girls.[32] Likewise, having an adolescent childbearing sister has an even stronger effect on the early initiation of sexual activity.[33] In addition, the sisters of pregnant and childbearing adolescents appear to be at a twofold elevated risk of adolescent childbearing themselves.[34] Precisely how these influences work remains to be seen, although it does seem clear that family processes play a great part and may be inferred from the composition of the family.[35] As socializing agents, parents may affect their children in a similar way as they may set standards of conduct or act as role models who shape the development of sexual attitudes and sexual norms.[36] Thus although parents may have an affect on adolescent sexual activity, the affect is far from simple and not necessarily within parents' control.

In addition to simply modeling through other children, parents influence adolescent sexuality through genetic inheritance. Parents provide genes that affect appearance, which influences attractiveness, which, in turn influences opportunities for sexual encounters.[37] Further, there is a genetic aspect to early puberty, and it is associated with early sexual experiences. For example, evidence indicates that girls whose fathers were absent from home during childhood begin menstruating earlier; and the presence of stepfathers or cohabitating men living with the girls' mothers tends to advance the age of maturation.[38] Evidence also indicates that girls who start menstruating earlier are more likely to commence sexual relations at younger ages.[39] And boys and girls with an early onset of puberty are more likely to enter into intimate partnerships or marry early[40] and to become parents sooner than their peers who mature later.[41] The research receives additional support from empirical investigations of adolescent pregnancy. Research indicates that whether an adolescent's mother had a child when she was an adolescent predicts her own teenager's trajectory into parenthood.[42] Likewise, a mothers's age at puberty is similar to that of her children, and the children of women who were sexually active at an early age also are more likely than other children to engage in sexual activity at an equally young age.[43]

A last important factor that remains beyond parents' direct control but also affects their children's sexuality involves parents' time spent in the home. For example, important studies find that the most significant, proximate maternal predictor for children to engage in early sexual activity (before 14) is the mother's employment: Children whose mothers spend more time at work are more likely to have had early sexual intercourse.[44] Precisely how maternal employment behavior affects child sexuality has yet to be clearly delineated. It remains to be determined if the links are a result of role modeling, parental supervision, or parental absence. However, other findings tend to support the latter; research indicates that much of an adolescent's sexual behavior occurs in homes.[45] The role-model hypothesis would suggest otherwise: Studies of factors associated with delays in sexual initiation identify the significance of a focus on achievement and models of economic competence to delay sexual activity.[46] However, it would seem inappropriate to conclude that the simple measure of employment would necessarily translate into models of economic achievement and competence, especially given the higher rates of poverty among single mothers who work.[47] In sum, it does seem that the relative unavailability of parents contributes to their children's early sexual debut.

Parental Factors Largely Within Parental Control

That parents largely control their children's sexuality and sexual development through indirect means does not negate their ability to control their children more directly. Two important areas of research reveal the potential significance of factors within parental control. The first area deals with the significant manner in which child maltreatment shapes children's sexuality and experiences. The second and most often suggested area deals with parental communications with their children. Both areas of research are worthy of emphasis, because they do not necessarily affect adolescent sexuality as much as popular beliefs suggest.

Although maltreating, abusive, and nonresponsive family environments do not figure prominently in discussions of adolescent sexuality, they actually play a critical role. Two areas of research are illustrative. The first area of research derives from research about adolescent sexual orientation. Commentators often note that discovery of a teenager's homosexual orientation further leads to parental rejection and verbal abuse: Nearly half of teens encounter strong negative attitudes from their parents when they disclose their sexual orientation, which places them at higher risk for psychological dysfunction.[48] Although parental reactions vary considerably,[49] these findings are important and have support from earlier research that highlighted that about half of the violence as a result of gay or lesbian sexual orientations comes from within the family[50] and that psychological maltreatment from family members is higher and has greater affects on gay and lesbian youth than any other group.[51] These findings are rather significant because they reveal the extent to which gay and lesbian adolescents have greater difficulty obtaining support from families. The continued finding of lack of family support becomes powerful in light of research that suggests teenagers abuse their gay and lesbian peers more than any other group.[52] These victimized teenagers may not only endure painful harassment from their parents but also are denied the familial support essential in a society that refuses to accept them. Unlike many members of minorities whose parents prepare their children for the harassment they may face in the world, families fail to provide support in these cases.[53] Gay and lesbian adolescents' outward behavioral patterns highlight the extent to which these youth do not have support and do experience emotional maltreatment within their homes. Compared to heterosexual adolescents, gay adolescents have higher rates of suicide,[54] homelessness (both as a result of being a throwaway and runaway),[55] substance abuse,[56] prostitution,[57] and HIV status.[58] Although it is difficult to determine whether these behaviors are the direct result of parental maltreatment, peer harassment, or wider societal rejection, research points the clearest link to parents. Negative consequences would abate if parents provided warmer emotional environments. For example, family troubles are the most often reported cause for suicidal attempts in gay adolescents[59] and up to half of gay adolescents kicked out of their homes engage in prostitution to support themselves.[60] Likewise, lack of support increases their vulnerability to relationship violence because they have difficulty obtaining assistance.[61] The complicated picture of sexual orientation, then, provides a clear example of the role healthy family environments play in securing healthy outcomes.[62]

The second area of research that links family environments to adolescent sexuality deals with the significant role sexual maltreatment and lack of familial support plays in teenage pregnancy and relationship violence. The effects reverberate simply because all forms of violence tend to be related. For example, teenage pregnancy relates to sexual abuse by a boyfriend[63] and family member;[64] and researchers have long noted that the risk of violence to both adult and adolescent women either begins or intensifies when boyfriends learn of pregnancy,[65] and abusive family dynamics lead children to engage in early coitus and early dating relationships[66] and to sexual revictimization.[67] In addition, extensive investigations of the development of antisocial behavior indicate that even when relationships do not seem abusive, certain child-rearing environments, such as those marked by negative affect and use of arbitrary, restrictive, and punitive parenting strategies fail to promote cooperative or healthy relationships and do not foster empathic or altruistic responses to and from others.[68] Evidence of the significance of more indirect forms of emotional maltreatment accumulates, particularly in the area of witnessing and living with domestic violence.[69] Research increasingly reveals that the experience of emotional violence remains hidden and revealed circuitously by adolescents' behaviors, which range from aggressive and violent behavior, pregnancy, suicide, to victimization outside the home.[70] It seems difficult to overemphasize the link between adolescents' "problem" behaviors and their home environments.

Instead of focusing on maltreating practices, policy makers and those interested in controlling adolescent sexuality focus on potentially positive steps parents may take to affect their children's sexuality. These efforts often exhort parents to take more seriously their responsibilities as children's guides to sexual development and values. The most frequent message from those who wish to affect adolescents' sexual behaviors includes the need for parents to discuss sexual matters with their children.[71] Although the approach may seem judicious, research actually indicates that the attempt remains limited in four ways that demonstrate the limited extent to which parents directly control their children's sexual development and experiences.

First, despite the belief that parents should actively guide their children's sexual development, parents generally find initiating and sustaining discussions about sexuality with their teenagers difficult. Parents generally feel that they lack knowledge, are embarrassed by the topic, and often misperceive their adolescents' behaviors. As their children develop and their need for information regarding the interpersonal, erotic, or moral aspects of sexuality increase, parents feel significantly challenged and less able to communicate comfortably and effectively.[72] The result is that as children reach adolescence, sexual discussions tend to be rare.[73] Much like parental reports, children's reports indicate that sexual discussions are difficult, and that the most difficult tend to be between fathers and sons.[74] Those who do find discussions more easy do not necessarily engage in more communication, however.[75]

Second, given the lack of overt communication, the possibility arises that rampant misperceptions and miscommunications exist. Parents generally find it difficult to believe that their own children might have experienced intercourse, even though parents recognize that similarly aged teenagers often engage in sexual activity.[76] For example, research finds that of the adolescents who have engaged in sexual intercourse, fewer than half of their mothers thought that they had done so.[77] These data are consistent with several studies that suggest that parents tend to underestimate the sexual activity of their children.[78] The findings also comport with numerous studies that report parent–child discrepancies in perceptions of family members regarding communication.[79] Parents tend to think they know more about their children's sexual activity than they actually do.

Third, even if families do discuss sexuality, research indicates that they are not necessarily effective in influencing adolescents' risk behavior. Fewer than half of sexually active teenagers surveyed reported having talked with their parents about sex and birth control.[80] Important early research suggests why: Adolescents and their parents who have discussed sex-related issues often contradict one another in descriptions of their own sex-related conversations.[81] Likewise, although children view parents' feelings as important, they are not as important as parents believe. Parents overestimate the value of their feelings to their child's engagement in sexual activity or use of protective measures.[82] For example, of adolescents who actually do talk with their parents, their discussions about birth control have little relationship to the consistency with which they use contraceptives.[83]

Fourth, parents and adolescents avoid conflicts about sexual matters. This area of research involves the burgeoning study of direct parent–child conflict. Despite popular beliefs that matters of sexuality infuse conflicts between parents and their children, familial conflicts tend to be about minor matters like dress and social life.[84] Parents and adolescents tend not to argue about some topics of greatest difference between them, such as sex, drugs, religion, and politics.[85] The overarching conflict of adolescence concerns different perspectives of parents and their offspring about how much control parents should have over various aspects of the lives of their adolescents. Parent–child relationships remain increasingly silent about the manner in which adolescents appear to regard an increasing range of issues to be under their own control, rather than those of their parents.[86] A primary example involves youth with homosexual orientations. Recent research reports that more than 80% of lesbian and gay youth experience severe isolation, and that the emotional isolation is especially high with regard to their families;[87] researchers report a "conspiracy of silence" that develops within the family, which makes an unspoken rule of not permitting anyone to discuss the issues.[88] The general belief that parents do and can control their offspring's sexual activity and protective behaviors has yet to survive rigorous empirical scrutiny.

Peer Relationship Influences on Sexual Debut

The failure to find consistent evidence of parental control of adolescents' sexual upbringing contrasts sharply with research that investigates the impact of peers on adolescent sexuality. Indeed, researchers frequently cite peer influence and peer pressure as one of the most influential factors that conducts adolescent sexual information, decisions, and activity.[89] Peers propel adolescent sexuality and experiences in a number of ways.

The first major way peers impact adolescent sexual matters is through the manner peers serve as primary sources of information. Peers serve as the most frequently sought source of information. For example, numerous research projects directly have asked adolescents whom they turn to for information about sex. Both boys and girls overwhelmingly report peers of the same sex more than parents and independent readings.[90] In terms of mere information, research about sources of information shows that peers make up for the minor role played by parents.[91]

The second way peers impact adolescent sexual debut involves their influence on sexual attitudes. A substantial research literature demonstrates the impact of perceptions of peers' behaviors and attitudes on young peoples' sexual activity. In terms of attitudes, one illustrative study found that relationships between peer measures and adolescents' attitudes were different for males and females and for virgins and nonvirgins. In all cases, friends' approval for engaging in sexual behavior related to premarital sexual attitudes, although sex differences temper the intensity of the peer influence.[92] In terms of perceptions of peer behaviors, a number of peer measures relate to adolescent sexual activity. These measures include peer pressure,[93] perceived approval of sexual behaviors,[94] peer acceptance and rejection,[95] and participation in a "deviant" peer network.[96] The consistent finding supports the rule that young people who believe that their peers are sexually active are more likely to be so themselves.[97] Likewise, the belief that their peers engage in certain sexual behaviors affects the extent to which youth view the practices as normal and appropriate.[98] Levels of communication with peers tend to increase the likelihood that adolescents will engage in risky behavior, although again important sex differences emerge in that peers influence males more than they do females.[99]

The third finding of peer impact on adolescent sexual activity involves the manner in which peers influence behaviors that relate to sexual activity. Several studies report that substance use powerfully predicts subsequent early sexual activity.[100] In fact, the increase in sexual experimentation over the last two decades of the 20th century parallels a concomitant increase in experimentation with illegal drugs. Increased rates in premarital sex and illicit drug use may be related, whether because one constitutes a risk factor for the other or because both are influenced by similar factors. Research indicates that illicit drug use and other nonnormative adolescent behaviors predispose adolescents to engage in sexual activity. The earlier the involvement in drugs, the greater the risk of sexual activity.[101] Again, it is important to note that drug use relates to peer activity and that both relate to sexual activity and link to other transitional behaviors, such as cigarette smoking, alcohol consumption, and delinquency.[102]

A fourth area of research that emphasizes the impact of peers on adolescent sexual activity involves the manner in which adolescent culture places value on sexual activity and teenagers' powerful desire to demonstrate adult-like behavior. Researchers show that a triumphant loss of virginity can mark the transition to a more mature and valued status. The significance given to sexual activity as a marker of the transition has reverberating effects. Adolescents and society view sexual intercourse as the major rite of passage to adulthood.[103] As a result, adolescents particularly are at risk for exaggerating reports to peers on the joys of sexual debut.[104] The effects of romanticized reports can be far-reaching, given the major role that peers play as models and as sources of information and reinforcement. Glamorized reports lead to increased attempts to seek similar experiences and contribute to the powerful influence peers exert on sexual activity.

Partners Affect Sexual Behavior

Although peers play a significant role in the sexual socialization and experiences of youth, partners arguably play an even greater role. Yet the role of partners in the sexual environment of youth remains ill-explored. Little empirical research explores the nature of adolescent relationships, the experience of sexual activity, the influence of partners on levels of sexual activity, and the influence of partners on resolutions of issues that may arise because of the sexual activity. This lack of empirical understanding supports the observation that, although we now know a great deal about who does what and what they do sexually, we have only partial information about how adolescents themselves perceive their sexual practices. Although existing research tends to ignore the impact of the relationship on sexual activity, findings that do exist highlight five significant ways partners should matter to those interested in understanding sexual debut.

The first important finding that links adolescent sexual debut to partners relates to the general rule that links increases in relationship commitment to an increasing desire for sexual involvement for both males and females. Despite the general belief that females are more reluctant than boys to engage in sexual activity, females approach males' level of sexual involvement with increasing age and increased commitment to the relationship.[105] This is significant because as relationships move from casual to committed, the likelihood of sexual experiences increases. Relatedly, the earlier the dating experience begins for an adolescent, the more likely they are to become involved in committed relationships and experience sexual activity.[106] The earlier the sexual experience, the more likely the adolescents are to have more sexual partners, older sexual partners, and participate in more frequent sexual activity.[107] Likewise, the earlier the dating experience, the more likely they are to experience earlier childbirth and marriage.[108]

The second finding derives from related research on risky sexual behavior and how it relates to the nature of relationships. Reviews of research about alcohol use and sexual behavior illustrate the significance of partners. Support for the alcohol–risky sex association emerges most consistently from studies that examine first-time sexual intercourse events.[109] Once relationships are established, researchers suggest the need to consider relationship dimensions such as trust, commitment, intimacy, and communication and their effect on behavior that places adolescents at risk.[110] It is important to note that sexual intercourse involving the first sexual event represents a significant and novel milestone and its correlates may not generalize to later experiences with new partners. However, it does seem that partners do directly influence levels of sexual activity.

The third evidentiary support derives from research on the dynamics of sexual coercion. Research consistently finds the powerful role partners play in determining sexual debut through their coercive behaviors, and young women seem apparently susceptible to coercive advances. Teenage girls who are sexually active, compared to their peers who have not had intercourse, are more susceptible to pressure form their male partners.[111] Sexual activity is high for girls who lack effective communication skills and perceive the expectation of sexual activity from their partner.[112] In the most recent, large-scale sex survey, 25% of the women claimed they did not want to have sex when they first did so.[113] That finding suggests the persistence of a long-standing pattern of pressure on women to engage in sexual activity at earlier stages in relationships. In spite of agreement as to what is appropriate and acceptable, researchers continue to find that boys still coerce and girls are coerced.[114] A substantial minority of adolescents report involuntary initiation into sexual activity.[115] Although it may be a minority, the coercion contributes to clear developmental outcomes, especially for girls coerced when they reach puberty. Nonvoluntary sex accounts for a large portion of all sexual exposure before the age of 14 among females.[116] Even among adolescents who experienced forced sex, virtually all later initiate voluntary sex during their teenage years.[117] Few teenagers have sex only once.[118] More than two thirds have sex again within six months of first intercourse. Likewise, coercion plays a significant role in high-risk sexual behaviors.[119] Partners, whether coercive or not, play a significant role.

The fourth point relates to issues of coercion but arises in the context of teenage pregnancy research. The interpersonal relationship of the adolescent boy–girl dyad has been found to relate more consistently and strongly with pregnancy risk than the quality of either peer or family relationships.[120] Likewise, those who continue the pregnancy report that partners have more influence on the decision than parents.[121] The greater the degree of involvement and commitment, the higher the frequency of sexual intercourse and contraceptive use. These findings relate to those that reveal an age disparity between girls and their past sexual partners. In general, the partners of young women who first have sex during their teenage years average about three years older than they are. On the other hand, teenage males' first partners average less than a year older.[122] Although the gap may be wider,[123] the disparity supports the proposition that partners play a critical and influential role in the initiation of sexual activity.

Lastly, adolescents who have the highest levels of sexual activity are those who are steadily dating one person, those who are dating several individuals have moderate levels, and those who date only occasionally have the lowest incidence of sexual activity.[124] Likewise, the initiation of sexual intercourse early in life associates with an increased number of sex partners.[125] However, it is important to note that young men have relatively few periods of multiple partners and that promiscuous behavior appears unusual. Having more than one partner a year generally indicates the instability of adolescent relationships, rather than adolescents' predatory and adventurous behaviors.[126] Although these findings may shed a different light on notions of promiscuity, they still support partners' significant role in the sexual socialization of youth.

The fundamental point that emerges from this research simply highlights that relationships matter. Characteristics of the relationship in terms of time in the relationships, commitment to the relationship, and relationship satisfaction affect levels of sexual activity. Over time, a couple takes on an identity of its own, one that overrides the pressures associated with parent and peer approval. Although the role played by partners generally remain ill-explored, research supports the expectation that partners may matter more than parents and peers.

Community Influences on Sexual Debut

Communities affect behavior; and adolescent sexuality does not provide an exception. Sociocultural norms strongly influence adolescent sexual behavior.[127] Researchers increasingly document how the communities and groups in which we live channel and constrain our behaviors. Those behaviors include those as profoundly intimate as sexual activity. Socially recognized norms guide the timing and sequencing of events associated with the transition to adulthood.[128] Thus although individuals themselves may ultimately decide life-course events, socially prescribed norms for transitions powerfully influence life events and decisions.

The area of community influence that attracts the most research involves the manner in which individuals from different ethnic and racial backgrounds perceive and actually pace life course events related to sexual behavior. The most well-documented findings reveal persistently different sexual, marital, and fertility patterns of Black and White adolescents.[129] For example, first intercourse occurs earlier among Blacks than Whites.[130] These patterns coincide with the normative beliefs held by White and Black adolescents. White teenagers are less accepting than Blacks of intercourse at younger ages and of nonmarital childbearing.[131] Recent research reveals that Hispanic and Southeast Asian youth exhibit yet other patterns of sexual debut and normative beliefs.[132]

Although much of the early research used race or ethnic status as a proxy for community differences, recent work extends this area of research to investigate two important predictors of sexual debut: community poverty and religiosity. Recent work addresses community and cultural effects on diverse sets of adolescent behaviors,[133] including sexual activity,[134] that arises from environments marked by poverty. Researchers have long associated living in poverty with both early sexual activity and early pregnancy. As socioeconomic status decreases, rates of sexual activity rise: Adolescents from economically disadvantaged backgrounds become sexually active at younger ages.[135] As we will see in chapter 4, these same variables play critical roles in resolutions of dilemmas that result from sexual activity and pregnancy, such as whether girls will abort, place the child for adoption, or get married. These findings relate to considerable research that suggests that girls who place little importance on or perceive little likelihood of achieving educational or work-related goals choose sexual activity and childbearing relatively early in the life course, and those who view school and career goals as important deliberately postpone sex and parenthood.[136]

Religiosity, often measured by frequency of attendance at services, either is related to or directly promotes the delay of sexual intercourse until a later age or until relationships stabilize.[137] Teenagers who report religion as important to them and who attend church more frequently are less likely to report having engaged in sexual intercourse.[138] The highest levels of premarital intercourse occur with those who have no religious affiliation.[139] The tendency to be devout and observant of religious custom and teaching is more predictive than any specific affiliation. However, it does seem that religions that teach sexual abstinence have a greater impact on delaying sexual behavior.[140] Yet even though that may seem laudable, religions linked to delays of first intercourse also link to risky behavior: When religious adolescents first engage in sexual intercourse, they are less likely to be protected with respect to both pregnancy and sexually transmitted diseases.[141] It is important that the community aspect of religion and the forces beyond families remains rather significant: A clear peer–religiosity interaction exists. Adolescents who attend church but who do not have any friends attending church are not different from those less religious in their likelihood of early sexual activity. However, children who attend church regularly and have peers attending the same church are less than half as likely to be sexually active by age 14 as their counterparts who do not attend church.[142] Again, the community in which youth live determines the impact of religion.

Preliminary Conclusion

The environment that most immediately affects the early upbringing of children who will become sexual adolescents remains under the legal control of parents. The legal standard for parental behaviors in terms of the way they treat their children remains remarkably low. This legal approach that relates parent–child relationships and the courts to adolescents' early relationships fails to reflect the empirical reality of adolescent life. Parents do not influence the debut of their children's sexual behavior in manners entirely within their control. Influences on adolescents cannot be approached independent of broad social contexts. The complexity of adolescent sexuality requires a complex response. The manner in which the factors work together suggests that attempts to disaggregate them and focus on one legal factor—the control of adolescents' rights by their parents—seems considerably inappropriate, which renders questionable the legal system's persistent effort to do so.

Regulating Access to Sexual Activity

Although parents legally control the family environments from which adolescents emerge, adolescents retain the ability to engage in sexual activity. Although adolescents do not necessarily have a ''right'' to engage in sexual activity, they generally remain free to engage in sexual behaviors and sexual intercourse, especially with adolescents of similar ages. The only legal limitations placed on these behaviors involve those that state criminal laws place on adolescents. Criminal law regulates sexual intercourse and sexual interactions in terms of sexual consent statutes. In addition to the usual consent statutes, most states also have laws that presume certain minors incapable of consenting to sexual intercourse and other sexual interactions; and such sexual conduct with unconsenting minors constitutes an array of criminal offenses. This section reviews and discusses notable aspects of these laws and then details the current empirical understanding of adolescents' consent to sexual activity.

The Law of Consent to Sexual Activity

Despite the general belief that minors cannot consent to sexual intercourse or other forms of sexual activity, the general rule is that the law actually assumes that most adolescents can consent to *and* may engage in sexual activity. The regulation of their consent and sexual experiences derives mainly from criminal law, particularly statutory rape and sexual assault laws. Although these laws generally are viewed as prohibiting sexual activity, they actually also do the opposite: The law renders permissible certain sexual activities and relationships that do not fall within statutory prohibitions. These relationships and activities are permissible, of course, only absent other forms of coerciveness. That is, laws that prohibit certain relationships and activities assume that adolescents are unable to make adult decisions in those contexts. Through these statutes, then, legal systems permit adolescents to engage in sexual activity and assume some forms of sexual behaviors are not necessarily coercive interactions.

Although we will consider issues of coercion and rape in chapters 8 and 9, at this juncture it is important to review parts of these laws that deal with issues of possible consent. Three points are noteworthy. First, the laws generally exclude from culpability those who fall within certain age ranges of the minor (often 2 to 4 years) who may consent to sexual activity; and the laws generally prohibit sexual activity between adolescents and older adults as well as with those in positions of authority over the minor. Second, the laws often differentiate between various forms of sexual activity the adolescent may engage in without holding the partner culpable for illegal sexual acts. Third, state laws vary in terms of the extent to which they disapprove of certain behaviors, as reflected in the penalties they would impose and the individuals they exclude from liability—statutes regularly exempt adolescents' spouses,[143] those who have sexual interactions with individuals deemed unchaste or promiscuous,[144] or those who reasonably may seem able to consent to sexual activity.[145] This section details these developments in the regulation of adolescents' consent to sexual activity that fall under two major areas of law.

The first major area of law that would control consent issues derives from statutory rape laws. These laws, which impose strict liability on those who engage in certain forms of sexual activity with certain groups of minors remain diverse and defy easy categorization. Statutes vary considerably in terms of the acts and relationships they potentially find impermissible. Given the diversity in laws and assumption about adolescents who legitimately may engage in sexual activity, it makes sense to approach the statutes in terms of what they allow adolescents of different ages to do. States range widely. For example, Louisiana permits adolescents between 11 and 17 to engage in some forms of sexual activity, such as sexual intercourse, so long as the male partner is not more than two years older than her and is less than 17.[146] Four states—Delaware, Kentucky, West Virginia, and Wyoming—allow for sexual activity at the age of 12.[147] Ten states permit 13-year-olds to consent to sexual activity.[148] Fourteen is the general age of consent for some forms of sexual activity in 20 states,[149] and five states place the age of consent at 15.[150] The next major group of states includes 12 that proscribe 16 as the age at which adolescents can engage in sexual activity.[151] Illinois prohibits any act of sexual conduct or sexual penetration with a person who is 17 or younger.[152] Two states—California and Oregon—go even further and prohibit all sexual contact until the adolescent is 18.[153] Note that the total actually exceeds fifty states because some states have more than one age of consent, which could vary according to the type of sexual activity and age ranges between partners.

The second series of statutes arises from sexual assault laws that combine age with relationship characteristics. These laws criminalize sex between adolescents of a certain age and persons in positions of authority or trust over them. Although it would seem that states would protect all adolescents from relationships that are most likely to involve vulnerability and abuse of power, fewer than half the states expressly enumerate provisions of this nature.[154] These statutes, like the statutory rape provisions discussed previously, vary considerably. For example, Colorado criminalizes sexual contact with a minor younger than 18 by anyone "in a position of trust with respect to the victim."[155] Oregon criminalizes sexual intercourse with a person under 16 years of age where the minor is the perpetrator's sibling, child, or spouse's child.[156] Other statutes more specifically define what would constitute positions of authority, trust, or supervision over the minor; Maine's extensive statute is illustrative of efforts to be as inclusive as possible.[157] These statutes reflect the notion that particular relationships may be so inherently authoritarian and hierarchical as to make any sex within these relationships criminally coercive.

In reading these statutes that aim to regulate adolescents' ability to consent and engage in sexual activity, it is important to keep in mind four points. The first point relates to the manner in which the age and type of sexual activity matters. Most states adopt a nuanced statutory scheme that penalizes by reference to both age and the type of sexual contact (e.g., penetrative intercourse or nonpenetrative contact). Where a state varies ages and types of contact, the state tends to allow younger adolescents to engage in sexual activity but not permit sexual intercourse until mid-adolescence. In addition, where ages vary within a state, the state tends to allow adolescents to engage in sexual activities with those closer in age, usually within two to four years.

A second point about statutes that regulate adolescents' ability to consent and engage in sexual activity involves issues of gender. Most statutory rape laws are now gender neutral in terms of those they will hold responsible. However, two important remnants remain. First, most states have repealed chastity and promiscuity defenses (only Florida and Mississippi retain the defenses).[158] The reforms are significant in that evidence of promiscuity or prior sexual activity negated the possibility of statutory rape. Second, most states also have removed distinctions between males and females in the extent to which they will be held accountable for certain actions. Yet three important exceptions remain. Alabama, Idaho, and New York all provide age-based rape as perpetrated only against a female by a male. In both Alabama and Idaho, age-based rape only can be committed by a male against a female.[159] New York's prohibition of sexual misconduct against a female under 17 assumes that such conduct can be committed only by a male (of any age).[160] It is important to note that one New York appellate court found the gender-specific aspect of the law unconstitutional,[161] despite direct Supreme Court authority finding such gender distinctions permissible.[162] In theory, therefore, the vast majority of states formally hold both sexes to the same standards of sexual conduct.

A third point about the statutory frameworks that regulates adolescent sexual activity involves the manner in which the Supreme Court has addressed the extent to which states may control adolescents' sexual activities. This has particular relevance in that, even though the previously discussed restrictions on adolescent sexuality may seem to matter, the issue is whether they matter enough to raise to constitutionally impermissible levels of infirmity. The Supreme Court directly confronted issues of statutory rape in *Michael M. v. Superior Court of Sonoma County*.[163] The Court upheld a California law that allowed for the prosecution of a 17 1/2-year-old man for the statutory rape of a 16 1/2-year-old woman. In theory, two arguments could have been made. The first challenge was the one the Court took seriously: whether the statute that treated adolescent males and females differently violated the equal protection clause of the Fourteenth Amendment. The Court's analysis applied a rather low level of scrutiny to the statute: the minimum rationality test, which finds intrusion on constitutional rights permissible so long as a reasonable argument could be made to link a compelling state interest to the imposition of different sanctions on male and female activities. Such a low standard was used in this case because gender, in this instance, did not need special protections: The Court noted that there is ''nothing to suggest that men, because of past discrimination or peculiar disadvantages, are in need of special solicitude of the courts.''[164] Given this low standard, the Court found that the challenged provision was not impermissible simply because the legislature acted reasonably within its authority when it accepted the rationale that the risk of pregnancy deterred female sexual activity and that the criminal sanction placed on males served to roughly equalize the deterrents on the sexes. The second challenge could have been from issues arising from the minor's right to privacy. Only the dissent considered whether a minor possessed a right to privacy that also would include the right to consensual sexual activity. Although noting that the right to privacy could include sexual activity, even the dissenting opinion realized that a juvenile's circumstances justifies a different constitutional standard and allows governmental intrusions in a minor's right to privacy if such intrusion rationally relates to a legitimate governmental interest. In this instance, again, numerous arguments could have been made to bolster the argument that the legislature had acted rationally. The result is that, since that decision, lower courts have relied on the Supreme Court's decision to deny adolescents the right to engage in consensual sexual activity; states now may regulate sexual activities as they pertain to minors.[165]

The fourth noteworthy consideration concerns the manner in which statutes may assume that adolescents are able to consent in some situations and less so in others. This rather controversial assumption relates to the pervasive finding that, even though the activity qualifies as statutorily impermissible, it does not mean that the laws are enforced. The failure to enforce statutory rape laws has been well-demonstrated in terms of police and prosecutorial discretion to ignore underage sex they deem consensual.[166] The failure to follow legal mandates also has been seen by two appellate courts that have refused to uphold statutory rape convictions for consensual sex despite clear statutory obligations.[167] Courts generally do not conduct meaningful inquiries into consent in relationships that are not deemed per se illegal. Thus even though laws differentiate, the reality remains considerably more complicated and difficult to apply in practice.

Realities of Adolescent Life

Few areas involve such significant personal choice as the choice to engage in sexual activity and intercourse. The choice signifies the entrance into a world of sexuality, responsibility, and potential danger. Although adolescents remain free to choose whether they will engage in some sexual behaviors, particularly with agemates, the law still regulates their sexual activity. The issue that concerns us at this point is whether the statutory rape and sexual assault laws that allow sexual activity reflect the realities of adolescent sexual behavior.

Through provisions of statutory and sexual assault statutes that differentiate between adolescents and adults or older adolescents, the law assumes at least some difference in the ability of some adolescents and adults to give meaningful, uncoerced consent to sexual activity. Both types of statutes consider age the proxy for the ability to consent to sexual activity and, like several laws guiding adolescent life, they presume adolescents who fall below certain ages as generally unable to consent to sexual activity. These assumptions have yet to be subjected to empirical scrutiny. There is no established literature on adolescents' abilities to consent to sexual encounters. The absence of such literature leads us to turn to other research to evaluate the current statutes. In this regard, existing research offers five important findings.

The first area of research relates to the manner in which statutes distinguish among various levels of sexual activity. For example, several statutes assume adolescents may consent to nonpenetrative sexual behavior at a younger age. At best, existing research suggests that such distinctions are dubious for at least three reasons. First, adolescent sexual development does not necessarily proceed in stages of sexual activity, as reflected in research about adolescent sexual timetables. Although some adolescents may proceed from kissing and petting toward sexual intercourse, others begin with sexual intercourse or have very short "less serious" stages.[168] Second, it is not clear why sexual activity that leads to more penetrative sexual behavior is permissible when penetrative behavior is forbidden. Although the distinction may reflect the difficulty of regulating nonpenetrative forms of sexual activity, it fails to reflect how intercourse necessarily links to nonpenetrative behaviors. Third, adolescents frequently engage in sexual intercourse while in relationships, and it is the level of relative commitment in the relationship that generally dictates levels of sexual activity. Characteristics of the relationship in terms of time in the relationship, commitment to the relationship, and relationship satisfaction affect levels of sexual activity.

The second general area of research deals with the coerciveness of adolescent sexual behavior. As discussed earlier, a substantial minority of young people report that initiation into sexual activity is involuntary.[169] Among girls who engaged in sexual activity before age 14, for example, involuntary sex accounts for a large portion of all their sexual experiences.[170] As we have seen, one quarter of women perceive their first sexual intercourse as involuntary.[171] Likewise, for women at least, sexual initiation is far from always a positive experience. Studies repeatedly show that a large majority of female adolescents report being overwhelmingly disappointed both physically and emotionally by their loss of virginity.[172] Some studies even report that more than half describe their experiences as painful and one third as "severely painful."[173] Girls tend not to be swept away with passion and sexual desire, despite popular beliefs to the contrary.[174] Girls are more likely to report that they engage in sexual activity because they feel pressured.[175] Males are clearly more likely to feel more positive than girls about initial intercourse.[176] Males also are more likely to be less emotionally attached to their partners.[177] These findings complement numerous studies that reveal how motivations for engaging in sex vary by gender: Boys aim for physical satisfaction and pleasure and girls seemingly aim for close emotional bonds.[178] Although these findings may remain controversial, they do suggest the need to reconsider the appropriateness of current schemes that leave consent to adolescents, distinguish between forms of activity, and differentially establish liability based on types of sexual relationships.

The third important area of research deals with sexually active teenagers. This area of research generally questions the ability of girls to consent to sexual activity. Sexually active teenage girls, compared to their peers who have not had intercourse, are more susceptible to pressure from their male partners.[179] Likewise, sexual activity is high for girls who lack effective communication skills and perceive the expectation of sexual activity from their partner.[180] This research is complemented by findings that few teenagers have sex only once and more than two thirds have sex again within six months of first intercourse.[181] Abusive behaviors set girls on early paths to sexual activity, a finding supported by research that suggests girls who have been victims of sexual child abuse begin to engage in sexual intercourse at an earlier age. Although it would seem important not to cast judgment on reasons adolescents engage in sexual activity, because adults frequently engage in such behaviors for similarly illegitimate reasons, findings relating to early sexual activity and amounts of pressure suggest that current statutes must adjust to the possibility of coercion that goes unnoticed.

The fourth important point relates to the current age disparities between partners in sexual relationships. As discussed earlier, in general the partners of young women who first have sex during their teenage years average about three years older than they are. For teenage males, their first partners average less than a year younger.[182] It is uncommon, though, for first partners to be substantially older: Only 9% of adolescent girls and 3% of adolescent boys reported that their first partner to be 23 or older.[183] By the time the relationships get more involved and lead to childbearing, more than one quarter of young mothers, those between ages 15 to 17, end up with partners at least five years older than themselves.[184] It is important to note that more than three quarters of that percentage will be married by the time they give birth,[185] which exempts them from statutory rape laws.[186] The findings, then, suggest that pressures and coercion occur in similar age ranges, which are not legally regulated, and for relationships that do fall within the proscribed age range, the offense no longer counts because of the manner marriage exempts offenders. The result is that the large number who may need protection receive none.

The fifth issue concerns whether the rationales for prohibiting sexual activity make sense. The extent to which youth suffer from the consequences of early sexual activity, whether consensual or not, is well-established. For example, for boys, a largely excluded group from discussions of the negative impact of early sexual activity, research indicates that males pay an emotional price for beginning a sexual relationship early. Early sexual activity brings a host of health hazards as well. Sexually transmitted diseases are well-known to affect both males and females; in fact, AIDS and other sexually transmitted diseases affect boys much more than they do girls.[187] Both teenagers often may be informed about the physical implications of engaging in sexual activity yet may not be fully aware of the emotional sacrifices associated with sexual activity.

It is important to note that although AIDS, unwanted pregnancy, and other negative consequences of illicit sexual activity can be used to justify statutory rape laws and the refusal to recognize a minor's right to consent to sexual activity, it is important to appreciate the limits of such arguments. The problem of using sex-related epidemics in support of a minor's capacity to consent to sex is fourfold. First, statutory rape laws have not had the deterrent effect they are designed to have; premarital sex is rampant and prosecutions rare. Second, with the onset of AIDS, teenagers are more informed about the nature and implications of engaging in early sexual activity and the importance of abstinence. Third, society places a great deal of responsibility in the hands of teenagers to make informed decisions regarding the use of condoms and other protective devices to reduce the spread of AIDS, although legal systems tend to limit access to devices and services that would help encourage responsibility. Fourth, society acknowledges that teenagers have a choice and that a majority choose to engage in sexual activities despite efforts to discourage them.

Preliminary Conclusion

Current legal approaches to adolescent sexual activity attempt to reflect the complexities of adolescent sexual behavior. Laws generally aim to recognize the ability of adolescents to consent to some forms of activities with some partners and assume other relationships are inherently coercive. The reality, however, seems to be that several adolescents remain unprotected: either their coercion is unrecognized or, if it is recognized as potentially problematic, it is justified and excused for other reasons (such as marriage). Thus in the first attempt made by law to recognize adolescents' potential legal independence in sexual matters, difficulties arise that offer no easy answers for a system that offers protection by distinguishing among people of different ages, their sexual activity, and sexual partners.

Regulating Access to Medical Testing and Treatment

Thus far the review notes that parents generally control the environment that gives rise to sexual activity. Parents, however, do not control adolescents' right to consent to certain sexual behaviors. To the extent legal control exists beyond the adolescent, state law regulates with whom the adolescent may engage in certain sexual activities. The law reflects a belief that some adolescents possess sufficient maturity to consent to sexual activity and that it is the state's role to determine if adolescents qualify as mature. These consent laws reflect similar attempts to respect adolescents' rights to autonomous and confidential decision making in the health care arena. The major rationale for allowing adolescents to control their health care decision making has been that the right belongs to those who are mature, or at least as mature as adults.[188] A close reading of the statutes reveals, however, that changes in the legal regulation of adolescents' rights do not necessarily reflect the adolescent's level of maturity or their own freedoms. Rather, statutory changes to increase access to services reflect basic societal concerns regarding the need to protect society from communicable diseases, to protect youth from those diseases, and to deter pregnancy. This section details the regulation of adolescents' rights to access to medical testing and treatment and the extent to which the law and its rationales properly reflect the realities of adolescents' experiences.

The Law and Adolescent Access to Services

The common law position regarding health care treatment for minors was that, until minors reached the age of majority, they lacked the legal authority to consent to their own health care.[189] Thus any treatment rendered to a minor absent parental consent could subject the health care provider to legal actions for assault and battery. Two reasons justify parents' authority, as reflected in the Supreme Court's guiding opinion, *Parham v. J.R.*,[190] that provides broad parameters to resolve conflicts between parent and child regarding mental health treatment. In *Parham* the Court noted how the broad parental authority "rests on a presumption that parents possess what a child lacks in maturity, experience and judgment required for making life's difficult decisions. More important, historically it was recognized that natural bonds of affection lead parents to act in the best interests of their children."[191] The general rule, then, holds that parental maturity and natural inclination to act in their children's best interests justifies granting parents legal control over their adolescents' access to medical services.

Despite that general rule, numerous exceptions allow minors to secure treatment without parental consent. The first exception arises in instances of emergency; in those situations doctors could treat a child of any age, even in the absence of parental consent. Such cases imply the guardian's consent because delay would jeopardize the minor's health. Although originally enunciated by courts, more than half the states now statutorily provide for medical treatment in cases of emergency.[192] Statutes that codify the emergency exception to parental consent rules take three general forms: They simply allow treatment without parental consent, relieve liability from those who would treat without consent, or find that minors may consent to emergency care.[193] An equally prevailing pattern, however, evinces no notification requirement.[194]

The second major exception derives from the rule that emancipated minors need not obtain parental consent. The exception operates on the rationale that parents surrender their duties and minors are responsible for themselves at this point. Given that the doctrine grew from common law, courts, without explicit statutory authorization, issue emancipation decrees under various situations in which parents relinquish their rights to the child. The main indicia of emancipation include the minor's marriage, induction into the armed forces, establishment of an independent home, or economic independence.[195] It is important to note that under common law doctrine, emancipation may be either complete or partial, which may require adolescents to obtain parental consent for certain services. Given the variability in judicial pronouncements, it is important to review the statutory frameworks in which courts operate, including the requirement that courts need not be involved in emancipated minors' access to medical services.

Less than half the states have statutes that provide for court-ordered emancipation for minors. These statutes vary in terms of the criteria for emancipation and the procedures to be followed. Only a few statutes explicitly find that court-ordered emancipations remove the requirement of parental consent for medical services.[196] Most statutes do not expressly provide that the effect of emancipation would be access to medical services without parental consent.[197] States that do not require judicial determinations view emancipation in terms of designated acts on the part of the parent, minor, or both;[198] however, all but one of those states explicitly finds that the minor may consent to health services.[199] In addition, several states, without specifying what constitutes emancipation or its determination, simply state that emancipated minors may consent to services.[200]

Although several states do not mention emancipation, it is important to note that the remaining states allow for access to medical services on the part of those who exhibit a degree of independence. For example, more than half the states statutorily allow minors who are parents to consent to health care;[201] approximately half the states statutorily allow minors who are or have been married to consent;[202] about one fourth allow consent by minors living apart from parents and managing their financial affairs;[203] and a few states provide minors in the military or those who have graduated from high school with the ability to consent to health services.[204] It is important to note that the statutes pervasively remain silent about whether parents should be notified when their emancipated children seek or obtain medical services.[205] Married minors,[206] minors who are parents,[207] minors living on their own and financially independent,[208] minors in the military,[209] and minors who have graduated from high school[210] generally do not require parental notification to obtain access to services. Thus the law tends to treat minors who exhibit considerable independence as adults. These adolescents can consent to their own health care and their parents need not be notified before or after treatment—a point of considerable significance because, in other instances, states have mandated parental notification when requiring parental consent was not legally permissible.

The third way certain groups of minors may obtain medical treatment is through the "mature minor" exception. This exception rejects the presumption of adolescent incompetency and lack of capacity supposedly inherent to chronological age. Despite the lack of accepted standards to determine maturity, minors eligible for the exception generally are able to understand the nature and importance of the medical steps that are characteristically not serious and complex.[211] Few state court decisions and few state statutes address the exception, even though the doctrine was enunciated in the early 1900s[212] and the Supreme Court applied the doctrine to a series of family planning services and abortion decisions.[213] Only five states—Arkansas, Idaho, Mississippi, Nevada, New Hampshire—codify mature minor provisions specifically for the purpose of medical care.[214] These statutes do not require parental consent; nor do they require parental notification unless under a very narrow set of conditions.[215] Note, however, that when medical procedures do become complex and the implications of the treatment arguably more serious, numerous states allow for a judicial by-pass for parental consent for specific medical services, such as abortion, and that alternative rests on the establishment of maturity.[216]

A fourth exception involves juvenile courts and child welfare agencies' power to provide youth access to medical care. This intervention is worthy of note for three reasons. First, all states bestow on their juvenile and family courts jurisdiction over abused and neglected children. As mentioned previously, the state's *parens patriae* power provides the authority to intervene and promote the welfare of children. Most enabling statutes expressly define neglect to include the failure to provide adequate medical care;[217] and those that do not expressly define medical care contain broad definitions of neglect that can be interpreted to cover failure to provide adequate medical–health care.[218] Second, although courts wield considerable power, intervention for medical care typically occurs when the minor's life is or will be threatened. That tendency relates to the general finding that, when courts do intervene, they do not do so to impose the wishes of the adolescent on the situation. The court intervenes to substitute its own judgment based primarily on societal mandates, as revealed in instances in which parents refuse to consent to care based on religious convictions or where the family and minor conflict in the refusal of life-sustaining treatment.[219] Third, personnel hold considerable power to consent to medical services for children under their own care, regardless of how they got into their care in the first instance.[220] The mental health setting already recognizes that parental consent is often precluded where minors need mental health assistance, especially with at-risk minors.[221]

The last major exception to the general rule that parents control adolescents' rights to consent to medical care derives from the specific problems or the specific services that are sought. Statutes typically concern themselves with two exceptions. The first exception deals with determinations of pregnancy. More than one half of the states expressly authorize minors to consent to pregnancy-related health services. These specific statutes permit female minors to obtain testing to determine pregnancy without parental consent and, if pregnant, allow them to obtain prenatal care and delivery services without parental consent;[222] and only one of these minor consent statutes imposes a minimum age requirement.[223] The many statutes that authorize minors to obtain pregnancy-related services without parental consent also do not require parental notification: Statutes specifically provide that no notification will be made,[224] have no provisions regarding parental notification,[225] or leave notification to the discretion of health professionals.[226]

The second exception that derives from the type of treatment sought deals with sexually transmitted and infectious diseases. Almost all states legislatively authorize minors to avoid parental consent to obtain medical treatment for venereal diseases or for sexually transmitted diseases. More specifically, more than two thirds of the states statutorily permit minors to consent to treatment of venereal diseases[227] and about one quarter of the states expressly permit minors to consent to health services for sexually transmitted diseases or to receive such services without parental consent.[228] The remaining states allow for minors to obtain delivery of health services for infectious, contagious, communicable, and other reportable diseases.[229] Note that these statutes generally do not require parental notification: Only one state requires notification under limited conditions[230] and the rest either do not contain notification provisions,[231] leave it to the discretion of professionals,[232] or simply state that services may be provided without notification.[233] The statutes often do not expressly include testing for HIV. However, states increasingly add HIV testing to the list of exceptions. Some states explicitly authorize minors to consent to HIV testing.[234] Other states take the capacity to consent further and directly authorize minors to consent to treatment for AIDS or HIV infection.[235] Other states define HIV as an STD, which allows minors the ability to seek tests and treatment under their STD exceptions.[236] As with the previous notification requirements for other services, the statutes do not generally require notification: States either leave it to the discretion of professionals,[237] contain no notification provisions,[238] or mandate notification if tests are positive.[239] Statutes generally allow minors to consent to services regardless of their age, although some do impose a minimum of 12[240] or 14 years of age[241] for minors to consent to services for sexually transmitted diseases.

The development of exceptions to the general rule that parents control their children's behaviors reflects remarkable progress to recognize the necessity of reaching adolescents. The sexually transmitted diseases exceptions are illustrative. Allowing minors' access to those services stems from a legislative recognition that society has a critical interest in facilitating and encouraging access to health services to reduce the spread of diseases among its citizens. These rules are justified by necessity, not by the actual maturity of minors or their inherent rights. As with the other aspects of the regulation of adolescents' sexuality, it remains to be determined whether the justifications for the rules reflect the reality of adolescent life and effectively deal with the apparent urgencies that contributed to legal reform.

Realities of Adolescent Life

Scant empirical research examines adolescents' rights in the context of medical testing and treatment. Despite limited research, existing findings and the realities of adolescent development are suggestive and serve to question the impact of several laws. Although numerous issues arise, the fundamental concern involves issues of access and the extent to which adolescents should, do, and can obtain certain services while still respecting the rights of parents to direct their children's upbringing. This general concern results in four points.

The first point involves the manner in which laws formally provide access. As we have seen, numerous exceptions allow adolescents to obtain medical tests and certain treatments for outcomes of sexual activity. Although numerous exceptions exist, states generally remain able to require, and often do require, parental consent or notification. Although legislatures and courts appear to regard the requirement of parental notification as less onerous than the requirement for parental consent, from the standpoint of the adolescent, it is not clear that they distinguish between these two requirements. Although research is unavailable that would suggest a difference in terms of the adolescents' perspective, three findings suggest that the manner in which parents find out may be immaterial to adolescents. First, the only study to examine the issue in terms of medical testing reveals that consent limits access to services. That research revealed that comparing one year before and after a new law that changed the need for parental consent (the new law no longer required it), the number of HIV tests increased twofold, and high-risk minors tripled their visits and requests for tests.[242] Second, related research on access to family planning services reports similar findings. Consent and notification requirements create access and utilization barriers. Third, other empirical research suggests that laws may not necessarily reach their other major goal—enhancing family participation. Parental notification and consent laws may not increase parental influence on adolescents' decision making simply because most minors actually do consult with their parents. For example, one study found that more than half had consulted with their mothers; by the time the determination of pregnancy status was made, more than 85 percent of pregnant adolescents had confided in their mothers.[243] Note that the number is even higher for teenagers living with their mothers: 90% confided in their mothers if they were living with them versus 66% who confided in them if they lived apart. More than 95 percent consult an adult; and those who make independent decisions about testing are older adolescents, who average nearly 17 years of age. These findings are significant. If there is a conflict between parents and children, the issue is whether consent and notification of parents will lead adolescents to be unwilling to reveal to their parents their need for health services related to sexual activity. These findings lead to the legitimate concern that laws may create barriers to access.

The second point of inquiry involves issues of competency. Considerable research investigates the extent to which minors may be competent to consent to treatment. Although the social policy issue goes beyond simple abilities, the law makes a distinction based on age: Adults are deemed competent as a matter of law to consent to health services. Thus the law assumes that adults, as a class, are competent to consent to health services resting on empirical assumptions that they have the requisite decision-making capacity; the assumption is that minors are incompetent. Research generally challenges the assumption that minors lack the requisite capacity to make health care decisions; and commentators seize on the findings to argue that laws inequitably deny minors the power to make their own determinations about obtaining health services.

Although the concept of competency is critical, much remains indeterminant in law and the social sciences. Legislatures and the courts have not furnished much guidance as to its content and meaning in terms of health care decision making. Legally, the standard tends to be low: Informed consent simply must be said to be informed and voluntary. To reach that standard, the assumption is that each minor should possess the intelligence, maturity, and relevant experience that their parents possess. Likewise, they must not be susceptible to pressures from others, unable to appreciate the long-term consequences of their decisions, and not make unwise decisions regarding their welfare. In terms of social science research, not much research directly speaks to the issue of competency to obtain tests. One of the few studies to do so investigated the decision-making competence of women seeking a pregnancy test and found that among those considering an abortion, women younger than 18 appeared as competent as legal adults aged 18–21.[244] Despite the general lack of research, other areas of inquiry are rather suggestive. Much of the research about competence or differences between adults or among adolescents has been conducted in studies regarding abortion decisions, which we will review in chapter 4. The general finding from that research suggests that adolescents, especially those 15 and older, are essentially not distinguishable in their decision making from adults. Despite these consistent findings, it is important to emphasize that competence remains only one rationale for parental consent and notification requirements—the law seeks several goals when it denies competent adolescents access to health services.

The third area of interest involves practical concerns that challenge the effectiveness of laws that even recognize adolescents' rights to access. Laws are not necessarily effective. Three practicalities arise. First, noncompliance remains an important concern. No research investigates the extent to which professionals actually comply with the legal mandates that do exist. Noncompliance may exist because the situation conflicts with ethical values and norms of their professional organization, and may result from misunderstandings or ignorance of the law. Second, even if the law does not require notification, service providers do not necessarily operate without parental consent. The major reason for this possibility deals with financial issues that may arise or the lack of parental consent may hinder the effectiveness of service delivery. Third, other research reveals that even at-risk youth do not know that they have the right to be tested anonymously. To affirm what increasingly becomes obvious in child welfare law, the existence of laws does not guarantee effectiveness.

The fourth area deals with the already existing laws. Given the extensive nature of the laws that allow minors to be tested, the concern for and focus on creating new laws that would allow adolescents to be tested would seem unwarranted. In the context of HIV testing, a close look reveals a host of barriers. Approximately half of adolescents who summon up the courage to be tested for HIV do not return for their results.[245] A major reason for the failure to return has been attributed to the lack of confidentiality.[246] Although this undoubtedly may be true, the most formidable barriers seem to be more practical in nature. For example, the cost of testing remains prohibitive.[247] In addition, once tested, effective treatment is not necessarily available.[248] Nor is there necessarily a right to learn about or obtain condoms to prevent further infection of others.[249] Nor are youths who would engage in high-risk behaviors and endanger their own lives likely to altruistically change their behaviors for others: Wishful thinking and attempts to forget disease are the most common way adolescents cope with sexually transmitted illnesses.[250] Simply put, the right to testing remains rather hollow without the concomitant right to services and treatment.[251] Thus instead of focusing on issues of testing, policy makers may better serve youth by focusing on alternatives to caring for HIV-infected youth.

Preliminary Conclusion

Adolescents' sexual rights relating to general access to medical testing and services present a complicated array of possibilities. Unlike the previously examined areas of law that regulate adolescent sexuality and that generally gave control of adolescents' right to parents, the state, or to adolescents themselves, no general consensus emerges in this area. The historical rule that parents control the rights of their children has been met by numerous exceptions that render it unrecognizable. The issue that has emerged now involves the impact of these laws in terms of access to testing and services, and whether the statutory changes that aim to open access actually achieve their ultimate goal for offering access in the first place. The general finding of policy analyses suggests that adolescents require more than mere access if they are to protect themselves and others.

Conclusion

Existing research on the influences of adolescent sexual attitudes and activities reveals the need to consider a diversity of factors. Sexuality does not develop in a void. Rather, it develops in the context of other developmental tasks of adolescence, such as establishing identity, developing autonomy, and forming intimate relationships. In dealing with these tasks, adolescents tend to rely on their parents, peers, and partners to different extents and at different times. Parents, communities, peers, and partners variously transmit tendencies toward certain types of behaviors.

The complexities of adolescent sexuality require a complex legal response. Regrettably, as important studies of adolescent sexuality and development continue to sharpen the understanding of minors' sexual lives, the legal system hesitates to acknowledge the realities of adolescent life. The legal system projects the image that parents control their adolescents, and society tends to work on the corollary assumption that parents pervasively direct their children's development. Despite that image, the allocation of power over various aspects of adolescent sexuality diverges considerably, depending on the nature of the activity or concern. These differences in the allocation of legal control over the transition to adolescent sexual behavior becomes even more pronounced in the next chapter's analyses of issues, which relate more directly to sexual intercourse.

Endnotes

1. Both society and the law generally perceive adolescent sexuality as dangerous and in need of control. Those perceptions often adopt a narrow view of sexual activity that equates sex with sexual intercourse and its negative outcomes. Frank C. Leeming, William Dwyer, and Diana P. Oliver, *Issues in Adolescent Sexuality* (Boston: Allyn and Bacon, 1996).
2. 262 U.S. 390 (1923).
3. *Id.* at 399.
4. 321 U.S. 158 (1944).
5. ALA. CODE §§ 13A-13-6, 26-15-1 to -3 (Michie 1992 & Supp. 1997); ALASKA STAT. § 11.51.100 (Michie 1996); ARIZ. REV. STAT. ANN. §§ 13-604.01, 13-1105(A)(2), 13-3619, 13-3623 (West 1989 & Supp. 1997); ARK. CODE ANN. §§ 5-27-203 to -204, 5-27-221 (Michie 1997); CAL. PENAL CODE § 273A (West 1996 & Supp. 1998); COLO. REV. STAT. ANN. §§ 18-6-401 to -401.2 (West 1990 & Supp. 1997); CONN. GEN. STAT. ANN. §§ 53-20, -21, -23 (West 1994 & Supp. 1998); DEL. CODE ANN. tit. 11, §§ 1101 to -1103 (Michie 1995 & Supp. 1996); FLA. STAT. ANN. ch. 827.03-.071 (Harrison 1991 & Supp. 1997); GA. CODE ANN. §§ 16-5-70, 16-5-72 (Michie 1996 & Supp. 1998); HAW. REV. STAT. §§ 707-750 to -751 (1993 & Supp. 1996); IDAHO CODE §§ 18-1501, -1506, -1506A (Michie 1987 & Supp. 1997); ILL. ANN. STAT. ch. 720, ¶ 5/12-4.3, 115/53, 150/4 (West/Smith-Hurd 1993 & Supp. 1998); IND. CODE ANN. §§ 35-46-1, -3 to -4 (Burns 1994 & Supp. 1998); IOWA CODE ANN. § 726.6 (West 1994 & Supp. 1998); KAN. STAT. ANN. §§ 21-3604 to -3604a, 21-3608 to -3609 (1988 & Supp. 1997); KY. REV. STAT. ANN. §§ 508.090-.120, 530.040, 530.060 (Michie/Bobbs-Merrill 1990 & Supp. 1996); LA. REV. STAT. ANN. §§ 14:92.1, :93, :93.2.1 (West 1986 & Supp. 1998); ME. REV. STAT. ANN. tit. 17-A, §§ 553-54 (West 1983 & Supp. 1996); MD. ANN. CODE art. 27, § 27-35A (Michie 1995 & Supp. 1997); MASS. GEN. LAWS ANN. ch. 265, § 13J (Law Co-op. 1994 & Supp. 1998); MICH. COMP. LAWS ANN. §§ 750.135, 750.136b (West 1991 & Supp. 1998); MINN. STAT. ANN. §§ 609.376-.378 (West 1992 & Supp. 1998); MISS. CODE ANN. §§ 97-5-1 to -3, 97-5-39 to -40 (Law. Co-op. 1994 & Supp. 1997); MO. ANN. STAT. §§ 568.030-.060 (West 1996 & Supp. 1997); MONT. CODE ANN. §§ 45-5-622, -627 (1997); NEB. REV. STAT. § 28-707 (1995 & Supp. 1997); NEV. REV. STAT. § 200.508 (Michie 1997); N.H. REV. STAT. ANN. §§ 631-2, 632-A:2, 639-3 (Butterworth 1994 & Supp. 1997); N.J. STAT. ANN. § 9:6-3 (West 1995 & Supp. 1998); N.M. STAT. ANN. § 30-6-1

(Michie 1978 & Supp. 1998); N.Y. PENAL LAW § 260.10 (McKinney 1989 & Supp. 1998); N.C. GEN. STAT. §§ 14-318.2, .4 (1993 & Supp. 1997); N.D. CENT. CODE §§ 14-07-15, 14-09-22 (Michie 1991 & Supp. 1997); OHIO REV. CODE ANN. § 2919.22 (Anderson 1994 & Supp. 1997); OKLA. STAT. ANN. tit. 21, §§ 843, 851-53 (West 1983 & Supp. 1998); OR. REV. STAT. §§ 163.545-.547, 163.575 (Butterworth 1990 & Supp. 1998); 18 PA. CONS. STAT. ANN. § 4304 (Purdon 1983 & Supp. 1998); R.I. GEN. LAWS §§ 11-9-5, 11-9-5.3 (Michie 1994 & Supp. 1997); S.C. CODE ANN. § 20-7-50 to -80 (West/Law. Co-op. 1985 & Supp. 1997); S.D. CODIFIED LAWS ANN. §§ 26-9-1, 26-10-1 (Michie 1992 & Supp. 1998); TENN. CODE ANN. §§ 39-13-202(a)(4), 39-15-401 to -402 (Michie 1997); TEX. PENAL CODE ANN. §§ 22.04-.041 (Vernon 1996 & Supp. 1998); UTAH CODE ANN. § 76-5-109 (Michie 1996 & Supp. 1998); VT. STAT. ANN. tit. 13, § 1304 (Michie 1974 & Supp. 1997); VA. CODE ANN. §§ 63.1-248.1 to -248.17 (Michie 1996 & Supp. 1998); WASH. REV. CODE ANN. §§ 9A.16.100, 9A.42.010-030 (West 1988 & Supp. 1998); W. VA. CODE §§ 61-8D-1 to -9 (Michie 1996 & Supp. 1997); WIS. STAT. ANN. §§ 48.981, 940.201 (West 1996 & Supp. 1997); WYO. STAT. § 6-2-503 (Michie 1997).

6. *See, e.g.,* Roger J. R. Levesque, ''Prosecuting Sex Crimes Against Children: Time for 'Outrageous' Proposals?'' *Law and Psychology Review* 19 (1995):59–91.

7. ALA. CODE § 26-16-2 (Michie 1992 & Supp. 1997) (defining child abuse as ''harm or threatened harm to a child's health or welfare by a person . . . which harm occurs or is threatened through . . . mental injury.'')

8. E.g., Wisconsin's statute defines ''mental harm'' as substantial harm to a child's psychological or intellectual functioning characterized by ''anxiety, depression, withdrawal or outward aggressive behavior.'' WIS. STAT. ANN. § 998.01 (West 1996 & Supp. 1997).

9. 431 U.S. 816, 862–863 (1977) (Stewart, J., concurring).

10. 405 U.S. 645, 657–658 (1972).

11. 455 U.S. 745, 769 (1982).

12. *Id.* at 753.

13. 117 S. Ct. 555, 569 (1996).

14. *Id.* at 560–564.

15. *E.g.,* Arizona holds parents responsible for their behavior that tends to cause their children to engage in certain conduct such as growing up to lead an ''idle, dissolute or immoral life''; ARIZ. REV. STAT. ANN. § 13-3612 (West 1989 & Supp. 1997). Other states have similarly broad mandates that hold parents responsible if their children habitually associate with ''vicious, immortal, or criminal persons''; R.I. GEN. LAWS § 11-9-4 (Michie 1994 & Supp. 1997), or acting in a way likely to ''injure or endanger the health or morals of himself or others''; OHIO REV. CODE ANN. § 2151.022 (Anderson 1994 & Supp. 1997). *See also* NEV. REV. STAT. ANN. § 201.090 (Michie 1997); VT. STAT. ANN. tit. 13, § 1301 (Michie 1974 & Supp. 1997).

16. ARIZ. REV. STAT. ANN. § 13-3612 (West 1989 & Supp. 1997); CAL. PENAL CODE § 272 (West 1996 & Supp. 1998); KY. REV. STAT. ANN. § 530.060 (Michie/Bobbs-Merrill 1990 & Supp. 1996); NEV. REV. STAT. ANN. § 201.090 (Michie 1997); N.Y. PENAL LAW § 260.10 (McKinney 1989 & Supp. 1998); S.D. CODIFIED LAWS ANN. § 26-9-1 (Michie 1992 & Supp. 1998).

17. *See* ALA. CODE § 12-15-13 (Michie 1995 & Supp. 1997) (''willfully''); ARK. STAT. ANN. § 5-27-205, 5-27-220 (Michie 1996) (''knowingly''); DEL. CODE ANN. tit. 11, § 1102 (Michie 1995 & Supp. 1998) (''knowingly'' or ''intentionally''); GA. CODE ANN. § 16-12-1 (Michie 1996 & Supp. 1998) (''knowingly and willfully'').

18. ALA. CODE §§ 30-3-150, -152 (Michie 1995 & Supp. 1997); ALASKA STAT. § 25.20.060 (Michie 1996); ARIZ. REV. STAT. ANN. § 25-403 (West 1989 & Supp. 1997); ARK. CODE ANN. § 9-13-101 (Michie 1997); CAL. FAM. CODE § 3100 (West 1996 & Supp. 1998); COLO. REV. STAT. ANN. § 14-10-124 (West 1996 & Supp. 1998); CONN. GEN. STAT. ANN. § 46b-59 (West 1994 & Supp. 1998); DEL. CODE ANN. tit. 13, § 722 (Michie 1995 & Supp. 1996); FLA. STAT. ANN. § 61.13 (Harrison 1991 & Supp. 1997); GA. CODE ANN. § 19-9-3 (Michie 1987 & Supp. 1997); HAW. REV. STAT. ANN. § 571-46 (1993 & Supp. 1996); IDAHO CODE § 32-717 (Michie 1987 & Supp. 1997); 750 ILL. COMP. STAT. ANN. 5/602 (West/Smith-Hurd 1993 & Supp. 1998); IND. CODE ANN. § 31-1-11.5-24 (Burns 1994 & Supp. 1998); IOWA CODE ANN. § 598.41 (West 1994 &

Supp. 1998); KAN. STAT. ANN. § 60-1616 (1988 & Supp. 1997); KY. REV. STAT. ANN. § 403.270 (Michie/Bobbs-Merrill 1990 & Supp. 1996); LA. CIV. CODE ANN. arts. 131, 136 (West 1986 & Supp. 1998); ME. REV. STAT. ANN. tit. 19, § 752 (West 1983 & Supp. 1996); MD. CODE ANN., FAM. LAW § 9-202 (Michie 1995 & Supp. 1997); MASS. GEN. LAWS ANN. ch. 208, § 31 (Law. Co-op. 1994 & Supp. 1998); MICH. COMP. LAWS ANN. §§ 552.501, 722.25 (West 1991 & Supp. 1998); MINN. STAT. ANN. § 518.175 (West 1991 & Supp. 1998); MISS. CODE ANN. § 93-5-24 (West 1992 & Supp. 1998); MO. ANN. STAT. § 452.400 (West 1996 & Supp. 1997); MONT. CODE ANN. § 40-4-217 (1997); NEB. REV. STAT. § 42-364 (1995 & Supp. 1997); NEV. REV. STAT. § 125.480 (Michie 1997); N.H. REV. STAT. ANN. § 458:17 (Butterworth 1994 & Supp. 1997); N.M. STAT. ANN. § 40-4-9 (Michie 1978 & Supp. 1998); N.Y. DOM. REL. LAW § 240 (McKinney 1989 & Supp. 1998); N.C. GEN. STAT. § 50-13.5 (1995); N.D. CENT. CODE § 14-09-06-1 (1993 & Supp. 1997); OHIO REV. CODE ANN. § 3109.051 (Anderson 1994 & Supp. 1998); OKLA. STAT. tit. 43, §§ 109, 112 (West 1983 & Supp. 1998); OR. REV. STAT. § 107.137 (Butterworth 1990 & Supp. 1998); PA. STAT. ANN. tit. 23, § 5301 (Purdon 1983 & Supp. 1998); S.D. CODIFIED LAWS § 25-4-45 (Michie 1992 & Supp. 1998); TENN. CODE ANN. § 36-6-101 (Michie 1997); TEX. FAM. CODE ANN. § 153.002 (Vernon 1996 & Supp. 1998); UTAH CODE ANN. § 30-3-5 (Michie 1996 & Supp. 1998); VT. STAT. ANN. tit. 15, §§ 650, 655 (Michie 1974 & Supp 1997); VA. CODE ANN. § 20-124.2 (Michie 1996 & Supp. 1997); WASH. REV. CODE ANN. § 26.10.100 (West 1988 & Supp. 1998); WIS. STAT. ANN. § 767.24 (West 1996 & Supp. 1997).

19. Roger J. R. Levesque, "Targeting 'Deadbeat' Dads: The Problem With the Direction of Welfare Reform," *Hamline Journal of Public Law and Policy* 15 (1994):1–53.

20. Susan Newcomer and J. Richard Udry, "Parental Marital Status Effects on Adolescent Sexual Behavior," *Journal of Marriage and the Family* 49 (1987):235–240; Frank F. Furstenberg Jr. and Julien O. Teitler, "Reconsidering the Effects of Marital Disruption: What Happens to Children of Divorce in Early Adulthood?" *Journal of Family Issues* 15 (1994):173–190; Robert L. Flewelling and Karl E. Bauman, "Family Structure as a Predictor of Initial Substance Use and Sexual Intercourse in Early Adolescence," *Journal of Marriage and the Family* 52 (1990):171–181.

21. Renata T. Forste and Tim B. Heaton, "Initiation of Sexual Activity Among Female Adolescents," *Youth and Society* 19 (1989):250–268; Brent C. Miller and C. Raymond Bingham, "Family Configuration in Relation to the Sexual Behavior of Female Adolescents," *Journal of Marriage and the Family* 51 (1989):499–506; Newcomer and Udry, "Parental Marital Status Effects on Adolescent Sexual Behavior."

22. Arland D. Thornton and Donald Camburn, "The Influence of the Family on Premarital Sexual Attitudes and Behavior," *Demography* 24 (1987):323–340.

23. Brent C. Miller and Kristin A. Moore, "Adolescent Sexual Behavior, Pregnancy, and Parenting: Research Through the 1980s," *Journal of Marriage and the Family* 52 (1990):1025–1044; *see also* Frank L. Mott, Michell M. Fondell, Paul N. Hu, Lori Kowaleski-Jones, and Elizabeth G. Menaghan, "The Determinants of First Sex by Age 14 in a High-Risk Adolescent Population," *Family Planning Perspectives* 28 (1996):13–18.

24. A substantial proportion of the putative effect of divorce on children's behavioral problems is evident prior to the occurrence of the marital breakup. Furstenberg and Teitler, "Reconsidering the Effects of Marital Disruption: What Happens to Children of Divorce in Early Adulthood?" That is, the break-up may simply crystallize or highlight longstanding family problems; or it may be a solution to longstanding family disruption and have beneficial effects, especially if there was high levels of conflict; Paul R. Amato, Laura Spencer Loomis, and Alan Booth, "Parental Divorce, Marital Conflict, and Offspring Well-Being During Early Adulthood," *Social Forces* 73 (1995):895–915.

25. The longitudinal study examined children from grade six to early adolescence four years later; *see* Susan Moore and Doreen Rosenthal, *Sexuality in Adolescence* (New York: Routledge, 1993).

26. James Jaccard, Patricia J. Dittus, and Vivian V. Gordon, "Maternal Correlates of Adolescent Sexual and Contraceptive Behavior," *Family Planning Perspectives* 28 (1996):159–165, 185.

27. S. Shirley Feldman and Nancy L. Brown, "Family Influence on Adolescent Male Sexuality: The

Mediational Role of Self-Restraint," *Social Development* 2 (1993):15–35; Grayson N. Holmbeck, Karen A. Waters, and Richard R. Brookman, "Psychosocial Correlates of Sexually Transmitted Diseases and Sexual Activity in Black Female Adolescents," *Journal of Adolescent Research* 5 (1990):431–448; Loretta Sweet Jemmott and John B. Jemmott III, "Family Structure, Parental Strictness, and Sexual Behavior Among Inner-City Black Male Adolescents," *Journal of Adolescent Research* 7 (1992):192–207.

28. Feldman and Brown, "Family Influence on Adolescent Male Sexuality: The Mediational Role of Self-Restraint''; Dennise B. Kandel, "Parenting Styles, Drug Use, and Children's Adjustment in Families of Young Adults," *Journal of Marriage and the Family* 52 (1990):183–196.

29. Nelwyn B. Moore and J. Kenneth Davidson Sr., "Guilt About First Intercourse: An Antecedent of Sexual Dissatisfaction Among College Women," *Journal of Sex & Marital Therapy* 23 (1997):29–46.

30. R. Jean Haurin and Frank L. Mott, "Adolescent Sexual Activity in the Family Context: The Impact of Older Siblings," *Demography* 27 (1990):537–557; Joseph Lee Rogers, David C. Rowe, and David F. Harris, "Sibling Differences in Adolescent Sexual Behavior: Inferring Process Models From Family Composition Patterns," *Journal of Marriage and the Family* 54 (1992):142–152.

31. Dennis Hogan and Evelyn M. Kitagawa, "The Impact of Social Status, Family Structure, and Neighborhood on the Fertility of Black Adolescents," *American Journal of Sociology* 90 (1985):825–836; Eric D. Widmer, "Influence of Older Siblings on Initiation of Sexual Intercourse," *Journal of Marriage and the Family* 59 (1997):928–938.

32. Widmer, "Influence of Older Siblings on Initiation of Sexual Intercourse," p. 936.

33. Patricia L. East, Marianne E. Felice, and Marcia C. Morgan, "Sisters' and Girlfriends' Sexual and Childbearing Behavior: Effects on Early Adolescent Girls' Sexual Outcomes," *Journal of Marriage and the Family* 55 (1993):953–963.

34. Patricia L. East and Marianne E. Felice, "Pregnancy Risk Among the Younger Sisters of Pregnancy and Child-Bearing Adolescents," *Journal of Developmental and Behavioral Pediatrics* 13 (1992):128–136.

35. Joseph L. Rogers and David C. Rowe, "Influences of Siblings on Adolescent Sexual Behavior," *Developmental Psychology* 24 (1988):722–728; Rogers et al., "Sibling Differences in Adolescent Sexual Behavior: Inferring Process Models From Family Composition Patterns."

36. E.g., virgin older brothers do not conform to the expectation of sexual activity associated with their gender in adolescence; being a virgin has significant meaning for a boy's identity and social status and might indirectly change a younger sibling's attitude toward sex in that it may have an additive effect to parental influence and may suggest to younger sibling that the parents' attitudes toward teenage sexual activity has relevance. Widmer, "Influence of Older Siblings on Initiation of Sexual Intercourse."

37. J. Richard Urdy, "Biological Predisposition and Social Control in Adolescent Sexual Behavior," *American Sociological Review* 53 (1988):709–722.

38. Terrie E. Moffitt, Avshalom Caspi, Jay Belsky, and Philip A. Silva, "Childhood Experience and the Onset of Menarche: A Test of a Sociobiological Model," *Child Development* 63 (1992):47–58; Avshalom Caspi and Terrie E. Moffit, "Individual Differences Are Accentuated During Periods of Social Change: The Sample Case of Girls at Puberty," *Journal of Personality and Social Psychology* 61 (1991):157–168; Lawrence Steinberg, "Reciprocal Relation Between Parent–Child Distance and Pubertal Maturation," *Developmental Psychology* 13 (1988):133–138. Note, though, that some studies do not find that relationship to be as strong. *See* M. P. M. Richards, "The Childhood Environment and the Development of Sexuality." In *Long Term Consequences of Early Environment,* ed. C. J. K. Henry and S.J. Ulijaszek (Cambridge, MA: Cambridge University Press, 1996).

39. Kathleen E. Kiernan and John Hobcraft, "Parental Divorce During Childhood: Age at First Intercourse, Partnership and Parenthood," *Population Studies* 51 (1997):41–55; Newcomer and Udry, "Parental Marital Status Effects on Adolescent Sexual Behavior."

40. Kiernan and Hobcraft, "Parental Divorce During Childhood: Age at First Intercourse, Partnership and Parenthood."

41. Kaye Wellings and Sally Bradshaw, "First Intercourse Between Men and Women." In *Sexual Attitudes and Lifestyles,* ed. Anne M. Johnson, Jane Wadsworth, Kaye Wellings, and Julia Field (Cambridge, MA: Blackwell Scientific, 1994).

42. Frank F. Furstenberg Jr., Jeanne Brooks-Gunn, and Lindsay Chase-Lansdale, "Teenage Pregnancy and Childbearing," *American Psychologist* 44 (1989):313–320; George W. Holden, Patricia Beatty Nelson, John Velasquez, and Kathy L. Ritchie, "Cognitive, Psychosocial, and Reported Sexual Behavior Differences Between Pregnant and Non-Pregnant Adolescents," *Adolescence* 28 (1993):557–572; Frank F. Furstenberg Jr., Judith A. Levine, and Jeanne Brooks Gunn, "The Children of Teenage Mothers: Patterns of Early Childbearing in Two Generations," *Family Planning Perspectives* 22 (1990):54–61.

43. Susan F. Newcomer and J. Richard Udry, "Mothers' Influence on the Sexual Behavior of Their Teenage Children," *Journal of Marriage and the Family* 46 (1984):477–485; J. Richard Udry, "Biological Predispositions and Social Control in Adolescent Sexual Behavior," *American Sociological Review* 53 (1988):709–722.

44. Mott et al., "The Determinants of First Sex by Age 14 in a High-Risk Adolescent Population"; Steven L. Nock and Paul W. Kingston, "Time With Children: The Impact of Couples' Work-Time Commitments," *Social Forces* 67 (1988):59–63.

45. *E.g.,* in an early study of never-married women between 15 and 19 who have engaged in sexual intercourse, 23 percent report that their most recent act of sexual intercourse took place in their own home, and 51 percent that it took place in their partner's homes; Melvin Zelnik and John F. Kantner, "Sexual and Contraceptive Experience of Young Unmarried Women in the United States, 1976 and 1971," *Family Planning Perspectives* 9 (1977):55–71; Melvin Zelnik, John F. Kantner, and Kathleen Ford, *Sex and Pregnancy in Adolescence* (Beverly Hills, CA: Sage, 1981).

46. Janet L. Lauritsen, "Explaining Race and Gender Differences in Adolescent Sexual Behavior," *Social Forces* 72 (1994):859–884; Robert D. Plotnik, "The Effects of Attitudes on Teenage Premarital Pregnancy and Its Resolution," *American Sociological Review* 57 (1992):800–811, Stephan A. Small and Tom Luster, "Adolescent Sexual Activity: An Ecological, Risk Factor Approach," *Journal of Marriage and the Family* 56 (1994):181–192. Likewise, focus on achievement, education, and work are associated with less sexual activity among both boys and girls; *see* Brent C. Miller and Karen R. Sneesby, "Educational Correlates of Adolescents' Sexual Attitudes and Behavior," *Journal of Youth and Adolescence* 17 (1988):521–530.

47. Kathryn Edin and Laura Lein, *Making Ends Meet: How Single Mothers Survive Welfare and Low-Wage Work* (New York: Russell Sage Foundation, 1997).

48. Ritch C. Savin-Williams, "Verbal and Physical Abuse as Stressors in the Lives of Lesbian, Gay Male, and Bisexual Youths: Associations With School Problems, Running Away, Substance Abuse, Prostitution, and Suicide," *Journal of Consulting and Clinical Psychology* 62 (1994):261–269; Gary Remafedi, "Male Homosexuality: The Adolescent's Perspective," *Pediatrics* 79 (1987):326–330.

49. Ritch C. Savin-Williams and Eric M. Dubé, "Parental Reactions to Their Child's Disclosure of a Gay/Lesbian Identity," *Family Relations* 47 (1998):7–13.

50. Emory S. Hetrick and A. Damsen Martin, "Developmental Issues and Their Resolution for Gay and Lesbian Adolescents," *Journal of Homosexuality* 14 (1987):25–43.

51. Paul Gibson, "Gay Male and Lesbian Youth Suicide." In *Report of the Secretary's Task Force on Youth Suicide,* U.S. Department of Health and Human Services (Washington, DC: Author, 1989).

52. Ritch C. Savin-Williams and Richard G. Roderiguez, "A Developmental, Clinical Perspective on Lesbian, Gay Male, and Bisexual Youths in Adolescent Sexuality." In *Advances in Adolescent Development,* ed. Thomas P. Gullotta, Gerald R. Adams, and Raymond Montemayor (Newbury Park, CA: Sage, 1993).

53. *Id.*

54. Douglas D. Durby, "Gay, Lesbian and Bisexual Youth." In *Helping Gay and Lesbian Youth:*

New Polices, New Programs, New Practice, ed. Teresa DeCrescenzo (New York: Haworth Press, 1994).

55. Gibson, ''Gay Male and Lesbian Youth Suicide.''

56. Savin-Williams, ''Verbal and Physical Abuse as Stressors in the Lives of Lesbian, Gay Male, and Bisexual Youths: Associations With School Problems, Running Away, Substance Abuse, Prostitution, and Suicide.''

57. Eli Coleman, ''The Development of Male Prostitution Activity Among Gay and Bisexual Adolescents,'' *Journal of Homosexuality* 17 (1989):131–149.

58. Roger J. R. Levesque, ''The Peculiar Place of Adolescents in the HIV-AIDS Epidemic: Unusual Progress & Usual Inadequacies in 'Adolescent Jurisprudence,''' *Loyola University Chicago Law Journal* 27 (1996): 701–739.

59. Gary Remafedi, James A. Farrow, and Robert W. Deisher, ''Risk Factors for Attempted Suicide in Gay and Bisexual Youth,'' *Pediatrics* 87 (1991):869–875.

60. Sonie Renee Martin, ''A Child's Right to Be Gay: Addressing the Emotional Maltreatment of Youth,'' *Hastings Law Journal* 48 (1996):167–196.

61. Carrie M. Renzetti, ''Violence and Abuse Among Same-Sex Couples.'' In *Violence Between Intimate Partners: Patterns, Causes and Effects,* ed. Albert P. Cardarelli (Needham Heights, MA: Allyn and Bacon, 1997).

62. The most recent review concludes that ''the most accurate generalization that can be made regarding factors that portend positive reactions is that a positive prior relationship between parents and child is a good omen for a healthy resolution.'' Savin-Williams and Dubé, ''Parental Reactions to Their Child's Disclosure of a Gay/Lesbian Identity.''

63. Mark W. Roosa, Jeann-Yun Tein Sein, Cindy Reinholtz, and Patrick J. Angelini, ''The Relationship of Childhood Sexual Abuse to Teenage Pregnancy,'' *Journal of Marriage and the Family* 59 (1997):119–130.

64. Abbey B. Berenson, Virginia V. San Miguel, and Gregg S. Wilkinson, ''Prevalence of Physical and Sexual Assault in Pregnant Adolescents,'' *Journal of Adolescent Health* 13 (1992):466–469.

65. Richard Gelles, ''Violence and Pregnancy: Are Pregnant Women at Greater Risk of Abuse?'' *Journal of Marriage and the Family* 50 (1988):841–847; Judith McFarlane, ''Battering in Pregnancy: The Tip of the Iceburg,'' *Women and Health* 15 (1988):69–84.

66. Debra Boyer and David Fine, ''Sexual Abuse as a Factor in Adolescent Pregnancy and Child Maltreatment,'' *Family Planning Perspectives* 24 (1992):4–11, 19; Philip Donovan, ''Can Statutory Rape Laws Be Effective in Preventing Adolescent Pregnancy?'' *Family Planning Perspectives* 29 (1997):30–34, 40.

67. David M. Fergusson, L. John Horwood, and Michael T. Lynskey, ''Childhood Sexual Abuse, Adolescent Sexual Behaviors and Sexual Revictimization,'' *Child Abuse & Neglect* 21 (1997):789–803.

68. Thoedore Dix, ''The Affective Organization of Parenting: Adaptive and Maladaptive Processes,'' *Psychological Bulletin* 110 (1991):3–25.

69. Einat Peled, ''Intervention With Children of Battered Women: A Review of Current Literature,'' *Children and Youth Services Review* 19 (1997):277–299.

70. Gregory A. Loken, '''Thrownaway' Children and Thowaway Parenthood,'' *Temple Law Review* 68 (1995):1715–1762.

71. James Jaccard and Patricia Dittus, *Parent–Teen Communication: Towards the Prevention of Unintended Pregnancies* (New York: Springer-Verlag, 1991).

72. Mary Jo Nolin and Karen K. Petersen, ''Gender Differences in Parent–Child Communication About Sexuality: An Exploratory Study,'' *Journal of Adolescent Research* 7 (1992):59–79.

73. Susan M. Moore and Doreen M. Rosenthal, ''Adolescents Perceptions of Friends' and Parents' Attitudes to Sex and Sexual Risk-Taking,'' *Journal of Community and Applied Social Psychology* 1 (1991):189–200.

74. Nolin and Petersen, ''Gender Differences in Parent–Child Communication About Sexuality: An Exploratory Study.''

75. *Id.*

76. Kristin Moore, James L. Peterson, and Frank F. Furstenberg Jr., "Parental Attitudes and the Occurrence of Early Sexual Activity," *Journal of Marriage and the Family* 48 (1986):777–782.

77. Jaccard et al., "Maternal Correlates of Adolescent Sexual and Contraceptive Behavior."

78. Jaccard and Dittus, *Parent–Teen Communication: Towards the Prevention of Unintended Pregnancies.*

79. Nolin and Petersen, "Gender Differences in Parent–Child Communication About Sexuality: An Exploratory Study."

80. House Select Committee on Children, Youth, and Families, 102 Cong., 1st Sess., *Risky Business of Adolescence: How to Help Teens Stay Safe — Part I* (Washington, DC: Author, 1991).

81. Susan F. Newcomer and J. Richard Udry, "Parent–Child Communication and Adolescent Sexual Behavior," *Family Planning Perspectives* 17 (1985):169–174.

82. Parental feelings alone may not be sufficient to counteract other influences. Jaccard et al., "Maternal Correlates of Adolescent Sexual and Contraceptive Behavior."

83. *Id.*

84. M. Ellis-Schwabe and H. D. Thornburg, "Conflict Areas Between Parents and Their Adolescents," *Journal of Psychology* 120 (1986):59–68.

85. For a review, *see* Patricia Noller and Victor Callan, *The Adolescent and the Family* (New York: Routledge, 1991).

86. Research in this area indicates that parents and children tend to agree which issues (moral, convention, or personal) should be under the increasing control of adolescents. However, they do not agree what behaviors and beliefs fall under those issues: Adolescents see sexuality as a personal issue, and parents see it as moral. Judith G. Smetana, "Adolescents' and Parents' Conceptions of Parental Authority," *Child Development* 59 (1988):321–335.

87. Martin, "A Child's Right to Be Gay: Addressing the Emotional Maltreatment of Youth."

88. Gary P. Mallon, "Counseling Strategies With Gay and Lesbian Youth," *Journal of Gay & Lesbian Social Services* 1 (1994):75–91.

89. James Jaccard and Patricia Dittus, "Parent–Adolescent Communication About Premarital Pregnancy," *Families in Society* 74 (1993):329–343.

90. Graham B. Spanier, "Sources of Sex Information and Premarital Sexual Behavior," *Journal of Sex Research* 13 (1977):73–88.

91. Moore and Rosenthal, *Sexuality in Adolescence.*

92. Dominique Treboux and Nancy A. Busch-Rossnagel, "Social Network Influences on Adolescent Sexual Attitudes and Behaviors," *Journal of Adolescent Research* 5 (1990):175–189; Ruth Andrea Levinson, James Jaccard, and LuAnn Beamer, "Older Adolescents Engagement in Casual Sex: Impact of Risk Perception and Psychological Motivations," *Journal of Youth and Adolescence* 24 (1995):349–364.

93. David Mechanic, "Adolescents at Risk: New Directions." In *Adolescents at Risk: Medical and Social Perspectives,* ed. David Rogers and Eli Ginzberg (Boulder, CO: Westview Press, 1992).

94. Robert W. Winslow, Louis R. Franzini, and Jimmy Hwang, "Perceived Peer Norms, Casual Sex, and AIDS Risk Prevention," *Journal of Applied Social Psychology* 22 (1992):1809–1827.

95. S. Shirley Feldman and Glen R. Elliott (Eds.), *At the Threshold: The Developing Adolescent* (Cambridge, MA: Harvard University Press, 1990).

96. Brent B. Benda and Frederick A. DiBlasio, "An Integration of Theory: Adolescent Sexual Contacts," *Journal of Youth and Adolescence* 23 (1994):403–420.

97. Frederick A. DiBlaiso and Brent B. Benda, "Adolescent Sexual Behavior: Multivariate Analyses of a Social Learning Model," *Journal of Adolescent Research* 5 (1990):449–466.

98. Doreen A. Rosenthal. "Understanding Sexual Coercion Among Young Adolescents: Communicative Clarity, Pressure and Acceptance," *Archives of Sexual Behavior* 26 (1997):481–493.

99. Deborah Holtzman and Richard Robinson, "Parent and Peer Communication Effects on AIDS-Related Behavior Among U.S. High School Students," *Family Planning Perspectives* 27 (1995):235–240, 268.

100. Mott et al., "The Determinants of First Sex by Age 14 in a High-Risk Adolescent Population"; Emily Rosenbaum and Denise B. Kandel, "Early Onset of Adolescent Sexual Behavior and Drug

Involvement," *Journal of Marriage and the Family* 52 (1990):783–798; Bernard I. Murnstein, Michelle J. Chapin, Kenneth V. Hard, and Stuart A. Vyse, "Sexual Behavior, Drugs, and Relationship Patterns on a College Campus Over Thirteen Years," *Adolescence* 24 (1989):125–139.

101. Rosenbaum and Kandel, "Early Onset of Adolescent Sexual Behavior and Drug Involvement."

102. Richard Jessor and Shirley L. Jessor, *Problem Behavior and Psychosocial Development: A Longitudinal Study of Youth* (New York: Academic Press, 1977); Denise Kandel, "Issues of Sequencing of Adolescent Drug Use and Other Problem Behaviors," *Journal of Drug Issues* 3 (1989):55–76; Frank L. Mott and R. Jean Haurin, "Linkages Between Sexual Activity and Alcohol Use Among American Adolescents," *Family Planning Perspectives* 20 (1988):128–136.

103. Ellen Porter Honnet, *Rites of Passage for College Students: The Psychological Meaning of the Experience of First Sexual Intercourse,* Doctoral Dissertation, Harvard University, 1989, Dis. Abstract, 51, 452b-453B.

104. Robin G. Sawyer and Nancy Gray Smith, "A Survey of Situational Factors at First Intercourse Among College Students," *American Journal of Health Behavior* 20 (1996):208–217.

105. Brent C. Miller, Cynthia R. Christopherson, and Pamela K. King, "Sexual Behavior in Adolescence." In *Adolescent Sexuality,* ed. Thomas P. Gullotta, Gerald R. Adams, and Raymond Montemayor (Newbury Park, CA: Sage, 1993).

106. Arland Thornton, "The Courtship Process and Adolescent Sexuality," *Journal of Family Issues* 11 (1990):239–273.

107. Priscilla Fay Carter Koyle, Larry Cyril Jensen, Joe Olsen, Bert Cundick, "Comparisons of Sexual Behavior Among Adolescents Having an Early, Middle or Late First Intercourse Experience," *Youth & Society* 20 (1989):461–476.

108. Brent C. Miller and Tim B. Heaton, "Age at First Sexual Intercourse and the Timing of Marriage and Childbirth," *Journal of Marriage and the Family* 53 (1991):719–732.

109. Bonnie L. Halpern-Felsher, Susan G. Millstein, & Jonathan M. Ellen, "Relationship of Alcohol Use and Risky Sexual Behavior: A Review and Analysis of Findings," *Journal of Adolescent Health* 19 (1996):331–336.

110. *Id.*

111. Miller and Moore, "Adolescent Sexual Behavior, Pregnancy, and Parenting: Research Through the 1980s."

112. *Id.*

113. Edward O. Laumann, John H. Gagnon, Robert T. Michael, and Stuart Michaels, *The Social Organization of Sexuality: Sexual Practices in the United States* (Chicago: University of Chicago Press, 1994).

114. Rosenthal, "Understanding Sexual Coercion Among Young Adolescents: Communicative Clarity, Pressure and Acceptance."

115. Kristin Anderson Moore, Christine Winquist Nord, and James L. Peterson, "Nonvoluntary Sexual Activity Among Adolescents," *Family Planning Perspectives* 21 (1989):110–114.

116. *Id.*

117. *Id.*

118. Miller and Moore, "Adolescent Sexual Behavior, Pregnancy, and Parenting: Research Through the 1980s"; Freya L. Sonenstein, Joseph H. Pleck, and Leighton C. Ku, "Sexual Activity, Condom Use, and AIDS Awareness Among Adolescent Males," *Family Planning Perspectives* 21 (1989):152–158.

119. Anthony Biglan, John Noell, Linda Ochs, Keith Smolowski, and Carol Metzler, "Does Sexual Coercion Play a Role in High-Risk Sexual Behavior of Adolescent and Young Adult Women?" *Journal of Behavioral Medicine* 18 (1995):549–568.

120. Stephen R. Jorgensen, Susan L. King, and Barbara A. Torrey, "Dyadic and Social Network Influences on Adolescent Exposure to Pregnancy Risk," *Journal of Marriage and the Family* 42 (1980):141–155.

121. Raye Hudson Rosen, "Adolescent Pregnancy Decision-Making: Are Parents Important?" *Adolescence* 15 (1990):43–54.

122. Miller and Moore, "Adolescent Sexual Behavior, Pregnancy, and Parenting: Research Through the 1980s."

123. Nine percent of adolescent females (ages 15–19) and 3% of adolescent males (ages 17–21) reported their first partner to be 23 or older. It is also important to note that the ages of both sexes averaged approximately 16 at the time of their first intercourse. *See* Melvin Zelnik and Farida K. Shah, "First Intercourse Among Young Americans," *Family Planning Perspectives* 15 (1983):64–70.

124. Brent C. Miller, J. K. McCoy, and Ted D. Olson, "Dating Age and Stage as Correlates of Adolescent Sexual Attitudes and Behavior," *Journal of Adolescent Research* 1 (1986):361–371.

125. Miller et al., "Sexual Behavior in Adolescence."

126. Sonenstein et al., "Sexual Activity, Condom Use, and AIDS Awareness Among Adolescent Males."

127. Susan Sprecher, "Premarital Sexual Standards for Different Categories of Individuals," *Journal of Sex Research* 26 (1989):232–248.

128. *See* Glenn Elder, "Age Differentiation and the Life Course." In *Annual Review of Sociology*, ed. A. Inkeles, J. Coleman, and N. Smelser (Palo Alto, CA: Annual Review, 1975).

129. Alan Guttmacher Institute, *Sex and America's Teenagers* (New York: Author, 1994).

130. Randal D. Day, "The Transition to First Intercourse Among Racially and Culturally Diverse Youth," *Journal of Marriage and the Family* 54 (1992):749–762.

131. Edward A. Smith and Laurie S. Zabin, "Marital and Birth Expectation of Urban Adolescents," *Youth & Society* 25 (1993):62–74.

132. Patricia L. East, "Racial and Ethnic Differences in Girls' Sexual, Marital, and Birth Expectations," *Journal of Marriage and the Family* 60 (1998):150–162.

133. Elijah Anderson, *Streetwise: Race, Class, and Change in an Urban Community* (Chicago: University of Chicago Press, 1990); Patricia L. East and Marianne E. Felice, *Adolescent Pregnancy and Parenting: Findings From a Racially Diverse Sample* (Mahwah, NJ: Lawrence Erlbaum, 1996).

134. For important studies, *see* Dennis P. Dennis and Evelyn M. Kitagawa, "The Impact of Social Status, Family Structure, and Neighborhood on Fertility of Black Adolescents," *American Journal of Sociology* 90 (1985):825–852; Dennis P. Hogan, Nan Marie Astone, and Evelyn M. Kitagawa, "Social and Environmental Factors Influencing Contraceptive Use Among Black Adolescents," *Family Planning Perspectives* 17 (1985):165–169; William D. Mosher and James W. McNally, "Contraceptive Use at First Premarital Intercourse, United States, 1965–1988," *Family Planning Perspectives* 23 (1991):108–116.

135. Patricia Voydanoff and Brenda W. Donnelly, *Adolescent Sexuality and Pregnancy* (Newbury Park, CA: Sage, 1990).

136. Christine McCauley Ohannessian and Lisa J. Crockett, "A Longitudinal Investigation of the Relationship Between Educational Investment and Adolescent Sexual Activity," *Journal of Adolescent Research* 8 (1993):167–182; N. M. Astone and D. M. Upchurch, "Forming a Family, Leaving School Early, and Earning a GED: A Racial and Cohort Comparison," *Journal of Marriage and the Family* 56 (1994):759–771.

137. Thornton and Camburn, "The Influence of the Family on Premarital Sexual Attitudes and Behavior."

138. Forste and Heaton, "Initiation of Sexual Activity Among Female Adolescents."

139. Brent C. Miller and Ted D. Olson, "Sexual Attitudes and Behavior of High School Students in Relation to Background and Contextual Factors," *Journal of Sex Research* 24 (1988):194–200; Thornton and Camburn, "The Influence of the Family on Premarital Sexual Attitudes and Behavior."

140. *Id.*

141. Elizabeth C. Cooksey, Ronald R. Rindfuss, and David K. Guilkey, "The Initiation of Adolescent Sexual and Contraceptive Behavior During Changing Times," *Journal of Health and Social*

Behavior 37 (1996):59–74. Likewise, religious faith has a reciprocal relationship with attachment to parents: Religious teachings that emphasize the importance of a strong parent–child bond and religious faiths that are often taught or reinforced by parents make the family influence significant; Brent B. Benda, Frederick A. DiBlasio, and T. Michael Kashner, "Adolescent Sexual Behavior: A Path Analysis," *Journal of Social Service Research* 19 (1994):49–69.

142. Mott et al., "The Determinants of First Sex by Age 14 in a High-Risk Adolescent Population."

143. *E.g., see* COLO. REV. STAT. ANN. §§ 18-3-403, 18-3-405 (West 1990 & Supp. 1997); GA. CODE ANN. § 16-6-3 (Michie 1996 & Supp. 1998); LA. REV. STAT. ANN. §§ 14:43.1, 14:43.3 (West 1986 & Supp. 1998); TEX. PENAL CODE ANN. § 21.11 (Vernon 1996 & Supp. 1998).

144. E.g., some states do not protect girls who were of "unchaste character." *See, e.g.,* Florida and Mississippi laws: FLA. STAT. ANN. § 794.05 (Harrison 1991 & Supp. 1997); MISS. CODE ANN. §§ 97-3-67, 97-5-21 (Law. Co-op. 1994 & Supp. 1997).

145. Mistake of age defenses still operate in the following states: ALASKA STAT. § 11.41.445 (Michie 1996); MONT. CODE ANN. § 45-5-511 (1997); ILL. ANN. STAT. ch. 720, ¶ 5/12-17 (West.Smith-Hurd 1993 & Supp. 1998); OR. REV. STAT. § 163.25 (Butterworth 1990 & Supp. 1998); IND. CODE ANN. §§ 35-42-4-3, 35-42-4-5, 35-42-4-9 (Burns 1994 & Supp. 1998).

146. LA. REV. STAT. ANN. §§ 14:80, 14:81 (West 1986 & Supp. 1998).

147. DEL. CODE ANN. tit. 11, §§ 768, 770, 762 (Michie 1995 & Supp. 1996); KY. REV. STAT. ANN. §§ 510-040, 510.050 (Michie/Bobbs-Merrill 1990 & Supp. 1996); W. VA. CODE §§ 61-8B-3 (Michie 1996 & Supp. 1997); WYO. STAT. § 6-2-303 (Michie 1997).

148. ALASKA STAT. § 11.41.440 (Michie 1996); MICH. COMP. LAWS ANN. § 750.520c (West 1991 & Supp. 1998); MINN. STAT. ANN. §§ 609.342, 609.344, 609.345 (West 1992 & Supp. 1998); MO. ANN. STAT. §§ 566.030, 566.040 (West 1996 & Supp. 1997); N.H. REV. STAT. ANN. § 632-A:3 (Butterworth 1994 & Supp. 1997); N.J. REV. STAT. ANN. §§ 2C:14-2, 2C:14-3 (West 1995 & Supp. 1998); N.M. STAT. ANN. §§ 30-9-11, 30-9-13 (Michie 1978 & Supp. 1998); N.C. GEN. STAT. §§ 14-27.2, 14-27.4 (1993 & Supp. 1997); OHIO REV. CODE ANN. §§ 2907.02, 2907.05, .07 (Anderson 1994 & Supp. 1997); TENN. CODE ANN. §§ 39-13-504, 39-13-522, 39-13-506 (Michie 1997).

149. ARIZ. REV. STAT. ANN. §§ 13-1404, 13-1410 (West 1989 & Supp. 1997); ARK. CODE ANN. §§ 5-14-102, 5-14-103, 5-14-104, 5-14-108, 5-14-109 (Michie 1997); CAL. PENAL CODE § 288 (West 1996 & Supp. 1998); GA. CODE ANN. §§ 16-6-3, 16-6-4, 16-6-5 (Michie 1996 & Supp. 1998); HAW. REV. STAT. §§ 707-730, 707-732 (1993 & Supp. 1996); IND. CODE ANN. § 35-42-4-6 (Burns 1994 & Supp. 1998); IOWA CODE ANN. §§ 702.17, 709.1, 709.3, 709.4 (West 1994 & Supp. 1998); ME. REV. STAT. ANN. tit. 17A, §§ 253, 254, 255 (West 1983 & Supp. 1996); MISS. CODE. ANN. § 97-3-65 (Law. Co-op. 1994 & Supp. 1997); MD. CRIM. LAW CODE ANN. §§ 463, 464A, 464B, 464C (Michie 1995 & Supp. 1997); NEB. REV. STAT. § 28-320.01 (1995 & Supp. 1997); NEV. REV. STAT. §§ 200.364, 200.368 (Michie 1997); OKLA. STAT. ANN. tit. 21, §§ 1111, 1112, 1114 (West 1983 & Supp. 1998); N.Y. PENAL LAW § 130.05-65 (McKinney 1989 & Supp. 1998); 18 PA. CONS. STAT. ANN. §§ 3102, 3121, 3122.1, 3123, 3125, 3127 (Purdon 1983 & Supp. 1998); TEX. PENAL CODE ANN. § 21.11 (Vernon 1996 & Supp. 1998); UTAH CODE ANN. §§ 76-5-402.1, 76-5-403.1, 76-5-404.1 (Michie 1996 & Supp. 1998); S.C. CODE ANN. § 16-15-140 (West/Law. Co-op. 1985 & Supp. 1997); VA. CODE ANN. § 18.2-370 (Michie 1996 & Supp. 1998); WASH. REV. CODE ANN. §§ 9A.44.073, 9A.44.076, 9A.44.079, 9A.44.083, 9A.44.086, 9A.44.089 (West 1988 & Supp. 1998).

150. CONN. GEN. STAT. ANN. § 53a-73a (West 1994 & Supp. 1998); COLO. REV. STAT. ANN. §§ 18-3-403, 18-3-405 (West 1990 & Supp. 1997); N.D. CENT. CODE §§ 12.1-20-03, 12.1-20-05, 12.1-20-07 (Michie 1991 & Supp. 1997); R.I. GEN. LAWS §§ 11-37-8.1, 11-37-8.3 (Michie 1994 & Supp. 1997); WIS. STAT. ANN. §§ 940.225, 948.09 (West 1996 & Supp. 1997).

151. ALA. CODE §§ 13A-6-62, 13A-6-61 (Michie 1995 & Supp. 1997); FLA. STAT. ANN § 794.011 (Harrison 1991 & Supp. 1997); IDAHO CODE § 18-1508 (Michie 1987 & Supp. 1997); KAN. STAT. ANN. § 21-3503 (1988 & Supp. 1997); MASS. GEN. LAWS ch. 265, § 23 (Law. Co-op. 1994 & Supp. 1998); MONT. CODE. ANN. §§ 45-5-501, 45-5-502, 45-5-503, 45-5-511 (1997); S.D.

CODIFIED LAWS ANN. § 22-22-1 (Michie 1992 & Supp. 1998); VT. STAT. ANN. tit. 13, § 3252 (Michie 1974 & Supp. 1997).

152. ILL. ANN. STAT. ch. 720, ¶¶ 5/12-13, 5/12-14, 5/12-16, 5/12-16 West/Smith-Hurd 1993 & Supp. 1998).

153. CAL. PENAL CODE §§ 261.5., 289 (West 1996 & Supp. 1998); OR. REV. STAT. §§ 163.415, 163.25 (Butterworth 1990 & Supp. 1997).

154. The states include ALASKA STAT. §§ 11.41.434(a)(2), (3), 11.41.436(a)(3), (5) (Michie 1995 & Supp. 1997); COLO. REV. STAT. § 18-3-405.3(1) (West 1990 & Supp. 1997); CONN. GEN. STAT. ANN. § 53a-71(a)(4), (8) (West 1994 & Supp. 1998); Id. § 53a-73a(a)(1)(D); FLA. STAT. ANN. § 794.011(8) (Harrison 1991 & Supp. 1997); 720 ILL. COMP. STAT. 5/12-13(a)(3), (4) (West/ Smith-Hurd 1993 & Supp. 1998); IND. CODE ANN. § 35-42-4-7(e) (Burns 1994 & Supp. 1998); IOWA CODE ANN. § 709.4(2)(c)(1)–(3) (West 1994 & Supp. 1998); ME. REV. STAT. ANN. tit. 17-A, §§ 253 (2)(F)–(H), 255(1)(F)–(G) (West 1983 & Supp. 1996); MICH. COMP. LAWS ANN. §§ 750.520b(1)(b), 750.520c(1)(b) (West 1991 & Supp. 1998); MINN. STAT. ANN. § 609.342(1)(b), (g) (West 1992 & Supp. 1998); Id. § 609.343(1)(b), (g); Id. § 609.344(1)(e)-(f) (West Supp. 1997); Id. § 609.345(1)(b), (e), (f) (West Supp. 1997) (read in conjunction with § 609.341(15)); N.H. REV. STAT. ANN. § 632-A:2(I)(j)–(k) (Butterworth 1994 & Supp. 1997); N.J. STAT. ANN. §§ 2C:14-2(a)(2), (c)(4), 2C:14-3(a) (West 1995 & Supp. 1998); N.M. STAT. ANN. § 30-9-13(A)(2)(a) (Michie 1974 & Supp. 1998); Id. § 30-9-11(D)(1); N.C. GEN. STAT. § 14-27.7 (1993 & Supp. 1997); N.D. CENT. CODE § 12.1-20-07(1)(e) (Michie 1991 & Supp. 1997); OHIO REV. CODE ANN. § 2907.03(A)(8), (9) (Anderson 1996 & Supp. 1998); OR. REV. STAT. § 163.375(1)(c) (Butterworth 1990 & Supp. 1998); S.C. CODE ANN. § 16-3-655(3) (Law. Co-op. 1985 & Supp. 1997); VT. STAT. ANN. tit. 13, § 3252(a)(4), (b) (Michie 1974 & Supp. 1997); VA. CODE ANN. § 18.2-61.1 (Michie 1996 & Supp. 1998); WASH. REV. CODE ANN. §§ 9A.44.093(1), 9A.44.096(1) (West 1996 & Supp. 1997).

155. COLO. REV. STAT. § 18-3-405.3(1) (West 1990 & Supp. 1997).

156. OR. REV. STAT. § 163.375(1)(c) (Butterworth 1990 & Supp. 1998).

157. ME. REV. STAT. ANN. tit. 17A, §§ 253(2)(F)–(H) (West 1983 & Supp. 1996).

158. FLA. STAT. ANN. § 794.05 (Harrison 1991 & Supp. 1997); MISS. CODE ANN. § 97-3-67, 97-5-21 (Law. Co-op. 1994 & Supp. 1997).

159. ALA. CODE §§ 13A-6-61(a)(3), 13A-6-62(a)(1) (Michie 1995 & Supp. 1997); IDAHO CODE § 18-1508 (Michie 1987 & Supp. 1997).

160. N.Y. PENAL LAW § 130.20(1) (McKinney 1989 & Supp. 1998) (in conjunction with § 130.05(3)(a)).

161. See In re Jessie C., 565 N.Y.S.2d 941 (N.Y. App. Div. 1991).

162. Michael M. v. Superior Court of Sonoma County, 450 U.S. 464 (1981).

163. Id.

164. Id. at 475–476.

165. Ferris v. Santa Clara County, 891 F.2d 715 (9th Cir. 1989), cert. denied, 498 U.S. 850 (1990); Jones v. State of Florida; State of Florida v. Rodriguez, 619 S.2d 418 (Fla. 1993), 619 So.2d 418 (Fla. App. 1993).

166. Michelle L. Oberman, "Turning Girls Into Women: Re-Evaluating Modern Statutory Rape Law," Journal of Criminal Law & Criminology 85 (1994):15–79.

167. See In re Jessie C., 565 N.Y.S.2d at 944 (N.Y. App. Div. 1991) (reversing a lower court's order that had found a 13-year-old boy delinquent because he violated a gender-based statutory rape provision where no evidence of force existed); In re Frederick, 622 N.E. 2d 762, 763 (Ohio Ct. App. 1993) (finding that consensual sex could not result in a charge of felony or rape even though the statute permitted such a charge).

168. Rosenthal, "Understanding Sexual Coercion Among Young Adolescents: Communicative Clarity, Pressure and Acceptance."

169. Moore et al., "Nonvoluntary Sexual Activity Among Adolescents."

170. Id.

171. Laumann et al., The Social Organization of Sexuality: Sexual Practices in the United States.

172. Julie M. Guggino and James J. Ponzetti Jr., "Gender Differences in Affective Reactions to First Coitus," *Journal of Adolescence* 20 (1997):189–200; Carol Anderson Darling, J. Kenneth Davidson, and Lauren C. Passarello, "The Mystique of First Intercourse Among College Youth: The Role of Partners, Contraceptive Practices, and Psychological Reactions," *Journal of Youth and Adolescence* 21 (1992):97–117.

173. David L. Weis, "The Experience of Pain During Women's First Sexual Intercourse: Cultural Mythology About Female Sexual Initiation," *Archives of Sexual Behavior* 14 (1985):421–438.

174. Sharon Thompson, "Putting a Big Thing into a Little Hole: Teenage Girls' Accounts of Sexual Initiation," *Journal of Sex Research* 27 (1990):341–361.

175. Sawyer and Smith, "A Survey of Situational Factors at First Intercourse Among College Students."

176. Darling et al., "The Mystique of First Intercourse Among College Youth: The Role of Partners, Contraceptive Practices, and Psychological Reactions."

177. *Id. See also* Zelnik and Shah, "First Intercourse Among Young Americans."

178. Young men most frequently endorse pleasure, desire, and physical satisfaction as their primary goals. Moore and Rosenthal, *Sexuality in Adolescence;* Susan Sprecher, A. Barbee, and Pepper Schwartz, "'Was It Good for You Too?': Gender Differences in First Sexual Intercourse Experiences," *Journal of Sex Research* 32 (1995):3–15. Young women tend to seek love, intimacy, and an emotionally close relationship; *see* Rodney M. Cate, Edgar Long, Jeffrey J. Angerra, and Kirsten Draper, "Sexual Intercourse and Relationship Development," *Family Relations* 42 (1993):158–163.

179. Miller and Moore, "Adolescent Sexual Behavior, Pregnancy, and Parenting: Research Through the 1980s."

180. *Id.*

181. *Id. See also* Sonenstein et al., "Sexual Activity, Condom Use, and AIDS Awareness Among Adolescent Males."

182. Miller and Moore, "Adolescent Sexual Behavior, Pregnancy, and Parenting: Research Through the 1980s."

183. *See* Zelnik and Shah, "First Intercourse Among Young Americans."

184. Laura Duberstein Lindberg, Freya L. Sonenstein, Leighton Ku, and Gladys Martinez, "Age Differences Between Minors Who Give Birth and Their Adult Partners," *Family Planning Perspectives* 29 (1997):61–66.

185. *Id.*

186. Four states explicitly exempt spouses from statutory rape; *see* COLO. REV. STAT. ANN. §§ 18-3-403, 18-3-405 (West 1990 & Supp. 1997) (any person who knowingly subjects another not his or her spouse to any sexual penetration or contact commits sexual assault on a child is a felony if the victim is under 15 and the offender is at least 4 years older than the victim); GA. CODE ANN. § 16-6-3 (Michie 1996 & Supp. 1998) (a person commits statutory rape when he engages in sexual intercourse with any female under 14 not his spouse, but no conviction can be had for this offense on the unsupported testimony of the female); LA. REV. STAT. ANN. §§ 14:43.1, 14:43.3 (West 1986 & Supp. 1998) (it is also a felony to touch the anus or genitals, using the mouth or any other instrumentality, when the victim is not the offender's spouse, is under 15, and is at least 3 years younger than the offender); TEX. PENAL CODE ANN. § 21.11 (Vernon 1996 & Supp. 1998) (A person is guilty of a felony if that person engages in sexual contact with a child under 17 and not the offender's spouse.) The small number of mandates is actually not as significant as unofficial policies that encourage pregnant teenagers to marry men who would otherwise be statutory rapists and that fail to pursue prosecutions for statutory rape cases where there have been established relations; *see* Kelly C. Connerton, "The Resurgence of the Marital Rape Exemption: The Victimization of Teens by Their Statutory Rapists," *Albany Law Review* 61 (1997):237–284.

187. Sevgi O. Aral and King K. Holmes, "Sexually Transmitted Diseases in the AIDS Era," *Scientific American* 264 (1991):62–69.

188. Court and commentators generally focus on maturity as the major reason and source of

exemption from the need to obtain parental consent to health care services; *see, e.g.,* Planned Parenthood v. Danforth, 428 U.S. 52, 74 (1976) (holding that minors have a right to demonstrate their maturity to make decisions with respect to obtaining abortions or contraceptives before the state imposes parental consent requirements).

189. John M. Shields and Alf Johnson, "Collision Between Law and Ethics: Consent for Treatment With Adolescents," *Bulletin of the American Academy of Psychiatry & Law* 20 (1992):309–323.

190. 442 U.S. 584 (1979).

191. *Id.* at 602–603.

192. ALA. CODE § 22-8-3 (Michie 1995 & Supp. 1997); ARIZ. REV. STAT. ANN. § 36-2271(C) (West 1989 & Supp. 1997); ARK. CODE ANN. § 20-9-603(1) (Michie 1997); DEL. CODE ANN. tit. 13, § 707(a)(5) (Michie 1995 & Supp. 1996); FLA. STAT. ANN. § 743-064 (Harrison 1991 & Supp. 1997); GA. CODE ANN. §§ 319-2, 31-9-3 (Michie 1996 & Supp. 1998); ILL. REV. STAT. ch. 111, § 4503 (West/Smith-Hurd 1993 & Supp. 1998); IOWA CODE § 147A.10 (West 1994 & Supp. 1998); KAN. STAT. ANN. § 65-2891 (1988 & Supp. 1997); KY. REV. STAT. ANN. § 214.185(3) (Michie/Bobbs-Merrill 1990 & Supp. 1996); MD. HEALTH-GEN. CODE ANN. § 20-102(b) (Michie 1995 & Supp. 1997); MASS. GEN. L. ch. 112, § 12F (Law. Co-op. 1994 & Supp. 1998); Minn. Stat. § 144.344 (West 1992 & Supp. 1998); MO. REV. STAT. § 537.037 (West 1996 & Supp. 1998); MONT. CODE ANN. §§ 41-1-402(1)(d), 41-1-405(1), 41-1-405(2) (1997); NEB. REV. STAT. § 71-5512 (1995 & Supp. 1997); N.Y. PUB. HEALTH LAW § 2504(4) (McKinney 1989 & Supp. 1998); N.D. CENT. CODE § 14-10-17.1 (Michie 1991 & Supp. 1997); OKLA. STAT. tit. 63, §§ 2602(a)(7), 2604 (Butterworth 1990 & Supp. 1998); PA. STAT. ANN. tit. 35, § 10104 (Purdon 1983 & Supp. 1997); R.I. GEN. LAWS § 23-4.6-1 (Michic 1994 & Supp. 1997); S.C. CODE ANN. § 20-7-290 (West/Law. Co-op. 1985 & Supp. 1997); S.D. CODIFIED LAWS ANN. § 20-9-4.2 (Michie 1992 & Supp. 1998); TENN. CODE ANN. §§ 63-6-222(a), 63-6-222(c) (Michie 1997); VA. CODE ANN. § 54-1-2969(C) (West 1988 & Supp. 1998); WYO. STAT. ANN. § 14-1-101(b)(iii) (Michie 1997).

193. FLA. STAT. 743.064(3) (Harrison 1991 & Supp. 1997); KY. REV. STAT. ANN. § 214.185(6) (Michie/Bobbs-Merrill 1990 & Supp. 1996); MD. HEALTH-GEN. CODE ANN. § 20-102(c) (Michie 1995 & Supp. 1997); MASS. GEN. L. ch. 112, § 12F (Law. Co-op. 1994 & Supp. 1998); MINN. STAT. § 144.344 (West 1993 & Supp. 1998); MONT. CODE § 41-1-403 (1997); NEV. REV. STAT. § 129.030(3) (Michie 1997); OKLA. STAT. tit. 63, § 2602(B) (West 1983 & Supp. 1998); TENN. CODE ANN. § 63-6-222(b) (Michie 1997); VA. CODE ANN. § 54.1-2969(G) (Michie 1996 & Supp. 1998).

194. ALA. CODE § 22-8-3 (Michie 1995 & Supp. 1997); ARIZ. REV. STAT. ANN. § 36-2271(c) (West 1989 & Supp. 1997); ARK. CODE ANN. § 20-9-603(1) (Michie 1997); DEL. CODE ANN. tit. 13, § 707(a)(5) (Michie 1995 & Supp. 1996); GA. CODE ANN. §§ 31-9-2, 31-9-3 (Michie 1996 & Supp. 1998); ILL. REV. STAT. ch. 111, ¶ 4503 (West/Smith-Hurd 1993 & Supp. 1998); IOWA CODE § 147A.10 (West 1994 & Supp. 1998); KAN. STAT. ANN. § 65-2891 (1988 & Supp. 1997); LA. REV. STAT. ANN. § 40:1299.54 (West 1986 & Supp. 1998); MO. REV. STAT. § 537.037 (West 1996 & Supp. 1997); NEV. REV. STAT. § 7105512 (Michie 1997); N.M. STAT. § 24-10-2 (Michie 1978 & Supp. 1998); N.Y. PUB. HEALTH LAW § 2504 (McKinney 1989 & Supp. 1998); N.D. CENT. CODE § 14-10-17.1 (Michie 1991 & Supp. 1997); PA. STAT. ANN. tit. 35, § 10104 (Purdon 1983 & Supp. 1998); R.I. GEN. LAWS § 23-4.6-1 (West/Law. Co-op. 1985 & Supp. 1997); S.C. CODE ANN. § 20-7-290 (West/Law. Co-op. 1985 & Supp. 1997); S.D. CODIFIED LAWS ANN. § 20-9-4.2 (Michie 1997); WYO. STAT. ANN. § 14.1-101 (Michie 1997).

195. In examining these issues, it is important to note that the minor's capacity to make decisions does not guide the analysis; it is the independence from parents which determines emancipation.

196. CAL. CIV. CODE §§ 62-69 (West 1996 & Supp. 1998); CONN. GEN. STAT. §§ 46b-150 to 46b-150e (West 1994 & Supp. 1998); MONT. CODE § 41-3-408 (1997); NEV. REV. STAT. §§ 129.080 to 129.140 (Michie 1997); N.M. STAT. ANN. §§ 28-6-3 to 28-6-8 (Michie 1978 & Supp. 1998); VA. CODE ANN. §§ 16.1-331 to 16.1-334 (Michie 1996 & Supp. 1998); WYO. STAT. §§ 14-1-101(b) (v), 14-1-201 to 14-1-206 (Michie 1997).

197. ALA. CODE §§ 26-13-1 to 26-13-8 (Michie 1995 & Supp. 1997); ALASKA STAT. § 09.55 (Michie

1996); Ark. Code Ann. § 9-26-104 (Michie 1997); Ill. Rev. Stat. ch. 40, §§ 2201 to 2211 (West/Smith-Hurd 1993 & Supp. 1998); Kan. Stat. Ann. §§ 38-108 (1988 & Supp. 1997); La. Civ. Code Ann. art. 385 (West 1986 & Supp. 1998); Me. Rev. Stat. Ann. tit. 15 § 3506-A (West 1983 & Supp. 1996); Or. Rev. Stat. §§ 109.510 to 109.565 (Butterworth 1990 & Supp. 1998); Tenn. Code Ann. §§ 29-31-101 to 29-31-105 (Vernon 1996 & Supp. 1998); W. Va. Code § 49-7-27 (Michie 1996 & Supp. 1997).

198. La. Civ. Code Ann. arts. 366, 368 to 384 (West. 1986 & Supp. 1998); Mich. Comp. Laws § 722.4 (West 1991 & Supp. 1998); Pa. Stat. Ann. tit. 16, § 2175(6) (Purdon 1983 & Supp. 1998); S.D. Codified Laws Ann. §§ 25-5-17 to 25-5-23 (Michie 1992 & Supp. 1998).

199. Mich. Comp. Laws § 722.4 (West 1991 & Supp. 1998) (when minor is in the custody of a law enforcement agency and his or her parent cannot be promptly located, the minor is considered emancipated for purposes of consenting to routine, nonsurgical medical care or emergency medical care).

200. Ariz. Rev. Stat. Ann. § 44-132 (West 1989 & Supp. 1997); Ark. Code Ann. § 20-9-602(6) (Michie 1997); Ind. Code § 16-8-12-2 (Burns 1994 & Supp. 1998); Ky. Rev. Stat. Ann. § 214.185(3) (Michie/Bobbs-Merrill 1990 & Supp. 1996); Miss. Code Ann. § 41-41-3 (Law. Co-op. 1994 & Supp. 1997); Mont. Code § 1-1-402 (1997); N.M. Stat. Ann. § 24-10-1 (Michie 1978 & Supp. 1998); N.C. Gen. Stat. § 90-21.5(b) (1993 & Supp. 1998); Okla. Stat. tit. 63, § 2602(1) (West 1983 & Supp. 1998).

201. Ala. Code § 22-8-5 (Michie 1995 & Supp. 1997); Alaska Stat. § 09.65.100(3) (Michie 1996); Ark. Code Ann. § 20-9-602(2) (Michie 1997); Colo. Rev. Stat. 13-22-103(3) (West 1990 & Supp. 1997); Conn. Gen. Stat. § 19a-285 (West 1994 & Supp. 1998); Del. Code Ann. tit. 13, § 707(a) (4) (Michie 1995 & Supp. 1996); Fla. Stat. § 743.065(2) (Harrison 1991 & Supp. 1997); Ga. Code Ann. § 31-9-2 (Michie 1996 & Supp. 1998); Idaho Code § 39-4303 (Michie 1987 & Supp. 1997); Ill. Rev. Stat. ch. 111, ¶ 4502 (West/Smith-Hurd 1993 & Supp. 1998); Kan. Stat. Ann. § 38-122 (1988 & Supp. 1997); Ky. Rev. Stat. Ann. § 214.185(3) (Michie/Bobbs-Merrill 1990 & Supp. 1996); La. Rev. Stat. Ann. § 40:1299.53(b) (West 1986 & Supp. 1998); Md. Health-Gen. Code Ann. § 20-102(a)(2) (Michie 1995 & Supp. 1997); Mass. Gen. L. ch. 112, § 12F (Law. Co-op. 1994 & Supp. 1998); Minn. Stat. § 144.342 (West 1992 & Supp. 1998); Miss. Code Ann. 41-41-3 (Law. Co-op. 1994 & Supp. 1997); Mo. Rev. Stat. § 431.061(3) (West 1996 & Supp. 1997); Mont. Code Ann. § 41-1-402(2) (1997); Nev. Rev. Stat. § 129.030 (Michie 1997); N.J. Stat. Ann. § 9:17A-1 (West 1995 & Supp. 1998); N.Y. Pub. Health Law § 2504(2) (McKinney 1989 & Supp. 1998); Okla. Stat. tit. 63, § 2602(A)(1), (4) (West 1983 & Supp. 1998); Pa. Stat. Ann. tit. 35, §§ 10101, 10102 (Purdon 1983 & Supp. 1998); R.I. Gen. Laws § 23-4.6-1 (Michie 1994 & Supp. 1997); S.C. Code Ann. §§ 20-7-300, 20-7-270 (West/Law. Co-op. 1985 & Supp. 1997); Utah Code Ann. § 78-14-5(4)(a) (Michie 1996 & Supp. 1998).

202. Ala. Code §§ 22-8-4 to 22-8-5 (Michie 1995 & Supp. 1997); Ariz. Rev. Stat. Ann. § 44-132 (West 1989 & Supp. 1997); Ark. Code Ann. § 20-9-602(3) (Michie 1997); Cal. Civ. Code § 25.6 (West 1996 & Supp. 1998); Colo. Rev. Stat. § 13-22-103 (West 1990 & Supp. 1997); Ga. Code Ann. § 31-9-2 (Michie 1996 & Supp. 1998); Ill. Rev. Stat. ch. 111, ¶ 4501 (West/Smith-Hurd 1993 & Supp. 1998); Ind. Code § 16-8-12-2(2) (C) (Burns 1994 & Supp. 1998); Ky. Rev. Stat. Ann. § 214.185(4) (Michie/Bobbs-Merrill 1990 & Supp. 1996); La. Rev. Stat. Ann. § 40: 1299.53(c) (West 1986 & Supp. 1998); Md. Health-Gen. Code Ann. § 20-102(a) (1) (Michie 1995 & Supp. 1998); Mass. Gen. L. ch. 112, § 12F (Law. Co-op. 1994 & Supp. 1997); Minn. Stat. § 144.342 (West 1992 & Supp. 1998); Miss. Code Ann. § 41-41-3 (Law. Co-op. 1994 & Supp. 1997); Mo. Rev. Stat. § 431.061(3) (West 1996 & Supp. 1997); Mont. Code Ann. § 41-1-402(a) (1997); Nev. Rev. Stat. § 129.030 (Michie 1997); N.M. Stat. Ann. § 24-10-1 (Michie 1978 & Supp. 1998); N.Y. Public Health Law § 2504 (McKinney 1989 & Supp. 1998); Okla. Stat. tit. 63, § 2602 (West 1983 & Supp. 1998); Pa. Stat. Ann. tit. 35, § 10101 (Purdon 1983 & Supp. 1998); R.I. Gen. Laws § 23-4.6-1 (Michie 1994 & Supp. 1997); S.C. Code Ann. § 20-7-270 (West/Law. Co-op. 1985 & Supp. 1997); Va. Code Ann. § 54.1-2969(E) (Michie 1996 & Supp. 1998); Wyo. Stat. § 14-1-101 (Michie 1997).

203. ALASKA STAT. § 09.65.100(a) (1) (Michie 1995 & Supp. 1997); CAL. CIV. CODE § 34.6 (West 1996 & Supp. 1998); COLO. REV. STAT. § 13-22-103 (West 1990 & Supp. 1997); IND. CODE § 16-8-12-2(2) (B) (Burns 1994 & Supp. 1998); MASS. GEN. L. ch. 112, § 12F (Law. Co-op. 1994 & Supp. 1997); MINN. STAT. § 144.341 (West 1992 & Supp. 1998); MONT. CODE ANN. § 41-1-402(1)(b) (1997); NEV. REV. STAT. § 129.030 (Michie 1997); OKLA. STAT. tit. 63, § 2602(A)(2) (Butterworth 1990 & Supp. 1998); TEX. FAM. CODE § 35.03 (Vernon 1996 & Supp. 1998); WYO. STAT. § 14-1-101(b) (iv), (v) (Michie 1997).

204. For minors in the armed forces, *see* CAL. CIV. CODE § 25.7 (West 1996 & Supp. 1998); IND. CODE § 16-08- 12-2(2)(D) (Burns 1996 & Supp. 1998); MASS. GEN. L. ch. 112, § 12F (Law. Co-op. 1994 & Supp. 1998); TEX. FAM. CODE ANN. § 35.03 (Vernon 1986 & Supp. 1998); WYO. STAT. § 14-1-101 (Michie 1997). For minors who have graduated, *see* ALA. CODE § 22-8-4 (Michie 1995 & Supp. 1997); MONT. CODE ANN. § 41-1-402(1)(a) (1997); PA. STAT. ANN. tit. 35, § 10101 (Purdon 1983 & Supp. 1998).

205. For statutes that remain silent, *see* ARIZ. REV. STAT. ANN. § 44-132 (West 1989 & Supp. 1997); ARK. CODE ANN. § 20-9-602 (Michie 1997); IND. CODE § 16-8-12-2 (Burns 1994 & Supp. 1998); MISS. CODE ANN. § 41-41-3(g) (Law. Co-op. 1994 & Supp. 1997); MONT. CODE § 41-3-408 (1997); N.M. STAT. ANN. § 24-10-1 (Michie 1978 & Supp. 1998); N.C. GEN. STAT. § 90-21.5(b) (1993 & Supp. 1997); WYO. STAT. § 14-1-101 (Michie 1997). For statutes that speak to the issue, *see* CAL. CIV. CODE § 63 (West 1990 & Supp. 1997); CONN. GEN. STAT. § 46b-150d (West 1994 & Supp. 1998); KY. REV. STAT. ANN. § 214.185(6) (Michie/Bobbs-Merrill 1990 & Supp. 1996); MONT. CODE § 41-1-403 (1997); NEV. REV. STAT. § 129.130(d) (Michie 1997); N.M. STAT. ANN. § 28-6-6 (Michie 1978 & Supp. 1998); OKLA. STAT. tit. 63, § 2602 (West 1983 & Supp. 1998); VA. CODE ANN. § 16.1-334 (Michie 1996 & Supp. 1998).

206. ALA. CODE § 22-8-4 (Michie 1995 & Supp. 1997); ARIZ. REV. STAT. ANN. § 44-132 (West 1989 & Supp. 1997); ARK. CODE ANN. § 20-9-602(3) (Michie 1997); CAL. CIV. CODE § 25.6 (West 1996 & Supp. 1998); COLO. REV. STAT. § 13-22-103 (West 1990 & 1997); GA. CODE ANN. § 31-9-2 (Michie 1996 & Supp. 1998); ILL. REV. STAT. ch. 111, ¶ 4501 (West-Smith-Hurd 1993 & Supp. 1998); IND. CODE § 16-8-12-2(2)(c) (Burns 1996 & Supp. 1998); KY. REV. STAT. ANN. § 214.185(5) (Michie/Bobbs-Merrill 1990 & Supp. 1996); LA. REV. STAT. ANN. § 40:1299.53(c) (West 1986 & Supp. 1998); MD. HEALTH-GEN. CODE ANN. § 20-102 (Michie 1995 & Supp. 1997); MASS. GEN. L. ch. 112, § 12F (Law. Co-op. 1994 & Supp. 1998); MINN. STAT. § 144.346 (West 1992 & Supp. 1998); MISS. CODE ANN. § 41-41-3(c) (Law. Co-op. 1994 & Supp. 1997); MO. REV. STAT. § 431.062(1.)(3) (West 1996 & Supp. 1997); MONT. CODE ANN. § 41-1-403 (1997); NEV. REV. STAT. § 129.030(3) (Michie 1997); N.M. STAT. ANN. § 24-10-1 (Michie 1978 & Supp. 1998); N.Y. PUBLIC HEALTH LAW § 2504 (McKinney 1989 & Supp. 1998); OKLA. STAT. tit. 63, § 2602(B) (West 1983 & Supp. 1998); PA. STAT. ANN. tit. 35, § 10101 (Purdon 1983 & Supp. 1998); R.I. GEN. LAWS § 23-4.6-1 (Michie 1994 & Supp. 1997); S.C. CODE ANN. § 20-7-270 (West/Law. Co-op. 1985 & Supp. 1997); VA. CODE ANN. § 54.1-2969(E) (Michie 1996 & Supp. 1998); WYO. STAT. § 14-1-101 (Michie 1997).

207. ALA. CODE § 22-8-5 (Michie 1995 & Supp. 1997); ALASKA STAT. § 09.65.100(3) (Michie 1996); ARK. CODE ANN. § 20-9-602(2) (Michie 1997); COLO. REV. STAT. § 13-22-103(3) (West 1990 & Supp. 1997); CONN. GEN. STAT. § 19a-285 (West 1994 & Supp. 1998); DEL. CODE ANN. tit. 13, § 707(a)(4) (Michie 1995 & Supp. 1996); FLA. STAT. § 743.065(2) (Harrison 1991 & Supp. 1997); GA. CODE ANN. § 31-9-2(2) (Michie 1996 & Supp. 1998); IDAHO CODE § 39-4303 (Michie 1987 & Supp. 1997); ILL. REV. STAT. ch. 111, ¶ 4502 (West/Smith-Hurd 1993 & Supp. 1998); KAN. STAT. ANN. § 38-122 (1988 & Supp. 1997); KY. REV. STAT. ANN. § 214.185(6) (Michie/Bobbs-Merrill 1990 & Supp. 1996); LA. REV. STAT. ANN. § 40:1299.53(b) (West 1986 & Supp. 1998); MD. HEALTH-GEN. CODE ANN. § 20-102(e) (Michie 1995 & Supp. 1997); MINN. STAT. § 144.346 (West 1992 & Supp. 1998); MISS. CODE ANN. § 41-41-3(b) (Law. Co-op. 1994 & Supp. 1997); MO. REV. STAT. § 431.062(3) (West 1997 & Supp. 1997); MONT. CODE § 41-1-403 (1997); N.J. STAT. ANN. § 9:17A-5 (West 1995 & Supp. 1998); OKLA. STAT. tit. 63 § 2602 (West 1983 & Supp. 1998); MASS. GEN. L. ch. 112, § 12F (Law. Co-op. 1994 & Supp. 1997); NEV. REV. STAT. § 129.030(3) (Michie 1997); N.Y. PUB. HEALTH LAW § 2504(2) (McKinney

1989 & Supp. 1998); PA. STAT. ANN. tit. 35, § 10102 (Purdon 1983 & Supp. 1998); R.I. GEN. LAWS § 23-4.6-1 (Michie 1994 & Supp. 1997); S.C. CODE ANN. §§ 20-7-300, 20-7-270 (West/ Law. Co-op. 1985 & Supp. 1997); UTAH CODE ANN. § 78-14-5(4)(a) (Michie 1996 & Supp. 1998).

208. ALASKA STAT. § 09.65.100(1) (Michie 1996); CAL. CIV. CODE § 34.6 (West 1996 & Supp. 1998); COLO. REV. STAT. § 13-22-103 (West 1990 & Supp. 1997); IND. CODE § 16-8-12-2(2)(B) (Burns 1994 & Supp. 1998); MASS. GEN. L. ch. 112, § 12F (Law. Co-op. 1994 & Supp. 1998); MINN. STAT. § 144.346 (West 1992 & Supp. 1998); MONT. CODE § 41-1-403 (1997); NEV. REV. STAT. § 129.030(3) (Michie 1997); OKLA. STAT. tit. 63, § 2602(B) (West 1983 & Supp. 1998); TEX. FAM. CODE § 35.03(d) (Vernon 1996 & Supp. 1998); WYO. STAT. § 14-1-101(b)(iv) (Michie 1997).

209. CAL. CIV. CODE § 25.7 (West 1990 & Supp. 1997); IND. CODE § 16-8-12-2(2)(D) (Burns 1994 & Supp. 1998); MASS. GEN. L. ch. 112, § 12F(iii) (Law. Co-op. 1994 & Supp. 1998); TEX. FAM. CODE § 35.03 (Vernon 1996 & Supp. 1998); Wyo. Stat. § 14-1-101(ii) (Michie 1997).

210. ALA. CODE § 22-8-4 (Michie 1995 & Supp. 1997); MONT. CODE § 41-1-403 (1997); PA. STAT. ANN. tit. 35, § 10101 (Purdon 1983 & Supp. 1998).

211. Gary B. Melton, ''Knowing What We Do Know: APA and Adolescent Abortion,'' *American Psychologist* 45 (1990):1171–1172.

212. Bakker v. Welch, 155 Mich. 632, 108 N.W. 94 (1906).

213. *See* chapter 4.

214. ARK. CODE ANN. § 82-363(9) (Michie 1997); IDAHO CODE § 39-4302 (Michie 1987 & Supp. 1997); MISS. CODE ANN. § 41-41-3 (Law. Co-op. 1994 & Supp. 1997); NEV. REV. STAT. ANN. § 129.030(2) (Michie 1997); N.H. REV. STAT. ANN. § 318-B:12-2 (Butterworth 1994 & Supp. 1997).

215. ARK. CODE ANN. § 20-9-602(7) (Michie 1997); IDAHO CODE § 39-4302 (Michie 1987 & Supp. 1997); MISS. CODE ANN. § 41-41-3(h) (Law. Co-op. 1994 & Supp. 1997); NEV. REV. STAT. § 129.030(3) (1987); N.H. REV. STAT. ANN. § 318-B:12a (Butterworth 1994 & Supp. 1997).

216. *See* chapter 4.

217. ALA. CODE § 26-14-1 (Michie 1995 & Supp. 1997); ALASKA STAT. § 47-10.010(a)(2)(B) (Michie 1996); ARIZ. REV. STAT. ANN. § 13-3620(A) (West 1989 & Supp. 1997); ARK. CODE ANN. § 9-27-303(4)(B) (Michie 1997); CAL. PENAL CODE § 11165.2(b) (West 1996 & Supp. 1998); COLO. REV. STAT. § 19-1-103(20)(d) (West 1990 & Supp. 1997); CONN. GEN. STAT. § 46b-120(iv) (West 1994 & Supp. 1997); DEL. CODE ANN. tit. 31, § 301(3) (Michie 1995 & Supp. 1996); FLA. STAT. § 39.01(37) (Harrison 1991 & Supp. 1997); HAW. REV. STAT. § 350-1(4) (1993 & Supp. 1996); IDAHO CODE 16-1602(n)(1) (Michie 1987 & Supp. 1997); ILL. REV. STAT. ch. 37, 802-3 (West/Smith-Hurd 1993 & Supp. 1998); IND. CODE ANN. § 31-6-4-3(a)(1) (Burns 1994 & Supp. 1998); IOWA CODE § 232.2 (6)(e) (West 1994 & Supp. 1998); KAN. STAT. ANN. § 38-1502(b) (1988 & Supp. 199); KY. REV. STAT. § 600.020(1) (Michie/Bobbs-Merrill 1990 & Supp. 1996); LA. REV. STAT. ANN. § 14:403(B)(5) (West 1986 & Supp. 1998); ME. REV. STAT. ANN. tit. 22, § 4002(6)(B) (West 1983 & Supp. 1996); MD. FAM. LAW CODE § 5-701(n)(2) (Michie 1995 & Supp. 1997); MICH. COMP. LAWS ANN. § 722.622(c) (West 1991 & Supp. 1998); MINN. STAT. § 626.556(2)(c) (West 1992 & Supp. 1998); MISS. CODE ANN. § 43-21-105(1)(i) (Law. Co-op. 1994 & Supp. 1997); MO. REV. STAT. § 210.110(5) (West 1996 & Supp. 1997); MONT. CODE ANN. § 41-3-102(3)(c) (1997); NEV. REV. STAT. § 432B.140 (Michie 1997); N.J. REV. STAT. § 9:6-8.21(c)(4) (West 1995 & Supp. 1998); N.M. STAT. ANN. § 32-1-3(L)(2) (Michie 1978 & Supp. 1998); N.Y. SOC. SERV. LAW § 371.(4-a) (McKinney 1989 & Supp. 1998); N.C. GEN. STAT. § 7A-517(21) (1993 & Supp. 1997); OHIO REV. CODE ANN. § 2151.03(c) (Anderson 1994 & Supp. 1997); OKLA. STAT. ANN. tit. 21, § 852 (West 1983 & Supp. 1998); OR. REV. STAT. § 418.740(1)(e) (Butterworth 1990 & Supp. 1998); R.I. GEN. LAWS § 40-11-2(2)(d) (Michie 1994 & Supp. 1997); S.C. Code Ann. § 20-7-409(c)(3) (West/Law. Co-op. 1985 & Supp. 1997); S.D. CODIFIED LAWS ANN. § 26-8-6(4) (Michie 1993 & Supp. 1998); TENN. CODE ANN. § 37-1-102(10)(D) (Vernon 1996 & Supp. 1998); TEX. FAM. CODE ANN. § 34.012(2)(ii) (Vernon 1996 & Supp. 1998); VT. STAT. ANN. tit. 33, § 682(3)(c) (Michie 1974 & Supp. 1997); VA. CODE

ANN. § 63.1-248.2(A)(2) (Michie 1996 & Supp. 1998); W. VA. CODE § 49-1-3(g)(1)(A) (Michie 1996 & Supp. 1997); WIS. STAT. § 48.981(1)(d) (West 1996 & Supp. 1997; WYO. STAT. § 14-6-201(a)(xvi)(A) (Michie 1997).

218. GA. CODE ANN. § 15-11-2(8)(A) (Michie 1996 & Supp. 1998); MASS. GEN. L. ch. 119, § 24 (Law. Co-op. 1994 & Supp. 1998); N.H. REV. STAT. ANN. § 169-C:3 (xix)(b) (Butterworth 1994 & Supp. 1997); PA. STAT. ANN. tit. 11, § 2203 (Purdon 1983 & Supp. 1998); UTAH CODE ANN. § 62A-4-502(4) (Michie 1996 & Supp. 1998); WASH. REV. CODE § 26.44.020(12) (West 1988 & Supp. 1998).

219. Courts remain reluctant to intervene in non–life-threatening situations; *see, e.g.,* James G. Dwyer, "Parents' Religion and Children's Welfare: Debunking the Doctrine of Parents' Rights," *California Law Review* 82 (1994):1371–1447.

220. States wield considerable power to intervene into family relations through child abuse and neglect laws, most of which include the failure to provide medical–health care as neglect. *See, e.g.,* CAL. PENAL CODE § 11165.2(b) (West 1996 & Supp. 1998) (defining general neglect as including negligent failure to provide medical care). A critical aspect regarding intervention is that once the child welfare system has intervened, the state is obligated to provide care for the minor; *see, e.g.,* CAL. WELF. & INST. CODE §§ 362, 369 (West 1996 & Supp. 1998) (providing that when a minor is adjudged dependent, the court may make any reasonable order for the care of the child). This protection has received the Supreme Court's imprimatur, DeShaney v. Winnebago County Dep't of Social Servs., 489 U.S. 189 (1989) (holding that due process protects children deprived of liberty by state actors).

221. Shields and Johnson, "Collision Between Law and Ethics: Consent for Treatment With Adolescents."

222. ALA. CODE § 22-8-6 (Michie 1995 & Supp. 1997); ALASKA STAT. § 09.65.100(4) (Michie 1996); ARK. CODE ANN. § 20-9-602 (Michie 1997); CAL. CIV. CODE § 34.5 (West 1996 & Supp. 1998); DEL. CODE ANN. tit. 13, § 708 (Michie 1995 & Supp. 1996); FLA. STAT. § 743.065(1) (Michie 1996 & Supp. 1998); GA. CODE ANN. § 31-9-2 (Michie 1996 & Supp. 1998); HAW. REV. STAT. § 577A-2 (1993 & Supp. 1996); KAN STAT. ANN. § 38-123 (1988 & Supp. 1997); KY. REV. STAT. ANN. § 214.185 (Michie/Bobbs-Merrill 1990 & Supp. 1996); LA. REV. STAT. ANN. § 40:1299.53 (West 1986 & Supp. 1998); MD. HEALTH-GEN. CODE ANN. § 20-102 (Michie 1995 & Supp. 1997); MICH. COMP. LAWS ANN. § 333.9132 (West 1991 & Supp. 1998); MINN. STAT. § 144.343 (West 1992 & Supp. 1998); MISS. CODE ANN. § 41-41-3(i) (Law. Co-op. 1994 & Supp. 1997); MO. REV. STAT. § 431.061 (West 1996 & Supp. 1997); MONT. CODE ANN. § 41-1-402 (1997); N.J. STAT. ANN. § 9:17A-1 (West 1995 & Supp. 1998); N.M. STAT. ANN. § 24-1-13 (Michie 1978 & Supp. 1998); N.Y. PUB. HEALTH LAW § 2504(3) (McKinney 1989 & Supp 1998); N.C. GEN. STAT. § 90-21.5(a) (1993 & Supp. 1997); OKLA. STAT. tit. 63, § 2602(3) (West 1983 & Supp. 1998); PA. STAT. ANN. tit. 35, § 10103 (Purdon 1983 & Supp. 1998); TENN. CODE ANN. § 63-6-223 (Michie 1997); TEX. FAM. CODE ANN. § 35.03 (Vernon 1996 & Supp. 1998); UTAH CODE ANN. § 78-14-5(4) (Michie 1996 & Supp. 1998); VA. CODE ANN. § 54.1-2969 (Michie 1996 & Supp. 1997).

223. DEL. CODE ANN. tit. 13, § 708 (Michie 1995 & Supp. 1996) (minor must be 12 years old to consent).

224. TENN. CODE ANN. § 63-6-223 (Michie 1997) (prenatal care without knowledge of minor's parent or guardian).

225. ALA. CODE § 22-8-6 (Michie 1995 & Supp. 1997); ALASKA STAT. § 09.65.100(4) (Michie 1996); ARK. CODE ANN. § 20-9-602 (Michie 1997); CAL. CIV. CODE § 34.5 (West 1996 & Supp. 1998); FLA. STAT. § 743.065(1) (Harrison 1991 & Supp. 1997); GA. CODE ANN. § 31-9-2(5) (Michie 1996 & Supp. 1998); KAN. STAT. ANN. § 38-123 (1988 & Supp. 1997); LA. REV. STAT. ANN. § 40:1299.53 (West 1986 & Supp. 1998); MISS. CODE ANN. § 41-41-3 (Law. Co-op. 1994 & Supp. 1997); N.M. STAT ANN. § 24-1-13 (Michie 1978 & Supp. 1998); N.Y. PUB. HEALTH LAW § 2504(3) (McKinney 1989 & Supp. 1998); N.C. GEN. STAT. § 90-21.5(a) (1993 & Supp. 1997); PA. STAT. ANN. tit. 35, § 10103 (Purdon 1983 & Supp. 1998); UTAH CODE ANN. § 78-14-5(4)(f) (Michie 1996 & Supp. 1998); VA. CODE ANN. § 54.1-2969(D)(2) (Michie 1996 & Supp. 1998).

226. Statutes provide for disclosure to minor's parent or guardian; *see* CAL. CIV. CODE § 34.6 (West 1996 & Supp. 1998); DEL. CODE ANN. tit. 13, § 708 (Michie 1995 & Supp. 1996); HAW. REV. STAT. § 577A-3 (1993 & Supp. 1996); KY. REV. STAT. ANN. § 214.185 (Michie/Bobbs-Merrill 1990 & Supp. 1996); MD. HEALTH-GEN. CODE. ANN. § 20-102 (Michie 1994 & Supp. 1997); MICH. COMP. LAWS ANN. § 333.9132 (West 1991 & Supp. 1998); MINN. STAT. § 144.346 (West 1992 & Supp. 1998); MO. REV. STAT. § 431.062 (West 1996 & Supp. 1997); MONT. CODE ANN. § 41-1-403 (1997); N.J. STAT. ANN. § 9:17A-5 (West 1995 & Supp. 1998); OKLA. STAT. tit. 63, § 2602 (West 1983 & Supp. 1998); TEX. FAM. CODE § 35.03 (Vernon 1996 & Supp. 1998).

227. ALA. CODE §§ 22-8-6, 22-11A-19 (Michie 1995 & Supp. 1997); ALASKA STAT. § 09.65.100(a)(4) (Michie 1996); ARIZ. REV. STAT. ANN. § 44-132.01 (West 1989 & Supp. 1997); ARK. CODE ANN. § 20-16-508(a)(1) (Michie 1997); COLO. REV. STAT. § 25-4-402(4) (West 1990 & Supp. 1997); CONN. GEN. STAT. § 19a-216 (West 1994 & Supp. 1998); GA. CODE. ANN. § 31-17-7(a) (Michie 1996 & Supp. 1998); HAW. REV. STAT. § 577A-2 (1993 & Supp. 1998); ILL. REV. STAT. ch. 111, § 4504 (West/ Smith-Hurd 1993 & Supp. 1998); IND. CODE § 16-8-5-1 (Burns 1994 & Supp. 1998); IOWA CODE § 140.9 (West 1994 & Supp. 1998); KAN. STAT. ANN. § 65-2892 (1988 & Supp. 1997); KY. REV. STAT. ANN. § 214.185 (Michie/Bobbs-Merrill 1990 & Supp. 1996); LA. REV. STAT. ANN. § 40:1065.1(A) (West 1986 & Supp. 1998); ME. REV. STAT. ANN. tit. 32, § 3292 (West 1983 & Supp. 1996); MD. HEALTH-GEN. CODE ANN. § 20-102(a), (c)(3) (Michie 1995 & Supp. 1997); MASS. GEN. LAW ch. 111, § 117 (Law. Co-op. 1994 & Supp. 1998); MICH. COMP. LAWS ANN. § 333.5257 (West 1991 & Supp. 1998); MINN. STAT. § 144.343(1) (West 1992 & Supp. 1998); MISS. CODE ANN. § 41-41-13 (Law. Co-op. 1994 & Supp. 1997); MO. REV. STAT. § 431.061(4)(b) (West 1996 & Supp. 1997); MONT. CODE ANN. § 41-1-402(c) (1977); NEV. REV. STAT. § 129.060 (Michie 1997); N.J. REV. STAT. ANN. § 9:17A-4 (West 1995 & Supp. 1998); N.M. STAT. ANN. § 24-1-9 (Michie 1978 & Supp. 1998); N.C. GEN. STAT. § 90-21.5(a) (1993 & Supp. 1997); N.D. CENT. CODE § 14-10-17 (Michie 1991 & Supp. 1997); OHIO REV. CODE ANN. § 3709.24.1 (Anderson 1994 & Supp. 1997); OKLA. STAT. tit. 63, § 1-532.1 (West 1983 & Supp. 1998); OR. REV. STAT. § 109.610 (Butterworth 1990 & Supp. 1998); PA. STAT. ANN. tit. 35, § 10103 (Purdon 1983 & Supp. 1998); S.D. CODIFIED LAWS ANN. § 34-23-16 (Michie 1992 & Supp. 1998); VT. STAT. ANN. tit. 18, § 4226 (Michie 1974 & Supp. 1997); VA. CODE ANN. § 54.1-2969(D)(1) (Michie 1996 & Supp. 1998); W. VA. CODE § 16-4-10 (Michie 1996 & Supp. 1997); WYO. STAT. § 35-4-131 (Michie 1997).

228. ALA. CODE §§ 22-11A-19, 22-8-6 (Michie 1995 & Supp. 1997); CAL. CIV. CODE § 34.7 (West 1996 & Supp. 1998); DEL. CODE ANN. tit. 16, § 710 (Michie 1995 & Supp. 1996); FLA. STAT. ANN. § 384.30(1) (Harrison 1991 & Supp. 1997); NEB. REV. STAT. § 71-504 (1995 & Supp. 1997); N.H. REV. STAT. ANN. § 141-C:18(11) (Butterworth 1994 & Supp. 1997); N.Y. PUB. HEALTH LAW § 2305(2) (McKinney 1989 & Supp. 1998); R.I. GEN. LAWS § 23-11-11 (Michie 1994 & Supp. 1997); TENN. CODE ANN. § 68-10-104 (Michie 1992 & Supp. 1997); TEX. FAM. CODE ANN. § 35.03(a)(3) (Vernon 1996 & Supp. 1998); UTAH CODE ANN. § 26-6-18 (Michie 1996 & Supp. 1998); WASH. REV. CODE § 70.24.110 (West 1988 & Supp. 1998); WIS. STAT. ANN. § 143.07(m) (West 1996 & Supp. 1997).

229. ALA. CODE § 22-8-6 (Michie 1995 & Supp. 1997); CAL. CIV. CODE § 34.7 (West 1996 & Supp. 1998); DEL. CODE ANN. tit. 13, § 708(a) (Michie 1995 & Supp. 1996); IDAHO CODE § 39-3801 (Michie 1987 & Supp. 1997); MONT. CODE ANN. § 41-1-402(c) (1997); OKLA. STAT. tit. 63, § 2602(A)(3) (West 1983 & Supp. 1998); PA. STAT. ANN. tit. 35, § 10103 (Purdon 1983 & Supp. 1998); TEX. FAM. CODE ANN. § 35.03 (Vernon 1996 & Supp. 1998); VA. CODE ANN. § 54.1-2969(D)(1) (Michie 1996 & Supp. 1998).

230. VT. STAT. ANN. tit. 18, § 4226 (Michie 1974 & Supp. 1997) (parent shall be notified if the condition of the minor requires immediate hospitalization).

231. ALA. CODE § 22-8-6 (Michie 1995 & Supp. 1997); ALASKA STAT. § 09.65.100(a)(4) (Michie 1996); CAL. CIV. CODE § 34.7 (West 1996 & Supp. 1998); IDAHO CODE § 39-3801 (Michie 1987 & Supp. 1997); IND. CODE § 16-8-5-1 (Burns 1994 & Supp. 1998); IOWA CODE § 140.9 (West 1994 & Supp. 1998); MASS. GEN. L. ch. 111, § 117 (Law. Co-op. 1994 & Supp. 1998); MISS. CODE ANN. § 41-41-13 (Law. Co-op. 1994 & Supp. 1997); NEV. REV. STAT. § 129.060 (Michie

1997); N.J. Rev. Stat. Ann. § 9:17A-4 (West 1995 & Supp. 1998); N.M. Stat. Ann. § 24-1-9 (Michie 1978 & Supp. 1998); N.C. Gen. Stat. § 90-21.5(a) (1993 & Supp. 1997); Ohio Rev. Code Ann. § 3709.24.1 (Anderson 1994 & Supp. 1997); Okla. Stat. tit. 63, § 1-532.1 (West 1983 & Supp. 1998); Pa. Stat. Ann. tit. 35, § 10103 (Purdon 1983 & Supp. 1998); R.I. Gen. Laws § 23-11-11 (Michie 1994 & Supp. 1997); S.D. Codified Laws Ann. 34-23-16 (Michie 1992 & Supp. 1998); Utah Code Ann. § 26-6-18 (Michie 1996 & Supp. 1998); Va. Code Ann. § 54.1-2969 (Michie 1996 & Supp. 1998); Wash. Rev. Code § 70.24.110 (West 1988 & Supp. 1998); Wis. Stat. § 143.07(m) (West 1996 & Supp. 1997); Wyo. Stat. § 35-4-131 (Michie 1997).

232. Ala. Code § 22-11A-19 (Michie 1995 & Supp. 1997); Ark. Code Ann. § 20-16-508(b) (Michie 1997); Del. Code Ann. tit. 13, § 708(c) (Michie 1995 & Supp. 1996); Colo. Rev. Stat. § 25-4-402(4) (West 1990 & Supp. 1997); Ga. Code Ann. § 31-17-7(b) (Michie 1996 & Supp. 1998); Haw. Rev. Stat. § 577A-3 (1993 & Supp. 1996); Ill. Rev. Stat. ch. 111, ¶ 4504, 4505 (West/Smith-Hurd 1993 & Supp. 1998); Kan. Stat. Ann. § 65-2892 (1988 & Supp. 1997); Ky. Rev. Stat. Ann. § 214.185(5) (Michie/Bobbs-Merrill 1990 & Supp. 1996); La. Rev. Stat. Ann. § 40:1065.1(c) (West 1986 & Supp. 1998); Me. Rev. Stat. Ann. tit. 32, § 3291 (West 1983 & Supp. 1996); Md. Health-Gen. Code Ann. § 20-102(e) (Michie 1995 & Supp. 1997); Mich. Comp. Laws § 333.5257(2) (West 1991 & Supp. 1998); Minn. Stat. § 144.346 (West 1992 & Supp. 1998); Mo. Rev. Stat. § 431.062(3) (West 1996 & Supp. 1997); Mont. Code Ann. § 41-1-403 (1997); Tex. Fam. Code Ann. § 35.03 (Vernon 1996 & Supp. 1998).

233. Conn. Gen. Stat. § 19a-216 (West 1994 & Supp. 1998); Fla. Stat. § 384.30(2) (Harrison 1991 & Supp. 1997); Neb. Rev. Stat. § 71-504 (1995 & Supp. 1997); N.H. Rev. Stat. Ann. § 141-C:18 (Butterworth 1994 & Supp. 1997); N.Y. Pub. Health Law § 2305(2) (McKinney 1989 & Supp. 1998); S.D. Codified Laws Ann. § 34-23-17 (Michie 1992 & Supp. 1998); Tenn. Code Ann. § 68-10-104 (Michie 1997); W. Va. Code § 16-4-10 (Michie 1996 & Supp. 1997).

234. Ariz. Rev. Stat. Ann. §§ 36-661(2), 36-663 (West 1989 & Supp. 1997); Cal. Health & Safety Code §§ 199.22, 199.27(a) (West 1996 & Supp. 1998); Colo. Rev. Stat. Ann. §§ 25-4-1405(6) (West 1990 & Supp. 1997); Del. Code. Ann. tit. 16, § 1202(f) (Michie 1995 & Supp. 1996); Fla. Stat. Ann. § 384.30 (Harrison 1991 & Supp. 1997); Iowa Code Ann. § 144.22 (West 1994 & Supp. 1998); Mich. Comp. Laws Ann. § 333.5127 (West 1991 & Supp. 1998); Mont. Code Ann. § 50 16 1007 (1997); N.M. Stat. Ann. § 24-2B-3 (Michie 1978 & Supp. 1998); N.Y. Pub. Health Law §§ 2780(5) & 2781(1) (McKinney 1989 & Supp. 1998); N.C. Gen. Stat. § 130A-148 (1993 & Supp. 1997); Ohio Rev. Code Ann. § 3701.24.2(B) (Anderson 1994 & Supp. 1997); Wis. Stat. Ann. § 146.02(2)(a)(4) (West 1996 & Supp. 1997).

235. Cal. Health & Safety Code § 199.27 (West 1996 & Supp. 1998); Colo. Rev. Stat. § 25-4-1405(6) (West 1990 & Supp. 1997); Del. Code Ann. tit. 16, § 1202(6)(f) (Michie 1995 & Supp. 1996); Iowa Code § 141.22 (West 1994 & Supp. 1998); Mich. Comp. Laws Ann. § 333.5127(i) (West 1991 & Supp. 1998); N.M. Stat. Ann. § 24-2B-3 (Michie 1978 & Supp. 1998); N.Y. Pub. Health Law §§ 2780, 2781 (McKinney 1989 & Supp. 1998); R.I. Gen. Laws § 23-11-17 (Michie 1994 & Supp. 1997).

236. States do so by allowing minors to obtain treatment for certain sexually transmitted diseases and classify HIV as a sexually transmitted disease; see, e.g., Ala. Admin. Code R. 420-4-1-.03 (Michie 1995 & Supp. 1997) (classifying HIV as an STD) and id. § 22-11A-19 (authorizing minors to consent to STD care); Fla. Stat. Ann. § 384.23 (Harrison 1991 & Supp. 1997) (requiring Florida Dept. of Health to consider HIV in designating STD) and id. § 384.30 (authorizing minors to consent to confidential treatment for STDs); Ill. Ann. Stat. ch. 111 1/2, ¶ 7403(3) (West/Smith-Hurd 1993 & Supp. 1998) (classifying HIV as an STD) and id. 4504-4505 (permitting minors age 12 or older to consent to VD diagnosis and treatment); Ky. Rev. Stat. Ann. § 214.185(2) (Michie/Bobbs-Merrill 1990 & Supp. 1996) (defining STD to include AIDS and HIV) and id. § 214.185 (giving minors ability to consent to diagnosis and treatment of VD); Mont. Code Ann. § 50-18-101 (1997) (defining AIDS as an STD); Mont. Admin. R. 16.28.202 (1997) (authorizing minors to consent to care for STD); Wash. Rev. Code Ann. § 70.24.017(13) (West 1988 & Supp. 1998) (defining STD to include HIV and AIDS); and id.

§ 24.110 (authorizing minors age 14 and older to consent to diagnosis and treatment of STDs); WYO. STAT. ANN. § 35-4-130(b) (Michie 1997) (defining AIDS as a reportable STD); and *id.* § 35-4-131 (authorizing minors to consent to examination and treatment for VD). Likewise, other states simply give authority to minors to seek treatment for sexually transmitted diseases; e.g., MISS. CODE. ANN. § 41-41-13 (Law. Co-op. 1994 & Supp. 1997) (permitting minors to obtain treatment for VD without parental consent); NEV. REV. STAT. ANN. § 129.060 (Michie 1997) (authorizing minors to consent to examination and treatment for VD); S.C. CODE ANN. § 20-7-290 (West/Law. Co-op. 1985 & Supp. 1997) (permitting minors to receive, without parental consent, health services the provider deems necessary to maintain the well-being of the minor); TENN. CODE. ANN. § 68-10-104 (Michie 1997) (authorizing minors to be examined, diagnosed, and treated for VD without parental consent); VT. STAT. ANN. tit. 18, § 4226 (Michie 1974 & Supp. 1997) (authorizing minors age 12 and older to consent to VD treatment).

237. COLO. REV. STAT. § 25-4-1405(6) (West 1990 & Supp. 1997); DEL. CODE ANN. tit. 16, § 1203 (Michie 1995 & Supp. 1996); MICH. COMP. LAWS § 333.5127(2) (West 1991 & Supp. 1998).

238. CAL. HEALTH & SAFETY CODE § 199.27 (West 1996 & Supp. 1998).

239. IOWA CODE § 141.22 (West 1994 & Supp. 1998).

240. ALA. CODE § 22-11A-19 (Michie 1995 & Supp. 1997); CAL. CIV. CODE § 34.7 (West 1996 & Supp. 1998); CAL. HEALTH & SAFETY CODE § 199.27 (West 1996 & Supp. 1998); DEL. CODE ANN. tit. 13, § 708 (Michie 1995 & Supp. 1996); DEL. CODE ANN. tit. 16, § 1202 (Michie 1995 & Supp. 1996); ILL. REV. STAT. ch. 111, ¶ 4504 (West/Smith-Hurd 1993 & Supp. 1998); VT. STAT. ANN. tit. 18, § 4226 (Michie 1974 & Supp. 1997).

241. IDAHO CODE § 39-3801 (Michie 1987 & Supp. 1997); N.H. REV. STAT. ANN. § 141-C:18(11) (Butterworth 1994 & Supp. 1997); N.D. CENT. CODE § 14-10-17 (Michie 1991 & Supp. 1997); WASH. REV. CODE § 70.24.110 (West 1988 & Supp. 1998).

242. Thera M. Meehan, Holger Hansen, and Waldo C. Klein, "The Impact of Parental Consent on HIV Testing of Minors," *American Journal of Public Health* 87 (1997):1338–1341.

243. Laurie S. Zabin, Marilyn B. Hirsch, Mark R. Emerson, and Elizabeth Raymond, "To Whom Do Inner-City Minors Talk About Their Pregnancies? Adolescents' Communication With Parents and Parent Surrogates," *Family Planning Perspectives* 24 (1992):148–154, 173.

244. Bruce Ambuel and Julian Rappaport, "Developmental Trends in Adolescents' Psychological and Legal Competence to Consent to Abortion," *Law and Human Behavior* 16 (1992):129–154.

245. Forty-seven percent of adolescents do not return for results; *see* Surgeon General, Antonia Novello, cited in Levesque, "The Peculiar Place of Adolescents in the HIV-AIDS Epidemic: Unusual Progress & Usual Inadequacies in 'Adolescent Jurisprudence.'"

246. *See, e.g.,* IOWA CODE ANN. § 144.22 (West 1994 & Supp. 1998). Protection of confidentiality is a critical element in adolescents' willingness to seek health care for HIV. A surprisingly high number of at-risk adolescents—84%—would agree to HIV testing if the test were anonymous and confidential; Lawrence S. Freidman, Lee Strunin, and Ralph Hingson, "Survey of Attitudes, Knowledge, and Behavior Related to HIV testing of Adolescents and Young Adults Enrolled in Alcohol and Drug Treatment," *Journal of Adolescent Health* 14 (1993): 442–445.

247. *See, e.g.,* OHIO REV. CODE ANN. § 3701.242(B) (Anderson 1994 & Supp. 1997) (minor may give consent for an HIV test, but parents are not liable for costs of test provided without their consent).

248. Mary Jane Rotheram-Borus and Cheryl Koopman, "Adolescents." In *Children and AIDS,* ed. Margaret L. Stuber (Washington, DC: American Psychiatric Press).

249. *See* chapter 4.

250. Susan L. Rosenthal, Frank M. Biro, Sheila S. Cohen, Paul A. Succop, and Lawrence R. Stanberry, "Strategies for Coping With Sexually Transmitted Diseases by Adolescent Females," *Adolescence* 30 (1995):655–666.

251. There is no general right to treatment. The major exception, of course, is if the adolescent is in the care of the state because they are in need of treatment.

Chapter 4
REGULATING SEXUALLY ACTIVE ADOLESCENTS

Having examined how laws relate to adolescents' transition to sexual activity, this chapter continues the social science analysis of legal responses to adolescents' sexual activity. The chapter examines laws that regulate contraceptive use, abortion, adolescent parenthood, and marriage. As with the previous chapter, the numerous concerns distill to one fundamental consideration: the manner the law should confer on adolescents, parents, and communities the legal power to control the outcome of sexual activity and the actual relationships that lead to sexual activity. The conclusion highlights that, although research in this area may still remain scattered and, as we have seen, conceptions of adolescents' rights remain variable and developed in a piecemeal fashion, the current understanding of the law and social science evidence does allow for important conclusions. These conclusions offer useful suggestions for alternative conceptions and developments in the laws that affect adolescents' sexuality and sexual development as the suggestions highlight the need to focus beyond laws that directly regulate adolescent sexuality. The alternative points of interest provide the basis for propositions developed in this chapter and the remaining seven.

Regulating Access to Contraceptives

The right to contraceptives reveals an attempt to ensure adolescents' rights to services. As adolescents gain increasing rights to obtain contraceptives, however, the right to access nevertheless still remains limited and curtailable by parental concerns and the extent to which the contraceptives will be made available by other parties. Social science evidence relating to pregnancy and sexually transmitted disease prevention suggests that concern about adolescents' access to contraceptives, although an important step in protecting adolescents and their rights, fails to address adolescents' needs and even fails to allow adolescents to make effective use of available contraceptives.

The Law and Adolescent Contraception

Although the right to privacy in intimate matters relating to reproductive rights is more frequently discussed in the abortion context, the Supreme Court first explicitly addressed the right to privacy in the context of access to contraceptives. About 35 years ago, in *Griswold v. Connecticut,* the Supreme Court held that the Constitution protects the right of married couples to seek contraceptives. The Court observed that the enumerated rights of the Bill of Rights have "penumbras" that extend to unmentioned protections necessary to protect the explicitly guaranteed rights.[1] In this instance, the right lied within the "zone of privacy created by several fundamental constitutional guarantees."[2] Having established that right, the Court then expanded the right to nonmarried couples in *Eisenstadt v. Baird*[3] Invoking an equal protection analysis, the Court found that the right extended to unmarried couples as well as to individuals. In an often-quoted passage, the Court found the right fundamental as it announced "the right of the *individual,* married or single, to be free from unwarranted governmental intrusion into matters so fundamentally affecting a person as the decision whether to bear or beget a child."[4]

The extension of the right to adolescents, those referred to as minors or juveniles by the legal system, came rather quickly and only once, in *Carey v. Population Services International.*[5] That case involved the constitutionality of a state ban on the sale or distribution of contraceptives to minors under 16 years of age. The plurality opinion explicitly extended the right of privacy to minors seeking contraception as it noted that "the right of privacy in connection with decisions affecting procreation extends to minors as well as adults."[6] Because the Court had previously asserted that states could not impose a blanket prohibition, or even a blanket requirement of parental consent, on the choice of a minor to terminate her pregnancy, the Constitution would also prohibit a blanket prohibition of the distribution of contraceptives.

Minors may have the right to contraceptives, but minors still may be treated differently than adults. Neither of the first two Supreme Court decisions dealing with access to contraceptives addressed whether and to what extent a state still could regulate an individual's access to contraceptives. The case that did extend the right to use contraceptives to minors, however, mentioned the possibility. Although the Court in *Carey* could have ended its discussion at the point that states could not impose a blanket prohibition on the distribution of contraceptives, because the statute in question had placed a blanket prohibition of distribution to minors under 16 years of age, the Court continued to assess the state's asserted interests in reducing sexual activity among minors. The Court noted that any restriction on the right to privacy in connection with procreation decisions would have to serve a "significant state interest . . . that is not present in the case of an adult."[7] Given that possibility, the Court sought to determine whether the state had demonstrated a sufficiently strong interest to uphold a ban on the distribution of condoms to minors. Likewise, and significantly, the Court interpreted the need to consider state interests in the context of parental consent requirements, and how they may be permissible in procreative rights contexts so long as there are no blanket prohibitions. The Court flatly rejected that the state could have an interest in deterring sexual activity by constricting access to contraceptives, finding that "it would be plainly unreasonable to assume that the State has prescribed pregnancy and the birth of an unwanted child as punishment for fornication."[8] In the end, it was only after the careful consideration of state interests that the Court rejected the ban.

Although the Court has not readdressed the issue of minor's access to contraceptives and most consider the matter closed, three points remain to be determined. Because *Carey* dealt with nonprescriptive contraceptives, it remains to be determined whether it provides a strong foundation to challenge parental consent or notice requirements as applied to prescriptive contraceptives, such as the oral contraceptive pill or the intrauterine device. What also remains to be determined is whether, and to what extent, a state may regulate *access* to all forms of contraceptives. A third issue involves the extent to which third parties may seek to make contraceptives available, regardless of the individual attempts of minors to seek, or parents to prohibit, access to contraceptive devices. Thus although the extent to which states may regulate minors' access to contraceptives remains an open issue, these three points are worthy of elaboration.

First, fewer than half the states statutorily provide that minors may obtain contraceptive services.[9] Although state statutes generally are silent on minor's access to contraceptive medical services, most states adopt policies that explicitly permit minors to obtain contraceptive services on their own consent.[10] Such treatment is significant given that some prescriptive methods have attendant health risks.[11] Note, however, that these statutes explicitly exclude sterilization and abortion or have been interpreted as doing so. These exceptions reflect the notion that sterilization and abortion are significantly different in terms of their impact on the minor and potential infringement on the rights and obligations of parents that states may regulate their access more strictly. Just as states have been free to offer access to contraceptive devices, they also remain free to limit the extent to which some contraceptives may be made available by the state. For example, several states actually prohibit the prescription, dispensation, distribution, or other dissemination of contraceptives in schools.[12] Other states prohibit the use of public funds to purchase or dispense contraceptives in school.[13] Note that states simply have the obligation not to impose a blanket ban on the availability of contraceptives, not to make such devices available.

Second, cases that have addressed issues of access have approached them on statutory grounds and in the context of parental challenges to their children's access to contraceptive services. The most notable series of these cases involves the "squeal rule" cases. These cases dealt with a rule that required family planning clinics that received Title X funding to notify parents of a minor seeking contraceptives before dispensing them to the minor.[14] That regulation was introduced to enforce Congress's amendment to Title X to include a provision that would encourage family involvement in efforts to seek family planning services from clinics funded by government monies.[15] Cases reviewing the challenges held that the regulation was outside of the authority of the agency because the regulation directly conflicted with congressional intent;[16] given that statutory basis, the courts did not have to proceed to constitutional issues. Again, although the federal regulations were not adopted, states remain free to impose parental notification. Despite that freedom, only a few of the state statutes that permit minors to consent to family planning services have provisions pertaining to parental notification for the minor's application for receipt of such services; and almost all of these statutes allow but do not compel notification.[17]

Third, cases analyzing constitutional grounds have found protection for minors. These cases have arisen in two contexts: in the context of family planning programs and school condom distribution efforts. In the context of federally funded family planning programs, only one case has decided the limits on access to contraceptives with the benefit of the landmark abortion decisions as existing legal precedent. Although the case also was decided on statutory grounds, its constitutional analysis is still illustrative. In *Planned Parenthood Ass'n v. Matheson*,[18] a federal court confronted the challenge to a Utah law that required parental notification before a minor could be provided with contraceptives. After linking issues of abortion and contraception in legal precedent and in terms of the decisions to obtain them, the court noted that the state could "not impose a blanket parental notification requirement on minors who seek to exercise their constitutionally protected right to decide whether to bear or beget a child by using contraceptives."[19] The court declared the statute unconstitutional on grounds that it failed to provide an adequate procedure whereby a minor could demonstrate that parental notification or consent was against her best interests to obtain contraceptives confidentially. Without the assurance of confidentiality, the fear was that adolescents would avoid clinics and suffer the consequences of sexual activity. Another case, this time from the perspective of parents who challenged, also illustrates the general trend. *Doe v. Irwin*[20] involved a challenge by parents who claimed that family planning clinics should abide by parental consent requirements. In that case, the federal court of appeals ruled that a publicly operated clinic's practice of distributing contraceptives to minors without notifying their parents did not violate parental rights. The court's reasoning was two-fold. First, the state did not require or prohibit the activity, unlike the facts presented in the "parental rights" cases of *Meyer, Pierce,* and *Yoder.* The court interpreted the program as one that did not impose "compulsory requirements or prohibitions which affect the rights of the plaintiffs" but one that "merely established a voluntary birth control clinic."[21] Second, the case involved an adolescent's individual rights to privacy, which includes the right to obtain contraceptives. In matters that involve obtaining contraceptives through clinics, then, minors have a statutory right to services. There is little dispute that clinics may distribute contraceptives to minors without parental notification.

Although there may not be disputes about the power of clinics to provide contraceptive services to minors, the issue remains far from settled in other contexts. In the environment adolescents most often find themselves, schools, the only two cases to confront the issue have taken fundamentally opposing approaches. The first case, *Alfonso v. Fernandez,* involved the adoption of a condom-availability program that did not include any parental consent or parental notification provisions.[22] Parents challenged the failure to have an opt-out provision on two grounds. The first involved the parental right to raise their children as they saw fit. The second proposed that implementing the program violated parent's constitutional right to the free exercise of their religion. The second argument was found unpersuasive; precedent clearly has established that a governmental requirement that a person exposed to an idea they find objectionable on religious grounds does not constitute a burden on free exercise as proscribed by the First Amendment. The first argument was found persuasive. The court construed the condom-availability program as a health service, a domain generally under the control of parental rights. The court reasoned that, given the well-recognized right parents have in rearing and educating their children in accord with their own views, the state would require a compelling state interest to justify departing from the common law and statutory prohibitions against providing medical treatment without prior parental consent. The court could not find a compelling state interest to justify the parents "being forced to surrender a parental right—specifically, to influence and guide the sexual activity of their children without State interference."[23] The court reasoned that, because minors could obtain condoms in nonschool clinics without their parents' knowledge, the block of parental involvement in the school distribution plan was not necessary to meet the state's compelling interest in preventing AIDS. The policy was invalid without a parental opt-out provision that allowed parental consent.

The second case, *Curtis v. School Committee,*[24] was factually identical to *Alfonso* in its design of a condom-availability program without any parental involvement provisions. Unlike the previous case, however, the highest court of the state unanimously upheld the program based on the failure of parents to demonstrate that the condom-availability programs placed a coercive burden on their rights. Using the element of compulsion as the decisive factor, the court concluded, "Although exposure to condom vending machines and to the program itself may offend the moral and religious sensibilities of the plaintiffs, mere exposure to programs offered at school does not amount to unconstitutional interference with parental liberties without the existence of some compulsory aspect to the program."[25] Even the "compulsory" nature of attendance laws did not create a sufficiently strong burden on parental rights.

The Supreme Court has denied certiorari—the discretionary device through which the Court selects the cases it wishes to hear—to the most recent case involving condom distribution programs, even though both cases squarely conflicted with one another in terms of fact.[26] In terms of law, the cases differed considerably. Although both opinions turned on the construal of state coercion and infringement on parental rights (not the rights of minors), they nevertheless involved infringement of allegedly different rights. The first case saw coercion in the form of medical service, and had been challenged on statutory grounds that gave parents rights to control medical service delivery. The second had no such statute and was thus more able to find no violated right because the content of educational matters could be construed as within the province of school officials. In addition, none of the cases seriously address the issue of blanket parental consent to have their children either "opt-in" or to have their children "opt-out;" nor do they consider blanket notification requirements.

Given current Supreme Court jurisprudence, states could be allowed to control without blanket bans or blanket control given to parents over their children's fundamental rights. The cases reflect the wide disparity in rights adolescents may enjoy, the continued power of parental rights, and why the Supreme Court will likely continue to condone efforts to restrict the rights of minors.

In sum, parents generally do not have direct control over the extent to which their children have access to contraceptives. When parents have challenged the state's attempts to make contraceptives available for use, the major rationale for limiting adolescents' access to contraceptives emerges from the parental right to provide guidance to one's children and to protect adolescents' health and morality. The limit and control of adolescents' rights in this context involves the extent to which this parental liberty interest enables parents to protest when the state does not overtly restrict parental choice but instead supplements and supplants what traditionally has been taught in the home. The legal mandates reflect the general rule that adolescents have rights so long as parents do not attempt to intrude or offer support to actually obtain services.

Realities of Adolescent Life

The realities of teenage sexual activity served as rationales to design and implement controversial programs that aim to ensure youth's access to condoms and other contraceptive devices. The prevalence of sexual activity has been reported in previous chapters. As we have seen, more than half of all high school students report engaging in sexual intercourse, and a significantly greater percentage report being sexually active. The Centers for Disease Control reports that more than 60% of male students and more than 50% of female students become sexually active before celebrating their 17th birthday.[27] In terms of contraceptives, it is difficult to underestimate the significance of high levels of sexual activity. Sexual activity places adolescents at risk for pregnancy. The high rates of pregnancy in the United States is unmatched by other industrialized societies, even though levels of adolescent sexual activity are about the same.[28] Since the late 1980s, however, it undoubtedly has been the AIDS epidemic that has led to an emphasis on the importance of protected sexual activity. Efforts to stem the tide of teenage pregnancy and the spread of sexually transmitted diseases, including AIDS, focus on condoms as the most effective preventative device.[29] Both of these public health issues, however, have resulted in efforts to encourage the diligent contraceptive use of sexually active teenagers as the major strategy to reduce rates.[30] The high rates provide states with a significant interest in preventing pregnancy and the spread of HIV among minors.

The most striking aspect of the AIDS epidemic and teenage pregnancy is that surveys repeatedly reveal that teenagers may know a lot about these issues, at least as much as adults, but that knowledge has yet to affect actual behaviors. Since the 1970s, sexually transmitted diseases, unintended pregnancies, and other problems that result from sexual activity have increased among adolescents in the United States.[31] The vast majority of sexually active teenagers do not regularly use condoms.[32] Moreover, one quarter to one third of sexually active adolescents never use any form of contraceptive.[33] The result is that teenage pregnancy rates remain high and rates of HIV infection among adolescents make them the fastest growing age group in contacting AIDS.[34] Thus the issue is not so much one of mere knowledge but one of practice. The problems associated with risky teenage sexual activity have not been significantly reduced despite relatively sustained efforts to do so.

Although the need may be apparent, efforts to encourage contraceptive use remain problematic in that parents feel, and the courts usually agree, that the state's encouragement of an activity that they oppose crosses the line between supplementing parental guidance and supplanting it. Despite that general tendency, the empirical evidence suggests that the fears may be unwarranted. The first fear that providing contraceptives increases sexual activity has yet to garner empirical support. For example, a major controversial issue is the belief that dispensing condoms in public schools will increase the rate of sexual activity among minors. The few studies that have been published indicate otherwise. In a recent review of knowledge of, and easy accessibility to, contraception and whether it promotes promiscuity, the authors characterized the association as ''myth.''[35]

The second fear involves perceptions of what constitutes distribution. The belief is that those empowered to distribute condoms and other contraceptive devices—for example, school nurses and medical personnel—do so aggressively. In reality, however, ''distribution'' is a misnomer for existing programs. For example, the notion that schools that adopt distribution programs actively distribute condoms is incorrect. Schools simply make them available to those students who request them, and make them available in a variety of ways such as through health clinics, health resource centers, licensed physicians, and trained school faculty advisors.[36] Students are not required to seek or receive them. The failure to require direct distribution and the use of third parties helps to ensure respect for parental rights: The services are not mandated and other adults may ensure that adolescents make careful decisions, two factors critical to legal analyses that support the proper recognition of adolescents' rights in a manner similarly recognized in other contexts.[37]

The third fear is that many parents do not approve of the distribution of contraceptives. However, a significant majority of American adults, in addition to minors, favor the distribution of condoms in public schools.[38] That public support for the distribution of condoms reflects not a shift in perceptions of morality so much as a belief that such a step will reduce the number of teenage pregnancies and the likelihood that students will contact AIDS or other sexually transmitted diseases.[39] Society, irrespective of cultural, moral, or religious values, supports the need for a serious educational defense mechanism.

The fourth fear derives from the proposition that constricting access to contraceptives deters sexual activity. Available evidence casts doubt on such suggestions. For example, studies of adolescents at family planning clinics indicate that parental involvement requirements will not significantly deter sexual activity: The decision to engage in sexual activity is made irrespective of the presence of contraceptives.[40]

The fifth issue involves the manner parental notification requirements keep youth away from services. Fear of such requirements or of parental knowledge contributes to keeping already sexually active teenagers from approaching clinics to receive the services they need.[41] Fear that parents may find out about clinic attendance or unfounded fears that clinics have parental-involvement requirements are cited by teenagers as major contributory factors in their typically lengthy delays between their initiation of sexual intercourse and attempts to receive family planning services.[42] On average, these delays are more than 16 1/2 months; and fewer than 15% of patients come to clinics as virgins.[43] These findings are rather significant. If those who were determined to practice family planning by attending a clinic postpone for more than half a year because of parental involvement requirements and about one quarter of those report that they would stop coming to clinics if parents had to be involved,[44] it is logical to conclude that youth less motivated to seek such services will be kept away even more.[45]

The sixth issue is the controversy that suggests that making contraceptives available leads immature adolescents to engage in sexual activity. Available evidence, however, suggests otherwise: Teenagers who seek contraception before engaging in sexual intercourse demonstrate a level of maturity and responsibility worthy of recognition. It would seem that the mature minor or one whose "best interests" would not be served by a notification requirement have a right to confidential services.[46] It seems, then, and as recognized by Congress and the courts, that assurance of confidentiality plays a critical role in attracting adolescents to clinics and that mandatory parental involvement deters adolescents from obtaining services.

The HIV/AIDS, abortion, pregnancy, and teenage childbearing crises have resulted in the need to ensure not only that adolescents are entitled to the contraceptives but also that they actually use them. This reality is that condom availability without parental consent in nonschool settings does not translate into condoms being readily available. The failure of existing methods by which contraceptives are available through drug stores and family planning clinics has not reduced rates of AIDS infection or pregnancy among adolescents. Public schools have the unique ability to reach large numbers of teenagers and can play a role in alerting those who are sexually active of the importance of using condoms to reduce the risk of disease and other negative outcomes of sexual behavior. In addition, condom availability protects those students who already are sexually active and might otherwise engage in unprotected sexual activity.

Although public schools may not have the duty to implement such programs, they may not then adopt a blanket parental consent requirement, which would confer on parents the power to veto their children's decision to seek contraceptives. If they do adopt such parental consent requirements, they must at least adopt some form of bypass procedures. The latest review of condom-availability programs reveals that 39% do not involve parents at all, 21% require prior parental consent, and 41% allow parents to opt their children out.[47] Thus despite sharing the same justification for dispensing condoms, schools vary in the ways they structure their programs. Likewise, it remains to be determined how many schools allow for blanket parental rejection of condom distributions, whether condoms are allowed in theory or actual practice.

Another point involves the issue that arises in the group of parents who remain disinterested. The state may have an interest in engaging them, which would lead to involving family members in contraceptives decisions. The lack of concern of indifferent parents does not necessitate placement of a burden on those parents who do care. The next critical issue that arises, then, is whether those who actually offer guidance and direction to their children have the impact that they are believed to have: Both pregnancy and AIDS research has addressed the issue and their findings are worthy of emphasis.

In terms of pregnancy, research suggests that communication with parents does lead to increased use of contraceptives. For example, research reveals that adolescents who reported that their mothers had discussed contraception with them were about three times as likely to have used an effective method at last coitus as were those who did not report such communications.[48] Although other studies have found that actual communication did not reflect contraceptive use,[49] sexually active students who do practice contraception tend to have higher quality communications with their parents.[50] Pregnant adolescents report that communication with their mothers does increase their likelihood of using contraceptives.[51] The fact that they are pregnant, though, is rather telling. Although teenagers who discuss contraceptive use with their parents may be more likely to use contraceptives, such discussions about birth control have little relationship to the *consistency* with which contraceptives are used.[52] In terms of the importance of family communication in the context of HIV infection and AIDS prevention, three recent studies suggest an important trend. Adolescents who have discussed AIDS with their parents and methods of protection are more likely to have attempted to avoid HIV infection through decreasing the number of sexual partners and using condoms.[53] Yet whether parents were effective in reducing the incidence of HIV infection remains to be determined. Although the likelihood of seeking protection may increase, the use of protective techniques remains inconsistent.

Researchers, however, have uncovered the factors that lead to consistent contraceptive use. One of the strongest and most consistent predictors of contraceptive use is the age of the adolescent.[54] In general, adolescents who experience intercourse at an early age (16 years or younger), are less likely to plan the event, less likely to use birth control, more likely to be in casual relationships, and more apt to use unreliable sources of information.[55] In addition and although little information exists about the conversations or events that lead to intercourse or the negotiations around the use of contraception, we do know that teenagers in stable relationships are more likely to use contraceptives.[56] That finding is significant in that adolescents typically proceed along different normative developmental patterns in the sequence of heterosexual behaviors.[57] Sexual situations that develop quickly from those that unfold more slowly would have an impact on contraception and protections from sexually transmitted diseases.[58] However, relationships often take different paths, with some groups of youth less likely to progress from kissing to petting and to intercourse and more likely to move more rapidly toward intercourse.[59] Groups have different normative expectations regarding intercourse, and how to protect them remains an unsettled area of public health concern.

Several studies associate pregnancy risk with such variables as family stress, family conflict, and family cohesion.[60] Other studies observe a relationship between the quality of the parent–child relationship and adolescents' sexual activity.[61] Research relating to AIDS/ HIV finds that family organization strongly relates to high-risk sexual behavior. Adolescents with limited family availability and low levels of parental monitoring and support are more likely to engage in high-risk behaviors.[62] In addition, sexually active adolescents with less family availability and less parental monitoring and support are less likely to use condoms.[63] Likewise, adolescents who engage in high-risk sexual behavior report more coercive family interchanges.[64] Thus sexually active adolescents with less supportive family environments engage in riskier sexual behaviors.

The finding that girls do not experience their first sexual experiences in a positive way and that they often feel pressured has serious implications for ways in which girls interpret sexual experiences. First, considerable evidence reveals that, to reduce their guilt and anxiety over early and ''causal'' sex, young women interpret these experiences in terms of ''love'' and forego condoms as precautions against HIV.[65] Researchers continue to show that reluctance to claim ownership of one's own sexual behavior and sexual guilt result in noncontraceptive use or use of less effective contraceptive methods.[66] Second, reports indicate little change in ''safer'' sex practices by girls, mainly because of a low sense of self-efficacy and control: Despite knowing more about sexual risks, change does not necessarily occur because girls rely on their partner's sexual behavior and view, for example, condom use as discretionary on his part.[67] Third, researchers report that girls who frequently feel guilt about sexual interactions experienced their first sexual intercourse at a younger age and are twice as likely to have been under the influence of alcohol or some other mind-altering substance at the time of their first intercourse.[68] The data support the proposal that alcohol offers youth an enabling script that allows them to avoid guilt about the sexual experience, which also places them at risk for less healthy responses of implied consent for first intercourse, rather than giving verbal consent,[69] and then the greater likelihood of casual sexual experiences with a greater number of sex partners and with recurring patterns of noncontraceptive use.[70] The negative consequences of guilt appear to be pervasive and highly interrelated with unhealthy sexual scripts. These findings suggest that, as much as the law may seek to encourage parental involvement, several forces challenge the potential effectiveness of such efforts and suggest a need for considering alternative approaches to dealing with adolescents' contraceptive needs and concerns.

Preliminary Conclusion

The realities of adolescents seeking contraceptives paint a bleak picture. High rates of sexual activity continue to be met with an increased incidence of AIDS and adolescents' low and inconsistent contraceptive use. As the legal systems concern themselves with efforts to ensure access, and find considerable opposition that justifies placing limits on access, research indicates that access simply does not ensure effective use. Effective efforts move beyond issues of access and seek to ensure basic skills and abilities to counter the forces that place adolescents in situations that increase the likelihood of sexual activity and decrease the likelihood of protection from the negative outcomes of ineffective contraceptive behavior.

Regulating Access to Abortion

The weight given adolescents' rights to medical testing, treatment, and contraceptives begins to wane when adolescents actually reach the stage in which they must resolve pregnancy decisions. At this point, the legal system generally allows parents a greater voice in matters affecting their children. The legal system allows for greater protection of parental rights as it attempts to ensure greater parental control and participation in adolescents' decision making. But as with other areas of adolescents' sexual rights, the empirical evidence questions the utility and effectiveness of these measures.

The Law and Adolescent Abortion

Since *Roe v. Wade*,[71] individuals' decisions to have abortions have been deemed a fundamental right protected under the Constitution. Although the Court held absolute prohibition impermissible, it explicitly abstained from deciding whether some forms of regulations may legitimately serve a state's interest and allow limits on the right to abortion.[72] A result of those cases was the promulgation of several statutes that attempted to regulate abortions and the subsequent attempt by the Supreme Court to define the permissible bounds of regulation that state legislatures may impose on an individual's right to obtain an abortion. Noting that "few situations in which denying a minor the right to make an important decision will have consequences so grave and indelible" as the decision to obtain an abortion, the Supreme Court has recognized that a pregnant minor has a substantial interest in being free to choose to have an abortion.[73] Moreover, the Court deemed the interest analogous to the constitutional rights possessed by adults, in the often repeated phrase that constitutional rights are not dormant until majority is attained: The right extended in *Roe* does not appear "magically only when one attains the state-defined age of majority[;] minors, as well as adults, are protected by the Constitution and possess constitutional rights."[74] Although the Court extends rights to minors, it still places a significant caveat on a minor's right to abortion. A state may legitimately restrict a minor's constitutional right if the restriction promotes a "significant state interest . . . not present in the case of an adult."[75] The issue and validity of state action regulating a minor's abortion decision depends on the specific interests that the state seeks to promote. Thus if a "significant" state interest is present, then "the constitutional rights of children cannot be equated with those of adults."[76]

In the context of abortion decisions and the regulation of minor's rights, the Supreme Court has acknowledged three "significant" state interests that may justify intrusion in minor's rights. These legitimate interests were explicitly explored in the foundational case of minor's rights, *Bellotti v. Baird,* to include three concerns: (a) protecting the unique vulnerability of children; (b) recognizing a child's diminished capacity to make intelligent decisions; and (c) facilitating the traditional parental role of child rearing.[77] Thus the Court recognizes the state action requiring parental consent or involvement in important decisions of minors to protect its youth from adverse governmental action and from a child's own immaturity. These protections essentially involve three practical concerns. The first concern regards the minor's limited constitutional right to choose an abortion. The second issue relates to a state's interest in ensuring that the parents are involved in the decisions. The last consideration pertains to the parent's interest in participating and aiding in their child's growth, development, and physical and emotional well-being. To balance these potentially conflicting interests, the Court has developed a framework that attempts to reach a proper resolution for each minor who seeks an abortion. If states decide to require pregnant minors to obtain one or both parents' consent to an abortion, it must provide an alternative procedure by which the authorization for the abortion may be obtained.

The Court noted that the procedure chosen by the state could not "in fact amount to the 'absolute, and possibly arbitrary, veto'" that the Court had found impermissible.[78] The Court entitles any minor to show that she is mature enough and well-informed enough to consult with her physician, independent of parental wishes. In the alternative, if she is not able to make the decision, then the abortion may be had if it is determined to be in her best interests. The statute in question in *Bellotti* only allowed a minor to obtain judicial consent on the condition that parental consent already had been denied. Because the statute was determined to unduly burden a minor's right to an abortion, the Court concluded that "every minor must have the opportunity—if she so desires—to go directly to court without first consulting or notifying her parents."[79] In essence, the Court held that the state does not hold the authority to give a third party, a parent, veto power over a minor's fundamental right, which in this instance involved the limited right to *seek* an abortion.

The Supreme Court has since reexamined, in numerous cases, the parameters within which a state may require parental consent for minors to explore the possibility of obtaining abortions and actually consenting to the abortive procedures. The matter is now settled law, as plainly stated by the Supreme Court in its most recent decision, *Planned Parenthood v. Casey.*[80] In that case, the Court firmly stated its position as settled: "We have been over most of this ground before. Our cases establish, and we reaffirm today, that a State may require a minor seeking an abortion to obtain the consent of a parent or guardian, *provided that there is an adequate judicial bypass procedure.*"[81] The Court, then, affirmatively has declared that minors have a right, although limited, to reproductive autonomy. Equally important, the cases limit the extent to which the state may intrude on the minor's decision-making process by prohibiting states from delegating absolute veto power to a third party.

The case reflects the extent to which adolescents will be treated differently. The *Casey* Court had confronted the constitutionality of state requirements that women consult their husbands or parents before terminating their pregnancies. The Court struck down the spousal notification statute on the grounds that it subjected married women to an effective spousal veto. The Court, however, upheld the one-parent parental consent statute for unemancipated young women under 18 so long as the statute provided a judicial bypass provision. Under these provisions, a minor may forego obtaining parental consent by petitioning a court for authorization on the grounds that she is either sufficiently mature to give informed consent or that obtaining an abortion is in her best interests. The Court requires an opportunity for case-by-case examination of each pregnant minor's maturity. The Court has ruled that when a minor chooses to exercise the judicial-bypass option, the judge must authorize the abortion if he or she deems the teenager mature enough to make the decision by herself, or if the adolescent is determined immature, that an abortion is in her best interests. The bypass proceeding must be confidential and, at least in theory, expeditious and the minor must have an opportunity to appeal denied petitions.

The Court also has held that a state may require a doctor to notify one or both parents of their daughter's plan to terminate a pregnancy.[82] The requirement may be imposed even if the parents are divorced or were never married and also if one of the parents has never known or supported the young woman. So far, the Court has specifically declined to rule on whether a state must provide a judicial bypass procedure if it requires the notification of only one parent.[83] However, the Court has held that a state must do so if it requires a doctor to inform both parents.[84] Ultimately, the Court resolved the issue by permitting states to require minors who seek abortions to obtain the consent of their parents so long as there was an alternative, such as a judicial bypass. In such instances, the minor must demonstrate that she is sufficiently mature to make her own decision regarding an abortion.

Although the constitutional permutations of an adolescent's right to obtain an abortion has become increasingly settled, the statutory frameworks that currently exist and respond to the constitutional doctrine regarding abortion are less clear. As we have seen, Supreme Court decisions do not allow states to require parental consent to abortions for all minors who wish to abort pregnancies. This constitutional floor leaves considerable room for differences in the manner in which states may treat the rights of minors who seek abortions. Two major variations dominate.

The first variation does not distinguish between minors' access to abortions and those of adults. Twelve states do allow minors access at least to the same extent that adults are allowed.[85] The second variation, involving the remaining states, requires some degree of parental involvement in minors' abortion decisions. This variation comes in three forms. First, three states require counseling for minors and provisions for counseling may require parental involvement in addition to the other two ways of involving parents.[86] Second, 23 states require parental consent but offer some form of "by-pass" for some minors.[87] Third, 14 states require parental notification.[88] The last two variations permit a by-pass if the minor is found mature and well-enough informed to make the abortion decision herself; if not found mature, the determination must be whether consulting her parents would be in her best interests.

In sum, the Supreme Court has been fairly consistent in its consideration of parental involvement legislation. The Court has found unconstitutional legislation in which one parent has the power to veto a teenager's abortion decisions. The justices continue to find troublesome the question of whether a minor's constitutional right to privacy equals that of adults. In addition, even though parental involvement is viewed positively, the Court has not allowed parental rights to carry more weight than those of teenagers. It remains ironic that as the Court insists on laws that allow adolescents leeway in demonstrating their maturity and making their own decisions, legislatures continue to limit teenagers' access to abortions while still crafting legislation that both meets their goal and remains constitutional.

Realities of Adolescent Life

Strong rationales support the recognition that parents retain a significant interest in controlling their children's access to abortive services. First, attempts to give adolescents greater control may send them the wrong message. Decisions about sexuality relate to other parts of adolescents' lives, which parents control. Likewise, statutes that give adolescents control affirm the adolescents' attitude that their sexuality is solely a private matter. Yet adolescents' sexual behaviors entail numerous public consequences. Parenthood, responsible sex with others, and responsibility to themselves to delay sexual activity until they are emotionally and psychologically prepared all impact society. In addition, encouraging proper parental involvement in their children's lives is a prudent measure. The law assumes that parents are situated to decide and act on their children's best interests and makes parents financially and socially responsible for their children.

These rationales, however, do not necessarily relate to the assumptions made by parental consent and notification laws and are not necessarily supported by evidence investigating those basic assumptions. As with other laws relating to adolescent sexuality, laws involving adolescent abortion make numerous assumptions that may be subjected to empirical analyses. In this area, six assumptions emerge as critical to current statutory frameworks that limit adolescents' access to abortions. These assumptions have generated much more empirical scrutiny of laws than any other assumptions made by the Supreme Court decisions and state legislations relating to adolescent sexuality.

The first area of inquiry involves assumptions that minors are necessarily incompetent decision makers. Significance of this assumption arises from the rationale that, with adults, the state may not interfere with the right to privacy in abortion decision making because adults presumably are able to consent for treatment and understand the consequences and implications of such decisions.[89] In contrast, minors may lack sufficient maturity to make informed decisions regarding pregnancy resolutions, a possibility that justifies parental involvement.[90] Thus the state may assume that adolescents need protections from their own immature and improvident decisions unless they can show that they are sufficiently mature to make decisions on their own. Yet the pivotal concept on which a minor's right to abortion rests—maturity—has yet to be defined by the courts and no reliable and valid measures exist. To further complicate matters, none of the statutes define maturity, even though that is the standard judges are supposed to use to determine whether to grant the girls' requests. This is problematic in that the unavailability of precise guidelines necessarily renders assessments of a minor's maturity to considerations based on the judges' own individual interpretations.

Controversies in law are not reflected in psychological research. Several factors may be used to assess adolescent's maturity. Researchers generally rely on whether the adolescent understands possible outcomes, is able to reason about positive and negative consequences of each outcome, understands how values are attached to different outcomes, and makes a proactive, uncoerced decision. Using these broad criteria, few differences exist between minors' and adults' decision-making abilities. Older minors (those ages 14 through 17) appear as mature as adults in their decision making processes and abilities.[91] Researchers also find that minors who are less able to make informed decisions are more likely not to consider abortions: Minors who choose to resolve their unwanted pregnancy, regardless of their age, demonstrate competency comparable to that of adults.[92] No research suggests that minors over the age of 13 are *unable* to make reasoned decisions.

The second major assumption made by policies and jurisprudence that regulates adolescents' access to abortions suggests that abortions psychologically harm minors. The presumed negative effects of abortion are another basis on which to limit the minor's right to abortions. In thinking of psychological harm, the Court centers on the abortion, not pregnancy in general. For example, the Court concluded that if the child is carried to term, the medical decisions to be made "entail few—perhaps none—of the potentially grave emotional and psychological consequences of the decision to abort."[93] Researchers who explore the psychological impact of abortions find that the psychological consequences are minimal in the vast majority of cases. The general finding, however, does not suggest that the decision is an easy one. Teenagers who abort, and who have control over abortion decisions and who have emotional support, report satisfaction with their decisions.[94] If anything, existing research points to the need to encourage positive support, protect youth from family conflict, and consider the psychological consequences of actually having children.[95]

The third assumption purports that parental involvement leads to positive outcomes. Parental involvement in decisions may be good to the extent it promotes family unity and family cohesion promotes good decision making. Legal justifications for this approach arise from the traditional state interest in protecting family integrity and the belief that the family works best when independent from governmental intrusion. The belief is that parental assistance is often desirable,[96] and that parental involvement best serves the interests of both the minor and the parent.[97] The assumption is that once parents are involved, they will make decisions that are in the child's best interest.[98] This assumption is related to the first in that, because legislatures may assume that minors are immature unless the minors can show otherwise, the state may assume that they are insufficiently mature to make a reasoned decision on their own, and thus will reach ''better'' decisions if assisted by a parent, and that the understanding of abortion arises from within the family.[99]

Research fails to support the notion that mandatory parental involvement promotes family unity. Four findings emerge from existing research. First, involvement is most beneficial with families that are healthy prior to pregnancies; and most likely harmful when families are experiencing crises and stresses prior to the minor's pregnancy.[100] Second, in the absence of legislation, younger teenagers do tend to discuss decisions with their parents, more so than those who are older and more mature.[101] Likewise, when bypass legislation exists, it is those who are older and more mature who seek judicial by-passes. The general rule is that young minors (15 and younger) tend to involve their parents, and more mature minors increasingly seek to avoid direct parental involvement.[102] Third, families' reactions tend not to be as negative and extreme as pregnant teens expect.[103] Yet teenagers report numerous repercussions, such as increased distrust, control, and attempts to sever ties with the potential child's father.[104] Likewise, teenagers report family situations that would be further disruptive and unhealthy if parents were involved.[105] Given that teenagers expect negative reactions and sometimes get them, even though they may generally receive more support than expected, they seek alternatives when parental notification and consent laws are put into effect.[106] Fourth, the U.S. Supreme Court case *Casey* distinguished itself from its predecessors because the justices relied on empirical data to document the plight of abortion-seeking married women in abusive households and the failure to consider the parallel vulnerability of unemancipated minor women's rights in similarly abusive households. Research indicates that a host of different forms of child abuse threatens the independent exercise of abortion rights by unemancipated minor women. The role of incest and sexual assault in the dynamics of early pregnancy illustrates the need to consider the violence minors may endure. Minor women are the most vulnerable to sexual assault.[107] In addition, the incidence of incest poses a multitude of risks to minor women seeking parental consent. These involve the issue of divided loyalty as it relates to the attitude the incest victim has toward family members coping with the admission. Likewise, an additional complication resulting from incest includes promiscuous sexual behavior, which suggests that although a teenage pregnancy may be a direct effect of incest, an indirect effect might also emerge because incest could lead to sexual activity that increases the risk of pregnancy. The hostile environment created by abusive households affects the exercise of minors' rights. Mandatory notification, then, does not necessarily seem to lead to family cohesion; and in some instances may be harmful to both youth and their families.

The fourth assumption supposes that adolescents would not notify and consult with parents and that those who would not are immature and in need of guidance from parents who would discourage abortions. Research tends to indicate otherwise. In reality, most minors left to their own devices do seek out the advice of an adult when contemplating abortion. In a study of jurisdictions without mandatory parental-involvement legislation, a representative sample of 1500 unmarried women having an abortion showed that 61% consulted their parents and 20% consulted aunts, teachers, or other adults.[108] More important, the research found that minors who did not tell their parents of their abortion decision did so because they had experienced domestic violence and feared further harm or estrangement from home.[109] Research continues to reveal that more than half (from 55 to 70%) do notify at least one parent that they intend to abort.[110] The number of those who consult parents tends to be higher when laws mandate notification.[111] However, even without such laws, more than 60% indicate that one or both parents know about the pregnancy by the time they seek abortions.[112] Minors also report that they tend to inform parents voluntarily, rather than rely on clinic notification procedures.[113] Factors associated with an increased likelihood of parental notification include younger age, living a greater distance from the clinic, good communication with the mother, anticipation of a supportive reaction, and less frequent attendance at religious services.[114] In addition, young women of lower socioeconomic status are less likely to use the court-bypass procedure and thus more likely to notify both parents.[115] And young women who view themselves as the primary decision makers—those who should control personal decisions—are less likely to notify either parent.[116] Those who do not notify parents report poor communication with their mothers and perceive that their parents exerted more control over their decisions.[117] Note, however, that the percentages (ranging from 30 to 45%) are misleading because older adolescents near 18 act more independently and are the ones most likely pregnant: Few of the youngest minors have abortions without the knowledge of either parent, even without laws.[118] The older ones tend to be living alone, already have a baby, are out of school, and employed on a full-time or part-time basis.[119] Reasons for not telling parents tend to be that they do not want to disappoint parents (73%), they fear the parents will be angry (55%), and they do not want the parents to know they have had sex (35%).[120] Less frequently cited reasons were fear of pressure to leave home (18%), punishment (15%), or physical harm (6%).[121] Other research findings report the involvement of high rates of potential violence: 28% report that they either fear violence between parents or their parents and themselves.[122] Adolescents tend to have accurate predictions of their parents' negative reactions. Their beliefs reflect actual parents' reactions to the pregnancy when parents are told: Parents are disappointed, fathers are likely to be angry. Unexpectedly, and unlike what adolescents assume, most parents—more than 90%—believe that the adolescent should have an abortion and more than 10% report that their parents pressured them to have an abortion.[123] Thus parents are more likely to urge abortion than continued pregnancy, adolescents are likely to tell their parents about possible abortions, and adolescents who would resist involving parents tend to be mature.

The fifth assumption suggests that the alternatives to parental notification and consent actually protect adolescents' rights. Although judicial alternatives seem a logical alternative, numerous problems have been identified with the use of judges and the judicial bypass. First, it imposes a delay in obtaining treatment. The problem with delay is that time is especially critical for adolescents who already are likely to postpone pregnancy resolution decisions, which results in more negative outcomes.[124] Second, problems with judicial standards arise. There is a problem with determining what exactly maturity is. Judges tend to focus on the presence of coercion, ability to understand benefits and risks, and the adolescents' age. Judges may apply the law unevenly within one jurisdiction and even within their own docket: Judges sometimes have little insight into their own judgment policies.[125] Third, there is a problem in terms of who actually uses the law. Compared to minors who notify their parents, minors who seek judicial bypasses report lower maternal support, are older (16 and above), from higher socioeconomic status backgrounds, more likely to be from a one-parent home, and attend religious services more frequently. Fourth, bypass procedures may outweigh any envisioned benefits. For example, when bypass legislation was implemented in Massachusetts, more than one third of abortion-seeking minors sought out-of-state treatment to avoid the bypass procedure.[126] In addition, several note the failure to justify the procedural burden because the procedures tend to function as rubber-stamp adjudications. Few minors are denied abortions: They either are found mature and competent enough to choose an abortion, or their lack of maturity suggests that it is not in their best interests to deliver and raise children.[127] Likewise, the bypass procedure has been described as demeaning and intrusive. Minors who petition courts for authorization must complete an intensive application, appear in court, answer personal questions, and wait as long as three days from the date of the application for a decision. Fifth, minor women seeking abortions are as able to make informed decisions as their adult counterparts;[128] those who decide to abort have a better ability to conceptualize the future, a greater feeling of control over their lives, less anxiety, and less traditional views of female sex roles than do those who opt for childbirth.[129]

The sixth assumption involves how the possibility and actual existence of family violence remains insufficient to grant adolescents rights, even though procedural alternatives would burden adolescents more than adults. What is remarkable is that the Court, in *Planned Parenthood v. Casey*,[130] acknowledged the constraining effect of domestic violence on a married woman's abortion rights while dismissing the relevance of that same barrier as it affects an unemancipated minor in a similarly abusive household. The Court painstakingly reviewed the extensive empirical evidence regarding the hazardous consequences of spousal notification as it ignored even more robust findings of violence in deciding the fate of parental consent. The disproportionate amount of text devoted to the issues reflects the treatment: The opinion contained six pages on the ill effects the spousal notification provision would have on a married woman's freedom to choose to have an abortion in an abusive household, but allocated only a half-page discussion to parental-consent provisions that merely reaffirmed the parental consent provision.[131] The Court discussed the possibilities without a comparative analysis of the mechanics of both the spouse and minor's alternatives to obtaining abortions. The statute reveals how the minor's alternative are far more intrusive and protracted than the relatively nontaxing spousal alternative.[132] Unlike the minor, the spouse simply would need to sign a statement; she would not need to go to court, withstand judicial interrogation and scrutiny, nor have her "statement" notarized.[133] The Court relied on its judicial assumptions regarding the indispensable role parents play in counseling their children.[134] Focusing on that role and the assumption that parents will act in their children's best interests[135] enabled the Court to ignore the status of unemancipated minor women seeking abortions in abusive households.

Preliminary Conclusion

State recognition of the need to increase adolescents' access to contraceptive and abortion services reflects important developments in the thinking of adolescents' rights. First, it recognizes that adolescents are competent to make health care decisions. Second, it installs a policy that grants adolescents autonomy to achieve greater sexual responsibility instead of a policy that requires parental involvement. Third, it reflects the concern for dealing with domestic violence and attempting to avoid conflict. Fourth, it recognizes how the burdens may have a more negative impact on girls than boys: The consent statutes are part of a whole package that ensures all women the right to procreative freedom and control over their own bodies. Fifth, it recognizes that certain adolescents already have access, such as emancipated minors, and that it would seem unfair to have those who live in families not have access to those services. Sixth, it does not hold adolescents to a higher standard than adults. For example, adolescents are seen as having children for selfish reasons, to strengthen relationships with boyfriends, to seek emancipation from parents, to have a child who loves them unconditionally. Some adults have children for some of the same reasons. Seventh, the developments still protect parental rights by having a judge or third-party adult ensure that the adolescent is mature enough to obtain the services.

Regulating Access to Possible Parenthood

The law that regulates rights that involve whether adolescents may beget children remains exceedingly complex. Complexities derive from three sources. Commentators and the courts generally fail to explore and define the rights of adolescents in these contexts. In addition, the jurisprudence that generally helps clarify the rights of minors—the rights of adults as well as the extent and manner they may be infringed—remains relatively ignored. Finally, the realities of modern technology and continued social crises ensure that even society remains ambivalent in the face of phenomena such as frozen embryos, egg harvesting, gestational surrogacy, and posthumous insemination, as well as major policy issues regarding whether certain groups (e.g., poor people, criminals, the mentally disabled, and minors) may be encouraged *not* to procreate both for their own sake and that of society. With these ill-explored complexities in mind, this section details the potential nature of adolescents' procreative rights and existing empirical research that may be used to shed light on implications of adolescents' right to parent.

The Law and Adolescent Parenthood

Given the unsettled nature of adolescents' legal rights in this context, it makes sense to begin with how the Supreme Court approaches the general right to procreation and addresses adolescents' right to procreation. The foundational case derives from criminal law and the sterilization of individuals as a means of punishment, *Skinner v. Oklahoma*.[136] In *Skinner* the Supreme Court declared that "marriage and procreation are fundamental to the very existence and survival of the race" and that issues surrounding procreation deal with "one of the basic civil rights of man."[137] Treating the right to procreation as a fundamental liberty, the Court invalidated a statutory program that called for sterilization of convicts who had committed crimes of moral turpitude. The Court reached its conclusion on equal protection grounds and found persuasive the argument that such prohibitions were impermissible because other crimes did not entail such penalties. Cases following *Skinner* have expanded and reinforced the contention that procreation involves an area of one's life in which the state must tread lightly. We have seen, for example, that the most notable extension of the freedom of procreation doctrine emerged in *Roe v. Wade*,[138] in which the Court upheld a woman's right to terminate her pregnancy; *Griswold v. Connecticut*,[139] in which the Court upheld a married couples' choices concerning contraceptives without state interference; *Eisenstadt v. Baird*,[140] which extended the freedom to unmarried individuals; and *Carey v. Population Services International*,[141] in which the Court found that the "right to privacy in connection with decisions affecting procreation extend to minors as well as to adults.''[142] Thus although not always dealing with the right to have or not have children, legal doctrine does reveal that individuals may make certain choices regarding procreation. Although the concept of freedom of procreation remains firmly rooted within our constitutional jurisprudence, the Court has held that the individual does not possess any *absolute* liberty interest that can never be restricted by law, when applied to either adults or adolescents. As with the right to abortion and contraceptive services, the fundamental right to privacy that protects procreative choices may find certain limits—most notably, society may not be unduly burdened.

The broad protections and limitations revealed in these cases suggest three important points worthy of our attention. First, as we have seen in the previous discussion of abortion rights, the law tends to approve of following pregnancies to term. For example, minor mothers do not need to prove to the state that they are mature enough to have children to procreate. Likewise, they need not show that motherhood is in their best interests. Furthermore, neither parents nor the state may force teenagers to obtain abortions. In addition, the putative fathers cannot force pregnant teenagers to have abortions or carry pregnancies to term against their will.[143] These are not contentious issues. Although the state may adopt policies that encourage or discourage pregnancies, they must not do so coercively. Likewise, the law generally does not grant parents or partners who may attempt to influence pregnancy resolutions the power to coerce decisions.

Second, the literature suggests that although men do not carry pregnancies, they nevertheless have procreative rights. As with the rights of women, however, the state may limit the rights of fathers and potential fathers. Although we will review seminal cases in greater detail in chapter 10, it is important to delineate at this point the factors that may protect an adolescent males' rights. Cases that are on point deal with unwed fathers, because once adolescents are wed, they are considered adults for the purpose of legal rights and generally have rights to the child once it is born. The relevant and long line of unwed father cases reveals that the Court protects an unmarried man's paternity by determining three factors: the unwed man's biological relationship to the child; his social relationship to the child; and his relationship to the child's mother.[144] The first two points are without legal controversy and grew from the first four cases that dealt with the rights of unmarried men to establish relationships with their children. The principle that emerged from these cases is that unwed biological fathers create liberty interests in their relationships with their children if they demonstrate ''a full commitment to the responsibilities of fatherhood.''[145] The last factor grew from the latest case, *Michael H. v. Gerald D.*,[146] which denied a putative father's request to seek paternity because the mother was married to another man. The ''marital presumption'' works to protect men's rights when they are in families; when biological fathers are outside of families and their children are in traditional ones, the Court allows states to not consider the rights of biological fathers. The rights of fathers, then, generally remain more limited than those of mothers.

The first two points in our discussion of adolescents' rights to parenthood deal with the extent to which rights may be limited or protected in contexts that involve pregnancy and birth. The third point of interest deals not with the resolution of pregnancies but with whether adolescents may get pregnant, or inseminate, in the first place. These laws deal with sterilization—the extent to which minors may be free to use sterilization as a form of contraception and the extent to which minors may be free from coercive sterilization. Regardless of these two possibilities, the concern generally tends to be whether parents and those acting as parents can use sterilization to control whether minors will beget children. Given that parents generally control the medical rights of minors, the issue fundamentally involves the extent to which minors may exercise their constitutional right to choose sterilization as a contraceptive measure or resist others who make the sterilization decision for them.

The Supreme Court has spoken to the issue of sterilization on three occasions. The first case dealt with the procreative rights of people with disabilities, *Buck v. Bell*,[147] in which the Court upheld a state's right to sterilize an allegedly mentally incompetent patient. The Court noted that the constitutionality of the sterilization could be challenged on both due process and equal protection grounds. However the Court found that the goal of improving the "welfare . . . of society"[148] sufficiently satisfied substantive due process challenges; likewise, the financial burden that would be placed on the state by the children of mentally incompetent people was found to justify the sterilization and thus did not violate equal protection standards. The second case, *Skinner v. Oklahoma*,[149] dealt with compulsory sterilization laws. As noted previously, the Supreme Court again supported states' rights to sterilize individuals. According to the Court, procreation may be among the "basic rights of man"[150] but states could sterilize people as long as certain requirements were met. Although establishing these requirements might seem to protect individuals from involuntary sterilization, the Supreme Court's most recent decision on sterilization undercut that possibility. In *Stump v. Sparkman*[151] the Court found that, despite several procedural inadequacies and the absence of an authorizing statute, a judge could not be held liable for ordering the sterilization of a 15-year-old girl.[152] The Court's opinion rested on the established rule that a judge has the "power to act on a petition for sterilization of a minor in the custody of her parents, particularly where the parents have authority under the Indiana statutes to 'consent to and contract for medical or hospital care or treatment of [the minor] including surgery.'"[153] These sterilization cases arguably remain "good law," because as recently as February 1995 the Court refused to grant *certiorari* to a case in which a physically and mentally disabled woman was sterilized.[154] The legal rule, then, is that parents may seek and obtain permission by the courts to sterilize their children in the absence of statutory or case precedents.

The *Sparkman* decision gains considerable significance when viewed in light of two points. The first reason for the case's significance is that only 17 states now statutorily regulate involuntary sterilization.[155] These state statutes generally involve institutionalized individuals and assume that sterilization is possible. The statutes generally focus on the person's due process rights, enumerate the factors that courts are to consider, and differ greatly in terms of protections. Requirements vary about who may initiate sterilization proceedings, ranging from the patient, parent, physician, or any interested party. All of the statutes define the factors to be weighed in the decision; the most frequent factors to be considered are the likelihood that the child will engage in sexual activity, the child's best interests, and the likelihood that the child will be sexually abused.[156] Even in these states, however, judges may still exercise considerable discretion. For example, the North Carolina statute recognizes the inability to care for children as the exclusive ground for sterilizing mentally disabled individuals. But in *In re Johnson*,[157] the North Carolina court of appeals allowed a foster mother to consent to the sterilization of her ward, even when the ward did not want sterilization. Although the court found that the petitioner could not "meet any acceptable standard of fitness to care for a child,"[158] the evidence dealt with other issues. In reviewing available evidence, the court heavily relied on a foster mother's testimony that Johnson "went out every night, had boyfriends, came in later than she was supposed to, slept most of the day and refused to take birth control pills" and that she had had an abortion.[159]

The *Sparkman* decision also gains significance in that, without the statutes, judicial discretion rules. Given the general failure of states to design statutes, states essentially have left sterilization issues to the judicial process. Lower courts variously support involuntary sterilization because prohibiting sterilization: (a) would place unnecessary burdens on mentally disabled women; (b) interfere with familial or parental privacy rights; or (c) infringe on states' compelling interest to limit the birth of "defective" children.

Several lower-court cases illustrate well the rationales for prohibiting sterilization. A Supreme Court of California case, *Conservatorship of Valerie N.,*[160] best exemplifies the first line of reasoning. The court ruled that a statutory *prohibition* of sterilization denied "developmentally disabled persons . . . privacy and liberty interests protected by the Fourteenth Amendment."[161] In essence, the court found that fertility burdens the mentally disabled, and the law must liberate mentally disabled women from the burdens of fertility. As another court in another leading case put it, sterilization may be a necessary part of allowing a woman to exercise fully her "personal right to control her own body and life."[162] The second line of reasoning supports parents' rights to have their mentally disabled children sterilized. For example, in *Ruby v. Massey,*[163] the parents of a mentally disabled minor successfully argued that a Connecticut statute restricting sterilizations violated their parental right to familial privacy and denied their daughter equal protection of the laws. In a convoluted analysis, the court reasoned that denying parents the "right" to judicially ordered sterilizations violated the children's equal protection rights because the state failed to demonstrate a compelling state interest that justified the denial. A third line of reasoning holds that states' interests in authorizing sterilizations outweigh fundamental rights to procreation and provide a reasonable basis for creating legal classifications based on mental disability. For example, in *North Carolina Association for Retarded Children v. North Carolina,*[164] the court examined the constitutionality of the North Carolina involuntary sterilization statute in a way that paid little attention to the plaintiff's fundamental rights-to-procreate argument. Instead, the court focused on the state's "compelling" interest in deterring the birth of "defective" children for whom their parents could not care. The analysis never addressed whether the statute was "narrowly drawn" to the state's compelling interests—in other words, whether the state's goal required sterilization or whether there were less intrusive means of reaching those goals. Thus state's interests were found to outweigh mentally disabled women's interests in remaining autonomous and free from state interference; state's interests were also found to outweigh these women's rights of privacy and procreative choice.[165]

Only one line of reasoning has been advanced in lower court decisions to support the finding that involuntary sterilizations improperly invade fundamental rights because there are no corresponding state interests strong enough to justify the intrusion. Unlike the courts cited previously, the court in *In re Eberhardy,*[166] a case that exemplifies this line of reasoning, strictly followed the two-pronged analysis appropriate for evaluating whether or not a state may intrude on a fundamental right. The court assumed that the mentally disabled have a fundamental right to procreate but examined (a) whether the state had a compelling interest to intrude on that right and (b) whether the state's statute was narrowly tailored to further the state's compelling interest using the least restrictive means. Moreover, unlike the other cases, instead of considering the state's interests in authorizing sterilization, the court recognized the state's interest in protecting mentally incompetent persons from the imposition of sterilization by parties with conflicting interests: "parents, guardians, or . . . social workers."[167]

In summary, although the right to parenthood remains ill-explored, some general rules emerge. The right to procreate, although fundamental, remains far from absolute. The law tends to encourage adolescents to carry pregnancies to term *if* they so desire. The law generally does not permit overtly forced abortions. Fathers have few rights to parenthood; their rights are generally respected if they are given the opportunity to parent and they attempt to do so. Sterilization of adolescents is permissible under a narrowly determined set of conditions. The law, then, generally aims to protect adolescents' rights to parenthood, with the notable exception that fathers and mentally incompetent adolescents may not enjoy the right as equally as others.

Realities of Adolescent Life

The extent to which the law reflects the realities of adolescents who may want to become parents remains largely uninvestigated. Despite the paucity of research, several points may be made. First, although adolescents need not show that they are mature enough to have children or that it would be in their best interests, minors who become parents place three generations at risk for numerous negative outcomes and produce considerable social costs. A wealth of documentation links minor motherhood with peril. Adolescent mothers experience direct costs of delayed or lost education, lost economic opportunities, and abrupt changes in their developmental trajectories.[168] Many adolescent fathers are negatively affected as well, although, as we will see in chapter 10, they are neglected by researchers. For children born to adolescent parents, the costs include an increased likelihood of a life in poverty, poor developmental prognosis (such as inordinately high infancy mortality rates and low birth weights), and increased probability of becoming adolescent parents themselves.[169] The parents of the adolescent parents also are affected. The surprise and disappointment that precedes acceptance of the pregnancy and their need to make room for additional family members simply begins their problems. The adolescents' parents typically provide monetary resources, time, and support for their daughters and grandchildren, which strains their own life-course pathways and developmental tasks.[170] Another category of consequences beyond the adolescents' families involves the impact of early pregnancy to society. These costs include those associated with children's health care, foster care placement, incarceration rates, and lower productivity.[171] From all indications, minor motherhood without social and economic support should be discouraged rather than encouraged by the state.[172]

Second, in terms of adolescents who follow through with the pregnancy, little research has examined the decision-making process among minors and their families. Existing research indicates that the proportion of teenagers who report that their mother influenced them was approximately the same among those in the abortion group as among those in the childbearing group.[173] When parents do exert direct pressure, they tend to urge their daughters to abort; and those daughters who did abort had felt more overt parental pressure and influence than had those who carried a pregnancy to term.[174] A related point of research involves the adolescents' satisfaction with their decision. Satisfaction appears not related to whether the minor consulted with her mother but highly associated with whether mothers support their children's decisions.[175] Thus the few who do not consult with mothers were as satisfied with their decision as those who did. In addition, young women who make the decision themselves are significantly more satisfied than those who feel the decision was made for them.[176] The decision to have the baby outside of marriage is affected by support for the decision from the mother and the partner.[177] It seems, then, that adolescent parents do not decide alone, and positive outcomes emerge from situations that support and foster their own decisions.

Third, adolescents rarely consider adoptions. Research that examines discussions of pregnancy outcomes reflect the failure: Adoption continues to be the least-discussed option.[178] Research that examined decisions to place children for adoption indicate that fewer than 3% of all unplanned pregnancies are resolved through adoption.[179] Likewise, researchers also tend to ignore adoption. A recent national survey of pregnancy resolutions ignores adoption as an option[180] and the most recent comprehensive text on "kids having kids" fails to mention the option.[181]

Demographic characteristics of those who place their children for adoption consistently reveal that those who keep their children are most likely to be the group of teenagers society would expect to place their children for adoption. The very young and poor keep their children; those who do place their children for adoption tend to be White,[182] older,[183] from higher socioeconomic backgrounds,[184] hold more traditional attitudes about family life,[185] and engage in less sexual risk-taking behaviors.[186] Likewise, those who place their children for adoption delay marriage, avoid subsequent pregnancy, and successfully complete educational training compared to those who maintain custody of their children.[187] In short, available data suggests that the young women who do place their children up for adoption resemble those who choose to have abortions.

Others who play significant roles in the resolution of pregnancies tend to discourage adoption. Although parents, especially mothers, highly influence the pregnancy resolution processes, they generally do not favor adoption.[188] The role of partners has been noted as inconclusive.[189] In terms of peers, the only study to examine directly the impact of peers found that one in five adolescents who placed a child felt that her peers would favor the idea of adoption.[190] Those who place children for adoption are likely to face peer reactions that view their behavior as "selfish, unloving and even incomprehensible."[191]

Cultural forces disfavor adoption. Adoption is viewed negatively by persons not involved in adoption experiences[192] and those who view the option as they project their own behaviors.[193] Negative attitudes have become even more forceful with the greater acceptance of single motherhood and legitimization of abortions.[194]

Even though the culture may view adoption in a negative light, the critical variable for placement is the positive attitudes toward adoption; and research suggests that those who place their children for adoption express regret but their overall psychological well-being remains.[195] Remarkably, few programs focus on the perceived costs and rewards accompanying adoption and alternatives to parenthood among adolescents who would benefit from them.[196] In short, although the belief may be that adoption provides a better alternative than others, adoption receives little consideration and actually remains stigmatized and little used.

Fourth, research relating to unwed fatherhood is relatively new. Although we will review the literature in chapter 10, two points are worth noting. A substantial proportion of children born to teenagers live with both a mother and a father at least some years of their childhood. Despite public rhetoric and popular stereotypes, a substantial proportion of teenage parents are married—in 1990 about a third of all babies born were to married teenagers; and the most recent data about out-of-wedlock births revealed that nearly half were married three years later.[197] The amount of out-of-wedlock births to teenagers is not necessarily worse than those that occur in adulthood; indeed, two out of three children born to an unmarried parent are born to a person who is *not* a teenager.[198] Despite these findings, it still seems difficult to overestimate the potentially negative outcomes of early marriage, or at least the conditions that would lead to early marriage.

Fifth, there is the least research on coerced sterilization and "forced" contraception. Although in theory the right involves the power to choose sterilization as a means of contraception, only about 1% of minors use sterilization as a contraceptive method.[199] Reviews of instances in which sterilization is more likely to be used suggest that they tend to involve mentally retarded individuals. The extent to which such measures are appropriate largely remains uninvestigated.[200] Yet these measures may be subject to numerous criticisms, such as the possibility that they are used to shield those who would sexually abuse mentally incompetent minors when even statutes use that possibility as a factor to allow sterilization.[201] The research on efforts to encourage contraception, such as the use of Norplant for teenagers on welfare, also remains limited, with the exception that Norplant does help reduce welfare rolls.[202]

Sixth, the effects of postponing parenthood are not likely to be as dramatic as hoped. Evidence suggests that those who do become parents earlier than others tend to come from impoverished lives. Rampant poverty, failure in school, divisions between the races, and gender-role expectations all lead to early pregnancy and contribute to lack of opportunities for personal and professional fulfillment.[203] Early pregnancy seemingly denotes poverty. Although intersections between poverty and early parenthood remain complicated, it does seem that poverty leads to early parenthood, and early parenthood simply continues the trend. The finding is increasingly less surprising as researchers realize that even adults who have children and who are single place economic constraints on their lives and are more likely to suffer from poverty, and the degree of suffering varies by race and ethnicity.[204]

Preliminary Conclusion

The right to parenthood generally extends to minors. Indeed, the law tends to protect and encourage access despite pervasively enormous costs to society and adolescents themselves. Efforts to limit access reveal that the healthier outcomes derive from efforts that support adolescent decision making, as revealed in levels of satisfaction with decisions not to abort and with decisions to place children for adoption. The significance of supports increases when access to parenthood results in negative outcomes for both adolescents and their social networks; parenthood exacerbates already difficult situations. The findings suggest that constraints on adolescents' lives places them on a path of further constraints and the law generally removes itself from efforts to discourage parenthood.

Regulating Access to Marriage

The uneven development in adolescents' rights finds equal inconsistency in the last aspect of sexual life that the law allows parents and society to control: marriage. Unlike previous areas of adolescent sexuality regulation, adolescents essentially do not control their right to marry. Their lack of control, however, is not absolute; for example, adolescents who become parents generally may marry. Thus although the right to marry may be among the most fundamental rights, adolescents generally do not control their own access to such rights. The extent to which parents and society should control the right remains essentially uninvestigated; but research does suggest that instances in which marriage is allowed and even encouraged tend to lead to negative outcomes. This section explores the diversity of controls over adolescents' right to marry and the ironic results that emerge from recognitions of that right.

The Law and Adolescent Marriage

In terms of the Constitution, the right to marry remains far from controversial. The judicial system has long supported the right to marry, including the right to have existing marital relationships protected. In the early 1920s, in *Meyer v. Nebraska*,[205] the Supreme Court noted that the liberties guaranteed by the Fourteenth Amendment extend to the individual's right to marry. Later the Court elaborated on that guarantee and explicitly granted the "freedom to marry" the highest protection: the freedom to marry became a "fundamental right" in *Skinner v. Oklahoma*[206] and *Loving v. Virginia*.[207] Although the two cases confirmed the fundamental nature of the right, the cases respectively held that despite the Supreme Court's strong endorsement of the "right to marry," states always have been allowed to regulate the entry into marriage. Thus, and as determined by the Supreme Court's first "family law" case in the end of the 1800s,[208] marriage is a social relation subject to the state's police power. Given state controls, an analysis of the right necessarily turns to statutes that all states have enacted to control marital unions.

In thinking of adolescents' rights, state statutes that regulate adolescents' access to marriage are important to consider. The statutes reveal the minimum age states view adolescents as capable of acting on their own to embark on this important decision. The analysis reveals who actually controls adolescents' rights: the adolescents themselves, parents, the state, or some combination of these possibilities. The extent to which marriage is allowed, it reveals how states condone sexual activity; for sexual activity within marriage vitiates the need for the adolescent to be able to consent to sexual activity. The analyses reveal alternative approaches to using the courts or parents to ensure not only adolescents' rights but also to consider the interests of society.

The most simple analysis of access to marriage laws involves the ages at which states consider adolescents legally competent to contract into marriage without consent from courts, parents, or other parties. In general, states set 18 as the minimum age at which adolescents may marry without consent from third parties. There are only three explicit exceptions to this general rule. Nebraska sets the age at 17; Ohio sets the age at 18 for boys and 16 for girls; and Mississippi sets the age at 18 for boys and girls at 15.[209] The fourth potential exception is New York state, which finds that a marriage is simply "voidable" (seemingly not absolutely void) by a court if one party is under 18;[210] but places the absolute minimum age as below 14.

A more complicated analysis involves the minimum age at which states allow adolescents to get married so long as they do so with third-party consent. States vary considerably in the extent to which parents, courts, or other persons are allowed to consent for adolescents. However, there are five major ways states regulate adolescents' access to marriage. The most common way by which marital age is set at a minimum is to have parents and the judiciary share the power to allow marriage between adolescents. Even this approach, however, varies. For example, three states require both court and parental approval for adolescents under 18 years of age;[211] nine require joint approval for adolescents under 16,[212] and two allow for marriage under 15 with both parental and judicial approval.[213] One state allows for underage marriage with court and parental approval for males below 17 and girls below 15,[214] and another sets the age at below 18 for males and below 16 for females.[215] Two states set the minimum age to the age at which the female partner is pregnant.[216] Also note that one of those states waives both the judicial and parental approval for males under 18 who have been arrested on a charge of sexual intercourse with a single, widowed, or divorced female of good repute for chastity who has thereby become pregnant.[217] Note that these ages were minimum ages at which youth who were under them could get married with parent and judicial approval. Only three states set a minimum age at which adolescents cannot be married and require parental and judicial consent when they are between those ages and the age of majority: Idaho sets the minimum age at 16[218] and Utah and Vermont set the age at 14.[219]

The next most common way to allow marriage is to provide for parental consent for minors. One state allows those age 17 to marry with parental consent,[220] and four bring the age down to 16[221] and yet another to 14.[222] One state poses no lower limit as long as they are under 17 and have parental consent.[223] Three allow for girls to be younger than boys (e.g., 14 and 13, 18 and 16, and 17 and 14) so long as they have parental consent.[224] Third, two allow for similar age differences but do not apply them if the partners are expecting or have children and have parental consent.[225]

Judicial waivers provide another common way to allow marriages with the consent of a third party. Again, these waivers are given to adolescents who may vary in age, and some special circumstances may allow for even lower ages than those explicitly stated in the statutes. For example, Florida and Indiana allow for judicial waiver of the age of majority in cases in which the female is pregnant.[226] Two states, Alaska and New York, limit the age of marriage to persons 14 and older with judicial waivers,[227] and Louisiana, Tennessee, and Washington do not specify minimum ages so long as there have been judicial waivers.[228]

The authority between parents and the judiciary can be split and thus allow minors to marry with the permission of either parents or the courts. For example, five states permit marriages when minors are at least 16 and have parental or judicial approval.[229] One state, Texas, lowers that age to 14.[230] A last state, Kentucky, allows for parental consent if under 18 but allows for judicial consent if the female is pregnant.[231]

Finally, minors may obtain permission when marriage involves instances in which their relationships concern pregnancy. In these situations, either parents may consent or a third party may suffice, such as a physician's certificate of pregnancy[232] or the permission of a director of social services.[233] Oklahoma allows for judicial consent and parental opportunity to be heard when the female is pregnant.[234]

In summary, the marriage laws reflect the extent to which adolescents may not act on their own. In general, the legal age of consent to marriage is 18. They reflect the extent to which adolescents who have become mature through parenthood may choose their own course. Marriage statutes reflect the power of parental rights. Parents provide the consent of very young adolescents who marry. The statutes reveal the increasing attempt by states to control both parental and adolescents' rights. States do so through using judges or other state officials as necessary to allow otherwise legally incompetent adolescents to marry.

Realities of Adolescent Life

Despite considerable interest in unwed parenting, research on teenage marriages remains significantly scant. Despite a dearth of knowledge, two general trends and findings from other studies of adolescent sexuality are worthy of observation. The most notable trend relates to negative links between early marriage and adolescent health. The general consensus is that early marriage leads to a host of negative outcomes. For example, early marriage links to early divorce, poverty, and increased childbearing.[235] However, just as with early parenthood, early marriage may not be a cause but rather a symptom of poverty, missed opportunities, and child maltreatment. The link is of considerable significance given the emerging trend in public policy, especially welfare reform laws, that seeks to marry adolescent girls to teenagers or older adults.[236] Such efforts are increasing and increasingly problematic. Although the directional nature of the links to negative outcomes of early marriage may be inconclusive, consistent findings emerge throughout the literature: young girls who become pregnant early in their life course and carry their children to term are not only likely to be poor but are also more likely to have been victims of violence and have been statutorily raped.

The second notable trend involves the manner in which individuals increasingly reject marriage as a viable option. More avoid or postpone marriage; and more choose not to marry during the prime family-building years.[237] Childbearing and childrearing increasingly disconnect from marriage.[238] Relatedly, individuals are less marriageable. The focus on marriageability has been on Black males who are not employed and unable to support families.[239] Recent research indicates that the patterns identified as critical for Black males increasingly link to all males and reduce the marriageability factor of Blacks and Whites alike.[240]

Preliminary Conclusion

Research relating to early marriage remains scant. However, available evidence suggests that early marriage continues to be linked to negative outcomes, individuals increasingly choose not to marry, and entire groups are increasingly rejected as potential marriage partners. Yet the only group the law allows to be encouraged to marry are the ones most likely to be at risk for negative outcomes. Although the issues certainly remain complex and uninvestigated, it is not difficult to imagine whose interests are at stake when adolescents are encouraged to marry when available evidence suggests that it is not in their interests. When adolescents do not have rights and others control the rights adolescents are deemed to possess, it does not necessarily follow that those in control act in the adolescents' short and long-term interests.

Conclusion

Despite the amassed empirical evidence, the belief persists that parents guide their children's sexual activities and consequences. The law pervasively continues to honor the myth of parental control at the same time it attempts to move away from it. The move away from parental rights comes most noticeable when differentiating the current legal configurations of adolescents' sexual rights as they relate to different aspects of adolescent sexuality. Viewed from this perspective, adolescents' sexual rights actually fluctuate considerably. The rights fluctuate in terms of the activity that is involved, with considerable rights to engage in sexual activity to fewer rights to obtain abortions and even fewer to get married. In addition to the variations across contexts, rights vary in terms of whether parents, states, or adolescents have discretion to control, with parents generally having considerable freedom and the state possessing the freedom to set the outer limits of parental rights. Likewise, the broad range of differences in the allocation of adolescents' rights generally fails to relate to adolescents' need for protection, regardless of whether it involves adolescents' need for autonomy or dependency.

Problems in current conceptions of adolescents' sexual rights, the existing failures, discrepancies, and disjunctions between law and reality suggest important conclusions. The current recognition counsels a need to shape adolescents' rights to take into account the power diverse social influences have on adolescent development. Such recognition requires a move toward increasing respect for adolescents' rights. Numerous problems arise from moving to an extreme that focuses on liberation and autonomy as the immediate goals of adolescent rights. Such goals are problematic, for example, when laws recognize adolescents' rights to engage in sexual relationships without offering concomitant access to medical and therapeutic services. Legal access to services without appropriate supports to guide adolescents to use the services and actually benefit from them renders developments in adolescents' rights laws ineffective. The current regulation of adolescent sexuality, then, reflects a slow move toward modernity, an increased recognition of the need to respect adolescents' individual rights and to design legal systems that foster adolescent development. Without doubt, systems of support lead to healthier outcomes. The remaining chapters chart possible pathways to developing such systems.

Endnotes

1. 381 U.S. 479, 485 (1965).
2. *Id.* at 485–486.
3. 405 U.S. 438 (1972).
4. *Id.* at 453.
5. 431 U.S. 678 (1977).
6. *Id.* at 693.
7. *Id.*
8. *Id.*
9. ALASKA STAT. § 09.65.100(a)(4) (Michie 1995 & Supp. 1997); ARK. CODE ANN. § 20-16-304 (Michie 1997); CAL. CIV. CODE § 34.5 (West 1996 & Supp. 1998); COLO. REV. STAT. § 13-22-105 (West 1990 & Supp. 1997); DEL. CODE ANN. tit. 13, § 708 (Michie 1995 & Supp. 1996); FLA. STAT. § 381.382(5) (Harrison 1991 & Supp. 1997); GA. CODE ANN. § 31-9-2(a)(5) (Michie 1996 & Supp. 1998); HAW. REV. STAT. § 577A-2 (1993 & Supp. 1996); IDAHO CODE § 18-603 (Michie 1987 & Supp. 1997); ILL. REV. STAT. ch. 111, ¶ 4651 (West/Smith-Hurd 1993 & Supp. 1998); KAN. STAT. ANN. § 23-501 (1988 & Supp. 1997); KY. REV. STAT. ANN. § 214.185 (Michie/Bobbs-Merrill 1990 & Supp. 1996); ME. REV. STAT. ANN. tit. 22, § 1908 (West 1983 & Supp. 1996); MD. HEALTH-GEN. CODE ANN. § 20-102 (Michie 1995 & Supp. 1998); MISS. CODE ANN. § 41-42-7 (Law. Co-op. 1994 & Supp. 1997); N.M. STAT. ANN. §§ 24-8-3, 24-8-5 (Michie 1978 & 1998); N.Y. SOC. SERV. LAW §§ 465 to 473 (McKinney 1989 & Supp. 1998); N.C. GEN. STAT. § 90-21.5 (1993 & Supp. 1997); TENN. CODE ANN. § 68-34-107 (Michie 1997); UTAH. CODE ANN. § 76-7-322 (Michie 1996 & Supp. 1998); VA. CODE ANN. § 54.1-2969(d) (Michie 1996 & Supp. 1998); WYO. STAT. § 42-5-101 (Michie 1997).
10. Mary Chamie, Susan Eisman, Jacqueline D. Forrest, Margaret Terry Orr, and Aida Torres, "Factors Affecting Adolescents' Use of Family Planning Clinics," *Family Planning Perspectives* 14 (1982):126–139.
11. *E.g.,* studies indicate that women who have never been pregnant and use an intrauterine device have an increased risk of infertility. *See* Daniel W. Cramer, Isaac Schiff, Stephen C. Schoenbaum, Mark Gibson, Serge Belisle, Bruge Albrecht, Robert J. Stillman, Merle Berger, Emery Wilson, Bruce Stadel, and Machelle Seibel, "Tubal Infertility and the Intrauterine Device," *New England Journal of Medicine* 312 (1985):941–947.
12. *See, e.g.,* GA. CODE ANN. § 20-2-773(a)(1) (Michie 1996 & Supp. 1998). (providing that "no facility operated on public school property or operated by a public school district and no employees of any such facility . . . shall . . . distribut[e] . . . contraceptives" to public school students); LA. REV. STAT. ANN. § 17:281A(3) (West 1986 & Supp. 1998) ("no contraceptive or abortifacient drug, device, or other similar product shall be distributed in any public school").
13. *See, e.g.,* ARK. CODE ANN. § 6-18-703(c)(1) (Michie 1997) ("'no state funds shall be used for the purchase or dispensing of contraceptives or abortifacients in public schools"); GA. CODE ANN. § 20-2-773(b) (Michie 1996 & Supp. 1998) ("the Department of education and local units of administration are prohibited from utilizing state funds for the distribution of contraceptives").
14. 42 C.F.R. § 59.5 (1983).
15. Title X, 42 U.S.C. § 300(a), was amended by the Omnibus Budget Reconciliation Act of 1981, Pub. L. No. 97-35, § 931(b)(1), 95 Stat. 357, 570 (1981).
16. *See* New York v. Heckler, 719 F.2d 1191, 1196–1197 (2d Cir. 1983); Planned Parenthood Federation v. Heckler, 712 F.2d 650, 655–656 (D.C. Cir. 1983).
17. *See, e.g.,* HAW. REV. STAT. § 577A-2 (1993 & Supp. 1996) (notification of parent at discretion of service provider after consulting with minor); KY. REV. STAT. ANN. § 214.185(6) (Michie/Bobbs-Merrill 1990 & Supp. 1996) (notification of parents by physician if it would benefit the minor's health).
18. 582 F. Supp. 1001 (D. Utah 1983).

19. *Id.* at 1009.

20. 615 F.2d 1162, 1169 (6th Cir. 1980) (not violating parental due process rights).

21. *Id.* at 1168.

22. 606 N.Y.S.2d 259, 261 (N.Y. App. Div. 1993).

23. *Id.* at 266.

24. 652 N.E.2d 580 (Mass. 1995).

25. *Id.* at 586.

26. Curtis v. School Community, No. 92518, 1993 WL 818795 (Mass. Supr. Ct. Oct. 7, 1993), *aff'd,* 652 N.E.2d 580 (Mass. 1995), *cert. denied,* 116 S. Ct. 753 (1996).

27. Centers for Disease Control, "Selected Behaviors That Increase Risk for HIV Infection Among High School Students—United States, 1990," *Morbidity & Mortality Weekly Report* 41 (1992):231.

28. Alan Guttmacher Institute, *Sex and America's Teenagers* (New York: Author, 1994), pp. 76, 77 fig. 55.

29. Philip Kestelman and James Trussell, "Efficacy of the Simultaneous Uses of Condoms and Spermicides," *Family Planning Perspectives* 23 (1991):226–227, 232.

30. Cheryl D. Hayes, *Risking the Future: Adolescent Sexuality, Pregnancy and Childrearing* (Washington, DC: National Academy Press, 1987). To ensure diligent use, for example, Congress established the National Research Counsel to further knowledge and advise the federal government, and recommended the removal of barriers to services, such as lack of confidentiality, costs, and convenience.

31. Centers for Disease Control, "Sexual Behavior Among High School Students—United States, 1990," *Morbidity & Mortality Weekly Report* 40 (1992):885–889.

32. Sally Guttmacher, Lisa Lieberman, David Ward, Alice Radosh, Yvonne Rafferty, and Nicholas Freudenberg, "Parents Attitudes and Beliefs About HIV/AIDS Prevention With Condom Availability in New York City Public High Schools," *Journal of School Health* 65 (1995):101–106; Leighton C. Ku, Freya L. Sonenstein, and Joseph H. Pleck, "The Association of AIDS Education and Sex Education With Sexual Behavior and Condom Use Among Teenage Men," *Family Planning Perspectives* 24 (1995):100–106.

33. Donna L. Richter, Robert F. Valois, Robert E. McKeown, and Murry L. Vincent, "Correlates of Condom Use and Number of Sexual Partners Among High School Adolescents," *Journal of School Health* 63 (1993):91–96.

34. Roger J. R. Levesque, "The Peculiar Place of Adolescents in the HIV-AIDS Epidemic: Unusual Progress & Usual Inadequacies in 'Adolescent Jurisprudence,'" *Loyola University Chicago Law Journal* 27 (1996):701–739.

35. Lucianá Lagana and David M. Hayes, "Contraceptive Health Programs for Adolescents: A Critical Review," *Adolescence* 28 (1993):347–359.

36. Douglas Kirby, "School-Based Programs to Reduce Sexual Risk-Taking Behaviors," *Journal of School Health* 62 (1992):283–287.

37. Religion provides a good example of the need to consider coercion and abortion, and third-party marital consent laws provide a good example of the manner in which third parties protect parental rights. *See* chapter 2.

38. For poll results, *see* Eugene C. Bjorklun, "Condom Distribution in the Public Schools: Is Parental Consent Required?" *Educational Law Reports* 91 (1994):11–21.

39. *See* Stanley M. Elam, Lowell C. Rose, and Alec M. Gallup, "The 24th Annual Gallup/Phi Delta Kappa Poll of the Public's Attitudes Toward Public Schools," *Phi Delta Kappan* 74 (1992): 41–53.

40. An early study reported that only 2% of adolescents stated that they would abstain from sexual activity rather than let their parents know of their clinic attendance. Aida Torres, Jacqueline Darroch Forrest, and Susan Eisman, "Telling Parents: Clinic Policies and Adolescents' Use of Family Planning and Abortion Services," *Family Planning Perspectives* 12 (1980):284–292. Other research shows that nine out of ten postpone the use of family planning services for about a year or more after having engaged in sexual activity. Laurie Schwab Zabin and Samuel D. Clark,

Jr., "Why They Delay: A Study of Teenage Family Planning Clinic Patients," *Family Planning Perspectives* 13 (1981):205–207, 211–217.

41. This has been recognized and explored by the courts. *See* Hodgson v. Minnesota, 648 F. Supp. 756, 763–769 (1986).

42. Zabin and Clark, "Why They Delay: A Study of Teenage Family Planning Clinic Patients."

43. *Id.* at 207.

44. Torres et al., "Telling Parents: Clinic Policies and Adolescents' Use of Family Planning and Abortion Services."

45. Zabin and Clark, "Why They Delay: A Study of Teenage Family Planning Clinic Patients."

46. As they do in the abortion context and in the leading case dealing with contraceptives that established that minors have a right to privacy; *see* Carey v. Population Services International, 431 U.S. 678 (1977).

47. Bjorklun, "Condom Distribution in the Public Schools: Is Parental Consent Required?" pp. 14–15.

48. Susan F. Newcomer and J. Richard Udry, "Parent–Child Communication and Teenagers' Contraceptive Use," *Family Planning Perspectives* 16 (1985):163–170.

49. E.g., in a longitudinal study involving a racially diverse sample of sexually active adolescents attending family planning clinics, 39% reported that they had discussed sex and birth control with their mothers. However, there was no association between communication about sex or birth control and the actual contraceptive practice at three points in time. Frank F. Furstenberg, Jr., Roberta Herreg-Baron, Judy Shea, and David Webb, "Family Communication and Teenagers' Contraceptive Use," *Family Planning Perspectives* 16 (1984):163–170.

50. C. D. Handelsman, R. J. Cabral, and Glenn E. Weisfeld, "Sources of Information and Adolescent Sexual Knowledge and Behavior," *Journal of Adolescent Research* 2 (1987):455–463.

51. Frank F. Furstenberg, Jr., "The Social Consequences of Teenage Parenthood," *Family Planning Perspectives* 8 (1976):148–164; Greer Litton Fox and Judith K. Inazu, "Patterns and Outcomes of Mother–Daughter Communication About Sexuality," *Journal of Social Issues* 36 (1976): 7–29.

52. Nearly 6 in 10 of sexually active teens who have discussed sex and contraceptive issues with their parents report consistent use of birth control. Levesque, "The Peculiar Place of Adolescents in the HIV-AIDS Epidemic: Unusual Progress & Usual Inadequacies in 'Adolescent Jurisprudence'"; James Jaccard, Patricia J. Dittus, and Vivian V. Gordon, "Maternal Correlates of Adolescent Sexual and Contraceptive Behavior," *Family Planning Perspectives* 28 (1996):159–165, 185.

53. The first study found that students with the least parental support (which included a communication component) were five times more likely to engage in high-risk behaviors than those with the most parental support. Heather J. Walter, Roger D. Vaughn, and Aalwyn T. Cohall, "Psychosocial Influences on Acquired Immunodeficiency Syndrome—Risk Behaviors Among High School Students," *Pediatrics* 88 (1991):846–852. Another important study found that compared with students who did not communicate with their parents about sex, those who did had fewer pregnancies, were less likely to be sexually experienced, were more likely to have attempted to avoid HIV infection through decreasing the number of sexual partners and using condoms. Nancy L. Leland and Richard P. Barth, "Characteristics of Adolescents Who Have Attempted to Avoid HIV and Who Have Communicated With Parents About Sex," *Journal of Adolescent Research* 8 (1993):58–76. In another study, reports indicated that students who discussed HIV with their parents were less likely than those who did not to have had multiple sex partners, to have had unprotected sexual intercourse, and to have ever injected drugs. Deborah Holtzman and Richard Robinson, "Parent and Peer Communication Effects on AIDS-Related Behavior Among U.S. High School Students," *Family Planning Perspectives* 27 (1995):235–240, 268.

54. Brent C. Miller and Kristin A. Moore, "Adolescent Sexual Behavior, Pregnancy, and Parenting: Research Through the 1980s," *Journal of Marriage and the Family* 52 (1990):1025–1044; Jeanne Brooks-Gunn and Frank F. Furstenberg, "Adolescent Sexual Behavior," *American Psychologist* 44 (1989):249–257.

55. J. R. Faulkenberry, M. Vincent, A. James, and W. Johnson, "Coital Behavior, Attitudes and Knowledge of Students Who Experience Early Coitus," *Adolescence* 86 (1987):321–332.

56. Sandra L. Hofferth, "Contraceptive Decision-Making Among Adolescents." In *Risking the Future: Adolescent Sexuality, Pregnancy, and Childbearing,* ed. Sandra L. Hofferth and Cheryl D. Hayes (Washington, DC: National Academy Press, 1987).

57. Marita P. McCabe and John K. Collins, "Measurement of Depth of Desired and Experienced Sexual Involvement at Different Stages of Dating," *Journal of Sex Research* 20 (1984):377–390.

58. Brooks-Gunn and Furstenberg, "Adolescent Sexual Behavior."

59. J. Richard Udry, "Biological Predispositions and Social Control in Adolescent Sexual Behavior," *American Sociological Review* 53 (1988):709–722; Edward A. Smith and J. Richard Udry, "Coital and Non-Coital Sexual Behaviors of White and Black Adolescents," *American Journal of Public Health* 75 (1985):1200–1203. For White youth, for example, the first sexual experiences leading to intercourse tend to progress from kissing to petting to intercourse. For Black youth, they are less likely to follow the progression, and thus are more likely to move rapidly toward intercourse.

60. Jawanda K. Barnett, Dennis R. Papini, and Edward Gbur, "Familial Correlates of Sexually Active Pregnant and Nonpregnant Adolescents," *Adolescence* 26 (1991):457–472; Sandra L. Hanson, David E. Myers, and Alan L. Ginsburg, "The Role of Responsibility and Knowledge in Rescuing Out of Wedlock Children," *Journal of Marriage and the Family* 49 (1987):241–257.

61. Brent B. Benda and Frederick A. DiBiBlaso, "An Integration of Theory: Adolescent Sexual Contacts," *Journal of Youth and Adolescence* 23 (1994):403–420; J. W. Scott, "African American Daughter–Mother Relations and Teenage Pregnancy: Two Faces of Premarital Teenage Pregnancy," *Western Journal of Black Studies* 17 (1994):73–81.

62. Anthony Biglan, John Noell, Linda Ochs, Keith Smolowski, and Carol Metzler, "Does Sexual Coercion Play a Role in High-Risk Sexual Behavior of Adolescent and Young Adult Women?" *Journal of Behavioral Medicine* 18 (1995).549–568.

63. *Id.*

64. *Id.*

65. J. Crawford, A. M. Turtle, and S. Kippaz, "Student-Favored Strategies for AIDS Avoidance," *Australian Journal of Psychology* 42 (1990):123–138.

66. Joan Murray, S. Marie Harvey, and Linda J. Beckman, "The Importance of Contraceptive Attributes of College Women," *Journal of Applied Social Psychology* 19 (1989):1327–1350.

67. Leo Carroll, "Gender, Knowledge About AIDSs, Reported Behavioral Change, and the Sexual Behavior of College Students," *Journal of American College Health* 40 (1991):5 12.

68. Nelwyn B. Moore and J. Kenneth Davidson Sr., "Guilt About First Intercourse: An Antecedent of Sexual Dissatisfaction Among College Women," *Journal of Sex & Marital Therapy* 23 (1997):29–46.

69. *Id.*; Carol Anderson Darling, J. Kenneth Davidson, and Lauren C. Passarello, "The Mystique of First Intercourse Among College Youth: The Role of Partners, Contraceptive Practices, and Psychological Reactions," *Journal of Youth and Adolescence* 21 (1992):97–117.

70. Moore and Davidson, "Guilt About First Intercourse: An Antecedent of Sexual Dissatisfaction Among College Women."

71. 410 U.S. 113, 152 (1973).

72. Roe v. Wade, 410 U.S. 113, 165, n.67 (1973) (remarking that it was not then deciding the status of spousal or parental consent statutes).

73. Bellotti v. Baird, 443 U.S. 622, 642 (1979).

74. Planned Parenthood v. Danforth, 428 U.S. 52, 74 (1976).

75. *Id.* at 75.

76. *Bellotti,* 443 U.S. 622, 634 (1979).

77. *Id.* at 640.

78. *Id.* at 644.

79. *Id.* at 647.

80. 505 U.S. 833 (1992).

81. *Id.* at 899 (emphasis added).

82. Ohio v. Akron Center for Reproductive Health, 497 U.S. 502 (1990). For the second proposition, *see* Hodgson v. Minnesota, 497 U.S. 417 (1990).

83. *Akron Center for Reproductive Health,* 497 U.S. at 502.

84. *Hodgson,* 497 U.S. at 417.

85. The states include California, Hawaii, Iowa, Nebraska, New Hampshire, New Jersey, New York, Oklahoma, Oregon, Texas, Vermont, and Washington.

86. CONN. GEN. STAT. ANN. §§ 19a-600 to -601 (West 1994 & Supp. 1998); ME. REV. STAT. ANN. tit. 22 § 1597-A (West 1983 & Supp. 1996); WISC. STAT. ANN. § 146.78 (West 1996 & Supp. 1997).

87. ALA. CODE § 26-21-3 (Michie 1992 & Supp. 1997); ALASKA STAT. § 18.16.010 (Michie 1996); ARIZ. REV. STAT. ANN. § 36-2152 (West 1993 & Supp. 1997); COLO. REV. STAT. § 18-6-101 et seq. (West 1990 & Supp. 1997); DEL. CODE ANN. tit. 24, § 1790 (Michie 1997); FLA. STAT. ANN. § 390.0111(4) (West 1991 & Supp. 1998); IND. CODE ANN. § 16-34-2-4 (Michie 1997); KY. REV. STAT. ANN. § 311.732 (Michie/Bobbs-Merrill 1990 & Supp. 1996); LA. REV. STAT. ANN. § 40:1299.35.5 (West 1992 & Supp. 1998); ME. REV. STAT. ANN. tit. 22 § 1597-A (West 1992 & Supp. 1998); MASS. ANN. LAWS ch. 112, § 12S (Law. Co-op. 1991 & Supp. 1998); MICH. COMP. LAW ANN. § 722.901-.908 (West 1993 & Supp. 1998); MISS. CODE ANN. § 41-41-53 (Law. Co-op 1993 & Supp. 1997); MO. ANN. STAT. § 188.028 (Vernon 1996 & Supp. 1998); N.M. STAT. ANN. § 30-5-1.C (Michie 1994 & Supp. 1998); N.C. Gen. Stat. § 90-21.7 (Michie 1997); N.D. CENT. CODE § 14-02.1-03.1 (Michie 1991 & Supp. 1997); PA. STAT. ANN. tit. 18, § 3206 (1983 & Supp. 1998); R.I. GEN. LAWS tit. 4C § 23-4.7-6 (Michie 96 & Supp. 1997); S.C. CODE ANN. § 44-41-31 (Law. Co-op. 1985 & Supp. 1997); TENN. CODE ANN. § 37-10-303 (Michie 1996 & Supp. 1997); VA. CODE ANN. § 18.2-76 (Michie 1996 & Supp. 1998); WIS. STAT. § 48.375 (West 1997).

88. ARK. CODE ANN. § 20-16-801 et seq. (Michie 1991 & Supp. 1997); GA. CODE ANN. § 15-11-112 (Michie 1994 & Supp. 1998); IDAHO CODE § 18-609 (Michie 1997); ILL. REV. STAT. ch. 720, ¶ 520-4 (West 1993 & Supp. 1998); KAN. STAT. ANN. § 65-6705 (1992 & Supp. 1997); MD. CODE ANN. HEALTH-GEN. § 20-103 (Michie 1996); MINN. STAT. ANN. § 144.343 (West 1998); MONT. CODE ANN. § 50-20-204 (1997); NEV. REV. STAT. § 442.255 (Michie 1996 & Supp. 1997); OHIO REV. CODE ANN. tit. 29 § 2919.12 (Anderson 1996 & Supp. 1997); S.D. CODIFIED LAWS ANN. § 34-23A-7 (Michie 1994 & Supp. 1998); UTAH. CODE ANN. § 76-7-304 (Michie 1995 & Supp. 1998); W. VA. CODE § 16-2F-3 (Michie 1998); WYO. STAT. § 35-6-118 (Michie 1997).

89. This was the rationale employed in Roe v. Wade, 410 U.S. 113 (1973).

90. *Bellotti,* 443 U.S. at 634–639.

91. Gary B. Melton, ''Knowing What We Do Know: APA and Adolescent Abortion,'' *American Psychologist* 45 (1990):1171–1172.

92. Bruce Ambuel and Julian Rappaport, ''Developmental Trends in Adolescents' Psychological and Legal Competence to Consent to Abortion,'' *Law and Human Behavior* 16 (1992):129–154. This research is significant in that competence does not necessarily transfer: Competence to determine medical procedures is not equivalent to competence to engage in sexual activity or competence to raise children. Commentators generally have assumed that decision making is similar across situations. Laura L. Finken and Janis E. Jacobs, ''Consultant Choice Across Decision Contexts: Are Abortion Decisions Different?'' *Journal of Adolescent Research* 11 (1996):235–260.

93. H. L. Matheson, 450 U.S. 398, 412–413 (1981).

94. Marvin Eisen and Gail L. Zellman, ''Factors Predicting Pregnancy Resolution Satisfaction of Unmarried Adolescents,'' *Journal of Genetic Psychology* 145 (1984):231–239.

95. Melton, ''Knowing What We Do Know: APA and Adolescent Abortion.''

96. Bellotti v. Baird, 443 U.S. 622, 633–639 (1979); H. L. Matheson, 450 U.S. 410 (1981); *Hodgson,* 497 U.S. at 417.

97. *Matheson,* 450 U.S. at 410; *Belotti,* 443 U.S. at 633–639.

98. *Akron Center for Reproductive Health,* 497 U.S. at 502.

99. *Id.*

100. David A. Baptiste Jr., "Counseling the Pregnant Adolescent Within a Family Context: Therapeutic Issues and Strategies," *Family Therapy* 13 (1986):163–176.

101. Torres et al., "Telling Parents: Clinic Policies and Adolescents' Use of Family Planning and Abortion Services."

102. Robert Wm. Blum, Michael D. Resnick, and Trisha A. Stark, "Factors Associated With the Use of Court Bypasses by Minors to Obtain Abortions," *Family Planning Perspectives* 22 (1990):158–160.

103. Everett L. Worthington Jr., David B. Larson, Malvin W. Brubaker, Cheryl Colecchi, James T. Berry, and David Morrow, "The Benefits of Legislation Requiring Parental Involvement Prior to Adolescent Abortion," *American Psychologist* 44 (1989):1542–1545.

104. For an early study, *see* Catherine Briedis, "Marginal Deviants: Teenage Girls Experience Community Response to Premarital Sex and Pregnancy," *Social Problems* 22 (1974):480–493.

105. Patricia Donovan, "Judging Teenagers: How Minors Fare When They Seek Court-Authorized Abortion," *Family Planning Perspectives* 15 (1983):259–267.

106. *Id.*

107. *See, e.g.,* David M. Ferguson, L. John Horwood, and Michael T. Lynskey, "Childhood Sexual Abuse, Adolescent Sexual Behaviors and Sexual Revictimization," *Child Abuse & Neglect* 21 (1997):789–803.

108. Stanley K. Henshaw and Kathryn Kost, "Parental Involvement in Minors' Abortion Decisions," *Family Planning Perspectives* 24 (1992):196–207, 213.

109. *Id.*

110. Blum et al., "Factors Associated With the Use of Court Bypasses by Minors to Obtain Abortions"; Torres et al., "Telling Parents: Clinic Policies and Adolescents' Use of Family Planning and Abortion Services."

111. Blum et al., "Factors Associated With the Use of Court Bypasses by Minors to Obtain Abortions."

112. Henshaw and Kost, "Parental Involvement in Minors' Abortion Decisions."

113. Torres et al., "Telling Parents: Clinic Policies and Adolescents' Use of Family Planning and Abortion Services."

114. Blum et al., "Factors Associated With the Use of Court Bypasses by Minors to Obtain Abortions"; Henshaw and Kost, "Parental Involvement in Minors' Abortion Decisions."

115. Blum et al., "Factors Associated With the Use of Court Bypasses by Minors to Obtain Abortions."

116. *Id.*

117. *Id.*

118. Henshaw and Kost, "Parental Involvement in Minors' Abortion Decisions."

119. *Id.*

120. *Id.*

121. *Id.*

122. *Id.*

123. By the time of the abortion, only 7% of mothers and 8% percent of fathers still wanted their daughters to continue their pregnancy. *Id.*

124. Donovan, "Judging Teenagers: How Minors Fare When They Seek Court-Authorized Abortion," e.g., noted that because teenagers must go to court, there is a delay in obtaining an abortion. The problem, of course, is that time is critical because delays may advance the pregnancy and increase the risk and cost of abortions. Delays also increase the likelihood that the adolescent will end up in a more tightly regulated trimester—when mothers reach the second and third trimesters, states have more freedom to limit access to abortions in the name of protecting the interests of society and the future child.

125. Christine Cregan Sensibaugh and Elizabeth Rice Allgeier, "Abortion and Judicial Bypass," *Politics and Life Sciences* 15 (1996):35–47.

126. Donovan, ''Judging Teenagers: How Minors Fare When They Seek Court-Authorized Abortion.''

127. Sensibaugh and Allgeier, ''Abortion and Judicial Bypass.''

128. Catherine C. Lewis, ''A Comparison of Minors' and Adults' Pregnancy Decisions,'' *American Journal of Orthopsychiatry* 50 (1980):446–451.

129. Robert Wm. Blum and Michael D. Resnick, ''Adolescent Sexual Decision-Making: Contraception, Pregnancy, Abortion, Motherhood,'' *Pediatric Annals* 11 (1982):797–801.

130. 505 U.S. 833 (1992).

131. Planned Parenthood v Casey, 505 U.S. 833, 887–901 (1992).

132. 18 PA. CONS. STAT. ANN. § 3206(1)-(g) (1992 & Supp. 1992).

133. *Id.*

134. *Casey,* 505 U.S. at 833.

135. *Id.* at 833.

136. 316 U.S. 535 (1942).

137. *Id.* at 541.

138. 410 U.S. 113 (1973).

139. 381 U.S. 479, 485–486 (1965).

140. 405 U.S. 438, 453 (1972).

141. 431 U.S. 678, 693 (1977).

142. *Id.*

143. The few times in which these cases have reached the courts have been in instances in which fathers refused to pay child support when they had told the mother to have an abortion. The claim is that because it was then her choice to have the child, it would not be reasonable to require him to support it. The argument has been entirely unsuccessful; *see, e.g.,* Harris v. Alabama, 356 So.2d 623 (Alabama, 1978); People of the Interest of S.P.B., 651 P.2d 1213 (Colo. 1982).

144. Roger J. R. Levesque, ''Targeting 'Deadbeat' Dads: The Problem With the Direction of Welfare Reform,'' *Hamline Journal of Public Law and Policy* 15 (1994):1–53.

145. Lehr v. Robertson, 463 U.S. 248, 261 (1983).

146. 491 U.S. 110 (1989).

147. Buck v. Bell, 274 U.S. 200 (1927).

148. *Id.* at 207.

149. Skinner v. Oklahoma, 316 U.S. 535 (1942).

150. *Id.* at 541.

151. Stump v. Sparkman, 435 U.S. 349 (1978).

152. C. W. v. Wasiek, 640 A.2d 427, *cert. denied,* 513 U.S. 1183 (1995).

153. *Stump,* 435 U.S. at 358.

154. *Wasiek,* 640 A.2d at 427, *cert. denied,* 513 U.S. at 1183.

155. ARK. CODE ANN. §§ 20-49-101 to -304 (Michie 1997); CAL. PROB. CODE §§ 1950 to 1969 (West 1996 & Supp. 1998); COLO. REV. STAT. 15.22 § 27-10.5-132 (19) (West 1990 & Supp. 1997); CONN. GEN. STAT. ANN. §§ 45a-690 to -700 (West 1994 & Supp. 1998); DEL. CODE ANN. tit. 16, §§ 5701 to -5716 (Michie 1995 & Supp. 1996); GA. CODE ANN. §§ 31-20-1 to -20-6 (Michie 1996 & Supp. 1997); HAW. REV. STAT. §§ 560.5-601 to -612 (1993 & Supp. 1998); IDAHO CODE §§ 39-3901 to -3910 (Michie 1987 & Supp. 1997); ME. REV. STAT. ANN. tit. 34-B, §§ 7001 to -7017 (West 1983 & Supp. 1997); MISS. CODE ANN. §§ 41-45-1 to -19 (Law. Co-op. 1994 & Supp. 1997); N.C. GEN. STAT. §§ 35-36 to -50 (Michie 1997); N.D. CENT. CODE §§ 25-01.2-09 & 25-01.211 (Michie 1991 & Supp. 1997); OR. REV. STAT. §§ 436.205 to -.335 (Butterworth 1990 & Supp. 1998); UTAH CODE ANN. §§ 62A-6-101 to -116 (Michie 1996 & Supp. 1998); VT. STAT. ANN. tit. 18 §§ 8705 to 16 (Michie 1975 & Supp. 1997); VA. CODE ANN. §§ 54.1-2976 to -2980 (Michie 1996 & Supp. 1998); W. VA. CODE §§ 27-16-1 to -4 (Michie 1996 & Supp. 1997).

156. For analyses of these statutes, *see* Roger J. R. Levesque, ''Regulating the Private Relations of Adults With Mental Disabilities—Old Laws, New Policies, Hollow Hopes,'' *Behavioral Sciences & the Law* 14 (1996):83–106.

157. 263 S.E.2d 805 (N.C. Ct. App. 1980).

158. *Id.*

159. *Id.* at 807.

160. 707 P.2d 760 (Sup. Ct. Cal. 1985).

161. *Id.* at 771–772.

162. *In re* Grady, 426 A.2d 467, 474 (N.J. Sup. Ct. 1981).

163. 452 F. Supp. 361 (D. Conn. 1978).

164. North Carolina Ass'n for Retarded Children v. N.C., 420 F. Supp. 451 (M.D.N.C. 1976).

165. *See also In re* Moore, 221 S.E.2d 307 (N.C. 1976).

166. 307 N.W.2d 881 (Wis. Sup. Ct. 1981).

167. *Id.* at 896–897.

168. Rebecca A. Maynard, "The Costs of Adolescent Childbearing." In *Kids Having Kids: Economic Costs and Social Consequences of Teen Pregnancy,* ed. Rebecca A. Maynard (Washington, DC: Urban Institute, 1997).

169. *See* chapter 10.

170. Much of this literature derives from investigations of poor and minority grandparents; Rebekah Levine Coley and P. Lindsay Chase-Linsdale, "Adolescent Pregnancy and Parenthood: Recent Evidence and Future Directions," *American Psychologist* 53 (1998):152–166.

171. Maynard, "The Costs of Adolescent Childbearing."

172. *Id.*

173. Raye Hudson Rosen, "Adolescent Pregnancy Decision-Making: Are Parents Important?" *Adolescence* 15 (1990):43–54.

174. Raye Hudson Rosen, Twylah Benson, and Jack M. Stack, "Help or Hinderance: Parental Impact on Pregnant Teenagers' Resolution Decision," *Family Relations* 31 (1982):271–280.

175. Laurie S. Zabin, Marilyn B. Hirsch, Mark R. Emerson, and Elizabeth Raymond, "To Whom Do Inner-City Minors Talk About Their Pregnancies? Adolescents' Communication With Parents and Parent Surrogates," *Family Planning Perspectives* 24 (1992):148–154, 173.

176. *Id.*

177. Miller and Moore, "Adolescent Sexual Behavior, Pregnancy, and Parenting: Research Through the 1980s"; Katherine Trent and Eve Powell-Griner, "Differences in Race, Marital Status, and Education Among Women Obtaining Abortions," *Social Forces* 69 (1991):1121–1141.

178. Kerry J. Daly, "Adolescent Perceptions of Adoption: Implications for Resolving an Unplanned Pregnancy," *Youth & Society* 25 (1994):330–350.

179. Christine A. Bachrach, Kathy Shepherd Stolley, and Kathryn A. Hatcher, "Relinquishment of Premarital Births: Evidence From the National Survey Data," *Family Planning Perspectives* 24 (1992):27–82.

180. Robert D. Plotnick, "The Effects of Attitudes on Teenage Premarital Pregnancy and Its Resolution," *American Sociological Review* 57 (1992):800–811.

181. Rebecca A. Maynard (Ed.), *Kids Having Kids: Economic Costs and Social Consequences of Teen Pregnancy* (Washington, DC: Urban Institute, 1997), pp. 285–337.

182. Debra Kalmuss, Pearila Brickner Namerow, and Linda Cushman, "Adoption Versus Parenting Among Young Pregnant Women," *Family Planning Perspectives* 23 (1991):17–23.

183. Maxine L. Weiman, Maralyn Robinson, Jane T. Simmons, Nelda B. Schreiber, and Ben Stafford, "Pregnant Teens: Differential Pregnancy Resolution and Treatment Implications," *Child Welfare* 68 (1989):45–55.

184. Brenda W. Donnelly and Patricia Voydanoff, "Parenting Versus Placing for Adoption: Consequences for Adolescent Mothers," *Family Relations* 45 (1996):427–434.

185. Kalmuss et al., "Adoption Versus Parenting Among Young Pregnant Women"; Michael D. Resnick, Robert Wm. Blum, Jane Bose, Martha Smith, and Roger Toogood, "Characteristics of Unmarried Adolescent Mothers: Determinants of Child Rearing Versus Adoption," *American Journal of Orthopsychiatry* 60 (1990):577–584.

186. Donnelly and Voydanoff, "Parenting Versus Placing for Adoption: Consequences for Adolescent Mothers."

187. Steven D. McLaughlin, Diane L. Manninen, and Linda D. Winges, "Do Adolescents Who

Relinquish Their Children Fare Better or Worse Than Those Who Raise Them?'' *Family Planning Perspectives* 20 (1988):25–32.

188. Kathleen M. Herr, ''Adoption Versus Parenting Decisions Among Pregnant Adolescents,'' *Adolescence* 24 (1989):795–799; Daly, ''Adolescent Perceptions of Adoption: Implications for Resolving an Unplanned Pregnancy.''

189. Daly, ''Adolescent Perceptions of Adoption: Implications for Resolving an Unplanned Pregnancy.''

190. *Id.*

191. Resnick et al., ''Characteristics of Unmarried Adolescent Mothers: Determinants of Child Rearing Versus Adoption,'' 583.

192. David J. Kallen, Robert J. Griffore, Susan Popovich, and Virginia Powell, ''Adolescent Mothers and Their Mothers View Adoption,'' *Family Relations* 39 (1990):311–316.

193. Daly, ''Adolescent Perceptions of Adoption: Implications for Resolving an Unplanned Pregnancy.''

194. Brenda W. Donnelly and Patricia Voydanoff, ''Factors Associated With Releasing for Adoption Among Adolescent Mothers,'' *Family Relations* 40 (1991):404–410.

195. Kalmuss et al., ''Adoption Versus Parenting Among Young Pregnant Women''; Donnelly and Voydanoff, ''Parenting Versus Placing for Adoption: Consequences for Adolescent Mothers,'' 195.

196. Donnelly and Voydanoff, ''Parenting Versus Placing for Adoption: Consequences for Adolescent Mothers.''

197. Kristin Luker, *Dubious Conceptions: The Politics of Teenage Pregnancy* (Cambridge, MA: Harvard University Press, 1996).

198. In 1990, for example, teenagers had 30% of all births out of wedlock. *See* Statistical Abstract of the United States (Washington, DC: Government Printing Office, 1994), table 101, ''Births to Unmarried Mothers, by Race of Child and Age of Mother, 1970–1990.''

199. Jacqueline Darroch Forrest and Susheela Singh, ''The Sexual Reproductive Behavior of American Women, 1982–1988,'' *Family Planning Perspectives* 22 (1990):206–314.

200. The only law review article written on the sterilization of minors was a short comment that simply laid the contours of their possible due process rights and the need for a state to adopt a statute; *see* Mark A. Small, ''Involuntary Sterilization of Mentally Retarded Minors in Nebraska,'' *Nebraska Law Review* 68 (1989):410–429.

201. *See* Levesque, ''Regulating the Private Relations of Adults With Mental Disabilities—Old Laws, New Policies, Hollow Hopes.''

202. Maynard, *Kids Having Kids: Economic Costs and Social Consequences of Teen Pregnancy.*

203. Coley and Chase-Linsdale, ''Adolescent Pregnancy and Parenthood: Recent Evidence and Future Directions.''

204. E. Michael Foster, Damon Jones, and Saul D. Hoffman, ''The Economic Impact of Nonmarital Childbearing: How Are Older, Single Mothers Faring?'' *Journal of Marriage and the Family* 60 (1998):163–174.

205. 262 U.S. 390 (1923).

206. 316 U.S. 535 (1942).

207. 388 U.S. 1 (1967).

208. Maynard v. Hill, 125 U.S. 190 (1888).

209. NEB. REV. STAT. § 42-102 (1995 & Supp. 1997); OHIO REV. CODE ANN. § 3105.01 (Anderson 1994 & Supp. 1997); MISS. CODE ANN. § 93-1-5 (Law. Co-op. 1994 & Supp. 1997).

210. N.Y. DOM. REL. LAW § 7 (McKinney 1989 & Supp. 1998).

211. CAL. FAM. CODE §§ 302 (West 1996 & Supp. 1998); KAN. STAT. ANN. § 23-106 (1988 & Supp. 1997); MASS. GEN. LAWS ch. 207, § 25 (Law. Co-op. 1994 & Supp. 1998).

212. ARIZ. REV. STAT. ANN. § 25-102 (Michie 1997); CONN. GEN. STAT. ANN. § 46b-30 (West 1994 & Supp. 1998); ME. REV. STAT. ANN. tit. 19, § 62 (West 1983 & Supp. 1996); NEV. REV. STAT. §§ 122.020, 122.025 (Michie 1997); N.J. STAT. ANN. § 37:1-6 (West 1995 & Supp. 1998); N.M. STAT. ANN. §§ 40-1-6 (Michie 1978 & Supp. 1998); PA. CONS. STAT. ANN. 23 § 1304 (Purdon

1983 & Supp. 1998); W. VA. CODE § 48-1-1 (Michie 1996 & Supp. 1997); WYO. STAT. § 20-1-102 (Michie 1997).

213. HAW. REV. STAT. §§ 572-1, 572-2 (1993 & Supp. 1996); MO. ANN. STAT. § 451.090 (West 1996 & Supp. 1997).

214. MISS. CODE ANN. § 93-1-5 (Law. Co-op. 1995 & Supp. 1998).

215. R.I. GEN. LAWS § 15-2-11 (Michie 1994 & Supp. 1997).

216. ARK. CODE ANN. §§ 9-11-102, 9-11-103 (Michie 1997); VA. CODE ANN. §§ 20-45.1, 20-48 (Michie 1996 & Supp. 1998).

217. N.J. STAT. ANN. § 37:1-6 (West 1995 & Supp. 1998).

218. IDAHO CODE § 32-202 (Michie 1987 & 1997).

219. UTAH. CODE ANN. §§ 30-1-2, 30-1-9 (Michie 1996 & Supp. 1998); VT. STAT. ANN. tit. 18, § 5142 (Michie 1974 & Supp. 1997).

220. OR. REV. STAT. § 106.060 (Butterworth 1990 & Supp. 1998).

221. MICH. COMP. LAWS ANN. § 551.103 (West 1991 & Supp. 1998); N.D. CENT. CODE § 14-03-02 (Michie 1991 & Supp. 1997); S.D. CODIFIED LAWS ANN. § 25-1-9 (Michie 1992 & Supp. 1998); WIS. STAT. ANN. § 765.02 (West 1996 & Supp. 1997).

222. ALA. CODE §§ 30-1-4, 30-1-5 (Michie 1995 & Supp. 1997).

223. NEB. REV. STAT. § 42-105 (1995 & Supp. 1997).

224. N.H. REV. STAT. ANN. §§ 457:4, 457:6 (Butterworth 1994 & Supp. 1997); OHIO REV. CODE ANN. § 3105.01 (Anderson 1994 & Supp. 1998); S.C. CODE ANN. § 20-1-250 (West/Law. Co-op. 1985 & Supp. 1997).

225. DEL. CODE ANN. tit. 13, § 123 (Michie 1995 & Supp. 1996); GA. CODE ANN. § 19-3-37 (Michie 1996 & Supp. 1998).

226. FLA. STAT. ANN. § 741.0405 (Harrison 1991 & Supp. 1997); IND. CODE ANN. §§ 31-7-1-6, 31-7-1-7, 31-7-2-2 (Burns 1994 & Supp. 1998).

227. ALASKA STAT. §§ 25.05.171 (Michie 1996); N.Y. DOM. REL. LAW §§ 7, 15a (McKinney 1989 & Supp. 1998).

228. LA. REV. STAT. ANN. art. 1545 (West 1986 & Supp. 1998); TENN. CODE ANN. § 36-3-107 (Michie 1997); WASH. REV. CODE ANN. § 26.04.010 (West 1988 & Supp. 1998).

229. COLO. REV. STAT. ANN. §§ 14-2-106, 14-2-108 (West 1990 & Supp. 1997); ILL. ANN. STAT. ch. 750, ¶ 5/208 (West/Smith-Hurd 1993 & Supp. 1998); IOWA CODE ANN. § 595.2 (West 1994 & Supp. 1998); MINN. STAT. ANN. § 517.02 (West 1992 & Supp. 1998); MONT. CODE ANN. § 40-1-402 (1997).

230. TEX. FAM. CODE ANN. §§ 1.52, 1.53 (Vernon 1996 & Supp. 1998).

231. KY. REV. STAT. ANN. § 402.020 (Michie/Bobbs-Merrill 1990 & Supp. 1996).

232. MD. CRIM. LAW CODE ANN. § 2-301 (Michie 1995 & Supp. 1997).

233. N.C. GEN. STAT. § 51-2 (1993 & Supp. 1997).

234. OKLA. STAT. ANN. tit. 43, § 3 (West 1983 & Supp. 1998).

235. Roger J. R. Levesque, *The Sexual Abuse of Children: A Human Rights Perspective* (Bloomington: Indiana University Press, 1999).

236. *Id.; see also* Kelly C. Connerton, "The Resurgence of the Marital Rape Exemption: The Victimization of Teens by Their Statutory Rapists," *Albany Law Review* 61 (1997):237–284.

237. U.S. Bureau of the Census, Marital Status and Living Arrangements, *Current Population Reports* Series P-20, no. 450 (1991), p. 1, Table A.

238. Larry Bumpass, "What's Happening to the Family: Interactions Between Demographic and Institutional Change," *Demography* 27 (1990):483–498.

239. The most noteworthy work in this area is by William J. Wilson, *The Truly Disadvantaged: The Inner City, the Underclass, and Public Policy* (Chicago: University of Chicago Press, 1987).

240. Luker, *Dubious Conceptions: The Politics of Teenage Pregnancy.*

PART III

Rethinking the Legal Control of Adolescent Sexuality

Chapter 5
SEX AND SCHOOLS

Despite the popular belief that parents and society pervasively object to formal sex education, they actually do not.[1] Society pervasively perceives schools as the proper forum to disseminate sexual information to adolescents. The majority of public school districts respond to the societal belief that schools must educate adolescents about some sexual matters. Schools that do attempt to fulfill their obligation to educate adolescents typically offer some traditional forms of sex education programs directed to disease prevention and some more contemporary educational programs aimed at sexual maltreatment prevention.[2]

The ubiquitousness and potential success of prevention efforts lead policy makers to view schools as the most efficient means to prevent major health and social problems confronting society.[3] Although schools do respond to the need to offer sex education, critics challenge the particular content of sex education programs and question claims of their relative effectiveness.[4] Existing sex education programs pervasively continue to fail adolescents and society.

Pervasive dissatisfaction about curricular content and the continued failure to design and implement effective programs reveal two important points about adolescents' sexual rights. Continuing debates confirm that sex education programs are morally charged. Whether explicitly or implicitly, sex education conveys images of gender roles, ethics of care, notions of normality, and conceptions of the good society. Thus although conflict over the content of sex education may be presented in terms of relative effectiveness, debates also fundamentally involve the clash over which set of moral norms related to sex shall be presented to adolescents.[5]

The discontent and moral clashes also reveal adolescents' precarious place in the U.S. legal system. Jurisprudence concerned with adolescents' sexual rights while in school remains one of the most undeveloped areas of law—that failed development contrasts sharply with measurable developments in numerous areas of adolescent rights, including the balance between adolescents' sexual rights against their parents' morals and demands in such controversial areas as abortion, contraceptives, and access to other forms of medical intervention relating to sexual activity.

A proper analysis of adolescents' sexual rights in the context of sex education requires analyses of both adolescents' educational rights and the profoundly moral nature of sex education. This chapter first reviews the state of the art in sex education and identifies reasons for reform, especially rationales and justifications that reach beyond traditional arguments. The analysis then examines adolescents' educational rights and finds that educators and state officials largely control the content of adolescents' rights, with the major exception that schools must not create programs contrary to ideals of a pluralistic, democratic society. Given states' broad discretion in determining educational content, the investigation of adolescents' educational rights continues with an analysis of existing state statutory mandates that guide sex education and reasons states could and should enact further legislation. The chapter then explores alternatives that may be taken to address adolescents' right to education that would ensure appropriate knowledge of sexuality and help adolescents deal with the nature and consequences of sexual activity. An important point of analysis centers on the extent to which education must be mandated, even despite objections from parents or students themselves.

The current social science and legal understanding of adolescents' educational rights in the context of sex education suggests that programs simply must provide basic information that the general public already deems noncontroversial and must focus on ensuring adolescents' eventual societal participation in a manner that simply reflects the traditional legal obligation of schools to inculcate adolescents and prepare them for citizenship.[6] The analysis underscores the need to remove sex education from divisive groups' conflicting views about how society should foster the next generation as the center of "culture wars." Instead, the analysis suggests that schools must address sexuality as it would any other important subject that prepares adolescents for their future and immediate societal participation. From this perspective, sex education is much more than about "sex." Sex education involves "sexuality" education—an approach that recognizes how sexuality plays a dominant role in adolescents' general education and place in society and that addresses the multiple forces that affect adolescent sexuality and its consequences. Although the perspective's benefits may not be intuitively obvious, several points signal its significance.[7] The focus coincides with laws regulating education and adolescents' citizenship as well as recent developments in adolescents' individual, human rights. The move also corresponds to research findings that relate to sound educational practice and to the manner in which adolescents develop and learn not only in schools but also in their families, peer groups, and communities. In addition, the refocus addresses moral systems that go beyond sexuality education and divisive ideologies that account for the relative failure of school reform efforts. Finally and unlike existing methods, the focus accommodates ideological pluralism, which remains necessary to maintain and further the societal commitment to basic democratic principles.

Sexuality Education

Movements to introduce different forms of sexuality education into public schools have a history that reaches back more than a century.[8] As could be expected, societal crises and shifting sensibilities contribute to the fluctuation and evolution of programs. Despite consistent and varied attempts to educate adolescents about sexuality, only the past few decades have witnessed dramatic changes in the scope, character, and philosophy of sexuality programs. Historically, sexuality education generally centered on disease prevention and reduction of sexual dysfunction.[9] Although those two concerns still remain, recent programs adopt more diverse approaches to protecting adolescents. Programs have moved from providing only basic information about ways to protect adolescents from pregnancy and sexually transmitted diseases, to offering opportunities for "value clarification" in addition to providing basic information, to not teaching students about prophylaxis and emphasizing abstinence instead of letting adolescents clarify their own values, to focusing on safer sex practices and pleasures of sexual behavior.[10] Without doubt, diversity in tone and content now marks the possible forms of sexuality education programs, even though they still tend to focus on preventing and reducing sexual dysfunction. Despite impressive diversity and eclecticism, the current character of sexuality programs vacillates between two extremes, which form the focus of the following analyses that explore the nature, effectiveness, and justifications of existing sexuality education programs.

The Nature of Sexuality Education Programs

The extremes in tone and character of current sexuality education programs reflect the extent of particular communities' commitments to divergent moral visions for humanity: the impulse toward restrictive orthodoxy and the impulse toward expansive liberalism.[11] Commentators reveal how these impulses operating in culture wars affect sexuality education programs. These two polarizing tendencies encompass broad sexual values that foster proposals to reform sexuality education and delimit visions and possibilities for further reform.[12] These extremes possess rather distinct tones and impressions of adolescents' sexual behaviors and champion different types of information that may be shared with adolescents. Given that much confusion may arise from value-laden terms used in this area of research, it is important to denote more precisely what each approach actually champions and seeks to accomplish through sexuality education.

The restrictive approach generally casts human sexuality in a negative light and seeks to subject sexual behavior to strict legal, social, and moral controls. The approach accepts only a narrow set of behaviors as moral and finds other behaviors destructive to the person and society. Advocates of this ideology generally disapprove of contraception and safer sex practices; they also condemn masturbation, homosexual behavior, and pre- and extramarital sexual relations. In terms of sexuality education, commentators generally characterize the approach as fear-based, antisex, and antiprophylactic.[13] The restrictive model encourages adolescents to avoid sexual activity and assumes that the majority of teenagers are incapable of making appropriately sound decisions about sexual activity. The model minimizes the instruction of sexual concepts and focuses on abstinence from sexual activity as the most effective route to eventual sexual maturity and health. Researchers who trace policy trends note that the model clearly has gained ground, as especially exemplified by the resurgence of abstinence-based national legislation.[14]

Advocates of the permissive approach generally view sexual behavior as a pleasurable aspect of life and propose that an active, pleasurable, and satisfying sexual life contributes to individual self-fulfillment and psychological health. Permissive ideologies generally view homosexuality as morally valid and accept many forms of nonprocreative sexual behavior. In terms of sex education, commentators characterize the approach as sex-positive, pluralistic, and comprehensive.[15] The approach operates under the belief that teaching abstinence alone remains ineffective and that using fear tactics hampers the eventual development of healthy, sexual adults. Programs influenced by permissive ideologies target students from kindergarten through high school and teach basic biological processes, the psychology of relationships, and the sociology of the family. More controversially, some programs cover materials on the sexology of masturbation and massage, contraception and condom use, as well as sexual pleasure.[16]

Although these two extremes guide existing programs found in most schools, they both face important challenges.[17] Some critics of the permissive approach propose that schools must solely instruct abstinence; and many fault the approach for encouraging adolescents to become sexually active and for not necessarily changing adolescents' protective behaviors. Some critics of the restrictive approach argue that teaching abstinence avoids reality, that it dangerously promotes fear and shame, and that it leads adolescents to engage in unprotected sexual behavior.

A most peculiar aspect of sexuality education debates is that critics of both approaches easily and readily garner support from research evaluations. A most notable example of the manner in which research may actually support both or neither of the dominant approaches to sexuality education (the restrictive or the permissive) involves the extent to which knowledge about sexual information from sexuality education courses affects sexual activity and attitudes. It is not surprising that students who take sex education classes do tend to know more about sexual matters.[18] More accurate knowledge of sexual behavior, however, fails to measurably affect sexual activity and attitudes.[19] The failure to change both practices and beliefs is most pronounced in the area that has been a major target in sexuality education: condom use. Research relating to adolescents' condom use reveals that most sexually active boys believe their partners would appreciate their offering to use a condom, feel less embarrassed about buying condoms, and increasingly report that condoms do not reduce sexual pleasure. Yet neither boys nor girls report a significant increase or proper use of condoms.[20] Evaluation studies reveal that nearly half of sexually active students would have intercourse without condoms. More problematically, too much knowledge of reasons condoms should be used (e.g., for AIDS prevention and birth control) as well as negative images associated with condom use (AIDS, promiscuity, homosexuality) actually decrease the likelihood of condom use because those images, for example, may conflict with the images partners may want to portray to one another.[21] Other measures of effectiveness also challenge the belief that sexuality-education programs reach their intended goals.[22] The general lack of positive findings that would indicate sustained and sustainable success in educational efforts leaves programs vulnerable to attacks from all sides.

Accounting for the Failures of Sexuality Education Programs

Several factors account for the failure to find expected results that would confirm the effects of sexuality education programs. Critics of evaluation studies generally attribute the failure to prove effectiveness to methodological problems evaluators face.[23] However, the failure to identify broadly successful programs, let alone those that would receive popular support, go beyond methodological and evaluative limitations. Several factors may limit success. Most current sexuality education programs are too limited in scope to increase significantly sexuality knowledge to the extent that it could affect behavior.[24] Despite calls for reform, current courses simply have not adapted to meet changing demands. Leading texts have not modified their contents to reflect changes in approaches to sexuality education.[25] Other schools simply do not offer courses and, instead, have made contraceptives available, despite strong evidence that increasing the ease of access to contraceptives does not increase their use.[26] As discussed in chapter 4, efforts to increase contraceptive use must address other reasons for not using them, such as the failure to plan ahead and the need to show trust in partners.

Sexuality education programs that have changed still remain limited. More comprehensive programs tend to be short: Sexuality education classes usually last a semester or less; and on average, schools allocate only 6½ hours a year on all sexuality education topics.[27] The short time would lead few to expect that even adults would modify behaviors, especially pleasurable ones, that place their health at risk. In addition, even though programs may have become comprehensive, they do not necessarily reach students who could affect the rates of sexual activity and their outcomes. Sexuality programs largely ignore males or provide them with much more limited information than they provide females. Even when sexuality topics are of mutual interest, gender differences still exist in the illustrations and representations of topics.[28] Some programs also separate males from females to teach different materials, despite claims that such efforts lead to imbalances in knowledge base and inhibit the development of proper interactions between the sexes.[29] Likewise, schools tend to introduce topics later than they are needed. For example, although those most at risk for negative consequences of sexual activity have engaged in risk behaviors by the eighth grade, it would make sense to start earlier, particularly because these adolescents also are most likely to drop out of school during eighth grade[30] and few social programs exist to assist them when outside of schools.[31]

Another major reason for the failure to effect changes in adolescent sexual behavior and beliefs derives from the manner in which schools deal with the moral issues presented earlier. Schools attempt to strike a balance between the two extremes by stressing abstinence, yet also teaching students safe sex practices and proper contraceptive use. These attempts to balance tend to make programs abstinence-only or abstinence-based; they remain concerned with the need to avoid controversial issues.[32] The result is that fewer than 5% of young people get complete comprehensive sexuality education; and no estimates exist that would indicate the number who do not have any form of sexuality education.[33] Concern with avoiding controversial issues also means that schools tend not to focus on actual sexual behavior, fewer focus on issues of diversity, gender roles, and the place of sexuality in society and culture.[34] The failure persists despite recognition that the majority of students are from some form of minority group and that some minority groups and those with special needs are at greater risk for experiencing the negative consequences sexuality education aims to prevent.[35]

Another important reason for the failure to find effective programs is that research on efforts to effect any behavioral changes reports that increased knowledge generally remains insufficient without a focus on other potential domains that influence behavior. In the context of sexuality education, this general rule would mean that they will remain ineffective as long as they do not also address peer behaviors and beliefs, family values, media exposure, and, often forgotten, the choice of partners and relationships with individual partners.[36] The programs that have addressed sexuality in such a comprehensive manner, though, also have proven ineffective in sustaining changes in sexual activities and attitudes. When relatively successful programs have been implemented—at least to the extent that some do alleviate some negative outcomes of sexual activity—for example, pregnancy and AIDs[37]—factions tend to develop and quickly dismantle efforts researchers find effective.[38]

The failure to find moderate and sustained effectiveness is of significance. Given the rampant failures of programs to decrease rates of sexual activity and increase the rates of safer-sex behaviors, proponents for sexuality education programs find it difficult to justify their existence. The failures of sexuality education programs also reveal that they tend to be justified for the wrong reasons, or at least reasons that are not demonstrably sound. The dismal picture emerging from research on sexuality education does not mean that programs should be abandoned, because proving effectiveness of any form of education proves considerably difficult.[39] Indeed, leading commentators emphasize that it is a mistake to promote sexuality education by promising to reduce problems.[40] The findings highlight how reasons and justifications for contemporary sexuality education programs must be reexamined, especially given the general acceptance that programs should exist.

Sexuality Education's Justifications

Adults and adolescents generally agree that adolescents' sexual activity runs the risk of placing adolescents in problematic circumstances and, as we have seen, most agree that schools could play a role in addressing the problem.[41] However, schools remain hampered by one fundamental limitation: Commitment to having schools deal with the problem does not necessarily translate into agreement on the nature of the problem. Widespread disagreement exists in beliefs about the nature of the ''problem'' and what constitutes problematic circumstances in which adolescents may find themselves.[42] Although these fundamental concerns remain largely ignored and the reasons for the existence of sexuality education are understood as homogenous, it is important to examine the dominant variations in current views of the nature of the problem, because perceptions of the problem necessarily dictate the nature of responses and the popular support for specific programs. It is not surprising that the problem is contested by those holding different views about the future direction society should take and the role formal education should play in its realization.

Many view the problem in terms of the increasing percentage of teenagers who engage in premarital, heterosexual activity at young ages. The fact that adolescents engage in sexual activity, regardless of whether they may be placing themselves at risk for certain negative consequences, serves as the central cause for concern.[43] The extent to which concern is placed on the number of adolescents who are involved in sexual activity seems well warranted: Adolescents do seem to engage in sexual activity, and a significant number will have had more than one partner. For example, according to the Centers for Disease Control, by the time adolescents reach 12th grade, more than 70 percent will report having had sexual intercourse.[44] Nearly one quarter of all high school students will have had four or more sexual partners by the time they reach 12th grade. Because early sexual activity and multiple partners places adolescents at risk for negative experiences, this perspective suggests that sexuality education, whether in schools or in the home, properly must focus on encouraging adolescents to abstain from premarital and other nontraditional sexual relationships. Rather than adopting a broad view of the need for sexuality education, others tend to focus more on specific issues that must be addressed to ensure more healthy adolescent development.

Perhaps the most dominant view of the problem involves perceptions of the frequency of unprotected heterosexual coitus and the potentially negative consequences associated with teenage pregnancy.[45] Again, given current statistics, the perception that a problem exists does seem warranted. Birth rates for unmarried teenagers have risen steadily over the past two decades and those rates still remain high.[46] These rates figure prominently in efforts to ensure that adolescents obtain accurate and useful sexuality information; they also are complemented by research that reveals sexually active adolescents fail to get reproductive care and basic sexuality information. Half of all teenage pregnancies occur within six months of the first sexual intercourse, one fifth within the first month; yet as has been discussed previously, teenagers generally wait one year before seeking reproductive health care.[47] These figures are often viewed as even more problematic in light of findings that almost half of those who become pregnant before they reach the age of majority obtain abortions.[48] From this perspective, sexuality education can either be abstinence focused or abstinence based but must at least include ways to protect sexually active adolescents from the consequences of pregnancy.

An increasingly dominant view perceives the problem in terms of the risk sexual activity poses for contacting sexually transmitted diseases.[49] Rates of sexually transmitted diseases (STDs) confirm that the concern is well-placed. One in four sexually active teenagers will be infected with an STD.[50] In addition, reports of the characteristics of people who are at risk for contacting AIDS place adolescents as one of the highest risk groups.[51] Defining these circumstances as problematic leads to a focus on providing adolescents with a more comprehensive education that would help them protect themselves. Although increasingly comprehensive, the programs that would assist adolescents and broaden their knowledge of AIDS and other diseases remain limited. Programs place emphasis on having adolescents protect themselves, and the relationships that are viewed as problematic are those in which adolescents voluntarily engage in sexual activity and find pleasurable.[52] Likewise, programs tend to ignore how to deal with infected adolescents and their classmates' reactions; nor do programs offer ''coping'' programs for adolescents from families with HIV-infected members.

Others view the major concern as the need to prepare adolescents to deal with coercive sexual behavior. Research relating to battering and rape that occurs in adolescent relationships illustrates the significance of the approach. Approximately 1 out of 10 high school students experiences physical violence in dating relationships.[53] Research also indicates that between 30 and 40% of girls who have dated report some form of sexual victimization during dating.[54] These findings from small samples are supported by estimates revealing that adolescent victims may account for more than 50% of rapes,[55] a finding supported by considerable research that reveals high levels of coercion involved in sexual activity.[56] From this perspective, sexuality education programs must be part of programs that offer skills to help students cope with and prevent aggressive behavior and provide adolescents with skills that will prevent them from engaging in coercive behaviors,[57] especially ways for adolescents to condemn violence committed by peers.[58]

Others view the problem more in terms of the manner the sexes generally treat each other and the manner in which heterosexual norms foster violence. The approach is most visible in terms of adolescent sexual harassment. A series of recent studies finds that more than 80% of female students experience behavior that would constitute sexual harassment if perpetrated by an adult.[59] Research reveals, however, very high victimization rates for both sexes. For example, although most researchers and commentators tend to assume girls are the only victims of harassing behavior,[60] a significant number of boys identify themselves as victims of sexual harassment: 75% of boys and 85% of girls report being the targets of sexually harassing behaviors.[61] Researchers also have identified a series of negative outcomes, including feeling embarrassed or self-conscious about incidents and fearing harassment to the extent that victims change their daily routines and drop out of school.[62] In addition to individual effects that produce fears significant enough to change everyday behavior, the sexual harassment endangers more than individual victims. For example, sexual harassment has been described as part of the hidden curriculum and has been linked to unequal access to education and general problems of gender bias and inequity in opportunities.[63] From this perspective, sexuality education must address all forms of violence, including systemic violence in schools,[64] and laws support the need for such education.[65]

Other commentators view the problem sexuality education must address in terms of the place sexuality has in the life cycle. The approach proposes that sexuality education simply be part of basic education that helps learners acquire information and begin to form attitudes that will help them lead full and productive lives.[66] The approach associates sexuality with other areas of personal development and highlights that knowledge of sexuality is important in today's changing world where many parents are unwilling to discuss sexuality and where adolescents receive distorted views of life from the media. The lack of appropriate information means that adolescents cannot gain insight and understanding to aid them in making responsible decisions.[67] The approach gains considerable support from many psychologists who highlight the significance of sexuality to adolescents' general well-being[68] that normally includes sexual desire, engagement in sexual behaviors, and the practice of safe sex.[69] The need to approach sexuality education from a life cycle perspective also receives support from research that highlights how adolescents generally are natural thrill seekers[70] and those who engage in risky sexual behavior also jeopardize their health and safety through problem behaviors (e.g., more physical fights and more smoking, alcohol, and drug use).[71]

Others view the problem in terms of the need to address inequalities and reconsider sexuality education part of moral education that would focus on respecting each students' own sexuality and sexual choices.[72] The significance of the approach emerges from the realization that social inequalities immensely affect sexual attitudes and behaviors. These commentators charge that programs deny reality when they assume that individuals are able to choose their behaviors freely within the context of coequal partnerships, or that they are committed to maintaining their own good health. They note, for example, that programs essentially ignore the manner socioeconomic inequities play a role in early pregnancy and largely ignore that relationships that place adolescents at highest risk for undesired conditions may not involve peers—for example, the partners of 15- to 17-year-old mothers average more than 3.5 years older (which generally means they are statutory rapists);[73] and pregnant teenagers are at higher risk of partner violence.[74] Others appropriately note how family violence, particularly sexual abuse, contributes to teenage pregnancy.[75] In addition, commentators highlight how programs ignore adolescents of nontraditional sexual orientations;[76] yet these adolescents are the ones who remain most likely to engage in self-destructive behaviors and who will be victimized by those who take advantage of their self-protective cloak of secrecy about being different.[77] Considerable research supports these commentators' claims: More than 80% of lesbian and gay adolescents experience severe isolation, and their emotional isolation is especially high with regard to their families.[78] The negative effects reverberate and place adolescents at risk for a series of destructive behaviors— for example, compared to heterosexual adolescents, gay adolescents have higher rates of suicide,[79] homelessness (both a result of having been thrown away by their families and of running away from their families),[80] substance abuse,[81] prostitution,[82] and HIV status.[83] These commentators emphasize that, because schools reproduce inequality that breeds violence in general and sexual violence in particular, programs must move beyond simply focusing on sexuality education.[84]

Regardless of the perspective, all associate sexual activity with potential harms and costs to individual adolescents. Yet the high costs of failed sexuality education actually affect more than those directly involved. For example, the harms also affect other pupils in that they may enforce the subordination of minority groups and dictate gender-role conformity. The harms also reach a greater societal level in the form of ignorance about human sexuality, which perpetuates social costs associated with violence, poverty, and illness. The harms also involve lack of understanding about adolescent life, which fosters the inadequate development of policies and reforms to deal with adolescents' problems. Simply put, ineffective and inadequate sexuality education disrupts the broader foundations of, and reasons for, a free public education—the development of a productive workforce, a harmonious society, and a responsible democracy.

Adolescents' Educational Rights and the Law

No fundamental source of law provides a solid threshold from which to analyze adolescents' sexual rights in the context of schools. No a priori standard exists to balance the rights and interests involved in tensions among adolescents' sexual rights, the rights and roles of parents involved in guiding their children's upbringings, and the roles and rights of schools in protecting adolescents and fostering certain qualities to prepare adolescents for adulthood. In addition to the general lack of guidance, existing jurisprudence fails to resolve tensions between individual liberty (of children and their parents) and communal concerns in schooling.

Although outcomes of conflicts among adolescents, parents, and schools' rights remain largely indeterminate, important trends emerge from a series of cases that deal with conflicts between parental, adolescent, and schools' rights. These cases reflect a shift from parental and student's rights to a current approach that bestows authority on school officials to make curricular and administrative decisions that reflect broader communal and societal values. As the analysis that follows reveals, the Supreme Court significantly limits adolescents' own sexual rights and curtails schools' considerable discretion in designing and implementing sexuality education programs. The major principle that emerges provides that schools may limit adolescents' right to sexual information only to the extent that states properly inculcate and prepare adolescents for citizenship and full participation in a democratic society. Although that shift becomes perceptible through an analysis of three distinct lines of cases, few state statutes that guide the implementation and nature of sexuality education harness the educational system's freedom and power to better respond to adolescents' needs. As we will see in the following sections, the extent of existing legal responses offers important opportunities and implications for those interested in rethinking sexuality education programs.

The Nature of Adolescents' Rights to Sexuality Education

The celebrated trilogy of parental rights cases provides the foundation for the first line of cases that address adolescents' educational rights in the context of sexuality education. Through these decisions, the Supreme Court furnishes the basis for claims by parents to control their children's education and be free from state intrusion. The first case, *Meyer v. Nebraska*,[85] actually involved the right of teachers to pursue their profession. Yet it is in *Meyer* that the Court announced that parents had a right to "establish a home and bring up children" and that the state had impermissibly interfered with the parents' venerable right to control their children's education.[86] In the second case, *Pierce v. Society of Sisters*,[87] a lower court had struck down a state law that had declared it a misdemeanor for a parent or guardian to send a child between the ages of 8 and 16 to school other than the public school in the district where the child resided. The Court reaffirmed and gave parents the power to direct their children's education, so long as education was provided. The *Pierce* Court found that "the child is not the mere creature of the State; those who nurture him and direct his destiny have the right, coupled with a high duty, to recognize and prepare him for future obligations."[88] Fifty years later, in *Wisconsin v. Yoder*,[89] the Court referred to *Pierce* as "a charter of the right of parents to direct the religious upbringing of their children"[90] to find that the "primary role of parents in the upbringing of their children is now established beyond debate as an enduring American tradition."[91] The *Yoder* Court upheld the challenge by parents of a state law that required all children under the age of 16 to attend public or private school; and the Court upheld the rights of parents to refuse to educate some children. As these cases strongly suggest, the parental right to control their children's educations has been well-entrenched. Bestowing on parents that right has two implicit outcomes: Firmly established parental rights minimize a school's inculcative function and diminish students' right to determine their own upbringing when balanced against the rights of their parents.

The second line of decisions aims to support students' rights and reflects the Court's specific recognition of students' right to protection from governmental intrusion into students' right to engage in speech and right to protection from government-compelled speech. In the first case, *West Virginia State Board of Education v. Barnette*,[92] the Court used unusually powerful language to find "that no official, high or petty, can prescribe what shall be orthodox in politics, nationalism, religion, or other matters of opinion or force citizens to confess by word or act their faith therein."[93] The Court found a schools' requirement that all students salute the U.S. flag an unconstitutional exercise of governmental authority. In the following cases, which also involved students' First Amendment rights, the Court further emphasized and reaffirmed its commitment to student's rights. In *Tinker v. Des Moines Independent Community School District*,[94] which involved a school's prohibition against students' wearing black armbands in protest of the Vietnam War, the Court found that students may not be confined to the expression of "officially approved" sentiments and struck down the ban.[95] According to this approach, schools should encourage students to participate in the learning process. After these cases, commentators have described the Court's educational ideology as discursive and analytical where both teacher and student actively examine data and as one that is "reciprocal rather than inculcative."[96] The cases contribute to the impression that students possess expansive educational rights. Yet few other cases explicitly affirm students' rights, as reflected in recent cases that seemingly backtrack away from students' rights and tip the balance in favor of school administrators' right to control curricular decisions.

The third approach reflects a move that accords school officials increasing power in educational policy making. The approach actually has important roots in the parental-rights cases and largely dominates the Rehnquist Court's approach to educational rights. For example, the *Pierce* Court, which had found in favor of parental rights, still had recognized the state's interest in regulating education and its inculcative functions. The Court acknowledged the "power of the State reasonably to regulate all schooling" and to require that "certain studies plainly essential to good citizenship must be taught, and nothing be taught which is essentially inimical to the public welfare."[97] The more recent cases that aim to bestow on school officials greater powers appeared more than half a decade later and quickly formed another foundational trilogy of cases. The first and transitional case, *Board of Education v. Pico*,[98] established the "right to receive information and ideas" in the context of school libraries.[99] The Court upheld the removal of library books, as it reasoned that school boards have discretion to remove books based on educationally relevant criteria but may not remove books based on partisan politics. The Court construed the school board's rights as "vitally important 'in the preparation of individuals for participation as citizens' and ... for 'inculcating fundamental values necessary to the maintenance of a democratic political system.'"[100] In curricular matters, the Court announced that school boards "might well defend their claim of absolute discretion" to transmit community values.[101]

If *Board of Education v. Pico* left any doubt about the state's power to control the information adolescents receive, the next two cases firmly balanced the right to control information in the direction of school officials. In *Bethel School District v. Fraser*,[102] a 17-year-old senior delivered a sexually charged speech nominating a fellow student for elective office. The Court affirmed that students' constitutional rights in public school settings are more narrowly defined than those of adults in other settings. The limitation allowed school officials to curb forms of speech deemed threatening to others, disruptive, and contrary to "shared values."[103] The Court reiterated its focus on community standards and the inculcative function of schools. According to the Supreme Court's interpretation of constitutional rights and obligations, public education must inculcate "fundamental values necessary to the maintenance of a democratic political system."[104] Included in these values are tolerance of diverse and unpopular political and religious views that must be balanced against the interests of society in teaching the bounds of "socially appropriate behavior."[105] The power of school authorities, acting as the inculcators of proper community values, was supported and developed further in *Hazelwood School District v. Kuhlmeier*.[106] In this instance, students alleged a violation of their free speech rights when their principal deleted two articles he deemed objectionable from their school paper. One article addressed issues of teenage pregnancy and the other examined the impact of parental divorce on students. The *Hazelwood* Court upheld the authority of school officials to control the content of school-sponsored speech based on "legitimate pedagogical concerns."[107] As in the *Fraser* opinion, the *Hazelwood* majority emphasized the role of schools as the primary vehicles for transmitting cultural values and their discretion in refusing to sponsor student speech that might be perceived as advocating conduct otherwise inconsistent with "the shared values of a civilized social order."[108]

The most recent cases that deal with students' educational rights reveal that the Court approaches them from two perspectives, one that reaffirms the authority of school officials to uphold the values of the community and another that emphasizes the mission of the schools as the promotion of fundamental, democratic values. Thus the Court accords the government considerable license to control public school classrooms in general and secular curriculum in particular to allow states, via schools, to fulfill their special responsibility to inculcate adolescents. The Supreme Court repeatedly has underscored the state's special responsibility and emphasized that the purpose of public education is the "inculcat[ion] [of] fundamental values necessary to the maintenance of a democratic political system;" that the school is a "principal instrument in awakening the child to cultural values, in preparing him for later professional training, and in helping him to adjust normally to his environment;" and that classrooms are a "market place of ideas" and "the Nation's future depends upon leaders trained through wide exposure to [these ideas.]"[109] The Supreme Court's decisions emphasize the inculcative or indoctrinative nature of schooling for a given purpose; according to these decisions, public schools not only may but *should* "influence their students to adopt particular beliefs, attitudes, and values."[110] Although other cases recognized and fostered the socialization function of schooling, the current approach looks to socialization as a mechanism both to preserve community interests and preferences and to prepare students for citizenship in the larger society.

The developments reflect how public school officials play the key role of arbiters and protectors of community values or preferences, both in the sense of common values shared throughout society and in a particular community. Taking their lead from the Supreme Court, lower courts also defer to school officials' decisions as they are granted comprehensive authority to manage the academic process.[111] Several lower court cases reflect the power schools hold. Indeed, challenges to school officials' discretion predominantly fail. For example, courts reject broad challenges to curriculum on the grounds that they advance secular humanism and inhibit theistic religion. Situations in which parents seek to remove materials from the curriculum and impose their religious views on the entire school community have followed the lead of *Smith v. Board of School Commissioners*,[112] which reversed a district court decision that had removed books from schools on charges of promoting the religion of secular humanism and found that school officials may seek to "instill . . . such values as independent thought, tolerance of diverse views, self-respect, maturity, self-reliance and logical decision-making."[113] Equally unsuccessful have been cases that have sought limited relief in the form of individualized accommodations to the free exercise of religion through exemptions or partial opting-out of some aspects of the curriculum. These cases, which generally deal with challenges to sex education or family life education programs, tend to find in favor of school authorities. The general rule was established in *Citizens for Parental Rights v. San Mateo County Board of Education*,[114] which held that sex education and family living courses did not impair the free exercise of religion or present an establishment of religion when the state provides for the parental right to remove children from instruction. Similar findings have been found with schools that offer access to contraceptive information.[115] The cases tend to provide some protection to parental rights when contraceptive services are provided without providing parents the power to opt-out their children.[116] However, when schools provide education without such services, courts tend to reject parental claims that schools violate the parental right to privacy and right to direct the upbringing of their children when schools compel students to attend extremely sexually explicit programs.[117] The finding comports with the general rule that parents have no fundamental right to educate their children free from reasonable governmental regulation. The Supreme Court's failure to review these lower court decisions confirms the immense power states wield in the regulation of school life.

States extensively regulate public schools. Two forms of regulation illustrate each state's broad power. All states statutorily govern public school teacher qualifications. For example, individual teachers need state-awarded credentials to reflect requisite training and meet determined standards.[118] In addition, all states exercise substantial control over the content of education. For example, states mandate that public schools teach certain subjects, follow state-prescribed curricular guidelines, and use only officially approved textbooks and other instructional materials.[119] Likewise, states require schools to administer standardized tests and other evaluative devices; and several states dictate the minimal requirements for progress to higher grades or for obtaining a high school diploma.[120] These powers are considerably broad, and state officials retain the power to inspect schools to ensure compliance with their directives.

Such statutory provisions reflect three important points about state educational mandates. First, mandates that govern the content of education and control who will deliver the content reflect a legislative judgment that children must develop certain habits, know certain materials, and be able to think and adapt to certain societal needs. Second, the provisions reflect how children's educational needs are likely to be fulfilled only by teachers with proper preparation under appropriate supervision that ultimately answers to the state. Third, the provisions reflect the legislative judgment that quality teacher training bears a close relationship to the development of students who mature into citizens who will reproduce or reconstruct a particular vision of the social order. These points reveal the extent to which states find certain educational experiences significant—states mandate basic educational standards when they are deemed significant enough to be worthy of state guidance.

State Statutory Mandates Regulating Sexuality Education

Given the bestowal of discretion to state officials, an analysis of adolescents' educational rights to sexuality education necessarily must turn to state protections and the extent to which state statutes guide sexuality education programs. Existing mandates are remarkable for their diversity. The diversity of statutory responses to ensuring educational rights to adolescents reflects the range of nomenclature used to describe what otherwise is broadly termed *sexuality education.* For example, programs have been labeled variously as family life education, sexual health, personal development, values clarification, sex respect, and human sexuality. The diversity in state guided programs reveals the wide range of curricula that differ in terms of aims, scope, implementation, and content. Although sexuality education is far from a unitary or homogeneous concept, state statutes that deal with sexuality education may be divided into three categories.

The first broad category involves the absence of mandates that would control the state's approach to sexuality education. These states have no statute to regulate what could be labelled as sex education or its equivalent, such as education relating to health, AIDS, or family life. These states offer the least statutory support and guidance for sexuality education programs in that these states do not even mention whether education relating to sex, AIDS, family life, or health may or should be taught at all. Fourteen states and the District of Columbia fall into this category.[121]

The second category includes states that do mandate some sexuality education by statutes that specify health, family life, or sex education, yet make no mention of AIDS or

HIV. Eighteen states have statutes that mention health, family life, or sex education but do not mention the need to educate children about AIDS or HIV.[122]

These statutes generally remain rather broad, vague, and fail to offer explicit guidance in terms of what instructors must teach. For example, Connecticut's statute simply states that the family life curriculum include human sexuality.[123] Likewise, some states limit what schools may offer as sexuality education. For example, Idaho defines ''sex education'' as the ''anatomy and the physiology of human reproduction'' and requires schools to emphasize that adolescents must control their sex drives.[124] When state statutes are explicit, their mandates tend to offer very broad guidelines. For example, Indiana simply requires that a state educational consultant develop a curriculum for health and physical education to encourage children to develop healthful living habits, an interest in lifetime health and physical fitness, and decision-making skills in the areas of health and physical fitness.[125]

Only two states, Michigan and South Carolina, provide more detailed mandates. In Michigan, the statute defines the aim of sex education as preparation for personal relationships between the sexes by providing appropriate educational opportunities designed to help a person develop an understanding, acceptance, respect, and trust for him- or herself and others. This includes knowledge of physical, emotional, and social growth and maturation, and understanding of individual needs; evaluation of men's and women's roles, responsibilities of each toward the other, and the development of responsible use of human sexuality.[126] In terms of content, the statute also is rather directive and explicit, yet still narrow in terms of what can be taught: Sex education includes family planning, human sexuality, reproductive health, and venereal disease; abstinence instructed as a responsible method of preventing pregnancy and sexually transmitted diseases and as a positive lifestyle for unmarried young people; prohibition of teaching of abortion as a method of family planning or reproductive health, prohibition of distribution of family planning drugs or devices; and parental exemption from instruction. South Carolina offers a similarly detailed program but still limits discussions.[127] For example, the state requires a comprehensive health education program that includes disease prevention, human physiology, illegal sexual conduct, and contraception in sex education. Yet the programs may not include discussion of alternate sexual lifestyles from heterosexual relations; nor may their programs include instruction regarding abortion counseling or abortion services or provision of assistance in obtaining abortion services. In addition, the programs must offer a parental exemption.

The last broad category includes states with statutes that specifically address sexuality education through mandating HIV/AIDS education. Eighteen states specifically provide for AIDS education in their statutory frameworks.[128] Despite the recognized need to react to crises involving HIV/AIDS, even these developments remain considerably far from being inclusive. Most of these statutes emphasize abstinence, and precisely what is mandated remains somewhat elusive; most states provide opt-out provisions for parents who do not want their children taught subjects covered by the statute.

Although undoubtedly limited in their conceptualizations of sexuality education and the need to provide adolescents with access to sexuality education, two of those states, California and Oregon, still offer strikingly comprehensive programs even though they offer parental exemptions. California's sex education program[129] emphasizes abstinence; provides information on condom reliability in preventing the spread of HIV; focuses on abstinence from sexual intercourse until readiness for marriage; and teaches honor and respect for monogamous heterosexual marriage. Although the view of relationships remains considerably limited, the programs stand out in terms of their unique focus on violence. Programs must instruct that it is unlawful for males of any age to have sexual relations with females under the age of 18 to whom they are not married; the statute includes rape and statutory rape provisions as it requires teachers to educate students to not make unwanted sexual advances, how to say ''no'' to unwanted sexual advances, and includes information about sexual assault, verbal, physical, and visual, including but not limited to, nonconsensual sexual advances, nonconsensual physical sexual contact, and rape by an acquaintance. The programs also include instruction on how to exercise good judgment and encourage adolescents to resist negative peer pressure. Oregon statutorily provides a much broader view of relationships and emphasizes responsibility. Under its statutes, the human sexuality curriculum in health education courses must be comprehensive, include information about responsible sexual behaviors and practices that reduce or eliminate risks of pregnancy, exposure to HIV and other infectious or sexually transmitted diseases; promote abstinence but not to the exclusion of other materials and instruction; acknowledge the value of abstinence while not devaluing those who have had or are having sexual intercourse; discuss consequences of preadolescent and adolescent sexual intercourse and consequences of unintended pregnancy, statistics and benefits and risks of all forms of contraceptives; advise about laws pertaining to financial responsibility for their children; advise that it is unlawful for persons 18 years of age or older to have sexual relations with persons younger than 18 to whom they are not married; teach that no form of sexual expression is right if it harms one's self or others; teach pupils not to make unwanted physical and verbal sexual advances; teach how to decline unwanted sexual advances or accept the refusal of unwanted sexual advances; assist in development of self-esteem, communication skills, and ability to resist peer pressure; emphasize that abstinence is the only method that is 100 percent effective against unintended pregnancy and sexually transmitted diseases.[130]

A statutory review of state sexuality education mandates reveals considerable diversity. The immense diversity among state statutory provisions reveals significant points worthy of emphasis. For our purposes, the diversity uncovers the relative failure of most states to address sexuality education, even though states have the mandate to do so. The diversity also affirms the result of challenges school systems face in their attempts to provide sexuality education; they must wrestle with the controversial and complex task of deciding what to teach and how to teach about human sexuality. Perhaps more important, though, the general failure amid some statutory mandates confirms that such mandates are at least within the realm of possibility. States with mandates indicate that all states may guide curricular matters regarding sexuality education, that they may do so with broad statutory mandates, and that mandates may also explicitly provide specific approaches and the delivery of services to adolescents. Given that states possess the authority to guide the actual implementation of adolescents' rights to sexuality education, it is important to understand why they also have the obligation to do so and how these very obligations provide opportunities for reform.

Opportunities for Reform

Thus far the legal analyses of adolescents' right to sexuality education reveal two important points. First, the Supreme Court has yet to recognize or explore the right. Like any educational right, however, it seems fair to conclude that the Court leaves determinations of the content of educational rights to the states, with the fundamental reservation that educational efforts must respect and promote democratic values. Second, even though the Court bestows determinations of the nature of the right to sexuality education on states, states generally have not made such determinations. Only a few states go beyond brief policy guides and enumerate explicitly the nature of sexuality education.

As currently framed, debates about the nature of sexuality education are not likely to end soon. The understanding that sexuality education debates are firmly rooted in polarized ideologies makes evident that no amount of discourse will develop consensus about which ideology should guide sexuality programs and that no single sexual ideology seems poised to assume a hegemonic position.[131] The alternative that emerges from the absence of consensus is to move toward a position of sexual pluralism. Although sexual pluralism may be discomforting when proposed as a policy move, a single look at current sexuality education programs reveals nothing but pluralism. As we have seen, teachers and administrators attempt to please constituents and generally offer a blend of abstinence-focused sexuality education programs along with programs that attempt to offer adolescents knowledge of protective behaviors.

This status quo results in immense diversity of content and information that schools convey to adolescents. The extent to which research has examined the diversity reveals that sexuality programs remain largely ineffective, even whether systematic programs are existent or nonexistent. As we have seen, efforts that seem to work often are dismantled when local political leaders change. The failure reveals the need to reconsider sexuality education practices that may better prepare adolescents to deal with sexual issues. The failure further reveals the need to consider the extent to which reforms can actually reach adolescents and the extent to which society can mandate sexuality education. This section explores these issues in light of the discussion that holds that society has an obligation to allow adolescents to develop into democratic citizens.[132]

Although society may never agree on values that relate to sexual beliefs and behavior, society formally shares values and aspirations that are not difficult to uncover and propose as fundamental to the education for living in democratic, pluralistic communities. In terms of educational practice, programs, like all effective educational programs, must (a) acknowledge and address adolescents' needs, concerns, and realities; (b) give students information and experiences needed to become critical thinkers and responsible decision makers; (c) create an environment in which students and teachers share responsibility and decision making within a broad framework of what must be learned; and (d) incorporate the development of skills into the entire curriculum.[133] The principles rest on the premise that, if society wants students to develop into democratic citizens who can function peaceably in a diverse society, it should allow students to experience democracy in the classroom and have their basic needs met in their learning experiences.

In terms of the actual content of sexual information, because sexuality education is first and foremost education, democratic principles require that programs use comprehensive and explicit educational materials and present divergent sexual beliefs and materials. Research indicates that explicit contraceptive education does not increase rates of sexual activity and does increase the likelihood of responsible sexual behavior. Indeed, the most recent study of condom distribution in schools reports the seemingly paradoxical finding that making condoms available in the context of efforts to educate adolescents about sexuality actually decreases the use of condoms, a finding that becomes less paradoxical in light of the other finding that students who had easy access to condoms and were counseled in health centers had less of a need for contraceptives.[134] Estimates suggest that greater educational efforts that move beyond discussions of sexual functions and also discuss sexual beliefs and behaviors would reduce the proportion of teenagers using protective methods by approximately 40%.[135] For maximum effectiveness, the interventions must be longer in duration, affect attitudes, and develop social skills.[136] In terms of types of behaviors, it would seem permissible to discuss societal perceptions of the broadest range of behaviors, including sexual behaviors that may be illegal (e.g., some types of homosexual and underage behaviors). The legality or immoral nature of sexual behaviors and beliefs would not necessarily permit exclusion (just as schools discuss violent behavior and drug abuse). To permit exclusion would be to compel public school administrators to conform their programs to the peculiar beliefs or values of particular students or parents, which would undermine, if not incapacitate, the "ideal of secular instruction."[137] Just as public schools may not promote a particular religion or political party, it would be improper to have derivatives of particular religious and political beliefs that appear in sexual ideologies control students' sexual or relational choices. Just as for any education, the goal must be to provide adolescents with the information and the opportunity to develop analytic tools and social skills by which to make independent and careful decisions about their immediate and future lives—all of which reduce rather than foster sexual activity and its associated harms.

Some states recently have enacted statutes that begin to reflect these needs. Oregon's efforts, reviewed in the previous section, are most illustrative of the needed reform and the breadth of statutory mandates. Such legislative directives are significant for several reasons.[138] The presence of statutes creates and helps reinforce state education agency policy so that programs will be subjected less to new and emergent streams of political capriciousness. In addition, statutory guidance assists in guiding curricular content, which helps ensure the presentation of important information. Legal mandates also help clarify administrators and teachers' roles. All but one state, Tennessee, explicitly recognizes that teachers must exercise their professional judgment and protects those who act in good faith to instruct individual pupils about sexual matters.[139] Further, support from statutory frameworks makes the task of implementing programs less daunting in the face of pressures from community groups. National levels of policy making regarding adolescent sexual behavior still remain conspicuously reticent to respond to sexuality education, and the guidance that does exist is very restrictive. Statutory frameworks assist researchers in their design of better interventions, help sustain interventions long enough to evaluate their effectiveness, and provide researchers with clear, measurable outcomes that have policy relevance (such as rates of violence, adolescent emotional development, and nature of sexual behavior). Finally, statutory guidance could help focus educational systems toward a more proactive, preventative stance.

Despite these efforts and their need, it remains to be determined if they will be taken seriously. In addition, the mandates are not without limitations themselves. Most sexuality education statutes allow for parental exemption of students from sexuality education. The extent to which states allow for this exception goes to the core of adolescents' rights to sexuality education. We now turn to that exception and propose how it may be restricted and approached like any other attempt made to shield adolescents from formal education.

We have seen how democratic principles appropriately may serve to guide the content and essential philosophy of sexuality education programs. Given that the very foundation of democracy rests on respect for diversity, tolerance, and restraint from compelling others to accept one's views, it remains to be determined the extent to which adolescents can be compelled to participate in sexuality education programs based on democratic values. Several possibilities may determine the extent to which adolescents may opt out, or be opted out, of programs or portions of programs. These variations deal with the extent to which parents, the state, and adolescents themselves may determine exposure to offensive sexual materials.

Where school officials direct education toward making students full participatory members of society, and if sexuality education is a necessary part of education and children are members of society, then neither parents nor adolescents may object to the education.

This scenario actually has considerable precedent in legal attempts to regulate adolescent life. A useful analogy involves medical services, an arena in which states may act paternalistically to protect adolescents from the objective harm to which their own decisions or those of parents might expose them. These cases include, for example, instances that involve religious objections to their adolescents' blood transfusions[140] or other life sustaining treatment.[141] The argument would be that the perpetuation of ignorance in an area so crucial to the adolescent's development would not be in the adolescent's interests and would therefore be contrary to the adolescent's own rights.

Another likely scenario could involve the provision of various opportunities for allowing parents and adolescents to opt out of programs. As we have seen, parents still possess the general right to control their children's upbringing.[142] Yet as venerable as they may be, parental rights still clearly lose their power when they place their children's lives at risk for injury and violence. Just as states may intrude in adolescents' lives to protect them from parental decision making, states have an obligation to infringe on parental rights in the name of protecting their children, especially when parents fail to do so. Instances in which the law allows for such intrusion generally involve three categories: a given minor's status authorizes his or her own consent to services, a particular medical condition (e.g., pregnancy, potential HIV status) gives him or her the right to services, or his or her level of maturity authorizes the minor to receive services if the adolescent is of sufficient maturity and intelligence to understand and appreciate the benefits and risks of the service.[143] Parents' defenses based solely on the free exercise clause of the First Amendment have not been persuasive enough to strike down prosecutions and convictions for parental failure to provide conventional medical care.[144] This does not necessarily mean that parents should be liable for prosecution for withholding information and access to services from their sexually active child, particularly because schools have not been held accountable for such failures as well.[145] The rule does reveal, however, the public recognition of the basic duties of parents to protect the health and well-being of their minor children and society's obligation to intervene and allow adolescents to exercise their rights when parents may not allow them.

Important alternatives exist to provide parents with a blanket option to remove their children from sexuality education programs. States may provide only strict conditions under which parents can opt their children out. For example, if parents propose that some aspects of the offered sexual curriculum conflict with their religious beliefs, they may be allowed to opt out as long as they indicate how their child will receive some form of sexuality education that meets minimal criteria. Students may be provided the right to challenge their parents' decisions to withdraw them from sex education. This approach would be consistent with Supreme Court jurisprudence that provides adolescents with access to services that affect their private lives and mandates that alternatives be available for adolescents to obtain services, such as commonly done through the provision of judicial by-passes that examine the minor's needs and competence.[146] Opting out could be allowed only for certain aspects of sexuality education. The major example involves the availability of condoms, which may be construed as a health service and may be under greater parental control.[147] The general rule in instances in which services are not construed as directly educational would be that students would not be compelled to avail themselves of those specific services but adolescents still would have access to a socially supportive environment. That environment would allow students to acquire the knowledge necessary to make safe decisions about engaging in sexual activity and, admittedly more controversially, the environment would allow exposure to perspectives different from those of their parents.

Although states may provide adolescents with considerable protections if they remain in public schools, the protections are not as secure if parents exercise their right to educate their children outside of public school systems.[148] State oversight and regulation of private schools, especially religious schools, remain minimal or nonexistent.[149] Indeed, private schools are essentially singled out of statutory mandates, and the Constitution prohibits states from using their funds to advance religion or otherwise become excessively entangled with religious schools.[150] The new trend toward creating charter schools rests largely on the belief that relieving schools from state and local regulations will allow them to experiment, innovate, and better educate adolescents.[151] Thus for both religious and charter schools, law and policy generally aim to limit state intrusion and regulation.

The failure of states to regulate private schools to any significant degree raises the question of whether states could do so if they wished. States have not attempted to regulate the content and nature of instructions in private schools to an extent that would set discernable precedents, and the Supreme Court has not set clear guidelines for halting states' intrusion into otherwise private matters. Yet three points suggest that states still retain considerable power, if they choose to exercise it. State and federal courts consistently uphold state laws regulating state approval of private school teachers, instruction in core subjects, and reporting of attendance information.[152] The Supreme Court has refused to review these cases that have imposed these obligations on private schools and thus at least approves of the states' regulating minimal requirements for all schools. In addition, states may condition government financial assistance to private schools on their compliance with requirements that the states might not otherwise be constitutionally permitted to impose.[153] The Supreme Court, for example, has upheld against First Amendment challenges to the federal government's conditioning of federal financial assistance on compliance with Title IX's provisions. In those cases, the Court has found that "Congress is free to attach reasonable and unambiguous conditions to federal financial assistance that educational institutions are not obligated to accept."[154] Furthermore, when the regulation connects to an important state interest relating to the children in these schools, the Supreme Court repeatedly has stressed that parents have no constitutional right to provide their children with a private school education unfettered by reasonable government regulation. Thus if states can demonstrate the importance of its regulations for children's well-being and the societal interest in that result, Court precedent would find that the state not only has the power but the "high responsibility . . . to impose reasonable regulations for the control and duration of basic education."[155]

In summary, so long as the programs are construed and construable as general education, school officials and the state maintain considerable control. For public schools, officials maintain control to the extent to which schools do not limit political and religious views or make partisan political and religious views the basis for sexuality education. As previously suggested, the analysis may lead to an uncomfortable outcome. The position allows for comprehensive discussions, but it does not allow for coercing objecting adolescents (whether objecting themselves or through their parents' objections) to take part in contraceptive delivery programs or other programs that may be construed as health services (e.g., although currently not even proposed in public schools, it is imaginable that some schools could provide needles to deal with dangers arising from drug use). For private schools, states could, at the very least, condition receipt of any financial aid a compliance with all important regulations presently applicable to public schools. State legislatures bear the full and only responsibility for setting and enforcing broad standards. As we have seen, an important part of those standards should include the development of sexuality education programs that respond to the needs of adolescents and those of a democratic society.

Conclusion

Complex, persistent social problems require complex, persistent social responses. Traditional justifications for sexuality education programs still exist; unintended pregnancies, dysfunctional relationships, sexual maltreatment, and the HIV pandemic all make for sound reasons students should be exposed to and have access to information. Broader societal changes increasingly complicate these traditional problems. The disintegration of families and communities, dwindling economic resources and educational opportunities, changing societal norms, and decline in the availability of social and health services all serve to emphasize that even exposure to sexual information will not suffice. The compelling need for sexuality education calls for change not only in sexuality education but also in opportunities adolescents have to obtain skills to survive in a constantly changing and even hostile world. Sexuality education, from this perspective, must be part of education even the Court envisioned as necessarily allowing adolescents to develop skills of critical thinking, analysis, judgment, skepticism, advocacy, and dissent, all of which prepare adolescents for responsible citizenship.

The review thus far suggests that the legal system may be harnessed to ensure adolescents' right to sexuality education. The proposal rests on the democratic notion that society must prepare adolescents for their future and immediate social participation. Taking that fundamental truth as a starting point allows for rethinking how schools prepare adolescents for responsible citizenship, which undoubtedly includes the manner in which adolescents treat others and themselves in their intimate relationships. The legal development is of significance in that it can no longer be proposed that schools are not the proper place for sexuality education and that available technology does not offer appropriate ways to foster sexual responsibility among adolescents. In addition to more responsive sexuality education programs, however, it is increasingly evident that they must be complemented by legal reforms that address the other ecologies of adolescent sexuality, most notably community attitudes toward sexuality and the relationships themselves. The next chapters focus on these potential sites of reform.

Endnotes

1. Jean Johnson and John Immerwahr, *Putting First Things First: What Americans Expect From Public Schools* (New York: Public Agenda, 1994).
2. Debra Haffner, "Sexuality Education: Issues for the 1990's," *New York Law School Law Review* 38 (1993):45–52; David Finkelhor and Jenifer Dziuba-Leatherman, "Victimization Prevention Programs: A National Survey of Children's Exposure and Reactions," *Child Abuse & Neglect* 19 (1995):129–139.
3. Joy G. Dryfoos, "Full Service Schools: Revolution or Fad?" *Journal of Research on Adolescence* 5 (1995):147–172.
4. Anne Grunseit, Susan Kippaz, Peter Aggleton, Mariella Baldo, and Gary Slutkin, "Sexuality Education and Young People's Behavior: A Review of Studies," *Journal of Adolescent Research* 12 (1997):421–453.
5. Sharon Lamb, "Sexual Education as Moral Education: Teaching for Pleasure, About Fantasy, and Against Abuse," *Journal of Moral Education* 26 (1997):301–315.
6. Roger J. R. Levesque, "Educating American Youth: Lessons From Children's Human Rights Law," *Journal of Law & Education* 27 (1998):173–209.
7. For further analyses of these rationales, see *id.*
8. Bonnie N. Trudell, "The First Organized Campaign for School Sex Education: A Source of

Critical Questions About Current Efforts,'' *Journal of Sex Education and Therapy* 11 (1985):10–16.

9. Douglas Kirby, ''School-Based Programs to Reduce Sexual Risk-Taking Behaviors,'' *Journal of School Health* 62 (1992):283–287.

10. For a brief review, *see* Evonne Hedgepeth & Joan Helmich, *Teaching About Sexuality and HIV: Principles and Methods for Effective Education* (New York: New York University Press, 1996).

11. James D. Hunter, *Culture Wars: The Struggle to Define America* (New York: Basic Books, 1991).

12. Alexander McKay, ''Accommodating Ideological Pluralism in Sexuality Education,'' *Journal of Moral Education* 26 (1997):285–300; Steven Seidman, *Embattled Eros: Sexual Politics and Ethics in Contemporary America* (New York: Routledge, 1992).

13. Leslie M. Kantor, ''Scared Chaste? Fear-Based Educational Curricula,'' *SIECUS Report* 21 (1993):1–15.

14. Cory L. Richards and Daniel Daley, ''Politics and Policy: Driving Forces Behind Sex Education in the United States.'' In *The Sexuality Education Challenge: Promoting Healthy Sexuality in Young People,* ed. Jody C. Drolet and Kay Clark (Santa Cruz, CA: ETR Associates, 1994).

15. Michelle Fine, ''Sexuality, Schools, and the Adolescent Female: The Missing Discourse of Desire,'' *Harvard Educational Review* 58 (1988):29–53; Debra W. Haffner, ''Sexual Health for American Adolescents,'' *Journal of School Health* 66 (1993):151–152.

16. Hedgepeth and Helmich, *Teaching About Sexuality and HIV: Principles and Methods for Effective Education.*

17. Haffner, ''Sexuality Education: Issues for the 1990's.''

18. Kirby, ''School-Based Programs to Reduce Sexual Risk-Taking Behaviors.''

19. For a comprehensive meta-analytic analysis, *see* Grunseit et al., ''Sexuality Education and Young People's Behavior: A Review of Studies.''

20. Joseph H. Pleck, Freya L. Sonenstein, and Leighton Ku, ''Changes in Adolescent Males' Use of and Attitudes Toward Condoms, 1988–91,'' *Family Planning Perspective* 25 (1993):106–110.

21. A. Odasuo Alali, ''Introduction: AIDS, Public Policy, and the Education of Students.'' In *HIV and AIDS in the Public Schools,* ed. A. Odasauo Alali (Jefferson, NC: McFarland, 1995); Marie Helweg-Larsen and Barry E. Collins, ''A Social Psychological Perspective on the Role of Knowledge About AIDS in AIDS Prevention,'' *Current Directions in Psychological Science* 6 (1997):23–26.

22. *See* Clint E. Bruess and Jerrold S. Greenberg, *Sexuality Education: Theory and Practice.* 3d ed. (Madison, WI: Brown & Benchmark, 1994).

23. For a review, *see* Cecilia D. Jacobs and Eve M. Wolf, ''School Sexuality Education and Adolescent Risk-Taking Behavior,'' *Journal of School Health* 65 (1995):91–95.

24. Donald E. Greydanus and Robert B. Shearin, *Adolescent Sexuality and Gynecology* (Philadelphia: Lea & Febiger, 1990).

25. Robert F. Valois, Nancy L. Roth, Ellen Montgomery, and Karthyn A. Waring, ''Sex Education Content of Ninth Grade Health Education Textbooks: A Rhetorical Analysis,'' *Journal of Sex Education and Therapy* 21 (1995):192–209; Christine E. Beyer and Roberta J. Ogletree, ''Sexual Coercion Content Curricula,'' *Journal of School Health* 68 (1998):370–375.

26. Douglas Kirby, Nancy D. Brener, Nancy Peterfreund, Pamela Hillard, and Ron Harrist, ''The Impact of Condom Distribution in Seattle Schools on Sexual Behavior and Condom Use,'' *American Journal of Public Health* 89 (1999):182–187.

27. Kirby, ''School-Based Programs to Reduce Sexual Risk-Taking Behaviors''; Bruess and Greenberg, *Sexuality Education: Theory and Practice.*

28. Donald E. Greydanus, Helen D. Pratt, and Linda L. Dannison, ''Sexuality Education Programs for Youth: Current State of Affairs and Strategies for the Future,'' *Journal of Sex Education and Therapy* 21 (1995):238–254; Christine E. Bryer, Roberta J. Ogletree, Dale O. Ritzel, Judy C. Drolet, Sharon L. Gilbert, and Dale Brown, ''Gender Representations in Illustrations, Text and Topic Areas in Sexuality Education Curricula,'' *Journal of School Health* 66 (1996):361–364.

29. Ruth Mayer and Leslie Kantor, ''1995–1996 Trends in Opposition to Comprehensive Sexuality Education in Public Schools in the United States,'' *SIECUS Report* 24 (1996):3–11.

30. Kirby, ''School-Based Programs to Reduce Sexual Risk-Taking Behaviors''; William A. Firestone, ''The Content and Context of Sexuality Education: An Exploratory Study in One State,'' *Family Planning Perspectives* 26 (1994):125–131.

31. Steven P. Schinke, Mary Ann Forgey, and Mario Orlandi, ''Teenage Sexuality.'' In *Finding Solutions to Social Problems: Behavioral Strategies for Change,* ed. Mark A. Mattani and Bruce A. Thyer (Washington, DC: American Psychological Association, 1997).

32. Bonnie N. Trudell, *Doing Sex Education: Gender, Politics and Schools* (New York: Routledge, 1993).

33. Haffner, ''Sexuality Education: Issues for the 1990's.''

34. Roberta J. Ogletree, Barbara A. Rienzo, Judy C. Drolet, and Joyce V. Fetro, ''An Assessment of 23 Selected School-Based Sexuality Education Curricula,'' *Journal of School Health* 65 (1995):186–191.

35. Michele A. Whitehouse and Marita P. McCabe, ''Sex Education Programs for People With Intellectual Disability: How Effective Are They?'' *Education and Training in Mental Retardation and Developmental Disabilities* 32 (1997):229–240.

36. Jacobs and Wolf, ''School Sexuality Education and Adolescent Risk-Taking Behavior''; Roger J. R. Levesque, ''The Peculiar Place of Adolescents in the HIV-AIDS Epidemic: Unusual Progress & Usual Inadequacies in 'Adolescent Jurisprudence,' '' *Loyola University Chicago Law Journal* 27 (1996):701–739.

37. Douglas Kirby, ''Research on Effectiveness of Sex Education Programs,'' *Theory into Practice* 28 (1989):191–197.

38. Helen P. Koo, George H. Dunteman, Cindee George, Yvonne Green, and Murray Vincent, ''Reducing Adolescent Pregnancy Through School- and Community-Based Intervention, Denmark, South Carolina Revisited,'' *Family Planning Perspectives* 26 (1994):206–207.

39. *Cf.* Bruess and Greenberg, *Sexuality Education: Theory and Practice.*

40. Carol Cassell and Pamela M. Wilson (Eds.), *Sexuality Education: A Resource Book* (New York: Garland, 1989).

41. Trudell, *Doing Sex Education: Gender, Politics and Schools.*

42. *Cf.,* William L. Yarber, ''Past, Present and Future Perspectives on Sexuality Education.'' In *The Sexuality Education Challenge: Promoting Healthy Sexuality in Young People,* ed. Jody C. Drolet and Kay Clark (Santa Cruz, CA: ETR Associates, 1994).

43. Trudell, *Doing Sex Education: Gender, Politics and Schools.*

44. Centers for Disease Control (CDC), *HIV/AIDS Surveillance* (October 1992).

45. For reviews of outcomes, *see* Lawrence M. DeRidder, ''Teenage Pregnancy: Etiology and Educational Interventions,'' *Educational Psychology Review* 5 (1993):87–107.

46. Barbara Tatem Kelley, Terence P. Thornberry, and Carolyn A. Smith, ''In the Wake of Childhood Maltreatment,'' *Juvenile Justice Bulletin* (Washington, DC: Office of Justice Programs, U.S. Department of Justice, August 1997).

47. Hedgepeth and Helmich, *Teaching About Sexuality and HIV: Principles and Methods for Effective Education.*

48. For statistics, *see* Stanley K. Henshaw, ''Teenage Abortion, Birth and Pregnancy Statistics: 1988,'' *Family Planning Perspectives* 25 (1993):122–126.

49. *See, e.g.,* Kristen S. Rufo, ''Public Policy vs. Parent Policy: States Battle Over Whether Public Schools Can Provide Condoms to Minors Without Parental Consent,'' *New York Law School Journal of Human Rights* 13 (1997):589–624.

50. For a review, *see* Alali, ''Introduction: AIDS, Public Policy, and the Education of Students.''

51. Richard A. Crosby, ''Combating the Illusion of Adolescent Invincibility to HIV/AIDS,'' *Journal of School Health* 66 (1996):186–190.

52. Terry Nicole Steinberg, ''Feminist Sex Education: To Reduce the Spread of AIDS,'' *Women's Rights Law Reporter* 17 (1995):63–78a.

53. James M. Makepeace, ''Courtships Violence as Process: A Developmental Theory.'' In *Violence*

Between Intimate Partners: Patterns, Causes and Effects, ed. Albert P. Cardarelli (Needham Heights, MA: Allyn & Bacon, 1997).

54. *See, e.g.,* Melissa J. Himelein, Ron E. Vogel, and Dale G. Wachowiak, ''Nonconsensual Sexual Experiences in Precollege Women: Prevalence and Risk Factors,'' *Journal of Counseling & Development* 72 (1994):411–415; Stephen A. Small and Donell Kerns, ''Unwanted Sexual Activity Among Peers During Early and Middle Adolescence: Incidence and Risk Factors,'' *Journal of Marriage and the Family* 55 (1993):941–952; Anthony Biglan, John Noell, Linda Ochs, Keith Smolkowski, and Carol Metzler, ''Does Coercion Play a Role in the High Risk Sexual Behavior of Adolescent and Young Adult Women?'' *Journal of Behavioral Medicine* 18 (1995):549–568.

55. Barrie Levy (Ed.), *Dating Violence, Young Women in Danger* (Seattle, WA: Seal Press, 1991).

56. Biglan et al., ''Does Coercion Play a Role in the High Risk Sexual Behavior of Adolescent and Young Adult Women?''; Ian M. Johnson and Robert T. Sigler, *Forced Intercourse in Sexual Relationships* (Brookfield, VT: Ashgate, 1997).

57. *See, e.g.,* Francine Lavoie, Lucie Vezina, Christiane Piche, and Michel Boivin, ''Evaluation of a Prevention Program for Violence in Teen Dating Relationships,'' *Journal of Interpersonal Violence* 10 (1995):515–524; Sharon K. Araji, *Sexually Aggressive Children: Coming to Understand Them* (Thousand Oaks, CA: Sage, 1997).

58. Martin D. Schwartz and William S. DeKeseredy, *Sexual Assault on the College Campus: The Role of Male Peer Support* (Thousand Oaks, CA: Sage, 1997).

59. Chantal Richard, ''Surviving Student to Student Sexual Harassment: Legal Remedies and Prevention Programs,'' *Dalhousie Law Journal* 19 (1996):169–197; Valerie E. Lee, Ribert G. Croniger, Eleannor Linn, and Xianglei Chen, ''The Culture of Sexual Harassment in Secondary Schools,'' *American Educational Research Journal* 33 (1996):383–417; Carrie M. H. Herbert, *Talking of Silence: The Sexual Harassment of Schoolgirls* (New York: Falmer Press, 1996).

60. *See, e.g.,* Herbert, *Talking of Silence: The Sexual Harassment of Schoolgirls;* June Larkin, *Sexual Harassment: High School Girls Speak Out* (Toronto: Second Story Press, 1994).

61. American Association of University Women (AAUW), *Hostile Hallways: The AAUW Survey on Sexual Harassment in America's Schools* (Washington, DC: Louis Harris, 1993).

62. Lee et al., ''The Culture of Sexual Harassment in Secondary Schools.''

63. Nan Stein, ''Sexual Harassment in School: The Public Performance of Gendered Violence,'' *Harvard Educational Review* 65 (1995):145–162.

64. Judith B. Brandenburg, *Confronting Sexual Harassment: What Should Schools and Colleges Do?''* (New York: Teachers College Press, 1997).

65. Amy M. Rubin, ''Peer Sexual Harassment: Existing Harassment Doctrine and Its Application to School Children,'' *Hastings Women's Law Journal* 8 (1997):141–168; Alexandra A. Bodnar, ''Arming Students for Battle: Amending Title IX to Combat the Sexual Harassment of Students by Students in Primary and Secondary School,'' *Review of Law and Women's Studies* 5 (1996):549–589.

66. Bruess and Greenberg, *Sexuality Education: Theory and Practice.*

67. Thomas Andre, Christine Cietsch, and Yu Cheng, ''Sources of Sex Education as a Function of Sex, Coital Activity, and Type of Information,'' *Contemporary Educational Psychology* 16 (1991):215–240; Thomas Andre, Rita Lund Frevert, and Dana Schuchmann, ''From Whom Have College Students Learned What About Sex?'' *Youth and Society* 20 (1989):241–268.

68. Susan Moore and Doreen Rosenthal, *Sexuality in Adolescence* (New York: Routledge, 1993).

69. Jennifer Neeman, Jon Hubbard, and Ann S. Masten, ''The Changing Importance of Romantic Relationship Involvement to Competence From Late Childhood to Late Adolescence,'' *Development and Psychopathology* 7 (1995):727–750.

70. Jeffrey Arnett, ''The Young and the Reckless: Adolescent Reckless Behavior,'' *Current Directions in Psychological Science* 4 (1995):67–71.

71. Jacqueline A. Pesa, Thomas R. Syre, and Quiang Fu, ''Condom Use and Problem Behaviors Among Sexually Active Adolescents,'' *Journal of Health and Behavior* 30 (1999):120–124.

72. Lamb et al., "Sexual Education as Moral Education: Teaching for Pleasure, About Fantasy, and Against Abuse."

73. David J. Landry and Jacqueline Darrocs Forrest, "How Old Are U.S. Fathers?" *Family Planning Perspectives* 27 (1995):159–161, 165; Philip Donovan, "Can Statutory Rape Laws Be Effective in Preventing Adolescent Pregnancy?" *Family Planning Perspectives* 29 (1997):30–34, 40.

74. Abbey B. Berenson, Virginia V. San Miguel, and Gregg S. Wilkinson, "Prevalence of Physical and Sexual Assault in Pregnant Adolescents," *Journal of Adolescent Health* 13 (1992):466–469.

75. Debra Boyer and David Fine, "Sexual Abuse as a Factor in Adolescent Pregnancy and Child Maltreatment," *Family Planning Perspectives* 24 (1992):4–11, 19; Kelley et al., "In the Wake of Childhood Maltreatment"; Mark W. Roosa, Jeann-Yun Tein Sein, Cindy Reinholtz, and Patrick J. Angelini, "The Relationship of Childhood Sexual Abuse to Teenage Pregnancy," *Journal of Marriage and the Family* 59 (1997):119–130.

76. Kellie Armstrong, "The Silent Minority Within a Minority: Focusing on the Needs of Gay Youths in Our Public Schools," *Golden Gate University Law Review* 24 (1994):67–97.

77. Alfred P. Kielwasser and Michelle A. Wolfe, "Silence, Difference, and Annihilation: Understanding the Impact of Mediated Heterosexism on High School Students," *The High School Journal* 77 (1994):58–79; Michael Radkowsky and Lawrence J. Siegel, "The Gay Adolescent: Stressors, Adaptations, and Psychosocial Interventions," *Clinical Psychology Review* 17 (1997):191–216.

78. Sonia R. Martin, "A Child's Right to Be Gay: Addressing the Emotional Maltreatment of Youth," *Hastings Law Journal* 48 (1996):167–196.

79. Douglas D. Durby, "Gay, Lesbian and Bisexual Youth." In *Helping Gay and Lesbian Youth: New Policies, New Programs, New Practice,* ed. Teresa Decrescenzo (New York: Haworth Press, 1994).

80. Paul Gibson, "Gay Male and Lesbian Youth Suicide." In *Report of the Secretary's Task Force on Youth Suicide* (Washington, DC: U.S. Department of Health and Human Services, 1989).

81. Ritch C. Savin-Williams, "Verbal and Physical Abuse as Stressors in the Lives of Lesbian, Gay Male, and Bisexual Youths: Associations With School Problems, Running Away, Substance Abuse, Prostitution, and Suicide," *Journal of Consulting and Clinical Psychology* 62 (1994):261–269.

82. Elijah Coleman, "The Development of Male Prostitution Activity Among Gay and Bisexual Adolescents," *Journal of Homosexuality* 17 (1989):131–149.

83. Levesque, "The Peculiar Place of Adolescents in the HIV-AIDS Epidemic: Unusual Progress & Usual Inadequacies in 'Adolescent Jurisprudence.'"

84. Jane Kenway and Lindsay Fitzclarence, "Masculinity, Violence and Schooling: Challenging 'Poisonous Pedagogies,'" *Gender and Education* 9 (1997):117–133.

85. 262 U.S. 390 (1923).

86. *Id.* at 399, 401.

87. 268 U.S. 510 (1925).

88. *Id.* at 535.

89. 406 U.S. 205 (1972).

90. *Id.* at 233.

91. *Id.* at 232.

92. 319 U.S. 624 (1943).

93. *Id.* at 642.

94. 393 U.S. 503 (1969).

95. *Id.* at 511.

96. William B. Senhauser, "Education and the Court: The Supreme Court's Educational Ideology," *Vanderbilt Law Review* 40 (1987):939–982, at 956.

97. *Pierce,* 268 U.S. at 534.

98. 457 U.S. 853 (1982).

99. *Id.* at 867.

100. *Id.* at 864.

101. *Id.* at 869.

102. 478 U.S. 675 (1986).

103. *Id.* at 683.

104. *Id.* at 681.

105. *Id.* at 681.

106. 484 U.S. 260 (1988).

107. *Id.* at 273.

108. *Id.* at 272.

109. *See* Ambach v. Norwick, 441 U.S. 68, 76–77 (1979); Brown v. Bd. of Educ., 347 U.S. 483, 493 (1954); Keyishian v. Bd. of Regents, 385 U.S. 589, 603 (1967).

110. Mary Harter Mitchell, "Secularism in the Public Education: The Constitutional Issues," *Boston University Law Review* 67 (1987):603–746, at 700.

111. *See* Rosemary C. Salomone, "Free Speech and School Governance in the Wake of *Hazelwood,*" *Georgia Law Review* 26 (1992):253–322.

112. 827 F.2d 684 (11th Cir. 1987).

113. *Id.* at 692.

114. 51 Cal. Rptr. 1 (Cal. Ct. App. 1975), *appeal dismissed,* 425 U.S. 908 (1976).

115. Curtis v. School Committee of Falmouth, 652 N.E.2d 580, 585–586 (Mass. 1995), *cert. denied,* 116 S. Ct. 753 (1996).

116. Alfonso v. Fernandez, 606 N.Y.S.2d 259, 265–266 (A.D. 2 Dept. 1993), *appeal dismissed without op.,* 637 N.E.2d (1994).

117. *See* Mozert v. Hawkins Country Bd. of Educ., 827 F.2d 1058 (6th Cir. 1987), *cert. denied,* 484 U.S. 1066 (1988); Brown v. Hot, Sexy and Safer Productions Inc., 68 F.3d 525 (1st Cir. 1995), *cert. denied,* 64 U.S.L.W. 3591 (U.S. Mar. 4. 1996) (No. 1158).

118. Robert C. O'Reilly and Edward T. Green, *School Law for the 1990s: A Handbook* (New York: Greenwood Press, 1992).

119. *See* Martha M. McCarthy and Nelda H. Cambron-McCabe, *Public School Law: Teachers' and Students Rights.* 4th ed. (Boston, MA: Allyn and Bacon, 1998).

120. *Id.*

121. Delaware, Hawaii, Kansas, Kentucky, Minnesota, Missouri, Montana, Nevada, New Hampshire, New Mexico, North Carolina, Oklahoma, South Dakota, and Wyoming.

122. ALASKA STAT. § 14.30.360 (Michie 1996); CONN. GEN. STAT. ANN. § 10-16c (West 1996 & Supp. 1997); IDAHO CODE § 33-1608-12 (Michie 1981 & Supp. 1997); IND. CODE ANN. § 20-1-1.1-7 (Burns 1992 & Supp. 1996); LA. REV. STAT. ANN. § 17:281 (West 1982 & Supp. 1997); ME. REV. STAT. ANN. tit. 20-A § 4723 (West 1993 & Supp. 1996); MD. EDUC. CODE ANN. § 7-401 (Michie 1997); MASS. GEN. LAWS. ANN ch. 71. § 380 (Law. Co-op. 1991 & Supp. 1997); MICH. COMP. LAWS ANN. §§ 380.1501, 380.1507 (West 1988 & Supp. 1997); MISS. CODE ANN. § 37-13-21, 131 (Law. Co-op. 1996); NEB. REV. STAT. § 79-712 (1996); N.Y. EDUC. LAW § 804-a (West 1988 Supp. 1997); N.D. Cent. Code § 15-38-07 (Michie 1993, Supp. 1995); OHIO REV. CODE ANN. § 3313.60 (Anderson 1997); PA. STAT. ANN. tit. 24, § 15-1511 (West 1992); S.C. CODE ANN. § 59-32-30 (Law. Co-op. 1990 & Supp. 1996); TEX. EDUC. CODE ANN. § 21.101 (West 1987); VA CODE ANN. § 22.1-207.1 (Michie 1997).

123. CONN. GEN. STAT. ANN. § 10-16c (West 1996 & Supp. 1997).

124. IDAHO CODE § 33-1608-12 (Michie 1981 & Supp. 1997).

125. IND. CODE ANN. § 20-1-1.1-7 (Burns 1992 & Supp. 1996)

126. MICH. COMP. LAWS ANN. § 380.1501 (West 1988 & Supp. 1997); *id.* 380.1507 (West 1988 & Supp. 1997)

127. S.C. CODE ANN. § 59-32-30 (Law. Co-op. 1990 & Supp. 1996).

128. ALA. CODE § 16-40-A-2 (Michie 1995 & Supp. 1996); ARIZ. REV. STAT. ANN. § 15-716 (West 1991 & Supp. 1996); ARK. CODE. ANN. § 6-18-703 (Michie 1993 & Supp. 1995); CAL. EDUC. CODE § 51553 (West 1989 & Supp. 1997); COLO. REV. STAT. § 22-25-101-106 (West 1990 & Supp. 1997); FLA. STAT. ANN. § 223.067, 223.067(2) (West Supp. 1994); GA. CODE ANN. § 20-2-143 (Michie 1996 & Supp. 1997); ILL. ANN. STAT. ch. 105, § 5/27-9.2 (Smith-Hurd 1993);

IOWA CODE ANN. § 256.11 (West 1996); N.J. ADMIN. CODE tit. §§ 18A, § 6:29-4.1, 18A:35-4.7 (West 1989 & Supp. 1997); OR. REV. STAT. § 336.035 (Butterworth 1995 & Supp. 1996); R.I. GEN. LAWS §§ 16-22-17, 16-22-18 (Michie 1996); TENN. CODE ANN. §§ 49-6-1005, 49-6-1008, 49-6-1301, 49-6-1303 (Michie 1996); UTAH CODE ANN. § 53A-13-101 (Michie 1997); VT. STAT. ANN. tit 16, § 131 (Michie 1989 & Supp. 1996); WASH. REV. CODE ANN. §§ 28A.230.070, 70.24.210-20, (West 1997); W. VA. CODE § 18-2-7b, 18-2-9(b) (Michie 1994 & Supp. 1997); WIS. STAT. ANN. § 118.019 (West 1991 & Supp. 1997).

129. CAL. EDUC. CODE § 51553 (West 1989 & Supp. 1997)

130. OR. REV. STAT. § 336.455 (Butterworth 1995 & Supp. 1996).

131. Jeffrey Weeks, *Invented Moralities: Sexual Values in an Age of Uncertainty* (Ann Arbor: University of Michigan Press, 1995).

132. For an analysis of that societal obligation and youths' right to it, *see* Levesque, "Educating American Youth: Lessons From Children's Human Rights Law."

133. Jerome Bruner, *The Culture of Education* (Cambridge, MA: Harvard University Press, 1996); Ann L. Brown, "Transforming Schools Into Communities of Thinking and Learning About Serious Matters," *American Psychologist* 52 (1997):399–413.

134. The researchers explain that health centers may have encouraged students to abstain from sexual activity and to have fewer sexual partners. Kirby et al., "The Impact of Condom Distribution in Seattle Schools on Sexual Behavior and Condom Use."

135. Jane Mauldon and Kristin Luker, "The Effects of Contraceptive Education on Method Use at First Intercourse," *Family Planning Perspectives* 28 (1996):19–24, 41.

136. *See, e.g.,* Nina Kim, Bonita Stanton, Xiang Li, Kay Dickerson, and Jennifer Galbraith, "Effectiveness of 40 Adolescent AIDS-Risk Reduction Interventions: A Quantitative Review," *Journal of Adolescent Health* 20 (1997):204–215; Richard P. Barth, Joyce V. Fetro, Nancy Leland, and Kevin Volkan, "Preventing Adolescent Pregnancy With Social and Cognitive Skills," *Journal of Adolescent Research* 7 (1992):208–232.

137. West Virginia State Bd. of Educ. v. Barnette, 319 U.S. 624, 637 (1943).

138. For a more in depth analysis of these reasons, *see* Roger J. R. Levesque, "Sexuality Education: What Adolescents' Educational Rights Require," *Journal of Psychology, Public Policy and the Law* (in press).

139. TENN. CODE ANN. § 49-6-1008 (Michie 1996).

140. Ann MacLean Massie, "The Religion Clauses and Parental Health Care Decisionmaking for Children: Suggestions for a New Approach," *Hastings Constitutional Law Quarterly* 21 (1994):725–775.

141. Jennifer L. Rosato, "The Ultimate Test of Autonomy: Should Minors Have a Right to Make Decisions Regarding Life-Sustaining Treatment?" *Rutgers Law Review* 49 (1996):1–103.

142. *See, e.g., Yoder,* 406 U.S. at 205.

143. Sharon Pomeranz, "Condoms Overturned on Appeal: Teens Stripped of Their Rights," *Journal of Gender and the Law* 4 (1995):219–247.

144. Massie, "The Religion Clauses and Parental Health Care Decisionmaking for Children: Suggestions for a New Approach."

145. Thomas G. Eschweiler, "Educational Malpractice in Sex Education," *SMU Law Review* 49 (1995):101–132.

146. Carey v. Population Servs. Int'l, 431 U.S. 678 (1977); Bellotti v. Baird, 443 U.S. 622 (1979).

147. Dede Hill, "Condom Availability Programs Belong in the Schools, Not in the Courts," *Wisconsin Law Review* (1996):1285 1317.

148. Pierce v. Society of Sisters, 268 U.S. 510 (1925).

149. Daniel J. Rose, "Compulsory Education and Parental Rights: A Judicial Framework of Analysis," *Boston College Law Review* (1989):861–902.

150. James B. Egle, "The Constitutional Implications of School Choice," *Wisconsin Law Review* (1992):459–510.

151. Jay P. Heubert, "Schools Without Rules? Charter Schools, Federal Disability Law, and the

Paradoxes of Deregulation,'' *Harvard Civil Rights-Civil Liberties Law Review* 32 (1997):301–353.

152. *See, e.g.,* Fellowship Baptist Church v. Benton, 815 F.2d 485 (8th Cir. 1987); New Life Baptist Church Academy v. Town of E. Longmeadow, 885 F.2d 940 (1st Cir. 1989), *cert. denied,* 494 U.S. 1066 (1990); Johnson v. Charles City Community Sch. Bd., 368 N.W.2d 74 (Iowa), *cert. denied sub nom.,* Pruessner v. Benton, 474 U.S. 1033 (1985).

153. Kline Capps and Carl H. Esbeck, ''The Use of Government Funding and Taxing Power to Regulate Religious Schools,'' *Journal of Law and Education* 14 (1985):553–574.

154. Grove City College v. Bell, 465 U.S. 555, 575 (1984).

155. *Yoder,* 406 U.S. at 213.

Chapter 6
SEX AND THE MEDIA

Adolescents live in an information-rich environment. Mass media, peers, families, and educational institutions bombard adolescents with information of varying quality and relevance. How to respond to these sources of information constitutes a critical part of healthy development. Whether to accept proffered information and how to act on it constructs values and moral judgments necessary for social functioning in a democratic society. The centrality of this task to adolescents and society ensures that attempts to address the role and regulation of the media in adolescent development necessarily remains problematic and controversial. The already controversial nature of information pertaining to sensitive and private issues with public consequences—such as sexuality and adolescents' access, use, and evaluation of sexual information—confirms that sexuality in the media remains an even more heated area of public debate and concern. The stigmatization of adolescent sexuality and the social and legal sanctions further complicate how to sort and respond to the information they receive and how society places demands on adolescents and adolescents place demands on themselves.

Although complex and fraught with legal and moral concerns, the media continues to provide sex in abundance.[1] Marketers use sex to hook adolescents into television or cable programs so that they provide an audience to sell to the advertiser. Likewise, sex provides a primary ingredient in popular music, video, and film and helps intensify interest in interactive and CD-ROM computer software. To complicate matters even more, legitimate societal issues and public health concerns prompt alarm. Popular media offers not only sex but also increasingly dysfunctional views of human relationships. Although this form of entertainment may not seem problematic for adults, it becomes troublesome when it serves as a leading source of sex education in the absence of widespread, effective sex education at home or in schools. Sociolegal responses fail to match the sexed media's dominating influences.

Given the media's current role in adolescents' sexual socialization, it is not surprising to find that the law and commentators increasingly seek to address crises exacerbated by new technologies and rapidly changing social structures that steer the media's influence. These attempts make sex in the media an important area to consider opportunities for developments in adolescents' sexual rights. In addition to the usual difficulties encountered in efforts to foster adolescents' rights, the area of law that deals with sex and the media recently has been subjected to fresh legal analysis and Supreme Court commentaries rooted in the First Amendment. Rather than being the mythic absolute bar to government regulation of speech, First Amendment doctrine now constitutes a complex set of rules. Diverse factors such as the effect and form of regulation, the purpose of the regulation, the relative value of the speech, and the type of media involved play into analyses that consider the appropriateness of the law in terms of legal doctrine. In addition to issues of law and adolescents' rights, analyses of adolescents' rights require determinations of whether regulations result in good law and effective policy. The central concern, then, becomes how the law may be harnessed to effect healthy outcomes in adolescents' access, use, and interpretations of sexuality in the media. Those concerns lead to broader considerations than the narrow issues of law that regulate adolescents' First Amendment rights in the media and aim to include adolescents' media rights into a more comprehensive approach to adolescents and the law. As with previous chapters, this chapter examines the eventual outcome of both legal and social science analyses and reconsiders the nature of adolescents' rights, adolescents' place in family life, and adolescents' citizenship in a democratic society.

Media Influences on Adolescents' Sexual Socialization

The degree to which diverse media shape popular culture has been researched frequently and in depth. A cursory look at the literature and a quick reality check reveals that adolescents live in an environment saturated with television, radio, films, books, and the "new" technologies—cable TV, walkmans, videodiscs, CDs, and computers.[2] Traditional and emerging mass media continue to change adolescents' everyday experiences, as they affect all of our lives.

Although the influence of media on adolescent life may be indisputable, precisely *how* the media influences adolescents actually remains relatively unknown. For example, considerable research has investigated the effects of violence in the media on children's aggressive and violent behavior. Although several find the evidence overwhelmingly supportive of a positive link between exposure to violence in the media and negative developmental outcomes, precisely how adolescents are influenced remains relatively uninvestigated, and even the more established findings about children continue to lead to more debates, challenges, and more violence in the media. In terms of sexuality, both lay commentators and researchers often cite sexualized media for high rates of sexual activity, teenage pregnancy, sexually transmitted diseases, and for continued damaging views of sex, gender roles, and family life. Authors of a compilation of chapters from leading scholars and researchers who report on adolescent sexuality concluded that television teaches sexual irresponsibility, that television programs provide "young people with lots of clues about how to be sexy, but they provide little information about how to be sexually responsible."[3] Yet remarkably little empirical attention has been directed to the interrelated concern of adolescents' exposure to sexually oriented media content and the more important issue of the manner and extent to which adolescents incorporate media information into their own attitudes or behaviors.

Sex in Television, Films, and Other Media

It is difficult to overestimate the amount of sex in the media. Numerous studies suggest a relatively high baseline. Several studies document well how incidents of sexual behavior on television are frequent, explicit, and generally irresponsible. In analyses of prime-time television, for example, one group of researchers reports 906 sexual incidents during one week of program coding and that sex is portrayed in humorous contexts when adolescents are most likely to watch.[4] Other researchers suggest that occurrences of "responsible" sexuality remain rare: Of 722 sexual encounters coded in one study, only 13 referred to contraception, 18 referenced prevention of sexually transmitted diseases (STDs; 13 of which related to AIDS), and no incidents of anyone contracting an STD were reported.[5] Sex on non–prime-time television also has become increasingly frequent and explicit. In an analysis of both prime time and afternoon television, for example, Louis Harris and Associates reported rapid increases in the use of sex from season to season, especially in the incidences of sexual behavior, deviant sexual activity, and explicit sex.[6] Even more telling, television sex made negligible references to sexuality education, STDs, birth control, and abortion.[7]

Although the findings may be striking, it is important to emphasize that the research remains controversial and that rapid changes in the use of sexuality in the media continue. The research remains controversial with regard to what constitutes sexual behavior, let alone irresponsible behavior, and also with regard to its portrayal of society and the media's impact. For example, and as several note, the media reflects gender roles and promotes the development and promulgation of sex-role stereotypes as sexist attitudes persist to play to the perceived fantasies of heterosexual models.[8] Although the impact of these stereotypes may be controversial, it does seem that television provides a distinctive vehicle for producing and reproducing meanings of gender and sexuality within natural social networks.[9] Television continues to depict women in weaker, subordinate roles relative to men. Women tend to be younger, more attractive, more nurturing, more concerned with romance, and more likely to be victimized than males.[10] The important finding about these programs and images is that the sexes seem differentially attracted to the programs that foster these views—for example, girls are more likely to seek movies and television programs that feature romance, the scriptwriter's euphemism for sex, and in that regard, exposes girls to more sexualized television than boys.[11] Likewise, those who do watch these programs tend to adopt similar traditional views of the gender's places in society.[12] The notion that audiences select content that reinforces previously held beliefs is not new; and research suggests that teenagers incorporate television messages into their own sex-role schemata, which relates to their involvement in sexual relationships.[13]

In terms of changes, the latest research reveals that the early and mid-1990s prime-time television programming experienced a drop in sexual behavior and references; and, perhaps more important, there was also a precipitous trend toward less explicit types of portrayals in increasingly prosocial contexts and nonviolent contexts, particularly humor.[14] Despite those noteworthy trends, sexuality still imbues television programming. Advertisements continue to use sex to sell a variety of products with the implicit message that people are sexually active and have no worries about pregnancy or STDs.[15] More strikingly, although prime-time television network commercials remain subject to more indecency restrictions and make less use of sex appeals than other media, female models regularly appear in some state of undress and feature sexually oriented conduct.[16] In addition, "talk shows," which may not be prime time but actually are available at key times for adolescents to view, increasingly provide extensive coverage of sexual activity and do so in the context of abnormal situations of abuse, addiction, and criminal behavior.[17] For example, from 80 talk show episodes from the summer of 1995, researchers recorded 126 disclosures of sexual activity (more than half of which related to pregnancy and infidelity), 98 disclosures of physical abuse and sexual abuse, and 59 discussions related to addiction.[18] Although the study, like others in this area, did not compare the frequency of these topics to those in other programming, these findings do support the assertion that talk shows cover materials labeled deviant, antisocial, and sexual. Despite notable changes, then, television still remains subject to considerable criticism for its failure to reduce its use of sexuality and foster less stereotypic and irresponsible attitudes.

Despite the volume of criticisms broadcast television faces, other media actually offer more sexual materials. Videos and music videos illustrate the increasingly frequent, explicit, and irresponsible sexual behavior found in the media. For example, even when they were only starting to be popular among teenagers, music videos presented adolescents with provocative clothing and sexually suggestive dance movements, including sadomasochism and sexual bondage.[19] Music videos simply incorporated the sexual content of explicit popular music, with all that entailed; and the sexed nature of music videos has yet to wane. On Music Television (MTV), in another study that is nearly 15 years old, 75% of the concept videos that told stories involved sexual imagery, more than half involved violence, and 80% combined the two to portray violence against women.[20] Likewise, the small fraction of direct sex appeals and various states of undress found in network television commercials pale in comparison from MTVs ads explicitly geared toward adolescents.[21] Follow-up studies reveal essentially little change: MTV broadcasts (including commercials) still depict female characters wearing revealing clothing, portray females as ''sex-objects,'' and continue gender-role stereotyping.[22] MTV continues to broadcast stereotypic and sexualized images that provide adolescents with restricted views of gender and sexuality.

Popular movies are also sexual in content and readily available.[23] Researchers report that 13- and 14-year-olds regularly have access to R-rated movies, and all who desire access are able to view whatever rental videos they wish.[24] Despite movie ratings, teenagers do have access to movies rated for adults; except for pornographic movies, the rules regulating access to theaters are imposed by the movie industry and do not have the force of law. In a real sense, the ratings simply are like those that appear on televisions to warn audiences about potentially harmful and disturbing content. In terms of sexual content, though, research has identified several important points. Although sex acts typically are not supposed to be common in films geared toward adolescents all the leading movies seen by adolescents during a denoted time period contained, on average, eight acts of sexual intercourse between unmarried partners, with a ratio of unmarried to married intercourse 32:1.[25] Although the majority of filmed references tended to be verbal, more than one third had visual components.[26] Likewise, characters were portrayed as overly interested in sexual activity. Films also frequently presented the use of alcohol, drugs, and profanity; every film studied made use of nudity, an average of approximately ten scenes per movie.[27] As expected, R-rated movies contain considerable sexual content; that content, however, tends to be much more coercive, violent, aggressive, and antisocial than other movies.[28] R-rated movies contain at least five times more violent behavior than movies rated X or XXX.[29] Thus the lower the rating, the higher aggression and violent sexual encounters, and the more access adolescents have to it.

Media does more than portray sexual activity, it has the potential to teach adolescents about sexual behavior, responsible behavior, and gender roles. Research has long supported the perception that the standard fare of songs, videos, and television programs constitutes provocatively clothed women in contexts filled with sexual aggression and types of sexual activity that cater to sexist attitudes and irresponsible behavior.[30] The availability of these sexualized media, however, does not necessarily indicate that they actually affect adolescents and that adolescents have access to them. Other research, however, suggests that adolescents do have access and that the media does have a significant effect on adolescents. We now turn to these two major findings, all of which reinforce the need to accept the teenage viewer as an active participant in his or her own socialization.

Patterns of Exposure to and Selection of Sexual Content

It seems difficult to dispute that the media contain sexually explicit materials and that they generally portray stereotypic gender roles. However, mere availability of sexual content or stereotypes do not necessarily produce learning. The period of adolescence is marked by dramatic changes in media use. Whether adolescents seek the media, select certain forms, and then pattern their behaviors remains the critical consideration.

Adolescents clearly spend much of their leisure time with their televisions. Adolescents typically spend about half of their daily leisure time watching television.[31] As adolescents approach the upper end of their teenage years, however, their amount of television watching decreases from approximately 30 hours to less than 20 hours per week.[32] When adolescents do watch, however, they are more likely to view sexual activity.[33] As mentioned previously, adolescents are thus more likely to view sexual activity associated with humor or violence and not likely to benefit from learning about birth control, sexually transmitted diseases, or sex education. The decrease in general TV viewing continues throughout the period of adolescent development, which reduces the exposure to sexual material on television. Adolescents, however, fill the void with increasing levels of music listening.[34] Adolescents trade one medium for another, and both contain significant levels of sexual content. Precisely how adolescents consume other media and incorporate them into the adolescent lifestyle remains unclear, with the general exception that males and females gravitate toward gendered media—for example, the magazine of choice for boys tends to be *Playboy* and it tends to be *Cosmopolitan* for girls.[35]

Research documents well the evident changes of adolescents' exposure to media. What leads to and influences the changes in media use, however, remains less clear. The number of influences on consumption patterns are virtually without limit. As with other areas of adolescent life, the influences change throughout adolescence. Without doubt, parents influence consumption patterns.[36] But that influence tends to wane as peers enhance the desirability of certain media or reduce the appeal of other media.[37] For example, for adolescents in the ninth grade, television viewing correlates to moods in relation to family members and negatively correlates with their moods with friends, which researchers interpret as television producing positive relationships with family members but not with peers.[38] Music becomes critical to peer relationships, including popularity, heterosexual attraction, dating, and sexual relationships.[39] Unlike television, music is negatively associated with moods with family members and positively associated with time spent with peers.[40] Thus as adolescents develop, their tastes change and the influences on those tastes in turn influence the changes.

The changes, however, tend to emerge not only in relation to age but also in relation to gender and dating status. Although the use of different media may be similar, boys and girls gravitate toward different content within the media. For example, boys are more likely to move toward heavy metal music whereas girls move toward softer rock.[41] Although adolescents' music tastes continue to change and now include rap, hip-hop, pop, as well as country and western, all musical styles portray high rates of sex and violence,[42] still appeal differently to the sexes,[43] and, as discussed later, affect the sexes differently. Likewise, although general television viewing decreases with age, watching television with a boyfriend or girlfriend is positively associated with more television time and more television sex content, as it is also related to more R-rated movie experiences with sexual content.[44]

Patterns of exposure to sexual content and selection of media complement well studies that estimate the amount and nature of sexual content on television and in other media. If anything, the patterns validate cause for concern. As adolescents develop, they increasingly select the forms of media that are least regulated and expose themselves to the least responsible and most explicit sexual content. These findings in and of themselves, however, do not necessarily amount to the need for concern. The actual effects of easy access to sexualized media determine their significance; and those findings, reviewed later, simply confirm that the media plays a powerful socializing role in adolescent life.

Responding to and Understanding Sexual Content

The effects of exposure to sexually oriented media remain a central area of concern, although not researched as much to match its purported significance. Basic research deals with the perceptions of the significance of the media as well as potential links between the sexualized content and actual behavior. In general, the research highlights cause for concern.

Adolescents incorporate televised sexual content into their perceptions of human sexuality. ''Cultivation studies''—research that examines how individuals seek and respond to media—suggest that those who view television more frequently than others adopt its world view, and exposure to sexually oriented materials biases a teenager's perceptions of the amount and kinds of sexual activity engaged in by other people. Research generally shows that television viewing distorts perceptions about several sex-related variables in the ''real world,'' such as the proportion of women who have abortions, men who have affairs, and perceptions of sex roles.[45] Current content of movies and television programs suggest other possible perceptions. Those who view television tend to view sex as important and as occurring frequently and often outside of marriage,[46] and the heaviest users provide the highest overestimation of activities adolescents allegedly do. Heavier viewers also perceive parenthood differently. Adolescent girls who watch soap operas, for example, have more idealistic views of single parenthood in that they view single mothers as well-educated, well-employed, and financially secure and view their children as healthy and cared for by adult men who are their mother's friends.[47] Adolescents who view movies also are more likely to view sex as a regular, popular activity, especially sexual intercourse, and that frequent discussion about sex are common. Likewise, they are more likely to believe that sex occurs outside of marriage, be overly positive about sex, and seldom consider contraception or potentially negative consequences.[48] The possibilities help explain the striking finding reported by researchers who report that ''after viewing less than an hour of MTV . . . adolescents were more likely to approve of premarital sex than were adolescents not having viewed MTV.''[49] Although their finding is now more than a decade old, like the majority of research examining adolescents' responses to sexuality in the media, it does reveal well the extent to which research has long supported the impact of media on adolescent sexuality. Adolescents who view sexually laden television programs and movies are more likely to believe that the media depicts the real world, or that the real world should conform to the media's rules.

Although the cultivation seems persuasive, important factors mediate the impact. Parents are the most significant mediating variable in the process of learning from television. Adolescents with parents involved in their television viewing show smaller relationships between the amount of viewing and degree of perceiving the world in terms of television portrayals.[50] Researchers have noted that direct parental mediation, coupled by discussion of parents' views of television content, successfully shapes their children's perceptions.[51] Conversely, adolescents without the benefit of parental mediation seem more inclined to seek out and accept TV portrayals as realistic. Note that adolescents who come from homes with their two natural parents watch significantly less television containing portrayals of and references to sexual activities; and those adolescents also are likely to see fewer R-rated movies.[52] Having step-parents does not lead to the same result as having natural parents; an adolescent of divorce or separation is more likely to watch and choose television programs that are sexier in both an absolute and relative basis.[53] Media, then, seemingly influences perceptions; but those influences are not necessarily immune from moderating influences.

Although sexual depictions in media may influence perceptions, the point of significance is whether they actually influence sexual behaviors. Theory suggests that distorted perceptions of the amount and kinds of sexual activity portrayed by the media affects teenager's behaviors. Evidence supports the link between perceptions of media influence and exposure to sexualized media. In terms of pressure toward sexual activity, adolescents consistently list television and music as a major source of pressure, and some studies list them as the most powerful force.[54] A variety of studies indicate that the media constitutes a major self-reported source of sexual information for adolescents.[55] In addition to these self-evaluations, it is important to note that media molds cultural norms; so even though some media remains highly rated as sources of information, their impact likely increases in light of the proposition that the other sources of information adolescents rely on are themselves influenced by the media. Investigations repeatedly demonstrate that exposure to televised programming increases the acceptance of certain sexual attitudes and stereotypes.[56]

In terms of media effects on actual behaviors, empirical research again links exposure to sexualized media and behaviors. Amounts of television viewing seemingly links with the likelihood of sexual intercourse. Although the links may not be direct, research indicates that, for females, viewing and sexual experience are positively related, whereas for males the heaviest users tend to have the highest incidence of reported sexual activity.[57] Likewise, adolescents who view more sex on television are more likely to have had sexual intercourse than those who viewed smaller portions of sexual content.[58] The links between sexualized media and adolescent sexual behavior, however, generally are far from linear, and this likely is the case for several reasons. As we will see later, consistent sex differences emerge among the amount, nature, and saliency of media influences.[59] The levels of viewing change throughout adolescence and the associations between viewing and sexual activity changes.[60] The viewing context, such as whether parents are present, has an important impact. For example, girls who watch television apart from their parents have more than three times the rate of sexual experiences than those who watch with their parents,[61] a finding consistent with the persistent finding that family satisfaction remains a constant moderator of the relationship between media variables and premarital sexual permissiveness among adolescents.[62] The amount of sexually oriented television, not surprisingly, thus also correlates with the probability that the adolescents are sexually active.[63] The extent to which media figures become salient role models has an impact as well: Those who identify media persons as their first choices of models of "responsible" sexual behavior report more permissive sexual attitudes and higher rates of sexual activity than those who report nonmedia personalities as role models.[64] Male students tend to identify even more with media characters as models of irresponsible sexuality, and this identification correlates with "more permissive sexual attitudes, higher rates of sexual intercourse, greater numbers of sexual partners, and lower rates of contraceptive usage."[65] The television media affects adolescents' sex-role stereotypes and eventually their sex-role behaviors at different points in development.[66] Media also affects adolescents differently when they have different educational and economic aspirations—for example, correlations for boys with the highest educational aspirations are near zero.[67] Different media have different effects: Research does support the contention that media, especially music videos, prime adolescents for stereotypical appraisals of social interactions and change what the sexes perceive when they meet.[68] Finally, differences in sexual experiences affect the relevance of sexualized media.[69] Biased perceptions and attitudes about sexual activity seemingly contribute to nonrealistic sexual activity portrayed in the media.

Although the earlier findings may be persuasive, research actually has yet to note *causal* links between media use and sexual activity.[70] However, the evidence does indicate that exposure to sexually oriented materials influences adolescent sexuality. Whether consumption of sexual content leads to high activity, or high activity leads to increased consumption remains an empirical question. Most likely, the relationship is circular. People's perceptions and behaviors are influenced by the media they consume. It should not be surprising to find that every meta-analysis to date that has examined the media's effects on both the attitudes and behaviors of individuals, finds an impact,[71] including links between pornography and rape-myth acceptance (skeptical attitudes toward rape victims)[72] and television violence on antisocial behavior.[73] In addition, research relating to music reveals that exposure to rap and pop music increases adolescents' (especially boys') acceptance of teenage dating violence and sexual harassment.[74] Again, although no causal links have been systematically demonstrated, the associations do indicate the magnitude of the media's influence on people's attitudes and behaviors, that social institutions affect people's development of various attitudes. Rather than acting in an immediate manner, different media seemingly act more indirectly by teaching, in the absence of other influences, certain values, language, and scripts that are consistent with and perhaps encourage certain forms of sexual activity.

Adolescents' Media Access and the Law

Despite the common view of the First Amendment right to freedom of speech and the press as paragons of American freedom, the Supreme Court has never considered the right absolute.[75] Laws may abridge the right of free speech to serve the perceived needs of governance. For example, "fighting words," advocacy of imminent lawless behavior, libel, and obscenity receive no First Amendment protection and sexually offensive speech generally lies at the periphery of First Amendment concerns.[76] In addition to categorical exclusions from protection, different broadcast mediums, such as television and radio, continue to receive only limited First Amendment protection.[77] And of course, political speech, even by minors, generally receives the utmost protection.[78] Different speech and speech in different contexts, then, may occupy a different place in the hierarchy of First Amendment protection. This section details adolescents' media rights as they relate to sexually charged materials in different media.

To understand the nature of adolescents' rights in the context of media regulations of sexuality, it is important to first distinguish between indecent and obscene materials.[79] Obscene materials essentially are offensive materials without political or social value and thus banned by law. Indecent materials are those that may be offensive but may have some redeeming social or political value and thus are not subject to being banned. The critical issue that arises is the extent to which some indecent materials actually may be obscene from the perspective of adolescents. For example, child pornography (reviewed in depth in chapter 7) is viewed as harmful and obscene for everyone and therefore it has been banned for everyone. Unlike the blanket ban on child pornography, bans on materials that are obscene only as to adolescents (e.g., adult pornography) are applied in a variable manner.

Adolescents and Access to Pornography

The Supreme Court first recognized the concept of variable obscenity, as applied to adolescents, in *Ginsberg v. New York.*[80] In *Ginsberg,* a mother enlisted her 16-year-old son to purchase two "girlie magazines," containing pictures of female nudity, from a "mom-and-pop" luncheonette so that the owners could be prosecuted. The New York courts held the sales to be in violation of a New York law that criminalized such sales. The Court noted that the magazines at issue were not obscene when sold to adults and that the appellant did not argue that the magazines did not meet the statutory definition of "harmful to minors."[81] The only issue presented to the Court involved the availability of a different standard for obscenity, one that varied according to age.

In determining whether double standards were permissible, the Court conducted a two-pronged analysis. The first issue was whether the statute intruded on whatever freedom of speech the Constitution grants to minors. The Court noted that a state has the power to regulate for the well-being of its children, both in support of parents in their upbringing of their children and based on the state's own interest in the character of its adolescents. In its analysis, the Court accepted "variable concepts of obscenity" to reject the proposition that the statute improperly prohibited the sale of materials "harmful to minors."[82] The Court thus adjusted the definition of obscenity to what it called "social realities" and the general rule "that the State has [the] power to make that adjustment seems clear, for we have recognized that even where there is an invasion of protected freedoms 'the power of the state to control the conduct of children reaches beyond the scope of its authority over adults.'"[83] The second issue emerged from the first and involved whether the legislature could rationally conclude that exposure to the restricted materials would harm adolescents. Given that low standard, the Court simply had to find that it was not irrational for the legislature to find that the exposure to the condemned material was harmful to minors. The Court then examined existing scientific material, found that the link had been neither proved nor disproved and that there was no need to satisfy a higher standard to uphold the statute. Given that the materials were not protected, there was no reason to require "scientifically certain criteria of legislation" that would link materials to harm."[84] In restricting minor's access to obscene materials, states need not demonstrate a causal link between materials determined obscene for adolescents and the degradation of the adolescents' morals. The statute simply reflected the community's judgment about what was appropriate for minors with regard to a form of expression that does not enjoy full First Amendment protection, and because minor's rights did not acquire full protection, the Court simply had to find that it was not irrational for the state to regulate adolescents' exposure to the materials. Furthermore, the Court argued that it could have rested its decision fully on Congress's interest in supporting "parents' claim to authority in their own household."[85] Thus although the Court has assumed that indecency is harmful to minors, its decisions have not relied solely on this mere supposition to limit adolescents' access to sexually indecent materials.

The *Ginsberg* rationale has served to support state efforts to restrict minor's rights to pornography. Since the *Ginsberg* opinion, several states have adopted statutes aimed to protect minors from sexually explicit material by adopting the New York approach that creates an "obscene as to minors" standard.[86] As long as states confine the scope of their regulations to works that depict or describe sexual conduct, appellate decisions routinely support efforts to limit adolescents' access to these "harmful materials."[87] Thus statutes that include materials that are harmful to minors but that are not sexual, such as excessive violence, tend to fall short of constitutional requirements.[88] With the permissible ends of the legislation thus construed, the issues in most cases turn on the means by which states elect to prevent minors from accessing the forbidden materials.[89]

Although the Court adopts a more lenient approach to regulations that restrict otherwise protected material from being viewed by minors, three Supreme Court cases reveal the limits of the leniency. The cases illustrate the need to restrict attempts to shield adolescents from sexually charged media, and all deal with the manner the regulation denies minors access to proscribed materials. The first case involved congressional efforts to eliminate "dial-a-porn" services through the Communications Act Amendment of 1988. That Act allowed the Federal Communication Commission (FCC) to place a blanket prohibition on indecent and obscene telephone messages.[90] The Court declared the section unconstitutional in *Sable Communications, Inc. v. FCC.*[91] Sable Communications had offered recorded, sexually oriented messages over the telephone and billed calls at a higher rate as it split proceedings with Sable and Pacific Bell Telephone. The Court concluded that a ban on indecent, but not obscene, material could not be justified. Given that nonobscene speech enjoyed First Amendment protection, the regulation required a compelling interest and the restriction had to be the least restrictive means of furthering that interest. Although the Court recognized the compelling interest in protecting the physical and psychological well-being of minors that extended to shielding minors from indecent material, the Court did not find the statutory attempt narrowly drawn. The Court noted that the total ban would unconstitutionally limit adult access to such materials and that minors' exposure was limited by the fee charged by the telephone services. Although the Court disapproved of the method of billing, it found that the interest in protecting minors could be addressed by the less restrictive means of screening through requiring credit cards or other similar means. The FCC could not justify a complete ban that far exceeded the level necessary to prevent minors from being exposed to such protected messages.

The second important case that attempted to shield minors from exposure to pornography was *Butler v. Michigan.* [92] *Butler* involved the appeal of a conviction for violating a Michigan statute that proscribed the possession for sale of publications that tended to "incite minors to violent or depraved or immoral acts, manifestly tending to the corruption of the morals of adolescents."[93] *Butler* simply made the materials available for the entire public and had not sold the materials to minors. Instead, he had sold a book to a police officer, an act the trial court found could have potentially deleterious effects on adolescents. The Court refused to accept Michigan's attempt to protect adolescents by preventing adults from obtaining materials that were not obscene, which would reduce the Michigan population to reading only what is fit for "children." The case enunciated a key principle that still affects the constitutional assessment of many of the proposals to restrict minors' access to obscene or indecent materials. The principle, that reductions of protections would lead to an impermissively chilling effect on adults' access to materials fit and protected for them, permeates all decisions that follow; the Court repeatedly returns to read *Butler* as leading to the conclusion that "the level of discourse reaching a mailbox simply cannot be limited to that which would be suitable for a sandbox."[94] That decision, and those that follow its approach, abide by what the courts call the "plain-brown wrapper" principle. Books, magazines, and the like that are clearly not intended for minors may be distributed by simply concealing their contents, thereby shielding minors from their indecent materials. When the unanimous Court struck down the statute, it did not discount the state's interest in protecting minors from harmful materials; rather, it rejected the manner in which the state sought to protect minors.

The limits to child protection as a result of the protection of adults' liberties comes equally obvious in the most recent attempts to regulate minors' access to pornographic and indecent materials through the Telecommunications Act of 1996.[95] Among other controversial provisions, the legislation contained the Communications Decency Act (CDA) that addressed indecent materials on the Internet.[96] The clear purpose of the CDA was to restrict access by minors to offensive depictions of sexual or excretory activities that may be available over interactive computer services, including materials over the Internet.[97] Note that under this statute the government could "completely ban obscenity and child pornography from the Internet. No Internet speaker has a right to engage in these forms of speech, and no Internet listener has a right to receive them."[98]

Although the CDA contained exceedingly broad language, the public and scholarly commentaries' focus narrowed to discussions that relate to protecting children from access to indecent materials that would be obscene as to minors. That form of speech occupies a more ambiguous place in First Amendment jurisprudence that leads to difficulties in determining when speech is obscene or indecent and that challenges statutory schemes deemed to too broadly restrict speech.[99] In this instance, the CDA was perceived as so broad that the statute never went into effect; less than a year after its enactment, the Supreme Court struck down the attempt to have Internet users limit their transactions for fear that exposure to minors would bring criminal sanctions.

The case that condemned the legislative attempt, *Reno v. American Civil Liberties Union*,[100] exemplifies how the Court seeks to balance the rights of adults with those of adolescents. The Court agreed that the statute swept too broadly and chilled the free expression rights of adults; the criminalization of indecent speech by the CDA improperly prohibited adults from accessing such material. The only dissenting opinion, by two Justices, concurred with the judgment but broke with the majority in its refusal to address the contention that the CDA did not unconstitutionally interfere with the First Amendment rights of minors. Although the CDA might reach some materials protected even as to minors, the dissenting Justices were not convinced that there was the real and substantial overbreadth required to prevail on a facial challenge to a statute. As with the *Ginsberg* decision that "zoned" minors out of adult bookstores, the dissenters would allow regulation if technology could "zone" the Internet in a way that preserves adults' Internet access to sexually explicit materials that are inappropriate for minors.

Efforts to curb minor's access to pornographic materials, then, remain permissible if they respond to adult's legitimate interests. As new technology emerges, regulations must also respond to the legitimate interests of both users and communication businesses. The need to balance continues and plays an equal role in the regulation of indecent materials not even considered pornographic as to minors.

Despite considerable concern with pornographic materials, indecent materials are at the center of regulation and controversies. Rather than focusing on the broad regulation of sexual materials in newspapers, magazines, books, videos, or movies, this section focuses on access to sexual materials on television. Although these media exhibit common characteristics that lead to regulation, television remains more useful to consider because it poses increasingly complicated problems and generates enduring debates, both in law and in terms of television's impact. The possible exception would be computers, the regulation of which has been addressed previously to find that, in terms of indecency, the Supreme Court broadly shields them from regulation.[101]

Adolescents and Access to Broadcast Materials

Regulation of broadcast materials pervasively falls within the power of the FCC. The FCC derives its statutory mandate from two somewhat contradictory provisions. The first prohibits the FCC from censoring broadcast communications,[102] and the second makes it a crime to "utter any obscene, indecent or profane language" via broadcast communications.[103] Although the regulation would appear rather complex and seemingly treads on important constitutional rights, in terms of indecent materials in broadcasting, the Supreme Court addressed the issue only once, in *FCC v. Pacifica Foundation*.[104]

Pacifica involved a complaint to the FCC by a man who allegedly stumbled onto a broadcast on his car radio while driving with his 15-year-old son. Both had heard a twelve-minute monologue by comedian George Carlin titled "Filthy Words," a discussion of the seven "words you couldn't say on the public . . . airwaves."[105] The comedian proved to be prophetic in his identification of words he could not say on the air. The Commission upheld the complaint against the New York radio station owned by Pacifica Foundation and found the language "patently offensive," broadcast at an inappropriate time, and thus indecent and prohibited by 18 U.S.C. § 1464. The Pacifica Foundation appealed to the D.C. Circuit, which reversed the Commission's decision.[106] The Supreme Court, however, reversed the circuit court's ruling and found that the Commission had the power to regulate and review the content of completed broadcasts.[107]

The Court proceeded on statutory and constitutional grounds. Statutorily, the Court had little trouble finding for the FCC. In resolving the apparent conflict between the rules that prohibit censorship and those that prohibit broadcasting of indecent materials, the Court simply held that the relevant language prohibiting censorship could not apply to prohibiting obscene, indecent, or profane material. Constitutionally, the Court also had no trouble finding for the FCC. The central constitutional issue involved the First Amendment. When the Court turned to First Amendment concerns, it found that, although speech generally gains protection, such language and references "surely lie at the periphery of First Amendment concern."[108] The Court noted that, because the monologue was not traced to political content, it required no First Amendment protection and thus could be regulated simply because the words offend for the same reasons that obscenity offends: The utterances were no essential part of any exposition of ideas and were of slight social value. The Court then explained how different media receive different levels of First Amendment protection, with broadcasting receiving the most limited protection in the indecency context for two reasons: First, broadcast media are uniquely pervasive in the lives of Americans, especially homes in which the individual has the right to be left alone from intruders, and second, broadcasting is uniquely accessible to minors and the government's interest in minors' well-being and in supporting parents' claim to authority in their own household justifies the regulation of otherwise protected expression.

Although the FCC had won a decisive victory, even it disavowed an expansive interpretation of indecency.[109] The FCC narrowly construed *Pacifica* as only allowing it to punish those broadcasters who repetitively used any of the "seven dirty words" before 10:00 P.M. It was only a decade later when the FCC began to apply the indecency definition as a generic standard and discharged three separate warnings against radio station broadcasts.[110] Several broadcasters challenged these three FCC decisions, which had followed the FCC's Public Notice summarizing its new enforcement policy and the Reconsideration Order affirming it.[111] The broadcasters appealed the warnings to the D.C. Circuit in *Action for Children's Television v. FCC*.[112] Among numerous challenges, the broadcasters asserted that the new mandates to create "safe harbors" (restriction of indecent broadcasts to late hours to limit the risk that minors are in the audience) were arbitrary and would reduce adults to seeing and hearing material fit only for minors. Although the court upheld the generic indecency standard, rejected a series of constitutional challenges, and offered a litany of restricted or regulated speech, the court still decided against the Commission for failing to provide adequate factual or analytical foundation in setting a time for the safe harbor for indecent programming without unduly restricting the rights of parents and more mature audiences. In response to the ruling, Congress quickly passed an amendment to an appropriations bill that required the FCC to "promulgate regulations in accordance with section 1464 ... to enforce the provisions . . . on a 24-hour a day basis."[113] FCC, in its own response, passed a total, 24-hour ban on indecent programming on broadcast television and radio.[114] The courts, in yet another case titled *Action for Children's Television v. FCC*,[115] responded by rejecting the absolute ban on grounds that the FCC failed to identify a reasonable time period to broadcast indecent materials. The Supreme Court denied *certiorari,* which then led Congress to enact another law, the Public Telecommunications Act of 1992, which ordered the FCC to promulgate regulations to prohibit the broadcasting of indecent programming between 6:00 A.M. and midnight, with the exception that some stations may begin broadcast at 10:00 P.M.[116] In yet another *Action for Children's Television v. FCC*,[117] the D.C. Circuit court affirmed the channeling regulations, with the minor modification that the FCC apply the less restrictive 10:00 P.M. cut-off to all broadcasters. In allowing for the regulation of otherwise protected speech, the court focused on the two compelling interests asserted by the Commission: the need to support parental supervision of their children and the general concern for children's well-being.

In the nine-year drama that culminated in allowing the FCC to regulate indecency in broadcasts, the courts consistently focused on the need to protect parental rights and the state's interest in minors' well-being. The most recent case emphasized both interests. In terms of the state's independent interests, the court accepted FCC findings about the prevalence of homes in which minors had radios or televisions in their own rooms to show that real parental control over what their children watched and heard was impossible. Thus the state had an interest in facilitating parental rights in controlling their children. The court also reaffirmed that the government had an independent and equally compelling interest in preventing minors from being exposed to indecent broadcasts. Although the limit in the time of broadcasts would infringe on the rights of adults, the court concluded that those rights "must yield to the imperative needs of the young."[118] The court focused on the data collected by the FCC as to the number of children under the age of 18 in the audience during the times of the ban, and found those numbers substantial enough to create a "reasonable risk that large numbers of children would be exposed to . . . indecent material."[119] The similarly large number of adults in the audience were not similarly situated; they had alternative means of satisfying their interest in indecent material and the relevant statutory mandate already had an inherently chilling effect on adult speech. The statute and its eventual implementation, then, allowed for restricting indecent materials to everyone.

In terms of the rights of parents, the Court has long protected parents' claims to authority in their own homes to direct the rearing of their children as they see fit. That right certainly includes what their children should and should not watch on television, free from governmental interference. The dissent in the first and only Supreme Court case to address the issue of indecent materials in broadcast media offered the only direct confrontation of the issue and argued that the principle of parental rights "supports a result directly contrary to that reached by the Court. . . . [P]arents, *not* the government, have the right to make certain decisions regarding the upbringing of their children."[120] The lone dissent in the D.C. District Court cases that followed the Supreme Court case also lamented how the FCC preempted, not facilitated, parental control.[121] Under the parental rights approach, the state's interest lies less with protecting children than it does with protecting parents. Parents would have the right to assess whether and how to regulate television watching of their children. The courts, however, construed the right as one that needed assistance because parents simply could not independently control their children's access to indecent media.

The content regulation in broadcasting departs from regulation of other media and other areas of free speech law. Indecent-but-not-obscene speech generally receives full First Amendment protection.[122] Yet no radio or television broadcaster may broadcast, between the hours of 6:00 A.M. and 10:00 P.M., programs containing "language or material that, in context, depicts or describes, in terms patently offensive as measured by the contemporary community standards for the broadcast medium, sexual or excretory activities or organs."[123] Although nonbroadcasted materials have received more protection, as we will see later, the Supreme Court recently held the indecency standards applicable to cable television in finding that "cable and broadcast television differ little, if at all."[124] The failure to find a difference between the media allowed the Court to apply the *Pacifica* standards of regulation to cable indecency and signalled a reluctance to eliminate *Pacifica's* rationales that allow for considerable censorship.

As with other regulation of fundamental rights, the pertinent issues to focus on are whether the interest that leads to the regulation is compelling, whether the regulatory means advance their ends, and whether less restrictive alternatives are available. Currently and in terms of broadcasts, the state interest is so compelling that other alternatives remain inadequate. For example, preprogram warnings, or warnings published in program guides, as to the content of the programs would seem effective institutional safeguards; but the case that upheld the ban on indecent materials involved a program that was preceded with similar warnings.[125] If technology could improve the ability of parents to censor adolescents' access to indecent media, blanket bans at even limited intervals would prove difficult to justify.

More recently, two approaches have been taken to narrow the intrusion into adults' rights and facilitate parental rights. Much emphasis has been placed on lock-out technology that enables parents to block particular programs or channels from being shown at particular times.[126] The Telecommunications Act of 1996 has offered two measures.[127] The first approach would be a ''V-chip'' that the Communications' Decency Act mandated for all televisions with a diagonal screen size of 13 inches or greater, and manufactured after a date set by the FCC.[128] If parents activate the chip, the television would not display certain programs accompanied by the signal. The second approach provides rating systems based on age appropriateness. Both approaches focus on putting the power in the hands of parents and theoretically provide the necessary protection of minors without limiting the choices of adults. As with pornographic books and magazines, the V-chip serves as the ''plain brown wrapper'' that allows adults to watch whatever is suited for them while, again at least in theory, eliminating minors from the audience. Although the Court hinted that these efforts offered less restrictive ways than blocking sexually explicit programming to adults, the Court did not explicitly rule that they would be constitutional.[129] Instead, the Court used the potential availability of technology to argue that the approach employed by Congress was not narrowly tailored.[130] Given that possibility, commentators have been quick to propose compelling arguments that would suggest that the V-chip would be both unconstitutional and impractical.[131] However, it is entirely imaginable that the First Amendment would be satisfied by increasing the power parents have over their minors' access to indecent materials and removing governmental controls over the content of television.

Broadcast television, radio, and cable television represent only a small part of the potential exposure of children to indecent images. Recognizing the problems encountered in attempts to shield children from indecency in new types of media, Congress recently enacted a series of statutes to regulate and limit adolescents' access to such materials. The most recent statute, the Communications Decency Act, reviewed previously, was roundly rejected by the Supreme Court for its broad intrusion on adults' rights. The other major statute dealt with the other medium left without much regulation, the cable television industry. The statute and its reception by the courts is worthy of emphasis, for it highlights principles similar to those that emerged from the Internet cases and, not surprisingly, suffered a similar fate by the Supreme Court's review.

The Cable Television Consumer Protection and Competition Act of 1992 (Cable Television Act)[132] addressed indecent materials on cable television. It is not surprising that the increasing maturity of cable television, with its numerous offerings, spawned heated disputes over allegedly indecent programming. The proliferation of court battles over indecent cable programming culminated in the relevant Supreme Court case, *Denver Area Education Telecommunication Consortium v. FCC*.[133] That case challenged the constitutionality of the Cable Television Act that addressed the issue of indecent material on cable programming. The consortium challenged congressional attempts to address the higher rates of ''adult situations'' and channels specifically aimed at an adult audience that were not covered by the FCC's regulations relating to broadcasts. The consortium objected to the need to have programmers provide 30-days notice to cable operators before presenting offensive programs, which would then allow operators to block access to customers who requested and then unblock access to those who would request the resumption of service. Despite the burdensome block and unblock requirements, the government sought to justify the statute as the least restrictive way to meet the compelling objective of protecting minors' physical and psychological well-being. The Court found the statute unnecessarily burdensome. Yet it is important to note that the Court still recognized the compelling interest in protecting the physical and psychological well-being of minors, it simply found that other methods would not be as cumbersome as the statutes' 30-day advance block requirements.

Solicitude for minors still justifies intrusion on adults' rights. In this case, even though it would be improper to reduce the adult population to view only the same sexually provocative materials that would be appropriate for minors, minors' vulnerabilities have consideration. However, the First Amendment remains a preferred freedom—one that, when balanced against other rights, gets the benefit of the doubt. Given that it is a preferred freedom, the Supreme Court requires narrowly tailored intrusions to achieve the goals of child protection without unduly curtailing the rights of adults. The Court contemplates numerous factors to determine whether speech would be protected: the minor's access to the expressive materials, whether minors are a captive audience, the restrictions placed on adults, the infringement on the role of parents in raising their children, the existence of potentially less intrusive means available to the government, and the regulation's reasonableness in its restrictions.

Opportunities for Reform

Analyses of media effects on adolescents' sexual lives reduce to three critical points. The multimedia environment adolescents inhabit simply cannot prevent adolescents' exposure to sexually charged materials, let alone the use of adolescents in sexually exploitative media. In addition, adolescents actively engage in and construct their own sexual socialization as they operate in their multimedia environment. Finally, the formal mass media is only one source from which adolescents learn about themselves and others as sexual human beings, and important factors may moderate the negative effects of media on adolescents. These three findings help highlight the limits of current approaches and suggest possible alternatives and opportunities for reform.

The Limitations of Current Legal Mandates

Legal analyses of adolescents and sexualized media generally reveal two efforts. The first area of interest focuses on limiting adolescents' access to media, particularly when the materials are obscene and when adolescents would be involved in their production, as in the ban on child pornography. The second area of regulation seeks to facilitate parents' abilities to raise their children as they see fit when materials are indecent as to adults but only potentially obscene as to minors, such as pornography and offensive television programming. In the latter instances, the law attempts to control the flow of information to minors while still allowing parents access and freedom to expose their children to the media and allowing adults general access to materials not obscene as to them. These two areas of focus largely account for the law's limitations.

Available evidence suggests that efforts to limit access are increasingly fruitless in two major ways. The effort seems fruitless because censorship makes the mass media untrustworthy for the majority of adolescents.[134] As a result, adolescents note that they would like to rely and actually would prefer the media as a source of information, they still pervasively rely on other sources of information.[135] The combination of lack of trust and deficit between the actual use of, and desire to use, the media suggests that the effectiveness of the mass media in health promotion with respect to dealing with sexual development, such as through promoting abstinence and preventing sexually transmitted diseases, may be limited and exacerbated by efforts to shield minors from improper programming.

The effort also seems fruitless given the wide range of media accessible to minors and their relative ease of access despite efforts to curb exposure to problematic materials. Adolescents regularly have access to numerous forms of media. The failure to address more properly diverse media sells short efforts to assist adolescents. For example, movies tend to be equally available as commercial network television and broadcast television's sexual content is tepid by comparison with film. Movies show what television suggests and discusses. Likewise, films feature salient role models who enjoy themselves, have no discussion of safe sex, have few negative consequences of sex, even aggressive and violent sex. In terms of television, MTV's music videos are more sexual than the usual television fare, and adolescents' orientation toward music intensifies as they enter middle adolescence. Movies and music videos not only vary from standard television in the quantity of their treatment of sex, but in the quality of their treatment as well. Movie sex scenes are longer, more passionate, visual, specific, and interesting. Thus current efforts fail to the extent that they ignore other media that gain increasing salience for adolescents but still remains generally regulated by those who provide the media.

Current efforts to address sexually charged matters in the media also remain limited in that they focus on sex as the problem, rather than concerning themselves with inappropriate sex. In general, the media creates socially inappropriate perceptions for young consumers. As with the concern with children's programming that may not have been appropriate for young children, there has been relatively no concern with creating programs suitable for adolescents. There has been a market failure for good programs, despite the decrease in use of sex in prime-time television. Thus efforts aim to limit the flow of sexualized media to adolescents, fail to do so, and fail to counter the potentially negative consequences of the failure to limit the flow.

In addition to being limited, current legal efforts also reveal the difficulties of reform. The courts remain ill-equipped to deal with sexuality in the media. For example, courts generally remain unable to impose liability on the networks for the content of their broadcasts for fear that it would chill speech and for the inability to prove that broadcasters were reckless in their programming.[136] Numerous cases follow these principles, even though the harms adolescents suffer seem linked to media effects.[137] In addition, when Congress does intervene to deal with materials obscene only as to minors, the general justification is that policies aim to assist parents; and the Supreme Court has relied on a similar rationale.[138] Yet Congress does not do so in a way that assists parents in addressing with children the issue of sex. Instead, laws simply aim to allow the removal of sex from the household. The pitfalls with this approach are enormous. The approach assumes that parents do moderate adolescents' media exposure when they increasingly do not. The approach ignores that warnings that trigger parents' need for caution in their adolescents' use of the media typically have no effects on adolescents, with the potential exception that it increases young teenagers interest in the materials that may contain indecent, violent, or sexually explicit content.[139] The approach fails to consider how parents still remain reluctant to discuss sexual mores with their children, which would heighten the need for increasing the availability of sexual matters in the family rather than limiting them. Finally, the approach improperly imposes constraints on adolescents' abilities to sort information, which removes opportunities to exercise meaningful maturity, autonomy, and control and, in the end, damages democracy and preempts the development of responsible citizenship. The reality of adolescent life, then, dictates the need for greater assistance, rather than policies of removal.

Blanket bans and the alternative that bestows the control of adolescents' media rights to parents ignore evidence that indecent materials as to adults actually play important roles in adolescent sexual development. For example, pornographic materials actually often play a part in adolescents' initiation into sexual maturity for both boys and girls.[140] Likewise, television and music remain among the most common sources of sexual information for boys and girls of all ages.[141] Arguably, access to sexually charged materials could benefit adolescents as they deal with the challenging issues of sexuality and sexual relationships. For example, current attempts to acknowledge and respect different sexualities necessarily increase the need to also respect their development. Gay adolescents, for instance, often suffer from harassment, ridicule, and lack of role models; they arguably could benefit from access to pornographic materials: commentators increasingly emphasize the significance of pornography to gay male's sexual development.[142] Likewise, although many assume that girls respond to erotic or provocative stimuli less readily than boys, gender differences are smaller than imagined, especially among sexually experienced adolescents.[143] Thus the titillating aspects of the adolescent culture, as exemplified in advertisements, music, rock videos, movies, and fashion may stimulate sexual arousal in both boys and girls and contribute to their sexual development.[144] These discussions raise highly controversial issues, yet they have become obvious and much needed points of discussion if society is to move toward tolerance and respect minors' individual right to self-determination.

Alternative Approaches to Regulating Adolescents' Media Rights

The boundaries of a state's power to regulate the First Amendment rights of minors delimit the boundaries of reform. However, rather than focus solely on limits to access, it is appropriate to conceive of alternatives. These alternatives inevitably involve the right to receive information and the need to reconsider and respond to what has been construed as the public interest in popular media regulation and the First Amendment itself.

In general, states may only abridge protected freedoms if they have an overriding interest in doing so. Furthermore, "It is not enough to show that the Government's ends are compelling; the means must be carefully tailored to achieve those ends."[145] In the area of free speech, the extreme value placed on complete freedom to publish ideas cannot be overstated; and the Court has carefully limited the First Amendment's scope. The Court, however, effectively has justified broadened regulation where minors are concerned. This new category of content regulation—minor's access regulation—was developed in *Ginsberg.*[146] The twin interests of supporting parents and the well-being of the state's adolescents provided the compelling interest to restrict minors' rights on less than "scientifically certain criteria of legislation."[147] Minor's access jurisprudence tends toward permissiveness in allowing states to address sexual problems facing adolescents without unduly interfering with the interests of the adult community in otherwise free speech.

Although the law allows permissive restrictions, it also limits restrictions to the extent the Court recognizes that the Constitution protects the right to receive information and ideas. Although that aspect of regulation tends to be ignored, it has received the Court's interest and resulted in important judicial commentaries.[148] The influential cases in which the Supreme Court touched on the right to receive ideas dealt with either sexuality or adolescents' rights. In *Stanley v. Georgia,*[149] the Court invalidated a state law making private possession of obscene materials by adults a crime, because it was "now well established that the Constitution protects the right to receive information and ideas."[150] In *Pacifica,* the dissent emphasized the interest of listeners who wished to hear broadcasts the FCC deemed offensive.[151] The last case dealt with the authority of school boards to remove books from the library, *Board of Education, Island Trees Union Free School District. No. 26 v. Pico.*[152] In

Pico, the Court proposed that the First Amendment rights of students to read the books limited the schools' authority to censor. The plurality opinion noted that the ''right to receive ideas is a necessary predicate to the *recipient's* meaningful exercise of his own rights of speech, press, and political freedom.''[153] In addition, the Court has recognized how students have a right ''to inquire, to study, and to evaluate, and to gain new maturity and understanding.''[154] The Court, then, recognizes the centrality of the right to adolescent development and to the exercise of other rights.

When applied to minors, two factors limit what the law allows in First Amendment restrictions and individuals' rights to receive ideas. First and to reiterate a prevailing theme in adolescents' rights, the law allows for parental control. Few dispute the right of parents to control the communications environment of their minor children, a right the Supreme Court has long recognized in parental liberty to direct the upbringing and education of their children as they see fit. For example, in *Ginsberg v. New York* the Court recognized that the parent's authority over their children means ''parents . . . who have this primary responsibility for children's well-being are entitled to the support of laws designed to aid discharge of that responsibility.''[155] From this perspective and from the view of materials that are indecent as to adults, the government has an interest in facilitating parenting, not a compelling interest in protecting children. In *Ginsberg,* the Court concluded that the legislature was not usurping the role of parents in raising their children but rather was merely providing a law that supported and respected the importance of parental guidance. Indeed, even those acting *in loco parentis,* such as schools, assume parental functions and may exercise great control over what speech students hear. In *Bethel School District No. 403 v. Fraser*[156] the Court upheld the punishment of a high school student for an indecent speech made at a school assembly as the Court emphasized the *in loco parentis* doctrine and the schools' educative mission, which could entail protecting children from exposure to sexually explicit, indecent, or lewd speech. Even the justice who had championed the rights of adolescents to receive information concurred with the judgment.[157] The most recent Supreme Court cases have found it unnecessary to accept or reject the contention that regulations violate the First Amendment by restricting materials with value for minors.[158] Indecency regulations may ignore minors' First Amendment rights by not exempting materials with serious value for adolescents. Parents may even do what the government cannot—adopt an overbroad prophylactic rule banning their children from accessing any media, which would allow adolescents access to what schools and other institutions offer.

The second factor that moderates the limits on adolescents' First Amendment rights reveals why rights are limited. In addition to protecting parental rights, the First Amendment protects the rights of society to make civil individuals. For example, public interests allow censorship in public schools. Censorship in broadcasting is allowed for a similar rationale; indeed, the FCC, which exercises regulatory authority over all forms of interstate communication via spectrum or wire, grants a license only ''if public convenience, interest, or necessity will be served thereby'' and the Commission may renew the license only on the basis of a similar finding that renewal would serve the ''public interest, convenience, and necessity.''[159] Indeed, the state's interest in producing healthy, productive citizens even overrules parental interests. Thus those institutions that hold licenses, such as television broadcasters, and those that do not, such as parents, must operate in the public interest when they deal with adolescents.

The public interests served by censoring adolescents' media environment serve several interests that distill to three simple concerns. The first two are relatively straightforward, whereas one requires elaboration. The first two reasons are explicit in cases that limit adolescents' access to sexually charged media: limits protect minors from harm and serve as facilitators of parental rights to raise their children. The third reason relates to the need to meet adolescents' need to prepare themselves a life of productive citizenship. The touchstone of the First Amendment is that it allows individuals to develop themselves through the communication of ideas, and the free flow of information, education, and association. Protecting free speech serves the goals of individual autonomy, self-realization, and human dignity.[160] The First Amendment reflects the state's commitment to democratic self-government. As for adults, the media should be the conduit of democratic values and decency for adolescents. The principles located in the First Amendment, then, are principles of governance that encourage the free flow of ideas and discourage the automatic restriction of speech to solve or prevent social problems. The Supreme Court often has asserted that the First Amendment "was fashioned to assure the unfettered interchange of ideas for bringing about of political and social changes desired by the people."[161] Free speech grants the right to give and receive and is essential to the very survival of democracy. Under this concept of a speech "marketplace," the "remedy" for dangerous expression is more and varied expression.[162] The interests served by the First Amendment lead to practical avenues and opportunities for reform.

The ultimate effect of what the social sciences suggest remains limited by what the law allows. Despite considerable limitations, several possibilities emerge. Unlike the current focus of policy efforts, however, the suggestions point to the need to look beyond parents' control of adolescents' media rights and champion a need to recognize ways to ensure adolescents' abilities to deal with much more than exploitative media. Laws also must aim to allow adolescents to deal with exploitative and damaging relationships. These points are worthy of emphasis and elaboration.

The omnipresent focus on parental rights necessitates a premium on parent education and support. This effort would depart from the current approach that focuses on preventing information from entering homes and adolescents' schools. Far from fearing what the media offer minors, efforts that support parents would provide the opportunity to discuss sex in a meaningful way with their children. Given the rampant and continued failure of parents to approach these issues with children, alternative approaches would need to be developed to deal with blanket censorship by either parents or communities. Material that, taken as a whole, has serious literary, artistic, political, or scientific value for minors is not obscene as to adolescents, yet these materials currently are subject to limitations simply because efforts to protect adolescents from sexual materials sweep broadly. Unlike other rights adolescents possess, the control wielded by parents poses an anomaly: Fundamental rights of minors generally must not be controlled solely by a third party, alternative means of protection must be allowed, such as the provision of judicial bypasses or other adults who are able to exercise the minor's rights when parents fail.

The focus on parents and the role of others in protecting adolescents' First Amendment rights suggest two other avenues of reform. The first would be to promote media literacy for adolescents. Although parents may play a preemininent role in creating media-literate children, school-based programs already have been developed that actually use media in developing effective adolescent health education.[163] The second avenue of reform would aim toward community efforts in the form, for example, of making more aggressive use of the media for health campaigns and prosocial purposes.[164] This seems rather difficult because of the heavy focus on making the media not credible when it comes to the majority of its programs. Media simply is seen as a less valued source of information even though it is in truth highly valued by adolescents. Yet in terms of sexuality, commentators and commissions already have proffered guides to responsible sexual content in the media.[165] Primary among the goals would be to recognize sex as a potentially healthy and natural part of life;

discuss the consequences of unprotected sex; depict how not all intimate relationships result in sex and indicate the essential nature of contraceptive practices; avoid linking violence and sex; recognize and respect the ability to say no; and encourage parent–child discussions about sex. To succeed, however, public education initiatives must give individuals permission and encouragement to challenge other people's actions that were once thought to be "none of their business." The central part of successful campaigns has been that citizens must take individual and collective action regarding social and public health issues, even if they are not directly involved in the problem. Personal accountability derives from believing the problem is widespread and of sufficient threat to the community fabric that it affects ones own life and thereby motivates one enough to take action.

Conclusion

States educate, regulate family life, and supervise adolescent development. Governments have an interest in raising healthy, well-rounded young people into mature citizens. Despite these interests, the current approach to adolescents' media rights seeks to limit adolescents' access to media, flatly fails to do so, and does not offer adolescents ways to protect themselves from potential harms. The analysis suggests that the media shapes more than individuals: It shapes society, its perceptions, and its definitions of culture. Properly used, it teaches adolescents about the complexities of life and may be used to ensure their participation in society, rather than ensuring that information be kept from them and that they be outsiders and nonparticipants in what otherwise would be their own cultural life. The proposal is actually not a new idea—the traditional First Amendment cure for social ills created by unsettling speech is more and varied expression. At its core, the First Amendment affirmatively encourages speech and demands that people participate in social life.

The expression of contentious materials provides an opportunity to respond to those ideas with other expression or with nongovernmental activity and provides opportunities for prevention of harms. Available evidence suggests that attention would need to be given to making young people's trust in media information highly selective so that inappropriate messages are not accepted and acted on. Although this may seem like a pipe dream, research indicates otherwise. Some adolescents rely on media more than others for determinations of norms and models. Adolescents also interpret content differently, given the social structure from which they come, previous sexual experiences, and their motives for using the media during particular points in their development. These motives and interpretations affect the incorporation of media messages into the adolescent's sexual identity and behavior.

Dealing with problematic media influences, then, necessitates dealing with the structure of adolescent life, most notably the position of adolescents in society and their eventual roles. Distal social contexts, such as race, gender, age, and social class play important roles in determining access and influence. Different teenagers have and see different opportunity structures, such as whether they intend to go to college, have a career, get married, and so forth. In addition, these social contexts are mediated by many institutions, such as peers, schools, and families. Research on media uses and gratifications suggests that, given the array of media, the one chosen depends on the motivations and the extent to which they become involved in the media. Thus the sexual content offered by various forms of media may constrain what adolescents learn and respond to, but the effect of that content depends on who adolescents are when they come to use the media and adolescents' rights shape who adolescents are.

Endnotes

1. *See* Victor C. Strasburger, *Adolescents and the Media: Medical and Psychological Impact* (Thousand Oaks, CA: Sage Publications, 1995); Dolf Zillmann, Jennings Bryant, and Aletha C. Huston (Eds.), *Media, Children, and the Family: Social Scientific, Psychodynamic, and Clinical Perspectives* (Hillsdale, NJ: Lawrence Erlbaum, 1994).

2. Aimee Dorr and Dale Kunkel, ''Children and the Media Environment: Change and Constancy Amid Change,'' *Communication Research* 17 (1990):5–25. *See also* Robert Kubey and Mihaly Csikszentmihalyi, *Television and the Quality of Life: How Viewing Shapes Everyday Experience* (Hillsdale, NJ: Erlbaum, 1990).

3. Cheryl D. Hayes (Ed.), *Risking the Future: Adolescent Sexuality, Pregnancy and Childbearing* (Washington, DC: National Academy Press, 1987), at 91.

4. Nancy L. Buerkel-Rothfuss, ''Background: What Prior Research Shows.'' In *Media, Sex and the Adolescent,* ed. Bradley S. Greenberg, Jane D. Brown, and Nancy Buerkel-Rothfuss (Creskill, NY: Hampton Press, 1993).

5. Dennis T. Lowry and David E. Towles, ''Prime Time TV Portrayals of Sex, Contraception, and Venereal Diseases,'' *Journalism Quarterly* 66 (1989):347–352.

6. Louis Harris & Associates, *Sexual Material on American Network Television During the 1987–88 Season* (New York: Planned Parenthood Federation of America, 1988).

7. The study found that American teenagers view nearly 14000 sexual references, innuendos, and jokes per year, yet only 165 of the references deal with such topics as birth control, self-control, abstinence, or STD. *Id. See also* Jane D. Brown, Kim Walsh Childers, and Cynthia S. Waszak, ''Television and Adolescent Sexuality,'' *Journal of Adolescent Health Care* 11 (1990):62–70.

8. Jennifer Herrett-Skjellum and Mike Allen, ''Television Programming and Sex Stereotyping: A Meta-Analysis,'' *Communication Yearbook* 19 (1996):157–185; Carolyn A. Lin, ''Beefcake Versus Cheesecake in the 1990s: Sexist Portrayals of Both Genders in Television Commercials,'' *Howard Journal of Communications* 8 (1997):237–249.

9. Melissa A. Milkie, ''Social World Approach to Cultural Studies: Mass Media and Gender in the Adolescent Peer Group,'' *Journal of Contemporary Ethnography* 23 (1994):354–380.

10. Nancy Signorielli, ''Children, Television, and Gender Roles: Messages and Impact,'' *Journal of Adolescent Health Care* 11 (1990):50–58; Nancy Signorielli, ''Sex Roles and Stereotyping on Television,'' *Adolescent Medicine: State of the Art Reviews* 4 (1990):551–561.

11. Kim Walsh-Childers and Jane D. Brown, ''Adolescents' Acceptance of Sex-Role Stereotypes and Television Viewing.'' In *Media, Sex and the Adolescent,* ed. Bradley S. Greenberg, Jane D. Brown, and Nancy Buerkel-Rothfuss (Creskill, NY: Hampton Press, 1993); Bradley S. Greenberg and Renato Linsangan, ''Gender Differences in Adolescents' Media Use, Exposure to Sexual Content and Parental Mediation.'' In *Media, Sex and the Adolescent,* ed. Bradley S. Greenberg, Jane D. Brown, and Nancy Buerkel-Rothfuss (Creskill, NY: Hampton Press, 1993).

12. Bradley S. Greenberg, Renato Linsangan, Anne Soderman, Carrie Heeter, Carolyn Lin, Cynthia Stanley, and Michelle Siemicki, ''Adolescents' Exposure to Television and Movie Sex.'' In *Media, Sex and the Adolescent,* ed. Bradley S. Greenberg, Jane D. Brown, and Nancy Buerkel-Rothfuss (Creskill, NY: Hampton Press, 1993).

13. Kim Walsh-Childers and Jane D. Brown, ''Adolescents' Acceptance of Sex-Role Stereotypes and Television Viewing.'' In *Media, Sex and the Adolescent,* ed. Bradley S. Greenberg, Jane D. Brown, and Nancy Buerkel-Rothfuss (Creskill, NY: Hampton Press, 1993).

14. Joan Gorham, ''Sex in Primetime Television: An Analysis of Content Trends, Context Categories, and Sampling Considerations,'' *Communication Research Reports* 11 (1994):171–181.

15. J. Kilbourne, ''Killing Us Softly: Gender Roles in Advertising,'' *Adolescent Medicine: State of the Art Reviews* 4 (1993):635–649.

16. Carolyn A. Lin, ''Uses of Sex Appeals in Prime-Time Television Commercials,'' *Sex Roles* 38 (1988):461–449.

17. Stacy Davis and Marie-Louis Mares, "Effects of Talk Show Viewing on Adolescents," *Journal of Communication* 48 (1998):69–86.

18. *See id.* at 70.

19. The research was conducted 15 years ago and showed the overwhelming nature of sex in music videos. Richard L. Baxter, Cynthia DeRiemer, Ann Landini, Larry Leslie, and Michael W. Singletary, "A Content Analysis of Music Videos," *Journal of Broadcasting and Electronic Media* 29 (1985):333–340.

20. Barry L. Sherman and Joseph R. Dominick, "Violence and Sex in Music Videos: TV and Rock 'n' Role," *Journal of Communication* 36 (1986):79–93.

21. Nancy Signorielli, Douglas McLeod, and Elain Healy, "Gender Stereotypes in MTV Commercials: The Best Goes On," *Journal of Broadcasting and Electronic Media* 38 (1994):91–101.

22. Steven A. Seidman, "Re-Visiting Sex-Role Stereotyping in MTV Videos," *International Journal of Instructional Media* 26 (1999):11–23.

23. Bradley S. Greenberg, Michelle Siemicki, Sandra Dorfman, Carrie Heeter, Cynthia Stanley, Anne Soderman, and Renato Linsangan, "Sex Content in R-Rated Films Viewed by Adolescents." In *Media, Sex and the Adolescent,* ed. Bradley S. Greenberg, Jane D. Brown, and Nancy Buerkel-Rothfuss (Creskill, NY: Hampton Press, 1993).

24. Bradley S. Greenberg, Renato Linsangan, Anne Soderman, Carrie Heeter, Carolyn Lin, Cynthia Stanley, and Michelle Siemicki, "Adolescents' Exposure to Television and Movie Sex." In *Media, Sex and the Adolescent,* ed. Bradley S. Greenberg, Jane D. Brown, and Nancy Buerkel-Rothfuss (Creskill, NY: Hampton Press, 1993).

25. Bradley S. Greenberg, Michelle Siemicki, Sandra Dorfman, Carrie Heeter, Cynthia Stanley, Anne Soderman, and Renato Linsangan, "Sex Content in R-Rated Films Viewed by Adolescents." In *Media, Sex and the Adolescent,* ed. Bradley S. Greenberg, Jane D. Brown, and Nancy Buerkel-Rothfuss (Creskill, NY: Hampton Press, 1993).

26. *Id.*

27. *Id.*

28. Ni Yang and Daniel Linz, "Movie Rating and the Content of Adult Videos: The Sex–Violence Ratio," *Journal of Communication* 40 (1990):28–42.

29. *Id.*

30. Barry L. Sherman and Joseph R. Dominick, "Violence and Sex in Music Videos: TV and Rock 'n' Role," *Journal of Communication* 36 (1986):79–93.

31. Buerkel-Rothfuss, "Background: What Prior Research Shows."

32. Michael Morgan, Alison Alexander, James Shanahan, and Cheryl Harris, "Adolescents, VCRs, and the Family Environment," *Communication Research* 17 (1990):83–106.

33. Robert Kubey and Reed Larson, "The Use and Experience of the New Video Media Among Children and Adolescents," *Communication Research* 17 (1990):107–130.

34. Jane D. Brown, Kim Walsh Childers, K. Bauman, and G. Koch, "The Influence of New Media and Family Structure on Young Adolescents' Television and Radio Use," *Communication Research* 17 (1990):65–82.

35. Buerkel-Rothfuss, "Background: What Prior Research Shows."

36. Brown et al., "Television and Adolescent Sexuality"; Morgan et al., "Adolescents, VCRs, and the Family Environment."

37. Reed Larson and Robert Kubey, "Television and Music: Contrasting Media in Adolescent Life," *Youth and Society* 15 (1983):13–32.

38. Reed Larson, Robert Kubey, and Joseph Colletti, "Changing Channels: Early Adolescent Media Choices and Shifting Investments in Family and Friends," *Journal of Youth and Adolescence* 18 (1989):583–599.

39. Larson and Kubey, "Television and Music: Contrasting Media in Adolescent Life."

40. Larson et al., "Changing Channels: Early Adolescent Media Choices and Shifting Investments in Family and Friends."

41. Peter G. Christenson and Jon Brian Peterson, "Genre and Gender in the Structure of Music Preferences," *Communications Research* 15 (1988):282–301.

42. Kenneth Jones, "Are Rap Videos More Violent? Style Differences and the Prevalence of Sex and Violence in the Age of MTV," *Howard Journal of Communications* 8 (1997):343–356.
43. Anthony B. Pinn, "'Getting Grown': Notes on Gangsta Rap Music and Notions of Manhood," *Journal of African American Men* 2 (1996):61–73.
44. Bradley S. Greenberg, Renato Linsangan, Anne Soderman, Carrie Heeter, Carolyn Lin, Cynthia Stanley, and Michelle Siemicki, "Adolescents' Exposure to Television and Movie Sex." In *Media, Sex and the Adolescent,* ed. Bradley S. Greenberg, Jane D. Brown, and Nancy Buerkel-Rothfuss (Creskill, NY: Hampton Press, 1993).
45. Michael Morgan and Nancy Rothschild, "Impact of the New Television Technology: Cable TV, Peers, and Sex-Role Cultivation in the Electronic Environment," *Youth and Society* 15 (1983):33–50; George Gerbner, Larry Gross, Michael Morgan, and Nancy Signorielli, "Living With Television: The Dynamics of the Cultivation Process." In *Perspectives on Media Effects,* ed. Jennings Bryant and Dolf Zillman (Hillsdale, NJ: Erlbaum, 1986); Nancy L. Buerkel-Rothfuss and Sandra Mayes, "Soap Opera Viewing: The Cultivation Effect," *Journal of Communication* 31 (1981):108–115; Davis and Mares, "Effects of Talk Show Viewing on Adolescents."
46. Bradley S. Greenberg, Cynthia Stanley, Michelle Siemicki, Carrie Heeter, Anne Soderman, and Renato Linsangan, "Sex Content on Soaps and Prime-Time Television Series Most Viewed by Adolescents." In *Media, Sex and the Adolescent,* ed. Bradley S. Greenberg, Jane D. Brown, and Nancy Buerkel-Rothfuss (Creskill, NY: Hampton Press, 1993); Davis and Mares, "Effects of Talk Show Viewing on Adolescents."
47. Mary Strom Larson, "Sex Roles and Soap Operas: What Adolescents Learn About Single Motherhood," *Sex Roles* 35 (1996):97–110.
48. Bradley S. Greenberg, Michelle Siemicki, Sandra Dorfman, Carrie Heeter, Cynthia Stanley, Anne Soderman, and Renato Linsangan, "Sex Content in R-Rated Films Viewed by Adolescents." In *Media, Sex and the Adolescent,* ed. Bradley S. Greenberg, Jane D. Brown, and Nancy Buerkel-Rothfuss (Creskill, NY: Hampton Press, 1993).
49. Larry E. Greeson and Rose Ann Williams, "Social Implications of Music Videos for Youth: An Analysis of the Content and Effects of MTV," *Youth and Society* 18 (1986):177–189, at 185.
50. Gerbner et al., "Living With Television: The Dynamics of the Cultivation Process."
51. Erica Weintraub Austin, Donald F. Roberts, and Clifford I. Nass, "Influences of Family Communication on Children's Television Interpretation Processes," *Communication Research* 36 (1990):545–564.
52. Bradley S. Greenberg, Renato Linsangan, Anne Soderman, Carrie Heeter, Carolyn Lin, Cynthia Stanley, and Michelle Siemicki, "Adolescents' Exposure to Television and Movie Sex." In *Media, Sex and the Adolescent,* ed. Bradley S. Greenberg, Jane D. Brown, and Nancy Buerkel-Rothfuss (Creskill, NY: Hampton Press, 1993).
53. Cynthia Stanley and Bradley S. Greenberg, "Family Structure and Adolescents' Orientation to TV and Movie Sex." In *Media, Sex and the Adolescent,* ed. Bradley S. Greenberg, Jane D. Brown, and Nancy Buerkel-Rothfuss (Creskill, NY: Hampton Press, 1993).
54. Marian Howard, "Postponing Sexual Involvement Among Adolescents: An Alternative Approach to Prevention of Sexually Transmitted Diseases," *Journal of Adolescent Health Care* 6 (1985):271–277.
55. Victor C. Strasburger, "Television and Adolescents: Sex, Drugs, Rock 'n' Role," *Adolescent Medicine: State of the Art Reviews* 1 (1990):161–194.
56. Herrett-Skjellum and Allen, "Television Programming and Sex Stereotyping: A Meta-Analysis."
57. Buerkel-Rothfuss, "Background: What Prior Research Shows."
58. Jane D. Brown and Susan F. Newcomer, "Television Viewing and Adolescents' Sexual Behavior," *Journal of Homosexuality* 21 (1991):77–91.
59. James L. Peterson, Kristin A. Moore, and Frank F. Furstenberg Jr., "Television Viewing and Early Initiation of Sexual Intercourse: Is There a Link?" *Journal of Homosexuality* 21 (1991):93–118.

60. *Id.*
61. *Id.*
62. *See, e.g.,* Jeremiah S. Strouse, Nancy Buerkel-Rothfuss, and Edgar C. J. Long, ''Gender and Family as Moderators of the Relationship Between Music Video Exposure and Adolescent Sexual Permissiveness,'' *Adolescence* 30 (1995):505–521.
63. *Id.*
64. Richard A. Fabes and Jeremiah Strouse, ''Perceptions of Responsible and Irresponsible Models of Sexuality: A Correlational Study,'' *Journal of Sex Research* 23 (1987):70–84.
65. *Id.* at 79.
66. Michael Morgan, ''Television, Sex-Role Attitudes, and Sex-Role Behavior,'' *Journal of Early Adolescence* 7 (1987):269–282.
67. Peterson et al., ''Television Viewing and Early Initiation of Sexual Intercourse: Is There a Link?''
68. Cristine H. Hansen and Roland D. Hansen, ''Priming Stereotypical Appraisal of Social Interactions: How Rock Music Videos Can Change What's Seen When Boy Meets Girls,'' *Sex Roles* 19 (1988):287–319; Crinstine Hall Hansen and Walter Krygowski, ''Arousal-Augmented Priming Effects: Rock Music Videos and Sex Object Schemas,'' *Communication Research* 21 (1994):24–47.
69. Peterson et al., ''Television Viewing and Early Initiation of Sexual Intercourse: Is There a Link?''
70. Nancy L. Buerkel-Rothfuss, Jeremiah S. Strouse, Gary Pettey, and Milton Shatzer, ''Adolescents' and Young Adults' Exposure to Sexually Oriented and Sexually Explicit Media.'' In *Media, Sex and the Adolescent,* ed. Bradley S. Greenberg, Jane D. Brown, and Nancy Buerkel-Rothfuss (Creskill, NY: Hampton Press, 1993).
71. Herrett-Skjellum and Allen, ''Television Programming and Sex Stereotyping: A Meta-Analysis.''
72. Mike Allen, Tara Emmers, Lisa Gebhardt, and Mary A. Giery, ''Pornography and Rape Myth Acceptance,'' *Journal of Communication* 45 (1995):5–26.
73. Haejung Paik and George Comstock, ''The Effects of Television Violence on Antisocial Behavior: A Meta-Analysis,'' *Communication Research* 21 (1994):516–546.
74. James D. Johnson, Mike S. Adams, Leslie Ashburn, and William Reed, ''Differential Gender Effects of Exposure to Rap Music on African American Adolescents' Acceptance of Teen Dating Violence,'' *Sex Roles* 33 (1995):597–605; Jeremiah S. Strouse, Megan P. Goodwin, and Bruce Roscoe, ''Correlates of Attitudes Toward Sexual Harassment Among Early Adolescents,'' *Sex Roles* 31 (1994):559–577.
75. The First Amendment states, in relevant part, ''Congress shall make no law ... abridging freedom of speech, or of the press.'' U.S. CONST. AMEND. I.
76. *See,* respectively, Chaplinsky v. New Hampshire, 315 U.S. 568, 571–572 (1942); Cohen v. California, 493 U.S. 15 (1971); New York Times v. Sullivan, 376 U.S. 254 (1954); Roth v. United States, 354 U.S. 476, 485 (1957); FCC v. Pacifica Found., 438 U.S. 726, 743 (1978).
77. FCC v. Pacifica Found., 438 U.S. 726, 748 (1978).
78. Tinker v. Des Moines Indep. Sch. Dist., 393 U.S. 503, 506 (1969); Bethel Sch. Dist. No. 403 v. Fraser, 4784 U.S. 675, 681–683 (1986).
79. FCC v. Pacifica Found., 438 U.S. 726, 740–741 (1978).
80. 390 U.S. 629, 638–639 (1968).
81. *Id.* at 634.
82. *Id.* at 631–633.
83. *Id.* at 638 (quoting Prince v. Massachusetts, 321 U.S. 158, 179 (1944)).
84. *Id.* at 643.
85. *Id.* at 639.
86. *See, e.g.,* ARIZ. REV. STAT. ANN. §§ 13-3501–3507 (Supp. 1986); ME. REV. STAT. tit. 17, §§ 2911, 2912 (West 1983 & Supp. 1995); MISS. CODE ANN. § 97-5-27 (1994); MO. ANN. STAT. §§ 573.060 (Vernon 1995).

87. *See, e.g.,* Soundgarden v. Eikenberry, 871 P.2d 1050 (Sup. Ct. Wash. 1994) (upholding constitutionality of definition), *cert. denied,* 513 U.S. 1056 (1994).

88. Davis-Kidd Booksellers, Inc. v. McWherter, 866 S.W.2d 520, 533 (Tenn. 1993) (upholding validity of statute only on striking the excess violence provisions from the definition of harmful to minors).

89. *Soundgarden,* 871 P.2d at 1050, *cert. denied,* 513 U.S. at 1056.

90. *Id.* at 117. *See* Communications Act Amendment of 1988, 47 U.S.C. § 223(b) (1994) (as amended by Departments of Labor, Health and Human Services, and Education, and Related Agencies Appropriation Act of 1990, § 521, Pub. L. No. 101-166, 103 Stat. 1159, 1192).

91. 492 U.S. 115 (1989).

92. 352 U.S. 380 (1957).

93. *Id.* at 381 (quoting Mich. Comp. Laws § 750.343 (Supp. 1954).

94. Most recently, the Justices cited the phrase in ACLU v. Reno, 117 S. Ct. 2329, 2346 (1997).

95. Pub. L. No. 104-104, 110 Stat. 133 (to be codified at 47 U.S.C. § 23 (a)–(h).)

96. Pub. L. No. 104-104, 110 Stat. 133 (codified as amended in scattered sections of 47 U.S.C.).

97. Telecommunications Competition and Deregulation Act of 1996, S. 652, 104th Cong., 2d Sess. §§ 501 et seq. The Act criminalizes the knowing use of "any comment, request, suggestion, proposal, image, or other communication that, in context, depicts or describes, in terms patently offensive as measured by contemporary community standards, sexual or excretory activities or organs." *Id.* § 502(e).

98. American Civil Liberties Union v. Reno, 929 F. Supp. 824, 865 (E.D. Pa. 1996).

99. The Supreme Court defines indecent speech as speech that "fail[s] to conform with accepted standards of morality," but that may have political or social value. *See Pacifica,* 438 U.S. 726, 740–741 (1978).

100. 117 S. Ct. 2329 (1997).

101. As seen previously in *American Civil Liberties Union,* 117 S. Ct. at 2329, the Communications Decency Act 1996, Pub. L. No. 104-104, 110 Stat. 133 (codified as amended in scattered sections of 47 U.S.C.) was unconstitutional for failing to protect adults' right to indecent materials.

102. 47 U.S.C. § 326 (1994): "Nothing in this chapter shall be understood or construed to give . . . the power of censorship over the . . . communications. . . ."

103. 18 U.S.C. § 1464 (1944): "Whoever utters an obscene, indecent, or profane language by means of radio communication shall be fined . . . or imprisoned."

104. 438 U.S. 726 (1978).

105. *Id.* at 729. The words Carlin so identified were "shit," "piss," "fuck," "cunt," "cocksucker," "motherfucker" and "tits," causing the case to be called the "seven dirty words case." *See Id.* at 751.

106. Pacifica Foundation v. FCC, 556 F.2d 9 (D.C. Cir. 1977), *rev'd,* 438 U.S. 726 (1978).

107. 438 U.S. 726, 735 (1978).

108. *Id.* at 743.

109. It actually did so in litigated cases; *see In re* Application of WGBH Education Foundation, 69 F.C.C. 2d 1250, 1254 (1978).

110. Action for Children's Television v. FCC 852 F. 2d 1332, 1336 (D.C. Cir. 1988).

111. New Indecency Enforcement Standards to be Applied to All Broadcast and Amateur Radio Licensees, F.C.C.R., 2, 2726 (1987).

112. 582 F.2d 1332, 1339 (D.C. Cir. 1988).

113. Departments of Commerce, Justice, and State, the Judiciary and Related Agencies Appropriations Act of 1989, Pub. L. No. 100-459, § 608, 102 Stat. 2186, 2228 (1988).

114. 47 C.F.R. § 73.3999 (1989).

115. 932 F.2d 1504, 1509 (D.C. Cir. 1991).

116. Public Telecommunications Act of 1992, Pub. L. No. 102-356, § 16 (a), 106 Stat. 949 (1992) (codified at 47 U.S.C. § 303 (Supp. IV 1992)).

117. 58 F.3d 654, 656, 660–663 (D.C. Cir. 1995) *(en banc),* *cert. denied,* 516 U.S. 1043 (1996).

118. *Id.* at 667.

119. *Id.* at 665.
120. *Pacifica,* 438 U.S. at 769–770.
121. In the third case: 58 F.3d 654, 670 (D.C. Cir. 1995) (Edwards, C.J. dissenting).
122. Sable Communications of Cal., Inc. v. FCC, 492 U.S. 115, 126–127 (1989) (refusing to uphold 24-hour ban on Dial-a-Porn service because commercial telephone communications were seen as substantially different from broadcasts).
123. Action for Children's Television v. FCC, 58 F.3d 654, 660 (D.C. Cir. 1995) *(en banc), cert. denied,* 116 S. Ct. 701 (1996).
124. Denver Area Educ. Telecommunication Consortium v. FCC, 116 S. Ct. 2374, 2388, 2386–2387 (1996).
125. FCC v. Pacifica Found., 438 U.S. 726, 748–749 (1978).
126. Newton N. Minow and Craig L. LaMay, *Abandoned in the Wasteland: Children, Television, and the First Amendment* (New York: Hill & Wang, 1995).
127. Pub. L. No. 104-104, § 551, 110 Stat. 56, 139 (1996) (to be codified at 47 U.S.C. § 303(w)).
128. 47 U.S.C.A. §§ 303(x), 330(c).
129. Denver Area Educ. Telecommunications Consortium, Inc. v. FCC, 116 S. Ct. 2374, 2392 (1996).
130. *Id.* The Court did the same in Reno v. ACLU, 117 S. Ct. 2329, 2348 (1997).
131. *See, e.g.,* J. M. Balkin, "Media Filters, The V-Chip, and the Foundations of Broadcast Regulation," *Duke Law Journal* 45 (1996):1131–1175.
132. Pub. L. No. 102-385, 106 Stat. 1460, 1486 (codified as amended in scattered sections of 47 U.S.C.)
133. 116 S. Ct. 2374 (1996).
134. Doreen A. Rosenthal and Anthony M. A. Smith, "Adolescents, Sexually Transmissible Diseases, and Health Promotion: Information Sources, Preferences and Trust," *Health Promotion Journal of Australia* 5 (1995):38–44.
135. *Id.*
136. *See, e.g.,* Olivia N. v. NBC, 178 Cal. Rptr. 888 (Ct. App. 1981).
137. McCollum v. Columbia Broadcasting Sys., 249 Cal. Rptr 187, 189 (Ct. App. 1988); DeFilippo v. National Broadcasting Co., 446 A.2d 1036 (R.I. 1982).
138. Both *Ginsberg* and *Ferber* well illustrate the point. In *Ferber,* the Court expressed utter confidence that the distribution of child pornography was harmful to minors and thus makes no mention of any supposed governmental interest in furthering parental discretion; 458 U.S. 747, 758 (1982). In *Ginsberg,* the Court acknowledged the lack of scientific support for the conclusion that the regulated material was actually harmful to children; 390 U.S. 629, 641 (1968), and then proceeded to uphold the ban on the sale of sexually explicit materials to children after specifically noting that "the prohibition against sales to minors does not bar parents who desire from purchasing the magazines for their children." 390 U.S. 629, 639 (1968).
139. *See, e.g.,* Marina Krcmar and Joanne Cantor, "The Role of Television Advisories and Ratings in Parent–Child Discussions of Television Viewing Choice," *Journal of Broadcasting & Electronic Media* 41 (1997):393–411.
140. The average age of exposure to pornography is 11 and nearly half of girls and 60% of boys report to have learned some or a lot from pornography. Gloria Cowan and Robin R. Campbell, "Rape Causal Attitudes Among Adolescents," *The Journal of Sex Research* 32 (1995):145–153.
141. Rosenthal and Smith, "Adolescents, Sexually Transmissible Diseases, and Health Promotion: Information Sources, Preferences and Trust."
142. *See* Jeffrey G. Sherman, "Love Speech: The Social Utility of Pornography," *Stanford Law Review* 47 (1995):661–705.
143. Herant A. Katchadourian, *Fundamentals of Human Sexuality.* 5th ed. (New York: Holt, Rinehart, and Winston, 1989).
144. Jean Brooks-Gunn and Frank F. Furstenberg Jr., "Coming of Age in the Era of AIDS: Puberty, Sexuality, and Contraception," *Milbank Quarterly* 68(Supp.) (1990):59–84.
145. Sable Communications, Inc. v. FCC, 492 U.S. 115, 126 (1988).
146. 390 U.S. at 636, 639–643.

147. *Id.* at 642–643.
148. Red Lion Bd. Co. v. FCC, 395 U.S. 367, 390 (1969). ("It is the right of viewers and listeners . . . which is paramount.").
149. 394 U.S. 557 (1969).
150. *Id.* at 564.
151. 438 U.S. at 766.
152. 457 U.S. 853 (1982).
153. *Id.* at 867 (plurality opinion of Brennan, J.).
154. Keyishian v. Board of Regents, 385 U.S. 589, 603 (1967).
155. 390 U.S. 629, 639 (1968).
156. 478 U.S. 675 (1986).
157. *Id.* at 687 (Brennan J., concurring in the judgment).
158. *See* ACLU v. Reno, 929 F. Supp. 824, 863, 864 (E.D. Pa. 1996), *aff'd,* 117 S. Ct. 2329 (1997); Reno v. ACLU, 117 S. Ct. 2329, 2348 (1997).
159. Communications Act of 1934, 47 U.S.C. §§ 151–152, 307(a)–(c) (1998).
160. *See* Martin H. Redish, "The Value of Free Speech," *University of Pennsylvania Law Review* 130 (1982):591–645, at 593 (proposing that the true value of free speech is "individual self-realization").
161. New York Times Co. v. Sullivan, 376 U.S. 254, 269 (1964).
162. Gertz v. Robert Welch, Inc., 418 U.S. 323, 339–340 (1974).
163. *See, e.g.,* Dorothy G. Singer and Jerome L. Singer, "Evaluating the Classroom Viewing of a Television Series, *Degrassi Junior High.*" In *Media, Children, and the Family: Social, Scientific, Psychodynamic, and Clinical Perspectives,* ed. Dolf Zillmann, Jennings Bryant, and Aletha C. Huston (Hillsdale, NJ: Lawrence Erlbaum, 1994).
164. Lawrence Wallack, Lori Dorfman, David Jernigan, and Makani Themba, *Media Advocacy and Public Health* (Newbury Park, CA: Sage, 1993).
165. Committee on Communications, "Sexuality, Contraception, and the Media," *Pediatrics* 95 (1995):298–300; Strasburger, *Adolescents and the Media. Medical and Psychological Impact.*

Chapter 7
Sexual Victimization by Adults

By the time they reach adulthood, more than 25% of girls and more than 15% of boys will have experienced sexual victimization.[1] Their abuse most likely will have started with the onset of early adolescence, between ages 10 and 12.[2] The abuse also likely will have persisted into the adolescent period, because victimization not only tends to recur within initially abusive relationships but also tends to transfer to other relationships.[3] Their abusive experiences also likely will have affected their sexual socialization beyond the immediate effects of victimization. Victimization places adolescents on developmental paths marked by higher rates of early onset of (consensual) sexual activity, teenage pregnancy, multiple sexual partnerships, sexually transmitted diseases, and sex offenses.[4] Victimization, then, significantly affects adolescents' sexual adjustment, a part of victims' lives that undoubtedly jolts their other developmental tasks.

As these findings suggest, the social sciences now have contributed greatly to our understanding of sexual victimization. Given the massive amount of research relating to this form of maltreatment,[5] this chapter tailors its discussion of sexual victimization to two forms of abuse readily associated with adolescents and their legal rights: prostitution and pornography. Although the abridged analysis clearly neglects considerable research that would relate to adolescents, six reasons lead to and justify the limited focus. First, addressing both prostitution and pornography requires considering how more common forms of sexual victimization foster and affect attempts to address these two forms of maltreatment. Second, attempts to protect adolescents from pornographic exploitation reveal the extreme to which society appears ready to limit the rights of those who would exploit adolescent sexuality. Third, efforts that respond to adolescent prostitution, which inevitably involves runaway and homeless adolescents, reveal how the legal system remains influenced (and hampered) by perceptions of what constitutes normal adolescent sexual and gender development. Fourth, responses to prostitution also reveal how laws designed to protect adolescents actually may contribute to adolescents' exploitation. Fifth, explorations of the two forms of abuse involve legal analyses that necessarily include laws relating to all other forms of abuse, particularly laws that address family violence. Sixth, although other forms of abuse may differ in significant ways, analyses of the nature of and legal responses to prostitution and pornography uncover themes that relate to all forms of maltreatment. Thus prostitution and pornography actually exemplify significant aspects of all forms of sexual victimization, reflect society's willingness to protect adolescents, and highlight the nature of much needed reform necessary to protect adolescents from harm.

This chapter presents the current social science understanding of prostitution and pornography, the dominant legal responses to these two forms of maltreatment, and the need for reforms consistent with a more expansive view of adolescents' rights. The analysis leaves for the next chapter the discussion of the actual nature and supporting rationales for the types of adolescents' rights needed to address adolescents' sexual victimization; for the nature of those rights become best understandable when presented in light of other forms of sexual victimizations that have yet to be taken seriously enough by legal systems.

Pornographic Exploitation

The place of adolescents in pornography remains generally unexplored and frequently equated with child pornography. The law may be simply stated: No jurisdiction legally permits the use of adolescents in pornography. Although this is a straightforward prohibition, the success of these prohibitions actually remains to be determined. The current social science understanding of the nature of pornographic exploitation and legal responses suggests a need to focus beyond current prohibitions and a need to expand protections by also focusing on other aspects of adolescents' legal rights.

Social Science Research

Social science analyses of the use of adolescents in pornography constitute an area subsumed under research dealing with child pornography. Research generally defines this form of exploitation as the law approaches it. Child pornography is the visual depiction of minors involved in sexually explicit activities.[6] Although this would seem to end the discussion—because sexual activities involving minors tend to be illegal—the matter does not stop there. Three key points warrant comment.

The first point involves the manner in which issues of consent reveal the exploitative nature of child pornography. If individuals could be involved legitimately in these activities, at least two forms of consent would be necessary: consent to being the subject of pornography and consent to the sexual acts and relationships. Adults currently are in a better position than adolescents to consent and enter into binding, legal contracts with their photographers or to engage in sexual activity. Indeed, contracts with minors generally are void *ab initio* (at inception).[7] In addition to adolescents' legal disadvantage, it remains unclear how even adults' performance of sexual (pornographic) acts for money fails to constitute legally prohibited acts of prostitution, as reflected by courts that arrive to opposite conclusions on the issue.[8]

The second critical point deals with the manner in which the uses of child pornography highlight its exploitative nature. The production of pornographic materials constitutes abuse. Maltreating conditions challenge any suggestions of consensuality.[9] In addition, child pornography serves as a tool to obtain other victims. Pornographic materials help lower other minor's inhibitions and encourage others to engage in activities similar to those depicted in pictures and magazines.[10] Child pornography also facilitates offenders' ability to legitimize abusive behaviors to themselves. Just as pornography allows victims to normalize abuse, it helps abusers normalize their behaviors by suggesting that minors are seductive, that they receive pleasure through sexual interactions, and that victims desire sexual relationships.[11] Child pornography also helps abusers increase their own sexual arousal before abusing minors and helps reinterpret their victim's behavior to support their abuse.[12] Finally, pornography contributes to conditions that foster offending behavior. Pedophiles expand their abuse as they record their abusive events and then sell, barter, or exchange materials with other abusers,[13] a process facilitated immensely by personal computers.

The third key point relates to the manner in which pornographic exploitation links to other forms of maltreatment. The most significant finding in this area involves how minors tend to suffer abuses in numerous ways, most notably through prostitution. The vast majority of adolescent prostitutes have been solicited to pose for pornographic photos or appear in films;[14] and adolescents who eventually do become prostitutes experienced childhood pornography for commercial purposes or the gratification of the photographer.[15] Even when researchers do not directly question adolescent prostitutes about the use of pornography, approximately one quarter of them incidentally volunteer the use of pornography by the adult before the sexual acts.[16] Child pornography, then, tends to be part of other abuses minors suffer.

The use of adolescents in pornographic media contributes several significant points to the investigation of media's effects on adolescents. It highlights how the problem is part of a complex dynamic in the way minors are used and abused. For example, family life affects how adolescents may become exploited subjects of pornography in that family dynamics may affect the risk of sexual abuse related to pornographic exploitation. In addition, responding to the problem entails dealing with other issues. For example, efforts to assist adolescents exploited through pornography actually may involve laws that prohibit sexual abuse and prostitution of children. Finally, sexual media play an important role in the manner people become sexual beings. For example, the manner in which child pornographers use materials to normalize certain sexual behaviors to themselves mirrors the pervious chapter's finding relating to adolescents' selective use of different media and the impact of those media on sexual socialization.

Adolescents and Pornography Law

Pornography law as applied to adolescents constitutes the most settled area of regulation of adolescents' rights in the media. The law construes adolescents' rights in terms of protection and generally bars the use of adolescents in pornographic media. Several leading Supreme Court cases recognize the need for protection, elucidate these laws' rationales, and provide guidance to state and federal efforts to address the pornographic exploitation of adolescents. Although a settled area of law, the actual effectiveness of this regulation remains to be determined.

In the groundbreaking 1982 case of *New York v. Ferber,*[17] the Supreme Court held that states may prohibit the depiction of minors engaged in sexual conduct. The purpose of the challenged New York statute at issue was "to prevent the abuse of children who are made to engage in sexual conduct for commercial purposes. . . ."[18] Although the law that was addressed dealt with the abuse of minors, the facts of the case involved a film that did not involve illegal or coercive acts. The film showed two adolescent males masturbating, a legal act that was apparently noncoercive. Rather than focusing on the actual film, the Court essentially focused on its potential use. The Court found the following dispositive: The film could encourage abuse if it were used to initiate minors into sexual activity; the prohibition properly dealt with the financial gain involved in selling and advertising child pornography to produce materials through activities that are prohibited throughout the United States; and adults' right to privacy and freedom of expression are overweighed by the potential harm to minors' physical and psychological well-being.[19]

The Court's findings are of considerable significance. *Ferber* distinguishes pornography involving minors from adult pornography and subjects the latter to less protection from regulation.[20] Likewise, the case recognizes the aggravated harm of repeated showings of films, and does so without any evidence of coercion between the parties. The case also recognizes that certain identifiable harms to minors outweigh the rights of adults. More significant in terms of legal doctrine, the case reflects an important move that allows intrusion into any individual's private life to restrict immoral behavior.

The move to restrict behavior in one's private affairs is pivotal and considerably broadened by prohibition of the actual possession of child pornography. The 1990 Supreme

Court case of *Osborne v. Ohio*[21] reflects well why statutory efforts may be allowed to actually reach into the privacy of one's life and criminalize the possession of child pornography. In that case, the Court held that the mere possession of child pornography could be criminalized because the state has a compelling interest in protecting minors from being exploited by pornography. The state's overriding need to protect minors from exploitation and harms involved in the production of pornographic materials provided the basis for intervention and created an important exception to the general rule established in *Stanley v. Georgia*.[22] In *Stanley,* the Court had ruled that an individual has a right to privately possess obscene materials in his or her own home because the government did not have the right to control the moral content of a person's thoughts and the government may not prohibit the mere possession of such materials on the grounds that it may lead to antisocial conduct. In *Osborne,* however, the Court accepted the state's three arguments for upholding the ban on the possession of child pornography to protect minors from sexual exploitation. The Court recognized that criminalization would lead to the destruction of existing child pornography, which would respond to the destructive effects of pornography that was seen as a permanent record of the minor's abuse and was believed to haunt minors for years to come. Criminalization would prevent pedophiles from using child pornography to seduce other children into sexual activity. Criminalization would decrease demand and supply of production that had been driven underground. Unlike the *Stanley* Court, which had rejected the state's interest in suppressing obscene materials largely for lack of empirical evidence that exposure would lead to deviant sexual behavior or crimes of sexual violence, the *Osborne* Court found the evidence dispositive. *Osborne* cited to *Ferber* to reason that banning the possession of child pornography could further the state interest in protecting the physical and psychological health of minors.

The Court's support for regulating child pornography has led states to enact legislation to deal with child pornography. For example, all 50 states and the District of Columbia have enacted legislation that makes criminal the production of materials depicting minors engaged in sexually explicit activity. These criminal statutes variously prohibit the production, promotion, sale, exhibition, or distribution of photographs of children in sexual activity.[23] Because child pornography has been deemed harmful, the focus on limiting its distribution has not been viewed as problematic. More problematic and controversial has been the series of new statutes that prohibit the possession of child pornography. These statutes appeared rather quickly after the *Osborne* decision; fewer than five years after the Court held that the possession of child pornography may be criminalized, more than half the states had passed laws to prohibit the possession of child pornography.[24]

In addition to state laws that prohibit the use of minors for pornographic purposes, the sexual use of minors in the media also has been part of important federal legislation that prohibits the sexual exploitation of minors. Prior to the enactment of laws specifically designed to address the problems of child pornography, federal laws prohibiting the transport of obscene materials served to pursue pornographers.[25] More specific legislation was enacted in 1977 to define exploitation, in part, as using a minor to engage in sexually explicit conduct for the purposes of producing any visual depiction of such conduct with the requisite knowledge that it was or would be transported in interstate or foreign commerce.[26] The legislation penalized the commercial production and dissemination of any visual or print medium of minors under 16 years of age engaging in sexually explicit conduct. After the *Ferber* decision, Congress passed more legislation to eliminate the requirement that materials be considered obscene before its production, dissemination, or receipt could be found criminal; raised the age limit of protection from 16 to 18 years of age; and eliminated the requirement that the production or distribution be for the purpose of sale.[27] The legislation was then amended in 1986 to ban the production and use of advertisements for child pornography[28] and again in 1988 to ban the use of computers to transport, distribute, or receive child pornography.[29] In 1990, in apparent response to *Osborne,* an amendment criminalized the possession of three or more copies of any materials that may be construed as child pornography.[30] In 1996 new amendments incorporated computer-generated definitions and proscriptions.[31]

These federal changes are notable for the move away from concern for specific harm to minors involved in the production of pornography. The new developments reflect the importance of strict regulation because child pornography potentially serves sex abusers' sexual appetites and desensitizes them to the pathology of child sexual exploitation, allows abusers to seduce other children into sexual activity, and sexualizes and eroticizes all minors, which detrimentally affects the moral fiber of society as a whole. Some, but not all, of these rationales find explicit support in Supreme Court doctrine, such as *Osborne's* rationale that child pornography serves to seduce other children and *Ferber's* proclamation that using minors as subjects was harmful to minors and society as a whole. The extent to which these justifications are sufficiently compelling and narrowly tailored to withstand First Amendment challenges against mere virtual depictions remains to be determined. The great latitude the Court grants states' efforts to protect minors, however, suggests that the Court will continue to grant states considerable freedom to attack the pornographic use of adolescents even when actual minors are not involved but may eventually suffer.

Despite great latitude given to states' efforts to combat this form of exploitation, the efforts' successes remain unclear. Without reliable prevalence estimates, it becomes difficult to determine the law's effectiveness in combatting this form of maltreatment. Arguably, the purposefully explicit and vivid sexual depiction of adolescents continues and even escapes legal censure.

The 1990s are known for much more than the extension of criminal laws' efforts to combat child pornography; they are known for the failure of legal prohibitions to address the new sexualization of adolescents in the media. The highly publicized and controversial examples of Calvin Klein's advertising campaign and Larry Clark's film *Kids* serve as prime examples of the availability and use of adolescents for depictions of sexual acts. The Calvin Klein ads presented young models in various stages of undress as they flashed their breasts or held their crotches.[32] The young models were poised to offer sexual pleasure and presented to fantasize their sexual availability as the ads evoked the dialogue of low-budget porn movies.[33] Yet the adds were withdrawn only because they aroused vituperative controversy, not because they had offended any laws. In yet other ads withdrawn solely because of the controversy they generated, Calvin Klein's campaigns showed men modeling underwear in what some said appeared to be a state of arousal.[34] Four years later, in 1999, it again voluntarily (because it was not illegal) pulled from circulation ads that drew criticism for showing children who appeared to be about 6 years old and were clad only in underwear.[35] *Kids* portrayed very young and explicit teenage sexual activity in the context of the spread of sexual diseases, drug use, violence, and predatory sexuality.[36] Framed in pseudodocumentary style, *Kids* purposefully presented a voyeuristic view of violent adolescent sexuality in a racial, hedonistic, diseased, socially decadent, and demonized manner. Unlike Klein's ads, *Kids* produced not only pornographic acts but also contributed popular misperceptions of adolescents' place in society, which in turn affect societal responses to acts of sex and violence. These two illustrations gain significance not for controversies stirred by portraying adolescent sexuality but by the law's response. The Supreme Court cases and legislation reviewed previously signaled the law's receptivity to social science evidence regarding the potential harm of pornography and society's willingness to intervene aggressively to protect adolescents. Yet despite the belief that adolescents' right to protection from pornographic exploitation readily outweighs adults' rights traditionally granted great reverence, pornographic acts continue in several forms that remain legal.

Although it would seem inappropriate to conclude that sexual acts depicted in popular media equate with those of pedophiles (and there are indeed key differences between portrayals of adolescents' sexual acts in popular media and in pedophile rings), four points suggest the need to consider their relationship. First, the legally permissible (or ignored) sexual depiction of adolescents in the media may be used by pedophiles. Second, as seen in the previous chapter, media images of adolescent sexuality affect adolescents' sexual socialization. Third, media depictions also affect society's images of adolescents' sexual behavior and contribute to the development of laws that actually may not reflect the reality of adolescent life. Fourth, they reflect how the extent to which adolescents actually gain protection arguably remains to be determined and continues to be surrounded by controversy. These points counsel a need to look elsewhere to complement current approaches to the use and portrayal of adolescents in the media to (a) prevent adolescents from involvement in exploitative pornographic materials; (b) help address the needs of those victimized through pornography; and (c) assist adolescents in understanding media presentations of adolescent sexuality.

Adolescent Prostitution

The prostitution of adolescents involves situations in which adolescents engage in systematic sexual activity for material gain for themselves or others. As with pornography, social science literature remains limited but does suggest that multiple forces sustain the lives of young prostitutes. That finding reveals that the legal system's most direct efforts to protect adolescents from exploitation actually may hamper efforts to offer assistance.

Social Science Research

Accurate data on the number of active prostitutes are difficult to obtain and statistics that do exist vary enormously depending on their source. The most conservative estimates, the Uniform Crime Reports, reveal only a modest number of juvenile prostitutes—for example, fewer than one thousand were arrested for prostitution in 1995.[37] These figures, however, necessarily underestimate actual rates of prostitution. Other estimates, including some from the federal government, suggest that there may be more than 900,000 juvenile prostitutes,[38] two thirds of whom are girls.[39] Other estimates focus on adolescents at risk for sexual exploitation—runaway, homeless, and thrownaway (i.e., those forced to leave home) adolescents—and report estimates slightly above 200,000.[40] These estimates also remain controversial. For example, the finding that two thirds are girls suggests a gross underestimate of the problem, because self-reports of trading sexual activities for money reveal that boys are five times more likely to do so than are girls.[41] Equally important, estimates that focus on risk factors, typically runaway behavior and homelessness, have yet to address how many adolescents at risk to engage in prostitution actually do engage in prostitution and how many not at risk do.[42] Despite wide disparities in statistical findings, mainly attributable to the sources of data and types of behaviors deemed indicative of prostitution, no source disputes the need to take seriously episodes in adolescents' lives in which they hire out their sexual services.

Although an important area of research, few actually have investigated the nature of adolescents' prostitution.[43] Yet existing social science evidence increasingly reveals important findings. The current body of research suggests that juvenile prostitution involves young people—more than 60% of whom are under the age of 16—running away from abusive homes.[44] Although it would be inappropriate to emphasize one causative factor, research consistently points to parental maltreatment as a central element in adolescents' runaway behavior.[45] The majority of young prostitutes—ranging from 40 to 75 percent— have been sexually abused or psychologically maltreated while they were growing up,[46] with female runaways more likely to be running away from sexual abuse than males (73% to 38%).[47] Runaway episodes also involve maltreatment as a precipitating event.[48]

Despite the overwhelming evidence that more than 80% of runaways experience very severe forms of abuse by parents and other adult caretakers,[49] it is important to emphasize that abuse actually may not be the sole precipitating cause for runaway behavior. Only 50% report running away *because* of abuse. Adolescents cite difficulty in getting along with caretakers and feeling unloved as equally important reasons for leaving.[50] These findings suggest that the psychological aspects of living in a dysfunctional family produce more negative consequences than the physical aspects of maltreatment.[51] Though evidence consistently points to high levels of rape, incest, and other kinds of sexual trauma in the backgrounds of young prostitutes, the purported link between sexual trauma and prostitution arises from failures of intergenerational attachments or inappropriate parenting behavior.[52] Prostituted adolescents are victims of their families' failure to integrate their children into their family system. Their families reveal poor conflict resolution, inadequate communication, and ineffective parental supervision.[53] The failed relationships tend to be so strained and severe that, for most types of violence experienced by runaway adolescents, the street actually seems to provide a haven of relative safety when compared to the abuse suffered at home by the runaways. Not only are homes more abusive, the abuse is more severe.[54] These findings highlight well the disruptiveness of several adolescents' home lives that push them to the streets. Yet it would be important to not minimize the disruptiveness of young prostitutes' street lives that place them at high risk for infectious diseases, drug use, and violence.[55] Likewise, it would be important not to minimize the role of peers; a recent line of research points to adolescents' maltreatment carried out by peers who reject them and the failure of parents and others to help adolescents deal with the rejection—a situation well illustrated by the experiences of gay adolescents.[56]

Although research does contribute the obvious point that families affect runaway and prostituting behaviors, the research still remains limited. The factors may explain why adolescents get to the street, but they do not necessarily dictate that adolescents will engage in prostitution. The most recent study to compare prostitute from nonprostitute adolescents revealed similarly high rates of prior sexual victimization for both, no difference in the experience of interparental violence, and the nonprostitute group reported higher rates of physical abuse and more physical violence.[57] The only differences that placed prostitutes into a higher risk category was their higher rates of runaway behavior and higher likelihood of having experienced homelessness; but again, no specific traumatic events in adolescents' backgrounds related to initiating prostitution activity.

Although victimization prior to leaving home may not directly affect prostituting behavior, it may still play important roles. The consequences of running away, such as involvement in crime or repeated victimization, appear more severe for those who have already experienced victimization at home prior to running away.[58] Likewise, sexually abused female runaways are more apt to engage in delinquent activities than nonsexually abused female runaways.[59] Sexual assault at home prior to running away increases the probability that both boys and girls will be sexually assaulted while on the streets.[60]

These findings support the proposition that the most common form of adolescent prostitution may be construed as "survival sex."[61] This form of prostitution involves trading sex for immediate needs such as shelter, food, or drugs.[62] This dominant form of prostitution reveals that engagement in prostitution depends on the length of time on the streets, the intensity of survival needs, previous encounters with sexual maltreatment, and the influence of friends and street peers.[63] Despite this dominant form of prostitution by those on the streets, it is important to note that adolescents not on the streets also report selling sexual services. For example, self-report surveys reveal that more than 1 in 20 adolescents has exchanged sexual activities for purely economic gain.[64] These findings suggest not only that many adolescents' engage in sexual activity for financial gain but also that many do so because they find themselves without viable alternatives.

Adolescent Prostitution and the Law

The United States possesses an unusually strong legal arsenal to combat prostitution. As with pornographic exploitation, all states forcefully criminalize prostitution.[65] Nevada provides the only exception to the blanket prohibition, as it permits counties to legalize prostitution under limited conditions.[66] In addition to state prohibitions, the federal government also prohibits prostitution through the Mann White Slave Travel Act of 1910, which originally concerned itself with protecting girls and women from interstate travel for immoral purposes but, since 1986, prohibits interstate travel for the purposes of ''any sexual activity for which any person can be charged with a criminal offense.''[67]

The legal system applies the criminalization of prostitution to adolescents and provides them with extra protections. Three examples illustrate how the legal system protects adolescents as it complements criminal laws with laws not applicable to adult prostitutes. The first and major efforts generally focus on runaway and homeless adolescents and the prevention of adolescent prostitution. For example, the federal Missing Children's Act[68] established a special national clearinghouse to facilitate identifications of missing and runaway minors as it aims to find runaways soon after they have left home. In addition, the federal Runaway and Homeless Adolescents Act[69] funds a national network of short-term shelters for adolescents and provides hotlines to call for assistance. In addition to these federal efforts, some states supplement the mandates and make specific statutory provisions for runaway and homeless adolescents' services.[70] The second major legal effort addresses the root causes of prostitution through the manner in which it seeks to prevent runaway behavior. The Child Abuse Prevention and Treatment and Adoption Reform Act, for example, includes juvenile prostitution as a form of child abuse that must be reported to appropriate agencies when the acts involve parents or caretakers.[71] The original objective of the legislation—to encourage reporting of abuse—also plays an essential part in preventing juvenile prostitution, because abuse is one of the primary factors contributing to runaway behavior and prostitution. As with the Missing Children's Act, the effort provides the hope that, with the prompt identification of missing or abusive conditions, the adolescent will be less likely to turn to prostitution.[72] The third example of existing laws that may be used to assist adolescents involves the manner in which the juvenile justice system allows for considerable control of adolescents' sexual behavior. For example, parents may use the juvenile justice system to exert parental authority over their children, either to return the children home or place them in the juvenile justice system.[73] Despite efforts to change the juvenile justice system's approach to those who commit status offenses (actions that are illegal simply because the individual is a minor) the system still controls adolescent sexuality (especially girls') as it seeks to protect adolescents from their own sexual acts.[74] Likewise, adolescents who sexually act out or act out because of their sexuality, particularly gay and lesbian adolescents,[75] are likely to be adjudicated as a person in need of supervision, or PINS (also referred to as child in need of services, CHINS), which allows family courts to place children in out-of-home care if they are habitually ungovernable, disobedient, and beyond parental control.[76]

Although impressive for their potential reach and effectiveness current laws have limits. Several problems are apparent with the criminalization approach. It may be simplistic to believe that punishment of customers will eliminate the problem, because even the most aggressive criminalization approaches have failed with adult prostitution.[77] In addition, applying the law to status offenders remains far from gender-neutral; runaway boys are more likely to be ignored by police.[78] When they are not ignored, boys are at greater risk of verbal and physical abuse from the police.[79] Policing also may lead to a loss of "safe" clients, hamper the development of informal support and warning networks, and actually increase the risks adolescents face.[80] Even crack-downs on pimps are not effective because often boys often operate with peers, not pimps.[81]

The social service approach that complements laws directed to adult prostitutes also reveals several limitations when addressing the needs of adolescent prostitutes. The two major relevant laws are remarkable for their limitations. The Child Abuse Prevention and Treatment and Adoption Reform Act[82] attacks acts of child prostitution by making them reportable offenses. Regrettably, only sexual exploitation perpetrated by parents, caretakers, or persons "responsible for the child's welfare" is a reportable condition. Acts of prostitution prompted by any other family member, or by extrafamilial third parties such as pimps, are outside the jurisdiction of the reporting legislation. The Missing Children Act also presents numerous limitations. It relies on family reports of missing children. Families that have disintegrated and abused children may not report; and thrownaway adolescents are not likely to be reached. In addition, the focus on returning minors home remains problematic. The approach assumes that adolescents will cooperate and want to return when they actually do not. Adolescents may actually stay away from shelters: On any given night, only 55% of available beds in adolescents shelters are occupied.[83] The focus on family reunification apparently discourages adolescents from reaching out to shelters. The focus on returning adolescents back home also hampers providing informal family and community shelter services to adolescents in need. As a result, although the largest resource of thrownaway and runaway children are nearby friends and relatives,[84] laws in most states as well as the federal law actively discourage this kind of assistance, as revealed, for example, by the manner in which some states still make it a crime or tort (civil offense) to knowingly or intentionally provide housing to a runaway minor.[85]

In addition to federal mandates, it is important to emphasize that, as we already have seen in chapter 3, all jurisdictions provide for state intervention to protect physically and sexually abused children; and new laws now include psychological maltreatment that allows for intervention even though parents may not have caused the harm.[86] In theory, the link between abusive family life and eventual adolescent prostitution suggests an important area of intervention to protect adolescents from exploitation. However, in practice these aggressive statutory mandates face enormous challenges, as illustrated by two difficulties. The first problem involves the typical child protection case. Rather than being victims of malicious beatings or even of sexual exploitation, at least half of the children who enter the child protection system are believed to have been neglected.[87] These live in families that experience multiple complex and serious problems. Solving their problems is substantially more difficult than "simple" attempts to ensure safety from brutal parents. These complicated circumstances have been made even more difficult by the backlash in child protection and attempts to curb state intervention.[88] The second major problem derives from the numerous deficiencies that cast doubt on the extent to which the rise in child protection statutes offer adolescents the necessary assistance.[89] All statutes remain limited in signifi-

cant ways that challenge the ultimate effectiveness of the legal mandates' efforts to deal with
the problems of maltreatment. All statutes do not allow for meaningful intervention until
substantial damage already has been done: All require demonstrable harm. Proof of harm or
other triggers for intervention may not become apparent until the victim is past adolescence.
Even when law can be invoked to intervene and curtail abusive behavior, intervention will
not necessarily alter underlying abusive relationships. A focus on symptomatic behaviors
cannot solve problems when parents do not understand the essence of a healthy relationship.
Concerns about privacy and protection of family autonomy also cause legal actors to err on
the side of nonintervention; social services focus on protection from abuse instead of
fostering healthy relationships and taking opportunities to channel normal interactions
toward the promotion of what some consider "wellness."[90] Several states still do not even
refer specifically to important forms of abuse (such as emotional abuse) and limit their
statutory language to intervene in instances in which impairment is a direct result of physical
injury or neglect.[91] Thus despite the attempt to assist adolescents in damaging relationships,
laws remain limited. These limitations are of significance—as we have seen, overall family
environment, more than specific abusive conditions, push adolescents to streets and into
prostitution.

Themes to Guide Reform

As we have seen, adolescents exploited through prostitution or pornography present a
complex social problem. This complexity partly results from the problems' interrelationship
with such other social problems as physical abuse, sexual abuse, family disruption, and
running away. Despite diversity and numerous challenges, at least three themes emerge and
provide potential areas for legal reform. Those themes are worth enumerating at this point
because they support the next chapter's approach to protecting adolescents from sexual
victimization.

A recurring theme that emerges from efforts to combat the sexual exploitation of
adolescents by adults highlights criminal law's failure to address the needs of adolescent
victims. Stricter penalties for adult participants, though an apparently needed response to
pressing problems, arguably do not have the broad intended impact. Although more
aggressive and harsh law enforcement has its place in protective efforts, simple criminalization leaves adolescents unprotected and arguably hampers adolescents' reintegration.
Increased criminalization may only work when coupled by, for example, antipoverty
programs to support families, communities, and particularly homeless adolescents. To a
large extent, the issue of adolescents' right to protection from exploitation fundamentally
remains an issue about resources and their distribution. The right to protection continues to
be undermined and eventually denied by poverty. It is not necessarily the parental or familial
poverty that matters—more than 70% of runaway adolescents who sell sex for economic
gain come from families of average or higher incomes,[92] and fewer than 10% come from
families on public assistance.[93] It is the adolescents' own poverty that places them at risk.
Despite federal calls for shelters, only 11 states statutorily provide for the manner in which
services will be directed to young runaways and homeless adolescents.[94] No more than one
in three adolescents ever receive shelter, and no more than 1 in 12 ever actually is identified
or cared for in any way by social service delivery systems.[95] Shelters that do provide refuge
do not offer transitional living services, intensive mental health and substance abuse
services, and other needs adolescents may require.[96] Equally important, shelters that may
exist may have unwritten policies that exclude adolescents in need: A recent federal study
revealed that the shelters investigated in the study had unwritten polices not to accept

individuals over the age of 12.[97] Thus both families and shelters leave homeless adolescents destitute and at risk for sexual exploitation.

A second theme involves the increasing recognition that an emphasis on prevention and treatment appears to be a necessary component of attempts to assist victimized adolescents as well as those at risk. As we have seen, few services currently exist that target adolescents themselves. Evidence supports the need to rethink services and consider adolescents' perspectives. To effectively combat exploitation, services must do more than reach adolescents while they are on the street. Services must also reach adolescents still in their families, schools, and communities. Prevention needs infusion of resources in the form of, for example, family support and adolescent services eluded to previously. Adolescents who engage in systematic prostitution reveal an inability to return to their homes, a situation that reduces the use of available resources that typically will result in automatic, involuntary returns to their families.[98] Not only do their homes lead them to the streets, then, they often keep them away from needed services and assistance. Exploited adolescents would benefit from law reform that enables them to obtain assistance from a variety of sources and that moves the legal system away from the foundational ideology that families are the best source of care and support for them.

A third important point involves the need to reconsider prevailing views of adolescents. Two examples are illustrative. The first example involves the tendency to regard adolescents who prostitute themselves as individual failures. This tendency shifts attention to them as it improperly draws attention away from the social institutions from which they flee—their families, foster homes, and schools, all of which play important roles in the encouragement of exploitation.[99] The second example relates to perceptions of gendered exploitation. Although self-report figures relating to prostitution vary widely, they do indicate that males are more than five times more likely to engage in sex for hire than are females.[100] That finding indicates that an important social issue defies stereotypes in the extent to which adolescent males dominate offenses traditionally considered "feminine." The result is that the laws aggressively seek to address girls' sexual behaviors, and may do so in an overly repressive fashion, while ignoring boys' victimization. The implementation of laws is marked by discrimination against girls who engage in sexual activity and gay and lesbian adolescents who act out in response to harassment from parents, peers, and social service agencies.

Conclusion

Existing evidence of the sexual victimization of adolescents by adults reveals a need to address this form of maltreatment. The issue affects much more than adolescents' sexual behaviors; it affects adolescents' entire development and place in society. Although numerous laws already seek to protect adolescents, an analysis of those legal reforms in light of existing social science evidence indicates a need for even greater reform. The analysis suggests a need to increase adolescents' independent right to legal protection from families and need to create environments in which adolescents may obtain necessary community supports and formal social services. That conclusion is of significance: It suggests that supportive services for adolescents must complement efforts that criminalize or otherwise prohibit adults' sexual victimization of adolescents. Before exploring more fully the nature of adolescents' rights to protection and access to sociolegal supports, it is important to understand how victimizations by peers—the next chapter's topic—further support the need to reconsider the current nature of adolescents' rights. The next chapter will present how the legal system may improve adolescents' access to community, social, and legal services and will provide responses to potential objections.

Endnotes

1. *See, e.g.,* David Finkelhor and Jill Korbin, ''Child Abuse as an International Issue,'' *Child Abuse & Neglect* 12 (1988):3–23.
2. Although no age grouping remains immune from sexual victimization, the peak age of onset of first abuse most commonly occurs near age 10 or 12. *See, e.g.,* David Finkelhor, G. Hotaling, I. A. Lewis, and C. Smith, ''Sexual Abuse in a National Survey of Adult Men and Women: Prevalence, Characteristics, and Risk Factors,'' *Child Abuse & Neglect* 14 (1990):19–28.
3. *See, e.g.,* David M. Ferguson, L. John Horwood, and Michael T. Lynskey, ''Childhood Sexual Abuse, Adolescent Sexual Behaviors and Sexual Revictimization,'' *Child Abuse & Neglect* 21 (1997):789–803.
4. For a review, *see id.*
5. For a comprehensive review, *see* Roger J. R. Levesque, *Child Sexual Abuse: A Human Rights Perspective* (Bloomington: Indiana University Press, 1999).
6. *See* 18 U.S.C. § 2256(2) (1996).
7. Larry A. DiMatteo, ''Deconstructing the Myth of the 'Infancy Law Doctrine': From Incapacity to Accountability,'' *Ohio Northern University Law Review* 21 (1995):481–525.
8. *See* Sarah H. Garb, ''Sex for Money Is Sex for Money: The Illegality of Pornographic Film as Prostitution,'' *Law and Inequality* 13 (1995):281–301.
9. Cudore L. Snell, *Young Men in the Street, Help-Seeking Behavior of Young Male Prostitutes* (Westport, CT: Praeger, 1995); Lesley A. Welsh, Francis X. Archambault, Mark-David Janus, and Scott W. Brown, *Running for Their Lives: Physical and Sexual Abuse of Runaway Adolescents* (New York: Garland, 1995).
10. U.S. Department of Justice, *Attorney General's Commission of Pornography: Final Report* (Washington, DC: Author, 1986), at 649.
11. Robert S. Wyer, ''Pornography and Sexual Violence: Working With Sex Offenders.''In *Pornography: Women, Violence and Civil Liberties: A Radical New View,* ed. Catherine Itzin (New York: Oxford University Press, 1992).
12. W. L. Marshall, ''The Use of Sexually Explicit Stimuli by Rapists, Child Molesters, and Non Offenders,'' *The Journal of Sex Research* 26 (1988):267–288; Daniel Lee Carter, Robert Alan Prentky, Raymond A. Knight, Penny L. Vanderveer, and Richard J. Boucher, ''Pornography in the Criminal and Developmental Histories of Sexual Offenders,'' *Journal of Interpersonal Violence* 2 (1987):196–211.
13. Tim Tate, ''The Child Pornography Industry: International Trade in Sexual Abuse.'' In *Pornography: Women, Violence and Civil Liberties: A Radical New View,* ed. Catherine Itzin (New York: Oxford University Press, 1992).
14. Gitta Sereny, *Invisible Children: The Shattering Tragedy of Runaways on Our Streets* (London: Pan, 1986).
15. Mimi Silbert and Ayala Pines, ''Pornography and Sexual Abuse of Women,'' *Sex Roles* 11/12 (1984):857–868.
16. *Id.*
17. 458 U.S. 747 (1982).
18. *Id.* at 753.
19. *Id.* at 756–764.
20. Pornography involving adults is not explicitly regulated, but it tends to be addressed under the rubric of obscenity; *see* Miller v. California, 413 U.S. 15, 24 (1973).
21. 495 U.S. 103 (1990).
22. 394 U.S. 557 (1969).
23. *See, e.g.,* ALA. CODE § 13A-12-197 (1996); ALASKA STAT. § 11.41.455, § 11.61.123 (Michie Supp. 1995).
24. *See* David B. Johnson, ''Why the Possession of Computer-Generated Child Pornography Can Be Constitutionally Prohibited,'' *Albany Law Journal of Science & Technology* 4 (1994):311–331.

25. The transportation involved mail, common carrier, and private conveyance. *See* 18 U.S.C. §§ 1461, 1462, 1465 (1994).

26. 18 U.S.C. § 2251 (1991 & Supp. 1996). Section 2252 further defines § 2251 by providing that a person knowingly transports, ships, receives, or distributes a visual depiction if the production involved the use of a minor engaged in sexually explicit conduct and the depiction was of such conduct. For the entire act, *see* the Sexual Exploitation of Children Act, Pub. L. No. 95-225, 92 Stat. 7 (1997) (codified as amended at 18 U.S.C. §§ 2251–2253 (1991 & Supp. 1996)).

27. Child Protection Act of 1984, Pub. L. No. 98-292, 98 Stat. 204 (1984).

28. Child Sexual Abuse and Pornography Act of 1986, Pub. L. No. 99-628, 100 Stat. 3510 (1986) (codified as amended at 18 U.S.C. § 2251(c) (1991 & Supp. 1996)).

29. Pub. L. No. 100-690, 102 Stat. 4486 (1988) (codified as amended at 18 U.S.C. § 2252 (1991 & Supp. 1996)).

30. *See* Child Protection Restoration and Penalties Act of 1990, Pub. L. No. 101-647, 104 Stat. 4818 (1990) (codified as amended at 18 U.S.C. § 2252(a)(4) (Supp. 1996)).

31. *See* Omnibus Consolidated Appropriations Act of 1997, Pub. L. No. 104-208 § 121, 110 Stat. 3009 (1996) (codified at 18 U.S.C. § 2252A, 2259) (Supp. 1996)).

32. *See* Henry A. Giroux, "Teenage Sexuality, Body Politics, and the Pedagogy of Display." In *Youth Culture: Identity in a Postmodern World,* ed. Jonathan S. Epstein (Malden, MA: Blackwell, 1998).

33. *Id.*

34. Andy Newman, "Calvin Klein Cancels Ads With Children Amid Criticism," *New York Times,* B19, Col. 1 (Feb. 18, 1999).

35. *Id.*

36. Giroux, "Teenage Sexuality, Body Politics, and the Pedagogy of Display."

37. For an analysis comparing current and historical rates, *see* Meda Chesney-Lind and Randall G. Shelden, *Girls, Delinquency, and Juvenile Justice* (New York: Wadsworth, 1998), at 13.

38. *Id.* at 38.

39. *See* R. Barri Flowers, *The Victimization and Exploitation of Women and Children* (Jefferson, NC: McFarland, 1994); D. Kelly Weisberg, "Children of the Night: The Adequacy of Statutory Treatment of Juvenile Prostitution," *American Journal of Criminal Law* 12 (1984):1–67.

40. David Finkelhor, Gerald Hotaling, and Anreas Sedlak, *Missing, Abducted, Runaway, and Thrownaway Children in America, First Report: Numbers and Characteristics National Incidence Studies, Executive Summary* (Washington, DC: U.S. Department of Justice, Office of Juvenile Justice and Delinquency Prevention, 1990).

41. Chesney-Lind and Shelden, *Girls, Delinquency, and Juvenile Justice.*

42. Gary L. Yates, Richard G. Mackensie, and Avon Swafford, "A Risk Profile Comparison of Homeless Youth Involved in Prostitution and Homeless Youth Not Involved," *Journal of Adolescent Health* 12 (1991):545–549.

43. The most notable research has been conducted by Weisberg and Snell; *see* D. Kelly Weisberg, *Children of the Night: A Study of Adolescent Prostitution* (Lexington, MA: Lexington Books, 1985); Snell, *Young Men in the Street, Help-Seeking Behavior of Young Male Prostitutes.*

44. Welsh et al., *Running for Their Lives: Physical and Sexual Abuse of Runaway Adolescents.*

45. Nathaniel Eugene Terrell, "Street Life: Aggravated and Sexual Assaults Among Homeless and Runaway Adolescents," *Youth and Society* 28 (1997):267–290.

46. Debra Boyer, "Male Prostitution and Homosexual Identity," *Journal of Homosexuality* 17 (1989):151–184; Weisberg, *Children of the Night: A Study of Adolescent Prostitution;* Flowers, *The Victimization and Exploitation of Women and Children;* Welsh et al., *Running for Their Lives: Physical and Sexual Abuse of Runaway Adolescents.*

47. Mark-David Janus, Arlene McCormack, Anne Wolbert Burgess, and Carol Hartmen, *Adolescent Runaways: Causes and Consequences* (Lexington, MA: Lexington Books, 1987).

48. Edward D. Farber and Jack A. Joseph, "The Maltreated Adolescent: Patterns of Physical Abuse," *Child Abuse & Neglect* 9 (1985):201–206.

49. Welsh et al., *Running for Their Lives: Physical and Sexual Abuse of Runaway Adolescents;*

Terrell, "Street Life: Aggravated and Sexual Assaults Among Homeless and Runaway Adolescents"; Les B. Whitbeck, Danny R. Hoyt, and Kevin A. Ackley, "Families of Homeless and Runaway Adolescents: A Comparison of Parent/Caretaker and Adolescents Perspectives on Parenting, Family Violence, and Adolescent Conduct," *Child Abuse & Neglect* 21 (1997):517–528.

50. Welsh et al., *Running for Their Lives: Physical and Sexual Abuse of Runaway Adolescents.*

51. *Id.*

52. Augustine Brannigan and Erin Gibbs Van Brunschot, "Youthful Prostitution and Child Sexual Trauma," *International Journal of Law and Psychiatry* 20 (1997):337–354. *See also* Les B. Whitbeck, Danny R. Hoyt, and Kevin Ackley, "Abusive Family Backgrounds and Late Victimization Among Runaway and Homeless Adolescents," *Journal of Research on Adolescence* 7 (1997):375–392.

53. Bill McCarthy and John Hagan, "Mean Streets: The Theoretical Significance of Situational Delinquency Among Homeless Youth," *American Journal of Sociology* 98 (1992):567–627; James Garbarino, Cynthia J. Schellbach, Janet M. Sebes, and Associates (Eds.), *Troubled Youth, Troubled Families* (New York: Aldine, 1986).

54. Welsh et al., *Running for Their Lives: Physical and Sexual Abuse of Runaway Adolescents.* The only exception to the rule that they suffer more assaults at home is that boys are more likely to be assaulted with a gun or weapon while on the streets.

55. Robert W. Deisher and William M. Rogers II, "The Medical Care of Street Youth," *Journal of Adolescent Health* 12 (1991):500–503; Yates et al., "A Risk Profile Comparison of Homeless Youth Involved in Prostitution and Homeless Youth Not Involved"; Anne Crowley and Gera Patel, "Accounting for 'Child Prostitution.'" In *A Case of Neglect? Children's Experiences and the Sociology of Childhood,* ed. Ian Butler and Ian Shaw (Brookfield, VT: Avebury, 1997).

56. Kelli Kristine Armstrong, "The Silent Minority Within a Minority: Focusing on the Needs of Gay Youth in Our Public Schools," *Golden Gate University Law Review* 41 (1994):67–97; Michael Radkowsky and Lawrence J. Siegel, "The Gay Adolescent: Stressors, Adaptations, and Psychosocial Interventions," *Clinical Psychology Review* 17 (1997):191–216.

57. Susan M. Nadon, Catherine Koverola, and Eduard H. Schludermann, "Antecedents to Prostitution: Childhood Victimization," *Journal of Interpersonal Violence* 13 (1998):206–221.

58. James Garbarino, Janis Wilson, and Anne C. Garborino, "The Adolescent Runaway." In *Troubled Youth, Troubled Families,* ed. James Garbarino, Cynthia J. Schellbach, Janet M. Sebes, and Associates (New York: Aldine, 1986).

59. Arlene McCormack, Mark-David Janus, and Ann Wolbert Burgess, "Runaway Youths and Sexual Victimization: Gender Differences in an Adolescent Runaway Population," *Child Abuse and Neglect* 10 (1986):387–395.

60. Terrell, "Street Life: Aggravated and Sexual Assaults Among Homeless and Runaway Adolescents."

61. *Id.*

62. *See* Chesney-Lind and Shelden, *Girls, Delinquency, and Juvenile Justice.*

63. *Id.*

64. *Id.*

65. Ala. Code 13A-12-110 (1997); Alaska Stat. 11.66.100 (1997); Ariz. Rev. Stat. Ann. 13-3201 (1997); Ark. Code Ann. 5-70-101 (1997); Cal. Penal Code 266-267 (1997); Colo. Rev. Stat. Ann. 18-7-201 (1996); Conn. Gen. Stat. 57a-82 (1997); Del. Code Ann. tit. 11, 1342 (1997); Fla. Stat. Ann. 796.03 (1997); Ga. Code Ann. 16-6-9 (1997); Haw. Rev. Stat. 712-1201 (1997); Idaho Code 18-5601 (1997); 720 Ill. Comp. Stat. 5/11-14 (1997); Ind. Code Ann. 35-45-4-2 (1997); Iowa Code 725.1 (1997); Kan. Stat. Ann. 21-3512 (1997); Ky. Rev. Stat. Ann. 529.010 (1997); La. Rev. Stat. Ann. 14:82 (1997); Me. Rev. Stat. Ann. tit. 17-A, 851 (1997); Md. Code Ann. art. 27, 16 (1998); Mass. Gen. Laws Ann. ch. 272, 2, 4B (1998); Mich. Comp. Laws Ann. 28.703 (1998); Minn. Stat. Ann. 609.321 (1997); Miss. Code Ann. 97-29-49 (1998); Mo. Ann. Stat. 567.020 (1997); Mont. Code Ann. 45-5-601 (1997); Neb. Rev. Stat. 28-801 (1997); Nev. Rev. Stat. 210.354 (1997); N.H. Rev. Stat. Ann. 544:1

(1998); N.J. Stat. Ann. 2C:34-1 (West 1997); N.M. Stat. Ann. 30-9-2 (1997); N.Y. Penal Law 230.00 (1997); N.C. Gen. Stat. 14-204 (1997); N.D. Cent. Code 12.1-29-01 (1997); Ohio Rev. Code Ann. 2907.21 (1997); Okla. Stat. Ann. tit. 21, 1029 (1997); Or. Rev. Stat. 167.007 (1997); Pa. Cons. Stat. Ann. 5902 (1997); R.I. Gen. Laws 11-34-5 (1997); S.C. Code Ann. 16-15-90 (1997); S.D. Codified Laws Ann. 22-23-1 (1997); Tenn. Code Ann. 39-13-512 (1997); Tex. Penal Code Ann. 43.02 (1997); Utah Code Ann. 76-10-1302 (1997); Vt. Stat. Ann. tit. 13, 2631 (1997); Va. Code Ann. 18.2-346 (1997); Wash. Rev. Code Ann. 9A.88.030 (1997); W. Va. Code 61-8-5 (1998); Wis. Stat. Ann. 944.30 (1997); Wyo. Stat. Ann. 6-4-101 (1997).

66. Nev. Rev. Stat. Ann. 201.353 (1997).

67. 18 U.S.C. 241 (1949) (amended 1986) (substituting in the 1986 amendment "individual" for "woman or girl" and deleting the language on "immoral purpose," adding criminal "sexual activity"). Child Sexual Abuse & Pornography Act, ch. 177, Sec. 5, § 2422, 100 Stat. 3510 (1986). *See* David J. Langum, *Crossing Over the Line: Legislating Morality and the Mann Act* (Chicago: University of Chicago Press, 1994).

68. 42 U.S.C. 5771 (1998).

69. Codified at 42 U.S.C.A. §§ 5701, 5702, 5731, 5751 (West 1995).

70. For a list, *see* Gregory A. Loken, "'Thrownaway' Children and Throwaway Parenthood," *Temple Law Review* 68 (1995):1715–1762.

71. 42 U.S.C. 5101–5106h (1994).

72. Weisberg, "Children of the Night: The Adequacy of Statutory Treatment of Juvenile Prostitution."

73. Chesney-Lind and Shelden, *Girls, Delinquency, and Juvenile Justice.*

74. *Id.*

75. *Id. See also* Colleen A. Sullivan, "Kids, Courts and Queers: Lesbian and Gay Youth in the Juvenile Justice and Foster Care Systems," *Law & Sexuality* 6 (1996):31–62.

76. *Id.* For examples of this power and how it controls youth who are not delinquent, *see* Maggie L. Hughey, "Holding a Child in Contempt," *Duke Law Journal* 46 (1996):353–385.

77. *See* Courtney Guyton Persons, "Sex in the Sunlight: The Effectiveness, Efficiency, Constitutionality, and Advisability of Publishing Names and Pictures of Prostitute's Patrons," *Vanderbilt Law Review* 49 (1997):1525–1575.

78. Julia M. Robertson, "Homeless and Runaway Youths: A Review of the Literature." In *Homelessness: A National Perspective,* ed. Marjorie J. Robertson and Milton Greenbaltt (New York: Plenum Press, 1992).

79. Crowley and Patel, "Accounting for Child Prostitution."

80. *Id.*

81. Weisberg, "Children of the Night: The Adequacy of Statutory Treatment of Juvenile Prostitution."

82. 42 U.S.C. §§ 5101–5106h (1994).

83. Jody M. Greene, Christopher L. Ringwalt, and Ronaldo Iachan, "Shelters for Runaway and Homeless Youths: Capacity and Occupancy," *Child Welfare* 76 (1997):549–561; Loken, "'Thrownaway' Children and Throwaway Parenthood."

84. Finkelhor et al., "Sexual Abuse in a National Survey of Adult Men and Women: Prevalence, Characteristics, and Risk Factors."

85. For example, Washington makes it a crime to "harbor" a homeless juvenile for four to six hours without notifying the parents or the police; Wash. Rev. Code. Ann. 13.32A.080 (1995). *See* Loken, "'Thrownaway' Children and Throwaway Parenthood."

86. Ala. Code § 26-16-2 (Michie 1992 & Supp. 1997) (defining child abuse as "harm or threatened harm to a child's health or welfare by a person . . . which harm occurs or is threatened through . . . mental injury.").

87. U.S. Department of Health and Human Services, National Center on Child Abuse and Neglect, *Child Maltreatment 1994: Reports From the States to the National Center on Child Abuse and Neglect* (Washington, DC: Government Publications Office, 1994).

88. John E. B. Myers, "Definitions and Origins of the Backlash Against Child Protection." In *The Backlash: Child Protection Under Fire,* ed. John E. B. Myers (Thousand Oaks, CA: Sage, 1994).

89. *See* Roger J. R. Levesque, "Emotional Maltreatment in Adolescents' Everyday Lives: Furthering Sociolegal Reforms and Social Service Provisions," *Behavioral Science and the Law* 16 (1998):237–263.

90. For an analysis of approaches that move from a repair mode toward a constructive, preventive, and fostering mode, *see* Roger P. Weissberg, Thomas P. Gullotta, Robert L. Hampton, Bruce A. Ryan, and Gerald R. Adams (Eds.), *Enhancing Children's Wellness* (Thousand Oaks, CA: Sage, 1997).

91. For example, New York's statute prohibits the "impairment of [a child's] emotional health." N.Y. Cons. Laws. Ann. Soc. Serv. § 26371.4-b(i)–(iii) (McKinney 1989 & Supp. 1998).

92. Mimi H. Silbert, *Sexual Assault of Prostitutes: Phase One* (Washington, DC: National Institute of Mental Health, 1980).

93. For a review, *see* Ilse Nehring, "'Throwaway Rights': Empowering a Forgotten Minority," *Whittier Law Review* 18 (1997):767–811.

94. Alaska Stat. §§ 47-10.300 to 47-10.390 (1999); Fla. Stat. Ann. § 409.441 (1998); Ill. Comp. Stat. Ann. ch. 705, § 405/3-5 (1999); Iowa Code § 232.196 (1977); La. Rev. Stat. Ann. § 46:1351-1256 (1999); Md. Ann. Code art. 83c, § 2-121 (1999); N.J. Stat. Ann. § 40:5-2.10(b) (1999); N.Y. Exec. L. §§ 532, 532-a through 532-e (1999); Ohio Rev. Code Ann. § 5119.65 (1999); Tenn. Code Ann. § 37-1-162 (1999); Tex. Hum. Res. Code § 141.0475 (1999).

95. House Committee on Education and Labor, Subcommittee of Human Resources, *Juvenile Justice, Runaway Youth and Missing Children's Acts,* Amendments, 98th Congress, 2d Sess., March 7, 1984.

96. Deborah Bass, *Helping Vulnerable Youths: Runaway and Homeless Adolescents in the United States* (Washington, DC: National Association of Social Workers Press, 1992).

97. Shiela A. Pires and Judith Tolmach Silber, *On Their Own: Runaway and Homeless Youth and Programs That Serve Them* (Washington, DC: CASSP Technical Assistance Center, Georgetown University Child Development Center, 1991).

98. Robertson, "Homeless and Runaway Youths: A Review of the Literature."

99. Armstrong, "The Silent Minority Within a Minority: Focusing on the Needs of Gay Youth in Our Public Schools."

100. Chesney-Lind and Shelden, *Girls, Delinquency, and Juvenile Justice.*

Chapter 8
SEXUAL VICTIMIZATION BY ADOLESCENTS

Society spends considerable energy controlling adolescents' sexual pleasures but not necessarily their distress associated with their sexual activity. As we have seen, society limits exposure to pornography, curbs access to "adult" entertainment, controls delivery of health services and prohibits interactions that may lead to sexual activity with adults and other minors. The control of adolescent sexual activity permeates social institutions so deeply that they continue despite controversies about their appropriateness and questionable impact, evidence that sexually charged activities may not necessarily be harmful, and the continued failure to convince adolescents about the wisdom of the control. Although pervasive, the controlling ethos fails to offer adolescents protection from *unwanted* sexual experiences and violent sexual relationships that involve victimization by other adolescents. Social and legal protections from blatantly harmful sexual advances, violent relationships and attacks against adolescents' sexual identity remain largely underdeveloped. These failures challenge the purported effectiveness of current protections and conceptions of adolescents' sexual rights.

This chapter presents the current social science evidence related to adolescent sexual victimization by adolescents and reviews existing laws and policies available for adolescents subjected to intimate violence. The analysis suggests that the proper development of protections from other adolescents remains fraught with obstacles simply because the victims are adolescents. The analysis reveals that, although current failures are not easily remediable, lack of progress to address adolescent sexual victimization mainly derives from the liminal nature of adolescence and the assumption that parents and other adults offer adequate protections.

The status of adolescence in the law that aims to protect adults derives from the legal values of adult autonomy, privacy, and neutrality. Each value is problematic when considering the violence adolescents endure. As the following analyses reveal, neutrality defines adulthood as the norm and adolescence as legally inferior, which constructs adolescents' victimization as less serious. Autonomy keeps adolescents' experiences individualized without recognizing the systemic nature of subordination; the legal system views "minors" as "always in some form of custody,"[1] which allows the law to assume that adults protect adolescents and that adolescents have a reduced need for independent access to the law or social services. Privacy keeps adolescents' experiences out of the public sphere; privacy allows adults to leave adolescents without protection and to define public violence as private. This unenviable place of adolescents in law signifies the need to reform social and legal perceptions of adolescents. Given this need, the following review seeks to create legal rules and policy responses out of adolescents' concrete personal experiences and better respond to adolescents' needs rather than foster values that contribute to adolescent victimization.

Sexual Harassment

Sexual harassment has been the subject of fervid social commentaries and significant legal reform. Although much of the most popular commentaries, detailed research, and legal reforms focus on adult experiences, recent efforts seek to expand these responses and apply them to adolescents' experiences. As applied to adolescent life, laws and social responses have been met with controversial and limited success. Consistent with our previous discussions and suggestions, existing responses pervasively fail to consider the peculiarities of the adolescent period. The sexual harassment of adolescents reflects the failure to properly mediate adolescents' restricted legal personhood, recognize the limits of legal reform, and offer protections from violence that goes ignored.

Realities of Adolescent Sexual Harassment

Properly addressing the issue of sexual harassment requires the ability to recognize behaviors that constitute sexual harassment. Researchers have only begun to move beyond that initial step and to understand the nature and dynamics of sexual harassment as applied to adolescents. As progress in recognition moves forward, sexual harassment as applied to adolescents increasingly becomes controversial. Despite benefiting from heightened public attention and research, adolescent sexual harassment continues to be poorly understood, poorly defined, and inadequately recognized as a problem adolescents encounter.

The term ''sexual harassment'' remains imprecise and the behaviors it denotes often are part of nonharassing behavior. Research definitions encompass many types of *unwanted* behaviors, ranging from bullying, both physical and verbal, to sexual aggression committed against individuals because of their gender, sexuality, or vulnerable position.[2] Other definitions limit the broad focus and emphasize the behaviors' persistency, impact, unwelcomeness, and the harasser's power over victims.[3] These definitions have been incorporated into the new definition adopted by the federal agency that receives and deals with the most official complaints of sexual harassment involving adolescents: the Department of Education's Office for Civil Rights (OCR). In 1997 the OCR included a broad range of behaviors but limited the definition so that, to qualify as harassing, the behavior must be severe, persistent, or pervasive enough to affect adolescents' abilities to participate in or benefit from schooling or to create an abusive or hostile educational environment.[4] The focus on persistency and its impact seeks to ensure that not all exchanges between adolescents discovering their sexual identities and gender roles is actionable and that the definition remains fluid enough to serve its purpose as guide in investigations of complaints.

Given the recent adoption of a definition that may now guide investigations, existing research that reports the extent of sexual harassment during adolescence tends simply to list behaviors, asks individuals to report if they ever have experienced such behaviors as unwanted or unwelcomed, and focuses on harassment as experienced in school.[5] This research reports high rates of sexual harassment. Estimates indicate that 75% of boys report being the targets of sexually harassing behaviors; girls report 85%.[6] Although these findings may overemphasize minor or infrequent events, it is important to emphasize four points that highlight the significance of these findings. First, the surveys explicitly state that the experiences must have been unwelcome or unwanted. Second, a high number report that they are harassed more than once: 58% of students report being sexually harassed often or occasionally, and boys make up almost half of that group.[7] Third, more than half of girls and boys admit that they have harassed another student.[8] Fourth, the most comprehensive research reveals that more than half of boys and girls report being both victims and offenders, even though they report finding their own victimization upsetting.[9] These findings serve to emphasize how sexual harassment remains widespread.

In addition to high prevalence rates, research reveals a need to respond simply because the experiences lead to significant consequences.[10] The leading study reported several key findings. Students who have experienced sexual harassment report being embarrassed or self-conscious about incidents: 64% of girls and 36% of boys have felt embarrassed.[11] Harassing behavior changes victims' daily routines. To avoid harassers, 69% of girls and 27% of boys alter their routines.[12] Both boys and girls fear harassment: 78% of girls and 30% of boys report being afraid of being sexually harassed.[13] Finally, these explicit, easily measured changes in behavior create environments that deny individuals access to education and exacerbate sexuality and gender inequity in social opportunities.[14] The consequences, then, are significant, as reflected by the cases (discussed in the next section) that have lead to litigation and formal complaints.[15]

Despite high prevalence rates and apparent consequences, harassing behavior goes unrecognized and ignored. Research analyses persistently reveal one theme: Adolescents and adults both tend to normalize and unconsciously accept sexually harassing behaviors as part of the reality of adolescent life.[16] The failure by adolescents to recognize and disclose unwanted sexual attention is multidetermined. A number of social pressures and expectations placed on female and male victims militate against disclosure. A first often identified factor that inhibits disclosure relates to issues of intentionality. Perceptions of the harasser's intent often are determinative. For example, victims are less likely to report if they feel the behaviors were intended to flatter or were done "by mistake." Harassing behavior confuses victims' perceptions of unwanted sexual attention and genuine and wanted attention. A second factor involves victims' lack of personal interpretations of the nature of harassment. Victims have difficulty identifying the behavior; adolescents typically have no name for annoying, teasing, and even abusive behaviors. Adolescents would be exceptional if they knew that the law requires them to expressly reject the harassment to invoke legal protection. Indeed, the failure to recognize the behavior as problematic and as serious ensures that victims may be unaware that legal protection could be possible. The language deficiency, the inability to communicate and recognize the existence of such problems, prevents victims from sharing the experience with others, which corners them into isolated, vulnerable, and silent positions. A third factor involves the difficulty of finding others in whom to confide, especially when the abusers are heterosexist and both genders are either involved in the perpetration or remain silent as the abusive behavior continues unchecked. A fourth factor simply relates to expectations of harassment: Girls may struggle with a desire to be noticed and accept uncomfortable overtures, and gay or feminine boys who are at increased risk of harassment simply expect to be subject to homophobic harassment. These reasons for failed recognition of victimization highlight the need to understand the diverse ways peers may have unequal relationships that may lead to unrecognized coercive behavior, such as when some have disparate self-images as a result of popularity, talents, competence, or relationships to certain adults.

The failure to recognize and respond to negative outcomes of sexually harassing experiences fuels its persistence. Offenders do not always realize that such abuses offend or hurt. Those who admit offensive behavior justify their harassment on the grounds that most students do it and that it simply is part of school life. The apparent normalness helps explain how both observers and victims remain silent when faced with harassing incidents. The toleration continues because of the prevailing attitude that "boys will be boys," "girls will be girls," and that behaviors are part of normal courtship and heterosexual gender-role socialization. The abusive behaviors go unchallenged, even behaviors that occur in front of individuals who occupy roles that mandate protecting adolescents.[17] Thus onlookers, perpetrators, and victims have become inured and may not see troubling behavior as abusive.

The current knowledge of adolescent development suggests a need for heightened awareness of sexual harassment experienced by adolescents. During adolescence, gender roles intensify and result in exaggerated and accepted extremes of how boys and girls are to interact with one another. Images of how boys and girls operate become embedded and form stereotypes that, if not followed, hold important consequences. Being labeled as having the opposite sex's characteristics are a common form of sexual harassment, just as adopting gender-role extremes may lead to harassing behavior or its acceptance. These gendered extremes affect both sexes and the extent to which both sexes will occupy both victim and perpetrator roles. The findings suggest that harassing behavior permeates adolescent life, highlight the extent to which the behaviors have been ignored, and support a special need for heightened awareness and reaction to the link between gender-role socialization, perceptions of heterosexuality, and harassing behavior. The links allow for an appreciation of how society broadly determines the nature of femininity and masculinity and largely influences what boys and girls can do.

Although appropriate to focus on adolescent behavior, two important findings emphasize how the societal silencing separates adults from adolescents and ignores parallels between their abusive experiences. The problem does not necessarily involve how adults actively maltreat adolescents.[18] Rather, the problem derives from the manner in which adults largely ignore adolescents' coercive sexual behaviors and allow the victimization of vulnerable adolescents to continue.

Peer abuse links to adult forms of harassing behaviors to the extent that those who hold dominant relationships structure relationships to maintain both personal and group power. Just as adult sexual harassment maintains power imbalances between individuals, the sexual harassment of adolescents maintains the adult-dominated society by devaluing and mistreating adolescents. Numerous examples support how experiences adolescents suffer would be deemed inappropriate if perpetrated by and on adults. The sexually demeaning insults, lewd gestures, demeaning attitudes, and cruel jokes adolescents tolerate are rarely viewed as inappropriate adolescent behavior; yet such invasive sexual comments, questions, and demands clearly could qualify as sexual harassment if the victims were adults. Likewise, if young victims were adults, physical forms of sexual harassment, such as roughing and grabbing, would be considered abusive. Comparing harassing behaviors adults endure to those that would be inappropriate if acted on adults illustrates the extent to which society generally holds adolescents to a different standard.

As we have seen, then, sexual harassment can constitute sexual violence against adolescents. Sexual harassment results in numerous and varied consequences. Its causes derive from the manner society views adolescents and socializes them into adult roles. For individuals, the cumulative effects of harassing behaviors can be as devastating and harmful as sexual assault; for society, the effects simply contribute to sustaining forces that condone and foster abuses.

Adolescent Sexual Harassment and the Law

Attempts to protect adolescents from sexually harassing behaviors from other adolescents and adults necessarily begin with existing legal mandates. Few legal mandates, however, directly apply to adolescent sexual harassment. Despite that void, important legal doctrine has developed both in the courts and through legislative efforts to counter sexual harassment. Much of the efforts have been brought under statutory titles that theoretically could impose liability on school boards for harms students suffer while in their care, and, more recently, attempts to protect have derived from state statutes to deal with all forms of harassing behavior experienced in schools. This section reviews these developments that seek to create affirmative duties to protect adolescents from sexual harassment and details practicalities that hamper the effective use of these legal mandates.

Civil Rights Actions Under Federal Tort Claims

Claims brought by students for the consequences of violent or harassing actions by other *students* often have been brought under 42 U.S.C. § 1983. That federal remedy allows imposing liability for failing to observe a constitutional duty.[19] The constitutional duty potentially placed on parties that deprive citizens of their liberties stems from the Fourteenth Amendment's protection from state deprivation of liberties without due process of law. The critical point of these arguments derives from the suggestion that students are in state custody and that those who act on the states' behalf must protect students from deprivations of their liberties—in other words, from harassment by other students.

Although the Supreme Court has dealt with section 1983 torts in a variety of contexts, three cases directly relate to the issue of a state actor's duty to protect a citizen. These cases serve as the appropriate starting point because they distinguish between the rights of victims based on whether they are in official state custody. The first two cases involved individuals in involuntary state custody, which allowed for the use of federal remedies under section 1983. The first case, *Estelle v. Gamble*,[20] dealt with a state's duty in relation to prisoners who, because of incarceration, could not care for themselves. Given that inability, the Court found the state had a duty to provide adequate medical care. The second case, *Youngberg v. Romeo*,[21] involved the state's duties to provide for involuntarily committed mental patients. As with *Estelle*, the Court found an affirmative duty to protect a citizen placed fully within the state's custody. The cases stand for the accepted principle that the act of state custody creates a "special relationship" that binds the state actor to protect those under the state's complete control.

The duty does not necessarily arise, however, when the citizen is not in full state custody. This general rule was the holding of the third case, *DeShaney v. Winnebago County Department of Social Services*.[22] In *DeShaney*, the Court refused to hold the state responsible for its failure to remove a child from a father's custody. In that case the state had received complaints of abuse and even had taken temporary custody of the child, only to return him home without adequate follow-up that allegedly could have prevented his disfigurement and severe disabilities. Although sympathetic to the child's plight, the Supreme Court found the obvious: "Nothing in the language of the Due Process Clause itself requires the State to protect the life, liberty, and property of its citizens against invasion by *private actors.* . . . Its purpose was to protect the people from the State, *not to ensure that the State protected them from each other.*"[23] Thus although it seemed obvious that the child had been in danger and that the state had taken steps to safeguard the child, the state still had no constitutional duty to protect the child from harm and even death unless it had taken him into custody. Only the custodial event gives rise to liability because it triggers the due process clause protections of a state's inability to deprive individuals of their liberties without due process of law because the state restrains the individual's freedom to act.

Some seek to derive a more liberal interpretation of the *DeShaney* rule that would attach liability when there would be "other similar restraint of personal liberty" than "incarceration or institutionalization"[24] or when the state renders the citizen more vulnerable to the dangers, even though the state did not create them.[25] However, the duty still only arises when there is a "special relationship" between the actors and the state formed when the latter takes the former into some form of custody. Despite the possibility of a more liberal interpretation of the *DeShaney* rule, the Court's open window to find control in other areas has proven difficult to lift. The lower courts follow a basic pattern in their logic.[26] The courts first determine whether custody exists, based on the amount of restraint of personal liberty. If the court does find requisite custody, the court then determines if the state somehow created or exacerbated the danger. Although the second determination may constitute a viable theory, it is not one courts generally accept; schools would have to place victimized students in tremendous and immediate peril that directly caused harm before a duty would arise from the school's official state action.

Attempts to impose sanctions on institutions that fail to protect students from other students consistently have proven unsuccessful. Relying on *DeShaney,* several circuits have found that sexual assault by another student does not give rise to a section 1983 claim.[27] Given that sexual assault has a venerable history of recognition, it is not surprising to find that the legal rule also offers no protection against sexual harassment. For example, in *Aurelia Davis v. Monroe County Board of Education,*[28] a case we will return to later, the court dismissed a case dealing with adolescent sexual harassment that continued over a period of months and stopped only with the harasser's guilty plea to criminal assault charges. The school, via the principal and teachers, allegedly had not responded appropriately to the victim's numerous pleas for assistance. The court found no cause for legal action on the grounds that the school did not have a special custodial relationship with its students and that the school thus had no special duty to protect them from other students. In dismissing the section 1983 claim, the court noted that, in spite of compulsory attendance laws and the common law doctrine of *in loco parentis,* no special relationship existed between the school district and victim that required an affirmative duty on the part of school officials to protect her from harassment. The case's legal analysis is rather significant in that, as discussed later, the Supreme Court eventually reviewed this case but only reversed it on other grounds.[29] Without the special relationships, schools have no duty under this legal approach to impose liability on the state and its actors.

In summary, school districts and their representatives generally owe no constitutional duty to protect schoolchildren from the acts of other students. Federal remedies arising from state actors' mandates to protect adolescents' constitutional rights are difficult to obtain. Although several may champion the need to recognize and expand the remedy, current jurisprudence severely limits its utility, and no case based on this legal theory has been won in the context of adolescent sexual harassment.

Federal Education Amendments

Actions on behalf of students have alleged a violation of Title IX.[30] These actions contend that schools allow a hostile environment that involves sexual harassment against students, which constitutes sex discrimination. The link between sexual harassment and discrimination is significant; otherwise, the statute does not apply and none of its remedies may be had. Title IX specifically only provides that "no person in the United States shall, *on the basis of sex,* be excluded from participation in, be denied the benefits of, or be subjected to discrimination under any education program receiving Federal financial assistance."[31] The link that allows some forms of sexual harassment to constitute sex discrimination, though, has been firmly connected and even has received the Supreme Court's imprimatur.

The Supreme Court first addressed the possible link between student sexual harassment and sex discrimination for the purposes of Title IX in *Franklin v. Gwinnett County (GA) Public Schools.*[32] *Franklin* involved the repeated sexual harassment of a high school student by a sports coach and teacher. The student alleged that when the school district became aware of the harassment and investigated it, the district took no action to halt it and discouraged Franklin from pressing charges. In a landmark 9–0 decision, the Court found that allegations of intentional discrimination that involve sexual harassment of a student *by a teacher* is a form of sex discrimination prohibited by Title IX. The Court stated its extension of suits in employment situations to school environments as follows:

> Unquestionably, Title IX placed on the Gwinnett County Schools the duty not to discriminate on the basis of sex, and "when a supervisor sexually harasses a subordinate because of the subordinate's sex, that supervisor 'discriminate[s]' on the basis of sex." We believe the same rule should apply when a teacher sexually harasses and abuses a student.[33]

The Court not only found that Title IX prohibits sexual harassment in public schools, it also held that a damage remedy is available for actions to enforce Title IX. The Court conceded that Title IX is enforceable through an implied right of action as it relied on the long-standing rule that, unless Congress specifically indicates otherwise or remains silent, the federal courts have the power to award any appropriate relief in a cause of action brought under a federal statute.

Commentators had been quick to use *Franklin* to signal the Court's approval of Title IX's use in sexual harassment claims and for allowing monetary compensation in such actions. However, four points warranted caution against using *Franklin* as an expansive doctrine on which to hook peer sexual harassment actions. First, *Franklin* actually had not been applied to student-to-student sexual harassment. Second, the case also had included rape, which is much more recognized as a form of violence. Third, the charges and suit for damages only had become actionable when the event alleged intentional, gender-based discrimination. Fourth, the Supreme Court had had the opportunity to review the implied right of action and had restricted its use: A student can recover under the implied right of action only when school district officials who have authority to institute corrective measures on the districts' behalf and who act with "deliberate indifference" to the violators' misconduct.[34] Thus *Franklin* had left disputable the fundamental issue at hand: whether, and under what circumstances, courts should impose Title IX liability on school districts in cases of peer sexual harassment.

The issue of whether Title IX supports a claim for a school official's failure to prevent student-to-student sexual harassment eventually was addressed in *Aurelia Davis v. Monroe County Board of Education*.[35] That case involved a fifth-grade student's repeated attempts to stop sexual harassment by another student. Her formal complaint alleged that school officials were slow to react and for a six-month period allowed harassing conduct by a boy who tried to touch her breasts, rubbed his body against hers, and used vulgar language. The harassing ended only after the mother filed criminal charges of sexual battery against the boy, to which he pled guilty. As a result of the behavior, the victim's grades had suffered and she had contemplated suicide. After a series of reversals, the Eleventh Circuit eventually affirmed the trial court's dismissal of the Title IX claim and held that Title IX does not allow a claim against a school board based on a school official's failure to remedy a known hostile environment created by student-to-student sexual harassment.[36] The Supreme Court, in a highly heated exchange between the majority and four dissenting justices, reversed. The Court found that Title IX actually *does* place a burden on schools to respond to student-to-student sexual harassment.[37]

To find liability under Title IX, the Court needed to find that (a) the statute allowed for imposing a right of action by victims against the school and (b) harassing behavior by peers could actually constitute discrimination for the purposes of Title IX. In its reasoning, the Court invoked *Franklin v. Gwinnett County Public Schools*[38] to find an implied right of action under Title IX, which allowed for private damages actions against schools that discriminated, in this instance the failure to respond to the student's harassment that deprived her of the school's educational opportunities.[39] In finding for the student, however, the Court also transposed from precedents a very high standard of misconduct on the part of the school and on the part of the harasser. In terms of the school, those seeking claims against schools must prove that the school had acted with "deliberate indifference to known acts of harassment."[40] The deliberate indifference must "'cause [students] to undergo' harassment or 'make them liable or vulnerable' to it."[41] To reach that high standard, the school must have exercised substantial control over both the harasser and the context in which the known harassment occurs.[42] In terms of harassing behavior that was not responded to appropriately by the school, the behavior must have been "so severe, pervasive, and objectively offensive" that it had undermined and detracted from the victim's educational experience so that they were "effectively denied equal access to an institution's resources and opportunities."[43] To reach that level, the Court explicitly noted that the behavior must be serious enough to have a "systemic effect" of denying the educational opportunity Title IX is designed to protect.[44]

The four dissenting justices in *Davis* objected on several grounds. Most notably, they objected on simple legal grounds that a case decided only the previous year[45] had emphasized the general illegitimacy of finding an implied private cause of action under a statute that has been silent on the subject; they reasoned that the silence meant that the Court had to defer to Congress and not infringe on the branches of state and federal government that make laws and allocate funds.[46] The justices also asserted that, for the purposes of Title IX's prohibitions, schools could only be held liable for harmful discriminatory actions when actually done pursuant or in accordance with school policy or action,[47] which essentially would make the schools not liable in peer harassment because it is not, for example, school policy to harass students. The justices also noted practical problems regarding the limited control schools have over their students, the need for schools to educate all students, the limitations placed on disciplinary measures against disruptive students, lack of resources to monitor students, and the difficulty of actually applying the legal notion of sexual harassment to normative adolescent sexual behavior.[48]

Despite the heated debates, a look at lower federal court cases reveals more support for the majority's view that, even though Title IX may provide a right of action against schools, the high standard set by the courts—that the harasser's actions be severe and persistent and that the schools be indifferent and discriminatory—ensures litigation and victims' success in only very serious cases. Before *Davis,* several circuit courts already had recognized the potential for Title IX's liability, yet none had found actual school liability in a peer sexual harassment case. The first case to address directly the issue of peer harassment through Title IX was *Doe v. Petaluma City School District.*[49] In *Petaluma,* the plaintiff's classmates subjected her to verbal obscenities.[50] Doe's complaint further alleged that the abuse lasted two years and that her counselor failed to take action to stop harassment, going as far as to say that "boys will be boys."[51] The counselor never told Doe or her parents that the school had a Title IX policy and representative. Only after Doe was slapped by a fellow student were her parents informed of Title IX grievance procedures. The district court elaborated on its ruling that a student seeking to obtain damages under Title IX must prove "intentional discrimination" based on sex, not just that the institution or "employee of the institution knew or should have known of a hostile environment and failed to take appropriate action."[52] Although it did seem that the claim could lead to eventual recovery, the suit was settled before the claim could be litigated.[53] In a second and highly cited case, *Seamons v. Snow,*[54] the alleged action involved taping a young man to a towel rack and involuntarily dragging a girl to view his naked body. The claimant did not file suit for the assault itself but rather for what ensued after he had reported the incident to school officials. On the student's report, the coach demanded that he apologize for betraying the team and, on his failing to do so, the coach dismissed him from the team. The school authorities were equally unresponsive and refused to discipline the players for the hazing; they too dismissed the behavior as appropriate. Seamons argued that the team ritual was well-known to the coach and school officials and that their actions were ''sexually discriminatory and harassing'' because officials expected him to ''have it like a man'' and the coach dismissed the incident as ''boys will be boys.''[55] Although the court recognized the ''hostile environment'' as a Title IX cause of action, it nevertheless found against the plaintiff for failing to show that the defendant's conduct was ''sexual in any way''[56] and that it constituted discrimination. In yet another important case, *Rowinsky v. Bryan Independent School District*,[57] two eighth-grade sisters rode a public school bus on a daily basis while a male student verbally and physically harassed them. The girls repeatedly complained to the school bus driver and their parents complained to the school principal who reported that they already knew about the incidents in question. Although the school then suspended the boy for three days, the remarks and behaviors continued. Later that year other students made crude remarks to the girls, groped the girls' genital areas, and, in a classroom, placed their hands under one of the girl's shirt and unhooked her bra. The school, in response to the classroom incident, suspended one of the boys for a day and a half. The girls' mother complained to various school officials and determined that they did not take appropriate action. She then sued the district and its employees on the claim that they ''condoned and caused hostile environment sexual harassment.''[58] The district court dismissed the claim and found that ''there was no evidence the [the school district] had discriminated against the students based on sex'' and that ''Rowinsky had failed to provide evidence that sexual harassment and misconduct [were] treated less severely toward girls than toward boys.''[59] The court relied on the fact that boys who assaulted girls were treated the same way as boys who assaulted boys and that any failure to train employees would harm male and female students equally. The Fifth Circuit agreed and reasoned that a plaintiff must prove that the school intentionally discriminated against students on the basis of sex. These cases reveal well the extent to which the legal system poses many formal obstacles to those who would use federal education mandates to pursue legal actions against schools.

State Statutes

Although federal statutes may not directly lead to viable outcomes, potential state remedies remain. The increased recognition of the need to protect adolescents from sexual harassment is reflected in state statutes that require school districts to instate sexual harassment policies that govern student behavior toward one another. Although recognition has increased in the past few years, five states have enacted statutes to address adolescent harassment and all deal with school contexts. Although not pervasive, these efforts are worthy of review, because they suggest important trends in recognition of adolescent sexual harassment.

Minnesota was the first state to enact a statute that recognized the need for schools to adopt antiharassment policies.[60] The statute provides that each school board will adopt a written policy that will apply to pupils, teachers, administrators, and other school personnel. In addition, the school policy will set forth disciplinary actions taken for violation of the policy and will be distributed to individuals, including students, through the student handbook. The statute also provides that each school must develop a process for discussing the schools' policy. The state provides a model curriculum for use in junior and senior high schools.[61] Under this statutory model, the state serves as guide.

Two other states have enacted policies that are similar in content and outcomes for those who harass. California requires that every school must (a) develop a written sexual harassment policy for staff and students; (b) display it promptly on campus; and (c) distribute a copy to each student and staff member.[62] The statute also permits principals to suspend or even expel students as young as the fourth-grade level who engage in sexual harassment.[63] Florida's statute provides for sexual harassment policies in a student handbook and for distribution to parents, teachers, staff, and students.[64] Like the California statute, Florida provides that violations of the policy by a student are grounds for suspension, expulsion, or imposition of other disciplinary action by the school and also may result in the imposition of criminal penalties. Although these two statutes do not provide curricular models, they do emphasize the need for taking decisive action against harassers and focus on punishment.

The last two states to adopt statutes that deal with sexual harassment by adolescents in public schools—Washington and Michigan—present polar opposites in their protections. Washington's statute requires the development of criteria for school district sexual harassment policies, grievance procedures, remedies, and disciplinary procedures.[65] In addition, and unlike the other statutes, the statute explicitly states that the harassment policy also applies to "students, including, but not limited to, conduct between students." The statute also provides that the school district policy be widely disseminated and that provisions and definition be discussed and addressed. The statute explicitly guarantees equal educational access and nondiscrimination standards to define sexual harassment as encompassing both *quid pro quo* and hostile environment standards. Michigan's statute simply provides that each school board of each school district "shall adopt and implement a written sexual harassment policy."[66] The statute does not direct implementation except to note that "at a minimum, the policy shall prohibit sexual harassment by school district employees, board members and pupils directed toward other employees or pupils and shall specify penalties for violation of the policy."[67]

Existing state remedies, then, remain considerably variable and undeveloped. Most states do not provide official, legal recognition of adolescent sexual harassment. The five states with provisions vary considerably in terms of the protections offered. In general, when protections exist, they simply suggest that schools create policies. The nature of those policies generally remains to be determined, as does how they will address the needs of adolescents.

Limitations of Current Recognition

Adolescents who seek redress for sexually harassing behaviors face enormous obstacles. Because most of the sexually harassing incidents are perpetrated while in school or are related to school activities, the first avenue of redress tends to involve in-school sexual harassment policies. Formal legal remedies tend to be sought only after exhausting internal school procedures. Regardless of the arena, several important legal and practical considerations hamper adolescents' efforts to seek and obtain redress.

The first consideration involves whether schools *have* policies. As we have seen, the five states with statutes that recognize peer sexual harassment in schools are notable for their limitations. The states offer no guidance for developing new sexual harassment policies; policies are left to school districts to be designed and implemented.[68] Likewise, statutes do not guide and support staff training for a curriculum that could help students define the boundaries of appropriate behavior. If, however, harassing behaviors are recognized, it does seem that the statutes provide for responses; they tend to focus on punishment of perpetrators. Note, though, that even with official mandates, several districts have developed official policies and increasingly do so in response to federal mandates that they do so.[69]

The second issue regarding the effectiveness of legal responses relates to whether victims will use available procedures. Whether adolescents will make use of grievance procedures remains debatable for four reasons. First, many students properly perceive that complaints to school authorities will not be treated confidentially and fear retaliation from alleged perpetrators or his or her friends and family. As with adults, adolescent victims think that they have a personal problem and blame themselves for having caused the harassment. Second, without school awareness and school programs, children and their parents may not even know of other avenues for redress. That is, victims who do report sexual harassment may be advised to drop charges. Or, out of ignorance, students may be advised to accept the behavior. Third, parents may not find the behavior disturbing and may contribute to the harassment. Fourth, despite existing mandates and the prevalence of sexual harassment in schools, relatively few complaints are filed, still fewer are heard, and even fewer are found actionable. When existing policies exist, they are not necessarily followed or enforced.

The third issue arises when school policies have failed, do not exist, or when school officials have failed to respond to harassing behaviors. In these instances, the first issue involves whether legal systems properly allow for such challenges to proceed through the legal system. Adolescents must use existing legal doctrine and place their experiences in predetermined legal categories that limit adolescents' avenues for redress. Despite numerous attempts to allow for liability, reviews find the possibility of students' succeeding in their legal challenges to stop sexually harassing behavior by another students as "remote."[70] The legal system continues to have difficulty in both evaluating harm and allocating responsibility when minors are involved. The burden of proof that must be met by the complainant undoubtedly constitutes an enormous challenge. Despite the liability standard set by the Supreme Court, how it could be met remains highly controversial. Typically, victims must show that the "reasonable person" would view the acts as unwelcome. Such standards are actually quite tricky to determine—in other words, whether conduct constitutes sexual harassment can be approached in terms of whether the reasonable person is a reasonable girl, reasonable boy, simply a reasonable child, or an expert in the field of child sexual harassment. To complicate matters, it remains unclear how victims' actions should be considered. The "normal" reaction tends to include laughing off such behavior or responding in kind, or because the victim experiences the behavior from a vulnerable position, she or he may blame her- or himself and not express disapproval of certain behaviors. A focus on conduct may also be problematic if the victim has had previous relationships with the harasser or has had amicable relationships where teasing was not originally unwelcome but later became problematic. In these situations, emphasis placed on the past conduct of complainants can be troubling. In addition, there may need to be a focus on overt violence and persistence, an application that leaves children unprotected: The focus on "repeated" behavior leaves several forms of harassment unaddressed and actions need not be overtly violent to be harmful. Finally, results from existing research reveal how sexual harassment by peers reveals more than its occurrence in public; it reveals that adolescents have no problem differentiating between sexual harassment and flirting: The difference is based on the *feelings* each behavior elicits. This subjective understanding, however, is not amenable to traditional legal responses that concern themselves with protecting individual rights and focus on objective, provable behavior.

The fourth issue relates to the necessary means to launch legal actions. Time and financial investment renders problematic the pursuit of sexual harassment claims. If those factors are problematic for adults, they are that much more so for adolescents. For students who only attend certain classes or schools for short spans, legal avenues are likely to be ineffective. Likewise, the sluggish process of legal action does not stop the behavior immediately. These difficulties are reflected in a plethora of important precedent-setting cases. Currently, these cases indicate that attempts to obtain redress are fraught with obstacles even though the right to proceed legally has been recognized for a narrow set of cases.

The fifth difficulty arises once legal obstacles to legal redress are met and remedies need to be considered. In theory, remedies can take several forms: compensatory awards, proactive remedies, or actual punishment of offenders. Again, however, several obstacles block such redress. For example, compensations for pain and suffering are difficult to determine; some plaintiffs simply want to ensure that school boards take more active stances. Legally, it also remains to be determined whether schools can actually take effective proactive measures to address the problem of sexual harassment within schools. Likewise, the harassing behaviors may be occurring outside of school grounds; and if so, protections are rather slim.

For extreme cases, the criminal justice system offers another, albeit limited, route. Although important controversies remain, cases of sexual harassment are not always so difficult. Cases involving physical harassment may be less difficult than the more ambiguous forms of harassment such as leering, sexual gestures, or inappropriate graffiti. Likewise, there are other forms of legal protections. When harassment escalates into more extreme physical and sexual violence, criminal codes may come into effect. For example, since 1990, 48 states have enacted specific stalking legislation that often define stalking in such broad terms as "harass" and "annoy." For example, Alabama defines "harasses" as engaging "in an intentional course of conduct directed at a specific person which alarms or annoys that person, or interferes with the freedom of movement of that person, and which serves no legitimate purpose."[71] However, these statutes require the communication to be a credible or even "terroristic" threat in addition to harassing behavior;[72] and statutes also generally include an objective standard that requires the harassing behavior to be severe enough to cause a "reasonable person to suffer substantial emotional distress."[73] However, some states have enacted statutes that expressly provide for recovery of civil damages from stalkers.[74]

Likewise, several criminal remedies also exist to respond to assaults. Despite progress in the availability of legal mandates to deal with harassing behavior, these more punitive alternatives also remain limited. They are available only if the abuse is recognized appropriately in the first place. In addition, the high burden of proof needed for criminal convictions makes harassing behavior even more difficult to prove. Also, the criminal justice system still focuses on punishing offenders rather than offering victims assistance. Finally, civil actions continue to be rare and only a few states recognize it as a possible remedy. Despite limitations, however, legal avenues still may be appropriate for extreme cases.

Obstacles to dealing effectively with harassing behaviors reveal important points. They reflect the extent to which statutes designed for adult behaviors are not readily adaptable to adolescents' actions. Further, they indicate the extent to which gender plays an important role, and how there may be a need to move beyond gendered analyses. In addition, they highlight the significance of addressing numerous societal forces that contribute to maltreating behaviors. Also, the obstacles highlight the need to focus on adolescents' own voices and priorities. They also reveal how some jurisdictions actually are responding and attempting to recognize harms adolescents suffer. Finally, the efforts remain consistent with traditional sexual harassment law that focuses on social change and the belief that sexual harassment essentially constitutes a societal issue requiring a larger scaled response that attacks societal forces leading to sexual harassment. These issues reflect the extent to which harassment law designed for adults has yet to be properly adapted to adolescents' lives and how attempts to equate the practices may enable the practice to continue.

Relationship Violence

The incidence and nature of violence between intimates has long been recognized as a significant symptom of the societal failure to protect its vulnerable citizens. Once recognized as a social problem worthy of consideration, however, the research community responded with an impressive number of studies to address domestic violence. Yet the proliferation of research and policies has remained limited in scope: Marital and adult-partner abuse has been the major focus of inquiry and concern in law, policy response, and social concern.[75] Despite the narrow focus, a small number of studies have examined adolescent relationships. These studies, coupled with considerable research about the nature of adolescence and violent relationships, enable us to draw themes and conclusions about adolescent relationship violence and suggest avenues for ensuring protection and broader societal responses to violence.

Realities of Adolescent Relationship Violence

Although social science researchers only recently turned their attention to adolescent relationship violence, several findings suggest cause for concern. Battering relationships appear to begin in adolescents' early teenage years, with the onset of dating relationships.[76] These episodes include slapping and pushing, beating, and threatening to use or actually using weapons.[77] In more extreme cases, violent relationships turn into stalking and homicide.[78] These forms of violence in adolescent relationships occur much more frequently than generally believed. National surveys reveal that more than 35% of both men and women inflict some form of physical aggression on their dating partners *and* sustain violence.[79] Smaller studies support these findings and indicate that between 20 to nearly 50% of adolescent relationships are marked by excessive physical violence.[80] Likewise, more than 70% of both dating males and females experience threatening behaviors, monitoring their actions, personal insults, and emotional maltreatment.[81] Nearly the same percentage perpetrate the same behaviors, and more than half of both males and females report injuries from the violence.[82] Other studies report similarly high rates, including nearly half of males and females reporting severe physical abuse.[83] As with other forms of violence, girls significantly experience higher levels of severe relationship violence.[84] In terms of the actual number of adolescents involved, approximately 1 out of 10 high school students experience physical violence in their dating relationships.[85] Although these estimates may seem high, they actually underestimate the violence reported in dating relationships, because they do not include instances of date rape and other violence occurring outside of long-term, committed relationships.

Although prevalence estimates do vary considerably from study to study, violence appears to be common to dating behavior. The high incidence and prevalence rates actually underestimate the magnitude of relationship violence.[86] The experience remains essentially invisible. Only a small fraction, as low as 7%, of violent episodes is ever reported to officials, authorities, and others who could render assistance, and almost half tell no one. Although the prevalence of battering may be less than harassing behaviors, the experiences seem remarkably similar in the extent to which victims resist outside assistance and the relationship dynamics render the violence essentially inevitable.

The hidden nature of violent adolescent relationships reflects the paradoxical behaviors victims exhibit.[87] Battered victims profess love for abusers, defend abusers even after severe beatings, blame themselves for the abuse done to them, and deny or minimize the threatening nature of the abuse. For example, almost half of dating violence victims report that their partner's violence was at least "somewhat justified" and a similarly high percentage take responsibility for initiating violence.[88]

The paradoxical behaviors help explain another remarkable aspect of physically violent dating relationships: their continuity. As many as 50% of dating relationships do not terminate after violent episodes.[89] Of the partners who continue and remain committed to their relationships after violent episodes, approximately half report no change or further deterioration.[90] Separated battered women report being battered 14 times as often as women still living with their partners.[91] Indeed, more than 75% of women involved in violent dating relationships expect to marry their abusers[92] and half that number of women actually do marry partners who have abused them before marriage.[93] The tendency to blame themselves, protect abusers, and remain in violent relationships has led researchers to conclude that victims "traumatically bond" to abusers.[94] Some adolescent victims, like individuals in psychologically comparable "hostage" situations (abused children, battered women, cult members, prisoners of war, etc.) adopt survival strategies that commit them to the relationship.[95]

Although research on domestic violence previously focused on adult partners, adolescents may be at higher risk for traumatic bonding.[96] For example, a consistent finding reveals that relationships are especially ripe for maltreatment when men and women respectively assume dominant and submissive roles. That finding suggests that adolescents may be more prone to violence as gender roles intensify during adolescence and adolescents tend to conform to extreme gender stereotypic roles. Intensified gender roles result in relationships that expect girls to be supportive and responsible for the success (and failure) of their relationships.[97] As with sexual harassment, adolescent relationships may be more prone to maltreatment because of intensified sexism seemingly inherent in gender norms. However, the pressure seems greater because it places limits on partners so that victims feel responsible for relationship maintenance. Adolescent girls may be more reluctant to leave abusive relationships.[98]

In addition to intensified gender roles and tendency to exhibit acceptance for traditional gender roles, adolescent partners' dependency on each other for social acceptance and self-esteem places them at risk for violence. Movement toward peer groups, attempts to conform to peer norms, and pressure to be involved in intimate relationships mark the normative transition through adolescence.[99] These social demands placed on adolescents, especially the need for conformity, render teenagers susceptible to battering. Social dependency and emotional attachment cement the hold to the batterer, a pattern that parallels to those of adult victims who are emotionally and financially dependent on abusers.[100]

In addition to considerations of gender dynamics during adolescence, adolescents are at risk because of adolescents' characteristic detachment from families.[101] The detachment is important to consider from the perspective of both adolescents and their parents. To be sure, adolescents still undoubtedly rely on families for important sources of support.[102] Yet the physical and emotional detachment places adolescents in precarious positions. Victims may be unable or unwilling to ask for assistance from their families. Turning to families may be more difficult for adolescents from cultures in which dating and sexuality, as well as alternative forms of relationships, are restricted and possible sources of shame.[103] Feelings of shame and helplessness keep adolescents from seeking assistance from familial sources, as reflected in the high number of adolescents who do not even disclose the sexual nature of dating relationships to parents who comfortably discuss sexuality.[104] The parents' perspectives of detachment also suggest a risk of maltreatment. Parents often fail to take adolescents' complaints seriously. Adults typically minimize the intensity of adolescent relationships, expect that adolescents can break bonds and date others, and fail to realize that adolescents could be involved in violent relationships.[105] To complicate matters even further, if parents do intervene when they suspect abusive behavior, intervention runs the risk of reinforcing the romantic bond.[106] The normative negotiation of movement away from family control contributes to adolescents' peculiar risks of relationship victimization.

In addition to the nature of abusive relationships and adolescent support groups, other hallmarks of the adolescent period indicate that the adolescent period provides an environment conducive to maltreatment. Adolescents characteristically test limits of self-control and risk-taking. A common manifestation of these normal developments includes experimentation with prohibited substances. Adolescent experimentation with these substances and attempts to "do adult things" invariably increase the risk of relationship violence. Research indicates that alcohol and drug use are highly associated with abusive episodes.[107] Although the use of alcohol and drugs may not cause the violence, they clearly help intensify abuse.[108] Evidence that alcohol has been a consistent risk marker for dating violence and that adolescents are beginning to experiment and learn to control their exposure to alcohol, then, suggests adolescents are at increased risk for relationship violence.

In addition to the nature of the adolescent period, the nature of adolescent relationships places adolescents at risk. Simply because adolescents are necessarily inexperienced in romantic relationships, they may not possess the ability to handle intense feelings. The inability to control new intense feelings plays a significant role in creating relationships known to be highly passionate, exciting, and possessive.[109] For example, the intensity of feelings may lead to interpreting jealousy as a normal way to express love and failing to recognize problems. Adolescents are particularly prone to experiencing normative confusion: normal becomes what happens in their relationships and their abusive relationships are experienced as neither problematic nor intolerable.[110] Proneness to normative confusion suggests that adolescents may not possess the "maturity" to deal with complex problems that may arise in relationships.[111] Faced with life-threatening situations, adolescents are prone to deny, rather than confront and systematically deal with the situation.[112]

In addition to the likely passionate aspect of adolescent relationships, courtships actually may be inherently violent and the violence increases in acceptability as relationships progress. The process of courtship violence emerges from the working out of relationship difficulties, such as jealousy and rejection.[113] Several studies report that jealousy provides the most frequent reason for partner violence;[114] and several studies document the significant role satisfaction with relationship power dynamics plays in the perpetration of dating violence.[115] As courtship progresses, relationships with more, and more frequent, problems increasingly experience violent episodes.[116] When relationship investment increases and attempts to leave the relationship are difficult and unwelcomed, episodes also become more injurious.[117] The increased rates and seriousness of violence become more acceptable by partners, as well as by outsiders, as the relationship becomes more serious and committed.[118] The process of breaking from violent and dependent relationships intensifies already difficult processes of breaking up, which even under normal conditions involves sophisticated interpersonal skills.[119] Although the process by which disengagements and disagreements degenerate to the point of physical aggression remains uninvestigated, the link indisputably exists.[120]

Although the nature of adolescent relationships may increase adolescents' vulnerability to relationship violence, certain types of relationships undoubtedly compound the risk. For example, research indicates that gay and lesbian adolescents report difficulty in obtaining assistance from anyone, let alone parents, school officials, and peers.[121] Yet violence against gay and lesbian adolescents remains pervasively ignored and their service needs unmet.[122] In addition, researchers have long noted that the risk of violence to both adult and adolescent women either begins or intensifies when boyfriends learn of pregnancy.[123] That pregnancy, motherhood, and homosexual orientations exacerbate risks remains quite understandable in light of the ecology of adolescent life and adolescent battering. These adolescents have fewer resources than adults and other peers, and the judgments and blaming received from adults and peers increase these adolescents' reluctance to seek assistance. Given the lack of support, the circumstances contribute to these adolescent victims' sense of helplessness and isolation and increase dependency on abusing partners. If there ever were instances in which a "vicious cycle" could be found, these adolescents' experiences would be prime candidates.

The problematic nature of the adolescent period and adolescent relationships becomes particularly eminent immediately prior to the period of legal emancipation.[124] The manner in which the legal system demarks childhood, adolescence, and adulthood does not reflect the social reality adolescents face. Many adolescents experience the approach of their 18th birthday with a mixture of great hopes and considerable trepidation. The formal "liberation" from parental accountability and compliance is coupled by other important moves and social opportunities for autonomy. For example, society marks the high school experience with rituals of closure and social entry into adulthood. The social and familial liberation intensify social activity. These activities, in turn, create incipient occasions for sexual, drug, alcohol, and other involvements that test courtship relationships. The sexual intimacy created in the ecology of adolescent liberation makes it difficult to exist without adverse and often violent consequences.

Equally important to understanding the victimology of adolescent relationship violence is the need to consider battering from the part of the adolescent batterer. Controlling adolescent perpetrators undoubtedly remains central to combatting adolescent and adult relationship violence.[125] Yet researchers essentially have ignored battering adolescents and their development into adult batterers.

Despite a general lack of focus on adolescent batterers, research that has examined adolescent relationship violence identifies various explanations for the batterers' violence. Numerous social influences particularly affect adolescents.[126] Adolescent batterers receive encouragement and approval from the media and friends. Peers and the media instill the belief that men should dominate women in relationships and that men have the right to use aggressive behavior. Battering teenagers tend to report their behavior to peer groups and actually receive support for it. Although the link between media and adolescent violence remains less clear, media portrayals of adolescent relationships do tend to be adversarial and affect adolescents' views of dating violence. Indeed, there is no need to resort to these specific influences: The pervasiveness of relationship violence indicates well how society continues to accept this form of violence, especially when relationships are considered serious, despite the belief that the violence should not be acceptable. Thus the condemnation of relationship violence is by no means absolute or universal; and numerous instances of relationship violence remain viewed as appropriate. When violence is not viewed as appropriate, outsiders simply believe that the relationships will end or that the couples will seek counseling.

A second research focus adopts a developmental perspective and suggests that adolescent relationship violence simply results from learned, maladaptive behavior. Family violence researchers often point to the "cycle of violence"—the view that individuals who experience or observe violence in their families are more likely to engage in violence in their families of procreation than individuals who do not have such experiences or observations.[127] This research indicates that parental abusive behavior and domestic violence place adolescents at risk for perpetrating domestic violence, both as adolescent victims and victimizers. Indeed, the major predictor of violent experiences in current relationships is their experiences in previous relationships. Although researchers only have started to link relationship violence to other groundbreaking research on the development of psychopathological behavior, the research does receive support from extensive investigations of the antisocial roots of human development. Child-rearing environments marked by negative affect, use of arbitrary, restrictive, and punitive parenting strategies fail to promote cooperative or healthy relationships; nor do they foster empathic or altruistic responses to and from others. These relational styles continue to be linked to antisocial behavior, including adult domestic violence.[128]

A third important research program focuses more on relationships themselves. This research reveals that the dynamics of abuse lead abusers to define and experience violence as rewarding. For example, being in control increases one's self-esteem and allows for the use of revenge for real or imagined wrongs.[129] Although undoubtedly subject to irrationalities, dating aggression relates to several underlying relationship difficulties, most notably jealousy and relationship breakdown.[130] Likewise, repeated emotional and physical violence ensures victim compliance with demands. This self-reinforcing pattern is likely to continue, especially because adolescent batterers may not experience negative consequences that might motivate them to alter their behavior. Even if a particular abusive relationship does end, there is the danger that an unhealthy pattern has been set, which helps rehearse roles that eventually most likely will be adopted in adult relationships.

The three emerging paradigms to help understand the perpetration of adolescent battering are significant. The vulnerability of adolescents to particular social influences, the developmental roots of antisocial behavior, the dynamics of violent relationships, and failed societal responses to adolescent relationship violence all perpetuate battering. These factors compliment the previously discussed literature that has identified factors that contribute to the victimization of adolescents: lack of dating experience, increase in peer pressure, need to conform to gender-role expectations, the vicissitudes of normal adolescence, and the nature of romantic relationships. It is difficult to underestimate the significance of these approaches. All locate personal violence in a larger social context, an approach that relates the structure of social arrangements to the structure of emotional relationships and violence between intimates.

The multidetermined nature of adolescent battering makes the personal, societal, political, and legal dimensions critical to consider. As a whole, research and policy responses suggest three reasons relationship violence constitutes an appropriate area of concern in investigations of adolescent sexuality. First, this form of violence constitutes a significant part of numerous adolescents' relationships; second, battering in relationships controls adolescents' sexual behavior and their sexuality; and third, battering poses special risks for adolescent victims and contributes to maladaptive patterns that allow victimization and offending to continue, even into other relationships. Given these findings, it is important to understand how the law responds to the need to protect adolescents from battering relationships.

Adolescent Relationship Violence and the Law

The growing body of theory and research that delves into family violence resulted in the recognition of domestic violence as an important legal problem.[131] The discovery quickly fueled the enactment of an impressive series of federal and state domestic violence statutes.[132] Although several components of these statutes certainly remain controversial,[133] the movement highlights what has been ignored: Victims need increased protection and the legal system could play a decisive role in intervention, prevention, and remediation efforts. The movement aims to take victims' rights seriously. Although they may vary in actual content and emphasis, the new statutes and policies have been buttressed by more than a billion dollars of victims' assistance federal funds in the hope of confronting relationship violence in essentially all relevant legal and social service arenas.[134] Regrettably and much like research, the proliferation of policies remains limited.

States tailor their domestic violence statutes to deal with the effects of *adult* relationship violence. Thus despite similarities in the social dynamics of adult battering and adolescent dating violence, dramatic differences remain in the availability and use of legal remedies. Thus adolescent victims and perpetrators are in relationships that are not statutorily recognized, the statutes simply do not apply, and adolescents are left without legal recourse and without mandated or otherwise available services. To obtain services, minors must overcome numerous, often insurmountable, obstacles to receive protection from new domestic violence policies. The most difficult obstacles adolescents encounter in domestic violence policy making involve the number of ways statutes systematically exclude dating adolescents from coverage.

Statutes in 18 states restrict "domestic violence" to relationships between individuals who possess adult-like qualities that essentially render adolescents adults from the legal system's perspective. The most common of these requirements limits access to participants who have reached majority; only those with adult-like qualities can receive protection and benefit from resources available to victims of domestic violence. Before assistance can be offered, 10 states require that participants be 18[135] and 3 require the age of 16.[136] A few of these states expand protections to spouses or former spouses of any age.[137] Requiring adulthood by age or marital status severely limits the ability of adolescents to benefit from legislative mandates. The great majority of adolescents in abusive relationships cannot receive protections because they are dating or are not old enough.

Another exclusionary mechanism requires that victims be current or former cohabitants or spouses. These restrictions aim to protect marriage-type live-in relationships. Eleven states use a variation of this restriction.[138] For example, Louisiana requires that victims be spouses, former spouses, or currently living with the defendant as a spouse. Maryland requires a sexual relationship and residence with the respondent for at least 90 days before filing the petition. Kansas requires that abusers and victims reside (or formerly reside) together *and* that both have legal access to the residence. Other states take a broader approach. Oregon, for example, defines a domestic violence victim as a person "who is related by blood, marriage or intimate cohabitation at the present or has been related at some time in the past." Residency and marital requirements make it unlikely that the domestic violence protections offered in these states could protect adolescent dating couples. Although some adolescents fit into these categories, many do not. Again, these statutes do not aim to protect teenagers who are simply dating.

The requirement that victims be either current or former spouses or current or former cohabitants or be coparents also functions to exclude adolescents. These states expand the previous approaches through the extra inclusion of parenthood.[139] For example, Kentucky defines domestic violence as abuse between "family members or members of an unmarried couple." Unmarried couples include those who have children in common. Unlike previous exclusionary mechanisms that require current or former marriage, the 13 states that adopt this approach at least include a very distinct group of adolescents at risk for maltreatment: teenage mothers. This recognition is important, given the high number of unwed teenage parents and the higher rates of violence reported for pregnant adolescents.

Only 13 states allow for the *possibility* of including dating adolescents in their definitions of domestic violence.[140] By not requiring parenthood, marriage, cohabitation, or other adult requirements, these states seemingly offer the most protection to adolescents. Some explicitly include dating as a condition that gives victims access to the protections under domestic violence policies. These states even distinguish between dating stages. Some states simply include dating, courtship, and engagement; others require "substantive dating" or engagement; and others require only dating or some form of sexual or intimate relationship. New Hampshire allows for the broadest inclusion of victims who would be able to seek protection from abusive relationships. Under New Hampshire law, domestic violence victims are "persons currently or formerly involved in a romantic relationship, whether or not such a relationship was ever consummated."[141] The broad approach taken by New Hampshire is significant. New Hampshire allows for inclusion of couples who date as "friends," nonexclusive couples, and couples with varying degrees of intimacy. Other approaches leave discretion to officials. For example, North Dakota's statute reaches "any other person with a significant relationship to the abusing person as determined by the court."[142] Although subject to interpretation, these attempts to include dating relationships at least *allow* for the inclusion of adolescents.

In addition to allowing or prohibiting minors to petition for relief, states also restrict the extent to which minors can be the subject of civil actions brought under the umbrella of domestic violence statutes. Only 10 states expressly allow civil protection orders to be brought *against* minors. Even these 10 states vary in their expansion of protection. Only five states[143] allow civil protections to be initiated against all minors. Other states limit actions against minors who are 13 and older[144] or 16 and older.[145] Eight states[146] expressly *prohibit* parties from bringing civil protection orders against minors. The remaining states are silent, but given that minors tend to be excluded from bringing orders, there is no reason to believe that they could be subjected to actions.[147]

Even in states that allow orders to be brought against minors, the statutory remedies still remain underdeveloped. Failure to address how orders are to be enforced against minor defendants constitutes a major difficulty for those who seek protection. Important consequences emerge from the failure to clarify the nature of enforcement. For example, the statutes do not indicate whether minors can be held in criminal contempt, and if so, whether those cases must be adjudicated in juvenile court. If minors are adjudicated in juvenile courts, the proceedings and dispositions tend to be more informal and flexible than those of criminal courts. The result is that the current focus on holding batterers accountable by relying on aggressive law enforcement[148] is not, nor may not be, practicable for adolescents.

Arguably, minors would be adjudicated in criminal courts only when charges are brought in states with criminal domestic violence statutes.[149] This venue is important, given that some states define victims of domestic violence differently in civil and criminal statutes. For example, different age or relationship requirements may be imposed in civil or criminal statutes. Several states limit the use of criminal codes by imposing age or relationship requirements that they do not require for civil codes.[150] On the other hand, some states have more inclusive criminal codes.[151] Despite these differences, it remains unclear how, and even if, juveniles will be adjudicated.

Consequences of Current Recognition

As we have seen, domestic violence legislation fails to include adolescents within its recognized jurisdiction. The tendency of domestic violence policy making to ignore adolescent relationships continues, even despite remarkable similarities in the nature and extent of adolescent and adult relationship violence and increasing evidence that both victims and perpetrators of adolescent relationship violence are likely to experience similar circumstances in adulthood. This section briefly highlights important legal and policy consequences deriving from the failure to include adolescent relationships in domestic violence legislation.

The exclusion effectively prohibits adolescents from obtaining relief from legal developments that aim to curb the incidence of violence and assist victims through harnessing the powers and resources of the legal system. For example, adolescents cannot benefit from several statutory reforms, such as mandatory arrest policies in domestic violence situations, restraining order violations, and more stringent penalties for batterers. The exclusion also means that maltreated adolescents may not avail themselves of critical services organized and funded by the state to care for domestic violence victims, including domestic violence shelters and nonresidential programs, that provide referrals, medical assistance, and counseling.

The general failure to include adolescents in domestic violence service provisions ironically denies benefits and services to a group that arguably exhibits the greatest need. For example, juvenile courts, in which minors are likely to be adjudicated, do not have victim-oriented services. Juvenile courts aim to rehabilitate offenders.[152] The focus on offenders means that they are the ones viewed as in need of services—not their victims. The lack of victim services for adolescent victims contrasts sharply with the victim and witness programs district and city attorney's offices have to assist adult battered women.[153] Recognizing adolescent relationship violence would let adolescents benefit from adult victim services. In addition to assisting adults to deal with out-of-court issues, the programs would guide adolescents through court processes that, as research indicates, may be more difficult for adolescent victims than adults.[154]

Even if court-related services were available, however, their practical utility remains questionable because adolescents may not even get to the court system. The law generally considers minors legally incompetent. That is, minors usually need an adult representative, usually a guardian or parent, to initiate a lawsuit or defend against one. Thus minors usually may not file civil cases or request restraining orders unless they have a guardian *ad litem* or parent who represents them in court proceedings. Fewer than half of the states allow guardians, parents, and other interested parties to bring civil protective order actions on behalf of minors.[155] The way the statutes are framed, however, reduces the likelihood that even they could assist victims of relationship violence. The statutes assume that minors are covictims of family violence, rather than potentially victims from their own dating relationships. Yet most states offer guardian *ad litems,* mandate the use of simplified forms or offer other forms of assistance in filing petitions when *adults* are victimized by relationship violence.[156]

In addition to exacerbating the usual rigors of proceeding through the justice system, the failure to recognize adolescents victimization also has important repercussions in terms of how legal actors perceive adolescent relationship violence. The failure is especially noticeable in the criminal justice system—the system adolescents must rely on when civil protections remain inadequate. For example, the lack of victim advocacy and understanding of adolescent relationships increases the likelihood that state officials will not appropriately understand adolescent violence. Without training, state officials arguably fail to understand how family and friends may pressure adolescent victims to drop cases or to understand that victims may be threatened by very young batterers. The significance of specialized training for prosecutors and the need for support services is not speculative. Victim support services dramatically increase the number of adult relationship-related violence prosecutions.[157] Yet the reforms have excluded adolescents.

The negative effects of the failure to prosecute reverberate, both in terms of apprehension of perpetrators and in the determination of dispositional alternatives.[158] For example, domestic violence statutes clearly reflect a trend toward a "preferred arrest policy." However, simply instructing officers to favor arrests does not lead to straightforward responses. Formal policies must be coupled with police training to counter negative attitudes toward use of arrest, and the outcomes of arrests must reinforce that they are effective. The eventual reaction of the criminal justice system, particularly of prosecutors, must be considered in reform attempts. Likewise, the role of juvenile court judges must be considered: They may not take adolescent relationship violence seriously, an obstacle to receiving assistance that may be exacerbated by the relative informality of the juvenile court procedures. The new trend toward sensitizing justice-system personnel to adult domestic violence reflects the extent to which law enforcement attitudes may be problematic. Yet adolescents are excluded from these domestic violence innovations. The concern remains focused on adult violence.

Another concern relates to the need for complementary changes in the civil and criminal justice system as well as social support services. Even if agreement existed about the need to strengthen law and policy as it applies to adolescent relationship violence, the rampant lack or inadequacy of secondary support services clearly would undermine the utility of more aggressive law enforcement action. Legal intervention remains relatively impotent when not coupled by support services. In terms of domestic violence, the most notable example has been the recent move toward proarrest policies that are effective only when police departments are part of a coordinated community response.[159] Policies only succeed with maximum participation in their formulation, implementation, and evaluation; yet those affected by policies tend to be ignored.

Existing policies, then, highlight the need to coordinate community responses and make full use of social service as well as civil and criminal justice innovations if we are ever to assist adolescents victimized by battering partners. The current lack of services available to adolescents throughout either social service or justice systems reveals a heightened need for recognition. Even though adolescents may make use of traditional forms of relief, such as cooperating for criminal prosecutions, those protective mechanisms remain inadequate without other support services. For adolescents, those supports simply are nonexistent. Only one state explicitly confirms that the minority of an individual does not preclude them from domestic violence program service provisions.[160] Adolescents' needs go unrecognized as the legal system essentially fails to confront adolescent relationship violence. Adolescents are left unprotected and society fails to address the root of domestic violence.

Sexual Assault

Unlike the study and legal responses to relationship violence and sexual harassment, sexual assault has been the subject of more sustained research efforts and legal change. Social reformers have sought to recognize the harms women suffer and enhance victims' access to justice. Although several of these reforms remain controversial, they continue to expand the range of persons protected by law, prohibit a wider range of sexual conduct, encourage victims to report and seek protection, and improve the treatment of assault victims by systemic responses. This section examines the extent to which these reforms and changing societal perceptions appropriately consider the place adolescents occupy in society and the law as well as the extent to which reforms actually assist victimized adolescents.

Realities of Adolescent Sexual Assault

Although much of the research on sexual assault addresses the plight of women, adolescent victims have been part of the greater movement to recognize sexual violence. The study of sexual assault has been one of the most fruitful and controversial areas of research dealing with adolescent sexuality. Research currently proceeds in four related fronts: the extent to which adolescents are victims of sexual assault, victims' responses to assault, reasons for those responses, and the impact of legal reforms.

As with sexual harassment, researchers tend to agree about what constitutes sexual assault but continue to use different definitions that complicate efforts to determine the prevalence of and needed response to problem behaviors. However, definitions of sexual assault generally require the following conditions: sexual acts against the person's will or without the person's consent, and with force, threat of force, or manipulation. Although all emphasize the notion of nonconsensual sexual conduct, researchers tend to include a broad range of behaviors that may be regarded as threats to victims and include a wide range of sexual acts. Behaviors included in research range from unwanted sexual contact, sexual coercion, and unwanted sexual intercourse.[161]

Regardless of the disparity in what constitutes sexual assault, using coercive and unwanted contact as the basis for inclusion as victimization leads to relatively consistent findings. Approximately one quarter of women report having been victims of rape or attempted rape.[162] More than 80 to 95% of those assaults involve acquaintances. In the most methodologically sophisticated national survey of sexual practices, only 4% of women who have been "forced to do something sexual that they did not want to do" were victimized by strangers.[163] Although researchers may differ in terms of what they study, then, results tend to concur that a significant percentage of women will be sexually victimized and that the vast majority will be victimized by someone they know.

The findings from national samples particularly relate to young victims' experiences. Estimates reveal that adolescent victims may account for more than 50% of rapes.[164] As with most assaults, the vast majority of adolescent sexual victimizations takes place in acquaintance or dating situations. One recent national project found that 92% of adolescent sexual assault victims were attacked by someone they knew, and more than half actually were raped while on a date.[165]

Although national findings confirm previous research estimates derived from smaller samples,[166] several challenge the finding of high assault rates. For example, critics assert that women's own views of whether or not they have been raped should determine whether their experiences count as rape, rather than applying legal or other interpretations to women's descriptions of their experiences.[167] Recognition of a particular incident as rape remains somewhat subjective. Victims themselves often are unable to define assaults as rape, and that failure has been identified as a critical part of the phenomenon of acquaintance rape.[168] Given that the failure to recognize is part of rape, it is understandable that researchers have sought to use measures that include instances in which even victims fail to recognize the violence. The use of broader definitions of sexual assaults by acquaintances leads to several important results, not the least of which is the inclusion of boys' experiences that, when investigated, reveal rates of coerced sexual activity similar to those experienced by girls.[169]

Despite controversies, researchers generally do not doubt the significance of sexual assault and do support the conclusion that many assaults go undetected simply because research suggests that victims remain silent about their abuse. Approximately half of the victims who identify themselves as victimized by sexually coercive acts never tell anyone.[170] These estimates, however, range widely.[171] According to federal victimization surveys, more than 60% of rape victims and approximately one quarter of attempted rape victims report the crime. According to another national survey that used a legal definition of rape or attempted rape, only 4% of sexual assault victims reported to the police. Despite the range in findings, it does seem that the vast majority of sexual assault victims do not report their victimization.

Considerable research has attempted to explain adolescents' failure to report and the system's attempts to respond to that failure. Research advances several reasons victims do not seek official societal responses.[172] Victims fail to report because they are embarrassed to answer a stranger's intimate questions about the incident, ashamed and do not want anyone to know about it, afraid of retaliation from the assailant, and seek to conceal their own behavior prior to the incident. When offenders are known to the victims, victims are even less likely to report. Victims of acquaintance rape are more likely to not report because they blame themselves or do not regard the crime as a "real rape." In addition to those two noncontroversial findings, researchers also report that victims of acquaintance rape do not report because they wish to establish a relationship with the offender: In one study, nearly 40 percent of victims of date rape did not report assaults because they continued to date and wanted to maintain relationships with the offender. The subjective recognition of rape poses one of the most troubling issues in the acquaintance rape context.

The process by which victims define themselves as having been assaulted has been the subject of important research. The process involves what the victims go through to ultimately recognize that they were victimized and how the process fits into the broader context of the relationship between the perpetrator and victim. A major reason for the silence is that adolescents tolerate coercive behavior in general. High school students find coercive sexual intercourse permissible in a variety of situations, most notably if the partners had previously engaged in sexual activity or if the girls wore revealing clothing or if the girls were otherwise responsible for sexually exciting the perpetrator.[173] These perceptions are highlighted by one study that found one quarter of female research participants agreed that a woman who refuses a date's advances and then is forced to have sexual relations has not been raped and only one fifth of the participants strongly believed that she has been raped.[174] In addition to research about perceptions of rape, a large body of research relating to "rape myths" reveals how adolescents adhere to rape myths even without understanding the meaning of rape.[175] This research is supported by recent investigations that reveal how slightly more than one quarter of rape victims view their victimizations as rapes even when their experiences fall under the legal category of rape[176] and how half of rape victims who are physically coerced blame themselves for the rape.[177] Given that the potential victims would not view physically *coerced sex* as sexual assault, it is not surprising that the same forces influence offenders and allow those who have raped to not believe that they have either been sexually coercive or committed a crime.[178]

Researchers attribute the silence about abuse, failure to recognize the actual experience of assault, and the broader culture of acceptance to social stereotypes that govern gendered social relationships. The major stereotype that arguably forms the basis of the abuse is one in which males dominate, control, and use power while women do the opposite.[179] Each gender expects disparate levels of aggressiveness and victimization and conditions those involved in violence do not even notice coercion. The adolescent culture accepts rape, an acceptability exacerbated by confusion that occurs in the context of paradoxical and adversarial expectation related to girls playing the role of "gatekeeper" and boys the "initiator" role surrounding sexual activity. As with battering relationships, sexual assault seemingly derives from the frustration of the desire to fulfill developmental normative prescriptions that is the principal cause of courtship violence. From this perspective, assault simply fulfills normal cultural dictates for intimacy during courtship and dating.

Research investigating the culture of acceptance and gender relations report important findings that go beyond highlighting how assaultive acts are silenced. Although the main research focus stresses the significance of gender and power dynamics, it is important to consider that males can be coerced by females. One study found 35% of females and 21% of males reported being victims of sexual coercion.[180] Another recent study found that 79% of females and 52% of males have been coerced sexually at least once by a partner.[181] The findings mirror more subtle coercion such as telling lies to have sex: Nearly half of the males and more than half of the females report having been lied to for sex.[182] These findings urge us to rethink the nature of sexual coercion and consent, let alone the causes and consequences of rape.

The second major finding involves the rampant distortion of nonverbal sexual cues. Perceptions of those cues vary, particularly by gender, age, ethnicity, attitudes toward sex, education, socioeconomic status, and other important variables.[183] The research reveals several consistent examples. One of the most consistent findings in the sexual communication literature is that males live in a more sexualized world than do females.[184] Likewise, research generally reveals that males read more sexual interest and intent into women's behavior than women interpret or intend.[185] In addition, men are more likely to attribute sexual connotations to mundane dating behavior than women are.[186] Finally, perhaps more significantly, males generally discount the truthfulness of women's rejections.[187] These findings highlight how sexual dating violence may stem from overconformity to certain sexualized roles in the socialization process.

The significance of variations in nonverbal contexts implicit in sexual courting operates at several points in responses to sexual assault. Although the process may be at work at dates' misinterpretations, the misperceptions continue and affect social reforms. Research suggests that social responses continue to abide by the same values that place adolescents at risk for perpetration and victimization—for example, juries may misinterpret the significance of the nonverbal context of the situation when attempting to discern the parties' intentions.[188] These findings have led commentators to propose that, although individuals operate as though rape is readily identifiable, mythic and stereotypical images of rape guide reactions to coercive situations and interpretations of those reactions. Given these forces, many rapes are viewed as miscommunications rather than a form of rape.

The third major finding relates to those who make "bad" victims. From the prosecution's point of view, acquaintance rapes are most difficult to prosecute and win if the victim engaged in consensual sex with the defendant at some time before the alleged rape or if the victim behaved in ways that challenge traditional norms of female propriety.[189] Researchers report several factors that make some victims less likely to be viewed as victims who may obtain redress. Common examples include engagement in promiscuous, runaway, or truant behavior. In addition, drinking heavily or wearing "sexy attire" contributes to difficulty in system responses.[190] Given these findings, it is not surprising to find that many scholars maintain that the reluctance of rape victims to prosecute largely results from social and official skepticisms toward victims of rape. Yet although these stereotypes may increase the likelihood that the victimization will not be addressed properly, it is important to place the failure of responses in context. Even though sexual assault may involve bad victims and present enormous difficulties in efforts to respond by using the criminal justice system, the system does not necessarily have better attrition rates for other felonious crimes.[191] Likewise, the differences in case attrition between crimes committed by strangers and crimes committed by acquaintances is not unique to sexual assault.[192]

The fourth major finding relates to informal responses to victims. Emerging literature suggests that the extent to which victims view themselves as assault victims depends on their personal network's reactions. Whether or not they have supportive friends who reassure them that they were not to blame and who help define the victimization as rape tends to be highly influential. Those whose friends interpret the experience as loving unanimously find that they were not victims of rape.[193] Thus social groups' support may not only lead to victimization in the manner in which it supports stereotypic attitudes and behaviors that may lead to rape, social support groups also help define the victimization experience.

In summary, large numbers of adolescents are sexually victimized. Contrary to popular perceptions of "real rapes," acquaintances, mainly dates, are the major source of victimization. That source of victimizations contributes several problems to efforts that address adolescents' victimization. Investigations reveal that victims, perpetrators, and others who may have knowledge of the behavior fail to understand the actions' coerciveness. Coercive behavior is interpreted as normal, as part of sexual relationships and gender-role development. As with the previous behaviors, then, it is important to consider the extent and nature of assault by intimate partners and the role it plays in the sexual maltreatment of adolescents.

Adolescent Sexual Assault and the Law

The current sociolegal response to adolescent sexual assault can be conceived in the context of statutes, now enacted in all states, that address sexual assault. These responses, previously viewed as the crime of rape, have been the subject of rapid reforms that adopt one of two approaches. The first approach reforms evidentiary laws and changes systemic responses to increase victims' willingness to report and pursue legal redress. The second effort changes the substance of rape laws and redefines the nature of rape itself to change both societal and legal system's views of what constitutes coercive sexual behavior. These two waves of reform continue to significantly affect the current character of rape law as it applies to adolescents.

Regulating System Responses

The first major effort to reform rape laws sought to reform difficulties in proving the occurrence of the crime. Reforms sought to counter the prevailing belief that complainants' credibility in rape cases were inherently more suspect and more subject to fabrication than in other cases. Reforms entailed removing from consideration several actions deemed relevant to determining the credibility or consent to the sexual acts. Courts and legislatures introduced several mechanisms designed to differentiate between consensual and nonconsensual sex. For example, most states previously required independent corroboration of the incident by witnesses and physical evidence of rape. Given the difficulty of producing a witness to a crime that typically takes place in private, states that strictly enforced this requirement exhibited comparatively low conviction rates.[194] Limits also now have been placed on the need for corroboration of the victim's testimony. In addition, laws now place limits on the need to prove resistance, the need to provide "fresh complaints" that immediately followed the rape, and the need to admit evidence of victim's prior sexual history.

The most notable and controversial example of reform efforts involves rape shield laws. This issue in the debate over rape legislation reform involves whether a victim's behavior prior to the assault has any probative value to the question as to whether rape occurred. Traditionally courts allowed evidence that reported the victim's past to determine the credibility of the complainant's character or whether she consented to the sexual acts. The new effort aimed to eradicate these archaic evidentiary rules to encourage rape victims to report crimes and end the practice of putting the *victim* on trial. Although all but three states have adopted some form of rape shield statute,[195] existing rape shield statutes vary widely in scope and procedural detail. To date, these statutes typically fall into four approaches that reject the previous automatic admissibility of the victims' previous sexual behavior.

The most dominant model follows Michigan's approach, adhered to by more than half the states.[196] Michigan's statute generally excludes all evidence of a victim's sexual history, but allows limited exceptions to its rule. The exceptions include evidence of the victim's "past sexual conduct with the actor" and "instances of sexual activity showing the source of origin of semen, pregnancy, or disease."[197] However, to allow sexual history evidence under either exception, a judge must weigh whether the evidence's probative value is not outweighed by its potential inflammatory or prejudicial nature.[198]

The second most dominant model for rape shield statutes follows the Arkansas approach.[199] Fourteen states trace this approach that provides for an *in camera* hearing (typically in the judge's chamber) that allows for judicial discretion.[200] The discretion the trial judge uses involves the traditional balancing test of whether the evidence's probative value outweighs its prejudicial effect. If the probative value prevails, then the evidence is admissible. Unlike the previous group of statutes, the judge weighs the probative value of admitting the evidence of the victim's sexual history against the degree of prejudice without any guidelines about what evidence should be relevant.[201]

The Federal Rules of Evidence provide the third model for six states.[202] This model is similar to the Michigan approach that renders evidence of an alleged victim's sexual history inadmissible, subject to limited exceptions. Federal Rule of Evidence 412 contains a broad exception for instances in which prohibiting the accused from introducing evidence would violate the accused's constitutional rights. Thus although the statute generally provides that evidence of an alleged victim's sexual history is inadmissible, the rule allows evidence of specific instances of the victim's past sexual conduct with the accused to show that the victim consented;[203] specific instances of the victim's sexual conduct with a person other than the accused when introduced to show that the accused was not the source of semen or injury;[204] and specific instances of the victim's sexual conduct when the Constitution requires it to be admitted.[205]

The final type of rape shield statute follows the California model.[206] Seven states allow evidence of the alleged victim's sexual history to be introduced for certain issues, but not others.[207] This approach uniquely divides past sexual history into two categories. The statute distinguishes between evidence that goes toward proving the defense of consent and evidence offered to attack the credibility of the accuser. Under the California model, the statute generally does not allow evidence of past sexual behavior offered for the issue of consent but admits it to attack a victim's credibility.[208] For example, four of those states allow evidence of the victim's sexual history so long as it is not introduced to show that the victim consented.[209] Two of the states exclude evidence of the victim's sexual conduct when introduced only to show the victim's lack of credibility.[210]

It is important to note that on two occasions the Supreme Court heard challenges to rape shield laws. In *Michigan v. Lucas,*[211] the defendant failed to inform the court of his intent to introduce evidence of the alleged victim's past sexual relations as required by the Michigan rape shield statute. Under Michigan law, the defendant was required to file written notice if he wished to introduce evidence of a victim's past sexual conduct within 10 days after arraignment. The lower court had held that the preclusion of evidence relating to previous sexual relations between a victim and a defendant was unconstitutional if founded solely on a defendant's failure to give timely notice as required by the statute. The Supreme Court found that the lower court's ruling created a per se rule that held as unconstitutional any attempt to use the notice requirement to preclude evidence of past sexual conduct. The Court then held that the notice and hearing requirements of the statute served a legitimate state interest and failure to comply justified preclusion. However, the Court refused to decide the larger question of whether such preclusion would violate a defendant's Sixth Amendment right to confrontation of witnesses, choosing instead to leave the determination to the state court. The Court noted that the "defendant's ability to confront adverse witnesses and present a defense is diminished. This does not necessarily render the statute unconstitutional."[212] A judge must weigh the item's relevance and probative value and then its prejudicial effect. The problem, of course, is that judicial discretion rules and trial judges, as they do in all cases, retain wide latitude to limit defendant's cross-examination of witnesses.

State discretion, though, does have its limits, which regards the need for strict statutory guidelines. In *Olden v. Kentucky,*[213] the Court reversed the decision of the Kentucky Court of Appeals that had upheld a trial court's discretion in excluding evidence. In that case, the defendant had sought to demonstrate that the alleged victim consented to intercourse, that she had a motive to fabricate charges, and that the prosecution witness cohabitated with the complainant. The trial court had excluded the evidence that the woman, who was White, was cohabitating with a Black man. The defendant wanted to introduce evidence that she fabricated the story so that her boyfriend would not find out that she had cheated on him. The court refused to admit the evidence because showing that the victim was cohabitating with a Black man would be highly prejudicial. The Supreme Court held that the exclusion was not based on rape shield law; the court had excluded the proffered evidence because of its sexual nature but the potential biracial evidence led the Supreme Court to conclude that the defendant's right of confrontation outweighed the state's interest in excluding prejudicial evidence.

Although both cases touch on issues concerning rape shield statutes, it is important to note that the Court has not ruled on the statutes' facial validity. *Olden* dealt with prejudice as a result of the biracial nature of the evidence involved and *Lucas* dealt with procedural rather than substantive aspects of rape shield laws. Neither decision addressed the constitutional validity of precluding evidence in a rape prosecution of past sexual conduct between a victim and a defendant when the issue of consent is involved. Yet both cases indicate two noteworthy points. First, they show that once a state interest has been established, trial judges have the right to sanction defendants who fail to comply by excluding all evidence offered in violation of the rule. Second, the Court consistently supports legislative efforts to remove power from the judiciary and holds that evidence specifically precluded by a rape shield statute should not be admitted and that some judicial discretion must be allowed, as was found in *Lucas.* By doing so, the Court recognizes how rape shield statutes serve the legitimate interest of protecting sexual assault victims from unfair invasions of privacy and supports legislative findings that such protections encourage sexual assault victims to report assaults, reduce gender bias in the courtroom, and respond to crimes that otherwise would go unaddressed.

The most innovative and recent moves in law and policy that address adolescent sexual assault involve attempts to rethink what constitutes consent. Some jurisdictions have addressed issues of consent by ignoring physical force and propose that the force inherent in sexual penetration meets the threshold requirement absent consent. Under this approach, the legal system finds that sexual assault occurs when the act of penetration was made without affirmative and freely given permission of the victim.[214] This makes for an important move. Traditionally courts have required victims' resistance, even when elements of the crime did not include resistance or force.[215] These reforms reflect the need to rethink burdens of proof and facilitate the ability to bring actions, particularly when parties were acquaintances.[216] These attempts, however, have yet to serve as models.

In summary, reformers aim to protect the privacy of victims and encourage victims to seek legal redress. These efforts ultimately seek to protect all women's autonomy by finding that a woman's sexual history does not dictate her willingness to reject other sexual activity. From this light and despite impressive reform efforts, the reforms are not really revolutionary, they aim to remove irrelevant and prejudicial evidence and, as the federal rules and several states explicitly emphasize, defendants still retain broad constitutional rights.

Redefining the Nature of Rape

Rather than focusing on reform to prove rape, the second wave questioned the very nature of rape itself. States essentially have abolished the crime of "rape" and graduated offenses into different degrees of sexual assault. These graded offenses include, for example, a focus on force, age differentials, nature of sexual acts, and the relationship between offender and victim. These reforms aim to draw attention to objective circumstances that would indicate the absence of consent and render unnecessary the need to prove victims' resistance or consent.

These changes are relevant for adolescents for two reasons. First, when sexual activity involves violence or lack of consent, sexual assault law makes the criminal justice system available for response. Second, in the absence of issues that involve coercion, force, or lack of consent, the law may still aim to protect adolescents through statutory rape laws. As discussed in chapter 3, states do not adopt a uniform approach. Regardless of the language and nature of protections, all states forbid certain sexual acts with adolescents. The manner in which states prohibit sexual interactions varies considerably and in three major ways: the nature of the prohibited assaults, those that the offenses apply to, and the punishment.

Statutes define sexual assault in three ways. Some statutes focus on penetration, such as sodomy, intercourse, and the use of objects.[217] Others broadly define sexual contact as an offense,[218] including the touching of intimate parts through clothing.[219] A third group of statutory offenses defines sexual assault by broadly prohibiting taking "immodest, immoral, or other indecent liberties" with minors.[220] Statutes generally combine these forms of assaults, although some simply use the third broad category.

Statutes impose strict liability largely based on the victim's age, a combination between the offender and victim's age, and the act. For example, in most states some minors may consent to sexual penetration with an adult, with most states placing the most common age of consent at 16, although they range from 14 to 18.[221] Some minors may also consent to sexual contact with adults, and the age at which they can do so tends to be uniformly lower than the age they may consent to sexual penetration, ranging from under 13 to under 18.[222] Finally, most states include a requirement of an age difference between the actors; and these offenses generally vary according to the nature of the offense.[223]

Statutes also vary in terms of punishment. If the minor is over 14 or 15, the penalty for contact offenses is more likely to be a misdemeanor; if the minor is younger, the penalty is more likely to be a felony.[224] Offenses involving penetration follow similar variations. Offenses that involve penetration may only constitute misdemeanors if perpetrated against older minors.[225] However, statutes generally provide that similar offenses become felonies if perpetrated against younger adolescents or those related to, or under the authority of, perpetrators.[226] Thus sexual penetration offenses are uniformly treated more seriously than sexual contact offenses, and older minors receive less protection to the extent that offenses against them receive less opprobrium.

Variations in punishment and prohibitions, although seemingly unjust for protecting some adolescents more than others, reflect attempts to deal with adolescent development. Statutory sexual assault laws aim to permit consensual sex for older minors and provide increased protection for younger adolescents. These goals are potentially contradictory and the law seeks to provide for them by graduating offenses, ages, and punishments.

Implications of Current Reforms

Unlike other areas of sexual victimization reviewed at the beginning of this chapter, sustained reform efforts deal with the sexual assault of adolescents. The legislative reforms and developments in legal doctrine present important developments. The efforts express, for example, a policy that the legal system should respect the privacy of assault victims and not force them to endure more violence in the courtroom. Likewise, reforms affirm that the victims' interests could be so significant as to infringe on defendants' rights to present their defenses. These developments reflect not only the extent to which society has moved to address the problem of adolescent sexual victimization, it also reflects the extent to which laws allow for addressing adolescents' needs. Systems can respond and place more priority on adolescents' needs, develop their rights, and aim to refashion systems to take adolescent victimization more seriously.

Although it is important not to minimize the importance of existing reform efforts, the ultimate significance of the reform remains debatable in terms of their impact.[227] Several findings support propositions that reforms have not been as fruitful as anticipated. These findings are important to consider, because they reveal the limits of law reform, even when states take the victimization seriously and enact comprehensive legislation.

Recall that a major rationale for reform was to encourage the reporting of rapes and to increase the use of prosecutorial efforts to ensure that sexual assaults would constitute a crime that could have real consequences for offenders. Although this constitutes a legitimate state interest, reforms have not necessarily met this objective. Studies indicate, for example, that rape shield statutes and other reforms that changed the substance of rape law have had little effect on reporting rates of sexual assault.[228] In addition, although the performance of the justice system in rape cases may have improved in the manner in which they treat victims, legal reforms generally have had little or no effect on the outcomes of rape cases or the proportions of rapists who are prosecuted or convicted.[229] Recent studies of rape-case processing report sharp case attrition for sexual assault crimes,[230] and as the Senate Judiciary Committee recently reported, 98% of rape victims "never see their attacker caught, tried and imprisoned."[231]

Second, despite reforms, sexual assault by acquaintances has very low rates of arrest and even lower conviction rates.[232] Sexual assaults perpetrated by acquaintances, although the most common form of sexual assault involving victims of all ages, still are viewed with suspicion and resist legal mandates aimed at reform.[233] These assaults typically involve less overt physical violence and result in less physical signs of abuse: Assaults by current or previous boyfriends or husbands are as violent and physically traumatic as assaults by strangers.[234] Because assaults involving acquaintances often do not include weapons or forceful struggle, victims are assumed to be able to prevent the attack and are thought to "want" or "deserve" their infliction.[235] Familiarity and wanting to be accepted by aggressors implies consent. Thus although efforts have been made to address sexual assault, much of the efforts have been aimed at "real rape" and have not necessarily addressed the more common forms of rape.

The third reason for the apparent limits of rape law reform is that despite progress, several jurisdictions have not embraced developments. For example, despite efforts to rethink the nature of rape and coercion, we already have seen that states generally do not criminalize nonconsensual sexual assault without force. Likewise, for example, the most common reform, rape shield laws, are consistent for their variation in protections. Most shield laws permit evidence of the victim's prior conduct with the accused, even though most other sexual history evidence is excluded. Likewise, statutes frequently differentiate evidence that attacks credibility and evidence that proves consent. Yet the forms of evidence tend to be functional equivalents: Evidence that establishes consent by the complainant will simultaneously impeach her credibility and evidence that impeaches her credibility will raise the perception of consent. Thus in instances in which sexual history is likely to prejudice, the law allows its entry into trial processes.

The fourth reason for the limits of reform is that, even *with* the reforms there are ways around legal mandates that aggressively respond to sexual assault. Three loopholes in the rape shield laws illustrate the limitations of reform. First, although rape shield laws prevent the use of sexual history evidence to show consent, sexual history may be allowed to show that the defendant mistakenly believed that the accuser consented and thus that the alleged offender lacked the requisite intent for rape.[236] The mistake-of-fact defense provides a back door entrance for evidence of a rape victim's sexual history. Honest and reasonably mistaken consent exonerate the defendant, and such mistakes may derive from the victim's prior sexual experiences to the extent that a reasonable person in the defendant's situation would not realize that the victim did not consent to sex. Second, and as recently found in a case of acquaintance rape, rape shield laws could not preclude evidence presented in support of a defense theory that the victim's prior sexual history may have influenced her decision to pursue fabricated rape charges, even though both parties agree that the victim said "no" throughout the sexual encounter.[237] Third, victim's clothing are admitted to show how "provocative" dress may reflect the mental state of both the victim and defendant. Such evidence is admitted if it would allow for a reasonable person to assume consent or that the victim actually consented. Alternatively, the same evidence may be used to impeach the complainant's testimony.[238] All approaches preserve the traditional "victim as suspect" approach to rape that modern statutes seek to remove from legal processes. These defenses are more likely to be permitted because of the recent move to eliminate resistance as a requirement of the crime of rape.[239]

The fifth reason efforts remain less effective than hoped is that courts continue to circumvent restrictions on their discretionary powers to accommodate the competing claims of defendants to introduce relevant evidence. The major impediment to reform is the consistent and strong recognition of the right of criminal defendants to present an adequate defense, especially regarding consent in a rape prosecution. Defendants' right may bow to accommodate other legitimate interests in the criminal trial process.[240] However, the legal system limits the extent to which a defendant will not be allowed to mount a defense. The Supreme Court has found the fundamental nature of due process in a criminal adjudication as the fair opportunity to defend against the state's accusations. The right to examine witnesses brought against the defendant, the right to offer testimony, and the right to be represented by counsel all have been found fundamental to the assurance of a fair trial under due process. If the rule of evidence prevents the introduction of evidence crucial to a defense, the rule must yield to the constitutional right of confrontation and due process of law. The defendant's rights to present relevant testimony restricts reform efforts.

The sixth reason for the limited success is that the reforms that have been made attempt to eliminate the most overt biases. The removal of biases leads to the misleading and superficial appearance that rape laws are now administered in a neutral and fair manner, an appearance that makes the legal system fail to confront the deeper problems created by the traditional perception that cause sexual assaults and allow them to continue. The acceptance of violence continues to color the manner in which rape laws are understood and implemented.[241]

When it comes to minors, the failure to protect is even greater, even though it is generally thought that laws automatically protect minors from all forms of rape. Statutory rape laws that do impose strict liability on those who would engage in sexual relations with minors provide a particularly powerful example of the failure to protect. Despite popular perceptions that these laws protect well, they fail because they essentially *exclude* peers from liability when those involved fall within statutory age limits.[242] For example, if the victim and perpetrator are both 14, or the perpetrator is two years older, their sexual interactions tend to be permissible in the absence of overt coercion. The rationale for excluding peers is that exclusion properly allows for sexual encounters and the difficulties that would arise if there were attempts to control voluntary sexual relationships of all minors. Yet the gap allows for not responding to certain forms of assault.

Admittedly, it often is difficult for victims, perpetrators, let alone legal systems, to distinguish between assault, aggression, seduction, and passion.[243] Despite the apparent need for such flexibility, three arguments may be used to challenge the statutes that exclude peer liability. First, adolescents' peer relationships may involve coercion that goes undetected. Peer pressure, the desire to be accepted, and other reasons for sexual interactions have been challenged as inappropriate.[244] Second, the existence of statutory rape law may result in the failure to recognize even overt coercion; coercion may be tolerated and seen as normal to adolescent sexual relationships.[245] Adolescents still interpret issues of coerciveness along prevailing myths, such as the belief that girls are sexually provocative, that provocative behavior generates consent, that females are naturally passive, and that girls are not to be trusted. Third, the existence of special laws for adolescents contributes to the failure to enact reforms that protect victims as much as those that protect adults. A prime example is the continued existence of the promiscuity defense that, in some jurisdictions, applies to juveniles but generally is improper when applied to adults.[246]

Sociolegal responses reflect the difficulty of responding to abuses suffered from acquaintances and adolescent offenders. It remains difficult to respond to the variety of ways adolescents may be coerced into unwanted sexual activity. Even when the coerciveness could be recognized, there remains the difficulty of addressing the prevailing culture of acceptance. Unlike developments that have dealt with sexual abuse perpetrated by adults, this area of law generally has not proposed and enacted efforts to minimize or negate the biases that would protect minors. Unaddressed cultural attitudes toward coercive sexuality perpetuate misconceptions of adolescents' lives and allow the practices to continue. Particularly problematic is the failure to respond more properly to consensual sexual activity. Efforts to criminalize sexual activity devoid of aggression continue even though the law also recognizes that minors have a right to privacy in intimate relations and that mature minors may be capable of consent to medical procedures related to their sexual activity.[247] The legal system simultaneously treats adolescents as mature and immature. The failure to respond appropriately continues despite rapid and extensive law reform relating to sexual assault.

Opportunities for Reform

This section discusses alternative responses to adolescents' sexual victimization that go beyond existing trends in legal reform. The analysis aims to increase access to services and addresses challenges that alternatives unduly extend the rights of adolescents at the expense of parental rights and social interests. Again, the discussion champions a participatory model that focuses on the need to include adolescents in their own protection not only in a formal legal system but also in societal arrangements that otherwise foster exclusion and victimization. Acknowledging adolescents' perspectives, and taking them seriously, means undertaking structural changes among parent–adolescent, adult–adolescent, and community–adolescent relationships.

Although adolescent jurisprudence has yet to recognize, in a broad manner, the right of adolescents to protections from sexual victimization, adolescents' place in the legal system could be expanded to recognize the right to protection. That recognition, however, would be subject to considerable criticisms; but the most significant concerns could be addressed by implementing realistic policy making and recognizing that adolescent's rights need not conform with adult models. The significance of the need to recognize the right requires elaborating on the precise nature of the right, delineating responses to likely objections, and envisioning alternative approaches to legal recognition of adolescents' own rights to protection from sexual violence.

Recognizing Adolescents' Right to Protection

Given the current invisibility of sexual victimization and the general lack of appropriate legal responses to the victimization of adolescents, small changes could dramatically enhance opportunities for intervention and prevention of sexual violence and the more overt forms of violence that contribute to victimization. To ensure greater protection, the most straightforward response would be to recognize adolescents' independent legal right to protection from maltreatment. Although commentators have yet to consider this position, the proposal is neither entirely unimaginable, impracticable, nor too radical to be worthy of deliberation.

Existing statutes and policies already recognize several of the forms of violence related to sexual victimization. Those legal mandates, however, essentially limit their reach to protecting and offering assistance to adults. Given the limited jurisdiction of existing mandates, one simple solution would be to expand the reach of existing legal protections and offer relief to all individuals victimized by sexual violence, regardless of where they occur and regardless of the age of victims and perpetrators. Three example are illustrative. First, greater access to legal intervention could be had by granting adolescents the explicit right to bring actions against other minors or adults. Such reform efforts aimed to improve adolescents' access to justice are not outside the realm of possibility, because some states already have bestowed on adolescents increased access to courts. In the context of relationship violence, for example, two of six states[248] that *explicitly* allow teenagers 16 and older to initiate actions on their own also have domestic violence statutes that arguably include adolescents who are in dating or sexually intimate relationships. Second, relationships that involve "noncoercive" sexual behavior could still be subject to legal intervention. The intervention, for example and as for adults in some jurisdictions, would require affirmative and voluntary consent to sexual interactions. Likewise, instead of focusing solely on the criminal justice system and punishing perpetrators, adolescents could be offered greater access to services that would help them cope with assault. Third, institutions that serve adolescents could develop policies that enumerate improper conduct, provide adolescents access to redress within that institution, educate adolescents about policies, and aim to provide adolescents with the skills to tailor their conduct to responsible behavior. Again, institutions dealing with adults have the obligation to develop and follow such policies, and few that deal with adolescents have policies and suffer little consequences when they do not. Providing adolescents with independent rights would ensure the institution of policies, recognition of adolescent maltreatment, and redress when systems fail to respond.

Considerable research buttresses the legal proposition that adolescents would benefit from the right to obtain protection on their own behalf. For example, as discussed earlier, adolescents in violent relationships and harassing environments could benefit from adult guidance, research consistently reveals that adolescents remain reluctant to involve adults. Indeed, the currently ignored rate of adolescent relationship violence and sexual harassment indicate well the undoubted failure of adults to protect adolescents. In addition to the more immediate benefit adolescents would derive from increased direct access to legal protection and services, other considerations highlight the need to offer adolescents greater access to protection. Statutes are more than practical tools to combat relationship violence. The recognition reinforces that adolescents know they can be victims and assistance is available to them. As we have seen, to address violence in abusive and assaultive relationships, adolescents must first combat "normative confusion" and realize the destructiveness of their relationships. Legal recognition would do considerably more than help victims realize the devastating impact of the abusive behavior. Just as important, legal recognition would help combat fears that prevent adolescents from seeking assistance. The recognition also would do more than send proper messages to victims; perpetrators also would receive a powerful message that the state disapproves. The disapproval could either lead to punishment or an offer of assistance to stop abusive behaviors. Beyond these important considerations, the legal recognition would indicate an important and necessary shift from defining sexual victimization as a personal or relational problem to recognizing harassing and assaultive behavior as a violent social problem and a broader human rights issue.

Although straightforward, a more comprehensive effort to provide adolescents direct access to legal and other social services that may be used by adults who are victimized by sexual violence would involve a radical turn in current adolescent jurisprudence. Any recognition of adolescents' rights to protection remains complicated and not without reverberating consequences. The recognition would mean more than recognizing the importance of adolescents' rights. Legally, the recognition essentially translates into the need to recognize and offer protection to alternative forms of relationships, rather than the currently privileged marital relationship. Although offering adolescents protection from sexual violence may not mean that all alternative relationships must be recognized, it does emphasize and require that all forms of violent relationships be addressed and that all citizens have a right to protection from violence, regardless of the form their relationships take.

Countering Objections to Adolescents' Right to Protection

Proposals that aim to give adolescents greater access to legal protections undoubtedly would encounter considerable resistance. Traditionally, efforts to offer minors greater legal autonomy and advance their civil rights have been challenged on grounds that increasing a minor's autonomy may cause irreparable harm to the child and may intrude impermissibly on parental rights to protect, control, and guide their own children's lives. The criminal and civil justice systems must also deal with similar concerns and with the additional fear that minors are more prone to fabrication. Although these arguments may be persuasive in some contexts, these common objections are unpersuasive in arenas that would confront the victimization of adolescents.

Fears of Adolescent Autonomy

The concern that including adolescents in efforts to prevent sexual, physical, as well as emotional violence would grant adolescents unfettered autonomy remains unwarranted. Three factors reveal the groundless nature of the fear. First, in the context of obtaining court protection, adolescents' rights to autonomy do not go unchecked. For example, protection orders against battering partners require judicial review. Second, in the context of obtaining nonjudicial support services, such as some involving schools and mental health services, several legal rules operate to give minors access to those services. For example, adolescents may have access to these services either because there is no need for parental notification (e.g., when parental rights are not infringed) or because their own special status gives them access. In the context of sexual and gendered violence, the problem tends to be that the services are simply nonexistent. Third, there is a fear that adolescents simply are not able to exercise good judgment. To the extent research remains inconclusive, as revealed by research on adolescent judgment and temperament,[249] sound policy would suggest that society err on the side of greater protection from *harm,* not from the use of the legal system.

Given that the usual fear that adolescents would be given unfettered autonomy remains unsound in the context of offering them greater legal protection from sexual victimization, it is clear that a first step in rethinking efforts would be to move toward increasing availability of services through the expansion of adolescents' legal rights. The efforts would seek to ensure mere access to actual availability and provision of services. The provision of such services is not within the realm of hopeless idealism. Schools, for example, could offer some of these services in classes and other opportunities already made available to students. Innovative research addressing school violence highlights the extent to which schools may be reformed.[250] Rather than discouraging and fearing adolescents' autonomy, these efforts recognize and attempt to capitalize on it to protect adolescents from violence.

Fears of Unjustly Restricting Parental Rights

Yet another traditional argument against expanding adolescents' rights rests on the parents' own right to control their children's upbringing. The right finds considerable support from numerous constitutional principles as society clings to the notion that parents are the primary caretakers of their children. Social science evidence and sound legal principles indicate that the fear that this venerable right will be inappropriately infringed is groundless. Indeed, if anything, the legal system's complacency regarding the sexual maltreatment of adolescents results from notions of parental rights deemed the very foundation of social order.

Regardless of the cultural attachment to childhoods determined by parental caretaking, social scientists continue to document the influences and need of communal institutions (e.g., schools) and informal peer groupings in determining successful child development outcomes.[251] Adolescence is characterized by a general detaching from families. Although adolescents rely on families for important sources of support, detaching from families places some adolescents in precarious positions. As we have seen, victims typically resist requesting assistance from their families, even when relationships take abusive turns.

Feelings of shame and helplessness keep adolescents from seeking assistance from familial sources, and adolescents who do seek assistance may not be taken seriously. The adolescent period provides an environment conducive to maltreatment simply because adolescents naturally detach themselves from familial matters. Bestowing adolescents with greater individual rights simply would reflect the needs and the realities of adolescent life.

As venerable as parental rights may be, parents' rights clearly lose their legitimacy when adolescents are subjected to violence. The public's interest in protecting adolescents and preventing escalating injury arguably outweighs parental rights. Just as states may intrude in adolescents' lives to protect them from parental decision making (e.g., as with abortion decisions and suicide prevention), states have an obligation to infringe on parental rights in the name of protecting their children, especially when parents fail to do so.

Allowing for intrusion does not mean that parental rights should be ignored. Practicalities require recognizing parental rights simply because ignoring them would allow parents to shirk responsibilities. For example, emancipation is a problematic alternative for most adolescents. Emancipation usually requires adolescents to have independent sources of income, does not address the minor's need for parental emotional supports, and does not address the underlying message regarding blame and responsibility.[252] The intervention, however, does mean that, like the judicial by-pass needed to protect adolescents' rights in other areas, legal systems should afford protection to those minors in danger and minors not willing to seek assistance if certain people need to be informed. Although adolescents caught in violent relationships, subject to harassing behavior, or victimized by acquaintance rape could benefit from parental or adult guidance, research consistently reveals that minors remain reluctant to involve adults. Indeed, the currently ignored rate of maltreatment in adolescence indicates well the failure of adults to protect adolescents.

Fears of False Accusations and Overwhelming Social Service Provisions

As suggested previously, several fear that false accusations will rise if legal systems offer victims greater access. Two areas of victimization research, child abuse allegations and sexual assault prosecutions, suggest that the fear is unwarranted. In terms of improper child abuse allegations and although some accusations and prosecutions may be unwarranted, the system has set protections against false accusations: The criminal and civil justice systems remain oriented toward providing defendants extensive due process rights even when balanced against society's strong interest in protecting victims from the rigors of legal intervention.[253] Likewise, children's motivational disincentives to claiming abuse at least counter the perceived incentives to accuse; and those in whom victims are most likely to confide, mothers, have many of the same motivations as their children to deny abuse.[254] For example, abused children are actually unlikely to disclose abuse because of shame, fear of reprisals, and the impact of accusations on loved ones (e.g., approximately 25% of those with medical evidence that indicates sexually transmitted diseases do not disclose abuse);[255] and mothers' reactions to disclosers tend to involve disbelief and a substantial proportion of nonoffending mothers (ranging from 55 to 70%) remain ambivalent, unsupportive, or hostile.[256] In addition, it remains true that children and adolescents do not fabricate more than adults do.[257]

In terms of sexual assault accusations, the fear of false accusations prevails despite strong evidence that false rape reports are no higher than for other crimes—5%—and the traumas inflicted by the judicial system guard against frivolous accusations.[258] There is also the general tendency to believe that teenagers, especially those who become pregnant, will be more prone to "cry rape." Again, however, evidence suggests that some pregnant teenagers who tell parents they were raped and then press charges to prove the assault to their parents actually tell prosecutors the acts were consensual.[259] This does not mean, of course, that the sexual interactions were free of coercion. It does mean, though, that victims' pathological disturbances and greed generally do not motivate victims to falsely accuse and systems to prosecute falsely.

In addition to concerns of fabrication, there is the related concern that recognizing sexual victimization, especially broadly defined, may mislead those entrusted in implementing mandates and result in ineffective policy making. The extent to which current laws are unable to respond to the mounting problem of child maltreatment certainly casts a shadow of futility over efforts to respond to the less immediately manifested dangers of an expansive view of adolescent maltreatment. Yet it does seem that narrowly delimited definitions could enhance responses if taken seriously. For example, addressing underlying factors that lead to and perpetuate abusive relationships makes more sense than addressing symptoms, as revealed by the child welfare system's focus on remedying and restructuring interpersonal bonds through mandated permanency planning, family preservation, and reasonable efforts requirements before terminating family bonds.[260]

Fears of Criminalizing and Pathologizing Normative Childhood

Researchers, practitioners, parents, and others who direct interactions with adolescents voice concern that a more expansive view of violence may make normal adolescent sexual and emotional explorations pathological or criminal.[261] Such criticisms are considerably potent given that the largely nascent body of literature that examines these concerns continues to have difficulty distinguishing between normative behaviors from other types. Even what would seem to be most obvious, overt aggressive sexual behavior, remains highly controversial and plagued by problems in distinguishing normal sex play from pathological conditions. Given these controversies, it is unsurprising that instances that do not involve overt violence find the most difficulty in gaining recognition as a legitimate cause for concern.

Although the concern certainly is well-founded and properly highlights the need to consider the effects of labeling and intervention in matters that may not need them, the current failure to recognize the harms adolescents suffer contradicts the major sociolegal principle that society must be vigilant in its efforts to protect adolescents and that minors are differently situated than adults. Case law is replete with decisions based on the need to protect children more than adults. As discussed in chapters 2, 3, and 4, these cases range from medical decision making to decisions regarding whether adolescents may see certain movies or play in certain public areas. As also discussed in those chapters, these cases are supplemented by considerable state and federal statutory schemes designed to offer special protections for minors, such as statutory rape, contract laws, and labor laws. These legal mandates reflect the basic policy that adolescents may need protection from themselves and others.

Legal recognition for the needed protection is of significance for three reasons. First, society recognizes a need to protect. Second, there is reason to recognize violence against adolescents, at least to the extent that it occurs between adults. Third, existing cases and statutes remain controversial for their protection—for example, it remains unclear exactly how much protection children should receive, the nature of that protection, and who should play the role of protector: parents, families, courts, social service agencies, criminal justice systems, or adolescents themselves. These points highlight the extent of agreement that adolescents need protection, of disagreement about what constitutes normal adolescent behavior, and the need to pathologize and criminalize some behaviors that currently go ignored.

Developing Sociolegal Alternatives

Efforts to recognize the legal rights of adolescents must consider two points. First, the traditional hostility toward recognizing adolescents' legal personhood suggests that both states and the federal government will hesitate to expand adolescents' rights. Even when adolescents' victimizations are recognized, systemic responses and views of adolescents, coupled with the limitations of criminal and civil justice systems, operate to limit the effectiveness of reforms. Second, legal reforms have their limits as revealed well by the experience with sexual assault laws.

Bearing in mind the slow process and inherent limits of sociolegal reform, alternative approaches to protecting adolescents still could be made available rather quickly. Jurisdictions that remain unwilling to grant minors direct legal protection could allow courts to appoint guardian *ad litems* or attorneys to bring or defend actions. For example, domestic violence statutes could expand to allow minors at least the ability to obtain protection orders with the assistance of an adult other than a parent. Although focusing on adults provides a limited remedy, it does begin to help address the needs of adolescents victimized by the very adults who are needed to assist in obtaining legal protection. Statutes also could expand to allow mature minors to obtain protections. Although reliance on determinations of maturity is problematic, this would at least allow some victimized adolescents to come under judicial scrutiny and increase the likelihood that services and protections may be provided.

Institutions that allow violence to flourish provide another site for legal intervention. For example, evidence suggests that personal violence often escapes the control of school officials, largely because schools tend not to address violence publicly and tend not to communicate a willingness or ability to respond.[262] Given increasing concerns about school violence, schools are becoming the sites for intervention and are held liable for failures to protect students from overt violence. These two points buttress the contention that schools can play a greater role in protecting adolescents from sexual violence. For example, to not be held liable, schools must (a) enhance awareness among students, teachers, and school officials; (b) provide students with an adequate complaint or reporting mechanism; and (c) take appropriate steps to react to reports of violence.[263] For sexual harassment, for example, remedial steps could include opening communication with students, expressing disapproval of certain types of behavior, developing formal grievance procedures, investigating allegations, removing harassers from classrooms, and enforcing sanctions. Although few schools have taken affirmative steps to prevent sexual violence, innovative programs suggest that several approaches can be taken to address violence and avoid liability. For example, successful relationship violence programs have been designed to help students increase nonviolent management of interpersonal conflict, develop means of coping with anger, jealousy and possessiveness, and alter attitudes that verbal and physical violence are acceptable means of conflict resolution, and these programs are in fact effective.[264] Likewise, several programs have been developed to help students and their schools identify and deal with sexually harassing behaviors.[265] Schools that are unable to develop intensive programs still could adopt a proactive stance aimed at broad prevention, much as several schools have done with drug abuse, sexual behavior, and general student aggression.[266] Some schools that have adopted broad prevention programs, coupled by support services, reveal that they are effective in reducing violence.[267] These innovative programs reinforce claims that existing knowledge can guide intervention efforts. These developments are important to consider. Counselors and school officials may otherwise try to ignore issues related to sexual relationships and how schools are critical sexual sites of students' coming of age.[268] The failed recognition results in the inability of victims to seek assistance from those who are entrusted by law and society to ensure adolescents safety.

Although intensive educational efforts are critical, such efforts may be insufficient by themselves in bringing about future long-term changes in destructive behavior once problem behavior patterns have been established. Yet few counseling and treatment services are available to help adolescents who are experiencing or perpetrating relationship and sexual violence.[269] The failed involvement of mental health professionals seems to be a result of extra legal considerations. Arguably, two reasons exist for the failure of professionals to offer assistance to victimizing and victimized adolescents. First, programs have not been tailored to adolescents. For example, few prevention programs are designed to help children develop nonviolent ways for resolving conflicts within their intimate relationships.[270] Likewise, mental health and social service providers tend to compartmentalize adolescents' problems; the result is that those who get attention for one problem are not identified as having other equally serious problems, and adolescents themselves tend to underuse professional support services that do exist.

The failures of the mental health system mean that victims do not seek formal support because they may be unaware of available opportunities for assistance, may rely on informal social networks, or, as we have seen, may define their violence as normative, as requiring no intervention. The underuse of formal support services indicates a possible role for the legal system. For example, as with adult victims of domestic violence who are brought to the attention of state officials, a burden could be placed on officials to direct adolescents to support services. Unlike adult-centered paradigms that rely solely on facilitating the use of the formal justice system, however, the burden would be placed on school officials and others acting *parens patriae*. Unlike for adults, however, these obligations essentially already exist when adolescents are victims; mandates simply need to be taken more seriously.

Because relying on schools and formal intervention remains a limited option, the legal system could aim to intervene in family life. Family intervention could seek to prevent victimizing behaviors and deal with victimization; as we have seen, family violence clearly increases the risk of victimization and perpetration outside the home. In terms of these forms of intervention, the legal system already is well-suited to play an important role. For example, child abuse and neglect laws could be enforced more strictly; parents could be offered services; and destructive relationships could be severed. Likewise, domestic violence statutes that enable parents to seek assistance and stop domestic violence in families with children undoubtedly could play a critical role; the statutes also may by used to protect children from the negative consequences of witnessing abuse.[271] In addition to more traditional methods of intervening in families, family intervention also would mean intervening to bolster family supports and transform social environments in which violent behaviors are learned or reinforced. Sexual violence only can be addressed by challenging attitudes that regularly generate, legitimize, and reinforce violence.

The alternatives, though, offer only limited protection. Education, access to services, and allowing for greater intrusion into family life will be ineffective unless reform also aims to alter social arrangements that overtly or subtly support violence against adolescents. To change social policies that perpetuate violence, legal rules and policy making must challenge adolescents toward social change. This challenge highlights the most devastating aspect of current legislation and jurisprudence: It ignores the power adolescents hold in determining their own lives. Recent legal and social science scholarship examining adolescents' issues emphasizes well the need to focus on the ways adolescents serve as resources to their families, schools, communities, and especially themselves. This approach imagines a jurisprudence that places less emphasis on punishing adolescents for their wrongdoings and more emphasis on responding to their victimization. This perspective suggests that adolescents must be supported with the information, resources, and skills needed to work toward prosocial change in their own lives, in the adolescent subculture and in broader society. Without doubt, the active agent in social change is participation by those who would benefit most by personal and societal reform.

The focus on active adolescents' involvement helps reemphasize the importance of not abandoning adolescents to their rights. Simply giving adolescents legal access to existing laws and services is hazardous. Recognizing sexual violence as another crime or as private relationship matters runs the risk of normalizing existing relations and failing to reach and transform social structural and political contexts that purposefully or unwittingly ignore or oppress adolescents. Recognizing the rights of adolescents will only ameliorate their plight if it also helps to adopt a more enlightened and realistic view of adolescent life.

Conclusion

The current reality facing sexually victimized adolescents is manifested by their behavior. To escape problems that result from familial victimization, adolescents often resort to drugs, alcohol, street life, suicide, or violent crimes. Those harassed by peers drop out of school and society. Those beaten by their partners often remain in maltreating relationships that further cycles of violence. Even sexually assaulted adolescents tend to seek to maintain relationships with aggressors. These adolescents could not send a clearer message to the legal system that they need assistance. The continued violence and failed responses derive from existing sociolegal frameworks that assume adolescents will not be victims of their own intimate sexual relationships or of their own peer groups. The belief is exacerbated by the liminal nature of adolescents' lives that fosters the assumption that parents and other adults offer adequate protections and enough freedom. Presumptions and misperceptions result in the failure to develop a sociolegal reaction to adolescent violence.

Realistic policy making can help meet minors' pressing needs. Policies must do more than simply protect; they must champion adolescent's sense of legal and social autonomy. Remedies that do not consider adolescents' needs for autonomy and protection, even remedies that include increases in support services and more aggressive law enforcement, will remain underused and not fully effective. Yet even without enough societal will to recognize adolescents' individual legal right to seek protection, several alternatives exist that may help restructure social arrangements that tolerate adolescents' victimization and denial of rights adults enjoy.

Endnotes

1. Schall v. Martin, 467 U.S. 253, 265 (1989).
2. Judith Berman Brandenburg, *Confronting Sexual Harassment: What Schools and Colleges Can Do* (New York: Teachers College Press, 1997).
3. This tends to be the approach adopted by courts. For a review of definitions, *see* Stacey R. Rinestine, ''Terrorism on the Playground: What Can Be Done?'' *Duquesne Law Review* 32 (1994):799–832.
4. Sexual Harassment Guidance Harassment of Students by School Employees, Other Students, and Third Parties, *Federal Register* 62 (1997):12034.

5. American Association of University Women, *Hostile Hallways: The AAUW Survey on Sexual Harassment in America's Schools* (Washington, DC: Louis Harris and Associates, 1993); Valerie E. Lee, Robert G. Croninger, Eleanor Linn, and Xianglei Chen, "The Culture of Sexual Harassment in Secondary Schools," *American Educational Research Journal* 33 (1996):383–417; Stanley D. Stratton and John S. Backes, "Sexual Harassment in North Dakota Public Schools: A Study of Eight High Schools," *The High School Journal* 80 (1997):163–172.

6. American Association of University Women, *Hostile Hallways: The AAUW Survey on Sexual Harassment in America's Schools,* at 7. Smaller studies report similar outcomes; *see* Stratton and Backes, "Sexual Harassment in North Dakota Public Schools."

7. American Association of University Women, *Hostile Hallways: The AAUW Survey on Sexual Harassment in America's Schools.*

8. *Id.* Sixty-six percent of the boys and 52% of the girls surveyed admitted to perpetration.

9. Valerie E. Lee, Robert G. Croninger, Eleanor Linn, and Xianglei Chen, "The Culture of Sexual Harassment in Secondary Schools," *American Educational Research Journal* 33 (1996):383–417.

10. The findings relate to those identified from adult samples that have led commentators to champion a "sexual harassment syndrome." Vita C. Rabinowitz, "Coping With Sexual Harassment." In *Ivory Power: Sexual Harassment on Campus,* ed. Michelle A. Paludi (Albany: State University of New York Press, 1990). The syndrome includes the following symptoms: general depression, as manifested by changes in eating and sleeping patterns, and vague complaints of aches and pains that prevent the student from attending class or completing work; undefined dissatisfaction with class; sense of powerlessness, helplessness, and vulnerability; loss of academic self-confidence and decline in academic performance; feelings of isolation from other students; irritability with family and friends; fear and anxiety; inability to concentrate, and so forth. *Id.* at 112–113.

11. American Association of University Women, *Hostile Hallways: The AAUW Survey on Sexual Harassment in America's Schools,* at 16–17.

12. *Id.* at 18. Up to a third of the students report that they did not want to attend, let alone participate in, classes because of the harassment. One third of the girls while thirteen percent of the boys reported these reactions. *Id.*

13. *See* Chantal Richard, "Surviving Student to Student Sexual Harassment: Legal Remedies and Prevention Programs," *Dalhousie Law Journal* 19 (1996):169–197.

14. Carrie M. H. Herbert, *Talking of Silence: The Sexual Harassment of Schoolgirls* (New York: Falmer Press, 1989).

15. *See* later discussion.

16. Herbert, *Talking of Silence: The Sexual Harassment of Schoolgirls;* June Larkin, "Walking Through Walls: The Sexual Harassment of High School Girls," *Gender and Education* 6 (1994):263–280; Peggy Orenstein, *School Girls: Young Women, Self-Esteem and the Confidence Gap* (New York: Doubleday, 1994); Kelli Kristine Armstrong, "The Silent Minority Within a Minority: Focusing on the Needs of Gay Youth in Our Public Schools," *Golden Gate University Law Review* 41 (1994):67–97.

17. For example, school personnel dismiss harassing behavior as normal courtship, even when the youth are not dating. Nan Stein, "Sexual Harassment in School: The Public Performance of Gendered Violence," *Harvard Educational Review* 65 (1995):145–162; Larkin, "Walking Through Walls: The Sexual Harassment of High School Girls."

18. Students are four times more likely to be harassed by other students than by school employees. American Association of University Women, *Hostile Hallways: The AAUW Survey on Sexual Harassment in America's Schools.*

19. According to 42 U.S.C. § 1983 (1998):

   Every person who, under color of any statute, ordinance, regulation, custom, or usage, of any State or Territory of the District of Columbia, subjects, or causes to be subjected, any citizen of the United States or other person within the jurisdiction thereof to the deprivation of any rights, privileges, or immunities secured by the Constitution and laws, shall be liable to the party injured in an action at law, suit in equity, or other proper proceedings for redress.

20. 429 U.S. 97 (1976).

21. 457 U.S. 307 (1982).

22. 489 U.S. 189, 195–200 (1989).

23. *Id.* at 195–196; emphasis added.

24. *Id.* at 200

25. *Id.* at 200, 201.

26. These cases follow *DeShaney's* analysis; *id.* at 200.; *see, e.g.,* D. R. v. Middle Bucks Area Vocational Tech. Sch., 972 F.2d 1364, 1371–1375 (3d Cir. 1992), *cert. denied,* 506 U.S. 1079 (1993) (finding no custody because the state did not restrict victim's liberty to access help after school hours).

27. The only exception thus far has been in the context of residential schools, in which one court has recognized the *possibility* that a "special relationship," and hence a duty to protect, could exist. Walton v. Alexander, 20 F.3d 1350 (5th Cir. 1994).

28. 862 F. Supp. 363 (M.D. Ga. 1994).

29. Aurelia Davis v. Monroe County Board of Education, 119 S. Ct. 1661 (1999).

30. Pub. L. No. 92-318, 86 Stat. 235 (1972).

31. 20 U.S.C. § 1681(a) (emphasis added). Title IX defines an educational institution as "any public or private preschool, elementary, or secondary school, or any institution of vocational, professional, or higher education." *Id.* § 1681(c).

32. 503 U.S. 60 (1992).

33. *Id.* citing Meritor Savings Bank F.S.B. v. Vinson, 477 U.S. 57, 64 (1986).

34. Gebser et al. v. Lago Vista Indep. Sch. Dist. No. 96-1866, 524 U.S. 274 (1998).

35. 119 S. Ct. 1661 (1999).

36. Davis v. Monroe County Bd. of Educ., 120 F.3d 1390, 1401 (11th Cir. 1997) *(en banc).* Of 11 judges, 6 concurred only in part and 4 dissented.

37. *Aurelia,* 119 S. Ct. at 1661.

38. 503 U.S. 60 (1992).

39. *Aurelia,* 119 S. Ct. at 1670–71.

40. *Id.* at 1671.

41. *Id.* at 1672.

42. *Id.*

43. *Id.* at 1675.

44. *Id.* at 1676.

45. *Gebser et al.,* 524 U.S. at 274.

46. *Aurelia,* 119 S. Ct. at 1677.

47. *Id.* at 1679.

48. *Id.* at 1680–1691.

49. 830 F. Supp. 1560 (N.D. Cal. 1993), *rev'd on other grounds,* 54 F.3d 1447 (9th Cir. 1995), *reconsideration granted,* 949 F. Supp. 1415 (N.D. 1996).

50. *Id.* at 1565–1566.

51. *Id.* at 1565.

52. *Id.* at 1564.

53. Before the case went to trial, however, the school settled for $250,000. "School District in California Settles Sex Harassment Suit," *New York Times,* Dec. 27, 1996, A24.

54. 864 F. Supp. 1111 (D. Utah, 1994).

55. *Id.* at 1130.

56. *Id.* at 1118.

57. 80 F.3d 1006 (5th Cir.), *cert. denied,* 117 S. Ct. 165 (1996).

58. *Id.* at 1010.

59. *Id.*

60. MINN. STAT. § 127.46 (1997).
61. Orenstein, *School Girls: Young Women, Self-Esteem and the Confidence Gap,* at 103 n.7.
62. CAL. EDUC. CODE § 212.6 (b)–(f).
63. Orenstein, *School Girls: Young Women, Self-Esteem and the Confidence Gap,* at 113.
64. FLA. STAT. ch. 230.23(6)(c)(2)(d)(8) (1997).
65. WASH. REV. CODE § 28A.640.020(2)(a)–(f) (1997).
66. MICH. COMP. LAWS ANN. § 380.1300a (West 1987 & Supp. 1999).
67. *Id.*
68. Florida, for example, mandates that "each code of student conduct shall be developed by the school board; elementary or secondary school teachers and other school personnel, including school administrators; students; and parents or guardians." FLA. STAT. ch. 230.23(6)(c)(2)(d)(8) (1997).
69. Amy M. Rubin, "Peer Sexual Harassment: Existing Harassment Doctrine and Its Application to School Children," *Hastings Women's Law Journal* 8 (1997):141–158.
70. Jeff Horner, "A Student's Right to Protection From Violence or Sexual Abuse by Other Students," *Educational Law Reporter* 4 (1996):110–114.
71. ALA. CODE § 13A-6-92(c) (1994).
72. ALA. CODE §§ 13A-6-92–94 (1994).
73. WASH. REV. CODE § 9A.46.110(1)(b).
74. CAL. CIV. CODE § 1708.7 (West Supp. 1996); MICH. COMP. LAWS ANN. § 600.2954 (West Supp. 1996); OR. REV. STAT. § 30.866 (1995); WYO. STAT. ANN. § 1-1-126 (Michie Supp. 1996).
75. *See* Albert R. Roberts (Ed.), *Helping Battered Women: New Perspectives and Remedies* (New York: Oxford University Press, 1996); Donald G. Dutton, *The Domestic Assault of Women: Psychological and Criminal Justice Perspectives.* Rev. ed. (Newbury Park, CA: Sage, 1995).
76. Research indicates that violence beings at about age 15. Teresa M. Bethke and David M. DeJoy, "An Experimental Study of Factors Influencing the Acceptability of Dating Violence," *Journal of Interpersonal Violence* 8 (1993):36–51.
77. Most of this research uses the Conflict Tactic Scales developed by Murray Straus; *see* Marie B. Caulfield and David S. Riggs, "The Assessment of Dating Aggression: Empirical Evaluation of the Conflict Tactics Scale," *Journal of Interpersonal Violence* 7 (1992):549–558; David S. Riggs, "Relationship Problems and Dating Aggression: A Potential Treatment Target," *Journal of Interpersonal Violence* 8 (1993):18–35.
78. Research indicates that personal relationships are at highest risk for such behavior; *see* Patricia Tjaden and Nancy Thoennes, *Stalking in America: Findings From the National Violence Against Women Survey* (National Institute of Justice Centers for Disease Control and Prevention, Research in Brief, U.S. Department of Justice, Washington, DC, April 1998).
79. Jacquelyn W. White and Marry P. Koss, "Courtship Violence: Incidence in a National Sample of Higher Education Students," *Violence and Victims* 6 (1992):247–256. Early research identified the surprising finding that relationship violence tends to be reciprocal; *see* James E. Deal and Karen Smith Wampler, "Dating Violence: The Primacy of Previous Experience," *Journal of Social and Personal Relationships* 3 (1986):457–471. Indeed, research indicates that dating relationships in which only one partner is abusive are short-lived; *see* Riggs, "The Assessment of Dating Aggression: Empirical Evaluation of the Conflict Tactics Scale," at 30–31.
80. Deal and Wampler, "Dating Violence: The Primacy of Previous Experience," at 467–468 (finding that 47% of respondents reported some experience with violence in a premarital dating relationship and noting that other studies ranged from 21.1 to 30 percent and as high as 42 percent). Ileanna Arias, Mary Samios, and K. Daniel O'Leary, "Prevalence and Correlates of Physical Aggression During Courtship," *Journal of Interpersonal Violence* 2 (1987):82–90. For a review, *see* David B. Sugarman and Gerald T. Hotaling, "Dating Violence: Prevalence, Context, and Risk Markers." In *Violence in Dating Relationships: Emerging Social Issues,* ed. Maureen A. Pirog-Good and Jan E. Stets (New York: Praeger).
81. Vangie A. Foshee, "Gender Differences in Adolescent Dating Abuse Prevalence, Types and Injuries," *Health Education Research: Theory & Practice* 11 (1996):275–286.

82. *Id.*
83. *See, e.g.,* David R. Jezl, Christian E. Molidor, and Tracy L. Wright, "Physical, Sexual and Psychological Abuse in High School Dating Relationships: Prevalence Rates and Self-Esteem Issues," *Child and Adolescent Social Work Journal* 13 (1996):69–87.
84. Christian Molidor and Richard M. Tolman, "Gender and Contextual Factors in Adolescent Dating Violence," *Violence Against Women* 4 (1998):180–194.
85. Bruce Roscoe and John E. Callahan, "Adolescents' Self-Report of Violence in Families and Dating Relations," *Adolescence* 20 (1985):545–553; Denise Gamache, "Domination and Control: The Social Context of Dating Violence." In *Dating Violence: Young Women in Danger,* ed. Barrie Levy (Seattle, WA: Seal Press, 1991). Despite statistics revealing high incidence and prevalence rates, only a small fraction, as low as 7%, of violent episodes is ever reported to officials, authorities, and others who could—in theory—render assistance. Chad LeJeune and Victoria Follette, "Taking Responsibility: Sex Differences in Reporting Dating Violence," *Journal of Interpersonal Violence* 9 (1994):122–140.
86. LeJeune and Follette, "Taking Responsibility: Sex Differences in Reporting Dating Violence."
87. Bethke and DeJoy, "An Experimental Study of Factors Influencing the Acceptability of Dating Violence."
88. *Id.*
89. About 50% of victims *do* terminate their relationships following violence; *see* Bethke and DeJoy, "An Experimental Study of Factors Influencing the Acceptability of Dating Violence," at 37.
90. This is the corollary to results presented, which indicates that about half report no change or improvement. *Id.* For victims who do not terminate relationships, "approximately 60% state no change or report an actual improvement in the relationship." *Id.*
91. Caroline Wolfe Harlow, *Female Victims of Violent Crime* (Washington, DC: Bureau of Justice Statistics, 1991).
92. Waiping Alice Lo and Michael J. Sporakowski, "The Continuation of Violence Dating Relationships Among College Students," *Journal of College Student Development* 30 (1989):432–439.
93. Bruce Roscoe and Nancy Benaske, "Courtship Violence Experienced by Abused Wives: Similarities in Patterns of Abuse," *Family Relations* 34 (1985):680–700.
94. Donald G. Dutton and Susan Painter, "Emotional Attachments in Abusive Relationships: A Test of Traumatic Bonding Theory," *Violence and Victims* 8 (1993):105–120.
95. Dee L. R. Graham and Edna I. Rawlings, "Bonding With Abusive Dating Partners: Dynamics of Stockholm Syndrome." In *Dating Violence: Young Women in Danger,* ed. Barrie Levy (Seattle, WA: Seal Press, 1991).
96. Peter J. Burke, Jan E. Stets, and Maureen A. Pirog-Good, "Gender Identity, Self-Esteem, and Physical and Sexual Abuse." In *Violence in Dating Relationships: Emerging Social Issues,* ed. Maureen A. Pirog-Good and Jan E. Stets (New York: Praeger, 1989); Nancy L. Galambos, David M. Almeida, and Anne C. Peterson, "Masculinity, Femininity, and Sex Role Attitudes in Early Adolescence: Exploring Gender Intensification," *Child Development* 61 (1990):1905–1914.
97. This is a clear example of sex differences; *see* Roger J. R. Levesque, "The Romantic Experiences of Adolescents in Satisfying Love Relationships," *Journal of Youth and Adolescence* 22 (1993):219–251.
98. Burke et al., "Gender Identity, Self-Esteem, and Physical and Sexual Abuse"; Galambos et al., "Masculinity, Femininity, and Sex Role Attitudes in Early Adolescence: Exploring Gender Intensification."
99. Susan Moore and Doreen Rosenthal, *Sexuality in Adolescence* (New York: Routledge, 1993).
100. Lenore E. Walker, "Psychology and Violence Against Women," *American Psychologist* 44 (1989):695–702.
101. Patricia Noller and Victor Callan, *The Adolescent in the Family* (New York: Routledge, 1991). Adolescents do rely on families for important sources of support; Robert M. Galatzer-Levy and Bertram J. Cohler, *The Essential Other: A Developmental Psychology of Self* (New York: Basic Books, 1993).

102. Robert M. Galatzer-Levy and Bertram J. Cohler, "The Psychological Significance of Others in Adolescence: Issues for Study and Intervention." In *Handbook of Clinical Research and Practice With Adolescents,* ed. Patrick H. Tolan and Bertram J. Cohler (New York: Wiley, 1993).

103. Turning to families may be more difficult for adolescents from cultures in which dating and sexuality, as well as alternative forms of relationships, are restricted and possible sources of shame. Caroline K. Waterman, Lori J. Dawson, and Michael J. Bologna, "Sexual Coercion in Gay Male and Lesbian Relationships: Predictors and Implications for Support Services," *Journal of Sex Research* 26 (1989):118–124. Feelings of shame and helplessness play a decisive role in keeping adolescents from seeking assistance from familial sources, as reflected in the high number of adolescents who do not even disclose the sexual nature of dating relationships to parents who comfortably discuss sexuality. Roger J. R. Levesque, "The Peculiar Place of Adolescents in the HIV-AIDS Epidemic: Unusual Progress & Usual Inadequacies in 'Adolescent Jurisprudence,'" *Loyola University Chicago Law Journal* 27 (1996):701–739.

104. Levesque, "The Peculiar Place of Adolescents in the HIV-AIDS Epidemic: Unusual Progress & Usual Inadequacies in 'Adolescent Jurisprudence.'"

105. Dating is simply not seen as an "official" form of relationship, legally or socially, in the sense that marital relationships are. In addition, from a developmental perspective, the relationships are viewed as transitional, as a phase between the family of orientation and family of procreation. It is assumed that relationships that do not work well will not be maintained. *Id.*

106. Richard Driscoll, Keith E. Davis, and Milton Lipetz, "Parental Interference and Romantic Love: The Romeo and Juliet Effect," *Journal of Personality and Social Psychology* 24 (1972):1–10.

107. LeJeune and Follette, "Taking Responsibility: Sex Differences in Reporting Dating Violence."

108. Sugarman and Hotaling, "Dating Violence: Prevalence, Context, and Risk Markers."

109. Levesque, "The Romantic Experiences of Adolescents in Satisfying Love Relationships."

110. Sugarman and Hotaling, "Dating Violence: Prevalence, Context, and Risk Markers."

111. This finding need not be particularly problematic for those who champion adolescents' maturity and adolescents' rights. Adults trapped in domestic violence also experience similar dynamics.

112. Levesque, "The Peculiar Place of Adolescents in the HIV-AIDS Epidemic: Unusual Progress & Usual Inadequacies in 'Adolescent Jurisprudence.'"

113. James M. Makepeace, "Dating, Living Together, and Courtship Violence." In *Violence in Dating Relationships: Emerging Social Issues,* ed. Maureen A. Pirog-Good and Jan E. Stets (New York: Praeger, 1989).

114. Maura O'Keefe and Laura Treister, "Victims of Dating Violence Among High School Students: Are the Predictors Different for Males and Females?" *Violence Against Women* 4 (1998):195–223.

115. Heidi M. Ronfeldt, Rachel Kimerling, and Ileana Arias, "Satisfaction With Relationship Power and the Perpetration of Dating Violence," *Journal of Marriage and the Family* 60 (1998):70–78.

116. Riggs, "Relationship Problems and Dating Aggression: A Potential Treatment Target," at 30–34.

117. Mary Reige Laner, "Competition and Combativeness in Courtship: Reports From Men," *Journal of Family Violence* 4 (1989):47–62.

118. This important finding parallels others that find that the seriousness of crimes are minimized when offenders are known or married to victims; *see* Bethke and DeJoy, "An Experimental Study of Factors Influencing the Acceptability of Dating Violence," at 47–49.

119. Roger J. R. Levesque, "Dating Violence, Adolescents, and the Law," *Virginia Journal of Social Policy and Law* 4 (1997):339–379.

120. It is surprising to note that only two studies have related dating problems to dating aggression. For a review, *see* Riggs, "Relationship Problems and Dating Aggression: A Potential Treatment Target," at 34.

121. Phyllis Goldfarb, "Describing Without Circumscribing: Questioning the Construction of Gender in the Discourse of Intimate Violence," *George Washington Law Review* 64 (1996):582–631; Suzanne Pharr, *Homophobia: A Weapon of Sexism* (Little Rock, AR: Chardon Press, 1988);

Claire M. Renzetti, *Violent Betrayal: Partner Abuse in Lesbian Relationships* (Newbury Park, CA: Sage, 1992).

122. Although consistently ignored in the provision and design of support services, gay and bisexual domestic violence exists; *see* Patrick Letellier, "Gay and Bisexual Male Domestic Violence Victimization: Challenges to Feminist Theory and Responses to Violence," *Violence and Victims* 9 (1994):95–106.

123. Richard Gelles, "Violence and Pregnancy: Are Pregnant Women at Greater Risk of Abuse?" *Journal of Marriage and the Family* 50 (1988):841–847; Judith McFarlane, "Battering in Pregnancy: The Tip of the Iceberg," *Women and Health* 15 (1989):69–84.

124. James M. Makepeace, "Courtship Violence as Process: A Developmental Theory." In *Violence Between Intimate Partners: Patterns, Causes, and Effects,* ed. Albert P. Cardarelli (Boston: Allyn & Bacon, 1997).

125. *See, e.g.,* Diane C. Dwyer, Paul R. Smolowski, John C. Bricourt, and John S. Wodarski, "Domestic Violence and Woman Battering: Theories and Practice Implications." In *Helping Battered Women: New Perspectives and Remedies,* ed. Albert R. Roberts (New York: Oxford University Press, 1996).

126. Martin S. Keseredy, "Women Abuse in Dating Relationships: The Relevance of Social Support Theory," *Journal of Family Violence* 3 (1988):1–14; Bonnie E. Carlson, "Dating Violence: Student Beliefs About Consequences," *Journal of Interpersonal Violence* 11 (1996):3–19; Victor C. Strasburger, *Adolescents and the Media: Medical and Psychological Impact* (Thousand Oaks, CA: Sage, 1995).

127. *See, e.g.,* M. L. Bernard and J. L. Bernard, "Violent Intimacy: The Family as a Model for Love Relationships," *Family Relations* 32 (1983):283–286.

128. Samuel Vuchinich, Lew Bank, and Gerald R. Patterson, "Parenting, Peers, and the Stability of Antisocial Behavior in Preadolescent Boys," *Developmental Psychology* 28 (1992):510–521; Donald G. Dutton, "Male Abusiveness in Intimate Relationships," *Clinical Psychology Review* 15 (1995):567–581.

129. Richard J. Gelles and Murray A. Strauss, *Intimate Violence* (New York: Simon & Schuster, 1988).

130. Riggs, "Relationship Problems and Dating Aggression: A Potential Treatment Target," at 22–30; Louise Foo and Gayla Margolin, "A Multivariate Investigation of Dating Aggression," *Journal of Family Violence* 10 (1995):351–377.

131. *See generally* Albert P. Cararelli (Ed.), *Violence Between Intimate Partners: Patterns, Causes, and Effects* (Boston: Allyn & Bacon, 1997).

132. Albert R. Roberts (Ed.), *Helping Battered Women: New Perspectives and Remedies* (New York: Oxford University Press, 1996); Catherine F. Klein and Leslie E. Orloff, "Providing Legal Protection for Battered Women: An Analysis of State Statutes and Case Law," *Hofstra Law Review* 21 (1993):801–1189.

133. *Id. See also* Eve S. Buzawa and Carl G. Buzawa (Eds.), *Do Arrests and Restraining Orders Work?* (Newbury Park, CA: Sage, 1996).

134. Albert R. Roberts, "Introduction: Myths and Realities Regarding Battered Women." In *Helping Battered Women: New Perspectives and Remedies,* ed. Albert R. Roberts (New York: Oxford University Press, 1996).

135. IND. CODE ANN. § 34-4-5.1-1(2) (West Supp. 1995); IOWA CODE ANN. § 236.2(2), 4 (West Supp. 1995); MICH. COMP. LAWS ANN. § 400.1501(c) (West 1995); MO. ANN. STAT. §§ 455.010(2),(5), 455.020 (Vernon Supp. 1996); MONT. CODE ANN. § 45-5-206(2)a–b (1995); N.J. STAT. ANN. § 2C:25-19(a),(d) (West 1995); R.I. GEN. LAWS § 12-29-2 (Michie Supp. 1994); TENN. CODE ANN. § 36-3-601(4) (Michie Supp. 1995); TEX. HUM. RES. CODE ANN. § 51.002(2) (West Supp. 1996); WIS. STAT. ANN. § 968.075(1) (West Supp. 1995).

136. N.Y. SOC. SERV. LAW § 459-a (McKinney 1996); UTAH CODE ANN. § 30-6-1(2) (Michie Supp. 1995); WASH. REV. CODE ANN. § 26.50.010(2), (3) (West Supp. 1993).

137. MICH. COMP. LAWS ANN. § 400.1501(c) (West 1995); MONT. CODE ANN. § 45-5-206(2)a–b

(1995); R.I. GEN. LAWS § 12-29-2 (Michie Supp. 1994); TENN. CODE ANN. § 36-3-601(4) (Michie Supp. 1995); WIS. STAT. ANN. § 968.075(1) (West Supp. 1995).

138. DEL. CODE ANN. tit. 10, § 901(9) (Supp. 1994); LA. REV. STAT. ANN. § 2132(4) (West Supp. 1995); MD. FAM. LAW CODE ANN. § 4-513 (West 1991 & Supp.1995); ARK. CODE ANN. § 9-15-103 (Michie Supp. 1995); HAW. REV. STAT. § 586-1 (West 1993); KAN. STAT. ANN. § 60-3102 (West 1993); MISS. CODE ANN. § 93-21-3 (West 1994); N.C. Gen. Stat. § 50B-1(a) (West 1994); OHIO REV. CODE ANN. § 2919.25 (Anderson 1995); OR. REV. STAT. § 108.710 et seq. (Butterworth 1992 Supp. 1994); VT. STAT. ANN. tit. 15, § 1101 (1989 & Supp. 1995).

139. ARIZ. REV. STAT. ANN. § 13-3001(3) (West 1980 & Supp. 1995); CONN. GEN. STAT. ANN. § 46b-38a(1)–(2) (West 1995); FLA. STAT. ANN. §§ 741.28(2), 415.602(5) (West Supp. 1995); GA. CODE ANN. § 19-13-1 (Michie 1995); IDAHO CODE § 39-6303(2) (Michie 1995); KY. REV. STAT. ANN. § 403.720(2), (3) (Michie 1994); ME. REV. STAT. ANN. tit. 19, § 762(4) (West Supp. 1995); NEB. REV. STAT. § 42-903(4) (1993); NEV. REV. STAT. ANN. § 33.018 (Michie 1986 & Supp. 1995); S.C. CODE ANN. § 16-25-10 (Law. Co-op. 1995); S.D. CODIFIED LAWS ANN. § 25-10-1(1)–(2) (Michie 1992 & Supp. 1995); VA. CODE ANN. § 16.1-228(2) (Michie Supp. 1995); WYO. STAT. § 35-21-102(a)(iii)–(iv) (West 1994).

140. ALA. CODE § 15-10-3(a)(8) (Michie 1995); ALASKA STAT. § 25.35.200(4) (West 1995); CA. FAM. CODE § 6211 (West Supp. 1996); COLO. REV. STAT. § 18-6-800.3(1),(2) (West Supp. 1995); ILL. ANN. STAT. ch. 750, § 60/103(6) (Smith-Hurd Supp. 1995); MASS. GEN. LAWS ANN. ch. 209A, §§ 1(e), 3(a) (West 1994 Supp. 1995); MINN. STAT. ANN. § 518B.01 subd. 2 (West & Supp. 1996); N.H. REV. STAT. ANN. § 173-B:1(I)–(IV) (Michie 1994 & Supp. 1995); N.M. STAT. ANN. § 40-13-2(D) (1993); N.D. CENT. CODE §§ 14-07.1-01(2), (4) (Michie 1991 & Supp. 1995); OKLA. STAT. ANN. tit. 22, § 60.1(1), (4) (West 1992 & Supp. 1995); PA. CONS. STAT. ANN. 23 § 6102(a) (Michie 1991 & Supp. 1995); W. VA. CODE § 48-2A-2(b) (Michie 1995).

141. N.H. REV. STAT. ANN. § 173-B(I)–(IV) (Michie 1994 & Supp. 1995).

142. N.D. CENT. CODE §§ 14-07.1-01(2), 4 (Michie 1991 & Supp. 1995).

143. ALASKA STAT. § 25.35.010 (1991); IDAHO CODE § 39-6306(4)(1993); ILL. ANN. STAT. ch. 750, § 60/214(a) (Smith-Hurd 1994); MASS. GEN. LAWS ANN. ch. 209A, § 3(a) (West 1994); R.I. GEN. LAWS § 15-15-5(b) (1994).

144. OKLA. STAT. ANN. tit. 22, § 60.1(1) (West 1995).

145. CONN. GEN. STAT. ANN. § 46b-38a(2) (West 1994); UTAH CODE ANN. § 30-6-1(2) (1990); WASH. REV. CODE ANN. § 26.50.020 (West 1994); WYO. STAT. § 35-21-102(a)(i) (1994).

146. ARK. CODE ANN. § 9-15-203(b) (Michie 1994); COLO. REV. STAT. ANN. § 14-4-101(2) (West 1994); IOWA CODE ANN. § 236.2(4) (West 1994); MO. ANN. STAT. § 455.020(1) (Vernon 1994); OR. REV. STAT. § 107.726 (1993); N.J. STAT. ANN. § 2C:25-19a (1994); TENN. CODE ANN. § 36-3-602 (1991); WIS. STAT. ANN. § 813.12(1)(a) (West 1994).

147. Roger J. R. Levesque and Alan J. Tomkins, "Revisioning Juvenile Justice: Implications of the New Child Protection Movement," *Journal of Urban and Contemporary Law* 48 (1995):87–116.

148. *See* J. David Hirschel and Ira Hutchinson, "Police-Preferred Arrest Policies." In *Woman Battering: Policy Responses,* ed. Michael Steinman (Cincinnati, OH: Anderson, 1991).

149. *See, e.g.,* ILL. ANN. STAT. ch. 725, § 5/112A-14(a) (Smith-Hurd 1994); OKLA. STAT. ANN. STAT. 22, §§ 60.4(A), 60.6(G) (West 1995); UTAH CODE ANN. § 77-36-1 (1994).

150. CA. FAM. CODE § 6211 (West Supp. 1996), CAL. PENAL CODE §§ 243e(1), 273.5 (West Supp. 1995); WASH. REV. CODE ANN. § 26.50.010 (West 1986 & Supp. 1996), 10.31.100 (West 1986 Supp. 1996); PA. CONS. STAT. ANN. 23 § 6102(a) (Michie 1991 & Supp. 1995), 18 § 2711 (Michie 1991 & Supp. 1995); MINN. STAT. ANN. §§ 518B.01 subd. 2, 629.341 (West Supp. 1996); R.I. GEN. LAWS § 12-29-2 (Michie Supp. 1994), 15-15-1 (Michie Supp. 1994); S.D. CODIFIED LAWS ANN. §§ 25-10-1(1)–(2) (1992), 23A-3-2.1 (Michie 1992 & Supp. 1995).

151. ARIZ. REV. STAT ANN. §§ 13-3601, 36, 3001 (Supp. 1995); ALA. CODE §§ 15-10-3(8); (Michie 1995), 30-6-1 (Michie 1995); MICH. COMP. LAWS ANN. §§ 400.1501(c) (West Supp. 1995), 764.15a (West Supp. 1995).

152. Levesque and Tomkins, "Revisioning Juvenile Justice: Implications of the New Child Protection Movement."

153. Naomi R. Cahn and Lisa G. Lerman, "Prosecuting Woman Abuse." In *Woman Battering: Policy Responses,* ed. Michael Steinman (Cincinnati, OH: Anderson, 1991).

154. Roger J. R. Levesque, "Prosecuting Sex Crimes Against Children: Time for 'Outrageous' Proposals?" *Law and Psychology Review* 19 (1995):59–91.

155. ALA. CODE § 30-5-5 (Michie 1989 & Supp. 1995); ARIZ. REV. STAT. ANN. § 13-3602A (West 1989 & Supp. 1995); ARK. CODE ANN. § 9-15-201(d) (Michie 1993 & Supp. 1995); CAL. FAMILY CODE § 6257 (West 1993 & Supp. 1995); DEL. CODE ANN. tit. 10, §§ 1041(3), 1042(a) (Michie 1989 & Supp. 1994); GA. CODE ANN. § 19-13-3(a) (West 1991 & Supp. 1995); HAW. REV. STAT. § 586-3(b) (1993); IDAHO CODE §§ 39-6304(2), 39-6306(1) (Michie 1993 & Supp. 1995); KAN. STAT. ANN. § 60-3104 (1993); KY. REV. STAT. ANN. § 403.725(3) (Michie 1993 & Supp. 1994); LA. REV. STAT. ANN. § 2133(4) (West 1996); ME. REV. STAT. ANN. tit. 19 § 764(1) (West 1981 & Supp. 1995); MD. CODE ANN., FAMILY LAW § 4-501(i) (Michie 1991 & Supp. 1995); MINN. STAT. ANN. § 518B.01(4)(a) (West 1991 & Supp. 1995); MISS. CODE ANN. § 93-21-7 (1995); N.H. REV. STAT. ANN. § 173-B:5 (1994); NC. GEN. STAT. § 50B-2(a) (1994); OHIO REV. CODE ANN. § 3113.31(c) (Anderson 1993); OKLA. STAT. ANN. tit. 22. § 60.2(A) (West 1995); PA. STAT. ANN. tit. 23 § 6106(a) (Michie 1991 & Supp. 1995); S.C. CODE ANN. § 20-4-40(a) (Law. Co-op. 1995); TEX. FAMILY CODE ANN. § 71-04(B) (West Supp. 1996); UTAH CODE ANN. §§ 30-6-3, 4 (Michie Supp. 1995); VT. STAT. ANN. tit. 15, § 1103(a) (1995); WASH. REV. CODE ANN. § 26.50.020(4) (West 1986 & Supp. 1996); W. VA. CODE § 48-2A-4(a) (Michie 1995).

156. States that offer the least social service assistance tend to be those that combat domestic violence through criminal laws; *see* ALA. CODE § 15-10-3(a) (1995); COLO. REV. STAT. § 18-6-800.3(1) (West Supp. 1995); N.J. STAT. ANN. § 2C:25-19 (1995); OHIO REV. CODE ANN. § 2919.25 et seq. (Anderson 1993); OKLA. STAT. ANN. tit. 22, § 60.1(1), (4) (West 1992); WIS. STAT. ANN. § 968.075(1) (West Supp. 1995).

157. Without such services, prosecution remains the exception rather than the norm. Marion Wanless, "Mandatory Arrest: A Step Toward Eradicating Domestic Violence, But Is It Enough?" *University of Illinois Law Review* (1996):533–586.

158. Hirschel and Hutchinson, "Police-Preferred Arrest Policies"; Lisa A. Frisch and Joseph M. Caruso, "The Criminalization of Women Battering: Planned Change Experiences in New York State." In *Helping Battered Women: New Perspectives and Remedies,* ed. Albert R. Roberts (New York: Oxford University Press, 1996); Casey G. Gwinn and Anne O'Dell, "Stopping the Violence: The Role of the Police Officer and the Prosecutor," *Western State University Law Review* 20 (1993):297–317.

159. Hirschel and Hutchinson, "Police-Preferred Arrest Policies."

160. N.H. REV. STAT. ANN. § 173-B:23-a (Michie 1994 & Supp. 1995).

161. Martin D. Schwartz and Walter S. DeKeseredy, *Sexual Assault on the College Campus: The Role of Male Peer Support* (Thousand Oaks, CA: Sage, 1997).

162. Mary P. Koss, "Hidden Rape: Sexual Aggression and Victimization in a National Sample of Students in Higher Education." In *Violence in Dating Relationships: Emerging Social Issues,* ed. Maureen A. Pirog-Good and Jan E. Stets (New York: Praeger, 1989).

163. Edward O. Laumann, John H. Gagnon, Robert T. Michael, and Stuart Michaels, *The Social Organization of Sexuality: Sexual Practices in the United States* (Chicago: University of Chicago Press, 1994).

164. Ida M. Johnson and Robert T. Sigler, *Forced Sexual Intercourse in Intimate Relationships* (Brookfield, VT: Ashgate, 1997).

165. Susan S. Ageton, "Vulnerability to Sexual Assault." In *Rape and Sexual Assault II,* ed. Ann Wolbert Burgess (New York: Garland, 1988).

166. Melissa J. Himelein, Ron E. Vogel, and Dale G. Wachowiak, "Nonconsensual Sexual Experiences in Precollege Women: Prevalence and Risk Factors," *Journal of Counseling and Development* 72 (1994):411–415.

167. *See* Neil Gilbert, "Realities and Mythologies of Rape," *Society* 29 (1992):4–10.

168. Martin S. Schwartz and Molly S. Leggett, "Bad Dates or Emotional Trauma? The Aftermath of Campus Sexual Assault," *Violence Against Women* 5 (1999):251–272.

169. Jill Rhynard, Marlene Krevs, and Julie Glover, "Sexual Assault in Dating Relationships," *Journal of School Health* 67 (1997):89–93. Although research now reveals high rates of coercion, actual figures regarding the incidence and prevalence of adolescent males' sexual assault remain elusive. See Paul J. Isely, Wilma Busse, and Peter Isely, "Sexual Assault of Males in Late Adolescence: A Hidden Phenomenon," *Professional School Counseling* 2 (1998):153–161.

170. Terry C. Davis, Gary Q. Peck, and John M. Storment, "Acquaintance Rape and the High School Student," *Journal of Adolescent Health* 12 (1993):220–224.

171. Bureau of Justice Statistics, *A National Crime Survey Report* (Washington, DC: U.S. Department of Justice, 1988), at 80; Mary P. Koss, "The Hidden Rape Victim: Personality, Attitudinal and Situational Characteristics," *Psychology of Women Quarterly* 9 (1985):193–212.

172. *See* Koss, "The Hidden Rape Victim: Personality, Attitudinal and Situational Characteristics."

173. Davis et al., "Acquaintance Rape and the High School Student." For example, if she led him on, 36% male and 18% female agree that the boy has a right to coerce sex; if she get him sexually excited, 37% male and 23% female; if they had sex before, 39% male and 12% female; if she wore revealing clothing, 27% male and 9% female. *See also* Susan K. Telljohann, James H. Price, Jodi Summers, Sherry A. Everett, and Suzanne Casler, "High School Students' Perceptions of Nonconsensual Sexual Activity," *Journal of School Health* 65 (1995):107–112.

174. *Id.* For an analysis of these studies in legal contexts, *see* Steven I. Friedland, "Date Rape and the Culture of Acceptance," *Florida Law Review* 43 (1991):487–527.

175. Jeanne Boxley, Lynette Lawrance, and Harvey Gruchow, "A Preliminary Study of Eighth Grade Students' Attitudes Toward Rape Myths and Women's Roles," *Journal of School Health* 65 (1995):96–100; Linda Cassidy and Rose Marie Hurell, "The Influence of Victim's Attire on Adolescents' Judgments of Date Rape," *Adolescence* 30 (1995):319–323. For a review, *see* Paul Pollard, "Judgements About Victims and Attackers in Depicted Rapes: A Review," *British Journal of Social Psychology* 31 (1992):307–326.

176. Martin D. Schwartz and Victoria L. Pitts, "Exploring a Feminist Routine Activities Approach to Explaining Sexual Assault," *Justice Quarterly* 12 (1995):9–31.

177. *See* Martin D. Schwartz and Walter S. DeKeseredy, *Sexual Assault on the College Campus: The Role of Male Peer Support* (Thousand Oaks, CA: Sage, 1997).

178. A characteristic found across several large samples studies is acceptance of interpersonal aggression. For a review, *see* Mary E. Craig, "Coercive Sexuality in Dating Relationships: A Situational Model," *Clinical Psychology Review* 10 (1990):395–423.

179. Makepeace, "Courtship Violence as Process: A Developmental Theory." For an analysis of these studies in legal contexts, *see* Steven I. Friedland, "Date Rape and the Culture of Acceptance," *Florida Law Review* 43 (1991):487–527.

180. Carol K. Sigelman, Carol J. Berry, and Katharine A. Wiles, "Violence in College Students' Dating Relationships," *Journal of Applied Social Psychology* 14 (1984):530–548.

181. Matthew Hogben, Donne Byrne, and Merle E. Hamburger, "Coercive Heterosexual Sexuality in Dating Relationships of College Students: Implications of Differential Male–Female Experiences," *Journal of Psychology and Human Sexuality* 8 (1996):69–78.

182. Susan D. Cochran and Vickie M. Mays, "Sex, Lies, and HIV," *New England Journal of Medicine* 322 (1990):774–775.

183. For a review, *see* Linda Brookover Bourque, *Defining Rape* (Durham, NC: Duke University Press, 1989).

184. David W. Bradley, Daniel S. Prentice, and Nancy E. Briggs, "Assessing Two Domains for Communicating Romance: Behavioral Context and Mode of Interaction," *Communication Research Reports* 7 (1990): 94–99.

185. Tracy D. Bostwick and Janice L. DeLucia, "Effects of Gender and Specific Dating Behaviors on Perceptions of Sex Willingness and Date Rape," *Journal of Social and Clinical Psychology* 11 (1992):14–25.

186. Robin M. Kowalski, "Inferring Sexual Interest From Behavioral Cues: Effects of Gender and Sexually Relevant Attitudes," *Sex Roles* 29 (1993):13–36.

187. Neil M. Malamuth and Lisa M. Brown, "Sexually Aggressive Men's Perceptions of Women's Communications: Testing Three Explanations," *Journal of Personality and Social Psychology* 67 (1994):699–712.

188. Jurors rely on their own social conditioning and gender biases to interpret relevant (and irrelevant) nonverbal cues. For example, to determine whether a situation is coercive, the presence of physical force is often used as a linchpin. See, for example, a study of 360 jurors who had decided rape cases that confirms the considerable role of latent gender bias in decision making. Gary D. LaFree, *Rape and Criminal Justice: The Social Construction of Sexual Assault* (Belmont, CA: Wadsworth, 1989).

189. For a review, *see* David P. Bryden and Sonja Lengnick, "Rape in the Criminal Justice System," *Journal of Criminal Law & Criminology* 87 (1997):1194–1384.

190. *Id.*

191. *Id.*

192. *Id.*

193. Victoria L. Pitts and Martin D. Schwartz, "Promoting Self-Blame Among Hidden Rape Survivors," *Humanity & Society* 17 (1993):383–398.

194. Note, "The Rape Corroboration Requirement: Repeal Not Reform," *Yale Law Journal* 81 (1972):1365–1391.

195. The exceptions are Arizona and Utah, which never enacted statutes, and Tennessee, which repealed its act. *See* TENN. CODE ANN. § 40-17-119 (1990) (repealed by Acts 1991, ch. 273, § 34).

196. States that follow the Michigan model include ALA. CODE § 12-21-203 (1995); FLA. STAT. ANN. § 794.022(2)-(5) (West Supp. 1996); ILL. ANN. STAT. ch. 725, § 5/115-7 (Smith-Hurd Supp. 1995); IND. CODE ANN. § 35-37-4-4 (West 1986); KY. R. EVID. 412; LA. CODE EVID. ANN. art. 412 (West 1986); ME. R. EVID. 412; MD. ANN. CODE art. 27, § 461A (1992); MASS. GEN. L. ch. 233, § 21B (1994); MICH. COMP. LAWS ANN. § 750.520j (West 1991)); MINN. STAT. ANN. § 609.347(3), (4), (6) (West Supp. 1996); MO. ANN. STAT. § 491.015 (Vernon Supp. 1996); MONT. CODE ANN. § 45-5-511(2), (3) (1995); NEB. REV. STAT. § 28-321 (1989); N.H. REV. STAT. ANN. § 632-A:6 (Supp. 1995); N.C. GEN. STAT. § 8C-1, R. 412 (1993); OHIO REV. CODE ANN. § 2907.02(D)–(F) (Baldwin 1994); PA. CONS. STAT. ANN. § 3104 (1983); S.C. CODE ANN. § 16-3-659.1 (Law. Co-op. 1985 & Supp. 1995); VT. STAT. ANN. tit. 13, § 3255 (Supp. 1995); VA. CODE ANN. § 18.2-67.7 (Michie 1988); W. VA. CODE § 61-8B-11 (1992); WIS. STAT. ANN. § 972.11(2) (West 1985 & Supp. 1995).

197. MICH. COMP. LAWS ANN. § 750.520j(1)(a), (b).

198. *Id.* at § 750.520j(1).

199. ARK. CODE ANN. § 16-42-101 (Michie 1994).

200. States that follow the Arkansas model include ALASKA STAT. § 12.45.045 (1995); ARK. CODE ANN. § 16-42-101 (Michie 1994); COLO. REV. STAT. ANN. § 18-3-407 (West 1990 & Supp. 1995); IDAHO CODE § 18-6105 (1987); KAN. STAT. ANN. § 21-3525 (1995); N.J. STAT. ANN. § 2C:14-7 (West 1995); N.M. STAT. ANN. § 30-9-16 (Michie 1994); R.I. GEN. LAWS § 11-37-13 (1994); S.D. CODIFIED LAWS ANN. § 23A-22-15 (1995); TEX. R. CRIM. EVID. § 412 (1997); WYO. STAT. § 6-2-312 (1988).

201. ARK. CODE ANN. § 16-42-101 (Michie 1994).

202. The following states have followed the federal approach: CONN. GEN. STAT. § 54-86f (1994); GA. CODE ANN. § 24-2-3 (1995); HAW. REV. STAT. ANN. § 626-1, R. 412 (1995); IOWA R. EVID. 412 (1995); N.Y. CRIM. PROC. LAW § 60.42 (McKinney 1992); OR. REV. STAT. § 40.210 (1988).

203. FED. R. EVID. 412(b)(2)(B).

204. FED. R. EVID. 412(b)(2)(A).

205. FED. R. EVID. 412(b)(2)(1).

206. CAL. EVID. CODE §§ 782, 1103(b) (West Supp. 1995).

207. States that follow the California model are CAL. EVID. CODE §§ 782, 1103(b) (West Supp. 1995); DEL. CODE ANN. tit. 11, §§ 3508, 3509, (1995); MISS. R. EVID. 412 (1995); N.D. CENT. CODE

§§ 12.1-20-14, -15 (1985); OKLA. STAT. ANN. tit. 12, § 2412 (West Supp. 1996). These statutes allow evidence of the victim's sexual history so long as it is not introduced to show the victim consented. NEV. REV. STAT. ANN. §§ 48.069, 50.090 (Michie Supp. 1995) and WASH. REV. CODE ANN. § 9A.44.0202(2)–(4) (West 1988)) exclude evidence of the victim's sexual conduct when introduced only to show the victim's lack of credibility.

208. CAL. EVIDENCE CODE §§ 782, 1103 (West 1995).

209. *Id.* These states include California, Delaware, Mississippi, North Dakota, and Oklahoma.

210. NEV. REV. STAT. ANN. §§ 48.069, 50.070 (Michie Supp. 1995) and WASH. REV. CODE ANN. § 9A.44.0202(2)–(4) (West 1998).

211. 500 U.S. 145 (1992).

212. *Id.* at 151.

213. 488 U.S. 227 (1988).

214. New Jersey stands as a prime example. *See In re* M. T. S., 609 A.2d 1266 (1992).

215. Cheryl A. Whitney, "Non-stranger, Non-consensual Assaults: Changing Legislation to Ensure that Acts Are Criminally Punished," *Rutgers Law Journal* 27 (1996):417–445.

216. Garthe E. Hire, "Holding Husbands and Lovers Accountable for Rape: Eliminating the 'Defendant' Exception of Rape Shield Laws," *Review of Law and Women's Studies* 5 (1996):591–610.

217. *See, e.g.,* ALA. CODE § 13A-6-60(2) (1994); ALASKA STAT. § 11.81.900 (Michie 1996).

218. *See, e.g.,* DEL. CODE ANN. tit. 11, § 761(f) (1995); HAW. REV. STAT. ANN. § 707-700 (Michie 1994).

219. *See, e.g.,* 720 ILL. COMP. STAT. § 5/12-12(e) (West 1993).

220. GA CODE ANN. § 16-6-4 (Supp. 1997) (defining child molestation as "any immoral or indecent act to or in the presence of any child"); N.C. STAT. § 14-202.1 (1993) (indecent liberties); S.C. CODE ANN. § 16-15-140 (Law. Co-op. 1985 & Supp. 1996) ("lewd or lascivious act"); WYO. STAT. ANN. § 14-3-105 (Michie Supp. 1996) (immoral or indecent touching).

221. For those under 14, *see* HAW. REV. STAT. ANN. § 707-730 (Michie 1994). For those under 18, *see, e.g.,* ARIZ. REV. STAT. ANN. § 13-1405 (West Supp. 1996); CAL. PENAL CODE § 261.5 (West Supp. 1997).

222. For under 13: N.H. REV. STAT. ANN. § 632-A:3 (1996); N.M. STAT. ANN. § 30-9-13 (Michie Supp. 1996); TENN. CODE ANN. § 39-13-504 (Supp. 1996); VA. CODE ANN. § 18.2-67.3 (Michie Supp. 1996). For under 18: ARIZ. REV. STAT. ANN. § 13-1405 (West Supp. 1996); CAL. PENAL § 288a (West Supp. 1997); IDAHO CODE § 18-1508A (Supp. 1996); N.D. CENT. CODE § 12.1-20-07 (1985); OR. REV. STAT. § 163.415 (1995); UTAH CODE ANN. § 76-5-404 (1995); WYO. STAT. ANN. § 14-3-105 (Michie Supp. 1996).

223. *See, e.g.,* ALA. CODE §§ 13A-6-61 to -67 (1994) (16 for most offenses; 19 for sexual contact offense with 13- to 15-year-old victim).

224. *See, e.g.,* ALASKA STAT. § 11.41.440(a)(2) (Michie 1996) (misdemeanor if child is 16–17 and defendant is in a position of trust), *Id.* § 11.41.438(a)(1) (felony if child is 13–15).

225. *See, e.g.,* CAL. PENAL CODE §§ 261.5, 286, 288a, & 289 (West Supp. 1997) (various penetration offenses if under 18).

226. *See, e.g.,* ARK. CODE ANN. §§ 5-14-106 & 5-14-120 (Michie 1993 & Supp. 1995) (under 16; 14–17 and defendant in position of authority); FLA. STAT. ANN. § 794.011(8) (West Supp. 1997) (12–17 and defendant in position of authority); *Id.* §§ 800.04(2) & (3) & 827.04(3) (under 16).

227. Jeanne C. Marsh, Allison Geist, and Nathan Caplan, *Rape and the Limits of Law Reform* (Boston: Auburn House, 1992); Cassia Spohn and Julie Horney, *Rape Law Reform: A Grassroots Revolution and Its Impact* (New York: Plenum Press, 1992); Ronet Bachman and Raymond Paternoster, "A Contemporary Look at the Effects of Rape Law Reform: How Far Have We Really Come?" *Journal of Criminal Law and Criminology* 81 (1993):554–574.

228. Marsh et al., *Rape and the Limits of Law Reform.*

229. For a review, *see* Spohn and Horney, *Rape Law Reform: A Grassroots Revolution and Its Impact.*

230. For a recent review of studies, *see* Ruth Tripletti and Susan L. Miller, "Case Processing in the

Harris County, Texas Criminal Justice System: A Comparison Across Crime Types," *Journal of Criminal Justice* 22 (1994):13–26.

231. Staff of Senate Comm. on the Judiciary, *The Response to Rape: Detours to Equal Justice,* 103d Cong. 1st Sess., Committee Print, 1993, at iii.

232. *Id.* Several note how not all forms of rape are viewed similarly; *see* Bachman and Paternoster, "A Contemporary Look at the Effects of Rape Law Reform: How Far Have We Really Come?"

233. Kathleen F. Cairney, "Addressing Acquaintance Rape: The New Direction of the Rape Law Reform Movement," *St. John's Law Review* 69 (1995):291–326.

234. Lana Stermac, Janice DuMont, and Sheila Dunn, "Violence in Known-Assailant Sexual Assaults," *Journal of Interpersonal Violence* 13 (1998):389–413.

235. Kimberly A. Longsway and Louise F. Fitzgerald, "Rape Myths: A Review," *Psychology of Women Quarterly* 18 (1994):133–164.

236. *See, e.g.,* Doe v. United States, 666 F.2d 43, 47–48 (4th Cir. 1981).

237. Commonwealth v. Berkwitz, 609 A.2d 1338, 1359, 1340 (Pa. Super. Ct.) *(per curiam), alloc. granted,* 613 A.2d 556 (Pa. 1992).

238. *See, e.g.,* Villafranco v. State, 313 S.E.2d 469, 471–474 (1984) (allowing testimony to rebut that the victim had not worn underwear at the time of the rape). For a review of similar but more sensational cases, *see* Alinor C. Sterling, "Undressing the Victim: The Intersection of Evidentiary and Semiotic Meanings of Women's Clothing in Rape Trials," *Yale Journal of Law and Feminism* 7 (1995):87–132.

239. Sakthi Murphy, "Rejecting Unreasonable Sexual Expectation: Limits on Using a Rape Victim's Sexual History to Show the Defendant's Mistaken Belief in Consent," *California Law Review* 79 (1991):541–576.

240. Chambers v. Mississippi, 410 U.S. 284, 295 (1973).

241. Lynne Henderson, "Rape and Responsibility," *Law and Philosophy* 11 (1992):127–178.

242. Michelle L. Oberman, "Turning Girls Into Women: Re-Evaluating Modern Statutory Rape Law," *Journal of Criminal Law and Criminology* 85 (1994):15–79.

243. *See* Leslie Francis (Ed.), *Date Rape: Feminism, Philosophy, and the Law* (University Park: Pennsylvania State University Press, 1996).

244. Heidi Kitrosser, "Meaningful Consent: Toward a New Generation of Statutory Rape Laws," *Virginia Journal of Social Policy and the Law* 4 (1997):287–338.

245. Oberman, "Turning Girls Into Women: Re-Evaluating Modern Statutory Rape Law."

246. Maryanne Lyons, "Adolescents in Jeopardy: An Analysis of Texas' Promiscuity Defense for Sexual Assault," *Houston Law Review* 29 (1992):583–632.

247. Alice Susan Andre-Clark, "Whither Statutory Rape Laws: Of *Michael M.,* the Fourteenth Amendment, and Protecting Women From Sexual Aggression," *Southern California Law Review* 65 (1992):1933–1992; Nicole A. Rapp, "Teenage Sex in California: Thirteen Years After *Michael M.,*" *Journal of Juvenile Law* 15 (1994):197–221. In *Michael M. v. Superior Court of Sonoma County,* 450 U.S. 464 (1981), the Court upheld a statutory rape statute that held only males criminally liable for acts of sexual intercourse for the purposes of the statute. In the facts presented to the Court, a 17 1/2-year-old male and a 16 1/2-year-old female had, as the dissent noted, engaged in apparently voluntary sexual activity. Yet the Court ruled that the law could permissibly distinguish between males and females and provide greater legal protection to girls by holding only males liable for their sexual relations.

248. Washington and Oregon explicitly allow minors access; the remainder do not. WASH. REV. CODE ANN. § 26.50.20(2) (1994); OR. REV. STAT. § 107.726 (1993); CONN. GEN. STAT. ANN. § 46b-38a(2)(D) (West 1994); OKLA. STAT. ANN. tit. 22, § 60.2(A) (West 1995); UTAH CODE ANN. § 30-6-1(2) (1990); WYO. STAT. § 35-21-102(a)(i) (1994).

249. Lawrence Steinberg and Elizabeth Cauffman, "Maturity and Judgment in Adolescence: Psychosocial Factors in Adolescent Decision Making," *Law and Human Behavior* 20 (1996):249–272.

250. Dorothea M. Ross, *Childhood Bullying and Teasing* (Alexandria, VA: American Counseling Association, 1996).

251. *See, e.g.,* Joy G. Dryfoos, "Full Service Schools: Revolution or Fad?" *Journal of Research on*

Adolescence 5 (1995):147–172; Judith R. Harris, "Where Is the Child's Environment? A Group Socialization Theory of Development," *Psychological Review* 102 (1995):458–489.

252. Carol Sanger and E. Willemsen, "Minor Changes: Emancipating Children in Modern Times," *University of Michigan Journal of Law Reform* 25 (1992):239–355.

253. J. A. Anderson, "The Sixth Amendment: Protecting Defendants' Rights at the Expense of Child Victims," *John Marshall Law Review* 30 (1997):767–802.

254. For a review, *see* Thomas D. Lyon, "The New Wave in Children's Suggestibility Research: A Critique," *Cornell Law Review* 84 (1999):1004–1087.

255. Stacy Gordon and Paula K. Jaudes, "Sexual Abuse Evaluations in the Emergency Department: Is the History Reliable?" *Child Abuse & Neglect* 20 (1996):315–322.

256. *See* Lyon, "The New Wave in Children's Suggestibility Research: A Critique."

257. Levesque, "Prosecuting Sex Crimes Against Children: Time for 'Outrageous' Proposals?"

258. Linda A. Fairstein, *Sexual Violence: Our War Against Rape* (New York: William Morrow, 1993).

259. *Id.*

260. Roger J. R. Levesque, "The Failures of Foster Care Reform: Revolutioning the Most Radical Blueprint," *Maryland Journal of Contemporary Legal Issues* 6 (1995):1–35; Jessica A. Graf, "Can Courts and Welfare Agencies Save the Family? An Examination of Permanency Planning, Family Preservation, and the Reasonable Efforts Requirement," *Suffolk University Law Review* 30 (1996):81–114.

261. Paul Okami, "Child Perpetrators of Sexual Abuse: The Emergence of a Problematic Deviant Category," *Journal of Sex Research* 29 (1992):109–140.

262. Stein, "Sexual Harassment in School: The Public Performance of Gendered Violence."

263. Kevin S. Mahoney, "School Personnel and Mandated Reporting of Child Maltreatment," *Journal of Law and Education* 24 (1995):227–239.

264. Walter B. Roberts, Jr., and Diane H. Coursol, "Strategies for Intervention With Childhood and Adolescent Victims of Bullying, Teasing, and Intimidation in School Settings," *Elementary School Guidance & Counseling* 30 (1996):204–212.

265. June Larkin, *Sexual Harassment: High School Girls Speak Out* (Toronto: Second Story Press, 1994).

266. Gilbert J. Botvin, Steven Schinke, and Mario A. Orlandi, "School-Based Health Promotion: Substance Abuse and Sexual Behavior," *Applied and Preventive Psychology* 4 (1995):167–184.

267. Einat Peled, Petter G. Jaffe, and Jeffrey L. Edleson (Eds.), *Ending the Cycle of Violence: Community Responses to Children of Battered Women* (Thousand Oaks, CA: Sage, 1995).

268. Mairt Mac an Ghaill, "Towards a Reconceptualized Sex/Sexuality Education Policy: Theory and Cultural Change," *Journal of Education Policy* 11 (1996):289–302.

269. Einat Peled, "Intervention With Children of Battered Women: A Review of Current Literature," *Children and Youth Services Review* 19 (1997):277–299.

270. Peled et al., *Ending the Cycle of Violence: Community Responses to Children of Battered Women.*

271. Peled, *Ending the Cycle of Violence: Community Responses to Children of Battered Women;* Joan Zorza, "Protecting the Children in Custody: Disputes When One Parent Abuses the Other," *Clearinghouse Review* (1996):1113–1127.

Chapter 9
SEXUAL OFFENDING

The history of the United States and of the place of adolescents in the law reveals an unending tradition of intolerance for adolescents' sexually deviant behavior. A sex crime committed in 1642 resulted in the first known execution on American soil for a crime by a minor. The offender was tried on Leviticus 20.15, which instructs death for bestiality, and was summarily hanged.[1] Although society still remains intolerant of sexually deviant behavior by adolescents, responses to the offense and the penalty would be different today.

The legal system's treatment of adolescents has changed much since the mid-1600s; but the most dramatic changes have been recent. The U.S. Supreme Court formally abolished the death penalty for some young juveniles (those under 16) only in 1988, although the recognition of the nature of adolescent sexual deviance occurred only in the 1970s. Concern for violent rapes committed by adolescents was part of broader legal transformations of sex laws that continue today. The implementation of laws in the 1990s focuses on adolescent sexual offending that society previously construed as byproducts of innocent curiosity. This recent view of adolescent offending and deviance undoubtedly constitutes one of the most significant findings to emerge from the study of adolescent sexuality. Prior to that recognition, society and the law generally ignored adolescents who engaged in forms of behaviors that are now both sexual and criminal.[2]

Although society and the law now object to a wider variety of sexually assaultive acts perpetrated by adolescents, much remains to be determined and gained by efforts to improve conceptualizations and responses to adolescent sex offenders. Despite agreement on the need to respond to adolescents who sexually offend, numerous controversies emerge from efforts to increase recognition. Among the most pressing problems are difficulties in reaching a consistent definition that transfers from research to social response, obtaining and deploying appropriate technology to deal with offending, determining the most appropriate response to young offenders, understanding and appropriately recognizing societal calls for reform, and embarking on intelligent policy directions to deal with sexually abusive events. These difficulties challenge the legal system to accept the peculiar needs of adolescents, which requires both support and control while still ensuring self-determination and social integration. How the legal system may balance these concerns remains an emotionally charged issue; unlike their victims, perpetrators neither arouse sympathy nor the desire to rehabilitate. Acknowledging, respecting, and responding to that punitive sentiment constrains attempts to revision legal responses to adolescent offenders. The punitive sentiment, however, simply complicates responses and still allows for effective intervention.

This chapter explores these complications through an analysis of current legal responses to adolescent offenders and of studies that examine the nature, etiology, treatment, and prevention of adolescents' offending. That analysis suggests opportunities for reform consistent with models that foster adolescents' competency development and active citizenship, a model that may counter objections to those who wish to punish at the expense of rehabilitation and those who champion the opposite.

Realities of Adolescent Sex Offending

A most interesting aspect of the study of adolescent sex offenders is that its recent recognition and responses to it proceed without a clear understanding of the prevalence and incidence of sexual behavior problems among adolescents. Few rigorous studies document the varieties of sexual offenses, characteristics of victims and offenders, and treatment alternatives. The latest reviews reveal that the vast majority of research in this area still remains exploratory, descriptive, and atheoretical.[3] Although existing research necessarily remains tentative, this section reviews attempts to evaluate current trends in responses to adolescent sex offending and to provide a basis to chart alternative approaches.

Scope and Significance

Estimates of the scope and analyses of the nature of adolescent sex offenses depend on definitional clarity. Researchers generally define juvenile sex offenses as involving coercion, force, or threats and sexual behavior that violates conventional norms and usually involves a younger child. The law, however, generally uses different standards; legal definitions tend to be broader and include noncoercive experiences and victims of any age. Regardless of definitional controversies and emphases, existing research, culled from several sources, form an important picture that provides an appropriate background to evaluate current policy trends and respond to sexually assaultive adolescents.

Prevalence Estimates

As we have seen, social science research and legal definitions often take different approaches to defining the activity of interest. In terms of existing research on juvenile sex offenders, researchers who examine rates from the view of adolescents who offend against younger children provide impressive statistics. Using this narrow definition, available evidence indicates that young perpetrators are an important source of sexual abuse against children. Juvenile sexual offenses actually are as common as those committed by adult offenders. Estimates reveal that adolescents commit more than 50% of sexual offenses perpetrated against children under 12 years of age.[4] Although these rates may appear relatively high, the figures actually may underestimate the magnitude of the extent of offending. Research relating to abusive adolescents relies mainly on official reports of sexual abuse against children, which often classify sexual offenses as assaults, ignore noncontact offenses, and, as with other offenses, involves underreporting to authorities.[5]

Research dealing with sexual assault also reveals high rates of adolescent sexual offending. The most conservative estimates, those that involve arrests, report that adolescents under the age of 18 account for a disproportionate number of arrests in light of offending over the life-span. In official statistics reported in the Uniform Crime Reports,[6] for example, young offenders account for 16% of all arrests for forcible rape and approximately one fifth of all arrests for every remaining sex offense other than prostitution. Moreover, 13- to 14-year-olds accumulate the largest number of arrests in both categories. Offenders 14 and younger account for 34% of forcible rapes and half of all other sex offenses committed by minors.[7] An understanding of adolescent sexual offending suggests that these rates also likely underestimate the magnitude of offending. As we have seen in the previous chapter, several forces militate against reporting to officials. Primary reasons for low report rates include the relationships between offenders and victims, the failure of victims to recognize abusive events, and the lack of social support systems for young victims. Even considering the official results at face value, however, leads to the conclusion that adolescent offenders constitute an important group of offenders.

Regardless of the statistical and methodological controversies, the prevalence of adolescent offending points to the need to consider the role young offenders play in sexual assaults. Adolescents account for a significant proportion of reported rapes and sexual abuse cases and likely account for even higher rates of unreported offenses. Adolescent sexual assault goes largely unrecognized by victims, offenders, and society; and the situations in which abuses occur tend not to lead to disclosure as much as other more clearly proscribed assaults perpetrated by adults.

Offenses and Offenders

Understanding the nature of adolescent offending remains complicated by the general failure to distinguish effectively between the age of offenders and their types of offenses. In general, however, existing research on adolescents who offend generally focuses on those who offend against younger children. Research dealing with adolescents who assault against peers generally remains limited, with the bulk of findings from studies of older adolescents. Despite these limitations, existing evidence does shed light on the nature of adolescent sexual offenses and has been rigorous enough to guide policy responses.

In terms of adolescents who assault against younger children, recent research reports consistent and important findings. In terms of offenders, boys in their early teens appear at highest risk for offending. Identified offenders tend to be male (95%),[8] and have reached their early teens (their modal age is 14).[9] In terms of victims, girls half the age of offenders tend to be at highest risk. The modal victim—the one most likely to be encountered in research and most described in commentaries—is likely to be a 7- or 8-year-old girl.[10] Both findings are significant in that the offenders have reached puberty but victims tend to be prepubescent—more than 60% are younger than 12 years of age and more than 40% of these are younger than 6.[11] Although the modal victim is female, several studies estimate that males account for a significant percentage of victims: Young males account from 40 to more than 60% of victims.[12] In terms of relationships between offenders and victims, evidence reveals that victims tend to know their offenders, who are likely to be siblings, babysitters, or adolescents who live in close proximity.[13]

In addition to findings relating to age and relationship differences, other important trends emerge from research that reports on the abusive events. Identified abusive behaviors tend not to be isolated events. Before they proceed to illegal behavior, young offenders already have explored sexuality in nondeviant ways.[14] Offenders also have repeated their offenses: The average number of victims of apprehended juvenile offenders is seven.[15] Nor are the behaviors results of innocent and curious exploration. Adolescent offenders tend to use verbal threats and bribes and other coercive measures.[16] Much like their adult counterparts, adolescent offenders do not predominantly use physical force; offenders of all ages use other means of coercive behaviors.[17] These findings are considerably significant; they help establish knowledge, intent, and culpability, which justify responses that take offending more seriously.

The limited information regarding adolescent offenders is more uneven when turning to adolescents who assault peers. Yet the limited research reveals two important and highly relevant conclusions. The first point involves differences that may exist in terms of offenders who offend against peers and those who offend against younger children. Those who offend against younger children tend to be more dependent, passive, avoidant, and more deviant than the former.[18] This evidence suggests that abused offenders have an earlier onset of offending, an increased number of victims, a tendency to predominantly abuse males, and a greater likelihood of exhibiting deviant sexual arousal.[19] These findings help explain the greater clinical focus on those more likely to be labeled adolescent pedophiles.

The second point to emerge from investigations of those who sexually assault peers reveals that these adolescents constitute a heterogenous group and actually appear considerably normal. Despite apparent normalcy, recent research, coupled with new developmental models of offending behavior, suggests two developmental trends.[20] The vast majority of adolescent sexual offenders who assault peers appear normal and constitute the first group of sex offenders. These adolescents typically assault acquaintances, including dates and girlfriends, rather than strangers. Researchers characterize these offenders as opportunistic and as limiting their coercive sexual activity to their own adolescence. Thus the group pervasively exhibits lower rates of assaults, later onset, and less chronicity. The second group consists of adolescents notable for their early onset of problem behavior and breadth of antisocial acts, including substance abuse and other criminal offenses. This group includes those who generally appear more pathological and who continue assaults during adulthood. These two models are important for two reasons. The delineation comports with recent developmental models of adolescent problem behavior that suggest dual pathways— one ''adolescence limited'' and seemingly less pathological; and another ''life-course persistent'' and considerably more antisocial.[21] Second, the groups reflect basic statistics regarding sexual assault: Acquaintances commit the majority of assaults and strangers commit the majority of more physically violent rapes.[22] Despite heterogeneity, then, important trends do emerge from research that describes adolescents who sexually offend against peers.

Although limited and in the process of development and further evaluations, existing findings present four related points that have immediate implications for responding to sexual offending by adolescents. First, behaviors tend to be difficult to uncover. Second, although offenders tend to be heterogeneous, some trends emerge and differences appear among adolescents who assault younger children, those who assault peers, and those who appear to have more antisocial personalities and assault strangers. Third, offenses tend to be rampant and repeated and, left unaddressed, continue for young offenders who commit pedophilic sex offenses.[23] Fourth, victims generally know offenders and offenses tend to be characterized as less violent, which exacerbates difficulties raised by the previous points. All these characteristics challenge efforts to understand the etiology of offending and hamper the development of effective responses to address victims' and perpetrators' needs.

Etiological Models

The most critical and frequent conclusion to emerge from research suggests that adolescent sex offenders are notable for one factor: diversity. That finding poses considerable challenges to understanding the roots of offending behavior. For example, social characteristics of adolescent offenders range considerably, from tough delinquent, social outcast, popular star athlete, to the honor-roll student.[24] Likewise, offenders tend not to suffer from mental illness, up to 95% of adolescent offenders present no identifiable pathologies beyond their sexually deviant acts.[25] Despite heterogeneity, common themes emerge in understanding the etiology of sex offending.

Many hypotheses explore the etiological roots that could explain why some adolescents turn to deviant rather than to appropriate means of sexual activity.[26] A dominant model suggests that the development of sex offenders results from, not surprisingly, a developmental impairment.[27] That approach suggests that those who offend are socially incompetent and have a poor self-image that frustrates attempts to satisfy sexual and emotional needs. These adolescents turn to children who are less threatening to serve as substitutes for sources of sexual gratification.[28] Relatedly, a more recent model emphasizes the cognitive distortions and faulty perceptions offenders bring to their interactions.[29] From this perspective, assaultive adolescents create distortions of reality to convince themselves of their desires' reality. In this manner, distortions allow them to rationalize behaviors that, in turn, allows adolescents to offend without feeling remorse or guilt. Both models find support from evidence that offenders have poor relationship skills and few peer relations, with significant numbers reporting no friends at all.[30] Indicators of shyness, timidity, withdrawal, and sexual isolation continue to be more frequent in adolescent offenders than other delinquents and other control groups.[31] These findings relate to clinical research that emphasizes the contribution of the lack of empathic experiences and sexualized patterns of coping to offending.[32]

Another model of sexual deviance, which also complements the previous approaches, relies on the basic principles of learning theory. This model suggests that adolescents learn their behavior through observation and modeling as they pair deviant thoughts with the reinforcement of sexual gratification. The model builds on evidence that young sex offenders's familial experiences are more likely to include assaultive and sexually deviant events, including child abuse, spousal abuse, and sexual molestation than the familial experiences of other adolescent offenders.[33] The model suggests that abusiveness emerges from an interaction of what individuals bring to their life experience and what surrounds them.[34] The approach gains support from three important findings. First, more than half of all juvenile offenders suffered from sexual abuse[35] and other sexually deviant environments.[36] Second, traumatic events tend to set children on a path to maladaptive adolescent development.[37] Third, 80% of adult sex offenders against children commit their first acts of sexual assault during their adolescent years.[38] Assaultive behaviors, then, seemingly derive from assaultive environments.

All approaches support the important finding that coercion and manipulation may be a common behavior pattern among offenders. Sexual offenders seemingly offend as part of coercive interactions, such as bullying.[39] These findings suggest that sexual deviancy is secondary to the abusive nature of the problem[40] and to research that highlights how beliefs, attitudes, and sexual interests of many nonoffenders are not so different from those of many abusive adolescents.[41] Such findings and hypotheses reveal a need to consider the developmental roots of what leads to adolescent sex offenders' distorted cognition about the effects of the offense, lack of empathy with others' needs, and a pattern of making demands on others.

The research reflects and receives empirical support from what we know about adults. Research that investigates the onset of what results in adult pedophiliac offending indicates that "we have no great insights"[42] into what might cause individuals to sexually assault children. However, evidence that does exist mirrors the findings for adolescents who offend. One extensive review of a wide range of factors related to sexual offending against children resulted in little success except the finding that a history of sexual aggression was the most accurate predictor of future sexual aggression.[43] As with adolescents, that finding tends to be consistent and complimented by findings of a history of victimization. Studies of pedophilia that compare different forms of pedophilia and sexual offenses to community control groups find child sexual and physical abuse common except for the control group.[44] In addition and still comparable to adolescents, researchers generally conclude that psychiatric, intellectual, and neurological problems characterize only a small minority of offenders,[45] that traditional categories of sex offenders essentially are meaningless[46] and that even the etiological backgrounds of "sexual predators" are not readily distinguishable from other types of offenders.[47] Available research suggests greater similarity than difference between sexual offenders and nonoffenders.[48]

Prevailing theories attribute the origins and maintenance of sexual offending to early childhood sexual gratifications, distortions, and social conditioning. These factors offer more comprehensive models of adolescent sex offending, focus on the multiple determinants of assaultive behavior, and attempt to explain the diversity of offenders in terms of their behavior, demographic characteristics, and history. Even these models, however, do not contribute markedly to the debate about the etiology of offending while in childhood. The genesis of deviant sexual behavior in childhood, adolescence, and adulthood still remains obscure despite a wide range of studies.[49]

Given the limitations of the search to identify singular causative variables, models respond to criticisms and focus more on understanding the processes that motivate, inhibit, and enable perpetrators to offend. Although not necessarily helpful in pinpointing direct causative factors, the approaches have been particularly influential to help guide research dealing with prevention and therapeutic efforts.[50] This area of research actually has been rather fruitful and has identified essentially four important points that need to be addressed to understand those who offend against children: *motivation* to relate sexually with young children and vulnerable peers, which finds support from research on cognitive distortions and social skill-deficits;[51] the need to overcome *internal inhibitors,* such as reduction of inhibitions by the use of alcohol, stressful life events (e.g., unemployment and divorce), emotional dysfunction, and lack of strong community sanctions;[52] reduction of *external inhibitors,* such as access to the victim and family dynamics that lack clear grasps of normal family relationships and find behaviors acceptable on some level even though they may not like their occurrences;[53] and overcoming the *victim's resistance,* by selecting vulnerable victims and using a variety of methods to ensure compliance and silence.[54]

This model and emerging findings reveal several important points. First, a focus on single factors and select groups of offenders does not further the appreciation of the wide variety of reasons and manners of those who offend.[55] Second, the focus on the inhibitors and motivators helps understand the need to take a broad view of sexual abuse. Third, efforts importantly place renewed interest in broader, sociocultural factors that foster distorted beliefs and support victimization.[56] These developments reflect the recognition of the difficulty of dealing with the occurrence of sexual assault against adolescents and children that is hidden from public life.

Treatment Modalities

The majority of published articles that report treatment alternatives for juvenile sex offenders reveals that childhood and early adolescence offers an opportune time to intervene if there will be hope to allow return to a more normative course of development and avoid further sexually abusive behaviors.[57] Although that proposition undoubtedly seems true, results from outcome studies tend to reveal cause for caution. Treatment efforts have yet to convince detractors that the therapeutic and rehabilitative community has the technology to help rehabilitate and reintegrate adolescents. Available evidence, however, provides three reasons for cautious optimism.

The first reason for guarded optimism derives from the failure to subject programs to rigorous scientific outcome evaluations. Indeed, few outcome studies exist and those that do report outcomes are open to several criticisms. Studies tend simply to describe treatment modalities, rely on very small samples, have short-term follow-ups, use outcome measures that do not necessarily indicate change, or use self-reports of aggressive acts after treatment.[58] For example, one ground-breaking therapeutic outcome study that receives considerable attention compared young sex offenders and a comparison group.[59] Although the results revealed the importance of taking multisystemic approaches, the study involved only 16 sex offenders. Another example deals with high rates of therapeutic success—for example, two robust studies reported that only 6 and 7.5% of released juveniles committed other sex crimes during long-term follow-ups.[60] However, juvenile sex offenders already have low rates of recidivism: Adolescent sex offenders, like adult offenders, have very low recidivism rates, seemingly regardless of the form of therapy or intervention.[61] These findings do not mean that attempts to treat sexually aggressive adolescents are necessarily unsuccessful, they simply mean that the clinical utility of interventions with these juveniles remains largely theoretical and extrapolations from adult literature.

The second reason for prudent enthusiasm is that treatment, and whether it works, depends on social as well as clinical constraints. Without doubt, programs and treatment modalities vary tremendously. Programs generally range from those offered in least restrictive environments to secure confinement at the most restrictive end of the continuum. Numerous possible treatment options exist within the range, such as therapeutic foster care, training schools, specialized treatment programs, and residential group homes.[62] In terms of actual therapeutic approaches, numerous protocols exist. Most therapeutic efforts make use of group therapy, familial therapy, and a host of psychosocio–educational modalities.[63] The major reason for caution is that treatment is not necessarily available and that the available treatment may not fit offenders' needs. The availability, context, and nature of therapeutic environments are important to highlight. These factors largely dictate the choice of treatment. It often is believed that the offense and offender dictate the treatment. In this regard, commentators note that several factors guide the choice of treatment. These factors typically include whether violence was involved, and if so, what level; whether the acts were ritualistic or otherwise bizarre; the offender's prior history of sexual or other offending; the offender's acknowledgement of culpability; and offender's family environment that could sustain the desired services.[64] However, given the availability of services, those who commit less violent offenses and lack complicating factors such as abusive families or other individual problem behaviors are the ones most likely to receive services, because they are candidates for the most frequently available forms of treatment: least restrictive environment programs that are community-based.[65] Thus those who are most violent and have fewer support services also have fewer options available; and, as we will see, they also are more readily transferred out of the juvenile justice system and go without treatment after adult court convictions. Note that, although seemingly unjust, it does seem that the group of adolescent sexual abusers who may not have the ingrained patterns of sexually aggressive behavior and may be the most amenable to treatment may be the first in line to receive it;[66] thus those who can benefit receive treatment and the others receive punishment.

The third reason for hope derives from research that deals with adult sex offenders. In a recent review of therapeutic approaches to the treatment of child sexual abusers, a leading expert concluded that ''the emerging literature is encouraging in terms of desired change for those individuals who are identified.''[67] Several comprehensive reviews reveal that appropriately tailored therapeutic approaches, particularly those with a cognitive–behavioral focus, report low recidivism rates for ''child molesters.''[68] Although research indicates that offenders are more amenable to therapeutic interventions than popular perceptions suggest, optimism remains guarded. Efforts to deal with adult offenders focus on incapacitation and a surging movement aims toward eliminating offender treatment programs, despite the fact that offenders eventually will be released from incarceration.[69] To further raise concerns, the current response to young sex offenders includes the tendency to transfer them to adult court, which then increases the likelihood of obtaining fewer rehabilitative resources.

In summary, although gaps in knowledge persist, available evidence indicates that multidimensional causal models of adolescent sexual offending point to the complex and reciprocal interplay between important characteristics of assaultive adolescents and their social systems. Moreover and in contrast to conclusions of early reviewers, research proposes that adolescent sexual violence may be treated effectively for a core group of offenders. Effectiveness, however, mandates providing treatment that flexibly addresses a broad range of social behaviors, including those that maintain problem behaviors, in adolescents' naturally occurring systems. Multidimensional problems, then, require multisystemic interventions to support offender's behavioral changes.

Prevention Programs

Given the scope of adolescent offending, difficulty uncovering abusive experiences, and obstacles to treatment and successful intervention, the expectation would be that prevention would be an area of keen interest. Yet little research focuses on preventing the development of young offenders.[70] Responses to sexual aggression against children and adolescents remain weighted toward victim-centered prevention.[71] However, given the considerable societal and empirical attention given to the prevention of sexual assault programs, new approaches develop rapidly and expand their reach to reflect the varied etiological and therapeutic emphases of multilevel intervention.

Prevention programs now focus on children, adolescents, parents, caretakers, and other community members. The majority of primary prevention measures have been school based and vary in their presentation of prevention information. Despite variability, consistency in program objectives converge along the following goals: They explain the forms of inappropriate relationships, describe perpetrators, focus on empowering children and adolescents through personal safety skills, and promote disclosure.[72] Although several note the danger of relying mainly on potential victims to defend themselves, research suggests that even most preschool age children can benefit from participating in developmentally appropriate personal safety programs.[73] Although children and adolescents may benefit, limitations associated with sole reliance on potential victims have been recognized and have led the prevention movement to include parents and other caretakers. Parent-focused efforts aim to inform parents about the problem of sexual abuse, offer ways for them to educate their children, have parents assist in identifying victims, and teach appropriate responses to disclosures of sexual abuse. Although it remains difficult to involve parents,[74] researchers continue to argue that parents could be highly effective in preventing and responding to sexual abuse.[75] Programs also now aim to include teachers, social workers, law enforcement, and medical professionals in prevention efforts, although the focus of their inclusion still tends to be on their duty to report suspected cases.[76] Although these experts continue to be underused in primary prevention efforts, researchers report considerable hope that they can assist.[77]

Despite progress, debates about prevention programs continue.[78] Some commentators propose that child- and adolescent-centered prevention programs are ineffective and essentially misguided;[79] others argue that students can and do learn important concepts and that prevention efforts are on the right track.[80] Others argue that current efforts focus too much on investigating and uncovering abuse rather than engaging in more preventive measures and adopting policies that will assist victims rather than focusing on punishing offenders.[81] Despite debates, however, it does seem that comprehensive efforts remain necessary. The general finding tends to be that children can benefit from participating in developmentally appropriate personal safety programs and that efforts must be expanded so that children do not shoulder the full responsibility of prevention.[82] Likewise, the focus on punishing offenders addresses important societal concerns that offenders "pay" for their crimes and serves as a way to ensure that children can be protected from people known to be dangerous to them and focuses public consciousness on the problem. In addition, children benefit from learning skills that may not only protect them from abusers but also begin a socialization process that helps ensure that they do not become abusive themselves. Finally, given what we have learned about motivators and inhibitors of abuse, it does seem that a comprehensive approach is more than a politically sound move; it seems to be a move necessary to combat different forces that factor into the largely silent ecology of sexual abuse.

Problems inherent to victim- and caretaker-centered programs have led to interest in preventive efforts with potential perpetrators of sexual aggression, not the small minority of aggressors who have been adjudicated. Program evaluators report promising interventions with adolescent sexual aggressors and their environments. These programs aim to teach adolescents who are at risk of abusing children about the nature and causes of child sexual abuse and help adolescents develop skills that relate to empathy, anger management, problem solving, decision making, and impulse control.[83] Commentators also emphasize the need to also reform societal attitudes about adolescents, male–female relationships, and sexuality.[84] These efforts focus more on the potential perpetrators' environment, such as preventing antisocial behavior via parent training[85] and molding peer environments in school settings.[86] Likewise, it is critical to note that other prevention efforts that aim to reduce delinquency also directly impact the development of adolescents who sexually assault;[87] for, as we have seen, for several adolescents, their sexual offenses are associated with bullying behavior and general delinquency. Although increasing, perpetrator-oriented interventions and broader community efforts have barely begun to move from focusing only on sexual aggressors who have been apprehended and convicted to a broader focus on all developmental levels of boys and girls.[88] Yet this is actually an important development that recognizes and confronts the finding that sexual abuse is engaged in by many more than the abnormal individuals who are apprehended and convicted.

Despite the general lack of research and the recency of efforts to tackle the development of offending, existing prevention efforts exhibit considerable promise. Preventative efforts now recognize the multifaceted nature of assault, which requires an equally complex response. The approaches no longer focus solely on victims; efforts aim to include more people and increase societal recognition that a greater number of individuals must support vulnerable individuals, including potential offenders. What remains to be determined is the extent to which the law may adjust to these emerging themes in studies of adolescent sexual offending.

Adolescent Sex Offenders and the Law

The Constitution does not require states to treat adolescents as juveniles (adolescents deemed minors by law). If anything, the Constitution requires states to treat adolescents more like adults and provide adolescents with significant protections prior to the deprivation of their liberties. The "constitutionalization" of the juvenile court contributes to recent transformations in the manner in which states treat allegations against adolescents who offend and those adjudicated as offenders.[89] That development in adolescents' rights affects the way society now treats sexually abusive juveniles and the current sway between two fundamental tensions in the manner in which the legal system responds to offenders. The first tension involves the need to balance the treatment of adolescents in terms of hoping for rehabilitation with holding adolescents accountable as adults who commit criminal acts. The second tension regards the need to balance the protection of vulnerable adolescents from aggressive and repressive intervention with the persistent need to ensure effective community protection. Current responses and emerging trends reflect a general move toward increasing community protection and enacting more punitive responses to adolescent violence. This section details these developments, which serve as a springboard to envision opportunities for further developments proposed in the section that will follow.

Juvenile Justice Responses

All states have a separate court system to adjudicate juveniles. These juvenile court systems have two-fold purposes. First, juveniles must not be treated as criminals. That orientation builds on the rationale that juveniles benefit from being removed from ordinary criminal courts and placed in forums that serve them as adolescents in need of treatment and rehabilitation. Second, the court deals with adolescents who have suffered neglect, abuse, or grown beyond their guardians' control. In those instances and because the adolescents are victims, the court again theoretically seeks to offer protection and treatment. The rationale for this orientation derives from the state's obligation to protect adolescents from their peculiar vulnerabilities as well as the state's interest in ensuring the production of competent citizens. The juvenile court, then, operates on the ideal that children, even those who break criminal laws, differ from adults and require different treatment in the law.

The rehabilitative ideals of the juvenile court have been subject to important transformations, particularly as the system relates to young offenders. Adolescents who commit otherwise criminal acts have troubled the juvenile justice system since its inception. Although troubling, it was not until the 1960s that both state and federal governments began to question seriously the juvenile court system's ability to deal with adolescent offenders and to begin dismantling some of the key features of the system. Three factors centrally contributed to the dramatic shift away from the traditional court that sought to rehabilitate adolescents and toward a more punitive, "just-desserts" model that treats adolescents more like adult criminals. First, the apparently constant increase in juvenile violence since the 1960s contributed to calls for more punitive reforms. Although the number of violent offenders was small, they were perceived as a sufficient threat to community safety to lead the President's Task Force on Violent Crime (Task Force) to recommend radical changes in juvenile justice policy.[90] The Task Force recommended a move from permissive to more punitive dispositions for violent and chronic offenders. The ensuing reforms culminated in more punitive dispositions for all offenders, nonviolent and violent alike. Second, at the time of the Task Force, policy makers were guided by early evidence from treatment research that "nothing works."[91] Although the nothing-works conclusion was aggressively debated,[92] critics of the juvenile justice system used the early work to attack lenient dispositions. These critics argued that research clearly refuted the juvenile court's rehabilitative ideal that coddled violent juveniles. The third factor that greatly contributed to current reforms was the effectiveness of the children's rights movement. The U.S. Supreme Court, in *In re Gault*,[93] a seminal juvenile rights case discussed in chapter 2, attacked the disparity between due process protections for adults and juveniles charged with crimes. The Supreme Court finding fueled reforms in two significant directions. First, it further raised concern about the *parens patriae* basis for the juvenile court system. The Court essentially replaced judicial discretion necessary for individualized, offender-oriented dispositions with a series of due process rights necessary for adjudicating offenses. Second, the new focus on ensuring due process allowed for more punitive and retributive sanctions. Because violent offenders were, at least in theory, accorded legal protections, the courts could then refocus on punishment philosophies and increase the severity of legal sanctions. The ultimate effect was a quick move toward circumscribing the jurisdiction of the juvenile court and applying criminal sanctions to violent delinquent behavior.

The same factors that contributed to calls for reform and recent efforts to abolish the juvenile court system still fuel calls for continued and more aggressive reforms and color the current recognition of adolescents who sexually offend. Lack of confidence in the effectiveness of juvenile court sanctions and rehabilitative dispositions, the need to protect adolescents' due process rights, and the necessity to ensure community safety all influence two key decision points in juvenile justice responses to adolescent sex offenders: whether adolescents make it into the system and the disposition of those who make it through the system. This section explores these two points of intervention.

Juvenile justice systems use two ways to gain jurisdiction over adolescents who sexually offend: statutory limits on the offenders' age at the time of the offense for the purposes of juvenile court jurisdiction and laws that regulate sexual offenses determine the threshold issue of whether adolescents come under the jurisdiction of the juvenile court. Both determinants of jurisdiction are fraught with complexities.

In terms of the juvenile courts' own jurisdiction, adolescents who offend generally come under the court's power in two ways. The first way to enter juvenile justice systems involves use of the offenders' age at the time of the offense. States provide upper age limits, usually age 17 for juvenile court jurisdiction. The ages, however, range widely—from 15 to 18—and often reach as high as 21 for penalties for crimes committed prior to the lower jurisdictional age.[94] Age limitations typically only limit maximum ages for jurisdiction. States do not absolutely exclude adolescents of certain minimum ages; those that do provide minimum ages typically do so as presumptions of capacity, with two states setting 10 as the minimum age and one setting 7 as the age of capacity for committing delinquent acts.[95]

The second way to determine juvenile court jurisdiction is significant yet often ignored. Young adolescent offenders may rely on the immaturity defense if it cannot be proven that they possessed sufficient mental capacity to appreciate the consequences of the acts charged. The possibility arises when statutes have no absolute age-based minimum and have discretionary jurisdictions for adolescents. In these instances, states require that adolescents possess sufficient intellectual and emotional maturity to justify a criminal conviction.[96] If adolescents succeed in their plea of infancy, the juvenile or family court may still gain jurisdiction for, in such instances, courts may invoke child protection laws and seek to provide family intervention to protect both adolescents and their victims.[97] These interventions are not limitless: the rights of adolescents and their parents limit child protection intervention, delinquency adjudications must be proven beyond a reasonable doubt,[98] and federal mandates restrict placements for both outcomes.[99] Despite different ways to intervene, the discussion will focus on juveniles as offenders instead of victims in need of services.

When juveniles potentially do come into court jurisdiction through their age or appropriate capacity, juvenile courts may gain jurisdiction over the offenders only to the extent that the adolescents violate any penal code. That determination is deceptively simple. States simply analogize adolescent misconduct to acts of adults and make use of adult penal statutes to determine legal responses. For example, states often define juvenile delinquents by age and then proceed to detail more particularized categories of offenses, such as mandatory, repeat, violent, and aggravated juvenile offenses.[100] Depending on circumstances, adolescent sex offenses may fall within any or all of these categories *depending* on the statutes that describe sexual assault.

Although apparently straightforward, the determination actually remains complicated and often ambiguous. The approach to jurisdiction over adolescent sex offenders depends on the scope of adult statutes that prohibit various forms of sexual conduct. In some circumstances, the reliance is obvious, and in others they are complicated by the traditional need to protect adolescents from societal intervention. Both the simple and more complicated approaches stem from the two ways statutes define sexual assault: through the presence of coercion or its proxy, age. (See chapters 7 and 8.)

The first and least complicated method involves the use of force, or threats of force, against unconsenting parties. In circumstances in which adolescents use force to attempt or accomplish sexual contact with others against their will, adult penal codes encompass adolescent behavior. Once the behavior falls into criminal code provisions, the juvenile justice system gains jurisdiction. The only major complication that may arise, as discussed later, is that the adolescent may be waived out of juvenile court and into the adult criminal justice system.

The second way statutes define sexual assault is through use of age as a proxy. Two approaches may be taken. First and as we have seen in the previous chapter, statutes may simply allow sexual conduct between juveniles based on a combination of various minimum ages for victims and maximum separation in ages between the victim and the offender. The approach complicates matters when juveniles are within statutory age limits and no overt threat or use of force was made. Culpability attaches only when the sexual contact entails abuse of someone who, because of specific infirmities, the law deems incapable of consenting to contact. The second approach makes use of child molestation statutes. These statutes simply look at the age of the victim as the trigger for *criminal* culpability. The vast majority of states have statutes that specifically criminalize child sexual abuse.[101] In defining and exercising jurisdiction over the offense, these statutes manifest neither concern with the age differential between parties nor the mental faculties of the victim or perpetrator. Ironically, these schemes do evince the policy decision that children under certain ages cannot legally consent to certain forms of sexual contact. Under this scheme, adolescents could be charged with an offense even when they themselves are young enough to fall within the age group that the relevant statute aims to protect. Even though the minor may fall within or under a specified age range singled out for protection, courts typically have no difficulty surmounting legal challenges to charging and sanctioning juveniles who would otherwise be protected from sexual activity. Courts generally hold that a minor defendant can be prosecuted for violating a statute prohibiting sexual activity with a minor in a specified age group even if the defendant falls within those age limitations.[102] This position rejects the argument that juvenile offenders should not be held accountable for sexual activity with children on the simple grounds that such a limitation would mean that some minors would essentially have a license to sexually molest others.[103] Courts will allow jurisdiction based on the minor's capacity and knowledge of wrongfulness.[104] Conversely, when minors do not have the requisite capacity for intent to commit the crime that would allow for jurisdiction, they may not be tried as juveniles.[105]

Regardless of the manner in which juvenile courts gain jurisdiction over adolescents, all existing approaches leave considerable discretion on those charged with enforcing statutory mandates. The statutory provisions allow prosecutors and judges to exercise significant freedom in their responses to adolescents. For prosecutors, the power is far from unusual; prosecutorial power has long been recognized and respected as it ranges over which cases to bring to trial, what charges to include in those cases, and what penalties to seek. Prosecutors have the discretion and ability to extend coverage to adolescents intended for protection. As long as the requisite age differential is present, nothing bars the state from pursuing a juvenile simply because he or she falls within a protected age group. As we will see, prosecutors also may avail themselves of an important reform measure: They increasingly may transfer offenders to adult court and seek adult penalties. Likewise, the juvenile court judge wields considerable power. Judicial discretion, despite attempts to eliminate it, necessarily makes an important part of judicial processes as judges control transfer hearings, adjudicate juveniles, and maintain control throughout the imposition of dispositions. Thus even though statutory clarity may be gained, its application remains considerably nuanced.

Once a juvenile court gains jurisdiction over alleged offenders and finds them culpable, the next phase involves imposing dispositional alternatives. The available array of potential dispositions (what in adult courts are called sentences or punishments) ranges along a continuum from no legal response to extreme legal consequences. The wide range in possible dispositions also ranges widely in effectiveness. Despite these wide ranges, existing research does suggest important directions as systems experience mounting pressure to reform.

Of available responses and trends, the most notable development involves making use of punitive and control measures developed to address sex predators. These measures, which include tougher sentencing, registration, and public notification, are part of the criminalization of juvenile justice responses and will be discussed later. These trends pose considerable difficulties for those who seek to keep the juvenile justice system faithful to its rehabilitative mission. Moves to hold adolescents accountable through incarceration generally contradict the philosophy of focusing on delinquent adolescents' treatment, privacy, confidentiality, and reintegration.

In addition to the new predator law measures, several dispositional alternatives remain available to deal with adolescents adjudicated delinquent.[106] Programs that currently deal with violent, and potentially violent, adolescents generally aim to remove them from their homes and communities. In addition to incarceration, these adolescents are institutionalized in detention centers, psychiatric hospitals, and more increasingly, paramilitary boot camps.[107] Less violent adolescents, including those who have been institutionalized, may also be placed in noninstitutional programs, such as excursion programs or community supervision. Some adolescents participate in a variety of these alternatives.

Despite the general move away from rehabilitation, there still exists a notable focus on treatment, which reflects the long history of the juvenile court's focus on rehabilitation and reintegration. In fact, the recognition of the existence of young sex offenders led to the rapid development of sex offender programs; even to the extent that programs that treat child and juvenile sex offenders have surpassed those that treat adults.[108] Likewise, adolescents who are not repeat offenders, who are not otherwise violent, and who have potentially supportive environments tend to remain in the juvenile court system and receive available rehabilitative services.[109] A wide range of service options exist that may be used to treat adolescent sex offenders in an effective manner. However, although options exist in theory and in statutory mandates, they are not always available in practice.

Adolescents may receive several modes of community-based therapy.[110] The most often used alternative to the incarceration of chronic (i.e., high-risk) adolescents is intensive probation supervision. Unlike regular probation, intensive supervision involves greater contact between officers and adolescents as well as regular contact with the adolescents' parents. Although programs differ greatly, these efforts enlist probation officers to help arrange for therapeutic and other services for both the adolescents and their families. More recently, efforts include police officers in the reintegration and control of adolescents returned to communities. In terms of actual therapy received, traditional psychotherapy remains the treatment of choice for juvenile offenders. Adolescents are either referred to an outpatient mental health setting for individual psychotherapy or, if it is deemed necessary, referred to a more restrictive environment for more intensive treatment in a residential setting. Both treatment modalities focus on providing individual therapy. In addition to using traditional treatment modalities, several systems have developed alternatives to confining violent adolescents and those potentially violent. As reviewed previously, one of these programs has been tailored directly to sex offenders and has found that comprehensive programs fashioned for adolescents' needs effectively reduce recidivism for both sexual and nonsexual crimes. Contrary to previous gloomy conclusions about the ineffectiveness of treating sex offenders, recent meta-analytic reviews of sex offender treatment programs reveal that comprehensive and properly administered programs with adolescents show the largest effect sizes.

The juvenile justice system continues to move toward providing other dispositional alternatives that range widely in terms of actual rehabilitative and reintegrative focus. These efforts reveal essentially one factor critical to establishing effective rehabilitative juvenile justice programs: Offer services in an ecologically sensitive manner that addresses the multidetermined nature of violent behavior. Developments in providing ecologically valid services during adolescence and before offenders develop chronic patterns of serious aggression continue to demonstrate considerable promise.

Criminal Justice Responses

It is not difficult to argue that the prevailing ethos in states' efforts to deal with problem adolescents centers on increasing and toughening sanctions. During the past several years, many states have responded to juvenile crime and violence by pursuing a strategy that emphasizes control, incarceration, and waiver to adult court. Given the rapid development and expansion of these responses to troubling adolescents, the punitive measures presumably effectively combat adolescent problem behavior. Yet available evidence casts doubt on the methods of transfer, modes of incarceration, and novel forms of control. Although combinations of these measures may be appropriate for some adolescents, existing evidence indicates a need to reconsider emerging punitive trends. This section details and evaluates these trends.

The law regulating the transfer of accused adolescents to adult court owes much to the seminal Supreme Court case that directly enumerated the nature of rights afforded in the process, *Kent v. United States*.[111] *Kent* involved the waiver of a 16-year-old male charged with numerous counts of rape and robbery. Despite Kent's motion for a waiver hearing, the juvenile court judge waived him to criminal court without an investigation on which to base decisions, without discussion of the grounds for waiver, and without a hearing. Reviewing the trial court's decision, the Supreme Court noted that the states' own statute did not endow judges with "a license for arbitrary procedure" or permit a judge to determine in isolation without representation or participation of the child the "critically important" question of whether a minor will be deprived of the juvenile court's special protections.[112] In sweeping language, the Court declared that "there is no place in our system of law for reaching a result of such tremendous consequences without ceremony—without hearing, without effective assistance of counsel, without a statement of reasons."[113] The Court then proceeded to entitle juveniles to a hearing before waiver, a statement of the reasons for the judicial determination, and access to the court's documents used in the transfer determination. The Court even went so far as to detail and approve of eight "determinative factors" for the judge's consideration in making the waiver decision, factors that range from public safety, seriousness of the offense, and the juvenile's personal circumstances.[114] Given the tenor of the Court's opinion, the case firmly stood to represent the Court's determination that states must bestow on adolescents extensive procedural rights if they are to deprive them of their liberties.

The states responded to the Supreme Court mandate to limit judicial discretion in two ways. First, judicial determinations of waivers now follow the Court's enumerated procedures. Juvenile courts that use judicial waivers of jurisdiction provide a formal hearing, address discrete factors regarding the juvenile's offense and circumstances, and document decisions. Second, states may opt out of using judicial waivers in favor of prosecutorial discretion to choose the forum or statutory exclusion of certain juveniles or offenses from juvenile court jurisdiction. This second option generally relegates the power to prosecutors, who have the decision to charge certain offenses, and removes the problem of judicial discretion identified by *Kent*. Thus despite the Supreme Court's pronouncements, states may waive juvenile offenders to adult criminal court without ceremony. By shifting focus, then, states could effectively rescind the rights previously given adolescents.

Although the different methods exist, proper consideration of adolescents' rights requires considering the pervasiveness of the methods. The states tend to use a combination of methods, depending on the age of the juvenile and the nature of the offense. The first approach, the judicial waiver, operates in 47 states.[115] Thirty-six states and the District of Columbia follow an alternative that involves an "automatic file" or a "legislative exclusion."[116] Under this alternative, charges are filed in the criminal court based on a combination of specified offense characteristics and offenders' ages, and most of these exclusions list sex crimes as a possible factor or come under its ambit through the broad umbrella of repeat offender designations. The last approach, followed by 11 states, provides prosecutors with the discretion to seek a transfer.[117] In these jurisdictions the prosecution simply files charges in criminal court when the state provides for concurrent jurisdiction with juvenile courts for certain crimes or repeated offenses. Thus although judicial waiver transfers still exist, states may circumvent that power by using other methods for particular adolescents and specific offenses, and states often have more than one method at their disposal.

These developments reveal important themes. First, all varieties of sexual assault may serve as the predicate acts for use of the various waiver statutes. Either the statutes explicitly highlight sexual assault as a qualifying offense or broadly state any offense qualifies as a possible predicate for transfers. The transfer for sex offenses is far from theoretical: Studies of transfers reveal that sex crimes and other serious felonies serve as the most frequent reasons for transfers and sex crimes receive the most severe punishments.[118] Second, the statutes generally provide the age of 14 as the minimum age for transfer, and several provide no age. The age range leaves a considerably wide net to catch juveniles for transfer. Third, transfers generally weigh the availability of community resources in the juvenile court system as they consider offenders' needs. Thus if services are not available, juveniles' chances of transfer increase. Fourth, the decision undoubtedly affects eventual dispositions. Transfer for sex crimes leads to fewer rehabilitative opportunities; adult courts aim to punish and place less focus on rehabilitation.

Even though transfers to adult courts allow for adult penalties, it is important to note that the criminal justice response trickles down to juveniles in other ways. Considered adults, juveniles are subject to typical adult sentences that now include several innovative developments that have been enacted under the rubric of "sexual predator laws." Once tried as adults, three measures now pervasively burden sex criminals in the interest of community protection. First, registration statutes, enacted in all states, oblige convicted sex offenders to provide law enforcement officials with their social security numbers, home addresses, photographs, fingerprints, and a slew of information relating to their past sexual crimes.[119] Second, community notification statutes, enacted in all but nine states, mandate law enforcement agents to distribute registration information to the general public; six of the remaining states do have some form of public disclosure on request; and the three remaining states have yet to statutorily prescribe notification. Third, civil commitment statutes may be used to confine involuntarily sex offenders adjudicated potentially dangerous; at least eight states have enacted new laws specifically aimed at using civil commitment to confine sex offenders *after* they have served their prison sentence.[120]

These efforts generally all seek the same goal: Restrict the freedom of convicted offenders. For example, registration provides law enforcement officials with a list of possible suspects to pursue when children have been harmed or missing.[121] Notification theoretically deters sex offenders from repeating their crimes by giving residents notice so they can warn and protect their families. Civil commitment laws immobilize offenders and thus promote immediate and long-term public safety by removing from society those determined to be ''sexually violent predators.''[122] These methods, then, all serve to ensure community protection and reflect the broad public health police powers in states' arsenals to combat sexual violence.

Although the statutory activity seems rather fervent at state levels, the recent slew of measures simply follow strict federal mandates. Federal legislation now requires more aggressive responses to sex crimes and binds states through withdrawal of funding. For example, the recent registration and notification requirements receive their impetus from the Jacob Wetterling Crimes Against Children Act.[123] The Act requires every state to enact laws governing the registration of sexually violent offenders. The laws require the creation of databases of known sex offenders. The federal government further requires states to share the information with the FBI and release it to government agencies as well as the public, if ''necessary to protect the public concerning a specific person required to register.''[124] The Act has been subsequently amended and now *mandates* community notification, by both state officials and the FBI, of the presence of individuals convicted of sex offenses against minors.[125] The federal government effectively binds the states through Congress's power to use conditional federal spending. For example, the Wettering Act[126] placed conditions on previous laws that, taken together, now read that states will lose 10% of criminal justice program block grants if they fail to comply with federal mandates. The withholding of federal monies provides powerful incentives; states can ill afford to ignore federal dollars to get tough on crime.

These statutes and trends are impressive for several reasons. They have been enacted with unprecedented speed across most jurisdictions. In addition, the federal government has spurred efforts without the usual state experimentation and statutes thus have been enacted without the benefit of social science evidence. The statutes also redefine the extent to which states will and can go to protect society. Finally, the statutes have been enacted despite persistent controversies and have spread in the face of growing evidence that challenge their effectiveness.

The current recognition of offenses committed by juveniles and the need to deal with deviant behavior invite juvenile and criminal justice system responses to adolescent sex offenders. The extent to which these responses reach effectiveness depends on their actual impact on adolescents and on efforts to protect children and the public from sex offenders. Evaluations of recent reform efforts based on these two factors often take widely variant positions. Although extremes do receive support, research also supports commonly defensible and desirable ends.

The most established and studied reform, the transfers to adult courts, gains considerable popularity. The major rationale for these reforms derives from the perceived need to be stricter on adolescents. Proponents of more aggressive use of waivers point to the satisfaction of the public's desire to get tougher on adolescents, the manner in which waivers appropriately respond to adolescents who cannot be rehabilitated, and how some crimes deserve longer sentences than what the juvenile system affords. If the goal of the system is to punish and incapacitate, then it becomes difficult to find transfer laws ineffective. Studies reveal that adolescents' sex crimes increasingly receive tougher sentences once transferred to adult courts; in one study, adolescents transferred to adult court and convicted of either rape or murder received nearly twice as much prison time for rape—adolescent offenders receive 11.8 years for murder and 19.8 years for rape.[127] Unfortunately for those who find these statistics encouraging, punishment is not the only goal of intervention in the lives of adolescents who offend.

Although incarceration figures suggest that the system effectively punishes some adolescents who offend, research reveals that the system achieves the goals at the expense of other critical ones. Five points for concern arise from considering available social science evidence that evaluates the long-term effects of transfer as well as the transfer itself. First, prosecutorial waivers, the major trend in reforms, creates several problems as it allows prosecutors to choose criminal or juvenile justice forums: It allows systems to ignore the best interests of the minor to protect immediate community interests and lacks procedural protections that judicial waivers otherwise afforded. Second, automatic or legislative transfers also are problematic as they remove case-by-case examinations of juveniles and fail to consider whether juveniles are potentially amenable to rehabilitation in the juvenile court. Third, judicial transfers do not necessarily ensure justice. Juveniles, particularly those 14 and younger, may not understand implications of their rights and may be less able to assist in trial processes.[128] Likewise, clinicians may not possess the requisite tools to inform the court about amenability to treatment and future risk for perpetration.[129] Fourth, and as reflected in the original mission of the juvenile court, adolescents may be less culpable and lose their rehabilitative opportunities with their transfer out of the juvenile court.[130] Fifth, transfers seemingly do make a difference in terms of recidivism but in a negative direction. Two main studies that report on the effects of transfer on recidivism rates reveal that transferred adolescents, even if incarcerated for longer periods of time, display a significantly higher rate of recidivism in a shorter time following incarceration than similarly situated adolescents who were not transferred.[131] In addition to higher recidivism rates, transferred offenders are more likely to commit subsequent felony offenses and more nontransfers substantially improve their behavior over time.[132] Transfers to adult court, then, may quickly incapacitate, but longer term consequences and their adherence to basic rights remain more debatable.

Given that juveniles transferred to adult courts generally become adults for the purposes of sanctions, no doubt exists that the sex-predator statutes can apply to transferred adolescents, unless statutes explicitly state otherwise. The more complicated issue that arises is whether juveniles adjudicated *delinquent* should be subject to restrictive laws that aim for long-term control of offenders. As with the transfer, however, even the adolescents who remain in the juvenile court are increasingly subject to the predator laws and, where laws do not explicitly extend to those adjudicated delinquents, the lowered protections adolescents receive in the juvenile justice system allow for their use.

The mandatory registration laws illustrate how predator laws increasingly extend to adolescent sex offenders. All states that have sex-offender registration laws do not necessarily extend them to adolescents adjudicated delinquent. Five states specifically mention that juveniles may be exempt from registration if they have been adjudicated delinquents or tried in adult systems.[133] Seventeen states specifically require juveniles to register as sex offenders even if adjudicated in the juvenile justice system.[134] Twenty-eight states remain ambiguous and may require adolescent sex offenders, regardless of which court they have been adjudicated, to comply with the same provisions as adults. Courts that have addressed the ambiguity allow the extension to juveniles who may need to register for periods of 15 years to life.[135] For the purposes of sex offenses, then, states treat juveniles who perpetrate sex crimes increasingly the same as adults.

Sex-predator laws reflect an important trend. Concern for public protection fuels the enactment of laws, not concern for the best interests of those who have been adjudicated sex offenders. Neither registration nor its accompanying notification requirement are objectionable when confined to local law enforcement. Such use remains consistent with the two fundamental concerns of the rehabilitative model: confidentiality and stigmatization. Predator laws become problematic, however, when they require the release of offender information to the public, which has become expansively defined by federal requirements that mandate notification.[136] Broadening notification requirements creates potential for public violence against juveniles; counters the rehabilitative goals of the juvenile court; and imposes obligations on adolescents who, unlike "normal" functioning adults and as recognized by the courts, may be less able to protect and care for themselves. The trend reveals a shift from rehabilitation to retribution and deterrence, and from guidance to punishment. Methods that may have been effective now expand to the extent that their effectiveness loses it potency and their use actually becomes counterproductive.

Opportunities for Reform

The current debate about the features of the juvenile justice system and responses to adolescent sex offenders is an emotional one. In this climate it has become increasingly difficult to move beyond symbolic gestures and quick fixes. It also has become difficult to have a rational examination of the issues. Nonetheless, a few conclusions give rise to opportunities for reform and address extreme positions to ensure both adolescents' rights and community interests.

Adolescents' Right to Differential Treatment

As we have seen throughout the previous chapters, the legal system's central concern relating to adolescents' place in the law involves the extend to which they should be treated as adults for the purposes of protecting them from others' actions, including actions by state officials. The trend in this area of adolescents' rights tend to treat adolescents as adults. That move entails a focus on a "justice model" that provides adolescents' rights as the state seeks to punish them as offenders instead of a focus on a "treatment model" that centers more on the difference between adolescents and adults to offer more opportunities to reintegrate offenders back into the community. A close look at social science analyses of the trend reveals a need to reverse orientations for the large majority of adolescent sex offenders. As experimentation and empirical evidence accumulates about the effects of the two approaches, the findings generally support the treatment over the justice model.[137] We already have seen how transfers to adult court exacerbate recidivism rates and fail to reintegrate adolescents. In addition, natural experiments that emerged from the move toward more punitive models and state policies also support treatment models.[138] The efficacy of treatment or justice models, however, have limited meaning if not linked to an understanding of the purposes of the juvenile justice system that frame the realities of service delivery and public policy.

The most recent understanding of delinquency and assaultive behavior leads to four preliminary points regarding needed policy moves. First, simply giving adolescents the same rights as adults will not solve the issue. Indeed, conferring adolescents with procedural rights arguably resulted in increasing the punitiveness of the juvenile court and stifled its rehabilitative and reintegrative mission. Second, a growing consensus emerges among reviewers of intervention efforts that family-based and other community-centered intervention with adolescents represents the most promising treatment for antisocial behavior. The innovations challenge the narrowly focused practices that currently dominate juvenile justice services and can serve as models for reforming current service delivery. Third, the nature of sex offenses and the increasing desire to punish offenders mandates responses that hold adolescents accountable and that place emphasis on community protection. Fourth, providing for the social welfare of young people ultimately remains a societal responsibility rather than a judicial one; addressing violence requires a whole host of social development programs that would affect the more basic needs of adolescents, children, families, and their communities.

In considering the nature of juvenile justice system responses to offending adolescents, the current success of treatment modalities and the understanding of adolescent sex offenders suggests a need to foster the juvenile courts' rehabilitative ideal and reconsider the place even violent adolescents may have in future visions of juvenile justice. Current understanding of sex offending suggests that a core of violent adolescents may be in need of extensive intervention and, on failure, transfer to adult court systems. The majority of adolescents who commit sex crimes, however, seemingly could benefit from more reintegrative modalities, which remains most promising but pervasively unavailable.[139]

Effective programs have the following characteristics in common: They assume a socioecological perspective that approaches problems in terms of key social contexts, deliver services to that natural social context, and provide individualized and flexible services.[140] However, the significance of the innovative approaches does not lie in their ability to present new forms of intervention but rather in their reminding us of the need to flexibly and creatively implement service plans tailored to the multiple needs of individual adolescents. The success of existing innovations moves us toward holding juveniles accountable while protecting society in a more cost-effective and humane manner.

Focus on juvenile justice and juveniles, however, tends to ignore links to other arenas adolescents contact. The singular focus on the juvenile justice system increasingly shortshrifts, if not entirely ignores, the very factors that in combination tend to predict juvenile offending and recidivism: dysfunctional family relations, school behavior problems, negative peer group influences, drug involvement, and deteriorating community supports. Thus the problem with the most serious, chronic, and violent offenders tends to be that they arise at the nexus of numerous social welfare problems and remedying the situation involves more than one state agency. Despite extensive needs, however, evidence does affirm that reintegrative strategies can address the needs of violent adolescents and societal protections. Although current trends seemingly aim in the opposite direction, several persuasive responses may effectively counter heated objections.

Responding to Objections Against Adolescents' Right to Differential Treatment

Several legitimate concerns and arguments face proposals that favor adolescents' rights to extensive reintegrative services. For example, the Supreme Court has long affirmed that states are under "no constitutional duty to provide substantive services within [their] borders."[141] In addition, adolescents have essentially no *federal,* legislative right to services.[142] Likewise, state courts disagree on whether juveniles actually have a right to treatment.[143] Finally, several legislatures have redefined the purpose of their juvenile courts to play down the role of rehabilitation and highlight the role of safety, punishment, and individual accountability.[144] Despite these legal trends, the argument does not necessarily fail and stop there. Although adolescents' positive rights may not be expanding, their negative rights remain. Likewise, economic, therapeutic, policy, and practical considerations support the focus on interventions tailored to adolescents' individual ecologies. These make for several important counterpoints to objections and help overcome obstacles.

Although federal mandates may not ensure the right to treatment, they nevertheless take adolescents' negative rights more seriously. For example, the Supreme Court grants minors, like adults, a "substantial liberty interest in not being confined unnecessarily for medical treatment."[145] The Court further has found that the same liberty interests are at stake in delinquency proceedings that could result in the deprivation of liberty and that the Constitution protects those interests. The bundle of rights involved in removals from homes, communities, and personal relationships have been expanded by federal legislative action. These rights result in the explicit state statutory mandates that require consideration of less restrictive alternatives before institutionalization of minors. State preference for least restrictive measures has been solidified by explicit federal mandates requiring the use of these alternatives. Thus before infringing on minor's liberties and freedoms, states must respect minors' rights to least restrictive intervention.

Parental and family rights also inevitably weigh in the equation. The legal system affords the best interests of the child priority when balancing child, parent, and state interests. As discussed in chapters 2 and 3, the Supreme Court bestows on parents primacy in child-rearing and recognizes parents' liberty interests in the care, custody, and management of their children are of fundamental importance. The Court has further recognized that state intervention directed toward the family should focus on rehabilitation and recognize that "parents retain a vital interest in preventing the irretrievable destruction of *their family life.*"[146]

The traditional nature of the juvenile court still exists and requires consideration of alternatives to punitive sanctions. Although juvenile courts increasingly have been characterized by their move toward punishment, enabling statutes still emphasize rehabilitation, treatment, and protective measures.[147] Taking rehabilitation and treatment seriously entails making meaningful attempts to provide services when and where they are most needed: when troubled adolescents have been identified and, where appropriate, in their own families or communities. All 50 states and the District of Columbia provide for in-home and community placements for juvenile offenders. These mandates typically are a statutory dispositional alternative open to the juvenile courts.[148] Thus despite punitive trends, no state accepts the punishment of juveniles as its sole mandate for juvenile court intervention in offenders' lives.

The costs of serving juveniles in their communities and homes remain considerably *less* than the costs of serving adolescents through institutionalization.[149] An often-cited estimate comparing in-home placement options that use intensive supervision of adolescents with institutionalization reports that in-home programs cost approximately one third the amount needed for institutionalization.[150] Other researchers have shown that placements in mental health facilities, such as a psychiatric institution, are even more expensive.[151] The viability of in-home programs has been shown in a number of recent studies demonstrating the effective and economical use of intense family preservation efforts.[152] Indeed, without intensive family preservation efforts, even serious *felony* offenders who are not institutional-ized but still under intensive supervision fare as well as institutionalized adolescents.[153]

Wise public policy demands limiting intrusions on the privacy of adolescents and their families. Even if the costs and general efficacy of the punitive/out-of-home-community and rehabilitative/in-home-community options were equivalent, public policy goals demand considering the human costs of avoiding institutionalization. In addition, future monetary savings, such as increased earnings and social productivity of exoffenders and averted criminal justice costs, demand considering policies aimed at helping young offenders in their families. Obvious social benefits accrue from programs resulting in crime reduction: The human costs of victimization are considerably high. A simple cost–benefit analysis, then, points to the conclusion that moving toward treating adolescents in their families is wise policy.

Prosecutors, courts, and child welfare officials all operate with wide discretion in execution of their duties. Historically, discretion was a critical part of the juvenile court's *parens patriae* orientation. Although task forces urge adoption of more objective risk assessment and classification systems to guide decisions at all points of the juvenile justice system, the Supreme Court infuses the process with efforts to limit discretion, and research identifies rampant abuses in discretion,[154] efforts to remove discretion remain controversial and plagued by institutional forces against them. Those with the most discretion tend to resist efforts to comply with strict guidelines. The resistance may not be entirely negative; to act in the best interests of the child requires discretion. Forces beyond those who would enforce the guidelines also arouse skepticism about the prospects of successful implementation and impact of guidelines. Decision making rests as much on the offender and the available resources as it does with the decision maker. And guidelines provide for discretion.[155] The tremendous discretion accorded to officials and the realities of implementation allow for the use of alternative sanctions.

Alternative sanctions hold adolescents accountable. Lost in the get-tough debate in juvenile justice is the notion that punishment, as well as control, can be exacted by means other than incarceration. Equally overlooked is the point that incarceration, while serving as one form of punishment, does not mean that all the other aims of sanctioning are unnecessary, unimportant, or irrelevant. The pursuit of punishment through incarceration makes all other aims, particularly rehabilitation and reintegration, more difficult to achieve. As we have seen, incarceration increases the risk of reoffending once released to the community. The manner secure correction facilities presently function directly challenges reintegration efforts.[156] Effective rehabilitative programs are found outside of custodial institutions, which at the very least suggest that confinement experiences disadvantage individuals on their return. Community- level interventions take advantage of one differ-ence: They are already in the community in which offenders need to achieve competent development. While in the community, offenders reintegrate by gaining accountability through a more active role in sanctions, accept more active responsibility, and begin the process of integrating with their communities to render them safe.[157]

Current prevalence estimates suggest that the most troubling adolescents, and those in most need of services, may not be transferred to adult court. Young adolescents, those younger than 14, constitute a majority of offenders identified by social science research as perpetrators of sexual abuse against other children. Figures on sexual assault arrests also reveal that very young adolescents commit a significant amount of sex crimes. These adolescents are unlikely to be transferred to adult court until their crimes are severely violent enough or they have become repeat offenders. Effective policy making would suggest that these adolescents would benefit from attempts at earlier intervention. Researchers continue to note that early aggressive and oppositional behaviors do not necessarily lead to delinquent, chronic, and antisocial life course outcomes; improved parenting, increased school commitment, and reduced affiliation with deviant peers all serve to mediate negative outcomes and place adolescents on positive developmental trajectories.[158]

When examining adolescents' rights to stay in their own families and communities it should be remembered that there is no dispute that they are entitled to a decent, stable environment. That entitlement is a human right memorialized in international declarations and conventions.[159] In addition to recognizing the rights and duties of children and families, the United Nations recently adopted The Riyadh Guidelines aimed at delinquency prevention.[160] The international community accepts the new focus on community-level sanctions and views institutionalization as a last resort. The right to reintegration into one's community is a basic human right that recognizes how unwise its seems to remove individuals from the conditions to which we hope to return them. More humane efforts ameliorate the real-world environmental conditions that led to adolescents' criminal behavior rather than remove adolescents from communities and natural community supports.

Conclusion

The horror, torment, and devastation associated with sex offenses provide states with the obligation and interest to prevent sex crimes, deter those who would otherwise commit such violent acts, and apprehend and hold accountable those who offend. In furthering that obligation, however, states may not disregard the rights of both victims and offenders and exacerbate already difficult situations. Yet the tendency to disregard those rights increases with significant policy transformations driven by public fervor.

The ironic response to public fears of crime has been to respond decisively but to embrace strategies proven to fail. As we have seen, calls for reform increasingly tend to result in the predictable failure to address the multiple causes and many consequences of offenses. The problem with juvenile sex offending is the same for all juvenile crime. Offending behavior relates to other problems that remain unaddressed by the increasing focus on the juvenile court as the means to deal with problem adolescents. The system increasingly serves as an escape hatch that deals with a small number of problematic offenders and fails to address the needs of those offenders, as well as the broader social problems that cause the behavior. As we have seen, the recognition and response to sex offenders remains limited in several ways. The offenses still remain largely hidden: Offenders average seven offenses before official reactions and identifications of abusive acts. Efforts to rehabilitate, even though consistent with the original mission of juvenile justice provisions, increasingly give way to more punitive sanctions. Systematic efforts to prevent the development of young offenders essentially do not exist. Existing trends weaken the primary ingredient to successful intervention; they reduce the juvenile justice system's ability to enable offenders to take responsibility for themselves.

The inability to recognize reintegrative responses need not lead to a sense of futility, which stifles more effective reform efforts. As we also have seen, punishment and rehabilitation are far from inconsistent goals and both still drive the juvenile court. Both goals may be reached and gain consistency by ensuring that reforms foster adolescents' rights while still ensuring community protection. Those rights include the need to consider a wide array of interventions, ranging from therapeutic services, intensive supervision, community-based confinement, and use of small facilities that foster reintegration.

Programs work when they address communities and offenders' multifaceted problems. As we have seen, the legal and political possibility of more appropriate responses are feasibly within reach. For the majority of offenders, the more reintegrative systems protect them and serve societal needs. For the minority of violent and chronic offenders, properly tailored sanctions also address the needs of society and the perpetrator. For the ignored perpetrators who do not make it to juvenile court, broader interventions that move beyond formal legal approaches can help prevent further assaults and address victim's needs.

Endnotes

1. The young offender, allegedly 16, had sodomized a cow, which was killed before he was. Victor L. Streib, *Death Penalty for Juveniles* (Bloomington: Indiana University Press, 1987), at 73.
2. National Adolescent Perpetrator Network, "The Revised Report From the National Task Force on Juvenile Sexual Offending," *Juvenile and Family Court Journal* 44 (1993):5–120; Gail Ryan, Thomas J. Miyoshi, Jeffrey L. Metzner, Richard D. Krugman, and George Fryer, "Trends in a National Sample of Sexually Abusive Youths," *Journal of the American Academy of Child and Adolescent Psychiatry* 35 (1996):17–25.
3. Judith V. Becker, "What We Know About the Characteristics and Treatment of Adolescents Who Have Committed Sexual Offenses," *Child Maltreatment* 3 (1998):317–329.
4. Ryan et al., "Trends in a National Sample of Sexually Abusive Youths"; Glen E. Davis and Harrold Leitenberg, "Adolescent Sex Offenders," *Psychological Bulletin* 101 (1987): 417–427.
5. Michael L. Bourke and Brad Donohue, "Assessment and Treatment of Juvenile Sex Offenders: An Empirical Review," *Journal of Child Sexual Abuse* 5 (1996):47–70.
6. United States Department of Justice, *Uniform Crime Reports* (Washington, DC: Author, 1993), at 222, 227.
7. Howard Snyder, *Juvenile Arrests 1996* (Washington, DC: Office of Juvenile Justice and Delinquency Prevention, U.S. Department of Justice, 1997). Estimates do not include prostitution.
8. Peter A. Fehrenbach, Wayne Smith, Caren Monastersky, and Robert W. Deisher, "Adolescent Sexual Offenders: Offender and Offense Characteristics," *American Journal of Orthopsychiatry* 56 (1986):225–233; Davis and Leitenberg, "Adolescent Sex Offenders." According to other researchers, the percentage of female offenders actually may be higher, as revealed by female offenders who admit offenses for which they have not been identified. Timothy J. Kahn and Mary A. Lanfond, "Treatment of the Adolescent Sex Offender," *Child and Adolescent Social Work* 5 (1988):135–148. When girls do offend, they are likely to do so with male cooffenders. Peter A. Fehrenbach and Caren Monastersky, "Characteristics of Female Adolescent Sexual Offenders," *American Journal of Orthopsychiatry* 58 (1988):148–151.
9. Fehrenbach et al., "Adolescent Sexual Offenders: Offender and Offense Characteristics."
10. *Id.*
11. *Id. See also* Judith Becker, Jerry Cunningham-Rathner, and Meg S. Kaplan, "Adolescent Sexual Offenders," *Journal of Interpersonal Violence* 1 (1986):431–435; Richard J. Kavoussi, Meg Kaplan, and Judith V. Becker, "Psychiatric Diagnoses in Adolescent Sex Offenders," *Journal of the American Academy of Child and Adolescent Psychiatry* 27 (1988):241–243.
12. Davis and Leitenberg, "Adolescent Sex Offenders."
13. Samples finding incestuous relationships range from 40 to 60 percent. Toni Cavanagh Johnson, "Child Perpetrators: Children Who Molest Other Children: Preliminary Findings," *Child Abuse & Neglect* 12 (1988):219–229; Lois H. Pierce and Robert L. Pierce, "Incestuous Victimization by Juvenenile Sex Offenders," *Journal of Family Violence* 2 (1987):351–364. For example, in a study of 350 young sex offenders, 95% were either siblings or children for whom the offender was babysitting. Kahn and Lanfond, "Treatment of the Adolescent Sex Offender." *See also* Leslie Margolin and John L. Craft, "Child Abuse by Adolescent Caregivers," *Child Abuse & Neglect* 14 (1990):365–373.

14. *Id.*
15. Judith V. Becker, "The Effects of Child Sexual Abuse on Adolescent Sexual Offenders." In *Lasting Effects of Child Sexual Abuse,* ed. Gail E. Wyatt and G.J. Powell (Beverly Hills: Sage, 1988). *See also* Judith V. Becker, Meg S. Kaplan, Jerry Cunningham-Rathner, and Richard Kavoussi, "Characteristics of Adolescent Incest Sexual Perpetrators," *Journal of Family Violence* 1 (1986):85–97.
16. Johnson, "Child Perpetrators: Children Who Molest Other Children: Preliminary Findings."
17. *Id.*
18. Roy J. O'Shaugnessy, "Clinical Aspects of Forensic Assessment of Juvenile Sex Offenders," *Psychiatric Clinics of North America* 15 (1992):721–735; Charlayne L. Cooper, William D. Murphy, and Mary R. Haynes, "Characteristics of Abused and Nonabused Adolescent Sexual Offenders," *Sexual Abuse: A Journal of Research and Treatment* 8 (1996):105–119.
19. Judith V. Becker and Robert M. Stein, "Is Sexual Erotica Associated With Sexual Deviance in Adolescent Males?" *International Journal of Law and Psychiatry* 14 (1991):85–95; Cooper et al., "Characteristics of Abused and Nonabused Adolescent Sexual Offenders."
20. *See, e.g.,* Michael C. Seto and Howard E. Barbaree, "Sexual Aggression as Antisocial Behavior: A Developmental Model." In *Handbook of Antisocial Behavior,* ed. David M. Stoff, James Breiling, and Jack D. Maser (New York: John Wiley, 1997).
21. Terrie E. Moffitt, "Adolescence-Limited and Life-Course-Persistent Antisocial Behavior: A Developmental Taxonomy," *Psychological Review* 100 (1993):674–701.
22. *See* chapter 8.
23. Howard E. Barbaree, Stephen M. Hudson, and Michael C. Seto, "Sexual Assault in Society: The Role of the Juvenile Offender." In *Juvenile Sex Offending,* ed. Howard E. Barbaree, William I. Marshall, and Stephen M. Hudson (New York: Guilford Press, 1993).
24. Gail Ryan, "Sexually Abusive Youth: Defining the Problem." In *Juvenile Sexual Offending: Causes, Consequences, and Corrections,* ed. Gail Ryan and Sandy Lane (San Francisco: Jossey-Bass, 1997).
25. *Id.*
26. For a review, *see* Eilana Gil, "Etiological Theories." In *Sexualized Children: Assessment and Treatment of Sexualized Children and Children Who Molest,* ed. Eliana Gil and Toni Cavanagh Johnson (Rockville, MD: Launch Press, 1993); Gail Ryan, "Theories of Etiology." In *Juvenile Sexual Offending: Causes, Consequences, and Corrections,* ed. Gail Ryan and Sandy Lane (San Francisco: Jossey-Bass, 1997); Brandt F. Steele and Gail Ryan, "Deviancy: Development Gone Wrong." In *Juvenile Sexual Offending: Causes, Consequences, and Corrections,* ed. Gail Ryan and Sandy Lane (San Francisco: Jossey-Bass, 1997); Sharon K. Araji, *Sexually Aggressive Children: Coming to Understand Them* (Thousand Oaks, CA: Sage, 1997).
27. Roger C. Katz, "Psychosocial Adjustment of Child Molesters," *Child Abuse & Neglect* 14 (1990):567–575.
28. *Id.*
29. Joyce F. Lakey, "The Profile and Treatment of Male Adolescent Sex Offenders," *Adolescence* 29 (1994):755–760.
30. Fehrenbach et al., "Adolescent Sexual Offenders: Offender and Offense Characteristics," found that 32% reported no friends and nearly two thirds showed evidence of social isolation. These results have been supported by several other researchers. *See* Kahn and Lanfond, "Treatment of the Adolescent Sex Offender"; Roger Graves, D. Kim Openshaw, and Gerald R. Adams, "Adolescent Sex Offenders and Social Skills Training," *International Journal of Offender Therapy and Comparative Criminology* 36 (1992):139–153.
31. Katz, "Psychosocial Adjustment of Child Molesters"; Jeffrey Fagan and Sandra Wexler, "Explanations of Sexual Assault Among Violent Delinquents," *Journal of Adolescent Research* 3 (1988):363–385.
32. It is these two themes that are important to understanding the abusive cycles and the manner in which children become abusive. For a review, *see* Sandy Lane, "The Sexual Abuse Cycle." In

Juvenile Sexual Offending: Causes, Consequences, and Corrections, ed. Gail Ryan and Sandy Lane (San Francisco: Jossey-Bass, 1997).

33. Steven Spaccarelli, Blake Bowden, J. Douglas Coatsworth, and Soni Kim, "Psychosocial Correlates of Male Sexual Aggression in a Chronic Delinquent Sample," *Criminal Justice and Behavior* 24 (1997):71–95; Fagan and Wexler, "Explanations of Sexual Assault Among Violent Delinquents"; Wayne R. Smith, "Delinquency and Abuse Among Juvenile Sexual Offenders," *Journal of Interpersonal Violence* 3 (1988):400–413.

34. William L. Marshall, Stephen M. Hudson, and Sharon Hodkinson, "The Importance of Attachment Bonds in the Development of Juvenile Sex Offending." In *Juvenile Sex Offending,* ed. Howard E. Barbaree, William I. Marshall, and Stephen M. Hudson (New York: Guilford Press, 1993).

35. Pierce and Pierce, "Incestuous Victimization by Juvenenile Sex Offenders"; Kahn and Lafond, "Treatment of the Adolescent Sex Offender."

36. R. Prentky, R. Knight, H. Straus, F. Rokous, D. Cerce, and J. Sims-Knight, "Developmental Antecedents of Sexual Aggression," *Development and Psychopathology* 1 (1989):153–169.

37. Colin Hawkes, Jilles Ann Jenkins, and Eileen Vizard, "Roots of Sexual Violence in Children and Adolescents." In *Violence in Children and Adolescents,* ed. Ved Varma (London: Jessica Kingsley, 1997).

38. For groundbreaking research in this area, *see* A. Nicholas Groth, Robert E. Longo, and J. Bradley McFaddin, "Undetected Recidivism Among Rapists and Child Molesters, *Crime and Delinquency* 28 (1982):450–458.

39. Gail Ryan, Sandy Lane, John Davis, and Connie Issac, "Juvenile Sex Offenders: Development and Correction," *Child Abuse & Neglect* 11 (1987):385–395.

40. National Adolescent Perpetrator Network, "The Revised Report From the National Task Force on Juvenile Sexual Offending."

41. Prentky et al., "Developmental Antecedents of Sexual Aggression."

42. Dennis Howitt, *Paedophiles and Sexual Offenses Against Children* (New York: Wiley, 1995), at 38.

43. Gordon C. Nagayama Hall, "Prediction of Sexual Aggression," *Clinical Psychology Review* 10 (1990):229–245.

44. R. A. Lang and R. Langevin, "Parent–Child Relations in Offenders Who Commit Violent Sexual Crimes Against Children," *Behavioral Sciences and the Law* 9 (1991):61–71.

45. Psychometric data do not distinguish perpetrators well, nor predict recidivism. Jean Proulx, Bruno Pellevin, Yves Paradis, Andre McKibben, Jocelyn Aubut, and Marc Ouimet, "Static and Dynamic Predictors of Recidivism in Sexual Aggressors," *Sexual Abuse: A Journal of Research and Treatment* 9 (1997):7–27.

46. Earlier approaches distinguished between two categories—*fixated* and *regressed* offenders, which were distinguishable by the former being less likely to be married, more likely to victimize strangers and acquaintances, and not exhibiting more mature forms of sexual expression. A. Nicholas Groth and H. Jean Birnbaum, "Adult Sexual Orientation and Attraction to Underage Persons," *Archives of Sexual Behavior* 7 (1978):175–181. This research mirrors more recent efforts to focus on distinguishing between abuse occurring either outside of or within families. Anne E. Pawlak, John R. Boulet, and John M. W. Bradford, "Discriminant Analysis of a Sexual-Functioning Inventory With Intrafamilial and Extrafamilial Child Molesters," *Archives of Sexual Behavior* 20 (1991):27–34. Despite the different focus and early belief that the abuses involved very different dynamics, research now finds increasing similarities: Both commit similar sexual acts, use similar methods to obtain sexual gratification, and have similar reasons for offending.

47. Rudolph Alexander, "Employing the Mental Health System to Control Sex Offenders After Penal Incarceration," *Law & Policy* 17 (1995):111–130.

48. W. L. Marshall, "The Sexual Offender: Monster, Victim, or Everyman?" *Sexual Abuse: A Journal of Research and Therapy* 8 (1996):317–335.

49. For a review of current theories and their criticisms, *see* Gordon C. Nagayama Hall, *Theory-*

Based Assessment, Treatment, and Prevention of Sexual Aggression (New York: Oxford University Press, 1996).

50. This work draws on Finkelhor's seminal work. *See* David Finkelhor, *Child Sexual Abuse: New Theory and Research* (New York: Free Press, 1984); David Finkelhor, "The Sexual Abuse of Children: Current Research Reviewed," *Psychiatric Annals* 17 (1987):233–241.

51. Lucy Johnston and Tony Ward, "Social Cognition and Sexual Offending: A Theoretical Framework," *Sexual Abuse: A Journal of Research and Treatment* 8 (1996):55–88; Larry Neidgh and Harry Krop, "Cognitive Distortion Among Child Sexual Offenders," *Journal of Sex Education and Therapy* 18 (1992):208–215; Vizard et al., "Child and Adolescent Sexual Abuse Perpetrators: A Review of the Research Literature"; Tony Ward, Stephen M. Hudson, Lucy Johnson, and William L. Marshall, "Cognitive Distortions in Sex Offenders: An Integrative Review," *Clinical Psychology Review* 17 (1997):479–507.

52. Nathan L. Pollock and Judith M. Hashmall, "The Excuses of Child Molesters," *Behavioral Sciences and the Law* 9 (1991):53–59; Patricia Phelan, "Incest and Its Meaning: Perspectives of Fathers and Daughters," *Child Abuse & Neglect* 19 (1995):7–24.

53. Rizwan Z. Shah, Paula W. Dail, and Time Heinrichs, "Familial Influences Upon the Occurrence of Child Sexual Abuse," *Journal of Child Sexual Abuse* 4 (1995):45–61.

54. Michele Elliott, Kevin Browne, and Jennifer Kilcoyne, "Child Sexual Abuse Prevention: What Sex Offenders Tell Us," *Child Abuse & Neglect* 19 (1995):579–594.

55. Little or nothing is known about pedophiles who are not convicted or who never enter the criminal justice system. Researchers indicate that men who do enter the system constitute only a small percentage of those who sexually abuse children. Betty N. Gordon and Carolyn S. Schroeder, *Sexuality: A Developmental Approach to Problems* (New York: Plenum Press, 1995).

56. Roger J. R. Levesque, "Prosecuting Sex Crimes Against Children: Time for 'Outrageous' Proposals?" *Law and Psychology Review* 19 (1995):59–91.

57. Barry Morenz and Judith Becker, "The Treatment of Youthful Sexual Offenders," *Applied and Preventive Psychology* 4 (1995):247–256; Kevin Epps, "The Residential Treatment of Adolescent Sex Offenders," *Issues in Criminological and Legal Psychology* 17 (1991):58–67; Janis F. Bremmer, "Serious Juvenile Sex Offenders: Treatment and Long Term Follow-Up," *Psychiatric Annals* 22 (1992):326–332.

58. For an empirical analysis of existing adolescent sex offender treatment programs, *see* Vizard et al., "Child and Adolescent Sexual Abuse Perpetrators: A Review of the Research Literature."

59. Charles M. Borduin, Scott W. Henggeler, David M. Blaske, and Risa J. Stein, "Multisystemic Treatment of Adolescent Sexual Offenders," *International Journal of Offender Therapy and Comparative Criminology* 34 (1990):105–113.

60. Bremmer, "Serious Juvenile Sex Offenders: Treatment and Long Term Follow-Up"; Timothy J. Kahn and Heather J. Chambers, "Assessing Reoffense Risk With Juvenile Sexual Offenders," *Child Welfare* 70 (1991):333–345.

61. Kahn and Chambers, "Assessing Reoffense Risk With Juvenile Sexual Offenders"; Davis and Leitenberg, "Adolescent Sex Offenders." One recent study found 9% of juvenile offenders were arrested for adult sex offenses. Ron Sipe, Eric L. Jensen, and Ronald S. Everett, "Adolescent Sexual Offenders Grown Up: Recidivism in Young Adulthood," *Criminal Justice and Behavior* 25 (1998):109–124.

62. Morenz and Becker, "The Treatment of Youthful Sex Offenders"; Epps, "The Recidivist Treatment of Adolescent Sex Offenders"; Bremmer, "Serious Juvenile Sex Offenders: Treatment and Long-Term Follow-Up."

63. For a review of treatment approaches, *see* Michael L. Bourke and Brad Donohue, "Assessment and Treatment of Juvenile Sex Offenders: An Empirical Review," *Journal of Child Sexual Abuse* 5 (1996):47–70; Vizard et al., "Child and Adolescent Sexual Abuse Perpetrators: A Review of the Research Literature."

64. Elissa J. Brown and David J. Kolko, "Treatment Efficacy and Program Evaluation With Juvenile Sex Abusers: A Critique With Directions for Service Delivery and Research," *Child Maltreatment* 3 (1998):362–373.

65. In a national survey of juvenile treatment programs, 80% were offered in community-based outpatient settings; the remainder operated in residential programs that included incarceration and mental health settings. Safer Society Program and Press, *1994 Nationwide Survey of Treatment Programs and Models Serving Abuse-reactive Children and Adolescent and Adult Sex Offenders* (Brandon, VT: Author, 1994).

66. Borduin et al., "Multisystemic Treatment of Adolescent Sexual Offenders."

67. David A. Wolfe, "The Role of Intervention and Treatment Services in the Prevention of Child Abuse and Neglect." In *Protecting Children From Abuse and Neglect: Foundations for a New National Strategy,* ed. Gary B. Melton and Frank D. Barry (New York: Guilford Press, 1994), at 280.

68. Judith V. Becker and John A. Hunter Jr., "Evaluation of Treatment Outcome for Adult Perpetrators of Child Sexual Abuse," *Criminal Justice and Behavior* 19 (1992):74–92.

69. Several states, most recently Massachusetts, Virginia, and Florida, have moved toward eliminating therapeutic programs. *See* Levesque, "Prosecuting Sex Crimes Against Children: Time for 'Outrageous' Proposals?"

70. Recent texts on sexually aggressive children ignore the issue; *see* Sharon K. Araji, *Sexually Aggressive Children: Coming to Understand Them.*

71. Gary B. Melton, "The Improbability of Prevention of Sexual Abuse." In *Prevention of Child Maltreatment,* ed. Diane J. Willis, William E. Holden, and Maurice S. Rosenberg (New York: Wiley, 1992).

72. Jan Rispens, Andre Aleman, and Paul P. Goudena, "Prevention of Child Sexual Abuse Victimization: A Meta-Analysis of School Programs," *Child Abuse & Neglect* 21 (1997):975–987.

73. Yet reviews also warn that children should not shoulder the full responsibility for prevention, particularly because the most difficult skill for young children to acquire is telling adults about inappropriate touching situations. *Id. See also* Sandy K. Wurtele and Julie Sarno Owens, "Teaching Personal Safety Skills to Young Children: An Investigation of Age and Gender Across Five Studies," *Child Abuse & Neglect* 21 (1997):805–814.

74. Recent research indicates that it remains difficult to get parents involved in prevention efforts: One study reported that only 1 out of 250 families explicitly discussed with their children the nature and proper reaction to unwanted sexual attention. Freda Briggs, "South Australian Parents Want Child Protection Programs to Be Offered in Schools and Preschools," *Australian Journal of Early Childhood* 12 (1987):20–25.

75. For a comprehensive review, *see* Sandra K. Wurtele and Cindy L. Miller-Perrin, *Preventing Child Sexual Abuse: Sharing the Responsibility* (Lincoln: University of Nebraska Press, 1992).

76. Roberta A. Hibbard and Terrell W. Zollinger, "Patterns of Child Sexual Abuse Knowledge Among Professionals," *Child Abuse & Neglect* 14 (1990):347–355; Deborah A. Daro, "Prevention of Child Sexual Abuse," *Future of Children* 4 (1994):198–223.

77. *Id.*

78. Jeffrey J. Haugaard and N. Dickon Reppucci, *The Sexual Abuse of Children: A Comprehensive Guide to Current Knowledge and Intervention Strategies* (San Francisco: Jossey-Bass, 1988).

79. Several criticize, for example, the focus on children as well as the untimely and inappropriate topics; *see* Leslie M. Tutty, "Developmental Issues in Young Children's Learning of Sexual Abuse Prevention Concepts," *Child Abuse and Neglect* 18 (1994):179–192.

80. Margot Taal and Monique Edelaar, "Positive and Negative Effects of a Child Sexual Abuse Prevention Program," *Child Abuse & Neglect* 21 (1997):339–410.

81. John E. B. Myers, "Adjudication of Child Sexual Abuse Cases," *Future of Children* 4 (1994):84–101.

82. Sandy K. Wurtele and Julie Sarno Owens, "Teaching Personal Safety Skills to Young Children: An Investigation of Age and Gender Across Studies," *Child Abuse & Neglect* 21 (1997):805–814; Leslie M. Tutty, "Child Sexual Abuse Prevention Programs: Evaluating *Who Do You Tell,*" *Child Abuse & Neglect* 21 (1997):869–881.

83. For a review of programs, *see* Wurtele and Miller-Perrin, *Preventing Child Sexual Abuse: Sharing the Responsibility.*

84. *Id. See also* Gordon and Schroeder, *Sexuality: A Developmental Approach to Problems.*

85. For a comprehensive review of efforts by a leading commentator, *see* Deborah Daro, *Confronting Child Abuse: Research for Effective Program Design* (New York: Free Press, 1988).

86. Several preschool and primary school programs report positive results in efforts to reduce delinquent behavior and deal with sexuality. *See* Joan McCord and Richard E. Tremblay (Eds.), *Preventing Antisocial Behavior: Intervention from Birth Through Adolescence* (New York: Guilford Press, 1992).

87. Edward Zigler, Cara Taussig, and Kathryn Black, "Early Childhood Intervention," *American Psychologist* 47 (1992):997–1006.

88. However, a recent review of primary prevention of perpetration reports that few efforts address primary prevention in community and family life, in relation to childhood sexuality, and intervention for high risk groups. Gail Ryan, "Perpetration Prevention: Primary and Secondary." In *Juvenile Sexual Offending: Causes, Consequences, and Corrections,* ed. Gail Ryan and Sandy Lane (San Francisco: Jossey-Bass, 1997).

89. Roger J. R. Levesque, "Is There Still a Place for Violent Youth in Juvenile Justice?" *Aggressive and Violent Behavior* 1 (1996):69–79.

90. President's Task Force on Violent Crime, *Final Report* (Washington, DC: Government Printing Office, 1982).

91. Robert Martinson, "New Findings, New Views: A Note of Caution Regarding Sentencing Reform," *Hofstra Law Review* 7 (1979):242–258.

92. Jeffrey Fagan, "Social and Legal Policy Dimensions of Violent Juvenile Crime," *Criminal Justice and Behavior* 17(1990):93–133.

93. 387 U.S. 1 (1967).

94. *See, e.g.,* Ga. Code Ann. § 15-11-2(2)(B) (Michie 1994 & Supp. 1998) (up to 21); 705 Ill. Comp. Stat. Ann. 405/1-3 (10) (West 1993 & Supp. 1998) ("minor" as less than 21); Ind. Code Ann. § 31-37-1-1(a)(1) (Michie 1997 & Supp. 1998) (21 years of age); N.D. Cent. Code § 27-20-02 (1991 & Supp. 1997) (up to 21); 42 Pa. Cons. Stat. Ann. § 6301 (West 1982 & Supp. 1998) (up to 21).

95. Kan. Stat. Ann. § 38-1601(a) (West 1993 & Supp. 1997) (10); Tex. Fam. Code Ann. § 52.027 (West 1996 & Supp. 1998) (10); Md. Code Ann., Cts. & Jud. Proc. § 3-805(c) (Michie 1989 & Supp. 1997) (7).

96. Gammons v. Berlat, 696 P.2d 700 (Ariz. 1985); *In re* R., 464 P.2d 127 (Cal. 1970); Commonwealth v. Walter R., 610 NE.2d 323 (Mass. 1993); *In re* Interest of J. M., 391 NW.2d 146 (1986); State ex rel. Juvenile Dept. of Mutnaomah County v. Wicjs, 776 P.2d 582 (Or. 1989); State v. S. P., 746 P.2d 813 (Wash. 1987).

97. For example, the state may file a Persons in Need of Supervision (P.I.N.S) petition against the child; *see, e.g.,* N.Y. Fam. Ct. Act § 711 (McKinney 1983 & Supp 1997). In the alternative, the state may file abuse or neglect proceedings against the parent(s); *see id.* at § 1011. Note that some states explicitly provide for the use of protective statutes; *see, e.g.,* Minn. Stat. Ann. § 260.015(10) (West 1992 & Supp. 1997) (defining child in need of protection or services as one who has committed a delinquent act before becoming 10 years old).

98. The Supreme Court found the standard necessary to protect minors from arbitrary state intervention in *In re* Winship, 397 U.S. 358, 368 (1970).

99. For example, states may no longer place children in detention facilities if there has not been a finding of juvenile delinquency, but only an adjudication that they are a P.I.N.S. *See* 42 U.S.C. § 5633(a)(12)(A)(B) (1998).

100. *See, e.g.,* Conn. Gen. Stat. Ann. §§ 46b-120(1), (5) (West 1995); Ky. Rev. Stat. Ann. § 6000.020 (Michie Supp. 1996); Minn. Stat. § 260.015 subd. 5 (1996); Colo. Rev. Stat. Ann. §§ 19-101-3(71), 19-2-516 (West Supp. 1997).

101. *See, e.g.,* Alaska Stat. §§ 11.41.434–.440 (1989 & Supp. 1994); Ariz. Rev. Stat. Ann. §§ 13-1404 to - 405, 13-1410, 13-1417 (1989 & Supp. 1994).

102. *See, e.g., In re* Oima County Juvenile Appeals, 164 Ariz. 25, 790 P.2d 723 (1990); L. L. L. v. State, 504 So.2d 6 (Fla. 1987); State v. Danny A., 536 A.2d 1136 (Me. 1988); Re Interests of R. J., 401 NW.2d 691 (Neb. 1987); *In re* P. M., 592 A.2d 862 (Vt. 1991).

103. *See, e.g., In re* John C., 569 A.2d 1154, 1156–57 (Conn. App. Ct. 1990).

104. *Gammons,* 696 P.2d at 700; *In re R.,* 464 P.2d at 127; *Walter R.,* 610 NE.2d at 323; *In re Interest of J. M.,* 391 NW.2d at 146; *Wicjs,* 776 P.2d at 582; *S. P.,* 746 P.2d at 813.

105. *See, e.g.,* In the Interest of C. P., 514 A.2d 850 (1986); *In re* M. D., 527 NE.2d 286 (1988).

106. *See* Melissa Sickmund, *Offenders in Juvenile Court* (Washington, DC: Office of Juvenile Justice and Delinquency Prevention, U.S. Department of Justice, 1997).

107. Levesque, "Is There Still a Place for Violent Youth in Juvenile Justice?"

108. Honey Knopp, Rob Freeman-Long, and Sandy Lane, "Program Development." In *Juvenile Sexual Offending: Causes, Consequences, and Corrections,* ed. Gail Ryan and Sandy Lane (San Francisco: Jossey-Bass, 1997).

109. *See* William H. Barton, "Resisting Limits on Discretion: Implementation Issues of Juvenile Dispositional Guidelines," *Criminal Justice Policy Review* 8 (1997):169–200.

110. For further analyses, *see* Nancy G. Guerra, Patrick H. Tolan, and W. Rodney Hammond, "Prevention and Treatment of Adolescent Violence." In *Reason to Hope: A Psychological Perspective on Violence and Youth,* ed. Leonard D. Eron, Jacquelyn H. Gentry, and Peggy Schlegel (Washington, DC: American Psychological Association, 1994); Charles M. Borduin, "Innovative Models of Treatment and Service Delivery in the Juvenile Justice System," *Journal of Clinical Child Psychology* (1994):19–25.

111. 383 U.S. 541 (1966).

112. *Id.* at 553.

113. *Id.* at 554.

114. *Id.* at 565–567. The factors include the seriousness and violence of the offense; whether it was committed against a person or property; whether probable cause exists; the desirability of trying the entire case in one court; the juvenile's personal circumstances and prior record; public safety; and the juvenile's likelihood of rehabilitation through the juvenile court.

115. ALA. CODE § 12-15-34 (1995); ALASKA STAT. § 47.10.060 (1995); ARIZ. R. JUV. P. 12, 14 (Supp. 1995); ARK. CODE ANN. § 9-27-318(d) (Michie 1993 & Supp. 1995); CAL. WELF. & INST. CODE § 707 (West 1984 & Supp. 1996); COLO. REV. STAT. § 19-2-806 (Supp. 1995); CONN. GEN. STAT. ANN. § 46b-127(b) (West 1995); DEL. CODE ANN. tit. 10, § 1010(b)–(c) (1975 & Supp. 1994); D.C. CODE ANN. § 16-2307(a) (1989 & Supp. 1995); FLA. STAT. ANN. § 39.052(2) (West Supp. 1996); GA. CODE ANN. § 15-11-39 (1994); HAW. REV. STAT. § 571-22(a)–(c) (1993); IDAHO CODE § 20-508 (Supp. 1995); ILL. ANN. STAT. ch. 705, ¶ 405/5-4 (Smith-Hurd 1992 & Supp. 1995); IND. CODE ANN. § 31-6-2-4 (Burns 1987 & Supp. 1995); IOWA CODE ANN. § 232.45 (West 1994 & Supp. 1995); KAN. STAT. ANN. § 38-1636 (1993); KY. REV. STAT. ANN. §§ 635.020, 640.010 (Michie/Bobbs-Merrill 1990 & Supp. 1994); LA. CHILD. CODE ANN. art. 857 (West 1995); ME. REV. STAT. ANN. tit. 15, § 3101(4) (West 1980 & Supp. 1995); MD. CODE ANN., CTS. & JUD. PROC. § 3-817 (1995); MASS. ANN. LAWS ch. 119, § 61 (Law. Co-op. 1994); MICH. COMP. LAWS ANN. § 712A.4 (West 1993); MINN. STAT. ANN. § 260.125 (West 1992 & Supp. 1996); MISS. CODE ANN. § 43-21-157 (1993 & Supp. 1995); MO. ANN. STAT. § 211.071 (Vernon 1983 & Supp. 1996); MONT. CODE ANN. § 41-5-206 (1995); NEV. REV. STAT. ANN. § 62.080 (Michie 1986 & Supp. 1995); N.H. REV. STAT. ANN. § 169-B:24 (1994 & Supp. 1995); N.J. STAT. ANN. § 2A:4A-26 (West 1987 & Supp. 1995); N.C. GEN. STAT. § 7A-608 (1995); N.D. CENT. CODE § 27-20-34 (1991 & Supp. 1995); OHIO REV. CODE ANN. § 2151.26 (Anderson 1994 & Supp. 1995); OKLA. STAT. ANN. tit. 10, § 7303-4.3(B) (West Supp. 1996); OR. REV. STAT. ANN. §§ 419C.349, 419C.352 (1995); 42 PA. CONS. STAT. ANN. § 6355 (1982); R.I. GEN. LAWS §§ 14-1-7 (1994), 14-1-7.1 (1994 & Supp. 1995); S.C. CODE ANN. §§ 20-7-430(3)-(6) (Law. Co-op. 1985 & Supp. 1995), 20-7-430(9) (Law. Co-op. Supp. 1995); S.D. CODIFIED LAWS ANN. § 26-11-4 (1992 & Supp. 1995); TENN. CODE ANN. § 37-1-134 (1991 & Supp. 1995); TEX. FAM. CODE ANN. § 54.02 (West 1986 & Supp. 1996); UTAH CODE ANN. § 78-3a-25 (1992 & Supp. 1995); VT. STAT. ANN. tit. 33, § 5506 (1991); VA. CODE ANN. § 16.1-269.1 (Michie Supp. 1995);

WASH. REV. CODE ANN. § 13.40.110 (West 1993); W. VA. CODE § 49-5-10 (1995 & Supp. 1995); WIS. STAT. ANN. § 48.18 (West Supp. 1995); WYO. STAT. ANN. § 14-6-237 (1986 & Supp. 1995).

116. ALA. CODE § 12-15-34.1(a)–(b) (1995); ALASKA STAT. § 47.10.010(e) (1995); CONN. GEN. STAT. ANN. § 46b-127(a) (West 1995); DEL. CODE ANN. tit. 10, §§ 921(2)(a) (1975 & Supp. 1994), 1010(a) (Supp. 1994); D.C. CODE ANN. § 16-2307(h) (1989); FLA. STAT. ANN. § 39.052(3)(a)(1), (3)(a)(3), (3)(a)(4)(d), (3)(a)(5)(b)(II), (3)(a)(5)(c)–(d) (West Supp. 1996); GA. CODE ANN. § 15-11-5(b)(2)(A) (1994); HAW. REV. STAT. § 571-22(c)–(d) (1993); IDAHO CODE § 20-509(1)–(2) (Supp. 1995); ILL. ANN. Stat. ch. 705, ¶ 405/5-4(3.1)–(3.2), (6)(a), (7)(a), (8)(a) (Smith-Hurd 1992 & Supp. 1995); IND. CODE ANN. § 31-6-2-1.1(b), (d) (Burns Supp. 1995); IOWA CODE ANN. § 232.8(1)(b) (West 1994); KAN. STAT. ANN. §§ 21-3611(a), (c) (1995), 38-1636(h) (1993); KY. REV. STAT. ANN. § 635.020(4) (Michie/Bobbs-Merrill Supp. 1994); LA. CHILD. CODE ANN. art. 305(A) (West 1995); ME. REV. STAT. ANN. tit. 15, § 3101(4)(G) (West 1980); MD. CODE ANN., CTS. & JUD. PROC. § 3-804(e)(1)–(4) (1995 & Supp. 1995); MINN. STAT. ANN. §§ 260.015(5)(b), 260.125(3)(a) (West Supp. 1996); MISS. CODE ANN. §§ 43-21-151(1)(a)–(b), (2) (1993 & Supp. 1995), 43-21-157(9) (Supp. 1995); MO. ANN. STAT. § 211.071(9) (Vernon Supp. 1996); MONT. CODE ANN. § 41-5-206(3) (1995); NEV. REV. STAT. ANN. §§ 62.040(1)(b)(1), 62.080(3) (Michie 1986 & Supp. 1995); N.H. REV. STAT. ANN. § 169-B:27 (1994); N.M. STAT. ANN. § 32A-2-3(H) (Michie 1995); N.Y. PENAL LAW § 30.00(2) (McKinney 1987); N.C. GEN. STAT. § 7A-608 (1995); OHIO REV. CODE ANN. §§ 2151.011(B)(1), 2151.26(B) (Anderson Supp. 1995); OKLA. STAT. ANN. tit. 10, §§ 7001-1.3(2), 7306-1.1(A)–(B) (West Supp. 1996); 42 PA. CONS. STAT. ANN. §§ 6322(a) (1982 & Supp. 1995), 6355(e) (1982); R.I. GEN. LAWS §§ 14-1-3(1), -7.1(c) (1994 & Supp. 1995); S.C. CODE ANN. § 20-7-390 (1985 & Law. Co-op. Supp. 1995); TENN. CODE ANN. § 37-1-134(c) (Supp. 1995); UTAH CODE ANN. §§ 78-3a-16(1), 78-3a-25(12) (Supp. 1995); VT. STAT. ANN. tit. 33, § 5505(b) (1991); VA. CODE ANN. § 16.1-269.6(C) (Michie Supp. 1995); WASH. REV. CODE ANN. §§ 13.04.030(1)(e)(iv), 13.40.020(14) (West Supp. 1996); WIS. STAT. ANN. § 48.183 (West Supp. 1995).

117. ARK. CODE ANN. § 9-27-318(b) (Michie 1993 & Supp. 1995); COLO. REV. STAT. § 19-2-805(1) (Supp. 1995); D.C. CODE ANN. § 16-2301(3)(A) (1989 & Supp. 1995); FLA. STAT. ANN. § 39.052(3)(a)(4)(a), (3)(a)(5)(a)–(b)(I) (West Supp. 1996); GA. CODE ANN. § 15-11-5(b)(1) (1994); LA. CHILD. CODE ANN. art. 305(B)(3) (West 1995); MICH. COMP. LAWS ANN. § 600.606 (West Supp. 1995); NEB. REV. STAT. § 43-247 (1993); VT. STAT. ANN. tit. 33, § 5505(c) (1991); WYO. STAT. ANN. § 14-6-203(c), (e)–(f) (1986 & Supp. 1995).

118. Mary J. Clement, "A Five-Year Study of Juvenile Waiver and Adult Court Sentences: Implications for Policy," *Criminal Justice Policy Review* 8 (1997):201–219; Eric J. Fritsch, Tory J. Caeti, and Craig Hemmens, "Spare the Needle but not the Punishment: The Incarceration of Waived Youth in Texas Prisons," *Crime & Delinquency* 42 (1996):503–609.

119. *See, e.g.,* ALA. CODE §§ 13A-11-200 to -203, §§ 15-20-22 to -24 (Michie 1995 & Supp. 1997); ALASKA STAT. §§ 12.63.010 ff., 18.65.087 (Michie 1996); ARIZ. REV. STAT. ANN. §§ 13-3821 to -3826 (West 1989 & Supp. 1997); ARK. CODE ANN. §§ 12-12-901 to -920 (Michie 1995 & Supp. 1997).

120. ARIZ. REV. STAT. ANN. §§ 13-4601 to 4609 (Supp. 1995); CAL. WELF. & INST. CODE §§ 6600-6608 (West Supp. 1996); IOWA CODE ANN. §§ 709C.1-.12 (West Supp. 1996); KAN. STAT. ANN. §§ 59-29a01 to a15 (1994); MINN. STAT. ANN. §§ 253B.02(7a), (18a), (18b), 253B.185 (West 1992 & Supp. 1996); N.J. STAT. ANN. § 30:4-82.4 (West Supp. 1996); WASH. REV. CODE ANN. §§ 71.09.010-.230 (West 1992 & Supp. 1996); WIS. STAT. ANN. §§ 980.01-.13 (West Supp. 1995).

121. *See* Michele L. Earl-Hubbard, "The Child Sex Offender Registration Laws: The Punishment, Liberty Deprivation, and Unintended Results Associated With the Scarlet Letter Laws of the 1990s," *Northwestern University Law Review* 90 (1996):788–862.

122. *See, e.g.,* WASH. REV. CODE ANN. §§ 71.09.030–.060 (West 1992 & Supp. 1996).

123. 42 U.S.C. §§ 14701, 14701(f)(1) (1995).

124. *Id.* at 14701(d).

125. Pam Lyncher Sexual Offender Tracking and Identification Act of 1996, Pub. L. No. 104-236, 100 Stat. 3093 (1996) (codified at 42 U.S.C. § 14072).

126. Jacob Wetterling Crimes Against Children and Sexually Violent Offender Registration Act, Pub. L. No. 103-332, Title XVII, § 170101, 108 Stat. 1796, 2038 (1994) (codified at 42 U.S.C. § 14071 (1994)).

127. Clement, "A Five-Year Study of Juvenile Waiver and Adult Court Sentences: Implications for Policy."

128. Thomas Grisso, "Society's Retributive Response to Juvenile Violence: A Developmental Perspective," *Law and Human Behavior* 20 (1996):229–247; Deborah K. Cooper, "Juvenile's Understanding of Trial-Related Information: Are They Competent Defendants?" *Behavioral Sciences and the Law* 15 (1997):167–180.

129. Ivan P. Kruh and Stanley L. Brodsky, "Clinical Evaluations for Transfer to Criminal Court: Current Practices and Future Research," *Behavioral Sciences & the Law* 15 (1997):151–165.

130. Levesque, "Is There Still a Place for Violent Youth in Juvenile Justice?"

131. Jeffrey Fagan, "Separating the Men From the Boys: The Comparative Advantage of Juvenile Versus Criminal Court Sanctions on Recidivism Among Adolescent Offenders." In *A Sourcebook: Serious, Violent & Chronic Juvenile Offenders,* ed. James C. Howell, Barry Krisberg, J. David Hawkins, and John J. Wilson (Thousand Oaks, CA: Sage, 1995).

132. *Id.*

133. ALA. CODE §§ 13A-11-200 to -203 (1994); KY. REV. STAT. ANN. §§ 17.500 to .540 (Michie 1996); LA. REV. STAT. ANN. §§ 540-549 (West Supp. 1998); NEB. REV. STAT. §§ 29-4001 to -4013 (Supp. 1996); VA. CODE §§ 19.2-298.1 to .4 (Michie 1995 & Supp. 1997).

134. ARIZ. REV. STAT. ANN. §§ 13-3821 to -3836 (West 1989 & Supp. 1997); CAL. PENAL CODE §§ 290 to 290.0 (West 1988 & Supp. 1998); COLO. REV. STAT. § 18-3-412.5 (1997); DEL. CODE ANN. tit. 11, § 4120 (1995 & Supp. 1996); IND. CODE ANN. § 5-2-12 (West Supp. 1997); IOWA CODE ANN. § 692.A (West Supp. 1998); MD. ANN. CODE art. 27, § 792 (1996 & Supp. 1997); MASS. GEN. LAWS ch. 6, § 178D (1996); MICH. COMP. LAWS ANN. §§ 28.721 to .732 (West Supp. 1997); MINN. STAT. ANN. § 243.166 (West 1992 & Supp. 1998); MISS. CODE ANN. §§ 45-33-1 to -19 (Supp. 1997); N.J. STAT. ANN. §§ 2C:7-1 to -11 (West 1995 & Supp. 1997); OR. REV. STAT. §§ 181.594 to .606 (1997); R.I. GEN. LAWS § 11-37-16 (1994); S.C. CODE ANN. §§ 23-3-400 to -490 (Law. Co-op. Supp. 1997); TEX. REV. CIV. STAT. ANN. art. § 4413(51) (West Supp. 1998); WIS. STAT. ANN. §§ 301.45 to .46 (West Supp. 1997).

135. *See, e.g., In re* B. G. 289 N.J. Super. 361, 674 S.2d 178 (App. Div. 1996).

136. 42 U.S.C. § 14071(d), amended by Pub. L. No. 104-145 § 2, 110 Stat. 1345 (1996).

137. Fagan, "Separating the Men From the Boys: The Comparative Advantage of Juvenile Versus Criminal Court Sanctions on Recidivism Among Adolescent Offenders."

138. Studies conducted in Massachusetts, Washington, and Utah end with the same conclusion: justice models do not reduce recidivism rates. *See* Thomas C. Castellano, "The Justice Model in the Juvenile Justice System: Washington State's Experience," *Law and Policy* 8 (1986):479–506; B. Krisberg, James F. Austin, K. Joe, and P. Steele, *The Impact of Juvenile Court Sanctions* (San Francisco: National Council on Crime and Delinquency, 1987); David Macallair, "Reaffirming Rehabilitation in Juvenile Justice," *Youth and Society* 25 (1993):104–125.

139. *See* Sipe et al., "Adolescent Sexual Offenders Grown Up: Recidivism in Young Adulthood."

140. Scott W. Henggeler, "A Consensus: Conclusions of the APA Task Force Report on Innovative Models of Mental Health Services for Children, Adolescents, and Their Families," *Journal of Clinical Child Psychology* 23 (1994):3–6.

141. Youngberg v. Romero, 457 U.S. 307, 317 (1982). For an examination of the right to services in community setting, *see* Michael L. Perlin, "Law and the Delivery of Mental Health Services in the Community," *American Journal of Orthopsychiatry* 64 (1994):194–205.

142. *See* Roger J. R. Levesque, "The Failures of Foster Care Reform: Revolutionizing the Most Radical Blueprint," *Maryland Journal of Contemporary Legal Issues* 6 (1995):1–35.

143. *See, e.g.,* Nelson v. Hyne, 491 F.2d 352, 358, 360 (7th Cir.), *cert. denied,* 417 U.S. 976 (1974); Morgan v. Sproat, 432 F. Supp. 1130, 1135–1136 (S.D. Miss. 1977). For authority to the

contrary, *see Nelson,* 491 F.2d at 360; *Morgan,* 432 F. Supp. at 1135–1136. Note, however, that the promise of rehabilitation is the *quid pro quo* for the historical denial of safeguards.

144. Eric J. Fritsch and Craig Hemmens, "Juvenile Waiver in the United States 1979–1995: A Comparison and Analysis of State Waiver Statutes," *Juvenile and Family Court Journal* 46 (1995):17–36.

145. Parham v. J. R., 442 U.S. 584, 599–600 (1979).

146. Santosky v. Kramer, 455 U.S. 745 (1982) (emphasis added); *see also* Smith v. OFFER, 431 U.S. 816, 862–863 (1977).

147. *See* Roger J. R. Levesque and Alan J. Tomkins, "Revisioning Juvenile Justice: Implications of the New Child Protection Movement," *Journal of Urban and Contemporary Law* 48 (1995):87–116.

148. *See id.*

149. Albert R. Roberts and Michael J. Camasso, "Juvenile Offender Treatment Programs and Cost–Benefit Analysis," *Juvenile & Family Court Journal* 42 (1991):37–47.

150. William H. Barton and Jeffrey A. Butts, "Viable Options: Intensive Supervision Programs for Juvenile Delinquents," *Crime & Delinquency* 36 (1990):238–256.

151. Ira M. Schwartz, *Justice for Juveniles: Rethinking the Best Interests of the Child* (Lexington, MA: Lexington Books, 1989).

152. Barry Krisberg and James F. Austin, *Reinventing Juvenile Justice* (New York: Columbia University Press, 1993). The authors describe Massachusetts's experience in removing thousands of youngsters from training schools and placing them in community programs and comparing the $170 per day for youths in secure treatment to $23 per day for youth in nonresidential outreach and tracking programs. *Id.* at 160–161.

153. These programs become increasingly cost-effective as the programs increase in size; Richard G. Wiebush, "Juvenile Intensive Supervision: The Impact on Felony Offenders Diverted From Institutional Placement," *Crime & Delinquency* 39 (1993):68–89.

154. James C. Howell (Ed.), *Guide for Implementing the Comprehensive Strategy for Serious, Violent, and Chronic Offenders* (Washington, DC: U.S. Department of Justice, Office of Justice Programs, Office of Juvenile Justice and Delinquency Prevention, 1995); Robert J. Sampton and John H. Laub, "Structural Variations in Juvenile Court Processing: Inequality, the Interclass, and Social Control," *Law & Society Review* 27 (1993):285–311; Barry C. Feld, "Justice by Geography: Urban, Suburban, and Rural Variations in Juvenile Justice Administrations," *Journal of Criminal Law and Criminology* 82 (1991):156–120.

155. *See, e.g.,* Barton, "Resisting Limits on Discretion: Implementation Issues of Juvenile Dispositional Guidelines."

156. *See* Michael Peters, David Thomas, Christopher Zamberlan, and Caliver Associates, *Boot Camps for Juvenile Offenders* (Washington, DC: Office of Juvenile Justice Delinquency Prevention, U.S. Department of Justice, 1997); Patricia Puritz and Mary Ann Scali, *Beyond the Walls: Improving Conditions of Confinement for Youth in Custody* (Washington, DC: Office of Juvenile Justice and Delinquency Prevention, U.S. Department of Justice, 1998).

157. This is the model, for example, of restorative justice that has been suggested for violent behavior. *See* Mark S. Umbreit, "Holding Juvenile Offenders Accountable: A Restorative Justice Perspective," *Juvenile and Family Court Journal* 46 (1995):31–42.

158. Ronald L. Simons, Christine Johnson, Rand D. Conger, and Glen Elder Jr., "A Test of Latent Trait Versus Life-Course Perspective on the Stability of Adolescent Antisocial Behavior," *Criminology* 36 (1998):217–243.

159. United Nations, "Convention on the Rights of the Child," *International Legal Materials* 28 (1989):1448.

160. United Nations Guidelines for the Prevention of Juvenile Delinquency (The Riyadh Guidelines), Resolution 45/112 of 14 December 1990, in *Human Rights: A Compilation of International Instruments,* E.93.XIV.1 (Vol. 1 I, Part 1) 346–355.

Chapter 10
ADOLESCENT CHILDREARING

Sociologists and economists essentially dominate the study of adolescent parenthood. Their dominance reflects the nature of the obstacles adolescent parents face in efforts to become productive societal members at an age when dominant societal norms expect them to be engaged in other activities. Although many adolescents eventually overcome obstacles, early parenthood negatively affects adolescents' educational, marital, and economic circumstances and often requires a disproportionate reallocation of societal resources to both parents and their children. That reallocation shapes societal responses to parenting adolescents and compels social scientists to study adolescent sexuality and early parenting; for both essentially aim to curb reallocations and deal with consequences of reallocations that fail.

Although the high costs of early parenthood fuel reform efforts and attract numerous commentaries, analyses have yet to focus on adolescents' rights. As with other social issues that affect both adults and adolescents, policies ignore the peculiar place of adolescents in law and generally assume parity in situations, outcomes, and in needed policy interventions. This chapter reviews these tendencies to highlight the need to reconsider the place of adolescents in the law and more effectively address adolescent parenthood. The analysis suggests that reforms consistent with recognizing adolescents' rights to protection, education, and medical services could help ameliorate adolescents' responses to sexual behaviors that may result in parenthood and also help alleviate the negative outcomes of early parenthood.

Realities of Adolescent Parenting

Despite important research and analyses that address the nature of adolescent parenting, attempts to decipher the causes and consequences of adolescent parenthood face familiar obstacles. Society and researchers do not necessarily distinguish among nonmarital, teenage, and schoolage parenthood. Researchers often draw from samples of teenagers that reach up to the age of 20 and include young and older parents into analyses of unwed parenthood. When minors are the subject of investigations, analyses often fail to distinguish among minors, even though recent research emphasizes the need to focus on preadolescents (up to 13), early adolescents (from 13 to 15), and those who are closer to the age of majority (16 and up). Most studies differentially focus on different ethnic, racial, and socioeconomic groups, document consistent differences in their findings, yet fail to temper generalizations.

Given that teenage parents who constitute these groups are distinguishable in law, policy, opportunities, and actual place in society, this review limits its scope. The analysis attempts to distinguish literature that uses the general age of majority as the cutoff age. Although limiting, using 18 as the important age for analyses of policy relating to adolescent childrearing leads to consideration of a significant part of the adolescent population. By their 18th birthday, 7% of White women, 14% of Latina women, and 26% of Black women have given birth.[1] Although the analysis will distinguish among adolescents based on their marital status, the discussion will highlight results for both unwed and wed adolescents. Teenage parents' marital status poses significant concerns for those interested in adolescent life, even though teenage parents account only for 3% of all nonmarital births in any given year.[2]

Adolescents' marriages tend to be more unstable and minor mothers are more likely to become single parents and raise their children in poverty, with all its attendant consequences for the mother, her children, their fathers, and society.[3] The analysis highlights important socioeconomic and cultural factors, for they interplay with age, marital status, and needed sociolegal responses.

Considering these factors leads to an analysis that finds how life outcomes are variable and tend to emerge from two different situations. The first group, those older than 16, constitutes the majority of unintended teenage births.[4] For this group, their parenting status tends to be accidental.[5] The second group (roughly, those 15 and younger) consists of those involved in sexual contact since puberty or before, a pattern that evinces a considerably more complex etiology. For two practical reasons, this analysis concerns itself most with the latter group. Comprehensive reproductive health could provide most of the social and medical support necessary to produce positive outcomes for the first group, such as reduction of the number of accidental conceptions.[6] The second group poses the most important policy issues that require much more than sex education and reproductive health services; the group of individuals who fit into this category require a response to harsh life circumstances and "toxic" social environments.[7] Simply put, addressing the second group necessarily entails alleviating the plight of the first, but simply addressing the first group's concerns fails to address the needs of the second. As we will see, policies, law, and society increasingly adopt the reverse approach in their broad policy initiatives: efforts tend to move toward addressing the situations of the first group and generally fail to alleviate the plight of the other.

Antecedents to Adolescent Parenthood

No single factor explains adolescent pregnancy; and numerous individual, family, and neighborhood characteristics predispose adolescents to become young parents. Researchers consistently identify several factors that correlate with early parenting. These factors frequently include poor school performance, early sexual activity, low socioeconomic status, high-risk neighborhoods, and parental attitudes and behaviors that condone the activity. The most important finding relating to these correlates is that they actually precede rather than stem from early parenthood. The finding is of significance. The many negative outcomes associated with adolescent parenthood essentially initiate the status that seemingly exacerbates already difficult situations. The reasons and processes behind these correlations are numerous, but hypotheses often center on experiences of poverty and resulting perceptions of limited life options and choices.[8] Life experiences associated with poverty—such as alienation at school, prevalent models of unmarried parenthood and unemployment, and lack of educational opportunities and stable career prospects—all serve to lower the perceived costs of early parenthood.[9] The experiences contribute to making adolescents unaware of the dramatic changes early childbearing will have on their lives.[10]

Given the links between life options and early parenting, the bulk of research aims to understand how community and cultural life predisposes adolescents toward early parenting.[11] As with numerous sex-related behaviors that differ with community and cultural contexts, the sociocultural context of teenage and nonmarital childrearing receives much scholarly and empirical attention.[12] Researchers attribute considerable weight to the impact of community factors. A leading study links social and economic variation among neighborhoods with levels of sexual activity and pregnancy among Black female teenagers.[13] Adolescents who reside in communities with high rates of poverty, welfare use, and single-mother households are at higher risk for early parenthood.[14] More than half of adolescent mothers live in poverty at the time of their baby's birth.[15] Similar findings have been reported for teenage fathers; adolescent males are more likely to become fathers if they live in more impoverished communities.[16] In addition to those studies, a number of structural arguments, such as the loss of stable blue-collar jobs in urban areas, explain the decreasing rates of marriage and financial responsibility of male adolescents and young men for the adolescents they impregnate and the babies they father.[17] Although the "culture of poverty" theory dominates and supports the assumption that poverty causes poverty and perpetuates it, the research is not without controversy. Recent research highlights the extent to which institutional forces shape gender, race, and class inequalities.[18] Although controversy surrounds how communities affect adolescent parenting, few doubt the impact of sociocultural forces. Neighborhood effects are unsurprising. Several recent studies report that neighborhood affects a variety of outcomes, including the likelihood that a teenager will drop out of school, not join the labor force, become sexually active or a parent, become involved in gang or criminal activity, or use drugs and alcohol.[19]

In addition to larger community situations marked by poverty and few options, several important studies report the impact of parenting, which does not necessarily emerge from cultural processes but may be influenced by them. Two examples are illustrative. First, recent studies report that a large proportion of teenage mothers have experienced sexual abuse and forced sexual intercourse prior to their early initiation of sex and teenage pregnancy; and that abuse tends to be at the hands of family members.[20] Second, adolescents prone to teenage parenthood also are more likely to have been raised by parents who obtain less education and who fail to emphasize *and* model the significance of education.[21] The failure of parents or other role models to emphasize the significance of education leads adolescents prone to early parenthood. Teenage parents tend to have low educational aspirations;[22] in fact, a sizeable number, fully one third of teenage mothers, drop out of school before becoming pregnant.[23]

These structural and familial forces constrict individuals' choices and actions. Teenage pregnancy and parenting (for both boys and girls) link to other problematic adolescent behaviors such as alcohol and drug use and, not surprisingly, to early initiation of sexual activity—all of which relate to familial and social conditions.[24] The links between parenthood and risks in social conditions are significant. No single risk factor results in teenage parenthood. Adolescents experiencing many risk factors in many life domains have high probabilities of becoming young parents, and those risks change as adolescents develop. To exacerbate matters, the numerous decision points adolescents must experience continue to shift toward increasing risk. Numerous examples highlight changes in situations that lead to parenthood. First, the experience of sexual activity has changed. The risk period for young childbearing has increased substantially through both decreasing age at first intercourse and rising age at marriage.[25] Second, adolescents who do engage in sexual activity do not protect themselves well from unwanted outcomes. For numerous reasons, younger teenagers tend not to use contraception effectively,[26] a failure attributed to the nature of adolescence and the lack of available services.[27] Third, teenagers' use of abortion and adoption have decreased in recent years, as have rates of marriage for pregnant teenagers.[28] Fourth, economic changes that reduce the availability of low-skill, high-paying manufacturing jobs foster negative outcomes of early parenting.[29] Although researchers tend to focus on the impact of the need for higher education on the stability of inner cities and the working poor, it also has changed the face of the teenage years and the early 20s. Only the middle-class population has accordingly adjusted its family formation activities by increasing median ages of school completion, marriage, and childrearing.[30] Thus adolescent childrearing, which earlier occurred mostly in the context of marriage with an employed husband, now occurs more with unmarried, divorced, or separated teenagers who, because of their impoverished backgrounds, have fewer immediate and longer term prospects for economic, social, and personal security.

Despite enduring debates, the social and economic characteristics of the community in which teenage parents live largely determine the likelihood that they will engage in risking pregnancy. Those who do become pregnant, impregnate, and become parents are more likely to have lower levels of educational attainment, less likely to find stable, remunerative employment, and as a consequence are more likely to be dependent on public assistance at some point in their adult lives to support either themselves or their children.[31] Birth of a child to an unmarried adolescent undoubtedly associates with the likelihood that she and her child, at some point, will rely on public assistance.[32] Major theoretical debates rage about the extent to which observed results occur by "accident or design."[33] As we have seen, although the research remains controversial,[34] differentials in adolescent childbearing are a function of social disadvantage that indirectly places adolescents at risk of first intercourse at earlier ages, fails to promote appropriate contraceptive use, and produces greater acceptance of early pregnancy for both sexes.[35]

Consequences of Parenthood for Adolescents

Teenagers who give birth during their adolescent years tend to function less effectively in numerous realms than their peers who delay childbearing. Until recently, social scientists generally assumed that childbirth and childrearing caused the lowered functioning. However, recent research now indicates that many of the negative outcomes of adolescent parenthood, such as low educational achievement and poverty, precede rather than stem from early parenthood. Nevertheless, teenage childbearing also adds to the limited prospects of already disadvantaged adolescents.

Compared with peers who postpone childbearing, outcomes include poorer psychological functioning, lower rates of school completion, lower levels of marital stability, additional nonmarital births, less stable employment, greater welfare use, higher rates of poverty, and slightly greater rates of health problems for both mothers and children.[36] The growing interest in understanding the impact on fathers reveals that they too become similarly disadvantaged by childrearing and that many of their disadvantages have roots that led to early parenting.[37] Thus as with the correlates and causes of adolescent parenthood, adolescents' circumstances largely dictate the effects of parenthood on the adolescents.

Four areas of research challenge the notion that early parenting, in and of itself, creates negative outcomes. First, studies of adolescent mothers no longer conclude that early parenthood has a strong negative effect on their educational attainment.[38] Recent studies find a narrow gap in educational outcomes.[39] New methodologies reveal that much of the difference in educational attainment may be due not to teenage parenthood itself but rather to preexisting differences between the groups.[40] The gap may be narrow but nevertheless the total still remains significant.[41]

Second, adolescent mothers experience more pregnancy and delivery problems and have less healthy babies overall than do older mothers. Again, recent research reveals how these differences may be less dramatic. The deleterious health outcomes seemingly relate more to the poverty and lack of prenatal care common to pregnant teenagers than to age per se.[42] Moreover, comprehensive prenatal care greatly reduces the frequency of adolescents' negative maternal health outcomes.[43] Again, however, even though it is important to note that the circumstances may not be as dire as previously thought and that other circumstances equally contribute to negative outcomes, some negative findings remain consistent. Those who begin to parent under the age of 15 experience many more negative outcomes, which leads researchers to conclude that young female adolescents provide an important exception to the risks associated with early parenthood.[44]

Third, unwed teenage parents are more likely to be on welfare and for longer periods.[45] That finding, however, obfuscates two factors that render the general finding deceptive. First, analyses of gender differences lead to different outcomes. Immediately after birth, adolescent teenage mothers make greater use of public assistance and have lower incomes. However, adolescent mothers are able to make up the disadvantage by increased employment and earnings in their late 20s and beyond, when their children reach school age and employment tends to be more lucrative.[46] The opposite tends to be true for boys. Adolescent fathers appear to work more hours and earn more money than their nonparent peers in the first years following the birth.[47] However, for boys the commitment also means that they obtain less education and, thus, have lower long-term labor market activity and earnings than their counterparts who delay parenthood.[48] The second point that obfuscates findings relates to cultural and ethnic differences. In general, the negative effects of teenage childbearing on later income and poverty rates are less severe for African Americans than for Whites and Hispanics. This difference likely results from high rates of single parenthood and poverty among all African American families, such that families headed by teenage mothers are not that different from African American families with older mothers.[49] In addition, African American teenage mothers are more likely than Whites or Hispanics to stay in their family home, continue in school, and delay marriage, practices that likely serve to increase their access to family help with child rearing and financial support.[50] Likewise, the finding that some women tend to earn more than their peers who did not become parents are even more dramatic for non-African American women; recent findings reveal that teenage childbearing actually increases a woman's eventual labor market earnings and hours worked compared with what they would have been had she delayed childbearing.[51]

Fourth, more positive trajectories are predictable. Being at a higher grade level when one becomes pregnant, coming from a smaller family of origin not on public assistance, and having high expectations from both one's family and one's self all help predict long-term success for young mothers.[52] These are the same factors that researchers identify as the most frequent backgrounds of those who avoid childbearing altogether yet come from similar life circumstances as determined by ethnicity, socioeconomic status, geography, and sexual activity.[53] The limited research on the family backgrounds and attitudes of teenage fathers mirrors those results.[54] Although parents are well-known to come from diverse backgrounds, it does seem that the vast majority share the dominant, mainstream American value of the importance of education, but it seems that many families of nonparent adolescents transmit the value and concretely reinforce and repeat it in a way that substantively influences adolescents' actual behaviors.[55] Even though these studies define success in terms of the ability to avoid poverty by achieving economic independence and obtaining the equivalent of a high school education, the rewards of education inevitably also affect nonmarket outcomes, most notably one's health, the cognitive development of one's children, and the broad social outcomes such as crime reduction.[56]

Without doubt, then, the economic and educational outcomes of young parents may not be as irreparable as expected. Evidence suggests, however, that the psychological consequences may remain. Both theory and research indicate that negative psychological outcomes may emerge, although these outcomes also may be remediable. Early parenthood generally impedes a number of psychological tasks of adolescence.[57] During the adolescent years, teenagers face the challenges of solidifying their sense of identity[58] and developing autonomy and independence from parents.[59] Early parenthood may challenge opportunities for exploration and appropriate individuation in areas of normative adolescent concern, such as peer relations, dating, schooling, career choices, and the ability to form mature, intimate relationships.[60] The effects of these stresses gain support from emerging research. For mothers, parenting results in heightened levels of psychological distress, as has been shown in studies of young mothers who express distress through higher rates of depressive symptomatology.[61] Again, younger teenagers may face greater obstacles, for they also tend to have slightly more children, often in quick succession, than do teenagers who postpone parenthood.[62] Like early motherhood, early fatherhood appears to have negative consequences on young fathers' future psychological functioning, although this issue has yet to be systematically investigated.[63] Strong associations exist between mental health and the assistance adolescent parents receive in caregiving.[64] Although it is difficult to underestimate the positive role played by personal support, even from unrelated individuals who simply mentor,[65] the psychological and family functioning of early parents appears more bleak over the long run. Although research has yet to address the psychological effects of unplanned early parenthood or the processes that allow some adolescent parents to overcome the disruptive experiences of this situation, evidence suggests that long-term negative outcomes may emerge simply based on what we know about marital patterns and parenting transitions. For example, early unwed births lead to a lower likelihood of marriage[66] and young mothers also are more likely to divorce.[67] Thus overall teenage mothers spend more of their parenting years as single mothers than do women who delay childbearing.[68] Although the psychological processes behind these marital and family formation choices are not well understood and currently hotly debated,[69] the stresses of single parenthood have been well identified. That research supports the view that young parents are at increased risk for negative psychological outcomes.[70]

Consequences of Adolescent Parenthood for Their Children

Despite longstanding interest in young parenting, attention only recently has moved toward the study of adolescents' children. Although generally limited in scope, two areas of research paint a complex picture of the impact of teenage parenting. Research generally focuses on either parenting practices or child functioning. As with the impact of early parenting on adolescents, studies that investigate the repercussions of early parenting find important negative outcomes but also highlight the important ameliorative opportunities appropriate social supports offer young parents and their children.

Numerous small-scale studies have examined the cognitive and behavioral functioning of children of teenage mothers.[71] Although the majority of these studies consider only the infancy and preschool periods, they provide important and often counterintuitive findings. Infants of teenagers tend to be little different than infants of older mothers. For example, infants born to teenage mothers appear no more likely to experience attachment problems than those of comparable high-risk older mothers (e.g., poor, minority single mothers).[72] Although potentially similarly situated in infancy, differences emerge and increase as children age. In the preschool years, delays in cognitive development emerge and continue into the early school years.[73] Preschoolers of teenage mothers also tend to exhibit behavior problems, including higher levels of aggression and lower impulse control, than their peers born to older mothers.[74]

When children of teenagers reach adolescence, their risks for negative outcomes increase and reach higher levels than those of peers born to older mothers. Two unusually long-term studies of adolescent mothers and their children found that adolescents experience higher rates of grade failure, delinquency, incarceration (for male adolescents), fertility (for females) and early sexual activity than their peers born to older mothers.[75] Other research reports similarly negative outcomes for adolescents of parents who began to parent early. A most notable finding highlights how children of teenage mothers are more likely to be recipients of reported child abuse and neglect and are more likely to be placed in foster care than are children of older mothers.[76] Thus children of adolescent parents not only are more likely to be delinquent, they also are more likely to be victimized. The effects on adolescents suggest that the cost of early parenthood seemingly are borne by the adolescents of early parents, not only adolescent parents themselves. Again, difficulties that arise during the period of adolescence, whether current or future ones, emerge as significant to address.

Research on children born to adolescent mothers rarely takes into account the roles of fathers. Existing evidence, however, remains highly suggestive. That research derives from a leading study of a 20-year follow-up of children of teenage mothers.[77] Those researchers found that the presence of a father in the home actually only had a modest impact; and regular contact with fathers outside the home led to no discernible positive outcomes for the children.[78] Although the findings may seem peculiar, they are not in light of the general rule that children only benefit from close relationships.[79] Thus for adolescents who lived with their biological fathers or stepfathers, those with strong attachments showed better educational, behavioral, and emotional functioning than adolescents with weak paternal bonds.[80] In contrast, highly involved fathers who subsequently decrease their involvement, or fathers who have poor relationships with their children throughout the child's life, prove more detrimental to their children than fathers who opt for no relationship at all. Although the findings comport with available theory, myriad questions remain concerning young fathers and their children, such as how fathers' availability, involvement, and interactions with their children affect child development. The lack of findings and the results that do exist parallel findings from research on fathering by parents who assume a more traditional role: Fathers tend to spend little time with their children and that factor generally leads to the conclusion that their impact remains much more negligible on children's psychological development than society and policy makers may want to admit.[81]

Although the findings tend to be consistent, several important caveats attach to the seemingly bleak picture of child outcomes. First, children, like their mothers, show diversity in their functioning. For example, although there is a perception that all children of teenage mothers are at high risk of early pregnancy themselves, most adolescents do not repeat their mothers' childbearing patterns.[82] Second, as for teenage mothers themselves, socioeconomic status and poverty appear to be more important predictors of children's and adolescents' functioning than is maternal age at birth.[83] Third, poor outcomes arise from common adolescent behaviors, such as failure to obtain adequate prenatal care, poor nutritional habits, and poor compliance with medical recommendations. These behaviors are amenable to intervention to improve outcomes, even though, ironically, it is those at highest risk for problems because of younger age and poverty status who receive less and less timely prenatal care.[84] In sum, the outcomes are not entirely negative, and several opportunities exist to ameliorate the negative consequences visited on the children of adolescent parents.

Regardless of age and background, stress marks the transition to parenting. As we have seen, for teenage parents, underprivileged and impoverished backgrounds typically compound these stresses. These conditions are further exacerbated by other normative changes that occur during adolescence, such as identity formation and the renegotiation of relationships with one's family of origin.[85] The stresses of parenting, social difficulties, and adolescence also become exacerbated by the likelihood that the younger adolescents will not marry and have additional children in quick succession.[86] These factors increase the already substantial difficulties such parents may have balancing child care, educational aspirations, and work responsibilities.[87] Thus it seems reasonable to expect that adolescents will have more difficulty with parenting than will older mothers.

Research generally supports negative expectations. Although teenage mothers have been found to be just as warm, studies report that they tend to be less verbal, less sensitive, and less responsive to their infants than nonteenage mothers.[88] Young mothers also generally provide a less stimulating home environment,[89] perceive their infants as being more difficult, and assert unrealistic expectations.[90] These factors may be related to their greater levels of depressive symptomatology in the year following childbirth and the circumstances that lead to the depression.[91]

Although the negative findings may appear dramatic, four recent lines of research and policy responses challenge their significance. First, the strength of the differences diminishes significantly when adolescent mothers are compared to groups from similar socioeconomic backgrounds, of similar ethnic origin, and of less drastic age gaps (e.g., when not comparing early teenagers with adults).[92] Studies that use more similar comparison groups, such as mothers in their early 20s who also live in poverty, find fewer differences in parenting styles.[93] Although differences attenuate when research more closely pairs comparison groups, differences do not entirely disappear altogether.[94]

Second, the vast majority of research on the parenting practices of adolescent mothers studies only the early years of parenting. The assumption has been that adolescent mothers' parenting would improve. Yet research suggests that adolescent mothers' parenting may decrease in quality or effectiveness as their children grow into adolescents. Researchers report that mothers have more problems in mothering when the infant reaches toddlerhood.[95] Toddlers pose considerable challenges when they attempt to control their own environments, become more autonomous, learn to control impulses, and deal with maturational changes. Those changes actually parallel the changes of the adolescent mother, which she has had difficulty overcoming or is going through herself with her own parents.[96] Thus as much as research indicates that early parenting negatively affects the care young children receive, research also reveals that it may actually have a more distal impact on parenting. As we have seen, child functioning appears to worsen over time.[97] These findings suggest an interaction pattern that deteriorates when societal responses fail to address more distal considerations.

Third, the negative findings related to mothers are reflected in the adolescents' environment, particularly their partners. Three findings are significant. First, the general rule tends to be that absent fathering does not necessarily mean uninvolved.[98] Teenage fathers tend to have high rates of child contact, more than 50% of teenage fathers live with their children sometime after birth,[99] but the situation does not necessarily last long.[100] If young fathers are not living with their children, they tend to visit regularly;[101] but again, these rates significantly decrease over time, such that fewer than a quarter of fathers who became fathers as teenagers see their schoolage children weekly.[102] Second, important ethnic and race differences exist. Contrary to popular perceptions, African American fathers do have very low rates of marriage and cohabitation, but they tend to remain more involved with their children over time than do White or Hispanic fathers.[103] Third, unstable or hostile mother–father bonds seem to interfere with unmarried fathers' positive involvement with their children, whereas positive intrafamilial relationships appear to support greater involvement by fathers[104] and mediate the relationship between father–child contact and child functioning.[105] Research on child support mirrors research on contact. Although most initially desire to provide for their children, their child support contributions are extremely low, although they may contribute in other ways—official statistics ignore unreported, irregular, and in-kind contributions.[106] Thus early parents may have greater opportunities to perform better early on, but supports deteriorate as the need increases. Again, the deterioration of supports mirrors the concomitant rise in negative outcomes for both the custodial parent and child.

Fourth, the negative outcomes generally remain unaddressed by attempts to offer services. Contrary to emerging evidence of the more serious negative consequences of teenage motherhood for older children, services remain directed to infants and toddlers.[107] Formal services, then, seemingly erode at the same time more informal supports deteriorate.

The erosion of support is of considerable importance. As the children of adolescent parents age, their cognitive and behavioral functioning seem to decrease as children age. These effects appear due to accumulated stress, increasing demands of parenting older children and adolescents, cumulative effects of long-term poverty, changes in living arrangements, and the transition of the offspring to school. Despite these impressive findings, it is important to distinguish effects of poverty from effects of the parents' age at birth on child development. A large research base already details the negative effects of poverty on family and child functioning, effects such as harsh parenting and parental depression, and for children, school failure, early sexuality, and delinquency.[108] As these outcomes are strikingly similar to the outcomes of teenage parenthood described previously, it seems plausible that poverty may account for much of the impact on children previously ascribed to teenage childbearing. Despite efforts to distinguish one from the other, it seems that both are inextricably related and one cannot be addressed without the other.

Intervention and Prevention Efforts

Public and political attention on teenage parenting and its effects results in several lines of intervention and prevention. Although the approaches may blur distinctions, three different approaches generally emerge. Efforts typically aim to prevent the occurrence of teenage pregnancy, address possible child outcomes, and support adolescents to ensure an opportunity for more positive life trajectories once they have become parents. These efforts vary in effectiveness and opportunities for improvement.

The first and broadest approach aims at primary prevention—the need to prevent adolescent pregnancy. As reviewed in chapter 5, existing programs remain limited and often adopt a number of tactics. Although historically inadequate, effective and innovative programs continue to emerge. The most successful programs provide knowledge of sexual reproduction and access to contraceptives; reinforce responsible values and teach abstinence; build decision-making and social skills; and increase other life options.[109] Key elements of the more successful programs also include targeting services based on developmental and experience level and providing comprehensive services with a variety of components.[110] The most effective efforts, though, emerge from community-based clinic programs, an important finding given that research and programs receiving the most attention are school-based and estimates suggest that 80% of school-based clinics do what community-based clinics do: Distribute contraceptives.[111] Although sexuality education programs increase in popularity, few programs aim to ameliorate the consequences of pregnancy. At best, programs focus on pregnancy prevention, and those efforts remain far from comprehensive.[112]

The second approach addresses the effects early parenthood may have for adolescent parents. Typically, these interventions seek to build adolescents' human and social capital and to improve their goals and life chances. The majority of these programs target poor parents, especially those who have dropped out of school. These efforts often include a broad array of services such as education and job training, free child care and transportation, and other support services.[113]

Although increasing in number and in the tendency to improve participants' educational attainment, the programs remain limited and report predominately limited successes.[114] Several factors contribute to the limited effectiveness. First, most of the increase in educational attainment has been in achievement of a GED, rather than high school completion or a college education, which does not necessarily increase teenage mothers' rates of employment or earnings, decrease their use of welfare, or decrease repeat pregnancies and births.[115] The general finding is that these programs face obstacles that render them unable to alter the lack of opportunities and harsh economic realities facing poor women and children of all races. Second, the programs serve young mothers who often are multiply disadvantaged. In addition to being young parents and living in poverty, these teenagers often lack basic educational skills.[116] Lack of academic skills often prohibit adolescent mothers from accessing job training and further educational services; and participants with higher education or skills at entry generally benefit more from programs.[117] Third, although programs attempt to coordinate a multitude of services, the services themselves are often of low quality or have requirements, such as minimum educational standards, that the teenagers do not meet.[118] Fourth, since the late 1980s programs have switched emphasis. Early programs focused on adolescent's health, education, and subsequent fertility. More recently, programs have focused on the young mother's employability and ability to avoid welfare dependency.[119] Early exit from welfare for adolescent parents often means that they will return and become "cyclers" (repeat users).[120] Fifth, programs tend to focus on teenage mothers and generally ignore familial needs and the needs of the fathers.[121] Sixth, programs assume that teenage pregnancy is an individual problem that can be treated outside the social and cultural context of young parents' lives.[122] All of these forces stymie efforts to assist young parents.

Although many efforts prove to disappoint, several report successes. Programs that report success take the different direction of current efforts and policies that tailor programs to narrow economic and educational needs. The lessons learned from failed service programs are relatively clear. Narrow interventions have proven ineffective over time.[123] Mothers and families that receive comprehensive services simply have greater opportunities for success. Broad consensus among service providers affirm the general rule and follow three principles that point to the best prospects for success. First, the most effective interventions emerge from closely coordinated services that include social support, educational assistance, and medical services.[124] Second, the services are easily accessible and free or offered at a very low cost. Leading examples offer programs in schools or community centers such as hospitals.[125] Third, the programs must be available so that the teenagers define the optimal time for intervention. The principle supports the finding that several critical stages for intervention provide an opportunity to assist, and that the intervention must be multifocused and geared to adolescents' needs.[126] Thus comprehensive, multilayered programming that addresses the relevant ecological systems in adolescent parents' lives result in effective intervention.

The third approach addresses child outcomes. As much as the efforts to approach teenage childrearing by addressing parents' life options remain rare, even more sparse are efforts that pay attention to the children of teenage parents. Most programs presumably believe that by aiding the prospects of teenage mothers, they inevitably improve the prospects of their children. Yet few programs or evaluations directly address the repercussions of intervention, either through services specifically for children or evaluations of program effects on children. Although scarce, some efforts aim to develop teenage parents' parenting skills and provide informative findings.

Services for ameliorating the outcomes of children born to adolescent parents take several forms and adopt different aims. Several programs have aimed to improve birth outcomes. Researchers report that programs have been successfully implemented in hospitals and community clinics that provide continuity of care through pregnancy, whereas other programs rely on home visits by nurses.[127] Home visiting programs have been viewed as having a positive impact on mother's relationships with their children and their children's fathers,[128] greater educational attainment, and fewer subsequent pregnancies.[129] Because adolescents often delay the use of prenatal care until later in pregnancy, schools increasingly provide programs tailored to adolescents' needs, including the creation of special schools for pregnant students.[130] Although researchers report positive outcomes for these developments, research remains methodologically weak and points to the failure to address the needs of those who drop out of school and those who refuse to seek prenatal care.[131] Likewise, it is important to note that neighborhood characteristics, the children's dispositions, and relationships with family members and children's fathers affect parenting behaviors and program successes.[132] Social support has multiple sources and multiple impacts; programs represent only one of many factors influencing teenagers.[133]

Despite persistent failures, solid evidence indicates that some programs are effective and that the most effective outcomes derive from those who follow mothers early in the pregnancy and continue postpartum.[134] As we already have seen, programs for children of adolescent mothers should go beyond infancy and the preschool years. Research does suggest that the effects of early intervention on cognitive and school outcomes for at-risk children (i.e., potential adolescent parents and their own children) positively affect the adolescent experience, and that the effects of extended childhood intervention lead to greater and longer lasting changes.[135] Although existing research indicates more negative outcomes for older versus younger children of teenage mothers, child-oriented services fail to reflect the significance of the finding.

Adolescent Parenting and the Law

Chapter 4 introduced the contours of adolescents' rights to parenthood. That analysis involved the right to *become* parents. Although the right remains significant, this section focuses on the rights of adolescents *as* parents. The pervasive theme that emerges from both adolescents' rights and policies that address adolescent childrearing focuses on ensuring personal responsibility for those who elect to either engage in sexual activity, if they are boys, and if they elect to become parents, if they are girls. This section explores this theme in light of developments in adolescents' rights to be parents and examines the implications of the current recognition. The analysis suggests that the most effective way to ensure that responsibility is to acknowledge and expand societal obligations.

Adolescents' Rights to Parenting

Mothers and fathers are differently situated for the purposes of family law related to parenting. In general, the right of mothers to parent is a nonissue. The mother generally controls whether she wishes to parent, place the child for adoption, or terminate the pregnancy. The rights of fathers are considerably more complicated. The most common issue involves the rights of unwed adolescents who have not committed the crime of statutory rape. In such instances, either the adolescents are legally permitted to engage in sexual activity or are married, which legally renders them adults. The more complicated analysis involves scenarios in which parents are not married. When adolescents are not married, then a series of Supreme Court cases delimits the threshold of adolescents' rights. This section explores these developments and highlights their significance.

Jurisprudence relating to adolescents' right to parent and parenting tend to deal with the rights of unwed fathers. Their rights have been litigated before the Supreme Court on six occasions.[136] In each of those cases, the Supreme Court examined whether an unwed father was entitled to the same protections as other parents. The contours of those decisions are delimited by the first case that set the trend, *Stanley v. Illinois,*[137] and the last, *Michael H. v. Gerald D.,*[138] which allowed states to block unwed fathers' claims to their children. Thus although explicitly about fathers, the cases are also about the rights of mothers, the rights of their children, and the rights of the state to limit or foster all of those rights when the state expresses a more compelling interest.

The facts and holdings of *Stanley* and *Michael H.* provide the basis on which to understand the parenting rights of adolescents. The petitioner in *Stanley* advanced the radical proposition that an unwed father had legally protected interests in his children. Stanley intermittently had lived with the mother of his three children for 18 years until she died and the children were placed into the custody of court-appointed guardians. Stanley appealed the decision on the basis that the law denied unwed fathers fitness hearings prior to denial of custody. The Supreme Court found the state statute unconstitutional on due process grounds.[139] The Court in *Michael H.* reached a conclusion that was largely the opposite. The petitioner had lived with the mother, had established a parenting relationship with his daughter, but the mother was married to another man. When the mother decided to return to her husband, she also decided to deny the natural father visitation rights. The father appealed and lost. The Court found that he had no protectable interest because the interest he claimed was not one that had been traditionally protected by society—the interest was not ''so rooted in the traditions and conscience of our people as to be ranked as fundamental.''[140] The majority of the Court found that *Michael* had misread the *Stanley* cases, that unwed fathers did not have cognizable interests, and that tradition dictated that the sanctity of the American family be maintained against claims like those asserted by *Michael.*[141] To allow a father such as Michael to disrupt a family would be adverse to the state's interest in legitimacy and protecting the integrity of the family unit. Thus even though fathers could have a substantial relationship, deemed determinative in the *Stanley* line of cases, that relationship fails to control when the interests conflict with those of a husband and a mother to whom an unwed father has no legal tie.

In terms of enumerating adolescents' parenting rights, the cases are notable for four reasons. First, the cases clearly distinguish between a mother and father's rights. In the balance, the Court allows states to view the mothers' rights as worthy of greater protection and allows states more flexibility in efforts to protect those rights. That trend is consistent with cases that give women greater rights in balancing whether fathers will become fathers at all, as in the case of abortions[142] and adoptions.[143] Second, the Court perceives fathers' rights as an opportunity. The *Stanley* cases view unwed fathers' rights as ''a foot in the door'' that grants fathers an attempt to establish relationships with their children and, in most circumstances, may entitle them to minimal procedural safeguards. Although the procedural safeguards emerge from opportunity, the state need not ensure that the father has the opportunity.[144] Third, although the Court moves away from tradition to recognize the rights of fathers with illegitimate children, the Court still focuses on tradition to limit the rights of biological fathers. The traditional nuclear family wins when pitted against the claims of outsiders; a state may entirely foil an unwed father's rights, even when he has had a relationship with the child.[145] Fourth, although the rights of parents have essentially been constitutionalized, the trend is to focus on state protections. If states want to provide greater protections to unwed fathers, states generally are free to do so; likewise, if states want to interfere in the relationship, they may do so in the presence of a substantial or compelling interest.[146]

Another right fathers have deals more with the absence of protections. Although a child's mother may unilaterally waive her parental rights and obligations by consenting to her child's adoption, a biological father may only waive his parental rights and obligations after the birth mother has already done so. Thus regardless of their age, fathers tend to be liable for child support. The obligation arises regardless of whether the fathers have had relationships with their children and also regardless of income.[147] Numerous cases require underage fathers, even when victims of statutory rape by a woman and even when they are as young as 13, to financially support the child.[148] These cases and the general rule reflect the judicial and legislative judgment that fathers, more so than society or even mothers who may break ties, must be responsible for their children.

In terms of parenting, then, jurisprudence of adolescents' rights generally remain weakly developed. Parents have a right to relationships, and the rights of fathers only arise when they have taken the opportunity to develop a bond and there are no other impediments that would give rise to a state interest to sever the bond. The other right essentially deals with the requirements of economic support. The remaining rights simply would comport with the rights of any other parent: Parents have the right to raise their children as they see fit.[149] In a sense, then, courts and legislatures have not tailored adolescents' parental rights to address their peculiar situations. Adolescents who become parents generally are treated as adults.

Current Policy Directions

Early parenting has been an issue that has posed serious and complex problems since colonial times, but it only has been in the past 30 years that the federal government has enacted systematic responses.[150] The 1970s witnessed the early response, which focused almost exclusively on providing contraceptives to sexually active teenagers. The late 1970s and early 1980s switched focus to emphasize postponing early sexual activity and helping mothers raise their children through welfare programs.[151] Programs focused on alleviating adverse consequences with economic support, education, job training, and fostering children's development.[152] The 1990s continued the trend, emphasized abstinence, and focused on teenagers in poverty. The developments manifest themselves most in the recent round of welfare legislation. Rather than assisting mothers raise their children, however, the mandates aim to abolish welfare and limit the role of the federal government by restricting the funds, services, and assistance that teenage parents may obtain. The trend increasingly shifts toward curbing the incidence of teenage parenting by eliminating economic support as an apparent incentive for nonmarital childbearing and by enforcing work among welfare mothers.

The Personal Responsibility and Work Opportunity Reconciliation Act of 1996[153] reflects the trend as it completely overhauled the United States's 60-year-old welfare system. The new effort eliminates the Aid to Families With Dependent Children (AFDC) program, and with it the federal guarantee of benefits to all eligible mothers and children.[154] As with the rights of adolescents in general, the federal legislation devolves considerable power to the states through "block grants."[155] Although these grants still require states to operate within broad parameters of the new federal law, states retain the primary responsibility to create and administer assistance programs and establish eligibility requirements and benefit levels. For adolescents, the new federal mandate includes important provisions that fall into three categories.

The first category involves the restrictions on teenage parents who wish to receive funding. Although efforts originally aimed to prohibit states from providing benefits to unwed minor mothers and their children, minor parents continue to be eligible for benefits.[156] The Act, however, does limit adolescents' eligibility. States are still free to deny benefits to minors if minors have children out of wedlock.[157] The new legislation also prohibits the use of funds to provide assistance to minor parents unless they live with a parent or in another adult-supervised setting.[158] The Act further prohibits states from paying benefits to teenage parents who do not participate in "educational activities directed toward the attainment of a high school diploma or its equivalent."[159] Thus although Congress rejected a blanket ban on denying benefits for unwed teenage parents,[160] it requires states to prohibit the use of federal funds for adolescents who do not comport with requirements set by either the state or federal government.

The second category involves provisions aimed to prevent adolescent pregnancy and childbirth. The Act uses three methods to approach teenage pregnancy. It requires states to provide state plans to reduce rates of out-of-wedlock pregnancies, with emphasis on teenage pregnancies.[161] These strategies must include ways to educate groups about statutory rape and expand teenage pregnancy prevention programs to include men.[162] These efforts are unfunded mandates, which significantly diminish the possibility that programs will be extensive and broadly implemented. Congress, instead, opted to fund the other two methods. The Act funds the second method to reduce teenage pregnancy: "abstinence education," defined as a program that has as its exclusive purpose "teaching abstinence from sexual activity until marriage."[163] Likewise, the Act funds the third approach, which consists of incentive programs; states that are most successful in reducing the number of out-of-wedlock births *and* abortion rates will receive extra funding.[164] Together, these efforts reflect the commitment to abstinence in dealing with sexuality education, reducing abortion rates, and early births—an orientation that, as discussed in chapter 5, principally fails to address those at highest risk and in need of more supportive environments.

The third category of welfare provisions does not specifically direct efforts to teenagers but to the welfare population as a whole. For example, the federal government requires that states not use the federal block grant funds to provide benefits to anyone who has received welfare benefits for a total of more than 60 months in his or her adult life.[165] The new law also requires states to improve their child support enforcement system.[166] Finally, the mandates provide child care block grants, which consolidate four federal child care programs.[167] The new Act prohibits states from penalizing any parent with children under the age of 6 who cannot meet work requirements because of a lack of available childcare and defines school attendance as "work" for the purposes of the exemption.[168]

Implications of Current Recognition

Although both research and reform efforts take increasingly new turns and aim toward different directions, available research does address several key components of current reforms that suggest future policy areas of focus. The general theme that emerges from this research is the failure to address properly the needs of adolescent parents. Even though the general thrust of reforms that focus on responsibility make intuitive sense and may be effective for adults, their current development renders them suspect when extended to adolescents.

Much of the recent policy reforms aim to encourage states to address the issue of unwed, separated, or divorced fathers who fail to pay child support.[169] Much hope has been attached to this effort. The belief is that provisions concerning fathers will increase the number of legally recognized father–child relationships and increase fathers' monetary contributions to their children and perhaps even improve the amount of interaction and the emotional bonds between fathers and their children. Although the financial status of young fathers may produce only limited support at first, it is believed that their status may improve over time for some, and thus enforcing child support payments could, in the long run, make a relatively large contribution to the care of children born to teenage mothers.[170]

Although intuitively appealing, rigorous efforts to require young fathers to provide for their children have several limits.[171] For some women and children, fathers may be a destructive presence. It also is possible that these increased paternal demands may actually decrease fathers' contributions and presence by interfering with private parental agreements. In addition, fathers may not have the ability to pay at the critical stage in the child's development. Men who were absent teenage fathers earn persistently and substantially less income than teenage fathers who lived with their children or those who postponed fatherhood, which leads researchers to suggest that they make poor marital prospects.[172] Finally, the hope that fathers may also be more attached and actually marry is problematic: Rates of martial disruption among those who wed as adolescents are high, and a greater likelihood of an earlier second pregnancy exists among those who marry, which actually increases the risk of becoming dependent on public assistance and challenges the solution of marriage.[173]

In addition to focusing on ensuring that fathers support their children, policies now aim to require grandparents to do so as well. The general focus has been to restrict eligibility for benefits to teenagers so that, with some exceptions reviewed later, mothers and their children will only receive benefits if they remain with their parents. The effort makes intuitive sense, especially because adolescents tend already to live with their parents when they have children of their own.[174] However, the impact the policy will have on those who otherwise would not live with their parents remains questionable.

The new coresidency requirements may be problematic. Forced coresidency may increase tensions between some mothers and grandparents and lead to poorer parenting, especially for older teenagers. Despite early findings of supportive family environments,[175] recent research that disentangles the effects of age reveals that the family of origin does not serve as a protective factor for parenting behavior. Living with grandparents does not improve the quality of the home environment provided by the young mother.[176] The findings reflect important points about social support networks and adolescent parenting.[177] As much as families and peers may provide support, such informal networks also provide important sources of conflict and interference with parental development and roles.[178] Family and friends may act as sources of conflict and their assistance may interfere with the mother's sense of independence as a mother.[179] This reflects the tendency to find that, despite the belief that families provide support, "poverty of relationships" from childhood lead to problems during adolescence as well as after: schools, parents, extended families, social services, and society at large fail to support those at highest risk.[180]

Although in its infancy, this area of research also suggests that, at least for older teenagers, teenage mothers may provide the most effective parenting and their children function best when they live apart from their grandparents but receive high levels of grandparent support or child care.[181] These findings present important implications for new welfare policies that require teenage mothers to reside at home to receive welfare benefits. The law explicitly provides for exemption from coresidency requirements if the minor parent or the child is or has been subjected to serious harm, if conditions present an imminent or serious harm, or if waiving requirements would be in either of their best interests.[182] These exemptions have been interpreted to not include less obvious conditions such as conflict and distressed family functioning that interfere with an adolescent's school progress, parenting abilities, and his or her children's development.[183] Even if removal from problematic home environments were noticed and were grounds for exemption, alternative adult-supervised living arrangements, as mandated by the new statutes, actually may not be available.[184] The failure to recognize adolescents' problems and to provide for those in need reflects what contributed to adolescents' problems in the first place. The difficulties of adolescent parenthood most likely arise because the adolescents were isolated from society and felt unwanted by everyone around them.

Although adolescent mothers are generally isolated and older teenagers and their children may not benefit from coresidency requirements, it is important to highlight that adolescent mother–grandmother relationships take several forms. Coresidency influences adolescent parents and their children in different ways. For example, supportive familial relationships benefit adolescents' mental health.[185] Under some conditions, coresidence improves the adolescents' educational outcomes and reduces their likelihood of poverty, premature marriage, and repeat unwanted pregnancies.[186] Grandmothers who are neither disengaged nor in total control of parenting responsibilities provide both the support and the autonomy adolescent parents need to assume healthy primary parental responsibility.[187] Young mothers' autonomy and emotional support systems seem to be important characteristics of healthier outcomes.

Given the state of social science evidence, the findings are important for five reasons. First, studies challenge the belief that adolescents are better off with their families. Second, the challenge comes in terms of the impact it has on the adolescent and their children. Third, the findings suggest a need to respect and promote autonomy. Fourth, results reveal that adolescent parents already are isolated from their families and that there would be a need to address the roots of that isolation as attempts increase to require teenage parents to coreside with grandparents. Fifth, coresidency requirements raise the need to still offer assistance and supports to families—community obligations remain despite efforts to eliminate them.

The argument behind welfare reform for adolescent mothers is largely economic. A most radical outcome of the argument is that a time-limited opportunity to raise children at home with governmental support will remove monetary incentives for pregnancy and disincentives for employment or marriage. Although somewhat appealing, research sheds light on this policy move and, again, questions the effectiveness of efforts to hasten the premature removal of adolescents from social supports.

The extent to which fiscal polices affect "unintended" pregnancies remains contentious. Recent reviews reveal that, at best, existing research remains equivocal.[188] Two reviews of the welfare incentive literature concluded that welfare benefits do not serve as a reasonable explanation of variations in pregnancy and childbearing among unmarried teens.[189] Studies since those reviews also find that decisions about pregnancy and childbearing are not as influenced by the availability of AFDC benefits as they are by career and marital opportunities[190] and the teenage mother's educational level, welfare receipt, and age at first birth.[191] Some studies do find associations between welfare benefit levels and nonmarital childbearing (but not teenage pregnancy) for White teenagers, but not for Black adolescents.[192] However, even those studies do not suggest that welfare variables are among the more important factors accounting for the increasing nonmarital birth rate.[193]

Despite more ardent attempts to eliminate public assistance, research unequivocally supports the view that such assistance helps even those who are persistently on welfare to eventually graduate high school, obtain work experience by combining work and welfare, and ultimately achieve self-reliance.[194] However, it does seem that those who cycle on and off assistance suffer most in terms of achieving independence. Those who persist obtain skills and resources, and those who exit quickly must struggle with fewer resources to remain off welfare and suffer more marital and job instability that seem to have long-term consequences.[195]

Because many teenage mothers receive welfare for 10 years or more, time limits present a major challenge. Opponents of welfare reform argue that mothers who enter the workforce or stay in school may have difficulty locating quality child care and may experience added stress from increased time demands. For other mothers who are unable to acquire stable jobs, their families thus could slide deeper into poverty and increase the risk of homelessness or child abuse and neglect. Research supports the possibility that those who persist in the system may not be able to exit within the allotted time. Those who exit early and are least likely to return to the system have more favorable family and individual resources and are among the oldest adolescents at first pregnancy, are more likely to graduate high school, and are more likely to enter stable marriages.[196] Persistent public assistance recipients come from more disadvantaged families and have fewer social supports and family resources. They are younger at first pregnancy, more likely to drop out of school, experience high additional fertility, and spend more time as a female head of household than other recipients. Given the diversity of young mother's needs for public assistance, time limits will not have simple and unidirectional effects; subsets of mothers will react in different ways.[197]

Little empirical research explores whether intervention programs might negatively or positively affect children's development. As with other issues adolescent parents face, the outcomes are likely to vary. For example, research does suggest that mothers with low education skills and poor functioning or with other family problems, such as a disabled child, may have great difficulty maintaining stable employment and thus may suffer a substantial loss in income.[198] As we have seen, mothers who begin to parent early place their children at risk for more needed services than their peers would require.

In summary, residence, school, and work requirements may provide a necessary incentive to aid some young mothers in finishing their education and obtaining employment. What remains to be determined are the impacts of these reforms on the adolescents' parenting to their children. Likewise, limits remain problematic in that those who can get off welfare actually do so when their environments present appropriate alternatives.[199] Diversity in recipiency requires diverse responses not easily found in efforts to eliminate formal public assistance.

Current policy efforts remain further problematic in that they provide no funds to target family planning or comprehensive programs to prevent teenage pregnancy. Instead, substantial funds have been set aside for new abstinence education programs for adolescents. The focus on abstinence remains problematic. Although sex education may be linked to knowledge about sexuality, conception, and contraception, the vast majority of programs that currently are used do not link to reduced rates of pregnancy.[200] The failure of the majority of programs currently in use is that they do not link efforts to other programs, ensure educational and economic opportunities, and take into account the important finding that those who have children do not necessarily want them. Programs fail to address important motivations when they simply address abstinence.

Opportunities for Reform

Two fundamental problems hobble programs that address adolescent childrearing. The first problem concerns the perceived lack of public consensus on what should be done. The second problem derives from individual-focused interventions that fail to maximize the necessary community level structural supports. These two problems fail to make the adolescent period one in which teenagers feel they are useful and productive members of their communities. That failure fuels negative consequences of adolescent parenting. Although previous chapters already have developed numerous ways to foster inclusion of adolescents into their communities, three are worthy of reemphasis in the context of early parenting. These three approaches highlight the relevance of legal approaches, demonstrate that community consensus persists on critical issues, and establish that protections already recognize adolescents' citizenship.

Legal systems exist to preserve fundamental levels of social justice and protect people from violence. This function and obligation serves as a necessary starting point to understand efforts that aim to ameliorate adolescent parents' circumstances. One of the most significant and determinative findings to emerge from studies of early parenthood involves the numerous forms of violence adolescents, their parents, and their children suffer. Although pervasive, the violence operates in several ways, all of which are amenable to intervention.

A most critical form of violence involves the victimization of adolescents for sexual purposes. As we have seen, the sexual maltreatment of adolescents often plays a critical role in early adolescent parenthood. Young female adolescents who become mothers disproportionately have been victimized by sexual maltreatment. Likewise, adolescents who become sexually active early and therefore are at risk for early pregnancy also are more likely to have been sexually victimized. In addition, mothers who are young, fail to use contraceptives effectively, decide to pursue the pregnancy to full term and keep their babies are more likely to have been victimized by their partners.[201] Although pervasive, all of these forms of violence are amenable to intervention, as we have seen in chapters 8 and 9.

In addition to sexual and relationship violence, research suggests a need to support families to prevent and respond more appropriately to child maltreatment. For early parents, evidence suggests two needs for supports. The first form of support involves providing community resources for families to prevent the maltreatment of adolescents. As we have seen, adolescents suffer from lack of resources and risk programs tend to ignore adolescents' needs. The second form of support involves direct support for adolescent parents who may place their children at risk for maltreatment when they have limited available means of social support.

The provision of these supports have been fraught with two frustrating beliefs: that policy makers do not possess the technology to protect adolescents and that, if the technology exists, resources simply are not available. The state of research and policy making, however, suggests otherwise. First and contrary to popular beliefs, those who evaluate intervention efforts essentially agree about the basic requirements of effective programs. Programs simply must be comprehensive and as extensive and long-term as clients' needs require. Second, effective programs need not be expensive, need not require massive infusion of only public funding, and actually would be a cost-effective use for public funds that are currently used for other programming. For example, educating schoolage children and adolescents about child-rearing roles and responsibilities prior to parenthood decreases the risk of child maltreatment by their children as adults.[202] Likewise, providing families with community supports alleviates child maltreatment rates.[203] Efforts to protect adolescents from violence, then, provide an essential ingredient that helps adolescents and society deal with the negative consequences of early adolescent parenthood.

If investigations of adolescents' early parenting suggest anything, it certainly is that early parenting and their antecedents truncate opportunities. That evidence suggests two points of intervention about which wide consensus already exists. The first area of consensus entails the need to deal with contraception, abstinence, and the provision of effective sexuality education; the second area of agreement encompasses the need to provide opportunities that generally only arise from educational achievement.

The first point of educational intervention, as discussed in chapter 5, suggests that current controversies surrounding sexuality education distort the wide consensus that already exists. In addition to broad consensus, where there is a failure to agree, legal rules already mandate the provision of educational services. Where laws do not mandate, experts and educators agree that education provides the foundation for effective intervention. With improved levels of program development, staff training, and assurance that the programs are actually implemented, educational initiatives provide the foundation of intelligent reproductive health care, not the least of which includes the reduction of violence that contributes to riskier life trajectories.

The second point of educational intervention reminds us that early parenting arises as a problem in the context of socioeconomic systems. Teenagers' decisions about sexual activity, contraception, and parenthood closely relate to their academic and career aspirations. Disadvantaged adolescents, who are most likely to become parents, do not believe that the consequences of pregnancy would negatively affect their lives. Although they may not ''want'' pregnancy, adolescents in difficult circumstances have no strong motivation to avoid it because they do not understand how their lives would be any different.[204] They fail, for example, to see how abstinence, contraception, childbearing, and childrearing are important issues for them and their future development and social conditions.

The substantial literature that finds how school failure and ineffective educational programs place adolescents at increased risk for parenthood and dire social circumstances is far from controversial. Expanding the life choices for adolescents through educational opportunities continues to be an area of wide societal concern, agreement, and commitment. Providing educational tools has been one of the earliest rights the Supreme Court recognized as belonging to adolescents, including those who historically have been denied educational opportunities.[205] As we have seen, however, it is the manner the right is provided that makes the difference for adolescents: Effective educational rights recognize adolescents' role in their development and emphasize education for citizenship.[206]

Few question the fundamental interest parents have to raise and direct the lives of their children. Those who challenge that interest do so to ensure greater protection to minor children. This consensus provides yet another opportunity to address the rights of young parents and to foster their own children's development. In thinking of adolescents' parental rights and the provision of healthy parenting environments, several important points emerge to highlight the necessary role of adolescents' rights and community obligations.

Just as with adults, minors have parental rights to raise their own children as they see fit. When adolescents fail to do so, community obligation arises to provide services, attempt to ensure that parents are able to provide their children with an adequate environment, and not hastily terminate parent and child bonds. All states recognize that terminating parent–child relations first generally requires fulfilling the families' right to support services to counter and prevent further negative outcomes. The protections come in the form of child abuse and neglect laws that support the fundamental constitutional rights of parents recognized by the Supreme Court. States sever family ties only after exhaustion of alternatives.

The position of adolescents in families and the law requires considering the rights and obligations grandparents have with respect to their children and grandchildren. As with much of the study of family law, it matters whether adolescent parents provide an intact family for the child. If the family is intact, then adolescents have greater rights to privacy that shield them from outside intrusion. Supreme Court decisions illustrate the emphasis on a "threatened harm" standard. Under this approach to delineating the rights of parents and children, a state must demonstrate a threatened harm to a child before intervening into the child's family or risk unconstitutional infringement of the parents' right to privacy to raise their children as they see fit. According to the Court, "absent a powerful countervailing interest, protection[,]" a parent possesses the right to "the companionship, care, custody and management of his or her children."[207] If the family is not intact, the state more easily may demonstrate a threatened harm and allow for intervention to mitigate the potential harm to the child. In such cases, courts may allow visitation and, if parents are found irremediably unfit, transfer custody. The emerging rule, then, confers on parents considerable autonomy, so long as it ensures the best interests and protection of the child.[208] Although the standard limits the rights of adolescent parents, it appropriately recognizes two points: (a) when parents are unable to parent, the state has the power to intervene, and (b) states have the obligation to allow others to support children's interest. The children's interest in intruding in parental rights simply serves to support the need to rethink the effects of policies that limit young parents' abilities to raise their children into healthy citizens.

An admittedly more controversial aspect of the right to parent involves the right not to have children. There is no doubt that access to contraception alleviates pregnancy rates and that widespread clinic networks play critical roles in averting large numbers of conceptions, births, and abortions. As we have seen in chapters 3 and 4, however, adolescents' access to services remains limited. Despite practical and legal limitations, analyses of adolescents' legal rights reveal that adolescents do have a right to access such services. Neither parental nor adolescents' rights prevent providing reproductive services. The irony of reproductive health assistance aimed to those at risk is that having a first child provides the ticket of admission to special initiatives closed to those who avoid conception.[209] Providing intensive services, ranging from educational interventions to intrusive medical technology (such as the use of Norplant), to those who become high risk serves to emphasize existing community commitment to providing services and the difficulty of balancing limited preventive strategies addressed to all adolescents and optimal, high-risk strategies addressed to adolescents and children who need them most.

In summary, the rights of adolescent parents as parents, as victims, and as citizens simply recognize the obvious. All aim to recognize the role adolescents have in their communities and the necessity of communities to foster adolescent development and provide them with opportunities for community commitment. Research suggests that the presence or absence of opportunities for valued participation within the social contexts of family and community associates with reduced rates of adolescent pregnancy and other successes.[210] That research, coupled with policy directives, does much to support the need to reorient current approaches and take adolescents' rights more seriously so as to address the plight of adolescent parents.

Conclusion

Research establishes the increasingly obvious point that early parenting results in high costs for adolescent parents, their own children and families, and society. Adolescent parenting results in a loss of human potential, and for many adolescents, the loss simply continues their downward trend emerging from their anteceding circumstances. Despite the bleak picture, existing evidence suggests that policies may be envisioned that would allow adolescents to alleviate many of the negative consequences for themselves and their children.

As we have seen in previous chapters, evidence suggests the need for law, policy, and society to take a greater interest in the needs of adolescents and ensure the rights that already have been recognized. Where social institutions protect adolescents and foster development, adolescents generally avoid behaviors that place them at risk and, when placed at risk, can position themselves on positive developmental trajectories. Where the environment fails to promote positive development, adolescents place themselves at risk and engage in behaviors that become damaging yet normative. Programs that recognize adolescents' needs and provide an array of accessible services can make a difference. The rights of adolescents may be tailored to ensure that those programs exist and suit adolescents' needs.

Endnotes

1. Annette Lawson and Deborah L. Rhode (Eds.), *The Politics of Pregnancy: Adolescent Sexuality and Public Policy* (New Haven, CT: Yale University Press, 1993).
2. Laura Duberstein Lindberg, Freya L. Sonenstein, Leighton Ku, and Gladys Martinez, "Age Differences Between Minors Who Give Birth and Their Adult Partners," *Family Planning Perspectives* 29 (1997):61–66.
3. Rebekah Levine Coley and P. Lindsay Chase-Linsdale, "Adolescent Pregnancy and Parenthood: Recent Evidence and Future Directions," *American Psychologist* 53 (1998):152–166.
4. Janet B. Hardy and Laurie Schwab Zabin, *Adolescent Pregnancy in an Urban Environment: Issues, Programs, and Evaluation* (Washington, DC: Urban Institute Press, 1991).
5. *Id.*
6. *Id.*
7. *Id. See also* Kathleen Mullan Harris, *Teen Mothers and the Revolving Welfare Door* (Philadelphia: Temple University Press, 1997).
8. Karin L. Brewster, John O. G. Billy, and William R. Grady, "Social Context and Adolescent Behavior: The Impact of Community on the Transition to Sexual Activity," *Social Forces* 71 (1993):713–740; William Julius Wilson, *The Truly Disadvantaged: The Inner City, the Underclass, and Public Policy* (Chicago: University of Chicago Press, 1987); Kristin Luker, *Dubious Conceptions: The Politics of Teenage Pregnancy* (Cambridge, MA: Harvard University Press, 1996).
9. Luker, *Dubious Conceptions: The Politics of Teenage Pregnancy;* Kristin A. Moore, Donna Ruane Morrison, and Dana A. Glei, "Welfare and Adolescent Sex: The Effects of Family History, Benefit Levels, and Community Context," *Journal of Family and Economic Issues* 16 (1995):207–237.
10. Patricia Voydanoff and Brenda W. Donnelly, *Adolescent Sexuality and Pregnancy* (Newbury Park, CA: Sage, 1990).
11. Elijah Anderson, *Streetwise: Race, Class, and Change in an Urban Community* (Chicago: University of Chicago Press, 1990); Elijah Anderson, "Sex Codes and Family Life Among Poor Inner City Youth," *Annals of the American Academy of Political and Social Science* 501 (1989):59–78; Linda M. Burton, "Teenage Childbearing as an Alternative Life Course Strategy in African American Families," *Human Nature* 1 (1990):123–143; Lawson and Rhode, *The Politics of Pregnancy: Adolescent Sexuality and Public Policy.*
12. For important studies, *see* Jonathan Crane, "The Epidemic Theory of Ghettos and Neighborhood Effects on Dropping Out and Teenage Childbearing," *American Journal of Sociology* 96 (1991):1226–1259; Dennis P. Hogan and Evelyn M. Kitagawa, "The Impact of Social Status, Family Structure, and Neighborhood on Fertility of Black Adolescents," *American Journal of Sociology* 90 (1985):825–852; Dennis P. Hogan, Nan Marie Astone, and Evelyn M. Kitagawa,

"Social and Environmental Factors Influencing Contraceptive Use Among Black Adolescents," *Family Planning Perspectives* 17 (1985):165–169; William D. Mosher and James W. McNally, "Contraceptive Use at First Premarital Intercourse, United States, 1965–1988," *Family Planning Perspectives* 23 (1991):108–116.

13. Hogan and Kitagawa, "Social and Environmental Factors Influencing Contraceptive Use Among Black Adolescents."

14. Wilson, *The Truly Disadvantaged: The Inner City, the Underclass, and Public Policy.*

15. Alan Guttmacher Institute, *Sex and America's Teenagers* (New York: Author, 1994).

16. Leighton Ku, Freya L. Sonenstein, and Joseph H. Pleck, "Neighborhood, Family, and Work: Influences on the Premarital Behaviors of Adolescent Males," *Social Forces* 72 (1995):479–503; Terence P. Thornberry, Carolyn A. Smith, and Gregory J. Howard, "Risk Factors for Teenage Fathers," *Journal of Marriage and the Family* 59 (1997):505–522.

17. *See, e.g.,* William Julius Wilson, *The Truly Disadvantaged: The Inner City, the Underclass, and Public Policy;* Wilson, *When Work Disappears: The World of the New Urban Poor* (New York: Knopf, 1996).

18. Elaine Bell Kaplan, *Not Our Kind of Girls: Unraveling the Myths of Black Teenage Motherhood* (Berkeley: University of California Press, 1997).

19. Karin Brewster, "Race Differences in Sexual Activity Among Adolescent Women: The Role of Neighborhood Characteristics," *American Sociological Review* 59 (1994):408–424; Jeanne Brook-Gunn, Greg J. Duncan, Pamela K. Klebanov, and Naomi Sealand, "Do Neighborhoods Affect Child and Adolescent Development?" *American Journal of Sociology* 99 (1993):353–395; Greg J. Duncan, "Families and Neighbors as Sources of Disadvantage in Schooling Decisions of White and Black Adolescents," *American Journal of Education* 103 (1994):20–53.

20. Debra Boyer and David Fine, "Sexual Abuse as a Factor in Adolescent Pregnancy and Child Maltreatment," *Family Planning Perspectives* 24 (1992):4–10; Janice R. Butler and Linda M. Burton, "Rethinking Teenage Childbearing: Is Sexual Abuse a Missing Link?" *Family Relations* 39 (1990):73–80; Moore et al., "Welfare and Adolescent Sex: The Effects of Family History, Benefit Levels, and Community Context."

21. Brewster et al., "Social Context and Adolescent Behavior: The Impact of Community on the Transition to Sexual Activity"; Andrew C. Cherlin, Kathleen E. Kiernan, and P. Lindsay Chase-Lansdale, "Parental Divorce in Childhood and Demographic Outcomes in Young Adulthood," *Demography* 32 (1995):299–318; Frank F. Furstenberg Jr. and Julien O. Teitler, "Welfare Benefits, Economic Opportunities, and Out-of-Wedlock Births Among Black Teenage Girls," *Demography* 27 (1994):519–535; Rebecca A. Maynard, "Teenage Childbearing and Welfare Reform: Lessons From a Decade of Demonstration and Evaluation Research," *Children and Youth Services Review* 17 (1995):309–332.

22. John Hagan and B. Whaton, "The Search for Adolescent Role Exits and the Transition to Adulthood," *Social Forces* 71 (1993):955–980.

23. Maynard, "Teenage Childbearing and Welfare Reform: Lessons From a Decade of Demonstration and Evaluation Research."

24. Sarah M. Horwitz, Lorraine V. Klerman, H. Sung Kuo, and James F. Jekel, "Intergenerational Transmission of School-Age Parenthood," *Family Planning Perspectives* 23 (1991):168–172, 177; Roberta L. Paikoff, "Early Heterosexual Debut: Situations of Sexual Possibility During That Transition to Adolescence," *American Journal of Orthopsychiatry* 65 (1995):538–568; J. Richard Udry, Judith Kovenock, and Naomi M. Morris, "Early Predictors of Nonmarital First Pregnancy and Abortion," *Family Planning Perspectives* 28 (1996):113–116; Thornberry et al., "Risk Factors for Teenage Fathers."

25. Andrew C. Cherlin, *Marriage, Divorce and Remarriage* (Cambridge, MA: Harvard University Press, 1992). Rates of adolescent sexuality prior to the age of 19 continue to increase. This proportion increased to 53% in the early 1970s, 66% in the 1980s, and 76% in 1995. *See* Levine and Chase-Linsdale, "Adolescent Pregnancy and Parenthood: Recent Evidence and Future Directions."

26. Data from 1990 to 1995 indicate that 33% of teenagers did not use contraception at first

intercourse, and the rates are higher for younger teenagers than for older teens. Levine and Chase-Linsdale, ''Adolescent Pregnancy and Parenthood: Recent Evidence and Future Directions.''

27. *Id.*
28. *Id.*
29. Wilson, *When Work Disappears: The World of the New Urban Poor.*
30. Cherlin, *Marriage, Divorce and Remarriage;* Margaret K. Rosenheim and Mark F. Testa (Eds.), *Early Parenthood and Coming of Age in the 1990s* (New Brunswick, NJ: Rutgers University Press, 1992).
31. Cheryl D. Hayes (Ed.), *Risking the Future: Adolescent Sexuality, Pregnancy, and Childbearing. Vol. 1* (Washington, DC: National Academy Press, 1987).
32. Arleen M. Leibowitz, M. Eisen, and W. K. Chow, ''An Economic Model of Teenage Pregnancy Decision-Making,'' *Demography* 23 (1986):67–77; Frank F. Furstenberg Jr., Jeanne Brooks-Gunn, and S. Philip Morgan, *Adolescent Mothers in Later Life* (New York: Cambridge University Press, 1987).
33. Laurie S. Zabin, Nan Marie Astone, and Mark R. Emeron, ''Do Adolescents Want Babies? The Relationship Between Attitudes and Behavior,'' *Journal of Research on Adolescence* 3 (1993):67–86, at 67; Frank F. Furstenberg Jr., ''As the Pendulum Swings: Teenage Childbearing and Social Concern,'' *Family Relations* 40 (1991):127–138; Frank F. Furstenberg Jr., ''Teenage Childbearing and Cultural Rationality: A Thesis in Search of Evidence,'' *Family Relations* 41 (1992):239–243; Arline T. Geronimus, ''Teenage Childbearing and Social and Reproductive Disadvantage: The Evolution of Complex Questions and the Demise of Simple Answers,'' *Family Relations* 40 (1991):463–471; Mark F. Testa, ''Introduction.'' In *Early Parenthood and Coming of Age in the 1990s,* ed. Margaret K. Rosenheim and Mark F. Testa (New Brunswick, NJ: Rutgers University Press, 1992).
34. For example, some posit that differentials in early and nonmarital childbearing may be viewed as outcomes of cultural differences and rationally planned adaptation to racial discrimination and social disadvantage. B. A. Haumburg and S. L. Dixon, ''Adolescent Pregnancy and Parenthood.'' In Margaret K. Rosenheim and Mark F. Testa, *Early Parenthood and Coming of Age in the 1990s,* (New Brunswick, NJ: Rugers University Press, 1992). This line of reasoning posits that those from disadvantaged backgrounds differentially desire early childbearing. Judith S. Musick, *Young, Poor, and Pregnant: The Psychology of Teenage Motherhood* (New Haven, CT: Yale University Press, 1993). S. Ruddick, ''Procreative Choice for Adolescent Women.'' In *The Politics of Pregnancy: Adolescent Sexuality and Public Policy,* ed. Annette Lawson and Deborah L. Rhode (New Haven, CT: Yale University Press, 1993).
35. The finding has been reported for both males and females across different ethnic groups, Furstenberg, ''As the Pendulum Swings: Teenage Childbearing and Social Concern''; *see also* William Marsiglio, ''Adolescent Males' Orientation Toward Paternity and Contraception,'' *Family Planning Perspectives* 25 (1993):22–31; Pamela I. Erickson, *Latina Adolescent Childbearing in East Los Angeles* (Austin: University of Texas Press, 1998).
36. Hayes, *Risking the Future: Adolescent Sexuality, Pregnancy, and Childbearing. Vol. 1.*
37. *See, e.g.,* William Marsiglio, ''Teenage Fatherhood: High School Completion and Educational Attainment.'' In *Adolescent Fatherhood,* ed. Arthur B. Elster and Michael E. Lamb (Hillsdale, NJ: Erlbaum, 1986).
38. Previously, the belief was that young mothers were unlikely to continue their education after childbirth and thus obtained lower total levels of education than their peers who delayed childbirth; *see, e.g.,* Kristin A. Moore and Linda J. Waite, ''Early Childbearing and Educational Attainment,'' *Family Planning Perspectives* 9 (1977):221–225.
39. This partly results from increasing general equivalency degree (GED) programs, schooling requirements for welfare receipt, and more progressive school policies on accepting pregnant students. The effects of teenage childbearing on educational attainment are also moderated by other variables, such as birth spacing and the decision to drop out of school. For example, if teenage mothers stay in school, they are almost as likely to graduate high school (73%) as are their nonparent peers (77%). In contrast, dropping out of high school is a strong risk factor for

pregnancy, and of adolescents who drop out of school either before or shortly after childbirth, only 30% return and eventually graduate, about half the rate of nonmother dropouts. Dawn M. Upchurch and James F. McCarthy, "The Timing of a First Birth and High School Completion," *American Sociological Review* 55 (1990):224–234.

40. Saul D. Hoffman, E. Michael Foster, and Frank F. Furstenberg Jr., "Reevaluating the Costs of Teenage Childbearing," *Demography* 30 (1993):1–13; Kristin A. Moore, David E. Myers, Donna Ruane Morrison, Christine Windquist Nord, Brett Brown, and Barry Edmonston, "Age at First Childbirth and Later Poverty," *Journal of Research on Adolescence* 3 (1993):393–422; V. Joseph Hotz, Susan Williams McElroy, and Seth G. Sanders, "The Costs and Consequences of Teenage Childbearing for Mothers." In *Kids Having Kids: Economic Costs and Social Consequences of Teen Pregnancy,* ed. Rebecca A. Maynard (Washington, DC: Urban Institute Press, 1997).

41. For example, *see* Hoffman et al., "Reevaluating the Costs of Teenage Childbearing"; Hotz et al., "The Costs and Consequences of Teenage Childbearing for Mothers."

42. For a review and meta-analysis, *see* Teresa O. Scholl, Mary L. Hediger, and Daniel H. Belsky, "Prenatal Care and Maternal Health During Adolescent Pregnancy: A Review and Metaanalysis," *Journal of Adolescent Health* 15 (1994):444–456.

43. *Id.*

44. *Id.*

45. Teenage mothers have lower incomes as adults and are more likely to be on welfare than their peers who delay childbirth; Moore et al., "Age at First Childbirth and Later Poverty." For example, the study by Hoffman et al., "Reevaluating the Costs of Teenage Childbearing," compared sets of sisters and found that a teenage birth nearly doubled the likelihood that a woman would be poor at ages 21–33, increasing the rate of poverty from 16% to 28%.

46. Furstenberg et al., *Adolescent Mothers in Later Life;* Hotz et al., "The Costs and Consequences of Teenage Childbearing for Mothers."

47. Michael J. Brien and Robert J. Willis, "Costs and Consequences for the Fathers." In *Kids Having Kids: Economic Costs and Social Consequences of Teen Pregnancy,* ed. Rebecca A. Maynard (Washington, DC: Urban Institute Press, 1997); Marsiglio, "Teenage Fatherhood: High School Completion and Educational Attainment."

48. *Id.*

49. Nan Marie Astone, "Are Adolescent Mothers Just Single Mothers?" *Journal of Research on Adolescence* 3 (1993):353–372; Moore et al., "Age at First Childbirth and Later Poverty."

50. U.S. Department of Health and Human Services, *Report to Congress on Out-of-Wedlock Childbearing* (Hyattsville, MD: Author, 1995); Rosenheim and Testa, *Early Parenthood and Coming of Age in the 1990's.*

51. Coley and Chase-Linsdale, "Adolescent Pregnancy and Parenthood: Recent Evidence and Future Directions."

52. Harris, *Teen Mothers and the Revolving Welfare Door;* Furstenberg et al., *Adolescent Mothers in Later Life.*

53. *See, e.g.,* Ellen W. Freeman and Karl Rickels, *Early Childbearing: Perspectives of Black Adolescents on Pregnancy, Abortion, and Contraception* (Newbury Park, CA: Sage, 1993).

54. Maureen A. Pirog-Good, *The Family Background and Attitudes of Teen Fathers* (Madison: University of Wisconsin, Institute for Research on Poverty, DP # 1006-93, 1993).

55. Naomi B. Farber and Roberta R. Iversen, *Transmitting Values About Education: A Comparison of Black Teen Mothers and Their Nonparent Peers* (Madison: University of Wisconsin, Institute for Research on Poverty, DP # 1094-96, 1996).

56. Barbara Wolfe and Samuel Zuvekas, *Nonmarket Outcomes of Schooling* (Madison: University of Wisconsin, Institute for Research on Poverty DP # 1065-95, 1995).

57. *See generally* Robert D. Kitterlinus, Michael E. Lamb, and Katherine Nitz, "Developmental and Ecological Sources of Stress Among Adolescent Parents," *Family Relations* 40 (1991):435–441.

58. Stuart T. Hauser, *Adolescents and Their Families* (New York: Free Press, 1991).

59. P. Lindsay Chase-Lansdale, Lauren S. Wakschlag, and Jeanne Brooks-Gunn, "A Psychological Perspective on the Development of Caring in Children and Youth: The Role of the Family," *Journal of Adolescence* 18 (1995):515–556.

60. Marguerite Stevenson Barratt, Mary A. Roach, Kari M. Morgan, and Karen K. Colbert, "Adjustment to Motherhood by Single Adolescents," *Family Relations* 45 (1996):209–215.

61. Gail A. Wasserman, Susan A. Brunelli, and Virginia A. Raugh, "Social Supports and Living Arrangements of Adolescent and Adult Mothers," *Journal of Adolescent Research* 5 (1990):54–66.

62. Hotz et al., "The Costs and Consequences of Teenage Childbearing for Mothers"; Moore et al., "Age at First Childbirth and Later Poverty."

63. Robert I. Lerman, "A National Profile of Young Unwed Fathers." In *Young Unwed Fathers,* ed. Robert I. Lerman and Theodora J. Ooms (Philadelphia: Temple University Press, 1993).

64. Barratt et al., "Adjustment to Motherhood by Single Adolescents."

65. Lynn Blinn-Pike, Diane Kuschel, Annette McDaniel, Suzanne Mingus, and Megan Poole Mutti, "The Process of Mentoring Pregnant Adolescents: An Exploratory Study," *Family Relations* 47 (1998):119–127.

66. Neil G. Bennet, David E. Bloom, and Cynthia K. Miller, "The Influence of Nonmarital Childbearing on the Formation of First Marriages," *Demography* 32 (1995):47–62.

67. *Id.*; Furstenberg et al., *Adolescent Mothers in Later Life;* Hayes, *Risking the Future: Adolescent Sexuality, Pregnancy, and Childbearing. Vol. 1;* Hotz et al., "The Costs and Consequences of Teenage Childbearing for Mothers"; Moore et al., "Age at First Childbirth and Later Poverty"; U.S. Department of Health and Human Services, *Report to Congress on Out-of-Wedlock Childbearing.*

68. *Id.*

69. Whether this decreased propensity to marry results from lowered marriage incentives for young mothers, less opportunity, or other reasons is still being debated. *See* Bennet et al., "The Influence of Nonmarital Childbearing on the Formation of First Marriages."

70. *Id.*

71. For a review, *see* P. Lindsay Chase-Lansdale and Jeanne Brooks-Gunn (Eds.), *Escape From Poverty: What Makes a Difference for Children?* (New York: Cambridge University Press, 1995).

72. Susan J. Spieker and Lilliam Bensley, "Roles of Living Arrangements and Grandmother Social Support in Adolescent Mothering and Infant Attachment," *Developmental Psychology* 30 (1994):102–111.

73. Furstenberg et al., *Adolescent Mothers in Later Life;* Kristine Anderson Moore, Donna Ruane Morrison, and Angela Dungee Greene, "Effects on the Children Born to Adolescent Mothers." In *Kids Having Kids: Economic Costs and Social Consequences of Teen Pregnancy,* ed. Rebecca A. Maynard (Washington, DC: Urban Institute Press, 1997).

74. *Id.*

75. Jeffrey Grogger, "Incarceration-Related Costs of Early Childbearing." In *Kids Having Kids: Economic Costs and Social Consequences of Teen Pregnancy,* ed. Rebecca A. Maynard (Washington, DC: Urban Institute Press, 1997); Robert H. Haveman, Barbara Wolfe, and Elaine Peterson, "Children of Early Childbearers as Young Adults." In *Kids Having Kids: Economic Costs and Social Consequences of Teen Pregnancy,* ed. Rebecca A. Maynard (Washington, DC: Urban Institute Press, 1997); Moore et al., "Effects on the Children Born to Adolescent Mothers."

76. Robert M. George and Bong Joo Lee, "Abuse and Neglect of the Children." In *Kids Having Kids: Economic Costs and Social Consequences of Teen Pregnancy,* ed. Rebecca A. Maynard (Washington, DC: Urban Institute Press, 1997).

77. Frank F. Furstenberg Jr. and Kathleen Mullan Harris, "When and Why Fathers Matter: Impacts of Father Involvement on the Children of Adolescent Mothers." In *Young Unwed Fathers: Changing Roles and Emerging Policies,* ed. Robert I. Lerman and Theodora J. Ooms (Philadelphia: Temple University Press, 1993).

78. *Id.*

79. *Id.*

80. *Id.*

81. Arthur B. Elster and Michael E. Lamb (Eds.), *Adolescent Fatherhood* (Hillsdale, NJ: Erlbaum, 1986).

82. In a Baltimore study, one third of the daughters became teenage mothers; Furstenberg et al., *Adolescent Mothers in Later Life.* The follow-up of the Young Mothers Program showed that one quarter of the daughters and 11% of the sons of participants became teenage parents; Horwitz et al., "Intergenerational Transmission of School-Age Parenthood."

83. Harris, *Teen Mothers and the Revolving Welfare Door.*

84. Voydanoff and Donnelly, *Adolescent Sexuality and Pregnancy.* Researchers report that only 36 percent of those under 15 and 53% of those between 15 to 19 receive care during their first trimester, compared with 76% of all pregnant women. *Id.* at 89. *See also* Sarah S. Brown (Ed.), *Prenatal Care: Reaching Mothers, Reaching Infants* (Washington, DC: National Academy Press, 1988).

85. Hauser, *Adolescents and Their Families.*

86. Coley and Chase-Lindale, "Adolescent Pregnancy and Parenthood: Recent Evidence and Future Directions."

87. *Id.*

88. Rea E. Culp, Mark I. Appelbaum, Joy D. Osofsky, and Janet A. Levy, "Adolescent and Older Mothers: Comparison Between Prenatal Maternal Variables and Newborn Interaction Measures," *Infant Behavior and Development* 11 (1988):353–362.

89. Tom Luster and Eric Dubow, "Predictors of the Quality of the Home Environment that Adolescent Mothers Provide for Their School Age Children," *Journal of Youth and Adolescence* 19 (1990):475–495; Moore et al., "Effects on the Children Born to Adolescent Mothers."

90. *See* Jeanne Brooks-Gunn and Frank F. Furstenberg Jr., "The Children of Adolescent Mothers: Physical, Academic, and Psychological Outcomes," *Developmental Review* 6 (1986):224–251.

91. Wasserman et al., "Social Supports and Living Arrangements of Adolescent and Adult Mothers."

92. Coley and Chase-Linsdale, "Adolescent Pregnancy and Parenthood: Recent Evidence and Future Directions."

93. April Ann Benasich and Jeanne Brooks-Gunn, "Enhancing Maternal Knowledge and Child-Rearing Concepts: Results From an Early Intervention Program," *Child Development* 67 (1996):1186–1205; Lauren S. Wakschlag, P. Lindsay Chase-Lansdale, and Jeanne Brooks-Gunn, "Not Just 'Ghosts in the Nursery': Contemporary Intergenerational Relationships and Parenting in Young African-American Families," *Child Development* 67 (1996):2131–2147.

94. Coley and Chase-Linsdale, "Adolescent Pregnancy and Parenthood: Recent Evidence and Future Directions."

95. Hardy and Zabin, *Pregnancy in an Urban Environment: Issues, Programs, and Evaluation.*

96. *Id.*

97. Coley and Chase-Linsdale, "Adolescent Pregnancy and Parenthood: Recent Evidence and Future Directions."

98. Sandra Danziger and Norma Radin, "Absent Does Not Equal Uninvolved: Predictors of Fathering in Teen Mother Families," *Journal of Marriage and the Family* 52 (1990):636–642.

99. Marsiglio, "Teenage Fatherhood: High School Completion and Educational Attainment."

100. *Id.*

101. In a nationally representative sample, Lerman, "A National Profile of Young Unwed Fathers," found that almost half of new young fathers visited their children weekly, and almost 25% had daily contact.

102. *Id.*

103. *Id.*; Marsiglio, "Teenage Fatherhood: High School Completion and Educational Attainment."

104. Frank F. Furstenerg Jr., "Fathering in the Inner City: Paternal Participation and Public Policy."

In *Fatherhood: Contemporary Theory, Research, and Social Policy,* ed. William Marsiglio (Thousand Oaks, CA: Sage, 1995).

105. Paul Amato and Sandra J. Rezac, "Contact With Nonresidential Parents, Interparental Conflict, and Children's Behavior," *Journal of Family Issues* 15 (1994):191–207.

106. Coley and Chase-Linsdale, "Adolescent Pregnancy and Parenthood: Recent Evidence and Future Directions."

107. P. Lindsay Chase-Lansdale, Jeanne Brooks-Gunn, and Roberta L. Paikoff, "Research and Programs for Adolescent Mothers: Missing Links and Future Promises," *Family Relations* 40 (1991):396–403.

108. *See, e.g.,* Vonnie C. McLoyd, "Socioeconomic Disadvantage and Child Development," *American Psychologist* 53 (1998):185–204; Greg J. Duncan and Jeane Brooks-Gunn, *Consequences of Growing up Poor* (New York: Russell Sage Foundation, 1997).

109. Several detailed reviews on teenage pregnancy prevention and intervention programs are available; *see, e.g.,* Jennifer J. Forst and Jacqueline Darroch Forrest, "Understanding the Impact of Effective Teenage Pregnancy Intervention Programs," *Family Planning Perspectives* 27 (1995):188–195; Douglas Kirby and Cindy Waszak, "School-Based Clinics." In *Preventing Adolescent Pregnancy: Model Programs and Evaluations,* ed. Brent C. Miller, Josefina J. Card, Roberta L. Paikoff, and James L. Peterson (Newbury Park, CA: Sage, 1992); Cynthia Franklin, Darlene Grant, Jacqueline Corcoran, Pamela O'Dell Miller, and Linda Bultman, "Effectiveness of Prevention Programs for Adolescent Pregnancy: A Meta-Analysis," *Journal of Marriage and the Family* 59 (1997):551–567.

110. *See* Forst and Forrest, "Understanding the Impact of Effective Teenage Pregnancy Intervention Programs"; Maynard, "Teenage Childbearing and Welfare Reform: Lessons From a Decade of Demonstration and Evaluation Research"; Miller et al., *Preventing Adolescent Pregnancy: Model Programs and Evaluations.*

111. Franklin et al., "Effectiveness of Prevention Programs for Adolescent Pregnancy: A Meta-Analysis."

112. Roger J. R. Levesque, "Sexuality Education: What Adolescents' Educational Rights Require," *Journal of Psychology, Public Policy and the Law* (in press).

113. Coley and Chase-Linsdale, "Adolescent Pregnancy and Parenthood: Recent Evidence and Future Directions."

114. Furstenberg et al., *Adolescent Mothers in Later Life;* Paula K. Braverman and Victor C. Strasburger, "Adolescent Sexual Activity," *Clinical Pediatrics* 32 (1993):658–668.

115. *See* Maynard, "Teenage Childbearing and Welfare Reform: Lessons From a Decade of Demonstration and Evaluation Research."

116. *Id.*

117. *See, e.g.,* Louise Warrick, Jon B. Christianson, Judy Walruff, and Paul C. Cook, "Educational Outcomes in Teenage Pregnancy and Parenting Programs: Results From a Demonstration," *Family Planning Perspectives* 25 (1993):148–155.

118. Coley and Chase-Linsdale, "Adolescent Pregnancy and Parenthood: Recent Evidence and Future Directions."

119. Lorraine V. Klerman & Sarah M. Horwitz, "Reducing Adverse Consequences of Adolescent Pregnancy and Parenting: The Role of Service Programs," *Adolescent Medicine: State of the Art Reviews* 3 (1992):299–316.

120. Coley and Chase-Linsdale, "Adolescent Pregnancy and Parenthood: Recent Evidence and Future Directions."

121. *Id.*

122. Luker, *Dubious Conceptions: The Politics of Teenage Pregnancy;* Erickson, *Latina Adolescent Childbearing in East Los Angeles.*

123. Richard Solomon and Cynthia Pierce Liefeld, "Effectiveness of a Family Support Center Approach to Adolescent Mothers: Repeat Pregnancy and School Drop-Out Rates," *Family Relations* 47 (1998):139–144.

124. Hardy and Zabin, *Adolescent Pregnancy in an Urban Environment: Issues, Programs, and Evaluation.*

125. Joy Dryfoos, *Full-Service Schools: A Revolution in Health and Social Services for Children, Youth, and Families* (San Francisco: Jossey-Bass, 1994).

126. Laurie Schwab Zabin and Sarah C. Hayward, *Adolescent Sexual Behavior and Childbearing* (Newbury Park, CA: Sage, 1993); LaWanda Ravoira and Andrew L. Cherry Jr., *Social Bonds and Teen Pregnancy* (Westport, CT: Praeger, 1992).

127. Victoria Seitz, "Adolescent Pregnancy and Parenting." In *Children, Families, and Government: Preparing for the Twenty-First Century,* ed. Edward F. Zigler, Sharon Lynn Kagan, and Nancy W. Hall (New York: Cambridge University Press, 1996).

128. *See, e.g.,* Tom Luster, Harry Perlstadt, Marvin McKinney, Kathryn Sims, and Linda Juang, "The Effects of a Family Support Program and Other Factors on the Home Environments Provided by Adolescent Mothers," *Family Relations* 45 (1996):255–264.

129. For comprehensive reviews, *see* David L. Olds and Harriet Kitzman, "Can Home Visitation Improve the Health of Women and Children at Environmental Risk?" *Pediatrics* 86 (1990):108–116; David A. Wolfe, N. Dickon Reppucci, and Stuart Hart, "Child Abuse Prevention: Knowledge and Priorities," *Journal of Clinical Child Psychology* 24 (1995):5–22.

130. Seitz, "Adolescent Pregnancy and Parenting."

131. *Id.*

132. *See, e.g.,* Luster et al., "The Effects of a Family Support Program and Other Factors on the Home Environments Provided by Adolescent Mothers."

133. Pamela S. Nath, John G. Borkowski, Thomas L. Whitman, and Cynthia J. Shellenbach, "Understanding Adolescent Parenting: The Dimensions and Functions of Social Support," *Family Relations* 40 (1991):411–420.

134. Luster et al., "The Effects of a Family Support Program and Other Factors on the Home Environments Provided by Adolescent Mothers"; *see also* David L. Olds and Harriet Kitzman, "Review of Research on Home Visiting for Pregnant Women and Young Children," *Future of Children* 3 (1993):53–92.

135. Frances A. Campbell and Craig T. Ramey, "Cognitive and School Outcomes for High Risk African-American Students at Middle Adolescence: Positive Effects of Early Intervention," *American Educational Research Journal* 32 (1995):743–772. *See generally* Edward Zigler and Sally J. Styfco (Eds.), *Head Start and Beyond: A National Plan for Extended Childhood Intervention* (New Haven, CT: Yale University Press, 1993).

136. Stanley v. Illinois, 405 U.S. 645 (1972); Quilloin v. Walcott, 434 U.S. 246 (1978).; Parham v. Hughes, 441 U.S. 347 (1979). Caban v. Mohammed, 441 U.S. 380 (1979); Lehr v. Robertson, 463 U.S. 248 (1983); Michael H. v. Gerald D., 491 U.S. 110 (1989).

137. 405 U.S. 645 (1972).

138. 491 U.S. 110 (1989).

139. *Stanley,* 405 U.S. at 657–658.

140. 490 U.S. 119, 122 (1989).

141. *Id.* at 124–126.

142. *See generally* Planned Parenthood v. Danforth, 428 U.S. 52 (1976), which held that a woman's right to terminate her pregnancy weighs heavier than her husband's rights to procreate and that the state may not delegate to the husband a power the state itself does not have.

143. Fathers have due process rights prior to a child's adoption; *see* Caban v. Mohammed, 441 U.S. 380, 389 (1979). However the state may limit that right, for the right usually requires that the father has established a relationship with the child. Stanley v. Illinois, 405 U.S. 645, 658 (1972).

144. Ruthe-Arlene W. Howe, "Legal Rights and Obligations: An Uneven Evolution." In *Young Unwed Fathers: Changing Roles and Emerging Policies,* ed. Robert I. Lerman and Theodora J. Ooms (Philadelphia: Temple University Press, 1993).

145. Michael H. v. Gerald D., 491 U.S. 110 (1989).

146. A prime example is when the father is a statutory rapist; *see* Pena v. Mattox, 84 F.3d 894 (7th Cir. 1996).

147. Esther Wattenberg, "Paternity Actions and Young Fathers." In *Young Unwed Fathers,* ed. Robert I. Lerman and Theodora J. Ooms (Philadelphia: Temple University Press, 1993).

148. *See, e.g.,* Mercer County Dep't of Social Servs. v. Alf M., 589 N.Y.S.2d 288 (Fam. Ct. 1992) (holding 16-year-old victim of statutory rape is legally responsible for the child); State ex rel. Hermesmann v. Seyer, 847 P.2d 1273 (Kan. 1993) (holding 13-year-old male victim of statutory rape must pay child support).

149. *See* chapters 2 through 4.

150. Maris A. Vinovskis, *An "Epidemic" of Adolescent Pregnancy: Some Historical and Policy Considerations* (New York: Oxford University Press, 1988).

151. *Id.*

152. Harris, *Teen Mothers and the Revolving Welfare Door.*

153. Pub. L. No. 104-193, 110 Stat. 2105 (codified in scattered sections 7, 8, 21, 25, and 42 U.S.C.A.).

154. 42 U.S.C.A § 601(b) (West Supp. 1999).

155. 42 U.S.C.A. §§ 601-619, amended by Balanced Budget Act, 5001-5504, 5501-5518, 111 Stat. at 577–594, 606–621.

156. *See, e.g.,* 42 U.S.C.A. §§ 608(a)(4), (5) (qualifying teenage parents' eligibility to welfare). H.R. 4, 104th Cong. (1995), the Republican-supported Personal Responsibility Act would have denied benefits to parents under the age of 18.

157. *Id.* § 602, amended by Balanced Budget Act of 1997, Pub. L. No. 105-33, 5501, 11 Stat. 251, § 606 (providing minimum requirements for state plans).

158. 42 U.S.C.A. § 608(a)(5). However, states may make some exceptions. *See id.* § 608(a)(5)(B).

159. *Id.* at § 608(a)(4) (West Supp. 1997).

160. *Id.* at § 608(a)(5)(B).

161. 42 U.S.C.A. § 602(a)(1)(v).

162. *Id.* § 602(a)(1)(vi).

163. *Id.* § 710(b)(1), 701(b)(2)(A).

164. *Id.* § 603(a)(2), amended by Balanced Budget Act, 5502, 111 Stat. 251, 606–609. *Id.* § 603(a)(2)(C)(i), amended by Balanced Budget Act, 5502(a)(2), 111 Stat. at 607.

165. 42 U.S.C.A. § 608(a)(7), amended by Balanced Budget Act, 50019d), 111 Stat. at 591.

166. 42 U.S.C.A. § 651–669(b) (West Supp. 1999).

167. 42 U.S.C.A. § 9858–9859n (West Supp. 1999).

168. *Id.* 607(e)(2); *id.* 607(d)(11).

169. Roger J. R. Levesque, "Targeting 'Deadbeat' Dads: The Problem With the Direction of Welfare Reform," *Hamline Journal of Public Law and Policy* 15 (1994):1–53.

170. Maureen A. Pirog-Good, *The Educational and Labor Market Outcomes of Adolescent Fathers* (Madison: University of Wisconsin, Institute for Research on Poverty, DP # 1014-93, 1993).

171. Sandra K. Danziger, Carolyn K. Kastner, and Terri J. Nickel, "The Problems and Promise of Support Policies." In *Young Unwed Fathers: Changing Roles and Emerging Policies,* ed. Robert I. Lerman and Theodora J. Ooms (Philadelphia: Temple University Press, 1993).

172. Maureen A. Pirog-Good and David H. Good, *Child Support Enforcement for Teenage Fathers: Problems and Prospects* (Madison: University of Wisconsin, Institute for Research on Poverty, DP # 1029-94, 1994).

173. *See* Vinovskis, *An "Epidemic" of Adolescent Pregnancy: Some Historical and Policy Considerations.* The most consistent finding is that early marriage often leads to either persistent or episodic spells of welfare receipt and high marriage dissolution rates. Harris, *Teen Mothers and the Revolving Welfare Door.*

174. Voydanoff and Donnelly, *Adolescent Sexuality and Pregnancy.*

175. Furstenberg et al., *Adolescent Mothers in Later Life;* Horwitz et al., "Intergenerational Transmission of School-Age Parenthood."

176. Spieker and Hensley, "Roles of Living Arrangements and Grandmother Social Support in Adolescent Mothering and Infant Attachment"; Leanne Whiteside-Mansell, Sandra K. Pope, and Robert H. Bradley, "Patterns of Parenting Behavior in Young Mothers," *Family Relations* 45 (1996):273–281. When young mothers coreside with grandmothers, both the mother and

grandmother adopt lower quality parenting practices, they are less supportive and authoritative, more negative and disengaged. However, in families where mothers were in their early teens when they gave birth, coresidence predicted warmer and more positive parenting by grandmothers. P. Lindsay Chase-Lansdale, Jeanne Brooks-Gunn, and Elise S. Zamsky, "Young African-American Multigenerational Families in Poverty: Quality of Mothering and Grandmothering," *Child Development* 65 (1994):373–393. Other researchers have noted similar effects: Coresidence among adolescent mothers and grandmothers was linked with higher mother–grandmother conflict and poorer child functioning. Patricia L. East and Marianne E. Felice, *Adolescent Pregnancy and Parenting: Findings From a Racially Diverse Sample* (Mahwah, NJ: Erlbaum, 1996).

177. Rachel A. Gordon, P. Lindsay Chase-Lansdale, Jennifer L. Matjasko, and Jeanne Brooks-Gunn, "Young Mothers Living With Grandmothers and Living Apart: How Neighborhood and Household Contexts Relate to Multigenerational Coresidence in African American Families," *Applied Developmental Science* 1 (1997):89–106.

178. Rhonda A. Richardson, Nancy Behman Barbour, and Donald L. Bubenzer, "Bittersweet Connections: Informal Social Networks as Sources of Support and Interference for Adolescent Mothers," *Family Relations* 40 (1991):430–434; Rhonda A. Richardson, Nancy Behman Barbour, and Donald L. Bubenzer, "Peer Relationships as a Source of Support for Adolescent Mothers," *Journal of Adolescent Research* 10 (1991):278–290.

179. Barratt et al., "Adjustment to Motherhood by Single Adolescents."

180. Kaplan, *Not Our Kind of Girls: Unraveling the Myths of Black Teenage Motherhood.*

181. Spieker and Bensley, "Roles of Living Arrangements and Grandmother Social Support in Adolescent Mothering and Infant Attachment"; East and Felice, *Adolescent Pregnancy and Parenting: Findings From a Racially Diverse Sample.*

182. 42 U.S.C.A. § 608(a)(5)(B)(ii)II)–(IV) (West Supp. 1999).

183. Ariel Kalil, Micheal S. Spencer, Susan J. Spieker, and Lewayne D. Gilchrist, "Effects of Grandmother Coresidence and Quality of Family Relationships on Depressive Symptoms in Adolescent Mothers," *Family Relations* 47 (1998):443–450.

184. *Id.*

185. Kalil et al., "Effects of Grandmother Coresidence and Quality of Family Relationships on Depressive Symptoms in Adolescent Mothers."

186. Katherine Trent and Sharon L. Harlan, "Teenage Mothers in Nuclear and Extended Households," *Journal of Family Issues* 15 (1994):309–337.

187. Nancy H. Apfel and Victoria Seitz, "Four Models of Adolescent Mother–Grandmother Relationships in Black Inner-City Families," *Family Relations* 40 (1991):421–429.

188. Brian L. Wilcox, Jennifer K. Robbennolt, Janet E. O'Keeffe, and Marisa E. Pynchon, "Teen Nonmarital Childbearing and Welfare: The Gap Between Research and Political Discourse," *Journal of Social Issues* 52 (1996):71–90.

189. Greg J. Duncan, Martha S. Hill, and Saul D. Hoffman, "Welfare Dependence Within and Across Generations," *Science* 239 (1988):461–471; Robert Moffit, "Incentive Effects in the U.S. Welfare System: A Review," *Journal of Economic Literature* 30 (1992):1–61.

190. Greg J. Duncan and Saul D. Hoffman, "Welfare Benefits, Economic Opportunities, and Out-of-Wedlock Birth Among Black Teenage Girls," *Demography* 27 (1990)519–535.

191. Chong-Bum An, Robert Haveman, and Barbara Wolfe, "Teen Out-of-Wedlock Births and Welfare Receipt: The Role of Childhood Events and Economic Circumstances," *Review of Economics and Statistics* 75 (1993):195–205; Moore et al., "Welfare and Adolescent Sex: The Effects of Family History, Benefit Levels, and Community Context."

192. Shelly Lundberg and Robert D. Plotnick, "Adolescent Premarital Childbearing: Do Economic Incentives Matter?" *Journal of Labor Economics* 13 (1995):177–200.

193. Wilcox et al., "Teen Nonmarital Childbearing and Welfare: The Gap Between Research and Political Discourse."

194. Harris, *Teen Mothers and the Revolving Welfare Door.*

195. *Id.*; Mary Jo Bane and David T. Ellwood, *Welfare Realities: From Rhetoric to Reform* (Cambridge, MA: Harvard University Press, 1994).

196. Harris, *Teen Mothers and the Revolving Welfare Door.*

197. For example, for young mothers with high school degrees and work experience, the benefit changes and time limits may provide the needed incentive to obtain and maintain stable employment. Mothers who continue their education, as opposed to beginning work earlier, reduce their risk of long-term welfare receipt. Harris, *id.* For young mothers, marital dissolutions are the most powerful determinants of initial entry into welfare; and exits through work are much more prevalent than exit through relationship changes. *Id.*

198. Maynard, ''Teenage Childbearing and Welfare Reform: Lessons From a Decade of Demonstration and Evaluation Research.''

199. Harris, *Teen Mothers and the Revolving Welfare Door.*

200. Voydanoff and Donnelly, *Adolescent Sexuality and Pregnancy;* Franklin et al., ''Effectiveness of Prevention Programs for Adolescent Pregnancy: A Meta-Analysis.''

201. From the information that is available, it is generally agreed that fathers tend to be 2 to 3 years older, on average, than teenage mothers. That age differential supports the claim that the pregnancy resulted from statutory rape. Lindberg et al., ''Age Differences Between Minors Who Give Birth and Their Adult Partners.''

202. Christine Wekerle and David A. Wolfe, ''Prevention of Child Physical Abuse and Neglect: Promising New Directions,'' *Clinical Psychology Review* 13 (1993):501–540.

203. *See, e.g.,* U.S. Advisory Board on Child Abuse and Neglect, *Neighbors Helping Neighbors: A New National Strategy for the Protection of Children* (Department of Health and Human Services, Washington, D.C: U.S. Government Printing Office, 1993).

204. *See* Freeman and Rickels, *Childbearing: Perspectives of Black Adolescents on Pregnancy, Abortion, and Contraception.*

205. Brown v. Board of Education, 347 U.S. 483 (1954).

206. Roger J. R. Levesque, ''Educating American Youth: Lessons From Children's Human Rights Law,'' *Journal of Law & Education* 27 (1998):173–209.

207. Lassiter v. Dept. of Social Services of Durham County, 452 U.S. 18, 27 (1981).

208. For a similar analysis, *see* David L. Walther, ''Survey of Grandparents' Visitation Rights,'' *American Journal of Family Law* 11 (1997):95–107.

209. Zabin and Hayward, *Adolescent Sexual Behavior and Childbearing.*

210. Robert Bickel, Susan Weaver, T. Williams, and Linda Lang, ''Opportunity, Community, and Teen Pregnancy in an Appalachian State,'' *Journal of Educational Research* 90 (1997):175–181.

PART IV

The Future of Adolescents' Rights

Chapter 11
REFORMING ADOLESCENTS' RIGHTS

The previous chapters revealed that inconsistency and incongruity mark the jurisprudence of adolescents' rights that relate to adolescent sexuality. Every formal regulation of adolescent sexuality varies considerably among states. States differ in terms of adolescents' age for sexual consent, ranging from age 10 to 18. States also diverge in terms of adolescents' permissible partners and types of sexual activity—some states set essentially no limits and others place strict limits on who may be potential partners; other states permit only minimal or no sexual touching whereas others allow sexual intercourse. States also widely vary in the extent that they provide adolescents' access to medical, mental health, educational, therapeutic, and criminal justice services. Some states do not allow minors access to some of these services, others require parental or other adult consent, others require a level of maturity, whereas others simply do not distinguish adolescents from adults who have freer access to services and assistance. Where there is less variation in legal regulation, the implementation of regulations still varies and often falters. For example, although laws generally permit the media industry to self-regulate and prohibit adolescents' access to certain media, adolescents freely gain access to sexually explicit and sexually violent media. Likewise, laws universally proscribe sexual assault; yet adolescent victims may receive less legal protection and access to services than adults who are recognized as independent legal actors. The considerably haphazard regulation of adolescent sexuality proceeds unabated and reflects adolescents' peculiar place in the law.

Although the differences in regulation may appear nonrational, they are not without justifications. Legal systems traditionally justify state and other local regulatory variations in terms of necessary experimentation and respect for fundamentally different social values. The vast differences in law, recognition of adolescents' rights, and legal protections offered adolescents, however, challenge the wisdom of these traditional justifications. In terms of adolescent sexuality, the incongruities reflect the legal system's failure to adapt to the complexity of forces that affect adolescent development and the resulting diversity of outcomes, expectations, and needs. Policies and developments in adolescents' rights lack coherency and guiding principles faithful to the current understanding of adolescent sexual development, adolescents' place in society, and the world adolescents inhabit.

Despite diversity, failures, and complexities, the previous chapters suggest that a sharper focus on adolescents' basic rights could better effect the desired outcomes of secure, healthy, and responsible development. Although potentially grouped in numerous ways, principles that emerged from the previous analyses of current law and suggestions for reform essentially propose five basic principles to guide policies and reform proposals. These principles involve the need to bestow on adolescents control over their own legal rights, expand legal notions of best-interests standards as applied to adolescents, situate adolescents so they can effect greater self-determination, increase adolescents' participation in matters affecting them, and appreciate the "processual nature" of adolescent development (how adolescents develop differently and at different rates depending on social, economic, physical, and psychological demands and changes). This enumeration, of course, is offered as an analytical strategy rather than absolute categorization. The principles are interrelated, rely on one another, and not necessarily distinct, Indeed, the principles all fundamentally rest on the need to champion respect for adolescents and ensure their membership in a society that takes adolescents' interests seriously and that fosters citizens who also take their own and societal interests seriously.

In light of preceding discussions of existing laws and realities of adolescent sexuality, this concluding chapter revisits the five guiding principles that emerged from our discussions of adolescents' sexual rights and enumerates the divergence of these principles from traditional law and policy. Although the principles extend innovations of adolescents' rights, the expansion remains far from radical and not beyond the realm of possibility. And although the approaches may be consistent with numerous legal mandates, legal structures that support the suggested approach remain largely undeveloped or simply ignored. In the end, the analysis reveals how legal and policy mandates may be developed and how they may better respect adolescents' basic rights and reflect the realities of adolescent life and healthy development.

Rethinking Adolescents' Legal Personhood

The preceding analyses of adolescents' legal rights reveal the continuing need to deal with the tension characteristic of adolescents' place in society. The tension involves the need to ensure protection for vulnerable, innocent, and immature adolescents while at the same time ensuring enough protection of their need for autonomy so that they may engage society as competent citizens. Currently, the legal system tends to balance protection over autonomous rights. Although we learn that adolescents do have some legal rights under the Constitution, the general rule has been that, when adolescents are deemed to possess rights, parents or the state (through its various officials) control those rights. This section highlights reasons adolescents' rights must shift away from the protective stance and aim to respect adolescents as subjects of their own rights and how states act more legitimately and appropriately if they seek to foster and affirmatively ensure adolescents' citizenship.

The Failures of Traditional Conceptions

Traditional attempts to protect minors against themselves by bestowing the control of their rights onto others are problematic in that adolescents do not enjoy the constitutionally guaranteed rights adults possess. The ultimate and practical result of that failure is that regulations involving the rights of adolescents need only satisfy a lower constitutional threshold. In legal parlance, issues involving adolescents' rights generally do not entail strict scrutiny: States generally remain free to infringe on the rights of adolescents so long as they provide a plausible rationale for doing so. Intrusive body searches, judicial by-pass procedures that require adolescents to obtain court support to exercise their rights, and the pervasive failure to provide adolescents direct access to the legal system represent well the consequences of applying a lower constitutional standard for adolescents. Even though rationales for different treatment may be devoid of empirical merit, states could plausibly make the arguments and thus discriminate against adolescents.

Another reason that renders the traditional balance problematic involves the extent to which family members or state officials actually can be trusted to act in the interests of adolescents. In terms of family life, what emerges in the courts' treatment of adolescent rights is a good faith parental standard. The standard is left to the discretion of the family, barring the extreme of abuse and neglect, and no one is in the position to second-guess parents. For courts, the important factors in protecting adolescents are preserving family sanctity and maintaining strong parental rights, with adolescents' interests presumed coterminous with parents' interests. The same standard applies when the minor is in the custody or control of the state. Where minors could be perceived as immature, and when a state's other interests suggest a need to recognize that immaturity, the courts will allow for special considerations and protections.[1] The failure of these standards to protect adolescents from maltreatment challenges the threshold for intervention and calls into question the assumption that substitute decision makers act to benefit adolescents' welfare. The legal system does not stray far away from the assumption that parents and state actors discharge their responsibilities in the minor's interests, despite evidence that minors' interests are not necessarily best served in that manner. Again, although those who control adolescents' rights may act to serve adolescents' interests, the legal system does not accommodate well for adolescents' rights when the system fails to protect adolescents.

Another difficulty posed by adolescents' traditional lack of control over their own rights lies in the extent to which it leaves their rights indeterminate. Although indeterminacy remains rampant throughout several contexts of adolescents' rights, two examples illustrate. Adolescents may not be as competent as adults and may need extra protections as they proceed through the criminal justice system. For example, a leading researcher and commentator on adolescents' capacity to waive their rights to counsel and on adolescents' capacities as trial defendants notes that adolescents generally fail to understand the significance of many of their rights.[2] Yet the law continues to act as though young adolescents do possess appropriate competence and the law even continues to reform itself to reach even younger adolescents and place them at greater risk for trial in criminal courts when their trial competence is impaired. On the other hand, leading researchers concur that adolescents generally are competent in their decision making and as mature as adults in their abilities to make informed decisions regarding abortions.[3] Yet laws increasingly aim to limit adolescents' access to abortions and require that they demonstrate competence and endure judicial obstacles from which adults are immune. The problematic nature of the traditional conception is that the different domains argue different conceptions of adolescents and offer considerably different images of the extent to which adolescents should be given more rights or treated differently from adults. Again, the legal system fails to tailor itself to adolescents' realities.

The traditional approach fails as a result of the manner in which the legal system, reflecting larger society, clings to the image of the nuclear family that separates vulnerable, immature, and dependent children from the harsh realities of adult life. The system also adheres to the traditional sociological notion that families serve as "the 'factories' which produce human personalities."[4] Yet rapid social, economic, and cultural changes continue to transform the structure of today's families and the intimate relationships adolescents enjoy within those families. The dramatic changes in the social realities alter attitudes about sex, marriage, and families and increase the extent to which adolescents engage in high-risk behavior that endanger their own health and well-being and that of others.[5] Likewise, community and family networks that sustained previous generations are less available because of massive family relocations that have resulted in a loss of social ties, community connections, and extended family support.[6] Yet the law still functions as though parents cared for and controlled their children as they did prior to these important demographic, sociological, and psychological transformations in adolescents' everyday lives.

Another reason the traditional conception of adolescents' rights remains problematic relates to the extent that the law already has adapted to social transformations and recognized the vulnerability of individuals within families. Current conceptions of adolescents' rights reflect the laws' continued understanding of adolescents in traditional terms while the law has redefined the legal rights and roles of other family members. The legal structures of family law that once made sense to approach adolescents in traditional terms have largely disappeared. Responding to shifts in the scope and meaning of family, the law increasingly recognizes *adult* family members as autonomous individuals vis-à-vis one another. Through a series of decisions that directly dislodged traditional notions of family privacy,[7] the Court has redefined family members as autonomous individuals whose separate preferences and shifting choices demand social respect and legal protection. These transformations mean that the strong common-law position that favored family privacy, and accordingly protected the family from "state intervention," makes less sense when even the legal system no longer views the family as a unit of social value apart from and encompassing the individuals who compose it. Traditional assumptions that families are private and they therefore best provide for their members without governmental interference can no longer be taken for granted; traditional notions of family privacy have dissolved and no longer necessarily protect vulnerable adolescents. Thus as the family no longer constitutes the only mediator between the person and the state and family privacy loses its sacrosanct status, traditional assumptions no longer serve to justify the current denial of adolescents' rights.

Yet another motivation to reconsider traditional views emerges from the theoretical and legal proposal that finds singularly untenable the view that minors are the property of parents or the state. Although the current rethinking of these laws direct their attention to children, a glance at the proposals reveals that they actually are more appropriate for adolescents. Children's rights advocates suggest that no one is entitled to control the life of another, that parental rights in fact only protect parents who harm children, and that all individuals have a right to self-determination.[8] The extent to which these arguments become increasingly persuasive for young children, they do debunk the myth that parents, or the state, should exert unilateral control over adolescents' everyday lives. The proposition derives considerable support from the history of the social construction of the adolescent period, which appropriately characterizes the development of the notion of adolescence as a history of contorted attempts to increase adolescents' dependency to exert more parental and social control over them and remove adult responsibilities.

The traditional conceptions of adolescents' rights derive from the Constitution and Supreme Court's failure to provide a readily usable framework to deal with the vulnerabilities of adolescents. The Constitution does not expressly consider adolescents; nor does it even consider the more general category of "children." The only possible mention of adolescents has been to exclude them from protection: Pursuant to Amendment XXVI, section 1, those under 18 are excluded from the right to vote. Despite the general invisibility of adolescents in the Constitution, the Supreme Court interprets the Constitution to include adolescents. Although an important move, the inclusion remains inconsistent in terms of what the Constitution protects. The Court grants broad authority to parents over their children,[9] yet limits that authority to protect state interests in adolescents.[10] The Court also interprets the Constitution to grant various rights to adolescents,[11] yet fails to grant them other rights.[12] The Court also interprets adolescents as autonomous individuals, free to make their own choices and control their lives;[13] yet in other instances the Court denies them the right to make choices or even the right to have choices made for them that differ from those of their parents.[14] How to deal with adolescents' vulnerability, then, remains to be determined even though the Court interprets the Constitution as protecting adolescents from vulnerability and also from not using vulnerability as a guise to control adolescents who do have rights.

The final consideration that leads to the need to reject the traditional legal position of adolescents emerges from what the reasons previously mentioned suggest: These considerations reveal the need to provide a standard that addresses the basis and rationale for the control of adolescents' rights. In thinking of that control, the current status of adolescents' rights suggests a need to redefine the nature of protection and develop principles that more accurately reflect the nature of adolescents' environments. Given the current development of adolescents' rights, the proposal that follows posits a need to view parents and others acting *parens patriae* not as powers that protect but as powers that develop, recognize development, and respond to adolescents' situations. Responding to those needs requires framing adolescents' rights as adolescents themselves develop and prepare for democratic, civil interactions.

Before exploring the basic principles the reasons for reform suggest and before detailing the reasons those efforts make sense, it is important to recap considerations that spur reform efforts. The rationale for reform is simple. Current conceptions of adolescent jurisprudence remain both limited and problematic. The nature of adolescents' rights remains indeterminate. Those in control of adolescents' rights do not necessarily act in adolescents' interests and the social realities adolescents face continue to challenge the legal reality of family and institutional life. Those changed realities reveal a need to focus on forces outside of family life and within the adolescent. Finally, the uneven development of adolescents' legal rights suggests that it would be disingenuous to propose that one theory either encompasses the existing approaches or that the Court, which lays the foundation for fundamental rights conceptions, envisions a consistent approach to adolescents' rights.

Moving Toward Modernity

The limits of adolescents' rights and the need to rethink the nature and control of existing adolescents' rights suggest the need for alternative conceptualizations. We have seen how the Court increasingly recognizes the period of adolescence. Yet neither the Court nor commentators have addressed how legal systems may approach adolescence in a more comprehensive manner that would provide principles applicable across legal domains. Despite that general failure, alternative approaches may be envisioned.

An appropriate starting point in thinking of alternative conceptions of adolescents' rights is to focus on the fundamental purpose of law. The role of law actually is rather straightforward, even with regard to adolescents. The law aims to regulate adolescents to allow and prepare them for societal participation, to foster law-abiding, civic-minded citizens. That is the rationale, for example, that both protects adolescents from and allows for intrusion into their privacy. The Court allows intrusion in adolescents' privacy interests in schools, for example, because officials act in *loco parentis* and have the duty to "inculcate the habits and manners of civility."[15] Likewise, the Court restrains state interference in family life because parents possess the right to control their children so long as they prepare them for civil society: The state has an interest in securing "healthy, well-rounded growth of young people into full maturity as citizens, with all that implies."[16] Ideally, then, the law seeks to produce democratic citizens, those who at least respect and even help foster the rights of others. At heart, the state's claim for all of its substitute-parenting authority rests on an assertion that important social values would be served if the state allowed adolescents to develop toward self-reliant adulthood.

Although the ultimate goal of law may be obvious, how to ensure that adolescents do become competent citizens remains less straightforward. Issues regarding citizenship and the general sociolegal structures that guide the practice of citizenship have yet to be explicitly applied to adolescents. Citizenship generally remains understood as an adult experience and commentators generally assume citizenship involves adulthood. Adolescents formally assume citizenship by proxy; the head of households assume the titular position that allows adolescents to have and benefit from citizenship. Yet adolescents experience citizenship in many ways and adolescents always have been part of concerted efforts to improve and, as discussed in chapter 1, even save civil society. Indeed, recent sociopolitical discourse aims to jolt perceptibly recalcitrant adolescents into more responsible citizenship.

The history and current manifestation of child welfare legislation and research essentially involves the history of adolescent citizenship. The history of schooling, child labor, and the development of the juvenile justice and child welfare systems reveals that these benevolent efforts are inseparable from, and actually constitute efforts to mold adolescents into, proper citizenship. In addition to contributing to the formation of those institutions, educational efforts consistently involved education for citizenship. The history of civic education provides an exceedingly rich array of approaches to instill civil values in adolescents. The field has developed from a basic focus on understanding political systems to the form of education that develops civic minded individuals who actively engage in community life.[17] The concern for developing adolescents' citizenship now reaches into much more systematic research and broader political efforts. In terms of research, efforts investigate adolescents' citizenship in the context of the transition from school to work and leaving the family home.[18] In terms of political movements, interest in adolescents' citizenship takes the form of calls to service and volunteerism to teach young people about their responsibilities to society.[19] These efforts all call for more active citizenship on the part of adolescents. The belief is that adolescents will learn tolerance and understanding through social mixing and about duties and obligations by undertaking socially useful work. The focus on adolescents' active citizenship and utility to society has been so significant as to deny issues of compulsion. Indeed, adolescents' civic "volunteerism" is viewed as necessary for adolescents' own good as opposed to benefits for others, a view that negates what otherwise would be prohibited as slave labor if the adolescents were adults.[20] Thus although not offered as an organizing concept of the way adolescents renegotiate society and the manner in which society confers full personhood, images of citizenship occupy a particularly significant part of child welfare research and regulation.

The focus on adolescent citizenship and need to foster public-minded citizens who do not shirk responsibilities contrasts sharply with the extent to which the legal system and society recognize adolescents' rights. As we have seen, inconsistency and incongruity mark the jurisprudence of adolescents' rights. Yet rights are critical to young peoples' social participation, willingness to undertake social responsibilities, and be active citizens.[21] The available research that directly addresses adolescents' rights reveals a clear link between the increase in rights and willingness to fulfill social responsibilities. For example, researchers link the recent erosion of rights adolescents already had, coupled by an increasing use of power by adults, to fewer opportunities for community and civil involvement that would allow adolescents to be more socially and civilly active.[22] Without such opportunities, adolescents increasingly do not feel the desire to undertake social responsibilities to either their local or national community. Likewise, without rights that protect relationships, or that protect adolescents from certain relationships, adolescents do not engage in responsible interpersonal relationships.[23]

Although social science research, history of child welfare, and current political concerns may support the view that adolescents' citizenship must be taken seriously, numerous reasons support the need to take seriously an approach to adolescents' rights that places a high premium on participation, self-determination, and socialization for democratic citizenship. These reasons spur the legal system toward a more modern system, yet ensure that new conceptions of adolescents' rights remain faithful to traditional jurisprudential concerns about the place of individuals in a changing democracy.

The first major reason to consider basic democratic concerns as a starting point to guide the development of adolescents' rights derives from the Constitution's basic protections. The Constitution sets the minimal floor on which to base and gauge individuals' legal protections. The extent to which the Constitution sets a minimal floor is important for two reasons. First, states can do more than what the Constitution allows, so long as they still protect the minimal rights guaranteed in the document. That point is actually simple to make and properly highlights that the Supreme Court's jurisprudence provides the constitutional floor on which to build adolescents' rights. That is, the Constitution simply sets the *minimal* floor on which to judge the treatment of *all* individuals. Second, the Constitution reflects the fundamental image of adulthood. Although the focus on "negative rights" (protections from state actions) has been the subject of considerable controversy, the image of democracy— in other words, the ideals of the U.S. system—is what guides it. The Constitution expects that people will operate in a democratic fashion and that even the Constitution remains subject to evolving interpretation. Because all other groups enjoy firmer protections guided in systematic and deliberate jurisprudence, there is a need for more explicit principles that would not render the treatment of adolescents subject to the whims of the times. Thus although the Constitution may allow for interpreting that adolescents' rights relate to their participation in society, it is important to emphasize that the Constitution actually calls for it. We live in a deliberative democracy that has as its central ethos individual self-determination and individual sovereignty.[24]

The second major reason to consider participatory and democratic citizenship to guide the development of adolescents' rights is that no legal rule prohibits the approach. The major limitation to increasing adolescents' rights is the notion of family privacy and parental rights. As we have seen, the failure to recognize adolescents' rights as distinct from parental and familial rights has been a major obstacle to the eventual success of the juvenile rights movement. As we also have seen, however, the history of adolescents' legal rights reveals the growing tendency to rebalance these interests against those of adolescents and society. Recent developments and apparent rise in adolescents' rights suggest that the limits placed on adolescents' rights no longer rest solely on adolescents because of their age. Recent efforts aim to alter adolescents' relationships with parents and the state. The extent to which the law recognizes mature minors is illustrative. Minors who are mature have been given greater access to health services, including access to therapeutic services. In addition and in terms of direct relationships to the state, minors have been determined to be sufficiently adult-like to be eligible for the death penalty—the ultimate control over adolescents granted to the state, not parents. As adolescents gain autonomous rights to act more freely from their parents and the *parens patriae* power of the state, the only other major limit is the state's police power to safeguard the interests of a democratic society.

The third proposal that supports the need to foster participatory citizenship derives from existing laws that reflect the need to inculcate adolescents and prepare them for societal membership. Existing child welfare laws are illustrative. The juvenile court, although subject to rapid reforms, still holds to the belief that rehabilitation serves its fundamental purpose: As we have seen, all enabling statutes still find rehabilitation central to their missions.[25] That mission remains intact and essentially reinforced as the more punitive trends aim to transfer adolescents from the juvenile to adult courts and leave the traditional juvenile court intact.

Family policies that aim to deal with child victimization also focus more on community involvement and establishing bonds outside the family, as reflected in the rise of community-based family support programs that offer families a comprehensive variety of services and activities designed to strengthen families and neighborhoods through social networking.[26] These proposals follow the ecological model that aims for intervention at multiple levels— for example, the individual, family, community, and society—and reject the notion that child maltreatment has a singular etiology. The goal is to empower families by promoting constructive child-rearing forces and reducing destructive ones, thereby enhancing the self-determining capacities of all individuals within families. These landmark laws reveal the legal system's commitment to produce appropriate institutions of socialization that regard adolescence as a time of tentative groping for self-identity, with room for exploration on the adolescents' own terms and with social circumstances that support and control that development so that adolescents will take their place in society.

The fourth major reason is that developments in law reflect changing times. The law is more ready to define adolescents in various contexts and for various purposes as autonomous individuals. Courts, asked to determine the boundaries and details of adolescents' domestic lives, are more and more frequently unable to rely on traditional assumptions about the character of domestic life and about the scope of parental authority. These changes reflect and encourage a series of clearly developing, though still incipient, shifts in the character of adolescents in contemporary society. Lives of adolescents and adults become increasingly indistinguishable. Because adults are expected to have voices in decisions that affect them, for example, it becomes increasingly difficult to justify the exclusion of adolescents' own voices in reaching decisions that will affect their lives. A review of the empirical reality of adolescent life reflects the approach's soundness. Considerable research reveals the significance of fostering adolescent participation in decisions that affect them.[27] Research suggests that the most healthy developmental outcomes derive from democratic relationships.[28] Research from family life, juvenile justice, and especially education reveals the extent to which the approach may be taken seriously.[29] That research simply reflects dramatic changes in social scientists' understanding of the role of parenting in the socialization of children. Regardless of the label—democratic, authoritative, warm, or psychologically autonomous—the common core of meaning that defines optimal parenting deals with the induction of adolescents into a system of reciprocity.[30]

The last reason emerges from responses to those who find the proposal problematic in the manner in which the alternative encourages participation by adolescents in matters that affect them. That is, although laws and research may encourage adopting the approach, a fundamental consideration involves the extent to which adolescents' right to dynamic self-determination for democratic citizenship gives most people cause for concern. The argument for denying participation rights has two interrelated themes. Critics either argue that adolescents are not rational or capable of making reasoned and informed decisions or that adolescents simply lack the wisdom born of experience. As a consequence adolescents are viewed as error-prone, a perception that legitimizes the rejection of their right to participate and make decisions for themselves. From those perspectives, the law benevolently acts as it protects adolescents from their own incompetence and even views them as having rights only to the extent to which families recognize such rights.

The centrality of these objections to proposals that encourage adolescents' participation and voice in decisions that affect them demands at least an abbreviated rebuttal at this point. Arguments used to deny adolescents' rights claims have been met in two ways. The first approach is to challenge current conceptions. Commentators either propose that adolescents do possess the qualities that critics allege they lack or concede that, if adolescents do lack the skills and qualities necessary for participating in decision making, they lack them to no greater degree than adults who are not disqualified from participation. An overwhelming amount of recent social science research supports *both* approaches.[31] Research suggests that

even infants engage in self-determined behavior, a finding that has revolutionized psychological approaches to child development,[32] and that adults' behaviors are not necessarily
self-determining; adults are far from being the mature individuals we often hold ourselves up
to be. The second reaction focuses on the misleading nature of critics' supposed difficulties
and obstacles that deny adolescents voices in important matters affecting their lives. The
approach appropriately emphasizes that efforts to foster self-determination do not stipulate
that decisions be foisted on adolescents and properly recognizes that adolescents already
make difficult decisions, even without the benefit of adult guidance. For example, the
adolescent competency debate has been narrowly constrained to "liberation" concerns,
such as those that involve access to reproductive materials and services. However, even in
that context that continues to dominate the self-determination debate, issues are far from
clear. Several have challenged the legitimacy of requiring judicial regulation of teenagers'
reproductive decision making.[33]

These propositions essentially distill to one point. It becomes increasingly untenable for
rhetoric to stress citizenship responsibilities while withdrawing opportunities to exercise
rights. Adolescents are the civil, political, and social citizens of the future. If adolescents are
to fulfill the obligations of citizenship as adults, they must be encouraged to learn their
responsibilities as adolescents. How people gain responsibilities and rights essentially
involves negotiations of citizenship. Those negotiations involve development, process, and
social circumstances, rather than simple age gradations that lose all sense of the processes
running through the early life course of individuals and the different life course of social
groupings.

Adolescents' Rights to Citizenship

Although the Court remains reluctant to guide the development of a jurisprudence
tailored to adolescents' rights, few have attempted to do what the Supreme Court has not
done: conceive and explicate conflicting rights of adolescents, parents, and society and
systematically rethink the nature and control of rights that may be held by adolescents. Given
the recent focus on responsibility, civil society, and citizenship, some commentators
envision a jurisprudence that reallocates the control of adolescents' rights to prepare
adolescents for eventual citizenship in a democratic society.[34] The proposal is actually
simple: The ultimate standard on which to base decisions affecting adolescents' rights
derives from the allocation of power among those who interact with adolescents so that the
negotiation of power would ensure the development of democratic citizens. The focus on
citizenship enables us to connect private life transitions with more general public processes
and deal with issues central to the period of adolescence: dependency and self-determination. Although the proposal may seem obvious, the focus on current and eventual citizenship
has yet to infiltrate discussions of the nature of adolescents' rights.

The current failure of law discussed previously and throughout the earlier chapters,
coupled with the transformations in the experience of adolescence discussed in chapter 1,
suggest that the law must recognize and address the peculiar place of adolescents both in
families and society. An appropriate starting point to reconceive adolescents' rights begins
with the most recent, global, ambitious, and comprehensive attempt to detail every
individuals' basic rights: the evolving human rights movement.[35] Just as in the United States,
though, human rights law does not contain a formal adolescent jurisprudence.[36] Despite that
notable absence in a movement that aims to include all of humanity, international developments enumerated through treaties offer new conceptions of children's rights; those

developments underscore important points that serve as a useful springboard to conceive adolescents' place in the law.

Human rights law now increasingly reconsiders issues involving the rights of children, parents, and the state with regard for parents and children's rights to autonomy and the state's interest in fostering autonomy. An interpretive analysis of human rights law suggests several considerations that may provide the necessary ingredients to both promote special protections against adolescents' vulnerabilities and foster their liberation.[37] Instead of focusing mainly on parental or state interests, international developments focus on every individual's inherent sense of human dignity. To recognize adolescents' peculiar place in society and ensure respect for adolescents' inherent dignity, the human rights movement encourages states to consider adolescents' own interests, recognize adolescents' voices in matters affecting them, and foster the development of adolescents and adults respectful of democratic ideals. For the purposes of our discussion, and as applied to U.S. law, these fundamental tenets essentially translate into five basic, indivisible principles that provide guidance to rethink adolescents' rights.

Recognize Adolescents as Legal Subjects

The need to view adolescents as subjects of rights emerges as the approach's first fundamental principle. From this perspective, adolescents are no longer possessions over which parents and others can exercise power and control. Instead of being conferred on parents or the state, rights are bestowed on adolescents. That is, adolescents no longer are mere *objects* of rights, they are the *subjects* of rights. Although the approach is not necessarily antithetical to recent developments in U.S. law, the orientation diverges considerably from the major jurisprudential trend in adolescents' rights as conceived in the United States.

Traditional jurisprudential trends in adolescents' rights generally bestow the control of adolescents' rights on parents. For example, parents generally control the context of family precursors to sexual debut, access to medical services, contraceptives, abortions, and marriage. Where parents do not have control, the state intervenes to act as parents otherwise would to control adolescents' rights, such as in the context of consent to voluntary sexual activity and access to abortions and contraceptives. Given that parents and the state control the nature of adolescents' rights, it is not difficult to imagine that a system that bestows on adolescents greater control over their own rights substantially differs from current approaches.

Two simple examples illustrate the significance of bestowing adolescents' rights on adolescents themselves. First, as subjects of rights, adolescents would hold greater power to determine their personal relationships. For example, adolescents would have a right to remain in their families and to maintain ties with their parents. This focus on relationships is likely to revolutionize family jurisprudence in that it would lead to the recognition of adolescents rights "in" and "to" relationships.[38] This approach allows for envisioning policies that aim to keep adolescents in their homes and with their families. A possible result could be, for example, giving adolescents a right not to be sent to institutions because it would violate their right to be with their families. This right could be ensured in several ways, most notably through prevention efforts that build community ties that support families and reduce the need for institutionalization. Regardless of *how* the right would be ensured, the fundamental difference would be that the right is recognized and society takes steps to affirm the right. Second, the significance of granting rights directly to adolescents also deals with the extent to which parents fail and adolescents would benefit from direct legal access to the courts or other social service systems. When parents do not support the rights of adolescents, legal systems would support either direct access to legal assistance or to another appropriate alternative. Numerous examples illustrate the significance of, and need to further develop, this approach to adolescents' rights. For example, when adolescents become runaways, the law would recognize their own right to services. Currently, the law, because of the focus on parental rights, seeks to return adolescents home and fails to offer protection to homeless adolescents. Likewise, the law fails to offer adolescents protection when parents do not recognize that adolescents are in abusive dating relationships. Currently, domestic violence laws that would provide adolescents access to shelters and systems that help them deal with abusers simply are unavailable because the law assumes that only adults need protection and that the only domestic violence adolescents would receive is through their parents. The reorientation of who holds the power to control adolescents' rights, then, provides adolescents greater access to protections that they would otherwise receive if they were adults.

Although the approach differs from traditional trends, the approach is feasible and far from radical. The approach still accepts the state's control of adolescents; it simply suggests that greater scrutiny be given to efforts that deny adolescents the rights others enjoy. That is, the effort demands that adolescents be treated with the respect given other groups and not suffer from invidious discrimination. For example, innovative policies ensure that adolescents have exit options in the form of judicial relief or social service delivery that allows for legal and social service access when parents fail to provide proper assistance to adolescents. The effort does not deny powerful bonds between parents and adolescents, but rather seeks to ensure that adolescents have options when those relationships fail to operate in adolescents' best interests. Controversial contraceptive programs exemplify the feasibility of the approach. The law permits adolescents to circumvent parental requirements that burden minors' rights to services many view as immoral; but the law has yet to foster adolescents' basic, accepted human rights, such as the rights to protection from violence, to basic sustenance, and to life.

It is difficult to justify the failure to provide assistance to victimized adolescents. It is even more difficult to justify denial of access to those resources simply because adolescents are not considered adults. For example, a focus on adolescents as holders of rights means that legal systems approach adolescent relationships differently, both in terms of partners and peers. Traditionally, when harm occurred in those relationships, adolescents did not receive services because they were not recognized as legal actors. The extent to which some states provide adolescents with direct access to courts and services reveals the approach's plausibility and feasibility.

Adolescents' increased control over their own rights as they become subjects of rights does not translate into abandoning them to their own rights. This proposition simply means that adolescents are entitled to the same consideration as adults. Although the thesis does not necessarily imply that adolescents always have *exactly* the same legal rights as adults, it does mean that adolescents' rights are not to be discounted because adolescents are not adults. The mere fact that they are adolescents would not necessarily translate into an inferior legal status. Because adolescents are persons, they are entitled to the same legal consideration to which anyone is entitled merely in virtue of being a person. Adolescents still remain social beings with social responsibilities. The fundamental issue that arises from the social nature of adolescents' rights involves the goals of socialization and how to achieve them. As revealed throughout the book, the fundamental goal of socialization from both social science and legal perspectives involves the need to integrate adolescents into responsible citizenship. To achieve that end, other principles emerge as critical components of adolescents' rights.

Expand Notions of Best Interests

In addition to viewing adolescents as persons in their own right with their own legal personhood, the movement to recognize adolescent personhood suggests a need to expand visions of the manner in which legal systems use the best-interests standard. The different manner in which the best-interests standard must be applied reveals part of the significance of recognizing adolescents as subjects of rights. The simple proposed rule suggests that those who control adolescents' rights should act in adolescents' best interests. For example, parental rights and responsibilities enjoin parents and legal guardians in exercising their primary responsibility for their children's upbringing and development to have the best interests of the child as their basic concern.[39] Currently, the best-interests standard tends to apply only to official actions of governmental bodies. Under this alternative conception, the best-interests standard applies to all actions involving minors.

The challenge to expand visions of what constitutes the best-interests standard is important. The effort challenges the notion of family privacy. The approach makes the family more visible to social regulation, not just from formal state structures but also from neighbors, relatives, communities, and even the international community. The approach capitalizes on the insight that states create and sustain the conditions under which adolescents are victimized and that states therefore should be accountable for the level of violence, much as the challenge to the public–private dichotomy that emphasizes the importance of state intervention to regulate violence in the private sphere of the family. Thus the alternative conception properly recognizes that states are far from being the greatest direct threat to the life and liberty of citizens, and that states reinforce the power that threatens adolescents' interests. Although the focus on opening up families is rather significant, it is important to note that the openness is not just limited to families. The approach also seeks to make practices of welfare professionals more visible and subject to new forms of monitoring and accountability. This effort provides a critical example of how human rights developments encourage attempts to rethink family and welfare paternalism. The approach confers on parents, the state, and every individual the duty to ensure that their children's rights are respected. Society arguably has an obligation to assist parents and families to ensure adolescents' rights. Although these general rights and obligations could be interpreted narrowly, parents and communities clearly have the responsibility to ensure adolescents' rights and the state gains powers of intrusion.

Numerous laws that regulate adolescent life and those who interact with adolescents already focus on adolescents' best interests. Parents already must act in their children's best interests. For example, the best-interests standard serves as the basic assumption that guides legal responses to family life—the standard provides the major rationale for allowing parents to control adolescents' access to medical services and prevents state intervention in families not viewed as abusive. In addition, not only does the law allow for interpretations that parents must act in adolescents' best interests, it actually mandates it, assumes that adolescents' best interests guides parent–child relationships, and views that guide as best for society.

Despite violent, abusive, and socially toxic communities, several legal rules require communities to address factors that lead to clear developmental deficits and require communities to act in adolescents' best interests. For example, several efforts directly aim resources to adolescents: Considerable allocations of what has been called "welfare" continues to be directed toward adolescents and children. In addition, laws indirectly reallocate access to resources through education and the need to capitalize on adolescents as societal resources. The effort is found in state mandates and laws that control educational rights and through other less visible efforts, such as mandates that broadcast media act in the best interests of society. The interests of adolescents allow communities and parents considerable power to regulate adolescents' sexual information and relationships. Again, legal mechanisms that foster adolescents' best interests appear when the law is approached in light of adolescents' rights.

Peers also must act to foster adolescents' best interests. Admittedly, developments in law still do not reflect the powerful role peers play in adolescent development and in efforts to foster healthy lifestyles. However, several avenues may be taken to ensure peer actions are more consistent with their peers' interests. At a minimum, efforts could aim to prevent direct harms perpetrated by peers. Efforts could encourage adolescents to treat each other with more respect and concern for other's interests and ensure that people act in others' interests as well as their own. Although these mandates may seem far-fetched, legal mandates already exist to develop peer relations along these two approaches. The two institutions that provide the environment for peer interactions and react to those interactions—schools and juvenile justice systems—already aim to encourage and foster healthy peer interactions. In terms of schools, their very existence rests on the rationale that they must foster responsible citizenship and moral citizens, a rationale accepted and expressed by the Supreme Court as well as several states' educational-enabling statutes. Likewise, the juvenile justice system aims to deal with problem adolescents and regulates peer interactions. Despite attempts to dismantle the juvenile justice system, the transfer of more hard-core offenders to adult courts allows the juvenile justice system to remain focused on rehabilitation and on fostering healthy relationships. Indeed, the major innovative policy trend counters "get tough" mandates and focuses on reintegration of adolescents into community life. Again, laws already exist that may be harnessed to help form peer relations consistent with healthy and supportive adolescent development.

An often ignored control and influence on adolescents are adolescents themselves. Healthy adolescents act in their own best interests. This is not to negate adolescents' profound role as social actors but to emphasize how adolescents actively contribute to their own development and how adolescents have responsibilities to themselves and others. This recognition demands legal reform to allow adolescents to act in their best interests, rather than foreclosing the possibility. Again, laws already adopt the rationale. Laws interfere and regulate adolescents' lives for the good of minors as well as to protect them from potential harm. That is the general rationale that allows legal systems to treat adolescents and children differently from adults. Laws that restrict adolescents' freedoms do so to ensure that adolescents' best interests are considered and acted on whenever practical.

Despite the slew of legal rules and principles, it still remains difficult and disingenuous to argue that society and individuals actually follow the numerous best-interest mandates. For example, states do not act on adolescents' best interests when they allow or encourage adolescent girls to marry older men to reduce welfare rolls, when state's deny sexually active adolescents access to counseling, when states refuse to provide adolescents with basic information about how to protect themselves from deadly diseases and impoverished futures, when states sterilize adolescents so that their sexual abuse will not result in pregnancy and thus essentially remain unknown, and when states do not provide meaningful access to protection from violence. When states deny the basic interests of adolescents in those circumstances, they pursue the best interests of parents, and institutional actors who deny adolescents' rights, rights that adolescents would otherwise enjoy but for their status as adolescents. As the state pursues those interests and denies adolescents' rights they would otherwise have but for their status as adolescents, the state's actions become increasingly difficult to justify. If anything, then, the focus on adolescents' best interests is far less peculiar than the failure to put adolescents' interests first when those interests arguably should—in theory, practice, and law—take precedence.

Foster Dynamic Self-Determination

The need to enhance dynamic self-determination modifies the need to view adolescents as subjects of rights and the need for everyone to aim toward acting in adolescents' best interests. This principle provides an important dimension that current conceptions of the best-interests standards lack. The central principle of dynamic self-determination refers to the manner rights are now framed and bestowed. The standard suggests that adolescents must receive more control over their own rights as they develop, that they should be bestowed autonomous rights consistent with their evolving capacities.[40] Most fundamentally, the principle demands that adolescents be allowed space within their personal relationships, families, and cultures to find their own mode of *individual* fulfillment.

A focus on self-determination highlights the need to optimally position adolescents so that they develop their own perceptions of their well-being as they enter adulthood, rather than foreclosing on the potential for such development. This is what is fundamentally meant by adolescents as rights-holders: Institutions concern themselves with furthering adolescents' own interests. The result is that socialization forces beyond the family are emphasized, as reflected in a strong emphasis placed on education, the sharing of ideas, and increasing access to information.[41] Arguably, for example, a community that would take this obligation seriously would protect adolescents who adopt different lifestyles from ridicule and violent harassment; such communities would not necessarily encourage, but at least allow, exploration without discrimination. Such communities also would recognize the numerous forms of violence adolescents endure in their families, especially emotional maltreatment that pervasively goes ignored.[42] Again, the recognition has important consequences. As discussed in the previous chapter, current welfare policy mandates that teenage parents live with their parents and provides clear-cut situations (such as exploitation, sexual abuse, or serious harm to the parent and his or her baby) as grounds for exempting them from coresidency requirements. Yet the less obvious conditions (such as emotional conflict and lack of emotional support from grandparents) produce the same negative outcomes for teenage parents and their children that policies aim to attenuate. The rationales that served for reforms in the first place—protecting adolescents from harm, preventing cycles of violence, providing healthy environments for children—support the need to provide for adolescents' self-determination needs.

The focus on adolescent self-determination constitutes a radical move and certainly moves against important social and political trends that aim to exert greater control over adolescents. However, the move makes considerable sense when developing programs that aim to protect and liberate adolescents. The dynamic self-determination principle does not aim to support a global view of socialization. It allows for cross- and intracultural differences and challenges essentialist, or singular representations of adolescents' experiences.[43] Taking self-determination seriously translates into a skeptical attitude toward decisions that will affect adolescents and the necessity to be more tentative and open-ended in the actual process of decision making. The presumption is that the best response to whatever issue has arisen may lie *within* the adolescent. This approach aims to help direct adolescents as they accommodate to their social world. Rather than manipulating the social world in hopes that adolescents will respond appropriately, the approach aims to include adolescents even though they may need direction to an accommodation with the social world that surrounds them.[44]

The central tenet of dynamic self-determination involves how to bestow and frame rights. The standard suggests that adolescents must gain more control over their own rights as they develop—that they should be bestowed autonomous rights consistent with their evolving capacities. Most fundamentally, the principle demands that adolescents be allowed space within their personal relationships, families, and communities to find their own mode of *individual* fulfillment. As conceived, self-determination encourages adolescents to develop their own perceptions of their well-being as they enter adulthood. Despite the focus on individual fulfillment, however, the principle also recognizes the social nature of development and seeks to involve adolescents in community membership and foster responsible citizenship. The focus on responsible citizenship emphasizes how the right to self-determination does not constitute the right to follow any whim that arises. Rather, the right involves the freedom and opportunity to choose a life-plan and to control its implementation. Adolescents' right to their own self-determination and right to be treated in accordance to their own best interests create a duty on the part of parents and society to educate and prepare adolescents for what it takes to choose and implement a lifeplan. That obligation remains key to understanding the extent to which adolescents freely make decisions that may affect the rest of their lives. Adolescents are caught between inequalities of opportunities and choice, based on their social class, gender, race or ethnicity, geographical location, and economic status. How to negotiate the impact of these inequalities remains the task of citizenship.

As with other legal developments discussed previously, legal systems already attempt to foster responses that consider adolescents' needs for self-determination and participation in civil society. The use of the maturity standard illustrates the utility of the approach. The standard, for example, has been used to determine access to marriage and medical services, including access to abortion, medical testing and treatment. Likewise, the maturity standard allows for adolescents' transfer to adult courts and adult punishments when they offend. Thus when adolescents' rights have been deemed fundamental and adolescents able to exercise these rights, the Court and state statutes increasingly allow adolescents access to services, courts, and extra procedural protections. In addition, the presence of potentially serious social consequences that would arise from denying access to social benefits adults enjoy, such as access to medical testing and treatment of sexually transmitted diseases, provides rationales for the legal system to protect adolescents' access and even to foster their self-determination. Lastly, adolescents' self-determination capacities are recognized so as not to hamper the state's police power, such as when adolescents are deemed able to waive their rights in criminal investigations and deemed mature enough (or their actions so adult-like) to be waived to adult criminal court, stand trial, and be subject to capital sentencing. The law clearly does recognize adolescents' self-determination needs and rights.

Although legal systems increasingly do recognize adolescents' right to self-determination for adolescents' own benefit, the principle remains applied narrowly and in limited contexts. For example, current conceptions of the maturity standard do not allow for more direct intervention into family dynamics and reallocation of familial dynamics consistent with adolescents' levels of maturity. Nor has the principle been used to regulate adolescents' sexual interactions with others, such as when the legal system presumes some adolescents incompetent to consent to sexual relations with some people but not others. Nor has the principle been used to expand adolescents' access to protective services when their own relationships place them in danger. In those instances, bright lines dictate how groups of adolescents gain rights. Few jurisdictions expansively recognize the need to better adolescents' sense of self-determination and respect for adolescents' individual rights.

Allow for Adolescent Participation

The focus on the need to accommodate adolescents' self-determination leads us to the next critical principle of participation. *All* adolescents must participate in decisions that affect them.[45] The right to participation in decision making may operate at several levels that include the rights to receive adequate information, be heard in matters that concern them, exercise freedom of expression, share in the decision-making process, and gradually control the outcome of decisions as the adolescent achieves independence. In practice the participation may also occur on several levels, ranging from manipulation, where adolescents are consulted but not given feedback, to actual participation that extends from passive assent, informed consent, to control over choices and decisions that have different consequences for the present and future. In any intervention in adolescents' lives, adults would need to ensure the provision of adequate information, provide opportunities for expression and exploration of options, report how adolescents' views will be considered, inform adolescents of decisional outcomes and explain decisions contrary to their wishes, and provide access to genuine avenues of complaint for situations in which the adolescents feel they may have been mistreated, ignored, or abused.

Although it may be difficult to include adolescents in decision making, the focus on participation provides several important contributions. It seeks to re-image adolescents' personhood. Adolescents are not necessarily passive, defenseless, and in need of protection by state agents who know what was in the adolescents' interests; nor are adolescents necessarily in need of protection from parents. The principle further challenges the assumption that the practices of states and families are inherently benevolent. Rather than assuming that they act in adolescents' interest, the principle assumes that they may not. For example, the interventions in family life are now to focus on individual family members, how their interests might diverge, and how those interests must be disaggregated to ensure that young family members may make distinctive rights claims. The focus on participation also breathes new life into the best-interests standard that already guides child welfare law. Adolescents would be able to help determine what is in their best interests through participation. Finally, the focus on participation recognizes the classic psychological bind of adolescence in which adolescents need guidance as they attempt to remain loyal to their own needs and rely on their own definition of those needs. For example, in efforts to evaluate claims to displace parents' control over their adolescents' rights, the approach would not demand that the adolescent be able to provide a clear expression of self-determination—either for or against his or her parents. Instead, the approach suggests that the ability to have an independent voice and ultimate self-determination should be the goal, not the prerequisite, for state interventions.

Both social sciences and the law recognize the central need for participation in decision making to develop decision-making skills that enable adolescents to become responsible societal members. In terms of social sciences, researchers emphasize the need to promote autonomous development through fostering participation in outcome determination. The finding emerges repeatedly in terms of family life and other social institutions that govern adolescents, especially schools and juvenile justice systems. The findings consistently indicate that healthy adolescent development results from social and familial contexts that support autonomy, provide structure, and supply warm and involved socializing agents. These contexts offer informational feedback, rationales, and administer consistent consequences as they encourage self-initiation, minimize use of controls, and adopt adolescents' perspectives. The healthy outcome of autonomy allows adolescents to act on their own volition while still relying on others for support, unlike the frequently fused and confused concept of independence, which implies detachment and minimal reliance on others.

In terms of law, the right to participation in decision making operates at several levels that include the rights to receive adequate information, be heard in matters that concern them, exercise freedom of expression, share in decision-making processes, and gradually control the outcome of important decisions as adolescents achieve legal independence. Although still in a limited manner, the law increasingly allows for participation. The right to participation most frequently involves efforts to provide adequate information in interventions and foster inclusion into society. For example, the law already mandates the principle in educational provisions, such as through the focus on inclusion, respect for cultural and religious differences, and recognition of students' rights to free speech. Likewise, laws provide adolescents in other settings with opportunities for expression and exploration of options, such as in requiring medical decision-making procedures that counsel before provision of services or materials. In addition, the law provides some adolescents with access to genuine avenues of complaint for situations in which adolescents feel mistreated, ignored, or abused. In summary, the basic principle reflected in due process—the right to be heard, recognized, and participate in governmental processes that impact one's rights—increasingly applies to adolescents and different parts of their lives that do not directly involve courts.

Appreciate the Processual Nature of Socialization

The last critical principle deals with the goals of socialization and the recognition that socialization continues throughout life. Contrary to the predominant view of adolescence portrayed by the legal system, socialization involves more continuation than actual achievement; people always are in the process of development, negotiate dependency and independency, and participate in their socioecological conditions. For example, terms such as *adolescence* or *adulthood* relate to life-course events and social relationships that are redefined and renegotiated. Leading researchers find it inappropriate to view socialization as the process whereby control of adolescents shifts from adults to adolescents themselves. Instead, they view, at every stage of life, relationships that involve coregulation, and individuals actually never graduate to being free of the regulatory requirements of intimate others unless they become social isolates.[46] As the relative inflexibility and inadequate explanatory power of traditional theories become apparent, attention shifts to the development of creative and interactive ecological and sociocultural theoretical schema.[47] As adolescents are viewed as social actors, their own views and desires become key concerns; viewing adolescents as passive subjects of social structures and processes results in paying little or no attention to the voices of adolescents themselves. To reflect reality, then, the law must move closer to the current understanding that adolescents actively construct and determine their own lives, the lives of those around them, and of the societies in which they live.

The processual aspect of human development highlights how development occurs in ecological contexts and focuses interest on ensuring societal, democratic participation. The focus on participation reinforces the need for children, adolescents, and adults to exist in peaceful community with others, assist in fostering a sense of community, develop healthy relationships, and respect others' sense of individuality and human dignity. The focus on process highlights the need to take into account the ways in which movement from one life stage to another remains subject to structural change over historical time, and the variation of experiences within cohorts according to their social and geographical locations. Thus although in policy terms adolescents are a very identifiable social group, the reality is that they differ and have vastly different experiences. Age has been structured as one dimension of inequality, but a focus on age should not result in ignoring other dimensions in the overall picture of inequality.

The extent to which society and legal systems recognize the processual nature of socialization generally serves not to foster adolescents' rights but to eliminate them.[48] For example, the antirights position is based on understanding personal relationships as processual; yet it ends with a view of rights that fosters two main dangers. The first is that rights create abstract, contractual, and impersonal relationships that run the risk of forging relationships that no longer give meaning to human existence. The second aspect of rights formulations that allegedly makes rights-talk detrimental to relationships is that they emphasize the separateness, independence, and autonomy of persons whereas relationships actually are about unions and dependent agents. It would be improper to propose that personal relationships and broader community relationships do not give a full meaning to life and are not seeded in dependency. However, the language and use of rights provide important advantages and certainly are not necessarily incompatible with relationships. The rights are not mere *prima facie* rights: Some may be overridden in particular cases, yet they do not vanish completely. Further, the conception moves adolescents in the public realm to offer protection. In addition, as with healthy relationships, the rights recognize and respect the unique value of persons. Finally, the processual nature of relationships insists that questions of rights, interests, and obligations remain open. When lines between the interests of parent, adolescent, community, and state seem clearly drawn, it is important to realize that none of the contestants clearly ousts the others. Thus state policy toward adolescent life revolves around attempts to answer whether adolescents will become what society wants and expects if the state actively guides or actively frees parents and plural subcultural groups to shape norms of adolescent life. The law simply accommodates disputes and offers guiding principles to deal with competing state, community, and parental claims over their adolescents.

Contrary to the traditional view of adolescence portrayed by the legal system, some innovative developments in adolescents' rights appreciate the processual nature of human development. Rather than fostering an adult status marked by individualism and ostensibly free from external constraints, the developments recognize how socialization involves more continuation and renegotiation of autonomous development. The developments recognize how people continuously develop, negotiate dependency and independency, and participate in their socioecological conditions. Innovative approaches to adolescents' rights consider the goals of socialization and recognize how socialization continues throughout life. The legal move is critical for two reasons.

First, the move appreciates changing influences on adolescent development. For example, age significantly structures the manner in which adolescents negotiate their informational environment. The developmental process of separation from parental influence with the increase in the role of peers rechannels the nature and saliency of sexual information. Although information from parents generally remains highly trusted throughout adolescence, adolescents who begin their early teenage years overwhelmingly do not prefer parents as a source of information. The information-seeking and receiving process affects decisions relating to sexual activity and the outcomes of sexual behavior, all of which range from purchasing cosmetics, dieting, worrying about pregnancy and sexually transmitted diseases, watching sexually explicit media, suffering violent relationships, and adopting or tolerating certain sex roles and types of sexual activity. Although the law assumes that parents guide adolescents' behaviors, an understanding of the process of adolescent development suggests that, as adolescents age, influences on them change, as do the predictors of sexual attitudes and behavior.

Second, the recognition acknowledges diversity of outcomes. The significance of this recognition comes in two forms. First, adolescents do not follow similar developmental paths. For example, adolescents engage in different forms of sexual activity, and the extent of sexual activity varies among groups of adolescents. The age at which adolescents engage in sexual activity, or progress from one activity to another, varies considerably within and between groups. Second, adolescents do not adopt and follow normative–traditional paths to sexual development. Adolescents who do not follow traditional paths suffer considerable consequences. Gay adolescents, for example, suffer both within families and peer groups. However, even adolescents who follow more traditionally accepted paths to sexual development suffer similar fates: Those who do not engage in sexual activity (as well as those who do) may suffer consequences, as revealed by the forces of peer sexual harassment.

Innovative laws respond to these developments in understanding adolescents' sexual development and recognize adolescents' diversity and diversity of influences on them. For example, some states statutorily mandate the development of sexual harassment policies in schools. Others statutorily provide adolescents access to social services when they become trapped in relationship violence. Still other laws recognize that adolescents mature earlier than others and accommodate their needs. Laws that regulate media and educational systems increasingly replace parents' failures to educate their children about important sexual matters. Although these emerging legal responses to adolescent sexuality remain controversial, they do reflect attempts to capitalize on the current understanding of the realities of adolescent life.

Conclusion

Available social science evidence and innovative laws indicate a need to rethink adolescents' rights and offer paths to greater legal recognition. Equally important, existing laws already provide mechanisms consistent with new conceptions of adolescents' rights, and the existence of several innovative efforts to address adolescents' rights suggests that efforts are far from futile. Effective efforts genuinely involve adolescents in planning and implementing programs and laws and recognize how groups and communities channel and constrain behaviors, even those as profoundly intimate as sexual activity. These developments reveal how it increasingly makes sense to ensure the fundamental democratic principle that all have a right to self-determination, to participate in society in a democratic manner that appreciates individuals' basic interests, and to control the rights that would benefit them.

The principles enumerated in this chapter and supported throughout the rest of the book clearly seek to revise societal approaches to adolescents' issues. As such, the approach requires us to rethink how different communities view adolescents and the place adolescents actually have in their own intimate relationships, especially those that involve romantic partners, peers, and families. The revisioning also requires the reallocation of resources and responsibilities not just in society but in families as well as interpersonal relations. Although the full import of this move has yet to be imagined, the principles aim to revision *all* approaches to adolescent life. Even though the proposed reforms would revision current approaches, it is critical to keep in mind that the principles that constitute the new approach already exist in current jurisprudence. The revolutionary nature of the move would be to make comprehensive and judicious progress toward an orientation that holds adolescents as significant actors who inappropriately may be denied rights they would otherwise enjoy if they were considered adults.

The proposed reforms advocate respect for adolescents as persons through recognizing that adolescents have identities, histories, and personal attachments. Identities, attachments, and developmental histories define everyone's humanity. The effort seeks to enshrine these considerations in the vocabulary of rights and to require society and individuals to treat adolescents as persons and accord them the moral status possessed by other persons. Given this broad vision, it is not surprising that basic respect for adolescents serves as a springboard to reconsider the laws relating to adolescent sexuality and to rethinking the place of adolescents in the law; both are central to humanity and everyone's place in society.

Endnotes

1. This proposal is highlighted, for example, by the established procedures directing young, pregnant teenagers to petition judges; *see* chapter 4.
2. Thomas Grisso, "The Competence of Adolescents as Trial Defendants," *Psychology, Public Policy, and Law* 3 (1997):3–32.
3. Gary B. Melton and Nancy F. Russo, "Adolescent Abortion: Psychological Perspectives on Public Policy," *American Psychologist* 42 (1987):69–72.
4. Talcott Parsons, *Family: Socialization and Interactive Processes* (London: Routledge and Kegal Paul, 1956), at 19.
5. Carolyn A. Smith and Susan B. Stern, "Delinquency and Antisocial Behavior: A Review of Family Processes and Intervention Research," *Social Service Review* 71 (1997):382–420.
6. Gary B. Melton, *The Individual, the Family, and Social Good: Personal Fulfillment in Times of Change* (Lincoln: University of Nebraska Press, 1995).
7. In Eisenstadt v. Baird, 405 U.S. 438, 453 (1972), the Court expressly recognized family members as autonomous individuals, connected to each other as such rather than as inseparable parts of a holistic social unit.
8. *See,* for an important review, James G. Dwyer, "Parents' Religion and Children's Welfare: Debunking the Doctrine of Parents' Rights," *California Law Review* 82 (1994):1371–1447.
9. Parham v. J.R., 442 U.S. 584, 620–621 (1979); Wisconsin v. Yoder, 406 U.S. 205, 207 (1972).
10. Bellotti v. Baird, 443 U.S. 622, 651 (1979).
11. *In re* Gault 387 U.S. 1, 29–31 (1967).
12. McKiever v. Pennsylvania, 403 U.S. 528, 545 (1971).
13. *Bellotti,* 443 U.S. at 643–644.
14. *Parham,* 442 U.S. at 603–604.
15. Vernonia Sch. Dist., 47J v. Acton, 515 U.S. 646, 655 (1995).
16. Prince v. Massachusetts, 321 U.S. 158, 168 (1944).
17. Roger J. R. Levesque, "The Politics of Schooling and Adolescent Life," *New York University Law School Review of Law & Social Change* (in press).
18. Gill Jones and Claire Wallace, *Youth, Family and Citizenship* (Philadelphia: Open University Press, 1992).
19. *See* Scott D. Minden, "The Constitutionality of Mandatory Community Service Programs in Public Schools," *Southern California Law Review* 68 (1995):1391–1416.
20. For example, the Supreme Court let stand mandatory labor by adolescents in and for public schools, such as working in school cafeterias and for nonschool organizations. These involuntary labor policies have been found permissible on the premise that they are noncoercive and for the students' own good. *See, e.g.,* Bobilin v. Board of Education, 403 F. Supp. 1095, 1104 (D. Haw. 1975) (upholding regulation requiring at least seven days of work in school cafeterias for children in grades 4 through 12 on the ground that the work requirement served the public need of defraying school costs).
21. Jones and Wallace, *Youth, Family and Citizenship;* Bob Coles, *Youth and Social Policy: Youth, Citizenship and Young Careers* (London: University College of London, 1995).

22. Alan France, "'Why Should We Care?' Young People, Citizenship and Questions of Social Responsibility," *Journal of Youth Studies* 1 (1998):97–111.

23. This may be seen at two levels. Although most discussions focus on family life, the approach also applies to those who are victims or victimizers. *See* Roger J. R. Levesque, "Emotional Maltreatment in Adolescents' Everyday Lives: Furthering Sociolegal Reforms and Social Service Provisions," *Behavioral Science & the Law* 16 (1998):237–263; Roger J. R. Levesque, "Future Visions of Juvenile Justice: Lessons From International and Comparative Law," *Creighton Law Review* 29 (1996):1563–1585.

24. James Bohman, *Public Deliberation: Pluralism, Complexity, and Democracy* (Cambridge, MA: MIT Press, 1996); David Held, *Democracy and the Global Order: From the Modern State to Cosmopolitan Governance* (Stanford, CA: Stanford University Press, 1995).

25. *See* Roger J. R. Levesque & Alan J. Tomkins, "Revisioning Juvenile Justice: Implications of the New Child Protection Movement," *Journal of Urban and Contemporary Law* 48 (1995):87–116.

26. James Garborino and John Eckenrode, *Understanding Abusive Families: An Ecological Approach to Theory and Practice* (San Francisco, CA: Jossey-Bass, 1997).

27. Eleanore E. Maccoby, "The Role of Parents in the Socialization of Children: An Historical Perspective," *Developmental Psychology* 28 (1994):237-293; Jones and Wallace, *Youth, Family and Citizenship;* France, "'Why Should We Care?' Young People, Citizenship and Questions of Social Responsibility."

28. For reviews in different contexts, *see* Levesque, "Future Visions of Juvenile Justice: Lessons From International and Comparative Law"; Levesque, "Emotional Maltreatment in Adolescents' Everyday Lives: Furthering Sociolegal Reforms and Social Service Provisions"; Levesque, "The Politics of Schooling and Adolescent Life."

29. *Id.*

30. Maccoby, "The Role of Parents in the Socialization of Children: An Historical Perspective."

31. Roger J. R. Levesque, "The Internationalization of Children's Human Rights: Too Radical for American Adolescents?" *Connecticut Journal of International Law* 9 (1994):237–293.

32. Daniel Stern, *The Interpersonal World of the Infant: A View From Psychoanalysis and Developmental Psychology* (New York: Basic Books, 1985).

33. Hyman Rodman, "Should Parental Involvement Be Required for Minor's Abortions?" *Family Relations* 40 (1991):155–160; Suellyn Scarnecchia and Julie Kunce Field, "Judging Girls: Decision Making in Parental Consent to Abortion Cases," *Michigan Journal of Gender and Law* 3 (1995):75–123.

34. Levesque, "Emotional Maltreatment in Adolescents' Everyday Lives: Furthering Sociolegal Reforms and Social Service Provisions;" Roger J. R. Levesque, "Educating American Youth: Lessons From Children's Human Rights Law," *Journal of Law and Education* 27 (1998):173–209.

35. *The Universal Declaration of Human Rights, GA Res 217A,* UN GAOR, 3d Sess (Part I. Resolutions), UN Doc A/810 (1948); *United Nations Covenant on Civil and Political Rights,* GA Res 2200, UN GAOR, 21st Sess (Supp No 16 at 52), UN Doc A/6316; 999 UNTS 171; 6 ILM 368 (1966); *United Nations Covenant on Economic, Social and Cultural Rights,* GA Res 2200 Annex, UN GAOR, 21st Sess (Supp No. 16 at 49), UN Doc A/6316; 993 UNTS 3; 6 ILM 360 (1966); *United Nations Convention on the Rights of the Child,* GA Res 44/25. UN GAOR, 44th Sess (Supp No 49 at 166), UN Doc A/44/49; 28 ILM 1448 (1989).

36. Roger J. R. Levesque, *Adolescents, Society, and the Law* (Chicago: American Bar Association, 1997).

37. *See* Levesque, "Educating American Youth: Lessons From Children's Human Rights Law."

38. Roger J. R. Levesque, "International Children's Rights: Can They Make a Difference in American Family Policy?" *American Psychologist* 51 (1996):1251–1256.

39. *United Nations Convention on the Rights of the Child.*

40. Several articles in human rights treaties make use of the variability; *see* Levesque, "Emotional Maltreatment in Adolescents' Everyday Lives: Furthering Sociolegal Reforms and Social Service

Provisions''; Levesque, ''International Children's Rights: Can They Make a Difference in American Family Policy?''

41. Roger J. R. Levesque, ''The International Human Rights to Education: The Lore and Lure of Law,'' *Annual Survey of International and Comparative Law* 4 (1998):205–252.

42. Levesque, ''Emotional Maltreatment in Adolescents' Everyday Lives: Furthering Sociolegal Reforms and Social Service Provisions.''

43. Jo Boyden, ''Childhood and the Policy Makers: A Comparative Perspective on the Globalization of Childhood.'' In *Constructing and Reconstructing Childhood,* ed. Alison James and Alan Prout (London: Falmer Press, 1990).

44. Levesque, ''Emotional Maltreatment in Adolescents' Everyday Lives: Furthering Sociolegal Reforms and Social Service Provisions.''

45. *E.g., United Nations Convention on the Rights of the Child,* Article 12.

46. For a brief review of the topic by the leading commentator as it applies to adolescents, *see* James Youniss, ''Social Construction of Adolescence by Adolescents and Parents.'' In *Adolescent Development in the Family: New Directions for Child Development,* ed. Harold D. Grotevant and Catherine R. Cooper (San Francisco: Jossey-Bass, 1983).

47. For the classic statement that started the trend, *see* Urie Bronfenbrenner, ''Developmental Research, Public Policy, and the Ecology of Childhood,'' *Child Development* 45 (1974):1–5.

48. For a clear statement of this position in terms of children and their parents, *see* Ferdinand Shoeman, ''Rights of Children, Rights of Parents, and the Moral Basis of the Family,'' *Ethics* 91 (1980):6–19. Similar criticisms have been made by feminist critics of rights; *see* John Hardwig, ''Should Women Think in Terms of Rights.'' In *Feminism and Political Theory,* ed. Cass Sunstein (Chicago: University of Chicago Press, 1990). Likewise, communitarians have lodged similar complaints. For a response, *see* John Tomasi, ''Individual Rights and Community Virtues,'' *Ethics* 101 (1991):521–536.

Table of Authorities

Numbers in italics refer to listings in the notes sections.

Federal Laws, Regulations, and Rules

State Laws, Regulations, and Rules

Cases

Author Index

Numbers in italics refer to listings in notes.

Subject Index

Abortion, 1–2, 5
    access to, 50, 79–80, 111–118, 297
    competency to make decisions, 114, 331
    family reactions and consequences, 115–117
    judicial bypass option, 112–113, 115–117
    media and, 168
    parental involvement, 112–116
    psychological consequences of, 114–115
    reduction of, 308
    spousal notification, 112, 117
    state control, 111–113
Abstinence education, 143, 145–146, 308, 311. See also Sex education
Abstract thinking, 23
Abuse of children. See Child abuse and neglect
Abuse of partners. See Dating violence; Domestic violence
Abuse of substances. See Substance use and abuse
Academic achievement. See School failure and dropping out
Acquaintance rape, 232–235, 239–240. See also Sexual assault; Sexual offending by adolescents
Acquired immune deficiency syndrome. See AIDS
Adolescence
    autonomy. See Autonomy in adolescence
    conceptions of. See Conceptions of adolescence
    criminal prosecution. See Juveniles tried as adults
    delinquency. See Juvenile delinquency
    dependency. See Dependency in adolescence
    employment. See Employment
    parental control. See Parental control
    parenthood. See Teen parenthood
    pornography. See Child and adolescent pornography
    pregnancy. See Teen pregnancy
    prostitution. See Prostitution (juvenile)
    rights. See Rights of adolescents

    sexuality. See Sexual activity; Sexual development
Adoption, and teen pregnancy, 122–123, 297, 307
Advertising. See Media
AFDC (Aid to Families With Dependent Children), 307. See also Welfare
African Americans
    sexual activity, 71
    teen parenthood, 299, 302, 310
    teen pregnancy, 299
Age
    adolescence, period of, 14, 23
    adolescent sexual offenders and victims, 265
    child pornography protections, 198
    domestic violence protections, 228
    gang membership, average age of, 24
    juvenile justice jurisdiction, 273
    juveniles tried as adults, 277
    marriage, legal age of consent, 125–126
    obscenity standard and, 174–175
    sexual consent, 73, 75, 238, 274, 329
    sexual maturity and activity and, 2–3
    sexual partners, age disparity among, 70, 73, 76, 148, 238–239, 241
Age-segregated activities, 19
Aggression. See Antisocial behavior; Violence
Aid to Families With Dependent Children (AFDC), 307. See also Welfare
AIDS, 2, 24. See also Sexually transmitted diseases (STDs)
    contraceptives and, 107–109
    early sexual activity and, 76–77
    homosexuality and, 66, 148
    incidence of, 107
    sex education and, 146, 153
    testing and treatment rights, 26, 80–82
Alabama, statutory rape law, 74
Alaska, marrying age, 126
Alcohol use and abuse. See Substance use and abuse
Alternative-care placements, 24, 203
    juvenile offenders, 282
    sexual offender treatment strategies, 269
    teen parenthood and, 309

ABOUT THE AUTHOR

Roger J. R. Levesque received a JD from Columbia University School of Law and a PhD in Cultural Psychology from the University of Chicago. Before joining Indiana University's Department of Criminal Justice, he was a Fellow in the Law & Psychology Program at the University of Nebraska—Lincoln. He has published more than 40 scholarly articles and book chapters that deal with family life, maltreatment, and the law. He is the author of *Child Sexual Abuse: A Human Rights Perspective* (Indiana University Press, 1999).